# Disaster Response and Recovery: Strategies and Tactics for Resilience

## SECOND EDITION

David A. McEntire, PhD

*Emergency Administration and Planning*
*Department of Public Administration*
*University of North Texas*

Published by John Wiley & Sons, Inc., Hoboken, New Jersey
Published simultaneously in Canada

For general information on our other products and services or for technical support, please contact our Customer Care Department within the United States at (800) 762-2974, outside the United States at (317) 572-3993 or fax (317) 572-4002.

Wiley also publishes its books in a variety of electronic formats. Some content that appears in print may not be available in electronic formats. For more information about Wiley products, visit our web site at www.wiley.com.

*Library of Congress Cataloging-in-Publication Data:*

McEntire, David A.
   Disaster response and recovery : strategies and tactics for resilience / David A. McEntire. – Second edition.
      pages   cm
   Includes index.
   ISBN 978-1-118-67302-7 (paperback)
1.  Disaster relief–United States.   I. Title.
   HV555.U6M394 2014
   363.34′80973–dc23

2014017668

Printed in the United States of America

10   9   8   7   6   5   4

*For emergency management students and professionals everywhere*

# CONTENTS

# ABOUT THE AUTHOR

Dr. McEntire is a Professor in the Emergency Administration and Planning Program (EADP) at the University of North Texas. He teaches emergency management courses in both the undergraduate and graduate programs. Previously, he served as the Coordinator for the EADP and PhD programs, and as the Associate Dean in the College of Public Affairs and Community Service.

Dr. McEntire's academic interests include emergency management theory, international disasters, community preparedness, response coordination, and vulnerability reduction. He has received several grants—funded by the Natural Hazards Center, the National Science Foundation, and other sources—that allowed him to conduct research in Peru, the Dominican Republic, Texas, New York, California, and Haiti.

Dr. McEntire is the author or editor of several books including *Introduction to Homeland Security* (Wiley), *Disciplines, Disasters and Emergency Management* (Charles C. Thomas), and *Comparative Emergency Management* (FEMA). His research has also been published in *Public Administration Review*, the *Australian Journal of Emergency Management*, *Disasters*, the *International Journal of Mass Emergencies and Disasters*, *Journal of Emergency Management*, *Journal of the Environment and Sustainable Development*, *Sustainable Communities Review*, *International Journal of Emergency Management*, *Towson Journal of International Affairs*, *Journal of the American Society of Professional Emergency Planners*, and the *Journal of International and Public Affairs*. His articles in *Disaster Prevention and Management* have received Highly Commended and Outstanding Paper awards.

Dr. McEntire completed an instructor guide on disaster response operations for the Federal Emergency Management Agency (FEMA). He has also published chapters in the *Handbook of Disaster Research* (Springer), the *Handbook of Disaster Management* (CRC Press), *Emergency Management: Principles and Practices for Local Government* (ICMA), *Critical Issues in Homeland Security* (Westview Press), *Handbook of Emergency Response* (CRC Press), *Preparedness and Response for Catastrophic Events* (CRC Press), and *Critical Issues in Disaster Science and Management* (FEMA).

Dr. McEntire received grants to conduct terrorism-response training for FEMA in Arkansas and Oklahoma. He has been a contributing author for a study of Texas Homeland Security Preparedness for the Century Foundation as well as three IQ reports for the International City/County Management Association. McEntire has presented papers in Mexico and Norway, at the National Science Foundation, at the National Academy of Sciences, and at the Higher Education Conference at FEMA's Emergency Management Institute in Emmitsburg, Maryland.

He is a member of Congressman Burgess' Homeland Security Advisory Board, FEMA Region VI Advisory Board, ICMA's Advisory Board, and the Fire Protection Publications Advisory Board. He has reviewed books for several publishers and is on the editorial staff for the *Journal of Emergency Management.*

Prior to coming to the University of North Texas, he attended the Graduate School of International Studies at the University of Denver. While pursuing his degree, he worked for the International and Emergency Services Departments at the American Red Cross.

Dr. McEntire was recognized as the 2010 Dr. B. Wayne Blanchard Award Recipient for Academic Excellence in Emergency Management Higher Education.

Contact information
Emergency Administration and Planning
Department of Public Administration
University of North Texas
1155 Union Circle, 310617
Denton, TX 76203-1340
(940) 565-2996
mcentire@unt.edu

# FOREWORD

Listen to the voices of family members. Listen to them describe the fear they felt and the protective actions they took just prior to their home being ripped apart by the tornado. When? Perhaps it was May, 2014. Perhaps it was a year or two before in Missouri. Or maybe it was Alabama or Tennessee. The locations and dates are less important than the fact that researchers were there to record their experiences and carefully juxtapose them with those of others. And collectively they are added to the scientific knowledge base about disaster response and recovery.

Dr. David A. McEntire has assessed and integrated these types of research findings from hurricanes like Katrina and, more recently, Sandy. We now marvel at the opening of the 9/11 museum dedicated to those who died and were injured during those terrible attacks. This structure, like so many others around the country, stands as a testament to the resilience of our nation, our national character. And as we hear of raging wildfires in California, miners dying again in places like Turkey, or those still struggling all these years after the destruction brought to Haiti, we are reminded again of why *Disaster Response and Recovery* are so important—so essential to resilience.

For decades, a slowly accumulating knowledge base was being constructed by scholars within numerous academic disciplines, especially sociology, geography, political science, and public administration. And today, those charged with the responsibility of preparing for, responding to, recovering from, and mitigating future disasters, explicitly recognize the need to transfer this knowledge base into their rapidly emerging profession.

The second edition of this outstanding book will assist in enhancing the resilience of communities as it brings this knowledge base to those of the front lines. Updated examples across the gamut of recent disasters, including earthquakes, hurricanes, tornadoes, wildfires and the like, will assist emergency managers, both those practicing and those preparing to enter the profession. Dr. McEntire outlines specific strategies and tactics for guiding the required interagency coordination that forms the very core of any disaster response. He skillfully takes the reader through both the horizontal and vertical layers of community organizations that link local jurisdictions to the resources of the state and federal governments. With this in-depth, but highly readable presentation of these and related topics, the entire profession may attain enhanced levels of competence and legitimacy.

Dr. McEntire directed the highly regarded emergency management program at the University of North Texas for several years. There he successfully blended the methods and theories of the academy with the needs of those working in local communities both in government agencies and in private organizations. Through his initial doctoral studies at the University of Denver, his superb work at North Texas, and numerous FEMA funded projects designed to assist other emergency management faculty worldwide, he has brought the perfect blend of experiences to this text. Self-evaluations are encouraged within each chapter; these are facilitated with careful specification of key concepts and lessons learned.

As such, this updated second edition of an excellent text will be an invaluable resource for all who practice this profession. They, like the public they seek to protect, are indebted to Dr. McEntire for this unique contribution.

**Thomas E. Drabek**
*John Evans Professor, Emeritus*
*Department of Sociology and Criminology*
*University of Denver*

# PREFACE

There is a growing sense among scholars and practitioners that greater emphasis needs to be placed on prevention and mitigation activities in the increasingly important profession of emergency management. Recurring hazards, new threats, rising losses, and further vulnerability all lead to the inescapable conclusion that a proactive approach to disasters is undeniably warranted.

At the same time, it is also necessary to recognize that response and recovery operations will always be required—to some degree or another—after earthquakes, hazardous materials spills, or terrorist attacks. Furthermore, as the reaction to Hurricane Katrina illustrates, there is ample room for improvement in how we deal with disasters. At least some of the mistakes made in New Orleans could have been avoided if the extensive disaster literature had been heeded by politicians, public servants, corporations, nonprofit agencies, and citizens alike. In addition, there is no doubt that postdisaster functions also have an immediate or long-term impact on the protection of life, property, and the environment as well as the minimization of human suffering and social disruption.

For these reasons, *Disaster Response and Recovery: Strategies and Tactics for Resilience* has been written. Its goal is to integrate the lessons provided by both researchers and professionals, updating the field with current studies and practical guidelines. Rather than address these reactive phases as if they were the only responsibilities of today's emergency managers, this book attempts to illustrate that successful warning, evacuation, and other disaster functions require careful implementation as well as advanced preparedness measures. Recovery likewise provides a prime opportunity to implement change, thereby reducing the probability and consequences of future disasters.

Of course, no book can provide sufficient or fail-proof ideas on how to react successfully to the complexities of today's disasters, and the reader should not consider the information in this text to be the best or only way to respond to or recover from deadly, destructive, and disruptive events. In spite of this fact, it is hoped that this volume will be of benefit to students, emergency managers, and others interested or involved in disaster management.

In order to meet these goals, *Disaster Response and Recovery* provides a thorough review of the challenges confronting emergency managers (and others) after disasters and discusses recommendations for their resolution.

▲ Chapter 1 shares background information about disasters, emergency management, and types of hazards and their interaction. Chapter 1 likewise discusses the consequences of disasters so you may know what to expect in their aftermath.

▲ Chapter 2 helps you recognize the large number of individuals and agencies that participate in response and recovery operations. This includes public servants, government departments, private and nonprofit organizations, and citizen volunteers.

▲ Chapter 3 covers human behavior in time of collective stress. It challenges widely held views and offers a more accurate view of disaster behavior.

▲ Chapter 4 identifies two theoretical approaches to the management of disasters. The advantages and disadvantages of the traditional and professional models are also explored.

▲ Chapter 5 mentions how the initial steps of hazard detection, warning, evacuation, and sheltering may protect people's lives.

▲ Chapter 6 discusses several disaster functions including search and rescue, emergency medical care, mass fatality management, and stress counseling. It describes how best to care for those who have been affected by disasters.

▲ Chapter 7 explains what can be done to successfully deal with the media, donations, and volunteers after a disaster. It will help you know how to manage public relations and community resources.

▲ At this point, the book transitions from response to recovery. Damage assessment, disaster declarations, and debris management are the topics covered in Chapter 8.

▲ In Chapter 9, the process of recovery is investigated along with its relation to mitigation. The types of disaster assistance programs are uncovered along with ways to reduce vulnerability.

▲ Typical problems during response and recovery operations are exposed in Chapter 10. The difficulties associated with communication, coordination, decision making, transportation, politics, special populations, legal issues, and record keeping are explained to help you fulfill your obligations as an emergency manager.

▲ Chapter 11 points out that technology and organization will improve disaster management and coordination among pertinent actors.

▲ Chapter 12 helps you understand the challenges of the future by looking at the lessons of prior disasters and the nature of emerging threats.

▲ The final chapter of the book focuses on how to develop disaster resilience. It underscores the value of preparedness, spontaneous planning, improvisation, leadership, and professionalism for you as an emergency manager.

## Learning and Teaching Aids

While reading each of the chapters, you will find helpful aids whether you are a student or an instructor.

**Starting Point/Pretest**: This assessment tool is an online test delivered through the book's companion web site. It enables you to focus reading comprehension on the areas where you are weakest.

**"What You'll Learn…" and "After Studying This Chapter…"**: These bulleted lists describe the topics to be covered in each chapter.

**Goals and Outcomes**: This bulleted list makes explicit the learning objectives for each chapter.

**For Example boxes**: Real-world cases or situations that illustrate the central points of each section of the chapter.

**Self Check Questions**: These inquiries help the student review the material presented in each section of the chapter before continuing on with the remainder of the text.

**Key Terms**: A list of major concepts, including definitions, is provided at the end of each chapter.

**Summary Questions**: True/false or multiple choice questions that capture the main points of each chapter to test student mastery of key issues and content.

**Review Questions**: Short-answer questions that remind the student of the central concepts and recommendations covered in each section of the chapter.

**Applying This Chapter Questions**: Short-answer questions that invite the student to consider new situations and how they would deal with alternative scenarios.

**You Try It!**: Open-ended questions that allow the students to go beyond the information presented in the text and examine how they would react to real-world experiences.

**Assess Your Understanding/Post-test**: This final test for the chapter is also online in the text's web site. It repeats the initial test questions in order to illustrate achievement made while reading the chapter.

# ACKNOWLEDGMENTS

Appreciation is expressed to several organizations and individuals that have helped significantly in the development of *Disaster Response and Recovery*. Although I alone am responsible for the content of this book, I am indebted first and foremost to the Federal Emergency Management Agency for a grant that made much of the research for this text possible. Gratitude is also conveyed to Wayne Blanchard, the former FEMA Higher Education Program Manager, for his ideas and insight regarding the theoretical and practical nature of postdisaster emergency management operations.

Special recognition is also warranted for the contributions of Siddik Ekici, Sarah Mathis, and Kristina Cramb, three graduate students in the Department of Public Administration at the University of North Texas. These dedicated research assistants eagerly assembled additional information and materials that were omitted during the initial literature review search. They also provided helpful case studies and worked on the extensive bibliography for this book.

I am also thankful for the knowledge and expertise of several scholars and practitioners that provided useful recommendations on earlier drafts of the book. These reviewers included Danny Peterson (Arizona State University), Phil Politano (Onondaga Community College), James Richardson (San Antonio Community College), William L. Waugh Jr. (Georgia State University), Cherlyn Wilhelmsen (University of Idaho), and Stacy Lynn Willet (University of Akron). The constructive advice of Gregg Dawson, Steve Reddish, Leland Baker, and other professional emergency managers is likewise noted.

I also wish to recognize my wonderful daughters, Ashley Layton and Kailey Birchall, for their assistance in developing the supplementary materials for the text. Their contributions have definitely made an overwhelming task more manageable.

Finally, Wiley's staff, including Karyn Drews, Laura Town, and Jorkill Almanza, and Project Manager, Sandeep Kumar of SPi Global deserve credit for their time-consuming preparation of this manuscript for publication. While every effort has been taken to produce an accurate portrayal of response and recovery activities and to incorporate appropriate citations, it is possible that mistakes or errors remain present. Should this be the case, the reader is encouraged to share thoughts on the book with the author.

**David A. McEntire, Ph.D.**
*Emergency Administration and Planning*
*Department of Public Administration*
*University of North Texas*
*1155 Union Circle, #310617*
*Denton, Texas 76203-5017*
*mcentire@unt.edu*

# 1

# KNOWING WHAT TO EXPECT
## Hazards, Vulnerability, and Disasters

## Starting Point

Pretest to assess your knowledge on hazards, vulnerability, and disasters.
*Determine where you need to concentrate your effort.*

## What You'll Learn in This Chapter

▲ Differences between accidents, emergencies, and disasters
▲ General emergency management responsibilities
▲ Types of natural, technological, and anthropogenic hazards
▲ The interaction of hazards and vulnerability
▲ The nature and impact of disasters
▲ The need for response and recovery operations

## After Studying This Chapter, You'll Be Able To

▲ Understand the diverse sizes and scope of disasters.
▲ Differentiate among the diverse hazard categories.
▲ Comprehend the relation among hazards, vulnerability, and disasters.
▲ Examine the overlap between response and recovery operations.
▲ Identify demands to be met in a disaster.

## Goals and Outcomes

▲ Compare and contrast different disaster magnitudes.
▲ Define and use basic disaster and emergency management terminology.
▲ Evaluate distinct types of hazards as well as common disaster characteristics.
▲ Predict changes resulting from disasters.
▲ Evaluate the importance of response and recovery operations.

*Disaster Response and Recovery: Strategies and Tactics for Resilience*, Second Edition. David A. McEntire.
© 2015 John Wiley & Sons, Inc. Published 2015 by John Wiley & Sons, Inc.

# INTRODUCTION

Welcome to the intriguing disaster discipline and the indispensable response and recovery profession! As a current or future emergency manager, it is crucial that you are aware of the important concepts relating to your vital duties and responsibilities. It is especially imperative that you are able to distinguish among differing disaster magnitudes as well as the factors that lead to and exacerbate these devastating events. For instance, it is vital that you understand natural, technological, and civil/conflict hazards as well as how they interact with the vulnerabilities humans create in society. Comprehending the consequences of disasters and the changes that take place when they occur is likewise necessary if you are to be able to react to them effectively. Being cognizant of the goals pertaining to response and recovery operations will also help you become a successful emergency manager. These topics are addressed in this introductory chapter of *Disaster Response and Recovery: Strategies and Tactics of Resilience*.

## 1.1 The Occurrence of Disasters

Everyday people around the world are impacted by events that produce injuries, cause death, destroy personal belongings, and interrupt daily activities. These disturbing experiences are categorized as accidents, crises, emergencies, disasters, calamities, or catastrophes. Such incidents adversely affect individuals, groups, communities, and even nations. Each of these events is similar in that they require action from government officials, businesses, nonprofit organizations, citizens and bystanders, and the victims and survivors themselves. However, these occurrences vary dramatically in terms of magnitude, extent of duration, and scope. For example, a traffic accident can typically be handled within minutes by a few police officers who file reports and a tow truck that removes wreckage. A structural conflagration may require one or two fire departments, but it can displace the resident or family for weeks or months. When a mass shooting occurs, resources are needed to neutralize the threat, investigate the incident, and address the longer-term psychological toll that may possibly result from these intentional acts of violence. Alternatively, an airplane crash may necessitate the participation of firefighters and emergency medical service (EMS) personnel as well as airline officials and government employees such as a coroner or public information officer. If the plane crash does not take everyone's life, the victims and survivors of the ordeal may be injured or permanently disabled and require long-term care. Finally, when a major earthquake or hurricane affects an urban area, many organizations will become involved. Besides first responders, additional personnel will be needed to remove debris, repair utilities, provide relief assistance, and coordinate rebuilding endeavors that could take years. Thus, the impact of a minor accident is both quantitatively and qualitatively different than a major disaster or catastrophe (see Table 1-1) (Quarantelli, 2006). While this book does discuss common emergencies and less frequent catastrophes, it focuses most of its attention on disasters.

**Table 1-1: Comparison of Event Magnitude**

|  | Accidents | Crises | Emergencies/ disasters | Calamities/ catastrophes |
|---|---|---|---|---|
| Injuries | Few | Many | Scores/ hundreds | Thousands/ more |
| Deaths | Few | Many | Scores/ hundreds | Thousands/ more |
| Damage | Minor | Moderate | Major | Severe |
| Disruption | Minor | Moderate | Major | Severe |
| Geographic impact | Immediate area | Local community | Regional | National/ international |
| Availability of resources | Abundant | Sufficient | Limited | Scarce |
| Number of responders | Few | Many | Scores/ hundreds | Thousands/ more |
| Time to recover | Minutes/ hours/days | Days/weeks | Months/years | Years/decades |

### 1.1.1 Important Concepts

**Disasters** are defined as deadly, destructive, and disruptive events that occur when a hazard interacts with human vulnerability. Disasters are significant societal events that injure and kill people, damage infrastructure and personal property, and complicate the routine activities people undertake on a daily basis (e.g., bathing, cooking, traveling, going to school, working, etc.).

There are two major types of variables that collide to produce a disaster. A **hazard** is the threat or trigger that initiates a disaster. Hazards include natural, technological, or anthropogenic (human-induced) agents like earthquakes, industrial explosions, and even terrorist attacks that negatively affect people or critical infrastructure. **Vulnerability**, on the other hand, refers to the proneness of people to disasters based on factors such as their geographic location, exposure of property, and level of income or other social variables. The ability of individuals, organizations, and communities to deal with disaster also determines the degree of vulnerability. Vulnerability is therefore closely related to the human element of disasters, while hazards may or may not always have a direct social cause.

While disasters result from the interaction of both hazards and vulnerability, the two concepts have distinct implications for practical application. Because hazards are not always controllable, people and organizations should give extra attention to efforts that reduce their vulnerability to disasters. For this reason, the knowledge and expertise of individuals that are employed in emergency management and

**Figure 1-1**

Emergency management personnel often attend meetings to discuss important emergency management issues and prepare for future disasters.
Michael Rieger/FEMA.

related professions are required to deal effectively with mass emergencies, disasters, calamities, and catastrophes (Figure 1-1).

From an academic standpoint, **emergency management** "is the study of how humans and their institutions deal with hazards, vulnerabilities and the events that result from their interaction" (Jensen, 2013). The emergency management discipline accordingly seeks to advance knowledge about what people and organizations can do to diminish the frequency and impact of disasters. From a practical perspective, **emergency management** "is the managerial function charged with creating the framework within which communities reduce vulnerability to hazards and cope with disasters" (Blanchard et al., 2007, p. 4). This suggests that highly educated and trained individuals have been given the responsibility to advance the goals of emergency management. These professionals are known as emergency managers.

**Emergency managers** are public servants that help jurisdictions reduce the liabilities and vulnerabilities that lead to disasters. These government employees work closely with many concerned stakeholders and endeavor to build capabilities to deal more effectively with hazards and disasters. Such efforts are commonly described as the disaster life cycle or the four phases of emergency management. This includes mitigation, preparedness, response, and recovery:

▲ **Mitigation** refers to several things, including risk reduction, loss minimization, or the alleviation of potential negative impacts associated with disasters. Careful land-use planning, improvements in building design and construction, and a reliance on insurance are examples of mitigation activities.

▲ **Preparedness** implies efforts to increase readiness for a disaster. Examples of preparedness initiatives include grant and resource acquisition, planning, training, exercises, and community education.

Mitigation and preparedness should be given the highest priority in the emergency management profession today. For this reason, emergency managers must not be seen solely as an extension of **first responders**—police, fire, and emergency medical personnel. The goals of emergency managers are more proactive and encompassing, even if they do overlap with the objectives and operations of first responders at times.

However, because it is impossible to eliminate all disasters, emergency managers must also be involved in disaster response and recovery operations. **Disaster response** is action "taken immediately before, during, or directly after an emergency occurs, to save lives [and] minimize damage to property" (Godschalk, 1991, p. 136). Examples of disaster response activities include:

▲ Warning people of severe weather
▲ Evacuating those considered to be at risk
▲ Sheltering the affected population

During response, it may also be necessary to provide emergency medical care, relay information to the public, and manage the arrival of donations and volunteers.

**Disaster recovery**, in contrast, consists of actions "to return vital life support systems to minimum operating standards and long-term activity designed to return life to normal or improved levels" (Godschalk, 1991, p. 136). This incorporates efforts to repair homes damaged by disaster and rebuild community infrastructure such as power lines, roads, and courthouses.

Each of the phases described in Section 1.1.1 is closely related to the others (Neal, 1997). For instance, it is difficult to separate mitigation from preparedness as both are proactive measures to reduce the impact of disaster. Preparedness also has a significant influence upon the success of postdisaster management since it enables a community to anticipate response and recovery needs. In addition, it is difficult to determine when response ends and recovery begins. For instance, are damage assessment and debris removal part of disaster response or disaster recovery operations? Also, during recovery, it is vitally important that steps be taken to prevent future disasters or minimize their potential impact. Instead of simply rebuilding homes that have been damaged by a flood or a tornado, it may be necessary to relocate them to safer areas or implement more stringent construction requirements. For these reasons, the word "phases" may be somewhat misleading. With this in mind, it may be advisable to substitute "phases" with the term "functional areas" or "functional activities." Also, these areas or activities of emergency management do not appear in a neat, linear fashion so it is difficult to separate them conceptually.

It is also imperative that emergency managers are aware of other important concepts related to their profession. New terms have been introduced recently in emergency management due to the rising threat of terrorism and the advent of homeland security. **Homeland security** was initially defined as "a concerted national effort to prevent terrorist attacks within the United States, reduce America's vulnerability to terrorism, and recover from and minimize the damage of attacks that do occur" (Office of Homeland Security, 2002, p. 2). This concept encompasses other important terms such as prevention and protection. **Prevention** refers to actions to stop the occurrence of terrorist attacks. It includes the gathering of intelligence, counterterrorism operations, and border control functions. **Protection**, on the other hand, is more concerned about actions that discourage attacks through increased security measures or efforts to minimize damage if such attacks cannot be prevented in the first place. The reliance on guards, fences, video surveillance, and access control falls into this category.

### 1.1.2  Preview of Disaster Response and Recovery

As indicated by the title, this book describes strategies and tactics to improve the management of disaster response and recovery operations. This decision is not meant to deny the value of functions relating to mitigation, preparedness, prevention, and protection. It is instead based on the assumption that there is a need for an up-to-date textbook about postdisaster activities. Although there are some great works on this subject already, some may lack current information or approach the material from an academic or practical standpoint only. Also, response and recovery operations have changed significantly over the last decade or two and even more substantially in recent years. The informative research generated by disaster scholars over the years likewise needs to be integrated with the extensive experience of professional emergency managers. Furthermore, there is a dire need to educate government leaders and public servants in order to avert the repetition of mistakes made after Hurricane Katrina and other disasters. Nevertheless, this book may also be of use to corporate personnel or humanitarian workers who are also involved in response and recovery operations.

In order to meet these goals, *Disaster Response and Recovery: Strategies and Tactics of Resilience* will provide a comprehensive discussion about postdisaster management issues and recommendations for their improvement. Chapter 2 will help you as an emergency manager identify the actors involved in response and recovery operations. This includes government officials and agencies as well as corporations, nonprofit organizations, and even ordinary citizens. Chapter 3 discusses human behavior in time of disaster. It dispels widely held myths and illustrates typical social reactions to collective stress. Chapter 4 compares alternative theoretical stances regarding the management of disasters. It acknowledges the strengths and weaknesses of traditional and professional approaches. Chapter 5 covers initial response measures, and it provides ideas on how to protect people through hazard detection, warning, evacuation, and sheltering. Chapter 6 lists steps that can be taken to care for those who have been adversely affected by a disaster. This chapter shares information about search and rescue, emergency medical care, fatality management, and psychological stress. Chapter 7 gives recommendations on how to manage public relations and community resources. In particular, it discusses how you can effectively manage the media, donations, and volunteers after a disaster. The transition from response to recovery is the subject of Chapter 8. It assesses functions such as damage assessment, disaster declarations, and debris removal. In Chapter 9, disaster assistance programs are discussed along with ways to reduce vulnerability. This chapter provides information on recovery and how this functional activity can be linked to mitigation. The challenges of response and recovery are exposed in Chapter 10. It will help you understand difficulties associated with communications, decision making, transportation, politics, special populations, legal issues, and record keeping. Chapter 11 points out tools that can be employed during response and recovery operations. These include technological equipment as well as organizational arrangements (e.g., incident command, emergency operation centers) that will improve coordination. Chapter 12 covers lessons from prior disasters along with new threats and reasons for rising vulnerability. It attempts to help you think critically about the future of emergency management. The final chapter of the book illustrates ways to foster disaster resilience. Chapter 13 discusses various aspects of disaster preparedness in addition to the importance of improvisation, leadership, and professionalism among emergency managers.

Before proceeding with the outlined direction of the book, the remainder of this initial chapter will provide additional information about the types of hazards and how they interact one with another. It also describes the impact of disasters and what you as an emergency manager can expect in their aftermath.

## SELF-CHECK

- What types of disruptive events can occur on a daily basis?
- How are they different from one another?
- What is a disaster and what are their causes?
- What is emergency management?
- How is response defined?
- What is recovery?

## 1.2 Types of Hazards

As an emergency manager who may be involved in disaster response and recovery operations, you must understand the nature of hazards if you are to be successful with your assigned responsibilities. As discussed earlier, a **hazard** is a physical, technological, or anthropogenic agent such as an earthquake, a chemical release, or a violent act. These hazardous events occur in the United States and around the world. Floods, tornadoes, and earthquakes occur, leaving buildings in rubble and other property damage. Vehicles collide due to careless drivers or in conjunction with poor weather conditions. Trains derail due to a mechanical failure of the tracks or human error by the engineer. Petrochemical facilities include large amounts of hazardous materials, sometimes leading to an explosion at the industrial complex. Terrorists detonate improvised explosive devices, producing carnage and fear in their wake. Hazards occur for many different reasons. Some hazards occur naturally in the environment, while others are the result of human activity, neglect of safety precautions, unanticipated mistakes, or malicious intent.

### 1.2.1  Natural Hazards

**Natural hazards** are those events originating from the physical environment, typically because of radiation from the sun, heat flow within the earth, or the force of gravity. Natural hazards occur in and across three arenas of action (Mileti, 1999):

▲ The atmosphere (the air surrounding the earth that is made up of various gasses)
▲ The hydrosphere (the earth's water system)
▲ The lithosphere (the earth's crust)

Natural hazards are classified as having atmospheric, geologic, hydrologic, seismic, volcanic, and wildfire origins. There are also other types of natural hazards that will be described in Sections 1.2.2–1.2.7.

### 1.2.2  Atmospheric Hazards

An **atmospheric hazard** is a hazard agent that is produced in or by the earth's atmosphere. A hurricane is one type of atmospheric hazard (Figure 1-2). Hurricanes begin as tropical depressions in the Atlantic Ocean and form as low-pressure systems due to the warm water that fuels them. When wind speeds top 74 mph, such

**Figure 1-2**

Hurricane Sandy and struck the northeast destroyed this roller coaster on the boardwalk in Seaside Heights, NJ. Liz Roll/FEMA.

**Table 1-2: Saffir–Simpson Hurricane Scale**

| Category | Sustained winds | Types of damage due to hurricane winds |
|---|---|---|
| 1 | 74–95 mph<br>64–82 kt<br>119–153 km/h | **Very dangerous winds will produce some damage:** well-constructed frame homes could have damage to roof, shingles, vinyl siding, and gutters. Large branches of trees will snap and shallowly rooted trees may be toppled. Extensive damage to power lines and poles likely will result in power outages that could last a few to several days |
| 2 | 96–110 mph<br>83–95 kt<br>154–177 km/h | **Extremely dangerous winds will cause extensive damage:** well-constructed frame homes could sustain major roof and siding damage. Many shallowly rooted trees will be snapped or uprooted and block numerous roads. Near-total power loss is expected with outages that could last from several days to weeks |
| 3 (major) | 111–129 mph<br>96–112 kt<br>178–208 km/h | **Devastating damage will occur:** well-built framed homes may incur major damage or removal of roof decking and gable ends. Many trees will be snapped or uprooted, blocking numerous roads. Electricity and water will be unavailable for several days to weeks after the storm passes |
| 4 (major) | 130–156 mph<br>113–136 kt<br>209–251 km/h | **Catastrophic damage will occur:** well-built framed homes can sustain severe damage with loss of most of the roof structure and/or some exterior walls. Most trees will be snapped or uprooted and power poles downed. Fallen trees and power poles will isolate residential areas. Power outages will last weeks to possibly months. Most of the area will be uninhabitable for weeks or months |
| 5 (major) | 157 mph or higher<br>137 kt or higher<br>252 km/h or higher | **Catastrophic damage will occur:** a high percentage of framed homes will be destroyed, with total roof failure and wall collapse. Fallen trees and power poles will isolate residential areas. Power outages will last for weeks to possibly months. Most of the area will be uninhabitable for weeks or months |

tropical depressions become known hurricanes. In the Indian Ocean, these storm systems are known as cyclones, and in the Pacific Ocean, they are labeled typhoons. The eye or center of these storms is somewhat calm, but it is surrounded by circling cloud bands that produce rain in large amounts. Some hurricanes may have winds in excess of 100 or even 200 mph, and they may produce a storm surge of up to 24 feet. In the Northern Hemisphere, hurricanes rotate in a counterclockwise direction and travel in a west–northwesterly direction. They frequently hit Atlantic states and those along the Gulf Coast. The strength of a hurricane is listed under the Saffir–Simpson scale. The **Saffir–Simpson scale** is a descriptive tool to explain the magnitude of a hurricane in terms of wind and storm surge. It includes five categories. Category 1 is the weakest, while Category 5 is the strongest (see Table 1-2).

This scale estimates potential property damage. Hurricanes reaching Category 3 and higher are considered major hurricanes because of their potential for significant loss of life and damage. Category 1 and 2 storms are still dangerous, however, and require preparatory measures. In the western North Pacific, the term "super typhoon" is used for tropical cyclones with sustained winds exceeding 150 mph.

Florida is one of many states that experiences hurricanes. Hurricane Andrew made landfall on August 24, 1992, and its strong winds devastated the Miami-Dade area. This hurricane produced dozens of deaths and left thousands of people without power and shelter. Weak building codes and poor enforcement resulted in major structural collapses and a debris management nightmare. Hurricane Andrew's impact on Florida was surpassed by four hurricanes and one tropical storm that hit Florida in 2004. This was one of the worst hurricane seasons on record. However, all of these hurricanes combined did not cause as many deaths as a cyclone that hit Bangladesh in 1970. It killed as many as 300,000 people.

A thunderstorm is another atmospheric hazard. Thunderstorms are produced when warm, moist air rises through convection (thermal uplift). They also occur along cold and warm fronts where different air masses collide or when clouds traverse mountain chains (i.e., orographic lifting). When a thunderstorm cell forms (cumulus and cumulonimbus clouds), air rises and then descends quickly leading to rain, sometimes in copious amounts.

## FOR EXAMPLE

### Hurricane Ike's Impact

In September 2008, Hurricane Ike became the third most costly hurricane in U.S. history. It affected a number of states including Mississippi, Louisiana, and Texas. In terms of impact, damage amounted to over $37 billion and fatalities numbered nearly 200. Obtaining food for those directly affected was a great concern following the disaster. Another major lesson was the need to improve communication and coordination between public agencies so that recovery could proceed smoothly. Even 2 years later, Texas was still working hard to rebuild what was destroyed by Hurricane Ike.

Depending on weather conditions and temperatures, the vertical movement of air also freezes water droplets that fall to the earth as hail. Most hail is small (pea size), but it can be large at times (baseball or even grapefruit size). Hail can damage the roofs of buildings, destroy car windshields, and even kill those that are struck by it. Some of the most costly natural disasters are hailstorms such as the one that hit Fort Worth, Texas, during a 1995 Mayfest celebration. It resulted in at least $1 billion in losses. Over 100 people had to be taken to area hospitals after being struck by softball-sized hailstones.

Thunderstorms also result in downdrafts and straight-line winds (which travel down to the ground and then move horizontally along the earth's surface). Such winds travel quickly and can slam airplanes to the ground and flatten fences and barns. Thunderstorms are common around the world. There are over 16,000 thunderstorms per year in all locations excluding the North and South Poles. In the United States, strong thunderstorms occur frequently along the Gulf Coast or in the Midwestern states. Such storms also generate lightning, which is the emission of electrical bolts from clouds as a result of the interaction of positively and negatively charged fields. Approximately 6000 lightning strikes occur every minute around the world. Lightning often hits buildings, trees, and the ground. Because the temperature of the bolt is extremely hot (perhaps up to 50,000 degrees Celsius), people can be killed. Burns, respiratory failure, and cardiac arrest result from lightning strikes. Forests may also be ignited with fire due to lightning.

Tornadoes are another type of atmospheric hazard. Tornadoes are closely associated with thunderstorms. In fact, the name "tornado" stems from the Spanish name for such storms. As warm, moist air collides against cool, dry air, winds may move in a circular or rotating direction. One portion of the rotating air shaft drops, while the other portion moves upward in a vertical manner. When the resulting funnel reaches the ground, it becomes known as a tornado. The speed of winds is the factor used to describe the strength of tornadoes under the Enhanced Fujita Scale. The **Enhanced Fujita Scale** is a scale used to categorize the size of a tornado, including the affiliated wind speed. (see Table 1-3). Small tornadoes (e.g., F0 or F1) are very common but possess slower wind speeds (e.g., 65 mph). Large tornadoes (e.g., F4 or F5) are infrequent, but their wind speed reaches over 200 mph. At such high speeds, windows are broken, roofs are ripped from walls, and even foundations can be sucked from their moorings. Glass, brick, two-by-fours, and even cars become missiles and may penetrate other structures. The large F5 tornado that struck Joplin, Missouri, in May 2011 became the costliest tornado in U.S. history. Damages in this disaster amounted to over $2.5 billion. St. John's Regional Medical Center was one of the larger building structures that received extensive damage. Over 150 people were killed due to this massive tornado.

Tornadoes are very common to the Midwest portion of the United States due to the movement of the jet stream and the collision of air from Canada and the Gulf of Mexico. In fact, 90% of the world's tornadoes take place in the United States (roughly 500–600 per year). Oklahoma has been especially hard hit, as was the case on May 3–5, 1999. Fifty-nine tornadoes were reported in central Oklahoma during this period, and many of them lasted several minutes and traveled great distances. At least 40 people were killed during the outbreak and 675 people were injured. Over 10,000 homes were also damaged or destroyed. Losses were estimated at $1.2 billion. Oklahoma has experienced numerous tornadoes, including three that traveled

### Table 1-3: Enhanced Fujita Scale for Tornado Damage

| | Fujita scale | | | Derived EF scale | | Operational EF scale | |
| --- | --- | --- | --- | --- | --- | --- | --- |
| F number | Fastest 1/4 mile (mph) | 3 second gust (mph) | EF number | 3 second gust (mph) | EF number | 3 second gust (mph) | |
| 0 | 40–72 | 45–78 | 0 | 65–85 | 0 | 65–85 | |
| 1 | 73–112 | 79–117 | 1 | 86–109 | 1 | 86–110 | |
| 2 | 113–157 | 118–161 | 2 | 110–137 | 2 | 111–135 | |
| 3 | 158–207 | 162–209 | 3 | 138–167 | 3 | 136–165 | |
| 4 | 208–260 | 210–261 | 4 | 168–199 | 4 | 166–200 | |
| 5 | 261–318 | 262–317 | 5 | 200–234 | 5 | Over 200 | |

**Important note about enhanced F-scale winds:** The enhanced F scale still is a set of wind estimates (not measurements) based on damage. It uses 3 second gusts estimated at the point of damage and estimates vary with height and exposure. The 3 second gust is not the same wind as in standard surface observations. Standard measurements are taken by weather stations in open exposures.

almost the same paths in the City of Moore in the past 15 years. While the central portion of the country is known as tornado alley, it should be pointed out that these storms have occurred in many locations around the United States.

Winter storms are atmospheric hazards that occur mainly in December, January, and February in the United States. Winter storms include snow, sleet, and ice and are associated with extremely cold temperatures (Figure 1-3). Snowstorms include fluffy flakes of water that has frozen as it falls to the ground. Sleet is sometimes difficult to distinguish from ice storms, although sleet has more water in liquid state than ice storms. In either case, sleet and ice storms will cause very dangerous conditions when they accumulate on the ground. Although winter storms occur most frequently in the northern, central, and western portions of the United States, it is possible for lower states to receive snow periodically. Even ice storms are not excluded from places like Louisiana and Texas.

A very damaging ice storm took place along the U.S.–Canadian border in January 1998. Ice piled up several times higher than prior records, and many power lines and transmission towers collapsed due to the excessive weight of thick ice. The storm revealed just how vulnerable infrastructure can be to the forces of nature. Similar problems occur with excessive snow. On January 28, 1977, Buffalo, New York, received 93 inches of snow. This is an amount greater than the average for that area during the entire year. Snowstorms can turn into blizzards if they are associated high winds. Such storms can leave several inches or feet of snow on the ground, making transportation difficult. When snow falls on steep slopes, the potential for avalanche may result. Avalanches are quick and violent movements of snow down the mountainside. They are common in Washington, Utah, and Colorado. The characteristics of snow, changing temperatures, wind, skiers, and

**Figure 1-3**

Severe weather can take people by surprise and cause damages to trees, homes, and infrastructure. This rare October 2011 nor-easter storm dumped massive amounts of snow in Connecticut. Darrell Habisch/FEMA.

snowmobiles can trigger avalanches. While snow and avalanches create several challenges, the cold temperatures also produce hypothermia in individuals who are exposed to such weather. In some cases, the heating or lighting of homes during winter storms may lead to fires that cause death and destruction.

A final atmospheric hazard to be discussed here is a heat wave. A heat wave is a prolonged period of high temperatures that may also be coupled with excessive humidity. Heat waves create loss of agricultural crops and also stress humans to the point that they cannot cool their bodies through the normal process of sweating. If relief from the weather or medical care is not given, coma, paralysis, and death will follow. For instance, around 700 deaths (mainly among the elderly) resulted from a prolonged heat wave in Chicago in July 1995. The danger of such events requires constant communication with the public. One of the things that need to be relayed is the **heat index**, which describes the severity of the situation. This index incorporates both temperature and humidity into a scale. It is used by meteorologists to help warn people to stay inside and drink lots of water.

### 1.2.3 Geological Hazards

**Geological hazards** are those hazard agents associated with the earth's soil and rock surfaces. Landslides are the most damaging kind of geological hazards. Landslides occur because of a number of variables such as slope angle, moisture content of the soil, and physiology of rock. The presence or absence of

FOR EXAMPLE

### Heat Wave in France

In August 2003, France experienced some of the highest minimum and maximum daily temperatures recorded in history. Because many families and physicians had taken time off from work during this typical vacation period, many elderly were left at home or without sufficient care in hospitals and nursing facilities. The lack of air-conditioning units in France combined with temperatures up to 104 degrees Fahrenheit and insufficient fluid intake resulted in the death of as many as 15,000 people. Heat waves such as this one are not always recognized as significant hazards, but their impact can be extensive as France discovered.

vegetation may also be a reason why landslides occur. Landslides may move swiftly and occur without warning or creep at a slow and perhaps unnoticeable pace. Such events are possible in any hilly or mountainous area but are probably most common along the Rocky Mountain region and the Pacific Coast. In 1983, a major landslide blocked a major highway in Thistle, Utah. The sediment and rock created an earthen dam that backed up a river and flooded a city. In 2005, a major portion of the mountain separated in La Conchita, California, and fell to the valley floor below. It buried 15 homes, damaged 16 others, and killed several individuals.

Besides landslides, there are also hazards related to subsidence and expansive soil. Subsidence occurs when the water table or underground rivers erode the soil around them and the earth collapses. This type of sinkhole is common in Florida (Figure 1-4). In August 2013, a sinkhole on Florida's surface swallowed parts of the Summer Bay Resort near Walt Disney World. The sinkhole was about 60 feet wide and 15 feet deep. Fortunately, those vacationing in the area were able to evacuate quickly as the building started to crumble and fall into the sinkhole. Another cause of subsidence is mining for coal and ore or the pumping of groundwater out of a certain geographic area. New Orleans and Mexico City are both sinking due to this latter activity. In contrast to subsidence, expansive soils may actually rise due to the presence of moisture in ground. This hazard is especially prevalent in locations that have clay soils. Although expansive soils are found most often in the south and west, they can be present in many parts of the United States. Expansive soils do not necessarily kill individuals, but they can create a large amount of property damage (especially to the foundations of buildings).

### 1.2.4 Hydrologic Hazards

**Hydrologic hazards** are hazard agents that emanate from the earth's water systems. There are four types of hydrologic hazards, one of them being floods. Floods are the most prevalent of any hazard—natural or otherwise. They are also among the most costly. Episodes of flooding occur when there is too much precipitation or where

Figure 1-4

This 45 foot-deep sinkhole formed in Monticello, FL, after Tropical Storm Debby produced excessive rains and flooding. David Fine/FEMA.

there is an inability for soil to absorb water that has fallen to the ground. Flooding can also result from melting snowpack, ice jams, and dam failures. Soil type, topography, and level of development have bearing on flooding. For instance, clay soils are more likely to produce runoff in comparison to sandy soils. Hills, valleys, and the use of cement in highly urbanized areas may also contribute to this type of hazard.

The 1993 great Midwestern flood is the most widespread and costly flood in U.S. history. Months of unusually wet weather and the seasonal snowmelt overwhelmed the Mississippi River Basin with water. Dykes, locks, and dams were eventually filled to capacity, and many of them were breached. The water emitted from broken levees only added to the flooding downstream. Thousands of people had to be evacuated and property losses totaled in the billions of dollars.

> ## FOR EXAMPLE
>
> ### The Sahel Drought and Famine
>
> From 1961 to 1990, several countries in the Sahel region of Africa experienced a significant decrease in rainfall. This transition zone between the Sahara Desert to the north and the tropical area to the south became even more arid, causing a sharp decline in agricultural production in the area. The large nomadic population, coupled with the overgrazing of animals, could not be sustained by the vegetation of the area. By 1974, over $350 in relief assistance had been provided by the international community. Nonetheless, 5 million head of livestock died due to the drought conditions. The situation was particularly devastating in that an estimated 300,000 people perished from the famine.

Storm surges and coastal erosion may result from hurricanes or other types of phenomena (e.g., low-pressure systems, strong winds, high tides, etc.). A storm surge is a temporary rise in the water level of an ocean or river estuary. Flooding is a product of storm surges, and it can take days and weeks before water recedes after such events. Coastal erosion may also occur as a result of storm surges, and it often damages roads, bridges, dunes, and beaches. Florida is frequently affected by storm surges and coastal erosion associated with hurricanes. Losses can amount to millions of dollars.

Droughts are another kind of hydrologic hazard. Low amounts of rainfall and high evaporation rates due to warm or hot temperatures lead to conditions of drought. Drought can have a major negative impact on agricultural output, thereby contributing to widespread famine. The Great Depression was triggered, in part, by severe drought. However, droughts do not typically result in a shortage of the overall food supply in the United States (although the provision of individual crops may be extremely low). In contrast, famines in other countries can be especially deadly. The lack of adequate food intake has resulted in malnourishment and the spread of fatal diseases in Ethiopia in the 1980s and Niger in the mid-2000s. Dust storms, desertification, and salinization of soil also result from droughts.

### 1.2.5 Seismic and Volcanic Hazards

**Seismic hazards** are hazard agents produced by the movement of tectonic plates that float on magma. Earthquakes are seismic hazards occurring along fault lines where landmasses move apart, collide, or slide against each other laterally. Earthquakes produce waves that travel in and on top of the earth. These waves emanate from the geographic origin of the earthquake, known as a focal point. The location on the earth's crust directly above the focal point is the epicenter. Earthquake intensity is measured with the **Richter scale**, a measurement of the registered shaking amplitudes. In contrast, the **Mercalli scale** is used to describe the physical observation of damages that result from the movement of the earth's crust (e.g., broken windows, cracked walls, falling pictures, etc.).

Earthquakes occur in every part of the world, although their probability is highest in places such as the ring of fire (around the Pacific Rim). In the United States, there are major fault lines in California, Utah, Illinois, and South Carolina and in New England. Earthquakes have likewise taken place along the New Madrid fault (stretching from Arkansas to Missouri and Tennessee) and have changed the course of the Mississippi River in the past. Additional destructive slips in this area are projected to occur in the future. Earthquake faults along the Pacific Coast are very active and have destroyed gas and water lines, roads and bridges, and homes and other structures. The 1989 Loma Prieta and 1994 Northridge earthquakes killed scores of individuals. Tens of thousands and even hundreds of thousands have perished in earthquakes in Mexico City, Russia, India, Iran, and Haiti. Building codes have historically been weak in these countries, resulting in additional building collapses when earthquakes occur and the crushing of their inhabitants. In 2013, the Sichuan province in China was the epicenter of a major earthquake. The movement of tectonic plates coupled with poor construction took 200 people's lives.

Tsunamis may be associated with underwater landslides and asteroids that impact the oceans, but they result most often from earthquake hazards. If fault lines slip under the ocean, the accompanying seismic waves displace water, which races vertically and horizontally away from the focal point. When these waves reach land, they become amplified on the surface. The resulting harbor waves may appear in a series of waves that may travel hundreds of feet to a few miles inland. These waves move rapidly (as fast as 500 mph) and may reach one or two stories in height. They level many of the buildings and much of infrastructure that lies in their path.

Tsunamis result in drowning and may sweep their victims out to sea as they recede. Hawaii and the northwestern coast of the United States are prone to tsunamis. One tsunami struck Hilo, Hawaii, in 1946 and another affected Alaska in 1964. Several deaths resulted in each event. The most powerful tsunami in history occurred on January 4, 2005. The Sumatra earthquake registered over 7.0 on the Richter scale; it sent powerful tsunami waves to over 12 countries surrounding the Indian Ocean. Over 300,000 people died from this tragic event. Another major tsunami occurred after an earthquake struck Japan in 2011. The tsunami that was generated had waves reaching over a 100 feet in some locations. The Tohoku earthquake and tsunami also damaged the Fukushima nuclear power plant and caused the release of radioactive material into the air. Almost 16,000 people were killed as a result of these combined hazards. This event illustrates how complex some disasters can be.

Volcanic activity is another type of natural hazard and it is closely related to earthquakes and the movement of magma within the earth's crust. Magma may bubble up through fissures in the earth surface, creating a cone with a reservoir of lava. These mountainous craters may vent superheated gasses and emit lava flows down the side of the cone. Volcanic eruptions can be particularly deadly, as was the case with Mt. St. Helens in 1980 (Figure 1-5). A bulge developed over time on the north face of Mt. St. Helens and eventually the growing pressure gave way in a violent explosion. Tons and tons of soil, lava, and mud were sent down the side of the mountain and into the valley and rivers below. Fifty-seven people were killed in the incident, being vaporized immediately, buried under volcanic debris, or drowned in lahars (violent mudflows). Volcanic ash also rained down on communities around the volcano and even in nearby states. This made some vehicles inoperable and caused a cleanup nightmare. In addition, the logging industry in this area was severely disrupted for a period of time due to the Mt. St. Helens eruption. In the United States, volcanic activity is present mainly in the Northwest and Hawaii.

## FOR EXAMPLE

### Nevado Del Ruiz

In November 1985, the 17,716 feet Nevado del Ruiz volcano in Western Columbia erupted, emitting an ash cloud that rose over 45,000 feet in the air. Superheated lava poured out of the crater, melting the snowcapped volcanic cone. The ash, lava, and water turned into a river of mud (known as a lahar) that raced down the mountainside toward the valley floor. This liquid avalanche was as high as 50 feet and moved up to 30 mph. It buried the city of Armero. Buildings were demolished and carried down the river channel or covered with tons of volcanic debris. When all was said and done, at least 20,000 were dead or missing. This volcanic hazard triggered one of the worst disasters in Columbia's history.

**Figure 1-5**

This picture of Mt. St. Helens on May 18, 1980, illustrates the significant risk posed by volcanic eruptions. NOAA News Photo.

### 1.2.6  Wildfire Hazards

**Wildfires** are hazards that result from lightning strikes and they can quickly envelop hundreds of acres of forest and brush. However, humans may also play a role in the ignition of wildfires due to carelessness with matches, cigarettes, grills, and campfires. High temperatures, drought conditions, low humidity in the air, and strong winds can cause wildfires to spread rapidly. This has been the case in major forest fires in Yellowstone National Park and in numerous other forested areas around the country. Increasingly, such wildfires threaten people's settlements due to the urban–wildland interface. For instance, in October 2007, wildfires in Southern California were extremely devastating. Some of the fires were started by power lines that were damaged due to strong Santa Ana winds or by a truck that overturned (causing sparks). Others were ignited by an arsonist and a boy who was playing with matches. The extreme fire conditions at this particular time of year resulted in over 500,000 acres being scorched in counties from as far north as Santa Barbara all the way down to San Diego. The fires destroyed over 1,500 homes and required the evacuation of up to 950,000 people. In addition, over 12,000 people had to be sheltered at Qualcomm Stadium. Many roads had to be closed as a result of the fast-moving flames, and responders from CAL FIRE, the National Guard, and even Canada were called in to extinguish the fires. Both ground and air crews were needed to get the fires under control by November 6. Fortunately, on other occasions, wildfires fires may die out as a result of topographic conditions (e.g., a gulch or river), weather changes (e.g., rain), and the lack of fuel (e.g., scarcity of trees and undergrowth).

### 1.2.7  Biological Hazards

**Biological hazards** are agents that spread disease or are otherwise poisonous. Such hazards pose a grave threat to humankind, and millions of people have died by coming into contact with them. Biological hazards may be broken down into two categories: pathogens and toxins. **Pathogens** are organisms that spread disease and may include anthrax, smallpox, plague, hemorrhagic fever, and rickettsiae. **Toxins** are poisons created by plants and animals. Ricin and botulism are examples of such toxins. Toxins are not likely to kill many people at a time. However, pathogens are far more devastating. For instance, the 1918 Spanish influenza pandemic killed more people in the United States than had died in combat in World War I. When famines occur and people are malnourished, disease epidemics are especially likely. In recent years, there have been growing agricultural and public health concerns related to hoof and mouth disease, hantavirus, SARS, and West Nile virus. The avian "bird" flu has also been a serious concern in Asia, Europe, and Africa. These biological hazards have created many worries for public health officials, particularly in light of our highly transient populations and the ease of modern travel around the world. Much more needs to be done to prepare for biological hazards.

## SELF-CHECK

- What is a natural hazard?
- What are the types of natural hazards?
- Are atmospheric and hydrological hazards related?
- How is a geological hazard different from a seismic hazard?
- What are the effects of biological hazards?

## 1.3 Technological Hazards

**Technological hazards** are hazard agents related to industry, nuclear materials, the built environment, computers, and transportation systems. These hazards abound in our modern, industrial world, and they range from hazardous materials releases and environmental degradation to structural failures and beyond.

### 1.3.1 Industrial Hazards

**Industrial hazards** are hazard agents produced by the extraction, creation, distribution, storage, use, and disposal of chemicals. Chlorine, benzene, insecticides, plastics, fuel, and other materials are released into the atmosphere when regulations are ignored, employees are untrained or careless, and equipment fails. Such materials in solid, liquid, or gas state may be toxic, flammable, explosive, or corrosive. They may react in very complex ways depending on temperature and the presence of water, oxygen, or other chemicals. The release of methyl isocyanate (MIC) in Bhopal, India, from the Union Carbide Company is regarded to be the most deadly industrial accidents in history. While the cause of this event has been under intense debate, it is believed that poor maintenance resulted in an accidental chemical release. Forty-five tons of gas was emitted into the city, killing anywhere between 2,500 and 10,000 people. While there is continued disagreement about the extent of fatalities and the cause of this hazard, the event had a profound impact on hazardous materials regulations in the United States and elsewhere. Unfortunately, industrial hazards continue to occur around the world. On October 4, 2010, a dike surrounding a sludge reservoir at the Hungarian Aluminum Production and Sales facility broke and released 1 million cubic meters of alkaline water and red sludge. It traveled down a creek and settled in three communities. The noxious flood killed 10 people, injured 286, and affected 358 homes (Ministry of the Interior, 2011). In 2013, a major industrial accident occurred in Texas (Figure 1-6). A stockpile of ammonium nitrate at the West Fertilizer Company exploded and killed 15 people, including many volunteer firefighters. Damage from the blast destroyed a school, a nursing home, and numerous homes and businesses in a 37-block area. The event prompted an investigation by the Chemical Safety Board and underscores the importance of land-use planning and emergency preparedness. Unfortunately,

**Figure 1-6**

The April 20, 2013, West Texas fertilizer plant explosion produced major damages, including to this apartment complex. Earl Armstrong/FEMA.

such events may not only result from mistakes; some may be intentional. There is always a potential that industrial hazards could be triggered by terrorists seeking to cause death and destruction.

### 1.3.2 Environmental Hazards

Careless industrial activity may have other negative effects. Pollution, degradation, and overuse of natural resources are types of ecological or environmental hazards. **Environmental hazards** are agents (such as pollution) that result in the degradation of our physical surroundings and pose a risk to people's health and well-being. Pollution involves the emission of wastes in the physical environment. This may include the distribution of solid, liquid, and gas wastes into landfills, rivers, and the atmosphere. Such activities harm the soil, contaminate water supplies, and poison the air. Pollution can also hinder farming and lead to health problems. It has also been suggested that the emission of pollutants into the atmosphere may add to global warming, although it should be noted that there is political controversy about the causes and consequences of climate change. In spite of this debate, alterations in climate would logically affect weather patterns and the nature of storms. For instance, flooding could become more severe and locations that had sufficient water in the past may later find themselves amid drought.

There are many other forms of degradation. One of the most salient environmental concerns is over fracking, which is a process of drilling into the earth and injecting a mixture of water, salt, sand, and other elements to obtain natural gas. While the search for cleaner fossil fuels is warranted, some believe chemicals injected into the soil may contaminate groundwater. Other types of environmental hazards include desertification and the salinization of the soil, which may accompany overfarming. This type of environmental hazard limits the production of agricultural goods and could lead to widespread famines in the future. While the depletion of natural resources is not always considered a primary issue for emergency management, the depletion of oil, gas, and coal would limit the heating of homes during the winter or the use of air conditioning during summer. This could put many lives in jeopardy, especially if renewable resources do not replace the fossil fuels we rely on currently.

### 1.3.3 Nuclear Hazards

A **nuclear hazard** results from the presence and potential threat of radioactive material. Nuclear power plants provide electricity for communities, businesses, and individual citizens. Although these facilities produce nuclear wastes that must be disposed of, they pollute less than the power plants running off of coal. Although nuclear hazards are rare, they can be extremely disruptive. Nuclear power plants create health risks because radiation can injure or kill people if it is accidentally released into the environment. This potential was witnessed in 1979 at the Three Mile Island nuclear power plant in Harrisburg, Pennsylvania. Because of a leak in the equipment that purifies water entering the turbines, a backup system should have been activated. Unfortunately, an employee had shut this secondary system off during maintenance, which caused the system to overheat. A warning light did not illuminate as it should have and radioactive material was released into the containment building. In time, an employee noticed what was taking place and was able to close a valve to reverse the unfolding chain of events. No one was killed in the incident. However, the public became alarmed at the lack of information during the warning and evacuation process. This was not the case at the Chernobyl reactor in the former Soviet Union. After similar mistakes and mechanical failures, many of those responding to the hazard died and thousands had to be evacuated. Nearby areas are still somewhat dangerous today, and cancer has affected those that failed to leave as requested by the government.

### 1.3.4 Structural Collapse Hazards

The collapse of structures is another potentially deadly hazard. **Structural collapses** are hazards that occur when gravity and poor engineering interact and result in the failure of buildings, roads, or other construction projects. These collapses may include the breaking of dams and dykes or the crashing down of buildings. There have been numerous dam failures throughout the history of the United States, including those in Johnstown, Pennsylvania (1889); Buffalo Creek, West Virginia (1972); and Teton, Idaho (1976). The failure of dikes and retaining devices has also occurred in the 1993 Midwest floods and after Hurricane Katrina in New Orleans. Thousands of lives and large amounts of infrastructure have been lost due to such hazards.

Structural failures are not limited to water retaining devices alone however. Buildings, bridges, and parking garages have also suffered from improper use, poor engineering, and inadequate construction. One of the most notable structural hazards was the 1981 Hyatt Skywalk collapse. While a dance was being held in the hotel atrium, the suspended walkway broke loose due to the dynamic load of those dancing on it. The walkway fell to the floor and on top of those dancing below. The event killed over 100 people, injured twice that amount, and posed

**Figure 1-7**

The aftermath of the I-35W bridge collapse is seen in this picture
from Minneapolis, MN. Todd Swain/FEMA.

extreme difficulties for those involved in search and rescue activities. Another
structural failure occurred in August 2007 over the Mississippi River near
Minneapolis. During rush hour traffic, the I-35W bridge suddenly gave way due to
what is speculated as a design flaw. The bridge and cars plummeted to the river
below. Nearly 150 people were injured and 13 were killed. In May 2013, a parking
structure that was under construction collapsed at Montgomery Mall in Maryland.
This event left one person dead and another injured. Structural failures are often
fatal, and they are very costly too (Figure 1-7).

### 1.3.5 Computer Hazards

Advanced technology increases productivity and provides many other benefits
to societies. However, modern computers have posed a technological hazard in
the past and will continue to do so in the future. A **computer hazard** is a disruptive hazard associated with computer hardware and software. One example
is the threat associated with Y2K. The system of recording dates created fears
that anything run by computers would fail. This included potential nightmare
scenarios relating to plane flight programs, public utility systems, and communications media. After conscientious efforts to change how dates were recorded
in computer coding and prepare for any eventuality, the arrival of the new
millennium came and went without any substantial disturbance. There have
been several situations, however, where computers have been affected by

freezing temperatures, floods, and fires. Such hazards shut down or disrupt power grids, traffic signals, communications capabilities, and online banking records. What is more, there is always a chance that a hacker will enter a supposedly secure website to steal information or cause mayhem. Businesses have had corporate information stolen and the Department of Defense firewalls have been breached. Hackers can therefore shut down or manipulate computer systems. For instance, people in other countries have interfered with 911 communication centers in the United States. Because of the knowledge and skills of today's hackers, cyberterrorism is a growing concern for the government and businesses alike.

### 1.3.6 Transportation Hazards

Because of the ease of moving people, goods, and services around the world, we are faced with several transportation hazards. A **transportation hazard** is an accident that occurs on roads or railways, at sea, or in the air. Such incidents may result from adverse meteorological circumstances, human error, or mechanical failure. For example, there may be mass vehicle accidents owing to fog or wet and wintery weather. At other times, tired or careless drivers may overturn their tankers, which carry hazardous materials and force the evacuation of neighborhoods and portions of cities. Train derailments are also common and may result from reckless young drivers trying to beat the safety gates, animals grazing on the tracks, and the expansion or contraction of rails due to heat and freezing temperatures. In July 2013, the conductor of a train in Spain was talking on a cell phone and failed to slow down as necessary for an approaching curve. The wreck claimed the lives of 79 people. Train derailments can also emit hazardous materials into the environment and create a cleanup nightmare for rail companies and surrounding communities.

Instances of cruise ships and ferries sinking, vessels crashing into docks, or oil tankers hitting jagged rocks and puncturing their hulls are transportation hazards that have occurred in the past and in more recent years too. Almost everyone is aware of the sinking of the Titanic, which killed over 1500 people in 1912. The event illustrated the impact of careless navigation, the danger posed by icebergs, and the need for sufficient lifeboats on ships. Unfortunately, there have been many other examples of shipping accidents at sea. In January of 2012, the captain of the Costa Concordia deviated from the designated route in the Mediterranean Sea and struck rocks. The Italian cruise liner sunk and 32 people died as a result. The sinking of ferries is also common in places like India or the Philippines, where they are often overloaded with people and supplies. On other occasions, captains have lost control of ships in harbors in New York and Canada. One of the most notorious incidents was the 2003 Staten Island Ferry crash. The vessel ran into a concrete pier, killing 11 people and injuring over 70. In some cases, extreme environmental damage may result from shipping accidents. The most notable transportation-related oil spill in U.S. history occurred on March 24, 1989, in Prince William Sound, Alaska. When the Exxon Valdez ran aground, more than 240,000 barrels of oil were deposited into the seawater, polluting the beach and killing thousands of animals.

## FOR EXAMPLE

### Ferry Sinking in Bangladesh

In July 2003, a ferry traveling to the southeast from the capital of Dhaka sank. The vessel encountered turbulent waters where two rivers merge. The boat, carrying between 500 and 800 people, capsized and quickly took on water. About half of those on the ship were rescued by fishermen or managed to swim to shore about 75 yards away. The overcrowded ferry and strong currents produced one of the deadliest transportation disasters in Bangladesh ever.

Wreckage from the Asiana Airlines Boeing 777 that crashed on July 6, 2013 while landing at San Francisco International Airport.

Airplane crashes are surprisingly less frequent than most other types of transportation accidents, but they may happen when pilots overshoot runways, when wind shear occurs, when runways are icy or wet, and when planes are not meticulously engineered and maintained. Plane crashes can be particularly devastating. In many cases, all passengers onboard will be killed. In November 2001, an Airbus A300-600 broke apart over Queens, New York, due to problems associated with the stress placed on the vertical stabilizer. Each of the 260 passengers and crewmembers died, and much of the fuselage landed in a neighborhood, which only added to the adverse consequences. In other cases, passengers may be fortunate to survive plane crashes. A Boeing 777 originating from South Korea crashed on July 6, 2013, at the San Francisco International Airport when it hit the seawall just short of the runway. The pilot was not sufficiently trained on the aircraft he was flying, and the guidance system was disabled at the airport at the time. While there were only 3 fatalities, nearly 200 people were injured. It is certainly amazing the outcome was not more severe.

## SELF-CHECK

- What is a technological hazard?
- What are the types of technological hazards?
- Why do technological hazards occur?
- How does industry and commerce influence hazards?
- What can be done to better prevent or deal with technological disasters?

## 1.4 Civil/Conflict Hazards

There are several types of **civil/conflict hazards**. Mass shootings, panic behavior, riots, terrorism, and war fall into this category. Each will be discussed in the following.

### 1.4.1 Mass Shootings

Mass shootings are one example of civil/conflict hazards. Unfortunately, it appears that these events have become more common in past years. The list of shootings at schools and other locations since the late 1990s is disturbing:

- ▲ Pearl, Mississippi (1997)—3 killed
- ▲ Paducah, Kentucky (1997)—3 killed
- ▲ Jonesborough, Arkansas (1998)—5 killed
- ▲ Springfield, Oregon (1998)—5 killed
- ▲ Conyers, Georgia (1999)—4 wounded
- ▲ Atlanta, Georgia (1999)—9 killed
- ▲ Pelham, Alabama (1999)—3 killed

Other events have been especially devastating. On April 20, 1999, two disgruntled students entered Columbine High School in Jefferson County, Colorado. Besides detonating several bombs in and around this educational facility, the students fired into the crowded cafeteria and library areas. By the time the perpetrators committed suicide, 12 students and 1 teacher were killed and 24

---

### FOR EXAMPLE

**Recent Mass Shootings**

On December 14, 2012, a horrific school shooting took place in Connecticut at Sandy Hook Elementary. Twenty children and six adults were murdered by a 20-year-old gunman. Those that survived the mass shooting and some emergency personnel that rushed to the scene to help have had an extremely difficult time coping with this traumatic event. On July 20, 2012, a similar crisis occurred inside a movie theater in Aurora, Colorado. A gunman used multiple weapons of weapons to attack his victims, ultimately killing 12 people and wounding over 50 others. On September 16, 2013, a man who was discharged from the military entered a Navy facility at a Washington Navy Yard. He opened fire, killing 12 and injuring several others. Each of these events has prompted additional discussion about gun control and mental health issues. They have also created a need for better prepared police officers, emergency medical technicians, and emergency management offices.

---

others were injured. The incident prompted a national review of how to respond to mass shootings, and the lessons gleaned have had a major impact on law enforcement policies and procedures. On September 15, 1999, a gunman walked into youth rally and discharged to weapons into the congregation at a church in Fort Worth, Texas. Seven people were killed. Numerous others were injured and had to be quickly taken to area hospitals. In October of 2002, there were several sniper shootings that occurred over a period of several weeks at numerous locations in Maryland, Virginia, and Washington, DC. One man and one minor were responsible for killing 10 people and injuring 3 others. These serial murderers prompted a massive investigation and illustrated the difficulty of capturing those involved in such episodes of violence.

### 1.4.2 Panic Flight

Panic flight, or the fleeing of many individuals from what appears to be imminent harm, is extremely rare. However, it has led to major emergencies under certain situations. Panic flight is most likely to occur when large crowds gather at concerts, sporting venues, and other large public gatherings. An example took place on February 20, 2003, in West Warwick, Rhode Island. The rock band Great White was performing at a nightclub. The road manager used pyrotechnics inside the building, causing the ceiling to catch on fire. As the fire spread quickly, the occupants headed for the doors. Because most people exited the same way they entered the building, a bottleneck ensued and many were trampled or became stuck. Around 100 people died in the blaze and over 187 were injured. The fire led to a drawn-out debate about who was legally liable. Was it the fault of the city inspectors, the building owner, or band manager? The tragedy also prompted a review of fire exits and sprinkler systems around the nation. Such events have occurred in countries around the world. In 2005, 841 people were killed and another 323 were injured while attending a religious gathering at a mosque in Baghdad.

> ## FOR EXAMPLE
>
> ### The Kiss Nightclub Fire
>
> In January 2013, flames ignited the Kiss nightclub in Santa Maria, Brazil, after band members lit a flare on stage. In an effort to escape the fire, a human stampede resulted. More than 200 people were unable to evacuate and died as a result of smoke inhalation. Another 150 were injured due to the rush of people trying to leave the burning nightclub. This fire was one of the worst emergencies in Brazil's history. It illustrated the dangers of panic flight, overcapacity in the nightclub, and insufficient signage for emergency exits.

Someone reported the presence of a suicide bomber, and people began to evacuate the building and area. Hundreds of people stampeded toward a bridge, which broke and fell into the Tigris River. Many people were killed or injured as a result. Panic flight does not occur very often, but it can turn deadly as these cases suggest.

### 1.4.3 Riots

Riots are another type of civil/conflict hazards. **Riots** are large disturbances where people engage in antisocial behavior. This conduct includes rock throwing, looting, tipping over vehicles, starting fires, and attacking law enforcement personnel. Social protesters and their opponents sometimes spark riots (perhaps because of political or economic circumstances). They can also result from racial tensions or cultural conflict. Other factors, such as the loss of a team in the Super Bowl, may also trigger riots. Whatever the cause, these events can disrupt business activities and hurt the economy. They may also produce a large number of injuries and even death.

There have been several notable riots in the United States, including the Watts Riot in Los Angeles in 1965. This episode began when an officer pulled over an African-American man who was alleged to have been driving erratically. In another racially charged situation, four police officers appeared to have used excessive force against Rodney King in Sylmar, California. The incident was caught on tape, but the police officers were not convicted of any crime. Many people believed that the police beating was unnecessary and brutal. Others believed the legal system was biased when the verdict was made public. On April 29, 1992, scores of people took to the streets to illustrate their dismay. Fifty people were killed, hundreds were injured, and thousands were arrested. Damage was in the millions of dollars. Another riot occurred in Seattle in 1999 when environmentalists and others protested the policies of the World Trade Organization. During a 4-day period, people marched, broke windows, disabled busses, and heckled police. Law enforcement agencies in Seattle were not fully prepared. They were caught off guard by the demonstration that turned violent. This was not the case after the George Zimmerman trial in 2013. The police in Florida and around the nation prepared for potential riots due to the death of a young black man, and fortunately, the resulting protests were limited in number and were generally peaceful.

### 1.4.4 Terrorism

Terrorism has been one of the most deadly civil/conflict hazards throughout history, and it has become even more pronounced in the past few years. **Terrorism** is the threat or use of violence to intimidate someone or a government. The perpetrators usually have ideological motives and a political objective to reach. For instance, terrorists engage in this behavior to seek independence, promote their religion, protest abortions, or protect the environment. Terrorists have used guns, arson, bombings, and other measures to kill and disrupt the activities of others. Their attacks have occurred around the world. Suicide bombings are common in the Middle East, particularly in Israel. Other major attacks have occurred in Spain, Germany, Russia, the United Kingdom, Iraq, Afghanistan, and Kenya.

The worst case of terrorism in the United States was on September 11, 2001. Islamic extremists hijacked four planes and used them as missiles against buildings symbolic of U.S. political, military, and economic interests. The World Trade Centers were the main targets of the planes. The towers collapsed after the ignited jet fuel weakened the structure. Thousands of people died and several buildings in New York were turned into a pile of broken glass, twisted metal, and other dangerous and unhealthy debris. The Pentagon was also struck during the attack, but few people died in this building than in the World Trade Centers in New York. One plane was crashed in Pennsylvania, and it is assumed that this aircraft was headed to the White House or Capitol Hill.

Terrorists are also seeking other novel ways to attack their enemies, including through the use of weapons of mass destruction (e.g., nerve, blister, blood, and choking and incapacitating agents). Shortly after 9/11, for example, envelopes containing anthrax were sent via mail to the headquarters of a newspaper in Florida and to Congressional leaders in Washington, DC. This attack disabled the postal service for days and killed a handful of people. In April 2013, a woman from East Texas sent an envelope containing ricin to President Obama. The individuals involved in these incidents were identified. The first person committed suicide and the other has been imprisoned for her actions.

## FOR EXAMPLE

### Manchester Bombing

In June 1996, terrorists parked a vehicle near a major intersection in the commercial district of Manchester, England. A local television station received word that a bomb would be detonated. A bomb squad was brought in, but team was not able to dismantle the explosives. However, the city was able to evacuate 80,000 people from the area. No one died in the attack, but it did injure over 200 people who were cut by glass, impaled by objects, or otherwise affected by the blast. Several buildings were damaged or destroyed, and many businesses and apartment dwellers lost office space or residences. This intentional disaster cost millions of dollars in direct and indirect losses. It prompted a major emergency response and criminal investigation.

A significant terrorist attack involved the use of sarin gas by the Aum Shinrikyo cult in Japan. This event, which occurred in a subway, killed several people. It also created massive medical care needs—whether real or imagined—for thousands of others. It illustrated the grave potential of biological, chemical, and nuclear weapons. The rising threat of terrorism has prompted a significant reorganization of the U.S. government and the establishment of the Department of Homeland Security. Billions of dollars have been poured into first responder training and public health preparedness measures as a result.

### 1.4.5 War

Conflict has occurred throughout history between different tribes, ethnic groups, and nation-states. With the advent of modern weaponry, however, the stakes of fighting have become much higher. Millions of people are killed when negotiations break down and violence ensues. Cities have also been leveled. Such was the case in World War II when London, Dresden, Hiroshima, and Nagasaki were bombed with conventional or nuclear explosives. Shortly thereafter and during the Cold War, the fear of a nuclear attack from the Soviet Union prompted the United States to invest heavily in civil defense initiatives. The goal was to prepare for such an attack, stockpile supplies, and evacuate and shelter citizens if required. Perhaps there is less interstate conflict today as compared to the past, but there are certainly notable exceptions. For instance, the United States intervened in Iraq to push back Saddam Hussein, and it also deposed the Taliban in Afghanistan. However, there is also the potential for major conflict in the Middle East due to ongoing tensions between Israel and its enemies or Iran and the United States. What is more, there has been a great deal of intrastate fighting as in places such as Somalia, Yugoslavia, Rwanda, Libya, and Syria. These internal civil wars are known as "complex emergencies." They typically involve ethnic cleansing, a failed government, and economic turmoil that are sometimes combined with natural and environmental disasters and especially famines. Those responding to such events have been targeted by the warring factions. For example, relief workers in Iraq have been kidnapped and killed by the belligerent parties.

## SELF-CHECK

- What is a civil/conflict hazard?
- What are the types of civil/conflict hazards?
- What is the role of humans in civil/conflict hazards?
- How is each type of civil/conflict hazard related to the other? Are they different? If so, how?

## 1.5 The Complexity and Impact of Disasters

Although it is useful to classify hazards in order to understand their unique features, it is also important for you to recognize that hazards are not mutually exclusive. In other words, each hazard may interact with others in convoluted and perhaps even unpredictable ways. Also, human vulnerability tends to complicate and exacerbate the impact of triggering agents. The examples are numerous:

▲ An earthquake may break a dam, cause a building collapse, and produce landslides.

▲ Degradation of the environment (e.g., deforestation) could exacerbate flash flooding and mudslides that are related to severe storms.

▲ Flooding and poor health conditions could lead to the spread of certain communicable diseases.

▲ Computer mishaps or cyberterrorism might lead to hazardous materials releases or infrastructure failures.

### FOR EXAMPLE

#### Hurricane Katrina

Hurricane Katrina will long be remembered as a complex disaster. In September 2005, Hurricane Katrina—a category four storm—slammed into the coast of Louisiana, Mississippi, and Alabama. Each of these states suffered severe losses. However, it was New Orleans that gained national and international attention. The winds of the hurricane damaged structures in the "Big Easy" and affected power and phone service. Nevertheless, the storm surge and heavy rains were most problematic. Lake Pontchartrain rose to historic levels and the levees set up to keep the waters from inundating the below-sea-level community were breached. New Orleans was flooded. Water, sewer, and gas lines were broken. The contents of numerous petroleum and hazardous chemical tanks were released. Homes and businesses were under water. Making matters worse, antisocial behaviors including looting and fights were reported around the city. The local, state, and federal response was slow and inadequate. The reaction was also hampered further when criminals began firing weapons at rescue helicopters and relief workers. Many evacuees sought shelter in the superdome where supplies were inadequate and conditions were filthy. Behavior was beginning to turn violent among some disaster victims about the time federal aid arrived at the superdome. The delivery of assistance was delayed because flooding severely affected the transportation system. Public health workers feared an outbreak of disease due to the squalid living conditions and requested an evacuation of the city. Katrina involved natural, environmental, biological, technological, and civil hazards. It was complicated by poor planning before the hurricane and insufficient communication during response and recovery operations (Figure 1-8).

**Figure 1-8**

This picture of boats impacting infrastructure illustrates why Hurricane Katrina was one of the most complex disasters to affect the United States. Robert Kaufmann/FEMA.

▲ A train derailment could result in the spill of dangerous chemicals and harm the natural habitat.

▲ Those participating in riots often set fire to nearby structures, which may trigger panic flight behavior.

▲ The failure of individuals and organizations to adequately plan and prepare for disasters often complicates response and recovery operations and aggravates disaster impacts.

As an emergency manager, you must appreciate the complex nature of hazards and vulnerability as it can have serious impact upon response and recovery operations. In most cases, you will be responding to multiple hazards and vulnerabilities in any given disaster. This creates serious challenges that you must be ready to deal with at a moment's notice.

### 1.5.1 The Nature of Disasters

As mentioned earlier, when a hazard or multiple hazards interact with humans and the vulnerability they create, disasters occur. People may be injured or killed as a result of these destructive events, and the impact is significant. From 2001 to 2012, natural disasters killed 1.9 million people worldwide and affected another 2.9 billion (UNISDR, 2013). Deaths are also significant in the United States. For instance, "it is estimated that natural hazards killed over 24,000 people between January 1, 1975 and December 31, 1994" (Mileti, 1999, p. 66). These statistics were collected from fires, flooding, or other hazards, although these numbers do not include the toll of disease outbreaks, which are also substantial. The number of injuries from disasters should not be overlooked either, as it averages about 100 per week in the United States (Mileti, 1999, p. 66). Such injuries may include superficial cuts from flying glass in a tornado or serious internal wounds due to the collapse of a building after an earthquake.

Property is likewise damaged or destroyed in disasters, costing billions of dollars each year. Homes and belongings can be covered by landslides, fishing vessels are sunk in hurricanes, and businesses are flattened by strong winds. Furniture, clothing, televisions, and cars are ruined in disasters. Losses average about $1 billion per week in the United States, and these figures are rising exponentially each decade (Mileti, 1999, p. 66). Hazardous materials spills, nuclear accidents, and other events can likewise degrade the natural environment, thereby affecting the health and well-being of people beyond the current generation.

Disasters also disrupt individuals and society as a whole. Routine activities such as cooking, sleeping, and bathing may be hindered due to the damages of one's appliances, bed, or home. Jobs are also lost, business transactions are prohibited, and traffic is snarled when hazards impact corporations and transportation systems. Disasters are also accompanied by building collapses, road closures, and downed power and phone lines. The infrastructure is often severely impacted. Simple tasks such as mailing a letter or having your trash hauled away cannot be performed because the government is also adversely affected. Disasters, including terrorist attacks, cause economic decline and can sometimes jeopardize mental health. Disasters of all types have even led to political turmoil at times and have changed the direction of policy in the United States (e.g., the creation of the Department of Homeland Security after 9/11). There is no doubt that disasters have a bearing upon taxes, insurance rates, and many other aspects of our lives.

### 1.5.2 Changes Associated with Disasters

During the immediate emergency period of a disaster, several significant changes occur that complicate the job of an emergency manager. Dynes et al. (1972), three well-known disaster scholars, have identified six of them:

1. **Uncertainty**. In the immediate aftermath of disaster, there is a lack of information about what has happened, why it occurred, the number of injured or dead, the extent of the devastation, and what should be done to deal with these problems.

2. **Urgency**. Seeing needs arise, most citizens and leaders desire to act quickly to issue warnings, treat injuries, and clear roads of debris as quickly as possible.

3. **Emergency consensus**. Individuals, groups, businesses, government departments, and political leaders generally work together (at least in the immediate aftermath of a disaster) to overcome problems.

4. **Expansion of citizen role**. People are not only more willing to cooperate in a disaster, but they are also likely to be involved in searching for neighbors trapped under debris, transporting the wounded to hospitals, and providing relief supplies to charitable organizations.

5. **De-emphasis of contractual relationships**. Because victims' needs must be met as soon as possible, written agreements are not relied upon. Verbal arrangements are made instead. Accounts and debts are settled when the situation calms down. It is also likely that supplies will be donated with no thought of reimbursement.

6. **Convergence**. People and material resources will flow to the scene of a disaster. This may include evacuees returning to the location and those wanting information about victims. It may also include volunteers, reporters, and researchers, people wanting to take advantage of the situation, groups cheering on the emergency workers, and others mourning those who have died in the event (Kendra and Wachtendorf, 2003c).

These changes can have a dramatic impact on those involved in the management of disasters. Decision making becomes difficult and postdisaster operations are stressful. Poor communications in disasters complicate the sharing of information. Many agencies and volunteers help to get things done quickly, but the arrival of too many organizations and donations can add to the overwhelming nature of disaster. Resources may be available, but they may not be shipped or tracked in an effective manner. Later on, blame may be placed on those considered to be at fault. Disagreements might arise about recovery policies, particularly in regard to disaster assistance and rebuilding priorities. Some of the changes that take place after a disaster have positive features while others are negative. In most cases, the changes resulting from disasters will provide benefits and drawbacks for those working in emergency management and related professions. For instance, more political and financial support may be given to emergency management after a disaster. However, disasters may require long hours for those working in this important endeavor.

### 1.5.3 The Need for Response and Recovery Operations

Besides understanding the consequences of disasters, you must be aware of the goals of response and recovery operations if you are to be an efficacious emergency manager. Such objectives include protecting lives, limiting property loss, and overcoming the disruption that disasters cause. There are other aspirations that must be considered as well. For instance, you must ensure care for special populations such as those in nursing homes. You must work to coordinate the efforts of all types of disaster participants, regardless if they are affiliated with the government or not. Another desire is to reduce further deterioration of the environment when a disaster occurs and rebuild with future hazards in mind. You may rely on both predetermined organizational arrangements and technology to complete these responsibilities. In most disasters, multiple activities will require your active attention and flexibility. Resources should be tracked to help cover expenses. Extreme care should be taken to avoid possible lawsuits. It will be important to record what has transpired so you can learn from your successes and shortcomings.

Your job during response and recovery operations is therefore extremely challenging. There are many demands that have to be addressed, and two of them have been identified by Ronald Perry (1991, p. 201):

▲ **Agent-generated demands** are the needs made evident by the hazard (e.g., problems resulting from the disaster agent itself). These demands appear immediately as the disaster unfolds, and some examples include sandbags to fight flooding, shelters to care for those made homeless, and the restoration of electricity owing to power outages.

▲ **Response-generated demands** are the needs that are made evident as individuals, organizations, and communities attempt to meet agent-generated demands. They are visible as people and agencies try to deal with the impact of flooding, earthquakes, and other hazards.

Acquiring sandbags, finding suitable shelter sites, and obtaining portable generators or electricians are examples of response-generated demands. Response-generated demands thus deal with the logistical issues pertaining to the reaction of people and organizations to agent-generated demands (Figure 1-9).

In addition to these demands, you should recognize that there will be other expectations placed upon you after a disaster:

▲ **Normalcy-generated demands** are the pressures to quickly get things back to predisaster conditions. Returning people to their homes and restarting business activity are types of normalcy-generated demands.

**Figure 1-9**

The damage of electricity infrastructure (an agent-generated demand) in Crystal Beach, TX, after Hurricane Ike created the need to replace power poles (a response-generated demand). Greg Henshall/FEMA.

▲ **Mitigation-generated demands** are the desires to prevent a recurrence of the disaster. Creating more stringent building codes and relocating residences to less-hazardous areas are examples of mitigation-generated demands.

▲ **Preparedness-generated demands** are expectations that the mistakes made evident in response and recovery operations will not be repeated in the future. Improvements in planning, training, exercises, and the allocation of additional resources fall into this category.

All of these disaster-related demands create priority problems for emergency managers. Normalcy-generated demands sometimes run in opposition to the mitigation- and preparedness-generated demands. As an example, people want to return to their homes even when it would be best to remove them permanently from the floodplain. Government officials may also desire to give attention to rebuilding schools rather than invest in emergency management personnel or planning activities. In spite of these conflicts, you must take advantage of the increased public concern disasters provide to promote change during response and recovery. All of these goals and functional activities are directed toward the goal of disaster resilience. **Resilience** may be described as the ability to react effectively and efficiently in time of disaster. It is the overarching goal of the remainder of this book.

## SELF-CHECK

- Do hazards interact with each other?
- What do we call hazards that occur in conjunction with other hazards?
- How are disasters different from hazards?
- What changes occur in society after a disaster?
- Why are response and recovery operations needed?
- What demands do emergency managers face after a disaster?

## SUMMARY

As an emergency manager, you should be aware of important concepts such as hazards, vulnerability disasters, emergency management, disaster response and recovery, and resilience. You must understand what types of hazards may occur including their natural, technological, and civil/conflict variants. It is also imperative that you comprehend how hazards interact with each other and vulnerability and how a myriad of variables may determine the impact of disasters. Successful emergency managers should know what changes to expect when a disaster occurs. They must effectively meet the demands that confront them and deal with the aftermath of a disaster in a successful manner.

# KEY TERMS

| | |
|---|---|
| **Agent-generated demands** | The needs made evident by the hazard (e.g., problems resulting from the disaster agent itself). |
| **Atmospheric hazards** | A hazard agent that is produced in or by the earth's atmosphere. |
| **Biological hazards** | Agents that spread disease or are otherwise poisonous. |
| **Civil/conflict hazards** | Violent events that have the potential to produce mass casualties. |
| **Compound hazards** | Multiple hazards that react to each other in chaotic fashion. |
| **Computer hazards** | A disruptive hazard associated with computer hardware and software. |
| **Disasters** | Deadly, destructive, and disruptive events that occur when a hazard (or multiple hazards) interacts with human vulnerability. |
| **Emergency management** | From an academic standpoint, "the study of how humans and their institutions deal with hazards, vulnerabilities and the events that result from their interaction." From a practical perspective, "the managerial function charged with creating the framework within which communities reduce vulnerability to hazards and cope with disasters." |
| **Emergency managers** | Public servants that help jurisdictions reduce the liabilities that lead to disasters. They also help built community disaster capabilities. |
| **Enhanced Fujita Scale** | A scale used to categorize the size of a tornado, including the affiliated wind speed. |
| **Environmental hazards** | Agents that involve the degradation of the environment, such as pollution, that pose a risk to people's health and well-being. |
| **First responders** | Public safety personnel such as police, firefighters, and emergency medical technicians. |
| **Geological hazards** | Hazard agents associated with the earth's soil and rock. |
| **Hazard** | A physical, technological, or intentional agent such as an earthquake, industrial explosion, or terrorist bombing. |
| **Heat index** | Incorporates both temperature and humidity into a scale to help warn people to stay inside and drink lots of water. |

| | |
|---|---|
| **Homeland security** | "A concerted national effort to prevent terrorist attacks within the United States, reduce America's vulnerability to terrorism, and recover from and minimize the damage of attacks that do occur." |
| **Hydrologic hazards** | Hazard agents that occur with the earth's water systems. |
| **Industrial hazards** | Hazards produced by the extraction, creation, distribution, storage, use, and disposal of chemicals. |
| **Mercalli scale** | A scale used to describe the physical observation of damages that result from the movement of the earth's crust (e.g., broken windows, cracked walls, falling pictures, etc.) |
| **Mitigation** | Risk reduction, loss minimization, or the alleviation of potential negative impacts associated with disasters. |
| **Mitigation-generated demands** | The desire to learn from the disaster and avoid making similar mistakes in the future. |
| **Na-tech hazards** | A combination of natural–technological hazards. |
| **Natural hazards** | Those events originating from the physical environment, typically because of radiation from the sun, heat flow within the earth, or the force of gravity. |
| **Normalcy-generated demands** | The pressures to get things back to predisaster conditions. |
| **Nuclear hazards** | A hazard resulting from the presence of radioactive material. |
| **Pathogens** | Organisms that spread disease and may include anthrax, smallpox, plague, hemorrhagic fever, and rickettsiae. |
| **Preparedness** | Efforts to increase readiness for disaster response and recovery operations. |
| **Preparedness-generated demands** | Expectations that the mistakes made evident in response and recovery will not be repeated in the future. Improvements in planning and the allocation of additional resources fall into this category. |
| **Prevention** | Refers to actions to stop the occurrence of terrorist attacks and includes the gathering of intelligence, counterterrorism operations, and border control functions. |
| **Protection** | Refers to actions that discourage attacks through increased security measures or efforts |

|  | to minimize damage if such attacks cannot be prevented in the first place. The reliance on guards, fences, video surveillance, and access control falls into this category. |
|---|---|
| **Recovery** | Activity to return the affected community to predisaster or, preferably, improved conditions. |
| **Richter scale** | A measurement of the registered shaking amplitudes of an earthquake. |
| **Resilience** | The ability to react effectively and efficiently in time of disaster. |
| **Response** | Activity in the immediate aftermath of a disaster to protect life and property. |
| **Response-generated demands** | The needs that are made evident as individuals, organizations, and communities attempt to meet agent-generated demands. |
| **Riots** | Large disturbances where people engage in antisocial behavior. |
| **Saffir–Simpson scale I** | A descriptive tool to explain the magnitude of a hurricane in terms of wind and storm surge. |
| **Seismic hazards** | Hazard agents produced by the movement of tectonic plates that float on magma. |
| **Structural collapse hazards** | Hazards that occur when gravity and poor engineering result in the failure of buildings, roads, or other construction projects. |
| **Technological hazards** | Hazard agents related to industry, structures, hazardous materials, computers, and transportation systems. |
| **Terrorism** | The threat or use of violence to intimidate someone or a government. |
| **Toxins** | Poisons created by plants and animals. |
| **Transportation hazards** | An accident that occurs in the air, on roads or railways, or at sea. |
| **Vulnerability** | Proneness to disasters or the inability of individuals, organizations, and communities to prevent them or deal with them effectively. |
| **Wildfire hazards** | Hazards that result from lightning strikes, which can quickly envelop hundreds of acres of forest and brush. |

# ASSESS YOUR UNDERSTANDING

Posttest to evaluate your knowledge on hazards and disasters.
*Measure your learning by comparing pretest and posttest results.*

## Summary Questions

1. A crisis is a much bigger problem than a catastrophe. True or false?
2. A disaster occurs when a hazard interacts with human vulnerability. True or false?
3. Emergency management is a profession that attempts to reduce the probability of disasters and be prepared to respond and recover effectively if they cannot be prevented. True or false?
4. There is no relation or overlap between response and recovery operations. True or false?
5. An earthquake is an example of a geological hazard. True or false?
6. Mass shootings and riots are civil/conflict hazards. True or false?
7. Disasters are not characterized by the disruption they cause to people's daily, routine activities. True or false?
8. A normalcy-generated demand is a desire to prevent the recurrence of a disaster. True or false?
9. Resilience is concerned about the effectiveness of emergency management, but not the efficiency of response and recovery operations. True or false?
10. A disaster is:
    (a) Smaller than an accident
    (b) Smaller than a crisis
    (c) Larger than an emergency
    (d) Larger than a calamity
    (e) Larger than a catastrophe
11. A winter storm is an example of:
    (a) A natural hazard
    (b) A technological hazard
    (c) A civil/conflict hazard
    (d) All of the above
    (e) None of the above
12. Tornadoes may be classified as:
    (a) An atmospheric hazard
    (b) A hydrologic hazard
    (c) A biological hazard
    (d) A civil/conflict hazard
    (e) None of the above

13. Disasters are complex because:
    (a) One hazard may trigger another hazard.
    (b) A hazard interacts with human vulnerability.
    (c) Low preparedness levels may exacerbate impact.
    (d) Answers a and b.
    (e) Answers a, b, and c.
14. Uncertainty:
    (a) Is defined as an urgent situation
    (b) Results from an expansion of the citizen role
    (c) Is associated with a lack of information
    (d) Is equated to a de-emphasis of contractual relationships
    (e) Answers a and b

## Review Questions

1. Explain the difference between an accident and a catastrophe.
2. Define the term disaster and note its relation to hazards and vulnerability.
3. What is an emergency manager and what does he or she do?
4. What are the four phases or functional areas of emergency management? How do these relate to homeland security?
5. List the major categories of hazards.
6. Provide one or two examples of hazards under each category identified in question 5.
7. What are the major changes an emergency manager can expect after a disaster?
8. What are the goals of disaster response and recovery?
9. What is an agent-generated demand?
10. What is a response-generated demand?
11. What is a normalcy-generated demand?
12. What is a mitigation-generated demand?
13. What is a preparedness-generated demand?
14. What is resilience?

## Applying This Chapter

1. After responding to a major apartment fire in Boise, Idaho, you become aware of the fact that a sprinkler system would have prevented much of the damage. How can you link recovery activities to the goals of mitigation?
2. Suppose you are expecting the arrival of a hurricane in Charleston, South Carolina. What hazards might be present along the coast, and how would they interact with each other? Give two examples.

3. A terrorist has just blown up a courthouse in Seattle, Washington. What changes might occur when this takes place? What can you as an emergency manager do to effectively deal with the unique challenges associated with such a disaster?

4. The mayor and city manager in Birmingham, Alabama, are questioning you about the value of your position in the government. Explain what types of disasters could occur in your city and justify the need for response and recovery operations.

5. A flood has destroyed many homes and businesses in Greenville, Mississippi. How can you help your community recovery from disaster while also promoting the necessary changes to prevent a recurrence in the future?

6. As an emergency manager, you are frequently invited to speak to various organizations in your community. While discussing the goals of response and recovery to a group of Boy Scouts, one of those in attendance asks, "What is resilience?" How would you define it to the young man and explain why it is necessary to pursue after disaster strikes?

# *YOU TRY IT*

## How Can I Get Information About Hazards?

Answer the following questions by providing a list of organizations and their contact information. If you wanted information about hurricanes, who could you contact? If you needed details about the impacts of earthquakes, who could assist you? If you need to learn more about volcanic hazards, what government agency could assist you? If you needed to understand tornadoes better, who could answer your questions? What if you needed to better comprehend hazardous materials incidents? Who could provide such information? What about terrorism? Who could help you understand terrorist behavior better?

## What Would I Do?

Suppose your community was affected by a tornado. What are the possible consequences of this hazard if it interacts with human vulnerability? What would you need to do to respond? What considerations should be taken into account for recovery?

## The Interaction of Hazards

You are the emergency manager for New Orleans. Hurricane Katrina has just struck your community. What are the hazards? Are the hazards related? If so, how? What are the implications of compound or na-tech hazards?

## Disasters and Change

Disasters result in a great deal of change. What are some of the changes you can expect? Are these good or bad? How would they impact your job as an emergency manager? Why is it important to be aware of them?

## Meeting Demands

What are the agent-generated demands, response-generated demands, normalcy-generated demands, mitigation-generated demands, and preparedness-generated demands? Make a list of the demands placed on you and categorize them. How do these impact your job as an emergency manager? Do they present difficulties for you? How could you overcome them?

43

# 2

# UNDERSTANDING THE ACTORS
## Roles and Responsibilities of Disaster Participants

## Starting Point

Pretest to assess your knowledge on roles and responsibilities of disaster participants.
*Determine where you need to concentrate your effort.*

## What You'll Learn in This Chapter

▲ Activities of local, state, and federal governments
▲ Roles of businesses and companies
▲ Responsibilities of the nonprofit sector
▲ Involvement of citizens in disasters
▲ How to work with different groups

## After Studying This Chapter, You'll Be Able To

▲ Compare and contrast the roles of the public and private sectors.
▲ Examine the activities of the nonprofit sector.
▲ Differentiate between the duties of the local government after a disaster versus those of the state and federal government.
▲ Discuss how corporations and faith-based organizations can assist with emergency management functions.
▲ Analyze how citizens form emergent groups address disaster demands.

## Goals and Outcomes

▲ Predict the responsibilities of the public, private, and nonprofit sectors.
▲ Evaluate the different services individuals and organizations may provide during postdisaster activities.
▲ Assess who can help you fulfill response and recovery operations.
▲ Analyze the challenges of coordination.
▲ Determine how groups and individuals interact during disasters.

*Disaster Response and Recovery: Strategies and Tactics for Resilience*, Second Edition. David A. McEntire.
© 2015 John Wiley & Sons, Inc. Published 2015 by John Wiley & Sons, Inc.

# INTRODUCTION

After Hurricane Andrew devastated Miami Dade County in 1992, one local emergency manager asked "Where's the cavalry on this one?" This so-called disaster "cavalry" includes many people and organizations. There are numerous individuals, groups, and agencies involved in response and recovery operations. By understanding these participants, you will be better able to use their knowledge, skills, and abilities after a disaster. Such actors include individuals and organizations from the public, private, and nonprofit sectors. The **public sector** is a segment of society that is made up of government offices, departments, and agencies. Indian tribes may also be considered a segment of the public sector, although there are some significant differences between federal and tribal governments. The **private sector** is the part of society that includes businesses and corporations. The **nonprofit sector** in our communities is comprised of humanitarian, charitable, religious, and voluntary organizations. Citizens also join in disaster response and recovery activities. A typology created by the Disaster Research Center (DRC) may help you comprehend the difference among the many organizations that are involved in postdisaster operations. Harnessing all of the participants involved in emergency management (EM) will help you to promote disaster resilience.

## 2.1 The Public Sector

As an emergency manager, you should be aware of the many participants involved in disaster response and recovery operations from the public sector. The public sector includes government entities at the local, state, and federal levels as well as tribal nations. No two government jurisdictions operate or are organized alike. However, city personnel, state agencies, federal officials, and tribal groups all form part of the public sector.

### 2.1.1 Local Government

Local governments are the first to react to disasters from the public sector. **Local governments** are city or county organizations that perform important public functions. These municipal governments employ emergency medical technicians (EMTs), firefighters, police officers, and emergency managers. Other departments and political leaders also play a role in response and recovery at the local level.

EMTs are paramedics who provide emergency medical care to the injured and transport disaster victims to hospitals. They often work as or with firefighters (but some may also be employed by private companies). Firefighters provide emergency medical care as well, but fire departments also extinguish fires and investigate their causes. Firefighters are also involved in responses to other types of disasters. They perform search and rescue operations after floods, for example. They may also clean up hazardous material spills when they occur. Police officers, or law enforcement personnel, join EMTs and firefighters as first responders. Whereas EMTs and firefighters deal with medical emergencies and fire suppression issues, the police provide traffic control after disasters and close off dangerous areas to the public. Police and other first responders are almost always sent to the scene of a disaster.

Official first responders – such as police officers and fire fighters – will be present at the scene of a disaster and will work together to help those in need. Bryan Dahlberg/FEMA.

If local first responders are not able to cope effectively with the disaster demands, mutual aid agreements can be activated. **Mutual aid** is the sharing of personnel, equipment, and facilities. The activation of mutual aid occurs when local resources are inadequate to meet the needs of the disaster. This may include the sharing of resources by nearby local governments. However, in major disasters, regional, state, and federal governments may also share resources as well. Mutual aid is vital after major disasters. Cities may not be able to cope without the assistance of unaffected jurisdictions. Even affected states may require aid from other states and the federal government to cope with the impact of disasters.

Within local governments are emergency managers who help communities prevent and prepare for disasters. When a disaster occurs, they issue warnings, oversee evacuation, and communicate with the leaders that supervise first responders. They also assemble statistics on damages, share public information with citizens through the media, and work with those in charge of shelters. Emergency managers also acquire resources for organizations that need them. These professionals make sure that departments are working together to address response and recovery challenges. The public servants known as emergency managers also help determine response and recovery priorities. They gather information about expenses so funds can be tracked and payments can be made. Their contributions are crucial during postdisaster operations. Emergency managers are in many ways like the hub in a wheel that has spokes. They are central to the coordination of EM activities before, during, and after disasters.

A host of other departments likewise play vital roles after disasters, and knowledgeable EM personnel are keenly aware of this fact. Public Works reestablishes public utilities such as water. They also clean up disaster debris from public areas (e.g., government land, government offices, and parks). The Department of Transportation assists with evacuation and removes debris from roads. This department makes repairs to signal lights and reconstructs damaged roads and bridges. Parks and Recreation has the specific responsibility of caring for its own facilities. However, it is a great asset in disasters as it loans out personnel as well as equipment and trucks to other departments for debris removal or transportation assistance. Public Health is in charge of caring for victims who have been infected by disease outbreaks or a biological terrorist attack. Public Health may also be involved in the health concerns related to natural or technological disasters, and it interacts frequently with hospitals to track patient bed availability. Public Health also issues orders to isolate patients when diseases spread. If there is not a Mental Health Department in the city, Public Health also counsels those who have been affected emotionally by the disaster.

There are many others that are involved in disasters at the local level. The coroner is responsible for gathering, storing, and identifying bodies of the deceased. He or she also releases the deceased to families and funeral homes so burial or cremation may take place. The Engineering Department inspects buildings to determine if they are habitable or if they should be condemned. This department also promotes more stringent building codes before reconstruction can begin. The Chamber of Commerce works with businesses to identify the financial impact of the disaster. It helps companies resume normal activities by representing their interests during recovery. The Department of Housing tells tenants if homes and apartments can be occupied after a disaster. This entity also facilitates the building of new housing during recovery. Development and Redevelopment Agencies may work with the Engineering Department, the Chamber of Commerce, and the Housing Department to make recovery decisions, rebuild urban areas, and implement mitigation measures. As an example, the New Jersey Economic Development Authority has been heavily involved in guiding recovery after Hurricane Sandy.

Elected civic leaders are also logically involved in postdisaster operations (Figure 2-1). Mayors declare emergencies and disasters, which is necessary if outside assistance is to be sought and obtained. These politicians work closely with city managers, city council members, emergency managers, and public information officers (PIOs) to establish priorities after a disaster, mobilize personnel and resources, and keep the public up-to-date about ongoing response and recovery activities.

Although many cities operate as described earlier, it must be recognized that no two communities are organized exactly alike. Some cities may rely on private ambulance companies but may have a dedicated emergency manager. Others may have volunteer firefighters and no emergency manager. In different cities, government departments may be organized in other ways, and this would require that they have distinct disaster responsibilities. For instance, in some cases, EM is located in the fire department, police department, or public works. In other situations, the EM office is independent or reports directly to the city manager. At other times, the Building Department and Public Works may be combined. It is therefore imperative that you understand your city organization and that of nearby jurisdictions. This will be vital if you are to harness local public resources after disasters.

Figure 2-1

Elective officials such as Freeport, NY Mayor, Andrew Hardwick, often meet with community members to discuss ongoing response and recovery efforts. Andrew Booher/FEMA.

### 2.1.2 County and Regional Governments

County/parish governments and regional governments are also heavily involved in postdisaster operations. Counties or parishes may have EM offices, and their employees often work with city EM offices. County/parish EM offices are typically responsible for unincorporated areas also. They typically have additional resources that can be deployed when disasters prove to be too much for local governments. In this case, a county judge or commissioner (or parish president in the State of Louisiana) may also declare a disaster and work with state and federal governments to acquire disaster assistance. In fact, presidentially declared disasters (those requiring federal assistance) are always initiated at the county level instead of at the local or state level.

Those involved in EM at the county-level work perform a variety of disaster functions. The sheriff's office may help with traffic control or other law enforcement functions after disasters. The Geographic Information Systems Department helps to plot the location of resources when EM activities are undertaken. Public Health helps to provide health services after all types of disasters, and they are key players in the distribution of medicines to affected communities. The County Economic Development Department may play a vital role in recovery. These county entities work with other agencies at the municipal level and cover unincorporated areas to ensure disaster funds are distributed and spent according to federal policy and regulations.

Regional governments are networks of local and county governments that address collective problems in large metroplex areas (e.g., Dallas/Fort Worth and Los Angeles) and across numerous counties in rural areas. These organizations focus on daily concerns that affect multiple jurisdictions like transportation and environmental issues. However, regional governments also give attention to disasters and may be the conduit by which the federal government distributes grant monies for EM. The federal government prefers to award grants to regional governments to avoid duplication of effort and unnecessary expenses. In return, regional governments are expected to share their resources (e.g., hazardous material teams or swift water rescue boats) with local jurisdictions in need.

The North Central Texas Council of Governments (NCTCOG) is one example of a regional governmental organization. This particular association attempts to strengthen local governments by assisting them in cooperative efforts across the Dallas/Fort Worth region. In terms of EM, the NCTCOG has a department dedicated to regional disaster planning and coordination. The Emergency Preparedness Program provides leadership to improve collaboration across jurisdictions in this geographic area.

### 2.1.3 State Government

Many state agencies are involved in response and recovery operations. The **state government** is the political unit comprised of numerous cities, counties, regional governments, as well as bureaucratic agencies and politicians. This includes departments similar to those at the local and county levels, but it has some notable differences as well.

For instance, the State Emergency Management Agency is somewhat similar to the local EM office. It works with all other departments at the state level in addition to local, county, and federal EM organizations. The State Emergency Management Agency may be an independent entity, or it can be affiliated with the governor's office or even a state homeland security agency. In fact, since 9/11, EM and homeland security offices have undergone several organizational transformations. Sometimes, these agencies are co-located, while in other cases they are separate entities. At times, they may be referred to as the Emergency Management Agency, the Department of Homeland Security, or the Homeland Security Agency. The important point to remember is that EM is typically more concerned with all types of disaster issues, while homeland security is generally geared toward crime and terrorist activity.

Besides EM and homeland security, there are many other state agencies involved in disasters. As an example, the Department of Forestry is in charge of suppressing forest fires (Figure 2-2). It is like a city fire department, but it is much larger and typically operates in rural areas instead of cities. The Department of Forestry also has large ground crews as well as air support (e.g., helicopters and tankers). The Department of Public Safety or Highway Department acts much like the local police department by handling traffic control after disasters. In some states, like Texas, the state Department of Public Safety plays an important role in assessing and declaring disasters.

In addition to these agencies, many other state departments participate in response and recovery operations. The Department of Transportation facilitates large-scale evacuations and rebuilds freeways after disasters. The Health Department at the state level assists with public and mental health issues. The Housing

Department addresses housing shortages made evident after disasters. The Environment Department protects the quality of natural resources such as soil and water if they are adversely affected by a hazard. The loss of crops and cattle is a priority of the state Agriculture Department. The state Department of Insurance and Department of Commerce may also become involved in disasters if there are conflicts regarding claim settlements or price gouging during recovery operations.

**Figure 2-2**

State firefighting resources will be utilized to extinguish blazes such as this one in Loveland, CO. Michael Rieger/FEMA.

## FOR EXAMPLE

### Evacuation before Hurricane Rita

After witnessing several weaknesses in Louisiana's response after Hurricane Katrina, Texas wanted to avoid going through similar problems. The Texas Division of Emergency Management and Department of Public Safety worked closely with local law enforcement officials to evacuate Houston citizens prior to the arrival Hurricane Rita. When the northbound side of the freeway became jammed with thousands of motorists, the southbound lanes were reversed. This increased traffic flow but required the coordinated assistance of police, sheriffs, and others from the highway patrol. The state also had to provide gas for vehicles that ran out of fuel. The state worked with north Texas communities to receive evacuees and open shelters. The evacuation was not without problems as some elderly residents died due to the stress of evacuation. However, hundreds of thousands of people were successfully moved from harm's way.

Much like a mayor or county judge (or parish president in Louisiana), the governor declares emergencies and disasters on behalf of the state. If the state is overwhelmed by the impact, the governor may seek internal or external assistance. This may include calling up the **National Guard**, which is a reserve military unit operated under the direction of the governor in each state. This civilian force may assist law enforcement personnel, conduct search and rescue operations, remove debris, or provide other types of assistance as required. The governor may also request relief from other states or the federal government. If the resources within the state prove insufficient, the governor may seek help from other states. For example, Oklahoma turned to Iowa for help from the May 2013 tornados, knowing that Iowa had utilized many capabilities to aid Louisiana after Hurricane Katrina. Upon the governor's request, the **Emergency Management Assistance Compact** (EMAC) can also be activated. This is like a local mutual aid agreement, but it is for states instead. For instance, personnel, equipment, and commodities can be sent from EMAC members to a state that is in need. EMAC is operated under the National Association of Emergency Managers, an EM organization for governors and state EM agencies. However, when the resources of neighboring states or EMAC are insufficient, the governor may also request assistance of the federal government (Figure 2-3).

**Figure 2-3**

Those responding to disasters will work together to respond to disasters. In this picture, personnel from the National Guard and U.S. Department of Wildlife are traveling in a flooded area in Minot, ND, to check on telephone towers and power stations. Andrea Booher/FEMA.

### 2.1.4 Federal Government

The **federal government** is the national political unit that is composed of many officials, departments, and agencies. The federal government includes political leaders who fulfill important disaster roles. For example, if state and local jurisdictions cannot cope with a large disaster, the president of the United States may declare a federal disaster and provide national resources to local and state governments. If this is the case, the Department of Homeland Security (DHS) and the Federal Emergency Management Agency (FEMA) also heavily involved.

DHS was created after the September 11, 2001, terrorist attacks. It includes 22 federal agencies and over 188,000 employees. DHS is responsible for public security in the nation, and it is organized around the Directorate for National Protection and Programs, the Science and Technology Directorate, the Directorate for Management, and other units. The main goal of DHS is to prevent terrorist attacks on American soil. It therefore relies heavily upon agencies such as Immigration and Customs Enforcement, the Transportation Security Administration, and the U.S. Coast Guard.

If a disaster or terrorist attack occurs, FEMA is given responsibility to assist local and state governments. FEMA was created in the late 1970s by President Jimmy Carter to coordinate the EM activities of the government. FEMA has a national office in Washington, DC, but it also has 10 regional offices spared around the nation (Figure 2-4). FEMA also has many functional divisions to promote mitigation and planning issues as well as other groups that address response and recovery activities (e.g., FEMA Incident Management Advanced Teams (IMAT) get deployed immediately before or after a disaster to assess what further resources will be needed). Among other things, FEMA helps direct large-scale search and rescue operations, reimburse local government for certain emergency operations, facilitate debris removal, and provide people with funds for rebuilding. FEMA works with many partners involved in the National Response Framework and the National Recovery Framework.

The **National Response Framework** is a planning document that describes what the government will do in catastrophic disasters. It deals with immediate needs made evident by a disaster. The **National Disaster Recovery Framework**, in contrast, is a guide to enable effective long-term rebuilding in disaster-stricken areas. It provides disaster recovery managers with a flexible structure to restore affected communities. Some of the organizations involved in these plans take on primary responsibilities, while others perform support functions. Several of these departments and agencies are listed in Table 2-1.

There are many other agencies and individuals that deal with disasters and EM besides those listed in the National Response and National Recovery Frameworks. Some agencies explore the causes and consequences of disasters, while others concentrate on specific types of events. For instance, the Federal Aviation Administration (FAA) controls flight traffic before and after aviation accidents occur. The National Transportation and Safety Board (NTSB) investigates transportation accidents such as plane crashes. For example, in fall 2001, a plane crashed in a residential neighborhood in New York. The NTSB traveled to the scene and determined that the accident was caused by turbulence. The

Figure 2-4

**FEMA Regional Offices**

| Region | Location | States Serving |
|---|---|---|
| Region I | Boston, MA | CT, MA, ME, NH, RI, VT |
| Region II | New York, NY | NJ, NY, PR, USVI |
| Region III | Philadelphia, PA | DC, DE, MD, PA, VA, WV |
| Region IV | Atlanta, GA | AL, FL, GA, KY, MS, NC, SC, TN |
| Region V | Chicago, IL | IL, IN, MI, MN, OH, WI |
| Region VI | Denton, TX | AR, LA, NM, OK, TX |
| Region VII | Kansas City, MO | IA, KS, MO, NE |
| Region VIII | Denver, CO | CO, MT, ND, SD, UT, WY |
| Region IX | Oakland, CA | AZ, CA, HI, NV, GU, AS, CNMI, RMI, FM |
| Region X | Bothell, WA | AK, ID, OR, WA |

FEMA has 10 regional offices around the United States. Source: FEMA.

Occupational Safety and Health Agency (OSHA) also probes the reason for accidents, but they look closely at injuries that result from the workplace. Another organization, the Chemical Safety Board, determines the cause of industrial explosions that result from safety violations. The Bureau of Alcohol, Tobacco and Firearms (ATF) and Federal Bureau of Investigation (FBI) are additional federal agencies that are involved in investigation. After the bombing of the Murrah Federal Building in Oklahoma in 1995, the ATF and FBI were on the scene to determine what happened and if it was an act of terrorism. The ATF and FBI also pursue and capture those who have violated laws relating to the possession of explosives and others who are considered suspected terrorists.

Other federal groups are involved in a myriad of activities including hazard detection and warning, fraud deterrence, and general oversight. The U.S. Geological Survey (USGS) is one example. It helps predict volcanic eruptions and determine the location and magnitude of earthquakes. The National Oceanic and Atmospheric Agency (NOAA) tracks hurricanes that form in the ocean and approach land. The

**Table 2-1: Federal Departments and Their Role in a Disaster**

| Department/agency | Disaster functions |
|---|---|
| U.S. Department of Agriculture (USDA) | Suppresses rural and urban fires |
| U.S. Department of Commerce (DOC) | Provides information and assists with planning, resource support, communications, and hazardous material incidents |
| U.S. Department of Defense (DOD) | Assists with public works and engineering, flood control, transportation, urban search and rescue, firefighting, mass care, and health and medical services. The DOD may also become involved in the detection and response to hazardous material spills and weapons of mass destruction |
| U.S. Department of Education (DOED) | Collects, processes, and disseminates critical information |
| U.S. Department of Energy (DOE) | Restores energy systems and reacts to nuclear power plant emergencies |
| U.S. Department of Health and Human Services (HHS) | Supplements local and state public health and medical operations |
| U.S. Department of Housing and Urban Development (HUD) | Provides or reestablishes temporary and permanent housing |
| U.S. Department of the Interior (DOI) | Supports with information and planning, emergency, communications, firefighting, and hazardous material functions |
| U.S. Department of Justice (DOJ) | Participates in information and planning, urban search and rescue, health and medical services, and hazardous material issues. Also ensures that all laws pertaining to disaster assistance are followed |
| U.S. Department of Labor (DOL) | Contributes to public works, engineering, resource support, urban search and rescue, and hazardous material areas |
| U.S. Department of State (DOS) | Takes part in transpiration, energy, and hazardous material services |

| Agency | Role |
|---|---|
| U.S. Department of Transportation (DOT) | Fulfills transportation, information and planning, energy, hazardous material duties after a disaster |
| U.S. Department of Treasury (TREAS) | Funds long-term recovery projects and mitigation measures |
| U.S. Department of Veterans Affairs (VA) | Seeks assistance for veteran needs after a disaster as well as mass care and health and medical services |
| U.S. Environmental Protection Agency (EPA) | Responds to and cleans up hazardous material spills and also works in firefighting, health and medical services |
| National Communications System | Facilitates communications after a disaster |
| General Services Administration (GSA) | Aids in logistical activities such as transportation, information and planning, mass care, and food distribution roles |
| National Aeronautics and Space Administration (NASA) | Completes urban search and rescue and other functions in reference to satellites and remote sensing |
| Nuclear Regulatory Commission (NRC) | Shares expertise in energy and hazardous material disasters involving nuclear plants |
| Office of Planning and Management (OPM) | Advances logistical and resource support to all other federal agencies involved in disaster response or recovery |
| Small Business Administration (SBA) | Offers financial assistance to individuals and businesses affected by disasters |
| Social Security Administration (SSA) | Supplies mass care, housing, and human services needs |
| Tennessee Valley Authority (TVA) | Makes available transportation, public works, engineering, and energy services |
| Agency for International Development (AID) | Supplies urban search and rescue resources |
| U.S. Postal Service (USPS) | Imparts transpiration support |

National Weather Service (NWS) deals with warnings pertaining to thunderstorms, flooding, tornadoes, hail, and other forms of severe weather. The Office of the Inspector General (IG) ensures that federal agencies and disaster victims are not misusing disaster assistance funds.

Besides government agencies, congressional representatives and senators often become involved in postdisaster activities. They bring visibility to disasters and attempt to get additional resources for victims and affected jurisdictions. After 9/11, for example, New York Senators Hillary Clinton and Charles Schumer gave several interviews about the needs of New York City and what assistance was still needed. Congressional representatives also help communities and states resolve problems made evident during response and recovery operations. Since Hurricane Katrina, congressional leaders from Louisiana have been determining how to improve their state's response capabilities. They are also working on measures that would make New Orleans safer, such as strengthening the levees. Senators and House of Representatives may also pass ad hoc legislation after a disaster to provide additional funding for disasters. The large number of agencies and officials involved in disaster response and recovery operations indicates that the federal government is a major player in EM activities.

### 2.1.5 Tribal Government

In addition to local, state, and federal government entities, there are also tribal governments that are involved in EM. A tribal government is "an Indian or Alaska Native tribe ... that the Secretary of the Interior acknowledges to exist as an Indian tribe pursuant to the Federally Recognized Indian Tribe List Act of 1994" (FEMA, 2012a). In the United States, there are 564 federally recognized tribes, and they have their own unique history, customs, language, and laws. Furthermore, each tribe has a unique relationship to the federal government. On the one hand, each Indian tribe is considered an independent nation. Indian tribes are, in essence, a

---

## FOR EXAMPLE

### FEMA AmeriCorps Teams

In September 2013, heavy rains caused flooding over 2000 square miles in 17 Colorado counties. Over 15,000 homes were damaged and nearly 2000 homes were completely destroyed. To address the needs of disaster victims, FEMA deployed 30 AmeriCorps Teams (affiliated with the U.S. Corporation for National and Community Service). These teams, comprised of over 240 members, included recent college graduates who want to make a difference while also gaining additional experience and credentials. These energetic individuals performed a variety of tasks including assistance regarding evacuation sites, sheltering locations, mass care, and donation staging and distribution. They also mudded and gutted flooded homes, and moved over 1.2 million pounds of furniture. The involvement of AmeriCorps cuts federal disaster costs and helps thousands of victims in need (Figure 2-5).

Figure 2-5

FEMA Corps members arrive in Jamestown, CO, on October 2, 2013. These government representatives went door to door to make sure residents were aware of the availability of FEMA disaster assistance. Michael Rieger/FEMA.

## FOR EXAMPLE

### Tribal Governments and Federal Aid

The Sandy Recovery Improvement Act of 2013 (SRIA) amended the Robert T. Stafford Disaster Relief and Emergency Assistance Act, as amended, 42 U.S.C. § 5121 *et seq.*, (Stafford Act) so federally recognized Indian tribal governments (tribal governments) have the option to request a presidential emergency or major disaster declaration independently of a state. A chief executive of a federally recognized tribal government may request that the president declare an emergency or major disaster for the tribal government *or* consider it as part of a state's declaration request.

separate country within the U.S. territory. On the other hand, the Indian tribe is somewhat like a state in that it may now receive funding from the federal government. In other words, federal EM assistance can now be given directly to Indian tribes and bypass the state in which it resides entirely. That being said, some tribal governments have more developed EM programs, while others do not. Those working in EM should make extra efforts to work with Indian tribes, based on the tribe's level of interest and needs.

## SELF-CHECK

- What are the different sectors that are involved in disaster response and recovery?
- What does the local government do when disaster strikes?
- How can the state help the emergency manager deal with disaster?
- Why is the federal government a major player in recovery operations?
- What are the major agencies involved in the National Response Framework and the National Recovery Framework?
- What makes tribal government unique from federal and state governments?

## 2.2 The Private Sector

As an emergency manager, you should understand that businesses will be involved in response and recovery operations. The first priority of any business is to seek profit through commerce of various types. However, companies also play important and varied roles after disasters (McEntire et al., 2003). On many occasions, those in the private sector will operate independently in disasters, taking care of their own needs and interests. However, at other times, the private sector will help the community to deal with the disaster and may be a vital asset for those working in EM. The responsibilities of the private sector are broad and range from emergency medical care to reporting and the settlement of insurance claims.

### 2.2.1 Emergency and Long-Term Medical Care

Providing emergency medical care is one of the first things the private sector will do after a disaster. As mentioned earlier, paramedics from both the public and private sectors will be dispatched to the scene. These paramedics, or EMTs, will assist those injured in the accident or disaster by providing basic first aid and other necessary medical procedures. This may include applying bandages to stop bleeding, treating shock, and setting broken bones. Postdisaster activities could also include giving intravenous fluids and medicines. After or while the patient is being stabilized, paramedics will transport the individual to the hospital by ambulance or helicopter. When several victims are involved in an event, many paramedics and transportation units will arrive. Field hospitals may be set up to care for anticipated mass casualties. At the hospital, the injured will receive more advanced assessments and treatments. This may include X-rays, surgery, and care for burns. The hospital will continue care and rehabilitation until the victim has recovered. If a patient dies, the private sector will become involved in mortuary services such as body cremation or preparation for burial and memorial services for the deceased.

### 2.2.2 Sheltering and Housing

Businesses also shelter individuals who evacuate from hazards such as hurricanes. For example, hotels provide shelter for those who leave the coast when a hurricane approaches. This could amount to thousands or hundreds of thousands of people moving inland to higher and safer ground. Hotels may also house emergency workers when they arrive from outside jurisdictions to assist the affected community. The private sector also shelters other people who lose their apartment or home in disasters. Manufacturers may produce and supply tents or mobile homes for temporary or semipermanent accommodations. This is especially important when disasters create serious housing shortages.

### 2.2.3 Media Reporting

The private sector informs the public about hazards and disasters. For example, it is the meteorologists and news anchors from radio and television stations that convey weather warnings from the NWS and relay information from the Emergency Alert System. When a disaster occurs, radio, TV, or other media outlets also report damages, deaths, and injuries. The media shares information about government response and recovery efforts and tells the public where to go for shelter and assistance. The media can be an important asset to you as an emergency manager. However, you will have to work closely with media personnel to ensure your message is heard and relayed correctly.

### 2.2.4 Volunteers and Donations

Companies support disaster response and recovery activities in a number of other ways. Businesses send volunteers and donations to those in need. This may include cooks and waiters from restaurants to distribute food. It may include sending construction personnel to tarp destroyed roofs. Heavy equipment operators may likewise be dispatched to assist with debris removal. Companies also give supplies to communities and individuals in need. For example, some beverage businesses deliver bottled water to hard hit areas. The private sector may also give or loan cell phones, flashlights, work boots, hard hats, gloves, generators, computers, vehicles, or anything else to first responders and EM officials. The private sector is a useful partner in disasters because of their impressive resources and logistical capabilities. Walmart was a major participant in the response to Hurricane Katrina. It could mobilize resources that the federal government did not possess.

### 2.2.5 Insurance Settlements

Because disasters result in the loss of life and property, insurance companies send teams of adjusters to the affected areas to settle claims (Figure 2-6). Local personnel will begin the claims process immediately. In the days and weeks that follow, other personnel will arrive to support the particular disaster operation in question. The services of insurance agencies are needed for several reasons. People are injured and they may acquire large medical bills. The breadwinner in a family may have died, and future income for the spouse and children may be jeopardized. Cars and homes are often destroyed, and other forms of personal property may be lost or rendered unusable. For this reason, State Farm, Allstate, and other insurance providers reimburse expenses, replace losses, and help disaster victims begin their path to recovery.

Figure 2-6

Insurance companies will send employees to disaster-affected areas
to begin processing claims. Micheal Rieger/FEMA.

### 2.2.6 Utility Restoration and Community Reconstruction

Major windstorms, earthquakes, and other hazards often impact utilities, homes, and other buildings. Phone and electrical poles may be downed in a disaster. Water and gas lines can be severed. Hundreds or millions of people may be left with limited or no services. Utility companies will therefore put their own employees to work or contract with others (even competitors) to get lines restored quickly. For example, Duke Power (based in North Carolina) sent workers to help Entergy (a New Orleans' utility provider) restore service in the affected areas after Hurricane Katrina. In many cases, these employees will work long hours and around the clock in shifts to reestablish utilities. Without their assistance, it would be impossible to respond successfully or resume routine activities. Electricity, for example, is required for emergency lighting, shelter operations, and the sharing of public information. Power is also essential to rebuild homes, businesses, and government facilities, and this construction could not occur without the private sector. The help of concrete companies, framers, plumbers, and electricians are needed to rebuild communities after disasters. In addition, the private sector also rebuilds roads, bridges, and other critical infrastructure. Utilities and construction companies play a vital role in economic development following a disaster, and cooperation across these organizations and with the government is a must.

### 2.2.7 Business Continuity

As can be seen, companies help others affected by disasters. But corporations also take care of themselves because disasters often affect and disrupt business activities. For instance, a manufacturing plant can be destroyed by an industrial explosion. A bank cannot issue loans if computer records are lost due to a power outage. A construction company cannot function if its employees cannot be contacted and told where to report for work. For this reason, business continuity plans are developed in the private sector. Continuity plans identify ways to reestablish facilities and ensure business transactions can continue when a disaster strikes. Exxon/Mobil, Raytheon, Marriott, Target, and many others have business continuity programs that can be activated in time of disaster. Some of the employees in this area are known as business continuity specialists or risk managers.

### 2.2.8 Transportation

Another role of businesses is transportation. Companies evacuate individuals before or after disasters. The private sector operates or contracts out taxis, shuttle vans, busses, trains, boats, and airplanes. These can all be used to move people to safer areas. Transportation companies may also be directly involved in an accident or crash. Such emergencies could result from adverse weather conditions, mechanical failure, or human error on land/rail, at sea, or in the air. If this is the case, employees from the affected company may be sent to the area to assist passengers and provide information to victims' families. Employees will also have to clean up wreckage, prevent or settle lawsuits, and answer questions from the media. At times, transportation accidents may result in the emission of hazardous materials. This will require remediation efforts to clean up the environment according to

---

## FOR EXAMPLE

### The Role of Businesses after 9/11

Corporations were integral to the response to 9/11. After two planes were intentionally flown into the World Trade Center, businesses facilitated the evacuation of the Twin Towers. They donated offices supplies for the make shift emergency operations center on pier 92 after building number seven was gutted by fire. Companies donated software to help emergency managers track personnel and resources. The private sector helped control the perimeter around ground zero with fences. Medical care was performed by private hospitals. The local and national media informed the public of the events and how to seek assistance. As recovery proceeded, many companies worked to restore phone, electric, and gas utilities. Others helped to clean up dust in buildings, remove debris, relocate those who had lost office space, and submit payments for life insurance policies. It is doubtful that response and recovery operations could have taken place as quickly as they did in New York City without the heavy involvement of the private sector.

DOT or EPA regulations. Specialized employees from the private sector are needed to follow such guidelines to prevent the company being fined.

### 2.2.9 Vending of Goods and Services

Some companies will make a great deal of money from disasters. Sandbags, personal protective equipment, fences, portable sanitation units, and heavy equipment are all needed during response and recovery operations. If available, businesses are willing to assist with these resources—especially true when a fee can be charged. Corporations also seek profits in other ways. There are companies that sell computer programs to communities so they can manage the disaster effectively. Some sell software that is utilized to manage first responders and other resources. Engineering firms also play a role after a disaster as they inspect damages to buildings to determine if they are safe for future habitation. Other companies remove debris after disasters. If a road or rail accident or disaster involves hazardous materials, firms like Cura Emergency Services and Hulcher Services Inc. may remove contaminated soil, complete required state and federal paperwork, or repair railways. When water or fire affects a building and its contents, companies like BMS Catastrophe sends employees to the site to pump out unhealthy air, remove mold and soot, and restore vital documents and waterlogged computer equipment. As can be seen, businesses are therefore vital partners in disaster response and recovery operations.

## SELF-CHECK

- Why are businesses involved in disaster response and recovery?
- How can the private sector help with emergency medical care?
- Who can help you manage public relations?
- Could insurance companies provide statistics on homes damaged in disasters and property loss?
- Why would it be necessary to work with utility companies involved in recovery?
- What else can corporations do to help you promote resilience after disasters?

## 2.3 The Nonprofit Sector

Many nonprofit organizations are involved in disaster response and recovery activities. Nonprofit organizations are charitable agencies that are prohibited by law from gaining financially for their humanitarian services to individuals and communities. While there are many nonprofit organizations that do not have a relation to EM, there are others that become heavily involved in disasters when they occur. A well-known example is the American Red Cross, but there are a host of other religious and community groups.

### 2.3.1 The Red Cross

The **American Red Cross** is a national member of the International Committee of the Red Cross (ICRC) and the International Federation of Red Cross and Red Crescent Societies (IFRCRCS). These organizations were created because of the caring leadership of Henry Dunant. As a young man from Switzerland, Dunant recognized the need to assist those wounded during an 1859 battle in Solferino, Italy. Thousands of soldiers were injured in the conflict between the Austrian Army and the Franco-Sardinian Alliance. Most lay helpless and dying in the battlefield. Dunant organized a relief effort among citizens to provide medical care to the military personnel in need. He also advocated that prisoners on both sides be treated with respect and dignity. These principles were ratified in 1863 by many European governments in Geneva, Switzerland (now the headquarters of the Red Cross movement). Today, the ICRC is based on several principles:

▲ **Humanity**. The Red Cross has a desire to help those in need.
▲ **Impartiality**. The assistance it gives will be provided without discrimination.
▲ **Neutrality**. No preference will be shown toward either side involved in hostility.
▲ **Independence**. Each society acts autonomously according to the laws of each nation.
▲ **Voluntary service**. Volunteers and charitable service motivate actions, not profit.
▲ **Unity**. There can be only one Red Cross organization in any particular country.
▲ **Universality**. All Red Cross societies are equal; none is more important than the other.

The Red Cross does not only deal with conflict-related events, however. Dunant himself thought that anyone in need of medical assistance should be given care, regardless of the cause. From its founding, the Red Cross has been involved in disaster relief activities.

As the Red Cross was being established abroad, Clara Barton (a nurse in the United States) was caring for the soldiers injured in the Civil War (Figure 2-7). She heard about the International Red Cross movement and traveled to Europe to learn more about the fledgling organization. She returned home and in 1881 established the American Association of Red Cross Societies. The American Red Cross—as it is known today—serves Dunant's and Barton's dual aims.

The American Red Cross was mandated by Congress to address citizen needs in time of disaster. The Red Cross has chapters and branches around the United States to prepare communities for disasters and give assistance after disasters strike. Their services, which are provided by both a small cadre of employees and a large number of volunteers, can be broken down into six areas:

1. **Disaster health services**. Provide first aid, fill prescriptions, and collect and distribute blood for those in need.
2. **Mental health services**. Support the emotional needs of disaster victims through counseling sessions and foster psychological recovery.

Figure 2-7

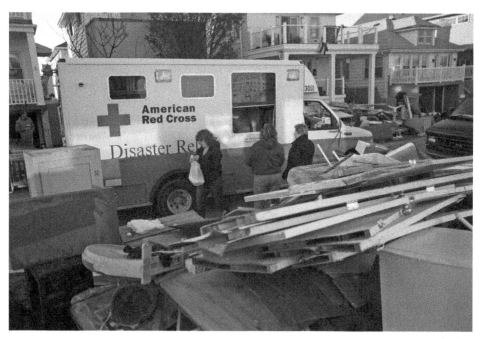

The Red Cross is present at almost any disaster or emergency, and it provides a variety of services to victims and survivors. Andrea Booher/FEMA.

3. **Disaster welfare inquiry**. Receive calls from loved ones who are worried about their loved ones, take steps to contact such individuals, and relay information back to the concerned family members.

4. **Family services**. Determine and meet the immediate and long-term needs of people including clothing, furniture, temporary housing, and even tools for work.

5. **Mass care**. Feed and establish shelters for emergency workers and the public.

6. **Other services**. Facilitate and support damage assessment, communications, volunteer management, logistics, interagency liaison, and public affairs.

For these reasons, the American Red Cross is an important part of EM in this country.

### 2.3.2 Faith-Based Organizations

**Faith-based organizations** perform some of the same functions as other nonprofits, but they are associated with religious organizations. One of the most notable is the Salvation Army. This religious movement was founded in England by William Booth in 1852 and was initially called the Hallelujah or Volunteer Army. The goal of the Salvation Army is to preach Christianity and care for the poor and needy. In 1879, this organization gained a foothold in the United States and established its headquarters in Alexandria, Virginia.

> **FOR EXAMPLE**
>
> **The Red Cross Responds to the Paso Robles Earthquake**
>
> A 6.5 magnitude earthquake struck the city of Paso Robles in central California on December 22, 2003. The Red Cross quickly mobilized to assess damages in residential areas. At least 10 teams of inspectors were sent into neighborhoods to determine the extent of destruction on homes and personal property. Their findings were shared with the local government that facilitated a federal disaster declaration. Without the Red Cross, the needs of victims would not be well known or quickly addressed.

Today, the Salvation Army is divided into four geographic areas around the country. It has developed memorandums of understanding to assist local and state governments when disaster strikes. Its 63,000 employees and thousands of volunteers take care of immediate and long-term needs of disaster victims. This includes the provision of physical, material, emotional, or spiritual necessities. Like the Red Cross, the Salvation Army provides food, water, and sheltering. These organizations are different in other respects however. The Salvation Army has religious motivations, whereas the Red Cross does not.

There are a number of other faith-based groups that participate in response and recovery efforts. They include the Baptist Men, Catholic Relief Services, Lutheran World Relief, Latter-Day Saint Charities, and the United Methodist Committee on Relief. Other groups that help after disasters include Muslim and Asian faith-based organizations. These agencies care for the physical needs of disaster victims and provide spiritual and mental health counseling. There are hundreds of similar organizations around the world that respond to disasters in developing nations.

### 2.3.3 Community Groups

Many community groups are involved in disasters and provide relief to those who have been negatively impacted. Such groups include the United Way, the Rotary Club, Goodwill Industries, and Boy and Girl Scout chapters, among others. These organizations donate food, water, clothing, and other necessities of life. They share financial resources and construction supplies with disaster victims and communities. In some cases, these community groups may provide translation services for those that have questions about relief programs or cannot read instructions regarding aid applications in English. Community groups also cover medical expenses that result from disasters. In addition, these groups attend to the long-term needs of victims including crisis counseling, physical therapy, transportation, and housing. Some groups address the needs of animals that have been adversely affected by disasters. Others may be interested in preserving artwork in museums affected by disasters. Thus, the involvement of community groups is broad and far-reaching. While such organizations are certainly helpful in disasters, they may inadvertently complicate response and recovery activities for others. For instance, volunteer groups may start rebuilding neighborhoods before new codes can be passed and enforced.

Coordination within and among community groups can be enhanced by the **National Volunteer Organizations Active in Disasters** (NVOAD). This organization brings such agencies together to promote various types of assistance after disasters. National VOAD consists of 110 member organizations across the United States that act according to core principles of cooperation, communication, coordination, and collaboration. Members are led by a board of directors, which oversees conferences, task forces, and other disaster functions.

## SELF-CHECK

- What are nonprofit organizations?
- Who are the most prominent nonprofit organizations that are involved in disasters and what do they do?
- What is a faith-based organization and how do they relate to disasters?
- What are the community groups in your community that could help with response and recovery operations?
- How could the NVOAD assist with coordination?

## 2.4 Citizen and Emergent Groups

Citizens are involved in a variety of postdisaster activities ranging from volunteering to the contribution of donations. They perform vital services after disasters and may be fairly organized or more spontaneous in nature. As an emergency manager, you must be aware that citizens will be some of the first people to respond to disasters when they occur.

Some citizens are members of Community Emergency Response Teams (CERTs). A **CERT** is a group of concerned citizens that receive some basic training about disasters from local governments (Figure 2-8). This enables them to care for their neighbors and coworkers after a disaster and buy time until formal assistance arrives. CERTs are different than certain types of nonprofit organizations in that they have no paid employees. They also have a greater interest in disaster issues than many other community groups.

CERTs first appeared in California in 1985. At this time, it was recognized that first responders would not be able to satisfy all of the needs of survivors who were affected by major earthquakes. Public officials realized that damaged roads, the large numbers of people impacted, and a shortage of trained professionals would prohibit or limit needed care for disaster victims. There was consequently a desire to educate citizens to be self-sufficient for at least 72 hours. The CERT program was created to provide this training to citizens.

Since this time, CERTs have been established around the nation by publicizing training opportunities and accepting applications from interested volunteers. CERTs are often created in areas that deserve special attention. This might include

Figure 2-8

Community Emergency Response Teams (CERTs) add flexibility to response and recovery operations. After a tornado affected Rowlett, TX, CERT members helped to remove debris. In other disasters, they may fill sandbags, direct traffic, or perform other important functions. FEMA.

a neighborhood that is located far away from city resources, an elderly community that has unique medical needs, and a community college or university that has a transient population. Participants accepted into the program then undergo training that usually consists of several 2½ to 4-hour classes over a 7 or 8-week period. Classes address types of disasters to be expected, basic preparedness measures, fire suppression techniques, search and rescue operations, disaster medicine, and disaster psychology. There is now more attention on terrorism and what to do about it in light of the 9/11 attacks.

The training of CERT teams is funded by government grants. This funding may also help CERT members obtain basic equipment such as hard hats, gloves, and other supplies that might be useful in time of a disaster. Because of this federal support, there are now hundreds of CERT programs in most states throughout the nation. The value of CERTs is increasingly recognized by those involved in EM since they may be able to help victims in need and ease the burden on official first responders.

Citizens are also involved in disasters in other ways. After virtually all emergencies and disasters, citizens create and participate in emergent groups. **Emergent groups** are individuals who work together to perform common goals but do not yet have a formalized organization (Stallings and Quarantelli, 1985, p. 84). Put differently, an emergent group is a collection of people that unite for the sole

---

**FOR EXAMPLE**

**Public Response to the Loma Prieta Earthquake**

On October 17, 1989, a massive earthquake shook the cities of Santa Cruz and San Francisco. The earthquake was a 7.1 on the Richter scale. Research by O'Brien and Mileti (1992) revealed that roughly 65% of citizens in these communities took part in disaster response activities. Nearly 200,000 people donated water and food to victims. 71,000 people supported the victims' emotional needs. Another 31,500 took part in search and rescue operations. Citizens also cared for the wounded, cleared debris, and sheltered those in need. The major lesson from this disaster is that people living in affected or nearby locations are resources that can and will be utilized to address urgent disaster needs.

---

purpose of addressing disaster needs. The people that make up emergent groups become involved in activities they have never performed before or do not participate in frequently. Emergent organizations are typically disbanded once the emergency situation is resolved. In some cases, however, the emergent organization is formalized and becomes a permanent part of the organizational landscape.

Scholars have long recognized the role of emergent groups in disasters. Samuel Prince, a doctoral student at Columbia University, examined an explosion that occurred when a French munitioner ran into a Belgian relief ship during World War I in a harbor in Halifax, Canada. His dissertation is the forerunner of modern disaster sociology. It illustrated that strangers, friends, relatives, neighbors, and even the victims themselves interact to care for the injured, gather the dead, and fulfill other important postdisaster functions.

Since the time of Prince's dissertation, emergent groups and the behavior they exhibit have been studied extensively. Their unique features and activities have been characterized in a variety of ways (see Drabek and McEntire, 2003, p. 98):

▲ **Therapeutic community**. Citizens come together to promote healing and rehabilitation.
▲ **Synthetic community**. People working together to resolve major challenges.
▲ **Mass assault**. A massive response that can be overwhelming.
▲ **Altruistic community**. Selfless acts to help and assist others.
▲ **Utopian community**. Harmonious relations that may exist only right after a disaster.
▲ **Emergence**. The appearance of new organizations in time of crisis.
▲ **Emergent behavior**. The pursuit of tasks that are new and unfamiliar.

Research also reveals that emergent groups are most likely to appear when there have been insufficient steps for preparedness, when disasters are especially severe, when there is a perception of dire need, and when people place blame for what has happened. Culture, socioeconomic status, and other factors may also determine the formation and purpose of groups. Such determinants may include religion, gender, and race and ethnicity.

Once formed, emergent groups may become involved in search and rescue operations, damage assessment, shelter provision, emotional support for victims, and other relief activities. As a result, these spontaneous organizations are beneficial for disaster response and recovery. They are always the first to arrive at the scene, even before official "first" responders. Emergent groups organize themselves quickly to address the needs made evident by disaster. Emergent groups possess diverse skills and have a deep commitment to the cause. They also provide an impressive number of volunteers that can be harnessed in times of disaster.

These groups are not without potential drawbacks however. Citizens may have no formal disaster training. They may unintentionally injure those people they are trying to help (e.g., by making mistakes when providing basic first aid). Emergent groups may also get in the way of professional responders as they go about their duties. Emergent responders may even create unique challenges for emergency managers. For example, after Hurricane Andrew, there were so many donations in terms of food and supplies that it was difficult for organizations to distribute the aid efficiently. Successful response and recovery operations require the harnessing of emergent groups while simultaneously minimizing their negative impact.

## SELF-CHECK

- What is a CERT?
- How could CERTs help you as an emergency manager?
- What are emergent groups and why do they form after a disaster?
- Are emergent groups beneficial or detrimental? Explain your reasoning.
- How is a "mass assault" different than an "altruistic community?"
- What can be done to utilize emergent groups effectively?

## 2.5 Working with Different Groups and the Whole Community

As an emergency management official, you must be aware how each of the agencies, individuals, and groups interacts during disasters. The people involved in disasters can be viewed holistically by means of the well-known disaster organizational typology (Dynes, 1970) (see Figure 2-9). This model was developed by scholars from the famous DRC at Ohio State University (now located at the University of Delaware). For this reason, it is called the DRC typology. Its purpose is to help scholars and practitioners comprehend the unique characteristics of organizations that become involved in disasters.

The DRC typology was developed by Russell Dynes and E.L. Quarantelli after they interviewed hundreds of people and practitioners who observed disasters or were involved in EM (Dynes, 1970; Quarantelli, 1966). They categorized these reports based on two dimensions and produced a fourfold typology of organizational involvement in disasters. The two dimensions of the model are tasks and structures.

**Figure 2-9**

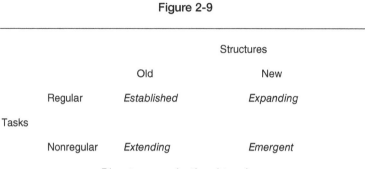

Disaster organizational typology.

Tasks refer to the activities of the organization. This may include functions that are routine (common to the organization) or nonroutine (unfamiliar to the organization). Structures refer to the organization's relationships and longevity. The organizational structure may be old (implying that it existed before the disaster) or new (implying that it was created after the disaster). Each type of organization has unique characteristics. For instance:

▲ **Established organizations** are groups that perform routine tasks with existing structures. A fire department falls under this category. It was present before the disaster and it fulfills fire suppression functions on a daily basis.
▲ **Expanding organizations** are groups that perform routine tasks with new structures. The Red Cross falls under this category. Its diverse workers from around the country are sent to a disaster site, but they complete their normal responsibilities.
▲ **Extending organizations** are groups that perform nonroutine tasks with existing structures. A possible example of the type of organization is a church. The pastor and congregation take new duties but were familiar with one another prior to the disaster.
▲ **Emergent organizations** are groups that perform nonroutine tasks with new structures. Citizens who were strangers prior to a disaster fall into this category if they are completing search and rescue activities for those injured in an earthquake.

The DRC typology should be considered as a useful tool by those involved in response and recovery operations. This model reveals that there are obviously many groups that participate in EM activities and they have distinct backgrounds, different goals, unique experiences, and varying lengths of existence. This complexity hinders coordination and often creates conflicts or problems. For instance, a fire department and police department may have an existing interagency rivalry (due to budgetary competition within a city), which may adversely affect cooperation in a disaster. Or nonprofit organizations may not wish to work with other humanitarian agencies in order to better highlight their individual accomplishments in a disaster.

However, it should be noted that the DRC typology has implications beyond descriptions of values and operational priorities. As an example, established organizations will most likely be aware of each other (e.g., fire department officials will know peers in the police department). This familiarity may better promote collaboration. Nevertheless, and in contrast, people in the expanding organizations and emergent groups may have never interacted before, and this limits the communication that could occur across people and agencies. Furthermore, an established organization most likely needs to follow strict laws and policies when it is performing the functions it has been assigned, and this fact may cause those affiliated with the organization to avoid interaction or have conflicting relations with emergent groups. For instance, an official search and rescue team may not want to have ordinary citizens involved in this activity due to liability concerns. Alternatively, those working in an existing business may know one another, but they may lack any expertise in disaster issues. This situation could cause others involved in EM to view them with suspicion or question their capabilities.

Knowing these sorts of interorganizational dynamics can help you better recognize potential problems in response and recovery operations and take measures to overcome them. With improved understanding of other organizations, you will be able to harmonize the interaction among them based on their unique skills and abilities in disasters. And this is a major principle in EM. In fact, FEMA's "**Whole Community**" concept acknowledges that a "government-centric approach to emergency management" is not sufficient to deal with a catastrophic disaster. All available resources must be collectively utilized at each level of government as well as within and across communities to prepare for and react to such an incident. Improved response and recovery operations will likely occur when all individuals and agencies fulfill individual roles and work collaboratively on responsibilities that span distinct organizational domains.

## SELF-CHECK

- What is the DRC typology?
- What are tasks?
- What are structures?
- What is the difference between an established organization and an extending organization?
- Can you give an example of an expanding organization?
- How can the DRC typology assist you in knowing what to expect when a disaster occurs?
- *What is the whole community?*

## SUMMARY

In order to promote disaster resilience, you must be aware of each of the participants in response and recovery operations. Local government departments and agencies are the first public organizations to respond to disaster. If needed, state and federal governments provide additional disaster assistance. Services, donations, and volunteers are made available by corporations and nonprofit organizations. Citizens—whether part of CERTs or emergent groups—also give of their time and energy to help victims affected by disasters. Awareness of the DRC typology can illustrate unique features of the organizations involved in disasters. It is imperative that you comprehend what types of conflicts may arise as multiple organizations react to disasters. It is imperative that you also understand who in the "whole community" can help you fill your role as an emergency manager when disasters occur.

## KEY TERMS

| | |
|---|---|
| **American Red Cross** | A national member of the International Committee of the Red Cross (ICRC) and a member of the International Federation of Red Cross and Red Crescent Societies (IFRCRCS). |
| **Community Emergency Response Team (CERT)** | A group of concerned citizens that receive some basic disaster training. |
| **Emergency Management Assistance Compact (EMAC)** | Similar to a local mutual aid agreement but it is for states. |
| **Emergent organizations** | Groups of individuals who work together to perform common goals but do not have a formalized organization (Stallings and Quarantelli, 1985, p. 84). |
| **Established organizations** | Groups that perform routine tasks with existing structures. |
| **Expanding organizations** | Groups that perform routine tasks with new structures. |
| **Extending organizations** | Groups that perform nonroutine tasks with existing structures. |
| **Faith-based organizations** | Nonprofit groups that perform some of the same functions as other nonprofits, but they are associated with religious organizations. |
| **Federal Emergency Management Agency** | Agency created in the late 1970s by President Jimmy Carter to help coordinate the activities of the government. |

| | |
|---|---|
| **Federal government** | The national political unit that is composed of many agencies and officials. |
| **Local governments** | City or county organizations that perform important public functions. |
| **Mutual aid** | The sharing of personnel, equipment, and facilities. This occurs when local resources are inadequate to meet the needs of the disaster. |
| **National Guard** | A reserve military unit operated under the direction of the governor. |
| **National Disaster Recovery Framework** | A guide to enable effective recovery in disaster-stricken areas. It provides disaster recovery managers with a flexible structure to restore affected communities. |
| **National Response Framework** | A document that describes what the government and whole communities will do in catastrophic disasters. |
| **National Volunteer Organizations Active in Disasters (NVOAD)** | An organization that brings agencies together to promote various types of assistance after disasters. |
| **Nonprofit sector** | The division of society that is comprised of humanitarian, charitable religious, and voluntary organizations. |
| **Private sector** | A part of society that includes businesses and corporations. |
| **Public sector** | The segment of society that is made up of government offices, departments, and agencies. |
| **State government** | The political unit comprised of numerous cities and counties and includes bureaucratic agencies and politicians. |
| **Tribal government** | "An Indian or Alaska Native tribe … that the Secretary of the Interior acknowledges to exist as an Indian tribe pursuant to the Federally Recognized Indian Tribe List Act of 1994." |
| **Whole community** | The idea that a "government-centric approach to emergency management" is not sufficient to face a catastrophic disaster. All available resources must be collectively utilized at each level of government to prepare for and respond to such an incident. |

# ASSESS YOUR UNDERSTANDING

Posttest to evaluate your knowledge of roles and responsibilities of disaster participants.

*Measure your learning by comparing pretest and posttest results.*

## Summary Questions

1. The public sector is subdivision of society made up of ordinary, everyday citizens. True or false?
2. A business would be categorized under the private sector. True or false?
3. An example of a nonprofit organization is a community-based agency that engages in humanitarian and charitable work. True or false?
4. Mutual aid involves the sharing of first responders or necessary supplies. True or false?
5. Mayors and other elected officials are responsible for declaring a disaster at the local level. True or false?
6. State governments will not become involved in disasters but will simply request assistance from the federal government. True or false?
7. The National Guard may help conduct search and rescue missions or remove debris after a disaster. True or false?
8. FEMA is the only organization at the federal level that gets involved in disaster activities. True or false?
9. Companies may provide donations but they do not have a bearing on sheltering and construction. True or false?
10. The Salvation Army is a faith-based organization. True or false?
11. Emergency management is most likely to be successful if all pertinent organizations perform their roles in disasters. True or false?
12. Which is not included in the public sector?
    (a) A firefighter that is a trained emergency medical technician
    (b) A company that supplies first responders with flashlights and batteries
    (c) Members of the city council
    (d) A local emergency manager
    (e) State and federal emergency management offices
13. What department is most likely to be able to assist you with traffic control issues?
    (a) Public Health
    (b) The coroner's office
    (c) Engineering
    (d) The police department
    (e) Department of Housing
14. Which person or entity may call up the National Guard?
    (a) The governor
    (b) The emergency manager
    (c) A representative from the Red Cross

    (d) The mayor

    (e) All of the above

15. The directorates of the Department of Homeland Security include:

    (a) Border and Transportation Security

    (b) Science and Technology

    (c) Information Analysis and Infrastructure Protection

    (d) Emergency Preparedness and Response

    (e) All of the above

16. Which federal agency or department may assist with hazardous material cleanup?

    (a) General Services Administration

    (b) Department of Agriculture

    (c) The Environmental Protection Agency

    (d) Department of Labor

    (e) Tennessee Valley Authority

17. Individuals that help companies recover from disasters are known as:

    (a) Private contractors

    (b) Business continuity specialists

    (c) CERT members

    (d) Members of emergent groups

    (e) None of the above

18. Under the principle of impartiality, the Red Cross tries to:

    (a) Help anyone in need

    (b) Serve out of charity and not for profit

    (c) Act autonomously in each nation

    (d) Provide assistance without discrimination

    (e) Remain neutral in armed conflicts

19. A major role of the Red Cross after a disaster is to:

    (a) Remove debris in the roads

    (b) Rebuild damaged infrastructure

    (c) Feed emergency workers

    (d) Shelter victims affected by disaster

    (e) Answers c and d

20. CERT stands for:

    (a) Civilian Emergency Repair Technician

    (b) Community Emergency Response Team

    (c) Civilian Emergency Response Technician

    (d) Community Emergent Recovery Team

    (e) Community Emergent Recovery Technician

21. An emergent group may be defined as:

    (a) The pursuit of tasks that are new and unfamiliar

    (b) Selfless acts of heroism

    (c) An organization that appears after a disaster to care for disaster victims (**d**) A department of the federal government

(**e**) A member of the National Volunteer Organizations Active in Disasters

22. An example of an extending organization is:

(**a**) A church

(**b**) A fire department

(**c**) The police department

(**d**) The Red Cross

(**e**) The local government

## Review Questions

1. Explain the difference between the public, private, and nonprofit sectors.
2. What are the responsibilities of the emergency manager?
3. If local resources are limited after a disaster, who could you contact for assistance?
4. How can the State Department of Public Safety help after a disaster?
5. What is the Emergency Management Assistance Compact?
6. What is the National Response Framework and how can it help you when a disaster occurs?
7. How is a tribal government similar and different than a state government?
8. What is the role of the National Weather Service in disaster response?
9. What businesses could you contact in the private sector if you had to evacuate thousands of people from a city?
10. What functions can be performed by the American Red Cross when a disaster occurs?
11. How could a CERT save lives and protect property?
12. Why is it necessary for an emergency manager to be aware of emergent behavior?
13. What is an established organization?
14. How can the DRC typology benefit those working in disaster response and recovery operations?

## Applying This Chapter

1. The National Weather Service predicts the arrival of severe weather in Chicago, Illinois. Your mayor is questioning who would be involved in response activities should a disaster occur. What are some of the participating organizations from the public, private, and nonprofit sectors?
2. An earthquake has damaged many of the homes and much of the infrastructure in Anaheim, California. What businesses from the private sector would logically be involved in the response to this disaster? How could you work with them to facilitate recovery?
3. A tornado has struck your community in the Midwest portion of the United States and left many people homeless. As a result, you have had to open up a shelter at a local church. Who could assist you with feeding and mass care issues?

4. You serve as a volunteer emergency manager in a small, rural community in Montana. Your town has been adversely affected by a major winter snow-storm—one that has shattered all of the prior records. Roads are impassible and you are worried about the elderly individuals in your jurisdiction. Could the state government assist you? Could faith-based organizations help? How would you call up their services?

5. Major events such as the Indian Ocean Tsunami generate impressive amounts of volunteerism. What do we call this type of behavior? Is this type of citizen involvement good or bad? How could you deal with it effectively?

### What Is a Local Emergency Manager?

Consider the position of an emergency manager. Write a one- or two-page paper that addresses the following questions: Where could it be located in the local government? Could it fall under the city manager's office? Fire department? Police department? What would the local emergency manager be in charge of? Who would he or she work with? What would he or she do on a daily basis? How would this change when a disaster occurs?

### The Need for Mutual Aid

A major fire has broken out at an industrial complex in a major metropolitan area near Los Angeles. Local firefighting resources are stretched thin and crews are beginning to tire. What could you do to get more personnel to the scene? What is the name we give to the sharing of such resources among neighboring jurisdictions or states? Why is this necessary?

### How Can a Business Help You?

Suppose a major hurricane swept over your community in Florida. The strong winds and storm surge downed power lines, deposited 2 feet of sand on roads, scattered boats blocks from the coast, and damages thousands of homes. Who could you contact in the private sector to help you resolve these problems created by the disaster?

### Have You Participated in or Witnessed an Emergent Group?

If a disaster has affected your city or state recently, did you participate in or see citizens respond? What did you or the others do? Did you or others perform a valuable role? What would have happened if you and others were not involved in that function? How important are citizens when a disaster strikes? Do you see any mistakes made or problems result from emergency groups?

### Consider How Organizations Interact

A terrorist attack has just occurred in a busy downtown area in Denver, Colorado. The police have cordoned off the area for safety. The Red Cross would like to provide snacks for firefighters, and business men and women would like to return to their buildings to retrieve their belongings. Spontaneous volunteers are arriving in the hundreds to donate blood and help remove debris. Are there any potential conflicts among these organizations? Can they be resolved? If so, how?

# 3

# ANTICIPATING HUMAN BEHAVIOR IN DISASTERS
## Myths, Exaggerations, and Realities

## Starting Point

Pretest to assess your knowledge on human behavior in disasters.
*Determine where you need to concentrate your effort.*

## What You'll Learn in This Chapter

▲ The impact of Hollywood and media portrayals about disaster behavior
▲ Research about human responses to disasters
▲ Reasons why researchers must study human behavior
▲ What people actually do in the aftermath of disaster
▲ The importance of understanding behavior correctly

## After Studying This Chapter, You'll Be Able To

▲ Compare and contrast the meaning of the words "myth" and "exaggerations."
▲ Examine what really happens in disaster situations.
▲ Identify ways to prevent the spread of incorrect views about human conduct after disasters.
▲ Explain how views about behavior affect response and recovery activities.

## Goals and Outcomes

▲ Evaluate the accuracy of Hollywood films and media broadcasts about disaster behavior.
▲ Assess fact and fiction about disaster behavior.
▲ Argue against inaccurate views about disaster response and recovery operations.
▲ Predict human behavior in disasters and respond accordingly.

*Disaster Response and Recovery: Strategies and Tactics for Resilience*, Second Edition. David A. McEntire.
© 2015 John Wiley & Sons, Inc. Published 2015 by John Wiley & Sons, Inc.

# INTRODUCTION

In order to react to a disaster effectively, it is imperative that you understand people's misperceptions about human behavior. Much of this comes from Hollywood films and the mass media. Unfortunately, the information presented in movies and by reporters focuses on sensational and unusual stories. For this reason, it is vital that you are aware of the research findings about human behavior in disasters. At the same time, you must also recognize that there is some degree of truth in the public's perception of postdisaster behavior. A recommendation to ensure successful response and recovery operations is to understand exactly how people behave after disasters.

## 3.1 The Impact of Hollywood and The Media

Most people get their views about human disaster behavior from films and the media (Fischer, 1998a). Movies are entertaining, of course, and media reports can keep one riveted to a disaster as it unfolds. Unfortunately, the perspectives from Hollywood and the media are almost always inaccurate (Eisenberg, 2003). Scholars have labeled these inaccuracies as "myths." A **myth** is defined in many dictionaries as a false belief. It is difficult to counter these incorrect portrayals about disaster behavior that are quickly spread through video footage and social media.

### 3.1.1 Hollywood

Hollywood is one of the major contributors to the public's perceptions about disasters. There are several movies that portray people's behavior in a negative and fictitious light.

*Dante's Peak* is a good example. This movie relays the story about a volcanic eruption in the Northwestern United States. After a number of deaths result from the emission of dangerous gasses from the volcano, community leaders hold a meeting to calm the public. During this gathering, an earthquake occurs and people panic as a result. They run haphazardly out of the building and begin to evacuate in droves as the volcano explodes from the mountain above them. Cars and trucks run into each other as their occupants drive frantically to escape the oozing lava and falling ash. Roads become clogged, and people do all they can to protect themselves while ignoring the needs of others. The movie suggests that when disaster strikes, people behave erratically.

*Volcano* is another disaster movie. It provides an amusing, but not completely accurate, view of human behavior in extreme events. After workers die in an underground utility tunnel in Los Angeles, a scientist named Dr. Amy Barnes discovers a growing volcanic threat. While investigating the source of deadly gasses below ground, the volcano becomes active. Dr. Barnes climbs out of the hole to save her life. When she arrives on the surface, she takes off her breathing apparatus and sets it down nearby. As she turns around, a bystander grabs her mask and runs off with it. This film gives the impression that theft and looting are common in disasters.

The movie *Asteroid* also provides an interesting portrayal of disasters. Upon learning that an asteroid is about to hit the United States, the government begins a massive evacuation. As people leave the area to be struck by the asteroid, one person becomes irate because of the government's decisions and shoots a FEMA official at an airport hangar. This movie, like many others, presents lawlessness and violence as the norm in disasters.

### 3.1.2 The Media

News reports, whether they come from television coverage, radio broadcasts, or newspaper articles, also portray human behavior in a dismal fashion. News reports and headlines tend to suggest that victims cannot care for themselves (Figure 3-1). After Hurricane Carla, several newspapers ran a headline noting "More than 100,000 Persons Flee in Near Panic." This title suggested pandemonium in spite of the fact that less than 1 percent of the evacuees were involved in a traffic accident (Quarantelli and Dynes, 1972, p. 70). Other stories frequently suggest that businesses price gouge the victims and survivors who need to make postdisaster purchases of goods and services.

To some extent, such reports are to be expected. The media is interested in abnormal events. For instance, if a dog bites a man, that is not particularly newsworthy. However, if a man bites a dog, this would certainly generate a great deal of publicity! Such unusual stories are the ones the media is infatuated with. They keep the viewers, listeners, and readers interested because of the drama being presented. Media ratings rise as a result.

**Figure 3-1**

Sometimes, media reports about disasters are inaccurate. FEMA has public information officers to ensure that correct and current information is given to the public. George Armstrong/FEMA.

---

**FOR EXAMPLE**

### Media Reports of Disasters

Turn on the television to any news broadcast and you will likely find at least one disaster-related story. News anchors or reporters will describe what occurred and the resulting impact. Chances are that they will also mention something about looting: it is occurring after the disaster, residents are worried about their property being stolen, law enforcement officials are out in force to discourage looters, etc. The media seems to be obsessed with looting, even though research reveals that it is uncommon, but not unheard of, in most disasters.

---

The media loves sensational stories. Nevertheless, the accuracy of such presentations may be in question. Since the media wants a unique angle on the human disaster-related activities, they are not always careful about gathering all of the facts. Truth is neglected because the media is not acquiring or providing the full story. For example, a study revealed that people sorting through debris after one disaster were not looters, but were good Samaritans who were trying to collect belongings so they could be returned to their rightful owners (Fischer, 1998a). The media, quickly reacting to the appearance of wrongdoing, incorrectly reported that a large group of people was engaging in looting behavior. This is an excellent, but disappointing, example of how the media erroneously educates the public about human behavior in a disaster.

## SELF-CHECK

- From where do most people get their understanding about disasters?
- How does Hollywood depict human responses to disasters?
- What is the role of the media in providing misrepresentations about disaster behavior?
- Does the media like sensational stories? How does this impact people's perceptions of disasters?

## 3.2 Research on Myths

Many sociologists have studied human behavior in disaster (see Table 3-1), and a great deal of literature has thus been written about the topic of disaster "myths." As an emergency manager, you should be familiar with this literature. Much of this research is dated, but prior studies reveal "most persons held preconceived notions about disaster behavior that were essentially untrue" (Quarantelli and Dynes, 1972, p. 67). In other words, "many common beliefs and perceptions

## Table 3-1:  Respondents' Beliefs about Disaster Response

| Statement | Agree | Disagree | Undecided or no response |
|---|---|---|---|
| A major problem community officials confront when faced with a natural disaster is controlling the panic of people fleeing from the danger area | 83.6% (296 respondents) | 10.2% (36 respondents) | 6.2% (22 respondents) |
| Looting rarely occurs after the impact of natural disasters | 27.7% (98 respondents) | 64.7% (229 respondents) | 7.6% (27 respondents) |
| When warned of an impending disaster, people are willing to cooperate and evacuate the area | 80.2% (284 respondents) | 13.6% (48 respondents) | 6.2% (22 respondents) |
| The crime rate of a community usually rises after it has experienced a natural disaster | 50.8% (180 respondents) | 34.7% (123 respondents) | 14.4% (51 respondents) |
| Immediately following the impact of a disaster, the disaster victims are in a state of shock and unable to cope with the situation by themselves | 73.7% (261 respondents) | 19.2% (68 respondents) | 7% (25 respondents) |
| The news media accurately portray the amount of devastation resulting from a natural disaster | 54.5% (193 respondents) | 35.6% (126 respondents) | 9.9% (35 respondents) |
| Martial law has never been instituted in a disaster area in the United States | 17.2 (61 respondents) | 60.2 (213 respondents) | 22.6% (80 respondents) |

Adapted from Wenger et al. (1975, p. 42).

about disaster response and post-impact behavior are not empirically valid" (Wenger et al., 1975, p. 33). Further research continues to reiterate previous findings (Tierney et al., 2001). New investigations were undertaken after Hurricane Katrina, and they add new insight into this matter (Barsky et al., 2006).

One of the most widely held myths according to the literature is that people act irrationally in disaster situations. It is believed that people always panic. **Panic** defined is people's inability to think clearly or their tendency to run frantically from buildings or the disaster scene. Another related belief is masses of people evacuating at once. The assertion is that everyone will evacuate and that they will compete to acquire safety.

It is true that many people will leave the scene of a disaster. This need not result in panic however. Research suggests that "despite the fact that people may well be terrified in disaster situations, even to the point of feeling that their lives are in imminent danger, they almost never resort to the kind of highly individualistic, competitive, headlong flight behavior that characterizes true panic" (Tierney, 2003, p. 35). Panic flight is rare, occurring only when there is an imminent threat to the well-being of the person or people evacuating. In addition, not everyone evacuates when requested to do so. Many people will ignore warnings and remain in the area that will be or has been affected by a hazard. This creates the need for dangerous search and rescue missions from police, fire, and military personnel.

A second major myth is in regard to antisocial behavior. This includes at least three aspects. First, people assume that **looting**—people searching debris or damaged homes with the intention to steal others' personal belongings—occurs rampantly after a disaster (Figure 3-2). Because doors and windows are broken, it is believed that people will automatically enter businesses and homes to steal food, electronic equipment, and other goods. This belief occurs even though much of the property is damaged beyond repair. Second, it is assumed that people will resort to violence to protect their interests. Guns are needed to fight off potential looters. Third, other types of deviant behavior, including price gouging, are viewed as predominant behavioral patterns. People think other individuals or groups will take advantage of victims to make money.

In most disasters, however, there are only reports of antisocial behavior. In other words, people think that looting might be taking place, but they have no evidence to support their assertions. In other cases, people expect there will be looting in

Figure 3-2

These individuals may be mistaken as looters. In reality, this group of volunteers was helping disaster victims recover personal belongings after the May 23, 2013, tornado in Moore, OK. Andrea Booher/FEMA.

disasters because it has occurred in riots and other forms of civil disturbance. Research reveals that this assumption is often erroneous.

**Price gouging**, or the selling of goods and services at a price higher than the normal market rate, is not a widespread phenomenon. Most citizens and business recognize that victims have experienced severe trauma. They would not think of adding to their problems. Some scholars even suggest that criminal activity may witness a decrease after a disaster. For instance, "in the month in which Hurricane Betsy struck New Orleans, major crimes in the city fell 26.6 percent below the rate for the corresponding month of the previous year. Burglaries reported to the police fell from 617 to 425. Thefts of over $50 dropped from 303 to 264, and those under $50 fell from 516 to 366" (Quarantelli and Dynes, 1972, p. 69). Similar drop in criminal activity may have been noted in Oklahoma City after the bombing of the Murrah Federal Building. There is a possibility that reporting of crime may be inaccurate, however, since police are concerned about bigger issues than petty theft after a disaster.

Another myth relates to people taking advantage of disaster victims to make money. For instance, it is reported that stores sell ice at inflated costs, as people need to keep food cool due to the loss of power to refrigerators. In other cases, it is commonly assumed that convenience stores raise the price of gasoline as people evacuate. Although such behavior does occur, it is probably the exception rather than the norm.

An additional myth is that emergency workers are unreliable in the aftermath of disaster. This is known as **role or post abandonment**. It is believed that police officers, firefighters, and EMTs will not fulfill their roles. They will leave their post when disaster strikes to take care of personal or family needs. Emergency workers are believed to fear the danger they face. Others are expected to quit their jobs to take care of themselves and their families. These views cannot be corroborated in the vast majority of cases.

People also have wrong or incomplete views about disaster victims. Some think that victims will always be in a state of **shock**—a period of disbelief after disaster, which renders them unable to think or take care of themselves. "The common belief is that shock leaves the victims dazed and disoriented, unable to cope with the immediate task of recovery" (Quarantelli and Dynes, 1972, p. 36).

Evidence suggests that victims exhibit shock symptoms in a minority of disaster cases. Most victims do not have long-lasting mental health effects. In addition, the vast majority of people will not require shelter or housing assistance. Typically, "congregate care utilization is likely to be in the range of 5–15 percent" (Tierney et al., 2001, p. 97).

---

### FOR EXAMPLE

#### Alleged Price Gouging

Two scholars traveled to Texas to study the community response to Hurricane Gilbert (Fischer, 1999a, p. 4). While watching media broadcasts of the event, news reporters claimed that local merchants were arrested for charging high prices for the plywood needed to protect windows from strong winds. The researchers called the police to see if this was accurate. The answer they received was "no." The media should have reported instead that city council had passed an ordinance to prevent such behavior.

**Table 3-2: Respondents' Beliefs about Effective Personal Aid to Disaster Victims**

| Respondents were asked to complete this statement: "What is the most effective assistance you as a concerned citizen can offer to the victims of natural disasters? Would you:" | Response |
|---|---|
| (a) Send supplies or money to the stricken community? | 35.9% (127 respondents) |
| (b) Go in person to the community to help? | 17.5% (62 respondents) |
| (c) Send money to disaster relief organizations? | 38.1% (135 respondents) |
| (d) Do nothing? | 3.4% (12 respondents) |
| (e) Undecided | 5.1% (18 respondents) |

Adapted from Wenger et al. (1975, p. 42).

There are other myths about disasters that should be mentioned. It is frequently assumed that the media provides an accurate portrayal of the disaster. It is believed that the statistics regarding the number of dead or injured are complete and trust-worthy. Because the media focuses excessively on destruction, the viewers are given an inflated impression about the extent of the situation. People therefore believe that a massive amount of aid is needed.

Research also indicates that the initial media reports are almost always inexact. No one, including the media, has a complete and accurate understanding about disasters initially because information is limited, sketchy, and uncorroborated. Estimates regarding those killed and otherwise affected are almost always over- or underestimated. Also, in their efforts to help disaster victims or increase interest in the disaster, reporters frequently request donations even though they may not be needed (see Table 3-2).

A final myth is that martial law must be imposed after disasters. **Martial law** is the replacing of civilian authority with that of the military. It involves the imposition of strict curfews and limitations on people's movement and activity. It is commonly held that the military and National Guard must be mobilized and utilized to maintain social stability when disasters occur. Research shows that martial law has yet to be imposed after disasters in the United States. "Press reports of martial law inevitably turn out to be entirely false or incorrect descriptions of limited emergency power usually given to local police by may-ors or city councils – usually to bar sightseers. In no way do such actions imply or involve cessation of regular civilian authority in the area" (Quarantelli and Dynes, 1972, p. 69).

To summarize, irrational behavior, antisocial behavior, unreliable emergency workers, the helpless state of disaster victims, and other myths are commonly held views about people's behavior in disaster. They do not appear to be correct in most cases.

SELF-CHECK

- What are the commonly held views about **panic** in disasters?
- Do most people **loot** after a disaster?
- Do all businesses **gouge** disaster victims?
- Is it wishful thinking to rely on emergency responders alone?
- Do communities always require relief assistance after disaster?
- Is it necessary to implement martial law after disasters occur?

## 3.3  Evidence of Exaggeration

Sections 3.1 and 3.2 raise some interesting questions about human behavior in disasters. Is the portrayal of disasters by Hollywood and the media completely wrong? Is the research literature entirely correct to assert that widely held views about disaster behavior are purely myths? The answer to both of these questions is somewhat complicated, although in both cases it is probably no. There is now research that seems to add to our prior understanding on the matter (see Table 3-3 taken from Barsky et al., 2006; as cited by John Handmer, 2006).

Films and media reports may have some element of truth, but the word "myth" could be slightly misleading. It might be more realistic, therefore, to alter our choice of words slightly. When speaking about people's perspectives of human behavior, we might want to use the term "exaggeration" instead of myth. An **exaggeration** is a simplistic overstatement about some type of phenomena. This term acknowledges that there could be some element of truth to the impression given by movies and news reports. This should not discount the predominant behaviors exhibited in disasters though. As an emergency manager, you should be aware of this fine point of distinction.

For instance, people have at times participated in "flight behavior" when a threat requires immediate action. As mentioned in Chapter 1, on February 21, 2003, the band Great White was performing in a nightclub in West Warwick, Rhode Island. The pyrotechnics used by the group caught ceiling on fire. The tiles on the ceiling were extremely combustible, causing the fire to spread rapidly throughout the structure. As the attendees noticed the dangerous situation, they scrambled to vacate the building. Because most exited the same way they entered, the hallways and doorways immediately became jammed, and over 100 people died as a result. Another example is from the 9/11 terrorist attacks. When the buildings collapsed, people ran down the streets to get out of harm's way. This, of course, may amount to rational behavior to save one's life. But it is often portrayed by Hollywood and the media as panic, regardless of the motive.

There are also several factual reports of a few individuals who have had their property stolen by the so-called looters after a disaster. As an example, when a computer failed due to the collapse of the World Trade Center, it was reported that

**Table 3-3: Disaster Myths, Reality, and New Orleans**

| "Myths" about what happens in a disaster | "Reality" as established by research and experience | New Orleans—what appeared to happen |
|---|---|---|
| Widespread looting is expected | There is no increase in criminal activity, and there is little or no looting | We all saw "looting," and there were numerous reports of this behavior by the media, local officials, people in the streets, blogs, etc. Some reports of looting and criminal behavior were confirmed. Others have been withdrawn. Looting has been redefined by some commentators to exclude much of the behavior (e.g., the hungry were feeding themselves, the addicted raided hospitals to access drugs, and so on) |
| Helplessness and abandonment of the weak | Disasters have differential impacts on the vulnerable. People help those in need | Over 100,000 did not have the means to evacuate and became dependent on others to keep them alive. Outside help was very slow to arrive and inadequate initially. Some in nursing homes and private hospitals were abandoned and died |
| Officials experience conflict between their official duties and family demands | Officials will do their job and not abandon their posts because of "role conflict" | Large-scale abandonment of officials' posts and duties. 50 officers were fired for going AWOL, and over 200 others were under investigation after Hurricane Katrina (Perlstein and Lee, 2005). A few police officers were also caught looting grocery and department stores. The situation seemed well beyond the capabilities of government leaders. First priority went to security rather than attending to those desperate for food and water and to those dying for want of medical attention. There were no public heroes |
| Large-scale demand for official emergency shelters | Little need for official emergency accommodation | The mass evacuation centers were overwhelmed. About 200,000 people were housed in official shelters a month and a half after the disaster. (There is a dispute over the actual figures with much higher numbers occasionally quoted) |
| People take advantage of disasters and the vulnerable | Postdisaster behavior is altruistic | There was evidence of price gouging and people being evicted from private rentals, thereby creating homelessness (Hartman, 2005). The town of Gretna, across the Mississippi from New Orleans, barricaded itself and at gunpoint prevented evacuees from entering their jurisdiction (Khaleej Times, 2005) |
| Outside rescue teams save many lives | Neighbors and nearby communities do the saving as outside help may take too long arrive | There were many reports of people assisting each other, but there was also general picture of an absence of rescue and help by neighbors initially |

Adapted from Handmer (2006, p. 32).

at least 66 people illegally withdrew $15 million from the Municipal Credit Union in New York City (Saulny, 2002). It was also illustrated that steel from the World Trade Center was being diverted illegally and attempted to be sold on the black market. After Hurricane Katrina, there was also a visible degree of looting in New Orleans as witnessed in many reports from journalists for local, national, and international media outlets. Most of the reports are considered to be inaccurate portrayals of looting because some people failed to adequately prepare for this disaster (for a variety of reasons) and therefore needed to take food and water from stores to sustain life. Under these conditions, the use of such resources could be understandable since people were attempting to care for their physical needs under dire circumstances. However, many others ran off with TVs, other electronic equipment, alcohol, and clothing or shoes that had little to do with immediate needs after the hurricane. Such behavior resulted in over 240 arrests for looting in New Orleans and Slidell (Barsky et al., 2006). Thus, it was clear that some people did take advantage of the disaster. Nevertheless, the findings about looting in Katrina need to be taken into context. The number of looting arrests after Katrina may have been lower than typical burglaries and thefts per day (Barsky et al., 2006). In addition, record keeping was problematic immediately after Katrina, and one police officer's view of what constitutes "looting" may be different than another's. Therefore, the findings about looting in Katrina are not conclusive.

Victims and communities may also be taken advantage of in some disasters. Vendors or contractors who get paid in advance will sometimes fail to complete their work. Businesses can also misrepresent their services and goods in advertisements. As an example, a scam promoted by one corporation promised consumers would be reimbursed by FEMA if they purchased air conditioners and purifiers after the 9/11 terrorist attacks. Flyers and websites implied that everyone would be eligible for this special offer. These advertisements did not mention the unique requirements for each federal grant. The FBI has also noted that there were several fraudulent websites claiming to collect donations for the Hurricane Katrina victims.

Post abandonment may not be a completely untrue perspective either (Figure 3-3). While this type of behavior is not typically witnessed after disasters, investigation after Hurricane Katrina illustrated that a few police officers did leave their duties unattended (Trainor and Barsky, 2011). Some were worried about having sufficient personal protection in a very unusual disaster situation. Some stopped patrolling the streets during the hurricane and went home to care for loved ones during the flooding. Others even participated in criminal behavior such as looting and lost their jobs as a result. In fact, one officer left his post, stole a car, and was arrested a short time later. This, however, is certainly the exception and not the rule.

It is also true that a minority of victims can be stunned by the death, the property destruction, and the social disruption caused by disasters. Victims may be emotionally distraught. Survivors may wander about aimlessly around their property trying to salvage anything worth retrieving. Some may cry and become depressed as a result of lost loved ones. Others may question their future in terms of housing and employment. This negative impact is to be expected. Who would not be overwhelmed initially with the grief and chaos that disasters produce?

Although the need for aid is regarded to be a myth, disasters always require at least some form of outside assistance. In fact, aid from nearby communities or from donors around the country is sometimes essential in major events. Food, water, supplies, emergency workers, and reconstruction specialists are therefore sent in to save lives and help the community recover. However, it is certainly doubtful that affected individuals and jurisdictions need everything. Politicians may overstate need in order to acquire as much free federal disaster assistance as possible.

## FOR EXAMPLE

### The Katrina Effect

Because the entire nation had witnessed the dangers of not evacuating after Hurricane Katrina, hundreds of thousands of people left the gulf coast region of Texas when Hurricane Rita neared. Even those some distance from the ocean got in their cars and left even though they were probably far enough inland to avoid major damage from the approaching storm. The presence of so many vehicles on the road clogged the major arteries leaving Galveston and Houston. The situation required that both lanes be opened for northbound traffic (a practice known as contraflow, which is common in Florida and other Gulf Coast states). Some people were stuck in traffic for 8 hours or longer. The fact that too many people were trying to evacuate has been labeled the "Katrina effect."

Figure 3-3

While some first responders may abandon their post in disasters, the overwhelming majority will make great personal sacrifices to fulfill their responsibilities. Andrea Booher/FEMA.

Finally, disasters may require a heavy law enforcement and military presence to maintain order. After Hurricane Katrina, lawlessness could be clearly observed in some areas. In addition to the occurrence of looting already mentioned, some people broke into hospitals to obtain narcotics for illicit drug use. Weapons were also being fired at those trying to prevent crime or rescue victims stranded on rooftops. Some people were angry because of the slow federal response, in spite of their own responsibility to care for themselves and others after the disaster. Citizens were also upset with those who were hoarding relief supplies. The city of New Orleans seemingly appeared to be under a condition of anarchy for several days after Katrina struck, but social order did not break down completely. However, the situation was so dire that some people called for martial law (although this was never carried out). Instead, curfews were established, and the streets were patrolled to purge them of criminals. This case, as well as the other evidence presented earlier, indicates that there might be a very small degree of truth in Hollywood movies and media reports. However, "while the stories may be factually correct, they are not representative" (Quarantelli and Dynes, 1972, p. 70). It may be wise for you to label these behaviors as exaggerations instead of myths.

## SELF-CHECK

- Have there been any cases of panic flight in disasters?
- Do some people take advantage of disaster victims through looting or price gouging?
- Are emergency workers always selfless during response operations?
- Are some victims incapacitated after a disaster?
- Do major disasters require outside assistance?
- Can a heavy law enforcement or military presence be beneficial for postdisaster operations?

## 3.4  Realities about Response and Recovery

The previous comments must not discount human behavior research. Studies do provide a dramatically different view than is commonly presented by Hollywood and the media (Quarantelli, 2008). During and after disasters, people act rationally and altruistically. Workers typically do not neglect their duties, and victims can do much to take care of themselves. Other common perceptions portrayed by the media—the need for disaster relief and use of martial law—are also overstated. In order to react successfully to a disaster, you must understand actual behavior better than anyone else in your community.

Instead of showing extreme panic in disasters, people are generally very rational (Quarantelli, 1986, p. 4). People typically respond with logical and calm behavior. They often know what to do to care for themselves and others, and they react accordingly. For instance, while the World Trade Center towers burned out of control on 9/11, people were seen walking calmly out of the building as if they were reacting to a fire drill. Rather than wait for emergency personnel to arrive at the scene, victims will often care for themselves and others.

What is more, the belief about mass panic is often overstated. It is true that many people do in fact leave an area when requested to do so. However, it is also likely that some people will not evacuate. These individuals will ignore warnings, potential risks, and requests for evacuation. Such people often require rescue during flooding incidents. Hurricane Katrina illustrated these points clearly (Figure 3-4). About 100,000 people did not or could not leave New Orleans. Many were rescued by the National Guard and the Coast Guard. Even with the imminent threat of Hurricane Sandy, many people would not leave coastal areas until Governor Christie told them emphatically "to get the hell out of there!" Therefore, "it appears that the major problem in an emergency is getting people to move, rather than preventing wild panic and disorderly flight" (Quarantelli and Dynes, 1972, pp. 67–68).

If there is looting or antisocial behavior during disaster, it is typically exhibited only among a very small minority of the population. In fact, some studies reveal that deviant behavior actually declines in times of disaster. The vast majority of people illustrate prosocial behavior. They work together to solve mutual problems. For example, coworkers help to evacuate the physically disabled if the building they are in is on fire. Taking this into account, Quarantelli (1986, p. 5) observes, "if disasters unleash anything it is not the criminal in us, but the altruistic."

The assertion that emergency workers will always fail to report to work is also ludicrous. Police, firefighters, and medical personnel often go to work or volunteer in times of disaster even when they have not been asked to report for duty. In fact, there are often too many emergency personnel responding to the disaster (Drabek, 1986). Emergency workers recognize the dangers inherent in their work, but they do it anyway. For instance, on 9/11, firefighters entered burning buildings to rescue those that were trapped. Furthermore, emergency workers do not always stop working to take care of their own personal or family needs. In contrast, many firefighters left home and arrived at the scene and began to help without reporting to incident commanders. Responders often work too long and frequently burn themselves out responding to the disaster. Some may fail to perform their assigned duties, but this is certainly the minority of cases.

Although some victims may be overwhelmed or otherwise incapacitated due to the disaster, most are not helpless. Those affected by disaster generally take care of themselves and others (Tierney et al., 2001). As an example, some may fight fires with extinguishers or garden hoses until firefighters arrive. Others provide basic first aid to the wounded. Victims are creative in how they respond to the needs. For example, people trapped in collapsed buildings eat gum to stay alive and whistle or tap debris (with fingers, hands, rocks, or other debris) to help emergency workers locate them.

Because the expected number of people needing shelters is often overestimated, many responding organizations set up and operate shelters after disaster. However, most victims will not use them. Evacuees tend to stay in hotels or visit friends and relatives (Quarantelli, 1995). They prefer to stay in comfortable accommodations

Figure 3-4

Many people did not or could not evacuate before Hurricane Katrina made landfall. Between 15,000 and 20,000 individuals therefore required shelter in the Superdome. Marty Bahamonde/FEMA.

with people they are familiar with. In fact, some people stay in hotels rather than shelters. They are subsequently surprised when they find out the federal government will not reimburse them for their hotel stay.

There is another reality that should be considered. The initial reports by the media are likely to be inaccurate, incomplete, and even misleading (Scanlon et al., 1985). For instance, the number of deaths reported by the media is often blown out of proportion. After the 9/11 terrorist attacks, it was believed that up to 50,000 people could have been killed. The actual number was around 3000. The number of deaths after Hurricane Katrina was also different than predicted.

Although specific types of assistance may be needed, certain types of relief are frequently unwarranted. Food, clothing, and other supplies are generally available

Figure 3-5

While certain types of aid may be insufficient immediately after disasters, large truck loads of supplies will make their way to the affected area. Jocelyn Augustino/FEMA.

to victims and emergency workers. If aid is not present initially, it is likely that it will be after the media reports the need. In many disasters, there is an overabundance of aid (Figure 3-5). Such aid may create additional problems because it has to be disposed of or sorted and distributed (Neal, 1994).

Finally, major disasters do occasionally require the services of the National Guard and armed forces. The governor or the president may request reservists and active-duty personnel to keep people away from dangerous areas or clean up debris. This is not martial law however. Although martial law has been imposed in wartime and due to disgruntled employees or workers on strike (see http://www.usconstitution.net/consttop_mlaw.html), "it has never been necessary to declare martial law following any U.S. disaster" (Tierney et al., 2001, p. 110). Even with the social chaos after Hurricane Katrina, martial law was not enacted. Some force was needed at times to reign in criminals toting weapons. But martial law was not imposed even in this dire situation. Americans are extremely hesitant to turn over total control to government officials, police, and the military. For example, the U.S. government has been criticized for wiretapping potential suspects after the 9/11 terrorist attacks.

All of this suggests that people tend to behave in ways that are not always consistent with Hollywood and media portrayals. Research findings on myths may also be questionable in regard to certain situations, although they are generally accurate most of the time. You should be cognizant of actual human behavior after disasters.

## FOR EXAMPLE

### The Reaction to Hurricane Katrina

Hurricane Katrina illustrated both the worst and best of people in New Orleans. Some people looted and engaged in violent behavior after the disaster. The deviant behavior after Hurricane Katrina may be a reflection of the continuities in society rather than a sharp break from daily life. "An orthodoxy discussed more among researchers than practitioners, is that disasters tend to highlight or sometime exacerbate existing trends, that than create entirely new circumstances. Given the 'normal' circumstances in New Orleans, what was seen and the fall out does not seem so surprising" (Handmer, 2006, p. 33). The case of New Orleans is somewhat unique. It is also complicated. "Press and agency apologies for exaggerating aspects of the extent of the crisis are emerging, although some evidence suggests that aspects were even worse than reported" (Handmer, 2006, p. 29). However, many people from inside and outside the community worked tirelessly to respond to victims' needs.

# SELF-CHECK

- Can fleeing the scene of a disaster be rational?
- Do all people leave when an evacuation request is made?
- Do many crimes decline after a disaster?
- Will emergency workers show up, even when they have not been requested?
- Are most people altruistic after disaster?
- Why do most individuals and families avoid public shelters?

## 3.5  The Importance of Understanding Behavior Correctly

Human behavior in disaster can be somewhat complicated. But does it really matter? The answer is an emphatic "yes!" You must base your postdisaster decisions and policies on what people are most likely to do. You should not make and implement decisions based on incorrect or incomplete beliefs. Doing so would unintentionally add to the problems associated with disasters. For example:

▲ The media's reporting of a "panicked evacuation" may make the emergency manager and government look incompetent. It could also postpone or complicate necessary evacuations.

▲ Inaccurate beliefs about human behavior may have led DHS to create an ineffective Homeland Security Advisory System for terrorist attacks (see Chapter 5).

▲ The belief that there will be massive amounts of looting and price gouging may take law enforcement officials away from more important work after a disaster (e.g., traffic control). Reports of criminal activity and law enforcement responses may also discourage victims from evacuating when required or returning to their homes to salvage their personal belongings.

▲ The assumption that responders will be unreliable may result in unnecessary communications to make sure emergency workers are doing their jobs. This ties up communication channels and interrupts other vital response activities.

▲ The assertion that victims cannot help themselves in disasters may also slow down the recovery of the community. This is because it is believed that the government and official disaster organizations must perform all disaster-related tasks.

▲ An overstatement of the disaster's impacts may result in the delivery of unnecessary donations. Volunteers may also show up at the scene when they are not needed.

▲ The perception that martial law will be imposed could cause some potential volunteers to refrain from participating in the response and recovery.

Fortunately, emergency managers are more likely to have accurate perceptions of reality today. Henry Fischer surveyed 54 local emergency managers in Ohio to assess their understanding of actual disaster behavior. His study indicates that education and training have helped emergency managers to gain "an increasingly accurate understanding of the actual behavioral response to disaster" (Fischer, 1998a, p. 94). Table 3-4 reveals the percentage of respondents that had correct views about human behavior in disasters. Progress has therefore been made over the past two decades. Fewer emergency managers accept the portrayals of Hollywood and the media than a decade ago.

However, inaccurate views of disaster behavior are sometimes still prevalent among some emergency managers (see the response statements in the lower half of Table 3-4). The public at large has even more room for improvement. They are even less educated about human behavior in disaster situations. Therefore, it is necessary to reiterate that Hollywood and the media frequently do not accurately

## Table 3-4: Emergency Managers' Views about Disaster Behavior

| Behavior statement | Percentage correct |
| --- | --- |
| Emergency workers will not be selfish | 98 |
| There will not be volunteer shortage | 85 |
| Local leaders will not panic | 83 |
| Local citizens will help each other | 80 |
| Local citizens do not price gouge | 74 |
| Local merchants do not price gouge | 72 |
| Local residents refuse to evacuate | 68 |
| EMS workers will not leave posts | 68 |
| Survivors will not behave selfishly | 67 |
| Shelters will often be underused | 63 |
| Residents will be looting | 61 |
| There will not be too few shelters | 54 |
| Citizens will not panic | 50 |
| Residents will not behave irrationally | 46 |
| Survivors will know what to do | 39 |
| Damage estimates not initially accurate | 37 |
| Death/injury estimates not accurate | 31 |

Adapted from Fischer (1998a, p. 102).

---

### FOR EXAMPLE

### Volunteers after the Loma Prieta Earthquake

After experiencing the Loma Prieta earthquake in October 17, 1989, relief agencies and citizens immediately began to respond collaboratively to the disaster. Within 30 minutes, the Local Amateur Radio Group set up communications among its members in the affected area. One of its main goals was to assist the operations of the American Red Cross. Volunteers from the Red Cross reported to headquarters and began to register victims and volunteers, establish shelters, feed victims and emergency workers, and take care of other pressing needs. The Salvation Army also distributed food as well as clothing, blankets, and other supplies to disaster victims. The Local Volunteer Coordination Council met to begin matching volunteers with community needs. According to Neal (1990, p. 94), "One staff member estimated that for every call that requested a volunteer, five people called to volunteer their services. For example, engineers, plumbers, daycare professionals, and businesses called to offer resources (e.g., personnel, expertise, equipment)." It appears that most organizations and people work diligently and cooperatively to help those affected by disasters. More people show up than needed.

portray human behavior in disasters. People tend to act rationally and exhibit a great deal of prosocial behavior. Emergency workers are generally selfless individuals that respond to the needs of disaster-affected communities. Victims are most likely to be proactive, and they take care of themselves and others. Media reports about disaster impacts are often overstated. Too much aid is frequently sent to the scene. The government has not imposed martial law when disaster strikes. The reality of disaster behavior is thus quite different than the exaggerations that are so commonly believed. Thinking otherwise adversely affects response and recovery operations. Nevertheless, more studies will be needed in the future. As an emergency manager, it is your responsibility to maintain awareness of this research.

## SELF-CHECK

- Could media reports of panic make response activities look unsuccessful?
- Do reports of looting keep police from other important responsibilities after a disaster?
- Is it necessary for superiors to always check on first responders?
- Do reporters influence the amount of donations that arrive in a disaster-stricken community?
- Can education and training change perspectives about human behavior in disasters?

## SUMMARY

Having correct views of disaster behavior is one of the best ways to promote successful response and recovery operations. Unfortunately, Hollywood films and the media often incorrectly portray human behavior in disasters. People tend to believe these sensational reports, which scholars label as myths. At times, human disaster behavior is less than desirable. But, for the most part, humans do try to assist one another in time of disaster. For this reason, you may wish to consider using the term exaggeration instead of myth. You should also develop a solid understanding of how people actually behave in disasters so your operations are effective and efficient. Failing to do so could jeopardize postdisaster activities.

## KEY TERMS

| | |
|---|---|
| **Exaggeration** | A simplistic overstatement about some type of phenomena. |
| **Looting** | Stealing others personal belongings. |
| **Martial law** | The replacing of civilian authority with that of the military. |
| **Myth** | A false belief. |

| | |
|---|---|
| **Panic** | People's inability to think clearly or their tendency to run franticly from buildings or the disaster scene. |
| **Price gouging** | The selling of goods and services at a price higher than the normal market rate. |
| **Role or post abandonment** | Not showing up to work during an emergency. |
| **Shock** | A period of disbelief after disaster, which renders them unable to think or take care of themselves. |

# ASSESS YOUR UNDERSTANDING

Posttest to evaluate your knowledge of human behaviors in disasters.
*Measure your learning by comparing pretest and posttest results.*

## Summary Questions

1. Most people get their understanding of disasters from movies and the media. True or false?
2. News reports often convey the impression that victims can care for themselves. True or false?
3. Anyone sorting through debris is a looter. True or false?
4. Most people panic when warned of an impending hazard. True or false?
5. Price gouging is not a widespread phenomenon. True or false?
6. Emergency workers cannot be counted on to get their job done. True or false?
7. Most people will not need some type of public shelter after a disaster. True or false?
8. Media reports may give a biased representation of the extent of the disaster damages. True or false?
9. The president always imposes martial law after disasters. True or false?
10. When the World Trade Center Towers fell, people ran. This is an example of:
    (a) Panic behavior
    (b) Rational behavior
    (c) Irrational behavior
    (d) Panic flight
    (e) Answers a and d
11. Vendors and contractors:
    (a) Will always be honest in their dealings with disaster victims
    (b) Will always be dishonest in their dealing with disaster victims
    (c) May sometimes be honest in their dealings with disaster victims
    (d) May sometimes be dishonest in their dealings with disaster victims
    (e) Will complete all work and never cheat the disaster victims
12. After a disaster, we should expect:
    (a) That all goods are sold at a higher price
    (b) That all goods are sold at a lower price
    (c) That some people might be emotionally distraught
    (d) That no people will be emotionally distraught
    (e) Answers b and d
13. After Hurricane Katrina:
    (a) There were no reports of looting.
    (b) There were some reports of looting.
    (c) There were no reports of violence.

(d) There were some reports of violence.

(e) Answers b and d.

14. In a disaster situation:
    (a) It is likely that not everyone will evacuate.
    (b) It is likely that everyone will evacuate.
    (c) It is likely that everyone will panic.
    (d) It is likely that all businesses will be involved in unethical behavior.
    (e) It is likely that all citizens will be in a state of shock.

15. Rather than stay in public shelters, most people will:
    (a) Try to ride out the disaster at home.
    (b) Try to ride out the disaster on the road.
    (c) Try to stay with family and friends.
    (d) Be involved in violent criminal activity.
    (e) Not be involved in violent criminal activity.

## Review Questions

1. Do people have erroneous views about disasters? If so, why?
2. What does the research say about disaster myths?
3. Do most people panic after a disaster?
4. What is a bigger challenge—panic flight or getting people to evacuate?
5. Is looting a common occurrence in every disaster?
6. Will police and fire personnel abandon their posts in disasters?
7. Can victims care for themselves after disaster?
8. Are media reports always accurate? Are they always inaccurate?
9. Do all victims need disaster donations?
10. Do disaster often require outside relief assistance?
11. Is martial law required after every disaster? Is it required in the vast majority of disasters?
12. Why is it preferable to use the term exaggeration instead of myth?
13. How do people really behave in disasters?
14. Could incorrect views have a negative impact on response and recovery operations?
15. What can be done to counter common but erroneous beliefs about human behavior in disasters?
16. What should the emergency manager do to make sure myths do not adversely affect response and recovery operations?

## Applying This Chapter

1. As a risk manager for a major business, you have just been notified that severe weather is approaching your corporate headquarters. One of the chief executive officers asserts that warning the employees will cause a great deal of panic. How would you deal with this situation?

2. An earthquake, registering 6.9 on the Richter scale, has just occurred in Salt Lake City, Utah. It has damaged thousands of homes and offices, which will take months to repair. It is January and winter temperatures are reaching record lows. The mayor has requested that you open up shelters for every-one that has been affected. Is this a needed action? What should you tell this community leader?

3. You are in charge of logistics for the American Red Cross. A major blizzard has just affected your community in Minnesota. The news media is request-ing that people outside the area send you donations of coats and blankets. Could these items be useful? Could you get too many of them? How would you deal with this situation?

4. While managing the response to a terrorist attack in the central business district in your city, you have been told that looting is taking place in nearby neighborhood. Would it be advisable to get additional information about this report from the media? Should you send police officers to the neighbor-hood? What concerns would you have about sending too many officers to this area?

5. An outbreak of a strange strain of flu has occurred in Boston, Massachusetts. Public health officials are concerned that they will have sufficient flu shots for citizens in this area. A medical official at a nearby hospital has requested that you implement martial law immediately. Is this a wise decision? What factors would you need to consider before proceeding with this choice?

## YOU TRY IT

### Debunking Myths

You just saw the movie *Titanic* with a friend. In one scene, an employee of the cruise line calls for order and shoots his gun into the air to get people's attention. Your friend comments that "disasters always bring out the worst in people." Write a four-page paper illustrating how you would deal with this situation. Be sure to discuss the media, Hollywood, disaster research, and actual behavior.

### Talking Points

While talking to the media about an upcoming disaster exercise, a reporter states, "people always panic when a hurricane approaches the coast." How would you respond as an emergency manager to help him/her understand human behavior accurately?

### Educating the Public

As you are engaged in community education about emergency management at a middle school, a student raises his hand and asks, "How many firefighters quit their job during disasters?" What would you say to give an accurate view of the situation?

### Verifying Sources

While responding to a disaster, the police chief comments that he needs to send some officers to stop looting in one particular neighborhood. The police chief is basing his comments on media reports. How can you ensure that the jurisdiction has sufficient officers to take care of traffic control issues after the disaster?

# 4

# RECOGNIZING ALTERNATIVE MANAGEMENT APPROACHES

## Disaster Response and Recovery Theory

## Starting Point

Pretest to assess your knowledge on management approaches.
*Determine where you need to concentrate your effort.*

## What You'll Learn in This Chapter

▲ The traditional perspective of response and recovery operations
▲ The professional approach to disaster, including its assumptions and conclusions

## After Studying This Chapter, You'll be Able To

▲ Identify strengths and weaknesses of the traditional and collaborative models.
▲ Determine which approach is most applicable for any given disaster situation.

## Goals and Outcomes

▲ Recognize traditional and collaborative models in response and recovery.
▲ Evaluate which approach to use in each disaster situation.

*Disaster Response and Recovery: Strategies and Tactics for Resilience*, Second Edition. David A. McEntire.
© 2015 John Wiley & Sons, Inc. Published 2015 by John Wiley & Sons, Inc.

# INTRODUCTION

Whether we recognize it or not, our lives are guided by theory. The same is true about disasters and emergency management. Our notions regarding disasters determine how we deal with them. In the past, people viewed disasters as acts of God. Accordingly, repentance or sacrifices were regarded as the means to appeasing deity. Later on, scientists equated disasters with the natural hazard agents that trigger them. Therefore, early warning systems and containment devices such as dams were seen as ways to give advanced notification of adverse weather or control rising floodwaters. In recent years, some have come to believe that technology will provide a "silver bullet" for all the disaster problems that confront us. Satellites, communication equipment, and improved engineering are all that is required for preparedness and mitigation. Today, many scholars currently argue that disasters are socially constructed. If we are to increase resilience, then we will need to alter our values, attitudes, and practices about disasters. One of the major theoretical recommendations associated with this view has to do with how we approach disaster management. There are two theoretical perspectives that may impact our resilience to disaster. These include what may be labeled as the traditional and professional models. The respective strengths and weaknesses of these two perspectives will be identified and compared in this chapter.

## 4.1  The Traditional Model

The **traditional model** for emergency management has been employed in many disasters in the United States. It has also been referred to as the civil defense, command and control, bureaucratic, or emergency service perspective. The traditional model is not always the preferred emergency management model among many scholars today, but it still provides useful insights into postdisaster operations. To understand this model, it is necessary to review the evolution of emergency management in the United States and the management strategies that have been promoted over time.

The participation of the federal government in disaster activities goes back over 200 years (Drabek, 1991). The involvement of national leaders and federal agencies in disasters was generally reactive and typically dealt with natural disasters such as floods and hurricanes. Things began to change after World War II when the world entered a new period of crisis. Political disagreements emerged between the Soviet Union and the United States. The conflict between these two superpowers was ideological in nature, with dictatorship and communism in the East pitted against democracy and capitalism in the West. Actual skirmishes occurred around the world as these rival nations vied for power, but the biggest concern resulted from the acquisition of nuclear warheads and the potential threat of **mutually assured destruction (MAD)**. This implied that the use of these weapons against one's enemy would invite massive retaliation that would result in the annihilation of most major cities in both countries and perhaps among allies as well (Figure 4-1).

In response to the threat of this "Cold War," emphasis in emergency management shifted from natural disasters to national security. Civil defense offices appeared in many cities around the United States. **Civil defense** was an effort by government officials to prepare for nuclear war. It included the building of underground shelters and the creation of plans to evacuate targeted urban areas of strategic value. The government thought there would be a great deal of panic on the part of the populace if nuclear war would occur and felt that social order would have to be maintained after a nuclear exchange. Although the distinction between civil defense and natural disaster relief activities created friction among agencies at times, the focus on civil defense was believed to be justified among federal policy makers. It was out of the context of the Cold War and fear of nuclear attack that the traditional model became popular.

Figure 4-1

Atomic cloud over Nagasaki, 1945 (NARA). Office for Emergency Management, Office of War Information, Overseas Operations Branch, New York Office, News and Features Bureau (1942–1945). Photographs of Allied and Axis Personalities and Activities. Record Group 208: Records of the Office of War Information, 1926–1951. National Archives Identifier: 535795. War and Conflict Number 1242.

The traditional model also became prevalent because the first emergency managers typically had military backgrounds. These individuals naturally gave priority to conflict disasters (e.g., war) and accepted the attitudes and structure of military organizations. Civil defense wardens were comfortable with the hierarchy of the armed forces, the centralization of decision making, and a reliance on standard operating procedures (SOPs). They applied this military model toward their planned disaster response operations.

Over time, first responders also began to support the traditional model. In many ways, it was logical that first responders would accept hierarchical organization and adherence to **SOPs**—rules and guidelines to complete disaster functions effectively and efficiently. Police and fire departments function under the direction of chiefs, and subordinates are supposed to respond according organizational policies for their own safety and the well-being of others. Police and fire departments and EMS also approach disasters from a mission perspective, focusing on what their organization can do to accomplish the functions they are tasked with. First responders are thus inclined to support the traditional model of emergency management.

### 4.1.1 Features of the Traditional Model

There are four major assumptions of the traditional model:

1. We need to give highest priority to war disasters.
2. Government is the most reliable actor because societal chaos will result after disaster.
3. It is best to adhere strictly to hierarchy and SOPs.
4. Emergency management is generally concerned with first responder issues only.

First, the traditional model of emergency management believed nuclear war would be the most devastating disaster imaginable. A fear of MAD caused civil defense directors and emergency managers to neglect the frequency and impact of other types of disasters. This model also heavily emphasized the role of government in disaster situations (Schneider, 1992). Emergency managers were comfortable with this approach, as it was relevant to the civil defense context in which they operated at the time. While it was natural that government officials viewed disaster response operations from their own perspective, this sometimes meant that the important roles performed by others were misunderstood and not integrated into the overall management of disasters.

In addition, the civil defense agencies that responded to disasters during this period were often organized in accordance with a chain of command. For example, the military has commissioned officers and others in the rank and file. Similarly, fire and police departments have chiefs, captains, sergeants, lieutenants, etc. In either situation, orders are given by superiors, and they are followed by those of lower rank. Disregarding requests made by leaders is not typically tolerated. The traditional model therefore accepts classical management theory (Britton, 1989a, p. 10). It assumed that decisions are made rationally by leaders who find solutions to the problem identified. Therefore, the traditional approach simplifies a complex process of policy making in times of disaster. Practitioners employing this model also relied on "clearly defined objectives, a division of labor, a formal structure, and a set of policies and procedures to fulfill disaster operations (Schneider, 1992)." The prevailing disaster management model did not allow people to adapt when performing tasks or functions (Figure 4-2).

The traditional model was also characterized by other assumptions, which were often incomplete or incorrect:

▲ Emergency management should always be located in fire or police departments.
▲ Emergency managers coordinate emergency service operations only.
▲ Politicians are nuisances and hinder disaster response.
▲ Information obtained or relayed by nongovernment personnel and agencies cannot be trusted.

**Figure 4-2**

Because of their hierarchical organization structures, military, police, and fire personnel are familiar with the traditional model of emergency management. Thomas R. Roberts/FEMA.

▲ Key leaders and decision makers thought emergency service personnel will neglect their duties in order to look after their own well-being and self-interest (or that of their friends and families).

▲ Laws, policies, and SOPs are always applicable and effective in any and every disaster situation.

▲ Failing to follow bureaucratic guidelines is detrimental to the response operation.

▲ Citizens do not respond to disasters or cannot do so effectively. Their behavior always involves panic, looting, or other antisocial activities.

▲ The spontaneous involvement of emergent groups hinders governmental response and recovery operations.

Such assumptions of the traditional model have several significant implications (Edwards-Winslow, 2002; Selves, 2002) (see Table 4-1). They rejected the need to deal with natural disasters, which have obviously been more frequent throughout history than nuclear attacks. The use of the traditional model also led to a situation where power and decision making became centralized in disaster situations. Bureaucratic expertise and strong government leadership were required to make sense out of the event and decide how best to respond. As a result, other responders were excluded from the decision making, and important functions such as media relations and resource coordination were consequently overlooked. Furthermore, hierarchy was needed to keep those operating in the field in line, while communications should be controlled to limit, filter, or interpret the flow of information. Finally, strict adherence to bureaucratic norms and procedures as outlined in emergency operations plans was valued, along with skepticism for creativity and improvisation (Britton, 1989, p. 13). In short, the traditional model advocated a limited and very rigid approach to the management of disaster response operations.

### 4.1.2  Strengths of Traditional Model

The traditional model has several strong points (see Table 4-2). First, it is true that war often produces more devastating consequences than many natural and technological disasters. A detonation of a single nuclear weapon could kill millions of people. We must therefore be prepared to respond to acts of war.

Another advantage of the model is that it recognizes that the government is a vital participant in disaster response operations. In our current efforts to promote homeland security, the government special responsibilities prevent terrorists from carrying out planned attacks (e.g., intelligence gathering and border control). The government is also typically involved in issuing warnings and evacuating people from hazardous situations. Public agencies also help to clean up debris and provide financial assistance to the victims of disaster. No one can doubt the vital role of public organizations in the emergency management context (Figure 4-3).

A third benefit deals with SOPs and hierarchy. SOPs help responders know what to do in case of a crisis situation. For instance, in order to protect workers from hazardous material spills, emergency responders are admonished to survey the scene of a tanker accident from a distance. Such SOPs can therefore be valuable in disaster responses. Hierarchy and orders are also advantageous. They can protect lives and help accomplish tasks based on prior experience. As an example, it is

### Table 4-1: Assumptions and Conclusions of the Traditional Model

| Assumptions | Implications/conclusions |
| --- | --- |
| War and civil defense disasters are of paramount importance | Other types of disasters are neglected |
| Emergency management should be located in emergency service depts. | Emergency management functions are only related to first responders |
| Emergency managers coordinate emergency services only | Disaster functions such as media relations are overlooked |
| Emergency managers need to have control, uniforms, emergency vehicles, and sirens | Turf battles and resentment build among first responders |
| Politicians are nuisances | Isolation from key leadership and other departments |
| Disasters result in a great deal of social chaos | The desire to bring order to disaster is natural and to be expected |
| Government is the main or only responder in times of disaster | Centralization of power and decision making is beneficial during disasters |
| Information obtained or relayed outside government cannot be trusted | Bureaucratic expertise and top-down communications structures are best |
| Emergency workers will leave their posts | A strong paramilitary leadership is required |
| SOPs will be effective in any and every disaster situation | Adherence to SOPs is preferred over creativity and improvisation |
| Failing to follow SOPs will be detrimental to the response | Same as above |
| Citizens do not or cannot respond effectively to disasters | Exclusion of others is viewed as the most effective type of response |
| Victim behavior includes panic, looting, and antisocial behavior | Same as above |
| Emergent groups hinder response operations | Same as above |

wise for firefighters to wait to enter a burning building until the chief has had enough time to conduct an initial evaluation of the situation. On 9/11, many off-duty first responders arrived at the World Trade Center to help. Instead of checking in with their fire chiefs, they entered the Twin Towers with their gear. Fire chiefs were not always aware of their involvement and had no way of communicating with the off-duty personnel. When it became apparent that the second tower would fall, an evacuation order was given. Ad hoc responders did not receive this message.

**Table 4-2: Strengths and Weaknesses of the Traditional Model**

| Strengths | Weaknesses |
|---|---|
| War may have the most adverse impacts of any disaster | Natural and technological disasters are more common |
| Government is an important factor in disaster response operations | Government is not the only actor in disaster response operations |
| SOPs provide logical guidelines for routine emergency situations | SOPs cannot provide guidance in all types of disaster situations |
| Hierarchy and orders may save lives and help to get things done | Top-down structures may slow down or hinder the response |
| The desire to bring order to disaster is natural and to be expected | There may be order in chaos and it is impossible control a disaster |

**Figure 4-3**

The federal government has vast resources to assist in time of disaster and this is a strength of the traditional model. Mark Wolfe/FEMA.

Had a chain of command been established and the order been heeded, fewer lives would have been lost in this disturbing terrorist attack.

The desire to respond to the disaster in the most efficient and effective manner is another benefit of this traditional emergency management model. As mentioned in Chapter 1, disasters are nonroutine social problems that pose significant challenges to responders and the community. Therefore, it is to be expected that emergency managers and first responders will desire to remedy the situation. They will naturally want to exert control over response personnel and deploy resources to where they are required.

### 4.1.3 Weaknesses of Traditional Model

The traditional model also has several weaknesses, and these failures have caused several scholars to disregard it as an effective approach. A major weakness of this model is a failure to appreciate the low probability of war-type disasters. Natural, technological, and other events are far more likely to occur. In 2005, there were numerous hurricanes that affected the United States. Each day, some type of hazardous material release occurs around the nation. Such disasters are far more common than conflict disasters.

Another weakness of the traditional model is the neglecting of other actors involved in response operations. Emergency managers and government agencies are not the only actors involved in disasters. Volunteers, hospitals, and businesses also play vital roles in search and rescue operations, medical care, utility restoration, and insurance claims after a disaster. The Red Cross also performs important functions such as emergency sheltering and mental health counseling. Churches also make important contributions in long-term recovery as well. Unfortunately, the traditional approach often overlooks the activity of other people and agencies outside the public sector.

A third weakness of the traditional model is the reliance on SOPs that do not work in every disaster. Disasters, by their very nature, create challenges that cannot always be predicted and planned for. For instance, an SOP may discuss guidelines about delaying the response to a hazardous material spill until the chief has conducted his or her size-up of the situation. Would this SOP be useful if an emergency worker determines that delaying the response could be dangerous as the spill is draining toward a crowded restaurant or an apartment complex? A real-life example of the need to disregard SOPs was seen on 9/11. The Coast Guard allowed more people to evacuate Manhattan on boats than was legally permitted in regulations at the time (Kendra and Wachtendorf, 2003b). This decision to fill up vessels beyond capacity allowed up to 500,000 to leave the island quickly. If regulations had been followed, it is likely that more lives would have been lost or affected. Thus, a reliance on SOPs

---

## FOR EXAMPLE

### The Role of the Military in Natural Disasters

After Hurricane Katrina devastated New Orleans and flooded the city, many wondered why the military did not arrive sooner. One reason for the delay was the failure of Louisiana Governor Blanco to request the military in a timely manner. The governor has to make a request for military involvement due to the Posse Comitatus Act of 1878. Under this act, the military cannot participate in state affairs unless requested by the governor. This is one of the many examples where SOPs delayed the arrival of needed resources for disaster-affected communities. However, it should be pointed out that the military was eventually deployed under a state declaration of emergency and the armed forces effectively assisted with evacuation and the maintenance of law and order.

according to the traditional model may not always allow you to effectively handle unpredictable or dynamic environments.

A fourth weakness is that the traditional model does not acknowledge that there may be order in situations that appear on the surface to be chaotic. While the involvement of numerous actors in disaster response operations often looks confusing, this does not necessarily mean that there is duplication of services or a lack of effectiveness. In fact, the participation of many organizations in the response may be necessary to effectively deal with the scope and nature of disasters. During Hurricane Katrina, for example, there were hundreds of organizations involved. The Coast Guard rescued people from flooded structures. The federal government and state agencies arrived to fulfill their roles. First responders were on the scene. Charities, such as the Salvation Army and the Red Cross, participated in relief and recovery efforts. The media worked to reunite separated families. Even ordinary citizens took in some of the displaced evacuees. Therefore, disasters are beyond the control of any single individual, department, or agency. In addition, people may behave in certain ways (e.g., donate goods and supplies) regardless of your efforts to promote or discourage those particular activities. During 9/11, for example, thousands of pounds of goods were collected for victims. Blankets, water, and food came by the truckload. More donations came in than were necessary and sat in warehouses in New York. Nevertheless, the abundance of supplies ensured that many needs were met in a timely manner.

Finally, the traditional model also relies on top-down communications. Unfortunately, organizational leadership may not have sufficient information to make correct decisions about the response, or it may take too long to relay problems up and down the chain of command before they can be addressed. For instance, the fire chief may not see an individual who is trapped in the burning building. It is the firefighter that will have to rescue the person immediately, possibly ignoring or delaying the initial requests of his or her commanding officer. Thus, the traditional model seems to imply that disaster response operations can be directed in an authoritarian manner. This model can be myopic, rigid, and cumbersome. In some circumstances, it can also be ineffective or inefficient.

## SELF CHECK

- What is the traditional model and why did it come about?
- What is MAD?
- What is civil defense?
- What does SOP stand for?
- What are the assumptions and conclusions of the traditional model?
- What are the strengths and weaknesses of this approach?

## 4.2 The Professional Model

A new model is now preferred by many scholars as a method for dealing with disasters. The **professional model** is an approach to emergency management that is based on interdependent organizational operations. It is known as the all-hazard, networking, collaborative, problem-solving, or public administration model. Understanding this model also requires an appreciation of how emergency management changed in the United States over time.

In 1979, emergency management underwent a major transformation. It was at this time that President Jimmy Carter created the Federal Emergency Management Agency (FEMA). The formation of FEMA combined several different civil defense and other disaster-related organizations under one roof. The programs incorporated into the new agency provided the basis for emergency management for local and state governments for the next 20 years. One of the major changes associated with FEMA was a recognition that the threat of nuclear war was diminishing as the Cold War appeared to be winding down. Government officials came to understand that natural and technological disasters were more common than wartime disasters. It was asserted that emergency managers must therefore be concerned with issues beyond evacuation and sheltering in the context of civil defense. Emergency management was beginning to formalize new responsibilities relating to donations management, debris removal, damage assessment and disaster relief, etc.

In addition, the traditional model seemingly exclusive concentration on military involvement did not work with the new FEMA organization. It was increasingly recognized that departments and agencies from all levels of government as well as nearby or distant communities will respond to disasters. Other organizations from the private and nonprofit sectors will also show up and participate in response and recovery operations when disaster strikes. Those espousing the professional model also began to acknowledge that society does not cease to function after disasters. The findings from disaster sociologists were increasingly recognized during this period. It was realized that people care for themselves and others and that they are resilient in spite of severe societal crises (Dynes, 1994). Thus, there was a growing acknowledgment that an organization's reaction to disasters is interdependent with the responses of others (Figure 4-4).

Those favoring the professional model also began to question the merit of following strict SOPs in disasters. Emergency managers became increasingly aware of the fact that disasters pose unique challenges that require departures from routine methods of dealing with smaller emergencies. Furthermore, while plans may serve as guidelines, they will not always be applicable to every disaster situation. Along these lines, laws and regulations may at times slow down response. This can make operations ineffective and/or inefficient. Creativity and improvisation began to be favored as bureaucratic procedures were seen as being too rigid. The professional model became a more flexible alternative to the traditional approach to disasters.

Finally, scholars and practitioners recognized over the past few decades that emergency management is more than emergency services (Selves, 2002). Emergency managers are not first responders, and emergency management includes more than life safety issues. It is increasingly recognized that disasters require warnings, volunteer management, and rebuilding among other activities. There are also important measures that emergency managers must pursue in order to mitigate and prepare for

Figure 4-4

The traditional model may miss the broad array of participants that get involved in emergency management. As an example, there are even individuals and agencies that address the needs of pets in disasters. Bob McMillan/FEMA.

disasters. Such proactive approaches may be far different than first responder activities in times of disasters. Furthermore, those in the field began to recognize that what one agency does or does not do may affect that ability of another to perform its functions. For instance, EMTs cannot transport the injured to hospitals if public works has not cleared the roads of disaster debris. Another example is an inability to communicate after a hurricane. Public officials, government agencies, private companies, and citizens might have to wait until utility companies establish or restore specific emergency phone lines. The professional model accepts the fact that no single group can respond to disasters alone or without the cooperation of others.

### 4.2.1 Features of the Professional Model

Like the traditional approach to disasters, the professional model is based on numerous assumptions. These expectations are as follows:

▲ Emergency managers will likely face many different types of disasters.
▲ Because of the unique nature of disaster, no single individual, group, or organization can respond alone.
▲ Disasters pose serious challenges to society, but individuals, groups, and organizations will—more than likely—meet the demands.
▲ Emergence cannot be prevented (Neal and Phillips, 1995, p. 334). People will respond to disasters whether they are invited to or not.

▲ The public is a resource. Public involvement is not necessarily a problem, although involvement may create challenges for emergency managers (e.g., coordination of volunteers).

▲ Disasters exhibit and exacerbate the weaknesses of SOPs. In addition, these events require and foster emergent norms. No emergency plan will account for all types of disaster issues; creativity may be needed when laws and regulations prove incomplete or cumbersome.

▲ Hierarchical and top-down relations among all responding entities are sometimes impossible when multiple organizations respond to disasters. Such **vertical relationships** involve information flow up and down government chains of command. A different approach is to stress horizontal relationships. **Horizontal relationships** are those in which parties communicate across departments and communities.

▲ Flexibility will be required in disaster situations. Departures from emergency operations plans are to be expected at times and will often prove beneficial.

▲ Emergency managers perform different roles than first responders.

▲ Emergency managers will not be able to get things done if they are isolated from decision makers and other departments' leaders.

There are several conclusions associated with the professional approach (see Table 4-3). For instance, it is now recognized that emergency managers must take an all-hazard perspective of the disaster problem. There are more hazards than nuclear war. Emergency managers must also work with the many actors that are involved in disaster response. In particular, they must maintain close relationships and work with politicians, other departments, and private, nonprofit, and emergent organizations. Emergency managers will continue to recognize the value of planning, but they are now more willing to depart from SOPs if needed. Finally, emergency managers are now aware of the need to see a much larger picture than that of the first responders.

### 4.2.2 Strengths of the Professional Model

The professional approach to disaster response operations and management has both strengths and weaknesses (see Table 4-4). One of the strengths of the professional model is that it takes an all-hazard approach to emergency management. It recognizes the fact that there are more types of disasters than war, and these should not be discounted. What is more, many types of disasters share similar response functions. For example, warning and sheltering may be required for hurricanes and hazardous material releases.

Because so many people and agencies are involved in a disaster, the professional approach also underscores the need to integrate activities. As an example, it is advisable that police, fire, and EMS officials collaborate with the media, Red Cross representatives, coroners, and crisis counselors at the scene of a major plane crash that kills hundreds of victims. These actors should work together to perform vital roles. They would help seal off the area. They would fight the fire. They would search and care for the wounded. They would keep the public informed about

## Table 4-3: Assumptions and Conclusions of the Professional Model

| Assumptions | Implications/conclusions |
| --- | --- |
| There are more types of disasters than civil hazards | Take an all-hazard approach to emergency management |
| Emergency managers cannot deal with disasters alone | Include politicians and the leaders of all departments in response activities |
| Disasters pose challenges; people will meet the demands | Emergency managers must be ready for a multiorganizational response |
| Emergence is not an aberration | Same as above |
| The desire to bring order to disaster is natural and to be expected | Same as above |
| Emergence cannot be prevented | Same as above |
| Emergence fills a void | Same as above |
| The public is a resource, not a liability | Same as above |
| Standard operating procedures do not always work | Flexibility is needed; departures from standard procedures are ok |
| No single responder can deal with disaster alone | Hierarchical relationships are not possible; stress horizontal relations |
| Emergency management is not the same as emergency services | Accept a broader view of the disaster |

## Table 4-4: Strengths and Weaknesses of Professional Model

| Strengths | Weaknesses |
| --- | --- |
| Takes an all-hazard approach | Downplays unique difficulties of wartime disasters |
| Acknowledges many actors | Downplays the role of government and first responders |
| Stresses integration of involved parties | Fails to recognize importance of hierarchical leadership |
| Allows for improvisation | Overlooks benefit of SOPs |
| Accepts a broad picture of disasters | Fails to see details of field-level operations |

> ### FOR EXAMPLE
>
> ### Improvising with Others to Help Disaster Victims
>
> DHL, a package shipment company, worked with American soldiers to set up shelter for the hundreds of thousands of victims of the 2005 Pakistan earthquake. One area where they concentrated their relief efforts on was Kashmir. The location of this community is remote, is mountainous, and does not have many roads or an airport nearby. DHL and the soldiers placed food and other supplies into the red polypropylene bags that DHL has been using for years. They then placed these bags on helicopters that could land in this affected region. In two weeks, the military delivered 6000 of these bags that had enough shelter supplies, food, and water to keep seven people alive for ten days (Simpson, 2005). This illustrates the value of partnership.

what is taking place. They would also identify the dead and console relatives. Many functions are therefore recognized under this model.

Third, the professional approach allows for flexibility in response. Every disaster is different. Therefore, SOPs will, on many occasions, be incomplete, ineffective, or inefficient. An example of this is trying to evacuate a hotel when the alarm systems or phone lines are not working properly. In normal situations, you could sound an alarm or call each room and ask the guests to leave the building immediately. Firefighters would also show up to take care of the problem. However, if the power is out or the phone lines have been rendered useless due to fire and if firefighters have not yet arrived, it might be necessary to send individuals to the rooms on each floor (assuming it is safe to do so). If guests are from foreign countries, additional measures will have to be taken to communicate in their language. The decision to warn and evacuate hotel guests can be situational. The professional model therefore advocates resolving the situation even if it means departing from the existing plan.

Finally, the professional model also sees the big picture and accepts modern principles of emergency management (see Table 4-5). Under this model, emergency management is not regarded to be the same as emergency services. Emergency managers work closely with police officers, firefighters, and paramedics. However, emergency managers also perform dramatically different functions than first responders. This is evident in routine response operations as well as in mitigation, preparedness, and recovery. The professional emergency management model thus recognizes these differences and appreciates their practical implications.

### 4.2.3 Weaknesses of Professional Model

Although there are strengths associated with the professional model, there are also some possible weaknesses that must be taken into consideration. By focusing on all hazards, the professional approach can miss the detail that is required in specific types of events. For example, the professional model may fail to acknowledge the threat and unique challenges associated with civil defense (or homeland security today). A nuclear attack, for example, could kill thousands of people. Responding to

## Table 4-5: Principles of Emergency Management

**Comprehensive**—emergency managers consider and take into account all hazards, all phases, all stakeholders, and all impacts relevant to disasters

**Progressive**—emergency managers anticipate future disasters and take preventive and preparatory measures to build disaster-resistant and disaster-resilient communities

**Risk driven**—emergency managers use sound risk management principles (hazard identification, risk analysis, and impact analysis) in assigning priorities and resources

**Integrated**—emergency managers ensure unity of effort among all levels of government and all elements of a community

**Collaborative**—emergency managers create and sustain broad and sincere relationships among individuals and organizations to encourage trust, advocate a team atmosphere, build consensus, and facilitate communication

**Coordinated**—emergency managers synchronize the activities of all relevant stakeholders to achieve a common purpose

**Flexible**—emergency managers use creative and innovative approaches in solving disaster challenges

**Professional**—emergency managers value a science and knowledge-based approach based on education, training, experience, ethical practice, public stewardship, and continuous improvement

http://training.fema.gov/EMIWeb/edu/emprinciples.asp.

a biological or chemical attack may be significantly different than providing medical care in a natural disaster. The intentional spread of disease or hazardous materials could possibly outpace the knowledge and ability of civilian medical personnel. The military may need to take a more active role in such situations. This is one of the reasons why homeland security tends to accept the traditional model of emergency management today.

Also, by stressing the involvement of others, the professional model reduces the importance of the government. This is problematic in that the government has access to wide variety of human and material resources. No other entity is more capable of fulfilling the diverse set of disaster needs on a long-term basis. The professional model may likewise fail to recognize the need for strong and decisive leadership in emergency situations. A vision of what needs to be accomplished and how it is to be done may help to unify the disparate actors involved in disaster response and recovery.

The professional model also overlooks importance of following strategies that have been developed in the past and tested over time. There may be no need to change public information operations in a current disaster if the methods proved effective in most previous events. Following prior guidelines can save time, ensure safety, and allow for an efficient allocation of resources.

Finally, by approaching disasters from a broader perspective, the professional model may downplay the importance of emergency services. However, when lives are on the line, it is the police and fire departments and EMTs that come to the rescue. Their vital contributions should not be underestimated in time of disaster.

## SELF-CHECK

- What is the professional approach to emergency management?
- Why did this model emerge?
- What are the features of the professional model?
- What conclusions are drawn from the assumptions of this model?
- What are the strengths of this model?
- What weaknesses are common to the professional model?

## 4.3 Comparison of The Models

As can be seen, there are both similarities and differences between the two models (see Table 4-6). A comparison of the two approaches involves examination of their:

▲ Respective goals
▲ Levels of analysis
▲ Assumptions
▲ Recommendations

Without a doubt, both the traditional and professional approaches were designed to foster beneficial outcomes in times of disaster. Each model was developed due to an awareness of the adverse effects of specific disasters. Both models try to resolve the problems inherent in emergency response and recovery operations. The two models try to resolve these problems quickly and in the most effective way possible. In spite of these similarities, there are significant differences between the alternative approaches.

For example, the traditional model is most applicable to routine emergencies and the activities of practitioners in the field at the scene of a disaster. In contrast, the professional model is more concerned about disasters and activities regarding the entire response and recovery system. One focuses on mission tactics, while the other is interested in overall strategy.

The different models also have their own unique assumptions and recommendations (Dynes, 1994). The traditional model assumes that all disasters result in chaos. Society may possibly break down during extreme events and important functions will be neglected. The traditional model recommends command and control as a way to resolve the situation. Centralized leadership is needed to make correct decisions about the event, and procedures must be implemented per the instructions of the figure or agency in authority.

The professional model, in contrast, has distinct assumptions and recommendations. This model presumes societal structures will likely continue in times of disaster. People and organizations deal with adverse situations in a logical and expected manner. The model recommends coordination and cooperation among responding entities. Individuals and agencies are most likely to resolve problems by communicating and assisting one another rather than simply telling others what to do.

As can be seen, the goals of the two models may be similar at times, but there are differences that must be recognized as well. Emergency managers should be aware of the traditional and professional models along with their respective strengths and weaknesses. It is imperative that emergency managers think critically about which model to employ in each particular disaster situation. At times, it will be necessary to operate under the traditional approach. In other situations, the professional approach will be desired.

Interestingly, some of the most recent research advocates blended approaches. Today's disasters warrant that all types of hazards must be taken into account, even if different agents require unique responses at times (McEntire, 2009). The government and first responders will continue to play important roles in disasters, but other functions will necessitate the involvement of emergent groups and others from the private and nonprofit sectors (Phillips, Neal and Webb, 2012). Disasters also create complex organizational challenges where both centralization and decentralization are required (Moynihan, 2009). Finally, standard procedures should be developed to anticipate common disaster consequences, but impacts may also necessitate a departure from the existing plan in certain situations (Webb and Chevreau, 2006). Knowing when to follow each model is one of the keys to successful postdisaster operations.

### Table 4-6: Assumptions of the Traditional and Professional Models During Emergency Response

| Traditional model | Professional model |
| --- | --- |
| Chaos in society | Continuity of society |
| Command over others | Coordination with others |
| Control over others | Cooperation with others |

Dynes (1994).

## SELF-CHECK

- How are the traditional and professional models similar?
- How are the models different?
- Why is it necessary to understand the traditional and professional models?
- Would it be beneficial to know when to apply each model? Why?

## SUMMARY

Theories guide our everyday lives and disaster response and recovery operations as well. Two models have been developed to guide emergency management. The traditional approach focused on civil defense issues during the Cold War. It gave priority to the military and the government, SOPs, and the activities of first responders. The professional model is more inclusive. It includes recognition of the threat of many hazards. It also recognizes that many different actors will participate in response and recovery operations and that plans and SOPs may not be pertinent in every disaster context. Comparing the strengths and weaknesses of the two models and knowing when it is best to operate under one versus the other will help you to deal effectively with disasters when they occur.

## KEY TERMS

| | |
|---|---|
| **Traditional model** | the civil defense command and control bureaucratic or emergency service perspective. |
| **Mutually assured destruction** | the use of nuclear weapons against one's enemy that invites massive retaliation and results in the annihilation of most major cities in both countries. |
| **Civil defense** | was an effort by government officials to prepare for nuclear war. It included the building of underground shelters and the creation of plans to evacuate targeted urban areas of strategic value. |
| **Standard operating procedures** | (SOPs) are rules and guidelines to complete disaster functions effectively and efficiently. |
| **Professional model** | the all-hazard networking collaborative problem-solving or public administration model. |
| **Vertical relationships** | involve information flow up and down government chains of command. |
| **Horizontal relationships** | those in which parties communicate across departments and communities. |

# ASSESS YOUR UNDERSTANDING

Posttest to evaluate your knowledge of management approaches.
*Measure your learning by comparing pretest and posttest results.*

## Summary Questions

1. Theory has no bearing on emergency management activities. True or false?
2. The traditional approach to disasters is known as the networking and problem-solving model. True or false?
3. Nuclear war was a major threat during the Cold War. True or false?
4. Civil defense was a government initiative to prepare cities for evacuation in case of a nuclear exchange with the Soviet Union. True or false?
5. The traditional approach to disasters disapproves of hierarchy. True or false?
6. There are no weaknesses associated with the traditional model. True or false?
7. The professional model is also referred to as the collaborative approach to emergency management. True or false?
8. When FEMA was organized, emergency management began to focus less on nuclear war and more on natural and technological hazards. True or false?
9. The professional approach to emergency management recognizes that the government is the only actor involved in response and recovery operations. True or false?
10. MAD stands for:
    (a) Management assistance device
    (b) Management assistance decision
    (c) Mutually assured destruction
    (d) Mutually assured devastation
    (e) Mitigation action device
11. SOPs are:
    (a) Flexible and rigid
    (b) Flexible
    (c) Espoused by the professional approach
    (d) Rigid
    (e) Related to improvisation and creativity
12. The professional model:
    (a) Gives highest priority to nuclear war
    (b) Focuses on cooperation with other organizations
    (c) Is similar to the emergency service model
    (d) Is similar to the public administration model
    (e) Answers b and d

13. The professional model:
   (a) Assumes that people will be a useful resource in disasters
   (b) Asserts that the government is not the only actor involved in response operations
   (c) Prefers horizontal relationships rather than a command and control mentality
   (d) All of the above
   (e) None of the above

14. A strength of the professional model is its flexible approach to disasters. A weakness of this model is that it:
   (a) Approaches disasters from an all-hazard perspective
   (b) Is extremely concerned about nuclear war
   (c) Is closely aligned with emergency service personnel
   (d) Cannot relate to private and nonprofit agencies
   (e) Has no relationship to emergent groups

## Review Questions

1. What are the two models of disaster response and recovery management?
2. Why did the traditional model of emergency management appear?
3. What are the other names of the traditional model?
4. What major assumptions are made by the traditional model?
5. The traditional model has numerous strengths and weaknesses. What are they?
6. How did the end of the Cold War and creation of FEMA lead to the professional approach to emergency management?
7. How is the professional approach different than the traditional model?
8. How does the professional model view hierarchy and SOPs?
9. Do the traditional and professional models overlap in any way?
10. Which model is related most to homeland security? Why?

## Applying This Chapter

1. While responding to a house fire, firefighters in El Paso, Texas recognize characteristics in the home that resemble a meth lab. How could standard operating procedures help protect firefighters in this situation?
2. While responding to a major fire, the fire chief notices that the media and Red Cross have arrived to film the incident and care for those fleeing the apartment fire. What concerns do you have about their presence at the scene of the disaster? Should you avoid working with them? What are the consequences of failing to communicate with them?

3. A major office building has been bombed in downtown Atlanta. Fire has engulfed many of the lower floors and the stairwells are filling with smoke. The elevator could be used, but the shaft is filled with dangerous fumes. 47 people are stranded on the roof waiting to be rescued. Helicopters from the fire department and a nearby military base are hovering overhead. Aviation regulations state that no more than 5 people should be inside the helicopters at any given time. Should you consider putting 7 people on the helicopters to speed up the evacuation? What are the dangers of doing so? Who could you talk to in order to see if this would be ok?

4. A major flash flood has affected a small community outside of Cheyenne, Wyoming. What are some of the organizations that might converge on this area? How would victim and bystanders behave? Would it be in your benefit as an emergency manager to consider what they are doing and if they could help you?

5. Suppose you were the emergency manager in Tokyo when the terrorist group Aum Shinrikyo released sarin gas in the subway. Many people died and thousands of people were affected. The event required a major medical mobilization, but it necessitated that other functions be performed (e.g., media relations, mass fatality management, criminal investigation). In what ways could the traditional approach help you? In what ways could the professional approach assist you?

## Working with Others

As a fire chief in Las Vegas, Nevada, you are responsible for property protection and for the safety of your crew. How can the traditional approach help you extinguish the fire and protect your firefighters? Are there issues relating to the fire you cannot address alone? Why would it be advantageous to work with other organizations?

## Standard Operating Procedures

You are the emergency manager for Oak Ridge, Tennessee. Oak Ridge is home to a nuclear power plant. What standard operating procedures might you have to deal with the leak of nuclear material? Could there be a situation where it would be advisable to deviate from SOPs?

## Representing Your Organization

You work in the transportation department and have been assigned to the local emergency operations center during a flood episode. Why would it be important to represent the interests of your organization in the EOC? Can your organization resolve all types of disaster problems alone? Why would it be important to work collaboratively with others? Do other organizations need the information you can provide? How do the priorities of other organizations influence the operations of your organization in times of disaster?

# 5

# IMPLEMENTING INITIAL RESPONSE MEASURES
## Hazard Detection, Warning, Evacuation, and Sheltering

## Starting Point

Pretest to assess your knowledge on initial response measures.
*Determine where you need to concentrate your effort.*

## What You'll Learn in This Chapter

▲ Methods to detect hazards during the initial period of the response phase
▲ The importance of warning systems
▲ Different evacuation methods
▲ Categories of sheltering and housing
▲ Typical human behavior during evacuation and sheltering

## After Studying This Chapter, You'll Be Able To

▲ Detect hazards and implement the community disaster plan.
▲ Develop effective warning messages.
▲ Compare and contrast alternative means to warn people about disasters.
▲ Understand human behavior during evacuation and sheltering.
▲ Evaluate evacuation and shelter options.

## Goals and Outcomes

▲ Understand ways to identify hazards.
▲ Assess the best way(s) to issue warnings.
▲ Implement the community's emergency operations plan.
▲ Evaluate and select the appropriate protective action for affected populations.
▲ Predict typical human behaviors during evacuation.
▲ Establish and maintain a shelter.

*Disaster Response and Recovery: Strategies and Tactics for Resilience*, Second Edition. David A. McEntire.
© 2015 John Wiley & Sons, Inc. Published 2015 by John Wiley & Sons, Inc.

# INTRODUCTION

When a disaster is about to occur, you, as an emergency manager, will have many significant responsibilities. The first step in response is to detect a hazard, and this may be accomplished through a variety of means. During or after this identification process, it will be imperative that you warn the population that could potentially be at risk. While warnings are being issued, you must also determine if evacuation and sheltering will be required. Do you need to move people to safer areas? Will they need a place to stay in the short or long term? This chapter provides guidelines on how to make and implement these difficult decisions that will have a profound impact on resilience.

## 5.1 Hazard Detection

Before you can respond to an emergency or disaster, you must know that one is about to occur or that it is currently taking place. Each emergency or disaster event is unique and may be detected in diverse and perhaps multiple ways. In some cases, emergency managers and other responders become aware of emergencies and disasters through technology that is hazard specific. For example, radar systems could alert you to the possibility of severe weather. Other events may be identified through many different strategies simultaneously. For example, a call from storm spotters may notify you about the possibility of flooding while you are reading an online report from meteorologists at the National Weather Service (NWS). There are several other means through which you may learn of an emergency or disaster. These detection methods include the following:

▲ **Senses**. You may actually experience the disaster first hand. The ground may shake violently due to an earthquake. Smoke from a building fire may be seen while you are driving to work. Or you could have a physical reaction to a release of hazardous chemicals. Sight, sound, and other senses may make you aware of a hazard.

▲ **Feedback from field personnel**. You may become aware of events that require response operations through city personnel. For example, while on patrol, a police officer may become cognizant of a serious accident or other incident because of unusually heavy traffic conditions or the gathering of people in a particular location. Firefighters, emergency service personnel, and anyone with a city uniform or vehicle may also become aware of emergency or disaster situations. These individuals drive around the jurisdiction frequently and are able to identify unique circumstances or situations. Citizens will also seek out these uniformed personnel and city employees in marked vehicles if public safety is at stake. If field personnel are aware of an event, they will share that information with dispatch and others (e.g., the police or fire chief).

▲ **Social media**. You may learn about unfolding disasters through various types of social media platforms like Facebook and Twitter. Instant status updates or tweets can inform you of events anywhere and everywhere.

For example, "social media was very helpful in the Virginia Tech shooting and the Southern California wildfires" (Pohl et al., 2012). Social media notified students, faculty, and citizens of these unfolding disasters so they could take protective action. It is important to note, however, that the information provided through social media may be faulty, incorrect, or incomplete because it can be easily manipulated by anyone. Nevertheless, social media can help emergency management personnel understand what is happening in their jurisdiction.

▲ **Dispatch**. Once an incident has been reported, the police and/or fire dispatch will notify you and other responders about the incident. Citizens will call 911 centers to report an emergency. Even major disasters such as the World Trade Center (WTC) terrorist attacks are often initiated by a 911 call (Figure 5-1). When information is received, the dispatch center will relay "alarms" to fire stations and send police officers to the scene. Additional units will be asked to report to the location of the incident if further resources are warranted (e.g., for 3-alarm fire or major traffic accident). Dispatch may contact you and other emergency management personnel if the services of the emergency operations center (EOC) will be needed.

▲ **Increased radio traffic**. As an incident occurs, emergency communications will become replete with discussions about the response among dispatch

**Figure 5-1**

Dispatchers like these individuals in Los Angeles County receive information about emergencies and send first responders to care for those in need. Jason Pack/FEMA.

personnel, incident commanders, and first responders. Anyone with a scanner may pick up these conversations (unless the communication is taking place on secured lines). The police or fire chief may notify the emergency manager or mayor directly, stating that an emergency has occurred and that assistance will be needed. Other key participants may be called to notify them of the incident. For example, a school shooting may require assistance mutual aid partners like a neighboring police department, a SWAT team, etc.

▲ **News media**. Reports from the news media will increase dramatically when a hazard has occurred or actual emergency is unfolding. Newspaper articles may discuss hurricanes that have formed and are approaching the coast. Radio stations will be interrupted by the Emergency Alert System (EAS). The EAS is a warning system that requires all media providers to comply with any requests from national officials to communicate to the public in the face of an emergency. Regular television programs will be interrupted for special reports about earthquakes, tornadoes, flash flooding, and other quick-onset hazards. Nightly news programs will cover the disasters in great depth. Internet news websites will also carry news stories and information about disasters will be updated quickly as things unfold.

▲ **Volunteers**. Volunteers will stay in contact with you when severe weather threatens and provide information about other types of disasters at times. For instance, members of the Amateur Radio Emergency Services (ARES) and the Radio Amateur Civil Emergency Services (RACES) will spot tornadoes and relay information to the EOC. They provide a boots-on-the-ground perspective of severe weather and can verify storm intensity.

▲ **Meteorological services and scientists**. Government agencies and natural scientists may notify emergency managers about impending disasters. The National Hurricane Center (located on the main campus of Florida International) monitors the development and tracking of cyclones. It provides daily forecasts of the storm's intensity as well as the time and location of projected landfall. The National Oceanic and Atmospheric Administration (NOAA) also tracks severe weather. Within the NOAA, the NWS has offices around the nation that will contact you with advisory bulletins and advisories when weather becomes dangerous. Volcanologists from the U.S. Geological Survey (USGS) also advise of potential eruptions based on past and current volcano activity (e.g., seismic activity and gas emissions).

▲ **Incident page network**. As an emergency manager, you might subscribe to paging services to learn about hazards and disasters (see http://www.incidentpage.net). These systems give you real-time information about severe weather, traffic accidents, major fire outbreaks, and other emergencies and disasters.

▲ **Hospitals**. Medical facilities such as doctor's offices, hospitals, and pharmacies may become aware of unique trends related to disease patterns and patient flow. Administrators may notify public health officials and emergency managers if large numbers of people exhibit similar symptoms.

Hospitals will play an especially crucial role in distributing information in the case of a biological weapons attack. However, some of the first reports of these attacks may come from special sensors that have been placed in classified locations in large cities throughout the United States.

▲ **Technology**. Modern computers and technology may help detect potential hazards. Satellites are used to track and monitor weather systems. Radar is also used to detect the formation of tornadoes and the location of rain and hail. The Collaborative Adaptive Sensing of the Atmosphere (CASA) radar outperforms the ability of traditional radar systems by predicting the specific time and location bad weather will hit. With better resolution, the CASA radar can pinpoint specific neighborhoods that are at risk. In other cases, buoys monitor the heat and level of the ocean to track the movement of water and tsunamis. Richter scales identify where earthquakes occur as well as their magnitude.

Thus, responders and emergency managers may detect emergency and disasters just as everyone else does through personal experience or through the news media. Responders and emergency managers may also receive advanced notice through weather reports, storm spotters, dispatch, and from field personnel and other professional associates or organizations. Regardless of what means are used to monitor hazards, it is important that responders and emergency constantly monitor circumstances in the jurisdiction for emergencies and disasters. There should always be someone who has been given this responsibility (or many individuals on a rotating basis). These people should be on call on a 24 hour basis—7 days a week, 365 days a year.

## 5.1.1 Initial Steps

Once you become aware of a hazard, emergency or disaster, it is imperative that you undertake several vital activities (often simultaneously in many cases). One of the first steps is to implement the community's emergency operations plan. An **emergency operations plan** is a document that describes how the jurisdiction might respond to a disaster. This typically involves alerting the leadership and asking them to meet in the EOC. This cadre of department supervisors plays an important role in the initial stages of the response. Department supervisors verify what has happened, determine the priorities, and manage the response.

These include seeking additional information, notifying and communicating with others, initiating the response, and activating the EOC.

### 5.1.1.1 Seeking Additional Information

When a hazard is imminent or occurring, it is always necessary to seek additional information. Having additional information will enable you to initiate the appropriate response and recovery operations. Possible questions to investigate include:

▲ What happened?
▲ Has the hazard/incident been verified?
▲ What are the consequences?

▲ How many people have been killed or injured?

▲ Has property been destroyed?

▲ What do the first responders need?

▲ What challenges must be overcome?

▲ Can the EOC provide support?

▲ What resources are needed now and in the long term?

▲ Do other individuals and agencies need to be involved?

▲ What can be done to remedy the situation quickly and effectively?

▲ Will the existing plan help the community respond to the event, or does it need to be adapted to the unique situation at hand?

▲ What contingencies need to be planned for as time unfolds?

### 5.1.1.2 Notifying and Communicating with Others

When an emergency or disaster is imminent or unfolding, it will be necessary to notify and communicate with others that will play important roles in response and recovery operations. This will not only assist in answering the questions posed above, but it will be required to formulate decisions and implement appropriate policies. Therefore, you will need to bring the emergency or disaster to the attention of key leaders. This includes mayors, city council members, city managers, department heads, and others in the private and nonprofit sectors. These individuals have responsibility to act in times of disaster and are given authority to mobilize resources and take all necessary actions.

You will also need to maintain communications with those individuals or organizations that notified you about the emergency or disaster. This may include dispatch, a fire chief, field personnel, etc. These individuals can provide additional information as it becomes available or answer the questions you ask of them. You will also want to communicate with others that have knowledge about what is taking place. This may include meteorologists, floodplain managers, storm spotters, field personnel, business owners, the Red Cross, etc. These people can verify what is happening and provide additional details and other perspectives about the emergency or disaster.

### 5.1.1.3 Activating the Emergency Operations Plan

As information is gathered and leaders communicate one with another, it may be necessary to implement initial response measures. Immediate activities may include:

▲ Dispatching additional fire units

▲ Warning the population

▲ Seeking mutual aid for mass casualties

▲ Evacuating the population

Such measures may be closely related to increased readiness conditions. Increased readiness conditions may be based on numerical numbers (e.g., 1–4) and denote the severity of an event along with appropriate measures to be taken. For instance, a level 1 or 2 event notes that a tornado is occurring/has occurred and that all necessary departments should be involved in the response. In contrast, a level 3 or 4 event implies that a tornado could occur and that department leaders should maintain awareness of weather reports. Thus, the nature and timing of disaster may determine what readiness level is chosen and acted upon. In addition, it is important to recognize that things can change quickly and require departure from standard operating procedures.

### 5.1.1.4  Activating the EOC

As part of the plan activation, and in accordance with the information received, the emergency manager, in consultation with the mayor or city manager, may decide to activate the EOC (Figure 5-2). The EOC is a central location where leaders can gather information, discuss options, make decisions, disseminate policy, communicate with involved parties, and seek and allocate resources (see Chapter 11 for further information about EOCs). EOC activation will help you understand the nature of the event and coordinate subsequent response and recovery operations. Activating the EOC may include bringing staff into the facility, turning on computers and communication equipment, and beginning to address the problems the disaster reveals. However, the EOC activation may be partial or complete, and this decision is dependent on the scope of the emergency:

▲ **Partial activation** may include some individuals, agencies, and functions.
▲ **Full activation** will include most people and organizations that are involved in typical response operations.

Figure 5-2

EOCs, like this one in Pulaski County, MO, will be activated
when disasters occur. Steve Zumwalt/FEMA.

Hence, a partial or full activation will be determined by the nature of the incident (type, scope, magnitude, etc.).

As the emergency or disaster unfolds, it is important for the emergency manager to understand who participates or should participate in response and recovery operations. Will the response require firefighters and search and rescue teams? Should the flood plan manager be notified? Are the services of the city's Engineering Department required for damage assessment? Could a faith-based organization help the victims and survivors who have been impacted? The point is to remember that the emergency or disaster will determine who is, will, or should be included in the EOC. A small emergency will require fewer people and agencies than a larger disaster. For example, a small forest fire will require different personnel than a major flood.

In addition, as you activate the EOC, it is good idea to recognize how others become involved in the incident or disaster. Some individuals will be integrated almost automatically (e.g., police or fire representatives), while others may need to be notified and asked to participate (e.g., officials in the Water Department). Furthermore, the people and organizations involved will not be static, but will expand and contract as response and recovery operations dictate. Meteorologists, for example, are vital before a tornado strikes, but may play a less salient role after the storm dissipates and moves elsewhere. Alternatively, a charitable organization may not do much during the first few hours of the disaster. However, it will play an increasingly important role as you transition from response to recovery.

## FOR EXAMPLE

### Detecting and Responding Terrorism

New Yorkers started their workday on September 11, 2001, seeing smoke billow up from the WTC after a plane crashed into the first tower. Immediately after this occurred, the event was initially reported by the news media as possible pilot error or mechanical malfunction. It was only when another plane struck the second tower and the Pentagon was attacked as well that the world realized the plane crashes were due to the actions of terrorists. Meanwhile, those working in and around the WTC called 911 to ask for help. Hundreds of first responders showed up to fight the fires, evacuate the buildings, and provide medical help. Mayor Giuliani held a news conference and put New York's disaster plan in motion. Unfortunately, the EOC (located in Building #7 at the WTC) could not be used because it was impacted when the twin towers fell to the ground. Those involved in emergency management had to undertake initial operations in response to the worst terrorist attack in U.S. history with no functioning EOC. In time, a makeshift EOC was set up in a pier along the Hudson River, and it was utilized for several months. 911 showed the importance of EOCs for response and recovery operations.

## SELF-CHECK

- What are the initial steps in disaster response and recovery?
- How are hazards detected?
- How can you obtain additional information about a hazard or disaster when it occurs?
- What steps are taken to initiate the plan or response and recovery operations?
- What is a full or partial activation of the EOC?

## 5.2 Issuing Warnings

After hazards are detected, one of the first and most important functions performed in times of disaster is warning the population about an impending hazard or actual disaster. **Warnings** are advanced notifications that allow people to take measures to protect themselves and their property. Most warnings occur before a hazard has occurred. However, warnings may take place after a disaster on an ongoing basis to help people to know the best way to prepare for or react in response and recovery operations.

Most warnings follow a similar pattern. According to E.L. Quarantelli, the process typically includes an assessment of the hazard and disaster as well as a dissemination of the warning message (1990, p. 1):

▲ The assessment phase is the phase when facts are gathered, decisions are made, and the message is formulated.

▲ The dissemination phase is when information is relayed to the public and those who will assist in delivering the warning to others.

Those receiving (listening and reacting to) the warning experience a related but perhaps broader process. Lindell and Perry (1992) include the following four steps:

1. Risk identification. Determining if a threat exists
2. Risk assessment. Determining if protection is needed
3. Risk reduction. Determining if protection is possible
4. Protective response. Determining what protective action is best and then taking that action

To help people prepare for hazards, the NWS uses the terms "watch" and "warning." People may not understand the difference between a watch and a warning, however. A **watch** indicates that conditions are ripe for a hazard to occur. The severe weather system may produce a tornado or flood. A **warning** indicates that the hazard is imminent, is taking place, or has occurred. A tornado warning suggests that a tornado has touched down or that the river is currently flooding.

People must fully understand the significance of warnings before they take protective action. A severe winter weather warning may allow people to buy additional groceries and supplies before the storm hits the area. Hurricane warnings encourage people to leave low-lying areas. Another example is a tornado warning. When people are given tornado warnings, they should take immediate shelter in a safe room (a small room in the center of a building on the lowest possible floor).

Warnings also provide vital information for the population at risk. This includes:

▲ When a hazard/disaster will occur
▲ How long a hazard/disaster will last in duration
▲ What the impact and severity of the disaster will be
▲ If there is a potential for power outages
▲ What damages are projected for homes and property
▲ If streets or neighborhoods have been closed

It is likewise essential for you to recognize that the warning function may be extremely complex. Depending on the type of hazard/disaster, warnings may or may not be possible. Earthquakes or terrorist attacks are extremely difficult to predict and therefore do not generally allow advanced warning. For example, the government wasn't able to warn citizens about the 9/11 terrorist attacks in advance. In contrast, severe weather systems can be monitored more effectively and generally permit advanced time for warning. Different hazards/disasters likewise permit dramatically different lead times for warning. A hurricane warning can be issued several days before landfall. However, a tornado warning may be issued only several minutes before touchdown or impact.

In addition, when a hazard is imminent or a disaster has occurred, you should take into account several issues to ensure a successful warning. Those issuing warnings should consider what criteria would serve as the basis of the warning decision. For example:

1. Do you issue a warning when there are signs that a tornado may form, or does the tornado have to touch down before you go public with this information?
2. Should you wait until the fire, accident, or chemical release been confirmed by a fire chief or police officer, or should you warn others if a citizen has reported the incident?
3. Is approval from higher sources (e.g., a mayor or your supervisor) needed before a warning for a hailstorm can be issued?

There are other factors to consider as well. What are the liabilities (e.g., deaths, property damage, lawsuits) if a warning is issued or not issued? How soon should the warning be issued and is additional information required before a warning can be made? What facts or advice should the warning message convey? Will the warning be followed by additional information? If so, when?

---

**FOR EXAMPLE**

**Warning about Hurricane Katrina**

Emergency management officials in Louisiana, Alabama, and Mississippi used many different warning systems to warn residents about the destructive impact of Hurricane Katrina. Warnings were given by local, state, and federal officials. Media reports discussed in depth the damage that could occur. Evacuation orders were given by all three states, although at different times. Local law enforcement went door-to-door in the most vulnerable areas asking people to leave. The EAS was used and warnings were issued in different languages. Despite all the warnings, some people stayed. Reasons why people did not evacuate are discussed later in this chapter.

---

You should also know that warnings could come from official and/or unofficial sources. The NWS—a formal government agency—may issue severe thunderstorm warnings. State and local emergency management organizations and personnel have involvement in the warning process. Politicians may issue warnings as well. For example, President Bush, Governor Blanco of Louisiana, and Mayor Nagin of New Orleans all issued warnings before Hurricane Katrina. In addition, the media plays an important role as well. Many of us have received warnings of severe weather by TV anchors, meteorologists, talk show hosts, and reporters. Other people and organizations also participate in the warning process. A friend may tell acquaintances about an approaching ice storm. Emergent groups may assist the fire department in warning others about a nearby forest fire that is approaching the neighborhood.

Although numerous individuals and groups are involved in issuing warnings, Golden and Adams (2000, p. 107) assert that the most important actors include the local NWS office, local emergency managers, and private forecasters/the news media. This group is known as the weather warning partnership.

### 5.2.1 Types of Warning Systems

There are many different types of warning systems, and the warnings that are issued may be performed with or without technology. Some may include door-to-door notifications for residents of an apartment complex that has caught on fire. Others could be issued from a police cruiser if floodwaters are anticipated to arrive downstream. Many warning systems today rely on modern computers and high-tech communication equipment.

Each type of warning system has strengths and weaknesses. It is important that you are aware of these strengths and weaknesses so you can make the correct decisions regarding the warning function. This is because the warning system you choose has an impact on the effectiveness of the warning message. However, emergency managers may use several warning systems in a single event. For instance, outdoor sirens are sounded when a tornado touches down in a residential area, while weather radios are activated at the same time in homes and businesses. The media is also alerted when severe weather moves in and people share perspectives of what is going on in social media. Thus, more than one method can therefore be utilized at a time. In fact, it is advisable to use as many means as possible to issue a warning as long as the message is consistent.

### 5.2.1.1 Sirens

Outdoor mechanical and electronic sirens are used for severe weather such as tornadoes or at industrial locations. Mechanical sirens can warn a large number of people provided that the individuals are able to hear the siren (Figure 5-3). People are most likely to be alerted by the siren when they are outside and in close proximity to this warning device. Much like a public address (PA) system, electronic sirens warn a large number people as well. The only difference is that electronic sirens produce numerous tones and allow voice warnings.

The weakness of a mechanical siren is that it produces a single tone, which may not be understood by those who hear it (they may not know the meaning of the siren). The drawback of an electronic siren is that the voice message may be muffled by outside noises or even the level of humidity in the air. Both electronic and mechanical sirens are not typically heard by people who are inside buildings. Finally, each of these systems can be very expensive and require significant maintenance.

### 5.2.1.2 Media

TV stations issue warnings as part of regular news broadcasts or may interrupt programming in times of emergency. Cable stations may also issue warnings through scroll text at the bottom of the television screen. Media reports quickly

**Figure 5-3**

Tornado sirens, such as this one in Greensburg, KS, warn residents of approaching severe weather. Leif Skoogfors/FEMA.

warn a large number of people if they are inside their home watching TV or listening to the radio in the car. TV anchors, weather experts, and reporters may provide detailed information about the hazard or disaster.

The source of the warning can make a big difference. Quarantelli suggests that "warnings sent via the mass media are more likely to be believed if delivered by governmental officials rather than by private citizens, or by personnel from emergency organizations than by members of other groups. Also, different mass media sources in a community are likely to have different degrees of credibility. Those with the most pre-disaster credibility are most likely to be seen as issuing a disaster warning" (Quarantelli, 1990, p. 4).

The weakness on relying on the media to issue warnings is that people may not be watching TV or listening to the radio when a hazard or disaster occurs. Also, power outages may render some forms of the media useless. Furthermore, the information relayed through the media might also be incorrect.

### 5.2.1.3 Emergency Alert System

As mentioned earlier, the EAS is used for a variety of hazards and may be issued by way of television or radio. It includes an announcement of what is occurring and what should be done for protection. The EAS quickly warns a large number of people. It also provides detailed and accurate information.

The weaknesses of the EAS are largely the same as the weaknesses of the media because the warnings are broadcast through the television and radio. People may not be in front of the television or in their car listening to the radio. Also, power outages can render the television and radio useless in time of disaster.

### 5.2.1.4 Reverse 911

Reverse 911 involves a call issued from a single site, which is transmitted by computer communication systems to homes and businesses in a designated jurisdiction. It is a computer system that can make a large number of calls to a designated area. Reverse 911 is able to warn a large number of people quickly and in a precise fashion. Recorded phone messages delivered through 911 can be simple or detailed.

Again, there are drawbacks with all warning systems. Hazards and disasters may result in inoperable telephone systems. In addition, some people may not have phones or answer their phone. Also, those answering the call may not believe a recorded message and may simply hang up before the information is relayed.

### 5.2.1.5 Intercoms, Teletype Writers, Telephone Devices, and Strobe Lights

Special warning devices are used to warn people in large buildings and to warn the deaf. This includes intercoms, teletype writers, telephone devices, and strobe lights. Such systems are good in that they warn people in buildings or those with hearing impairments. However, such systems generally warn a limited number of people only. Also, these warning systems may not provide adequate information (when compared to different systems like reverse 911).

### 5.2.1.6 Loud Speakers, Door-to-Door Notification and Weather Radios

Other warning systems may be relied on to notify others. For instance, bullhorns may be used by the police to warn people on a street of a nearby chemical release. Loud speakers are credible if mounted on an official vehicle like a police cruiser or fire engine. However, loud speakers may not be heard by people who are inside their homes.

Firefighters may also knock on the doors of nearby residents to encourage evacuation from hotels and high-rise buildings. Door-to-door warnings could theoretically permit the answering of questions. However, door-to-door warnings require significant manpower and are very time consuming. Before Hurricane Katrina, police went door-to-door in the low-lying parts of New Orleans to ask people to evacuate.

Weather radios are activated for weather watches and warnings and advise people of what to do in case of severe weather. Weather radios warn people in specific geographic areas about their weather. However, most people do not have weather radios—even though they are relatively inexpensive.

### 5.2.1.7 Social Media

Social media can be used by emergency managers to issue warnings to a large number of people quickly, who are likely to share such information with many more people. The major strength of social media is that an emergency manager can reach thousands or millions of people by posting updates electronically. The drawback is that not everyone is connected to or actively monitoring social media. Furthermore, some of the information sent through social media could be inaccurate and require correction.

### 5.2.1.8 Cell Phones/Smart Phones

Cell phones or smartphones can be used to issue important warning messages from government officials. As of 2012, wireless carriers must comply with a public safety system known as Wireless Emergency Alerts (WEA). Because of this law, the owners of new cell phones can receive warning messages about any hazards that may be threatening and specific to their geographic location.

### 5.2.2 Warning Considerations

In addition to considering the diverse types of warning systems that could be used, you should also take the following into account when you issue warnings:

▲ Warnings should be clear and contain accurate information. The more general a warning is, the less likely it will be perceived as a warning. The more specific a warning is, the more likely it will be heeded (Quarantelli, 1990, p. 4).

▲ Warning messages must be repeated often and be consistent in terms of content. People may not believe a message if it is only issued once and if the information changes over time.

▲ Warnings must be issued by a credible source. This may include a government official, a meteorologist, or other expert.

▲ People will perceive warnings differently based on the degree of the threat, prior experience in disasters, and interaction with others in society. If citizens can see the hurricane approaching (either in person or through television or a computer), they will be more likely to listen to the warning. If the warnings are issued and no disaster occurs, the less likely the warnings will be heeded in the future. This makes hurricane warnings especially problematic (hurricanes could be heading toward an area and then change track after people have already evacuated). Also, if someone's friends do not evacuate or take protective action, then these individuals are less likely to do so as well.

## FOR EXAMPLE

### The Ill-Fated Homeland Security Advisory System

After 9/11, the federal government created the infamous Homeland Security Advisory System. This is the color-coded warning system that was used to warn of possible terrorist threats and was the source of many jokes on late night TV. Unfortunately, those who created this system ignored much of the research on what makes warnings effective. The Homeland Security Advisory System did not provide clear information or make specific recommendations for those receiving the warnings. Consequently, it was discarded in April 2011 and replaced by the National Terrorism Advisory System. The new system issues alerts with as much practical information as possible and outlines measures to take to respond specifically to the threat at hand.

## SELF-CHECK

- What is a warning?
- How is a warning different than a watch?
- What are the different types of warning systems?
- What will make warning messages more effective?

**National Terrorism Advisory System**

# Alert

www.dhs.gov/alerts

DATE & TIME ISSUED: XXXX

## SUMMARY

The Secretary of Homeland Security informs the public and relevant government and private sector partners about a potential or actual threat with this alert, indicating whether there is an "imminent" or "elevated" threat.

## DURATION

An individual threat alert is issued for a specific time period and then automatically expires. It may be extended if new information becomes available or the threat evolves.

## DETAILS

• This section provides more detail about the threat and what the public and sectors need to know.

• It may include specific information, if available, about the nature and credibility of the threat, including the critical infrastructure sector(s) or location(s) that may be affected.

• It includes as much information as can be released publicly about actions being taken or planned by authorities to ensure public safety, such as increased protective actions and what the public may expect to see.

## AFFECTED AREAS

▪ This section includes visual depictions (such as maps or other graphics) showing the affected location(s), sector(s), or other illustrative detail about the threat itself.

## HOW YOU CAN HELP

• This section provides information on ways the public can help authorities (e.g. camera phone pictures taken at the site of an explosion), and reinforces the importance of reporting suspicious activity.

• It may ask the public or certain sectors to be alert for a particular item, situation, person, activity or developing trend.

## STAY PREPARED

• This section emphasizes the importance of the public planning and preparing for emergencies before they happen, including specific steps individuals, families and businesses can take to ready themselves and their communities.

• It provides additional preparedness information that may be relevant based on this threat.

## STAY INFORMED

• This section notifies the public about where to get more information.

• It encourages citizens to stay informed about updates from local public safety and community leaders.

• It includes a link to the DHS NTAS website http://www.dhs.gov/alerts and http://twitter.com/NTASAlerts

**If You See Something, Say Something™. Report suspicious activity to local law enforcement or call 911.**

The National Terrorism Advisory System provides Americans with alert information on homeland security threats. It is distributed by the Department of Homeland Security. More information is available at: **www.dhs.gov/alerts.** To receive mobile updates: **www.twitter.com/NTASAlerts**
If You See Something Say Something™ used with permission of the NY Metropolitan Transportation Authority.

This sample document illustrates the type of information that would be shared with the public under the National Terrorism Advisory System if there were a immanent or elevated threat.

## 5.3 Evacuation

In order to react effectively to a disaster, you must at times ensure that your population evacuates. **Evacuation**, or the movement of people away from potential or actual hazards for the purpose of safety, is very common after a warning has been issued or when an emergency or disaster has occurred. The purpose of an evacuation is to move oneself and other people to a safer location to reduce the loss of life and the chance for injury.

There are numerous examples of evacuation. A fire in a large building may require the occupants to leave the structure (because of the flames or resulting noxious fumes). An approaching hurricane poses danger to those on the coast, in low-lying areas, and within the projected path. People must leave these areas to avoid being adversely affected by storm surge and high winds.

Those responding to disaster should be aware that there are various types of evacuations. The vast majority of evacuations are **horizontal** in nature. These may include individuals and families fleeing a burning building. Another example of a horizontal evacuation is people moving inland when a hurricane approaches.

However, some evacuations may be **vertical**. Those in danger move from lower floors in a building to those above if there is a fire or flood. Some evacuees may move to higher floors or rooftops. Unfortunately, these vertical evacuations may prove deadly if waters continue to rise or if a fire cannot be extinguished (as smoke, flames, and heat rise to the floors above).

Evacuations are also of different durations. Some may be short term. People may be able to return to their homes or offices within hours or days if the danger has passed or the damage is minor. Nevertheless, many evacuations may be long term. This occurs when buildings are condemned due to the disaster or if a geographic area has been contaminated by poisonous chemicals.

### 5.3.1 Means of Evacuation

As an emergency manager, you should be aware of the various methods and means that can be utilized for evacuation. Each has respective strengths and weaknesses:

▲ **Walking**. Walking is common for hotel and office building evacuations. Walking is frequently a quick way to get people out of harm's way, and it may not require large numbers of emergency personnel. Walking is useful only when evacuation distances are short.

▲ **Automobiles**. Vehicles are relied on heavily in hurricane evacuations. Cars are useful when evacuation distances are far. The evacuating traffic may require large numbers of law enforcement personnel, prior planning, and close coordination. The number of evacuees involved may create serious traffic congestion problems however. Some hurricane evacuees, for example, will report being stuck on the interstate for 12 hours or longer. Also, evacuating in cars is not an option when roads and bridges are out.

▲ **Busses**. Busses are useful to move groups of people varying distances. Using busses is often the way of taking children away from a school that is at risk (Figure 5-4). Loading large numbers of people in busses also limits traffic congestion problems because each evacuee isn't driving his or her own automobile. Using this method to evacuate requires busses and drivers that may be difficult to obtain or schedule on short notice (e.g., from a school district). As with cars, evacuating by busses is not an option when transportation systems are damaged or destroyed.

Figure 5-4

Busses may be used to transport large numbers of people in case
evacuation is required. Robert Kaufmann/FEMA.

▲ **Boats**. Boats aren't always employed in evacuations, but they were used to
move people off of Manhattan Island after the 9/11 terrorist attacks. Boats
may be common to island areas and flood ravaged communities. Boats may
be one of the only ways to move people that have been isolated due to high
water. Evacuating this way requires boats and captains that may or may not
be available on short notice (e.g., from emergency services, a marina, or
transit authority).

▲ **Helicopters/planes**. Helicopters have been used to evacuate people off of
burning buildings or off of islands (e.g., volcanic eruption in Montserrat).
Evacuating by helicopter or small aircraft may be common to island areas,
flood ravaged communities, or other locations where roads have been
damaged or destroyed. Evacuating this way may be one of the only ways to
move people that have been isolated due to damaged roads and bridges. It
also requires helicopters, planes, and pilots that may be difficult to obtain or
schedule on short notice (e.g., from emergency services or an airport).

### 5.3.2 Evacuation Behavior

One of your concerns as an emergency manager is to understand evacuation
behavior. Contrary to what is presented in movies or on TV, there is typically very
little panic during evacuation or none whatsoever. However, as noted in Chapter 3,
some people will panic when it appears that their lives are in great danger. The fires
in a Chicago and Rhode Island nightclubs (on February 17 and 20, 2003, respec-
tively) illustrate that people may stampede the front exits to evacuate the premise.

During these mass exits, several people were killed because many were not aware of or forgot about the availability of other exits than the doors they entered.

In a natural disaster, some people will evacuate on their own without a recommendation from authorities. For example, after the destruction of Hurricane Katrina was widely reported, more people voluntarily evacuated during the hurricanes that came later in 2005. In other disasters, people will only evacuate when ordered to do so. Warnings and evacuation orders from officials are all that it takes for some people to evacuate. Others, as we see in many hurricanes, will not leave in spite of repeated warnings.

### 5.3.2.1 Why People Do Not Evacuate

There are many reasons why people will not evacuate when a hazard poses danger to their lives. As an emergency manager, you have to be aware of those reasons so you can try to convince people to leave. The main reasons people do not evacuate are listed below:

▲ **Not aware of the risk**. Many of those who do not evacuate are not aware of the request to evacuate. After a fire at a paint store in Ephrata, Pennsylvania, in 1990, Fischer reported that 79% of those who were not contacted did not evacuate (Fischer et al., 1995, p. 35).

▲ **Not taking risk seriously**. People downplay the risks. Those who do not believe they are in real danger will not evacuate.

▲ **Warning is unclear**. Many do not evacuate because the warning message was unclear. This is why it is so important that the warning issued is well understood and clear.

▲ **Fear of looting**. People are often afraid their homes and/or their businesses will be looted if they evacuate.

▲ **Age**. The elderly are often unable to evacuate on their own without help from family members, friends, or community members. Also, the elderly are often tied to their home emotionally and do not want to leave. Some New Orleans residents who did not evacuate before Hurricane Katrina had never left the city before.

▲ **Size and makeup of family**. People who live alone and who are only risking their own health are less likely to evacuate. In contrast, parents with young children are more likely to evacuate as they see protecting their children from death or injury as their main parental responsibility.

▲ **Missing family members and pets**. People who live with elderly parents or sick children that cannot be evacuated often will not leave their family members. Some people would not evacuate after Hurricane Katrina because shelters would not take their pets.

▲ **Neighbor's behavior**. People who do not see their neighbors or friends evacuate are also less likely to take the threat seriously and evacuate too.

▲ **Experience**. Those who have never been through a hurricane may downplay the risk and decide not to evacuate. They simply do not understand the threat. Others may rationalize staying home if the hurricane was not so severe in the past.

---

**FOR EXAMPLE**

### Window of Opportunity for Evacuation

It is understandable why some people do not evacuate. Evacuation orders have been issued in the past that were not necessary. Because severe weather such as hurricanes and tornadoes can easily change course, it is impossible to precisely predict if and how the weather will affect a specific area. However, it is vital that emergency managers point out the dangers of neglecting warnings and evacuation requests. If people decide to stay home until the threat is confirmed, it may be too late for them to leave. In fact, people may need to evacuate up to 36 hours before a hurricane makes landfall. If they do not leave early enough, they might be putting themselves at higher risk since strong winds and floodwaters will be present.

---

▲ **Education**. People who are less educated are most likely to ignore warnings. Alternatively, those with higher levels of education are the most likely to evacuate. These individuals are more likely to understand the threat and risk of staying behind during the disaster.

▲ **Type of housing**. Those living in homes may be less likely to evacuate. In contrast, mobile home dwellers are more likely to evacuate than any group. Mobile homes do not survive severe weather well and the mobile home owners recognize this.

▲ **Inconvenience**. Evacuations are difficult and troublesome. Not only do people have to gather their belongings and fight the traffic, but they also must face the prospect of living in a public shelter in the short-term or imposing on family members or friends.

▲ **Fear of reentry delays**. Those who are considering evacuating are often concerned that it will be several days, weeks, or months before they can return to their home and resume their normal life.

▲ **Distance from the incident location**. Those who live a distance from the threat may believe that they are not at risk. Consequently, they will not evacuate.

▲ **Other factors**. Other factors that may discourage evacuation include waiting for an evacuation order, insufficient financial reserves, no designated place for sheltering, and employment requirements (Figure 5-5).

### 5.3.3 Evacuation Considerations

When requesting an evacuation, there are several factors that must be considered. For instance, it is sometimes difficult to know if an area is or will be at risk. Weather patterns are extremely difficult to pinpoint. Hurricanes often look menacing and look like they are on a particular path before they alter direction. Thus, it is often

Figure 5-5

Traffic and reentry delays may discourage some people from evacuating.
Patsy Lynch/FEMA.

important to understand the need for evacuations clearly because incorrect decisions have negative consequences. "Unnecessary evacuations are expensive, disruptive and unpopular" (Baker, 1990, p. 3). The more often people have to evacuate when it isn't necessary, the less likely they will be to evacuate when it truly is required. Furthermore, safety concerns may ironically determine if an evacuation should be ordered. Depending on the type of hazard, it may be wise to shelter in place instead of evacuating. Also, evacuating can be dangerous. For example, many people die in floods while evacuating in automobiles (Sorensen and Mileti, 1988, p. 205).

Evacuation decisions to evacuate should be based on a number of variables.

**Risk**. If it appears that people could be injured or killed, and property will be damaged or destroyed, it is advisable to evacuate.

**The findings of decision aids**. For example, computer software can model hazards. HAZUS identifies vulnerable areas and potential for damage. CAMEO/ALOHA provides plume models for hazardous chemical releases. SLOSH generates storm surge and inundation areas (see Chapter 11 for further information about this software).

**Expert and political opinion**. NWS meteorologists predict storm intensity, direction, and speed for the evacuation decision. Building inspectors identify severely damaged buildings that should not be inhabited after earthquakes. Politicians consider many factors like access to roads and bridges and rely on the input of others, including that of emergency managers.

**Clearance times**. It may take hours and even days to evacuate people away from harm. Transportation officials may tell you that roads and highways will become congested with thousands of motorists.

### 5.3.4 Evacuation Procedures

There are routine processes of and methods for evacuation (Figure 5-6). Evacuations typically follow several steps:

1. Make the decision to evacuate. Fire chiefs, police chiefs, meteorologists, consultants, politicians, and the emergency manager must discuss the hazard and identify options to keep people safe.
2. Notify the population at risk. Use a warning system or a combination of the warning systems described earlier in this chapter.
3. Provide guidelines, instructions, and directions. People may not understand when to leave, what they should take, what evacuation route is recommended, how long they should be gone, how they will know when to return, etc. Assist evacuees as they leave homes, buildings, neighborhoods, and cities.
4. Direct traffic to avoid gridlock. Traffic may be unusually heavy during evacuation. Therefore, it may be necessary to open both lanes for sizable evacuating populations.
5. Ensure compliance and continued safety. Check for stragglers left behind. There is usually a small group of people that refuse to evacuate. These people often have to be rescued (e.g., from rising water) by emergency personnel.

**Figure 5-6**

Evacuations require significant planning and preparation, including this signs.
Jocelyn Augustino/FEMA.

6. Monitor the evacuation and traffic. It is important to make sure everyone is leaving and that vehicle bottlenecks are kept to a minimum. It may even be necessary to issue tickets if individuals are violating traffic laws.

7. Determine what steps need to be taken to help notify the population on when to return to their community (Lin et al., 2014; Siebeneck, 2013).

## SELF-CHECK

- What is evacuation?
- What are the different types of evacuation?
- How do people behave during evacuations?
- What should be considered when issuing evacuations?
- What will make evacuations more successful?

## 5.4 Sheltering

As people receive warnings and begin to evacuate, they will subsequently be faced with an important decision: where will they go for safety and rest? **Sheltering**, or the location or relocation of evacuees and others to places of refuge, is a function that is frequently required in many disasters (Figure 5-7). Disaster victims may need sheltering during a short-lived emergency such as a hotel fire, or they may have long-term sheltering needs because they have lost their homes in a fire or earthquake. Those affected by disaster will not be the only ones needing emergency or temporary shelters. Emergency responders, state officials, and FEMA employees may also need a place to stay and sleep while they respond to the disaster. For example, after the March 28, 2000, Fort Worth tornado, search and rescue teams stayed at the police and fire training facilities and at the city's Convention Center.

Emergency managers must remember that sheltering in place may be more advantageous than an evacuation to another area or shelter. There are many reasons for this decision. As an example, there may not be enough time to evacuate or it may be too dangerous to evacuate. In some cases, such as a hazardous chemical release, sheltering is the best course of action and will protect more lives than an evacuation would. When deciding whether to evacuate or shelter the population due to a hazardous material spill, there are several factors to consider (Hunt, 1989, p. 29):

▲ Actual or impending release
▲ The material itself (type/physical properties/chemical properties)
▲ Location of release
▲ Health/toxicological effects

Figure 5-7

The Houston Astrodome was used to shelter thousands of individuals
who had fled Hurricane Katrina. Ed Edahl/FEMA.

▲ Atmospheric conditions (wind direction, speed, stability, weather, temperature, dispersion patterns)
▲ Time of day
▲ Numbers and type of population at risk
▲ Estimated duration of release
▲ Emergency response resources and response time
▲ Notification systems
▲ Lead time and elapsed time necessary for evacuation
▲ Evacuation routes and terrain
▲ Ability to shelter in place
▲ Adequacy of shelters relevant to concentration of the release and duration

Thus, evacuation and sheltering decisions may be situational and require a great deal of anticipation and foresight.

### 5.4.1 Sheltering Types

As people will seek and need sheltering, it is important for you to be aware that there are different patterns of sheltering/housing. In an important study, Quarantelli (1982) identified four ideal types (or examples in pure form) along with their characteristics:

1. **Emergency sheltering**. It is the first place people go to seek shelter, and it usually lasts one night only (until more and more desirable shelter can be

located). This location may not have many services, at least initially. The Superdome in New Orleans was an emergency shelter during Hurricane Katrina. This shelter was not safe, well staffed, or supplied with enough food and water. The emergency management officials did not allow for as many people as they received and they did not realize that the shelter would be necessary for several days. There were reports of people dying in the Superdome, of crimes being committed, and people going hungry.

2. **Temporary sheltering**. Temporary shelters could be more established shelters, second homes, the house of a friend, or a motel. For instance, as people left New Orleans, thousands sought refuge in hotels or in the Astrodome in Houston. Such temporary shelters provide basic necessities such as food and water. Other activities may be allowed on a modified basis. For example, bathing may be allowed on a rotating basis. Evacuees might be able to wash their clothes or take their clothing to the Laundromat for cleaning.

3. **Temporary housing**. Temporary housing could include mobile homes, rented apartments, and tents. After Hurricane Katrina, FEMA brought in several mobile homes for disaster victims. Such temporary housing could extend for months, if not years. Temporary housing allows normal household routines including sleeping, food storage and preparation, dishwashing, waste disposal, and bathing.

4. **Permanent housing**. Permanent housing is the long-term solution to the housing problem that was created by the disaster. Victims may rebuild their homes or move to new homes. Victims may or may not return to the city they lived in. After taking temporary shelter in Houston, many Hurricane Katrina evacuees moved to Houston permanently even though they had lived in New Orleans their entire life. Permanent housing allows all household routines to be reestablished. Unfortunately, because of financial constraints, some people may not be able to obtain permanent housing after a disaster.

Also, those who need sheltering do not enter each type of shelter or housing at the same time. A portion of the Hurricane Katrina evacuees, for example, were taking emergency shelter in the Superdome in New Orleans, while some evacuees were already in temporary housing, having decided to live with relatives for an extended period.

## 5.4.2 Shelter Use and Characteristics

It is commonly believed that massive numbers of people will require sheltering. The reality is that most people will not use public shelters at all or will use them only as a last resort. People prefer to stay with friends and family if they can. The majority of people will also stay in shelters as briefly as possible because no one likes living with hundreds of strangers. Large disasters like the Indian Ocean Tsunami are an exception to the limited need for shelters in other disasters. The nature of that disaster required that hundreds of thousands be sheltered during and after the event. This was still only a portion of the population however.

Emergency managers should also be aware of the fact that no two shelter operations are exactly alike. Some shelters will "spring up" automatically and without prior intention as people try to find a safe place to relax and ride out the disaster event. Mileti et al. (1992, pp. 30–33) provide other characteristics regarding the use of shelters:

▲ Shelter use in cities will be higher than in rural areas.

▲ Shelter use is highest for hurricanes than other disasters.

▲ Shelters are more likely to be used when publicized.

▲ The larger the size of the disaster, the larger the relative number of people seeking shelters.

▲ People will be more likely to seek shelter if the disaster strikes at night.

▲ Those from lower socio-economic groups will be more likely to use shelters.

▲ Older people are more likely to use public shelters than younger individuals.

### 5.4.3 Working with Others to Establish and Manage Shelters

Emergency managers will need to work with a number of organizations that participate in the management of sheltering operations. Putting the local government in charge may ensure that sheltering takes place in accordance with municipal and leader priorities in mind. It may also help ensure that official information about the disaster is being given to disaster victims. However, the local government will already be burdened heavily after a disaster and sheltering responsibilities will only add to the many functions that it oversees after a disaster.

In addition to government emergency management agencies, many nonprofit and religious groups are involved in sheltering and housing. According to a congressional mandate, the American Red Cross has been given the responsibility for sheltering under the National Response Framework (Figure 5-8). However, this is not always known or accepted at the local or state level. For example, the Salvation Army is officially in charge of mass care in the State of Texas (even though the Red Cross also provides sheltering services in almost every disaster).

Emergency managers must therefore have involvement in who will participate in sheltering operations. The American Red Cross and Salvation Army have their own method of providing sheltering, which may not meet community objectives (e.g., location of shelter or time of closing). Also, voluntary organizations have expertise in sheltering functions and they can reduce the demands placed upon the local government. Regardless of who is in charge of the shelter, you must ensure that they are given important information about the disaster and unfolding relief operations.

In addition, the decision of where to open shelters must include a consideration of multiple hazards. A shelter should be opened in geographic areas that are not vulnerable to hazards (e.g., inland, out of the floodplain, away from the fault line, or a space that has been cleared of vegetation). All too often, shelters will be opened up in churches and schools that may not be located in safe areas. Hurricane Katrina illustrated the dangers associated with placing people in harm's way. The Superdome was used for shelter (but the roof was damaged by wind and it was surrounded by floodwaters).

Figure 5-8

The Red Cross plays a very important role in establishing and running shelters after disasters. Greg Henshall/FEMA.

Furthermore, it is not always advisable to use trailers or mobile homes for sheltering. These types of shelters are generally not safe places to stay in times of hurricanes or tornadoes. Also, some people do not accept mobile homes (because of the stigmatism associated with them), but prefer rental assistance instead (Quarantelli, 1995, p. 49). Trailers may likewise pose long-term problems, in that people may use them permanently and fail to leave them when requested to do so (Bolin and Stanford, 1991, p. 31).

There are many pitfalls that must be avoided in shelters. These problems include:

▲ Lack of adequate medical care
▲ Volunteers who aren't properly trained and are unaware of policies and procedures
▲ Uneven distribution of supplies and volunteers across shelters and within the shelter
▲ Shelters located in unsafe areas
▲ Inconsistent and changing policies
▲ Lack of record keeping as to who is using the shelter
▲ The failure of disaster victims to obey staff and follow shelter rules
▲ Disaster victims who may not get along with other individuals or groups staying in the shelter (e.g., those from other races, cultures, or neighborhoods)

You can avoid many of the problems listed above with some planning and preparation. For instance, it is imperative that shelters be well stocked with supplies. Some individuals died unnecessarily after Hurricane Katrina because the shelter was not adequately stocked with food and water.

The process of sheltering is typical for most disasters. It includes:

1. Assessing demand by examining the number of people needing shelter (including evacuees, victims, and emergency workers) and comparing it to available shelters and housing stock
2. Identifying potential shelters and developing additional shelter agreements (if not already in place)
3. Ensuring shelter is located in a safe area and has electricity, adequate water supply, restrooms, parking, etc.

You will also need to conduct a brief training session before shelters open. You will need to make sure the shelter:

▲ Is publicized
▲ Is adequately staffed
▲ Has sufficient food, cots, and blankets
▲ Has personnel who can provide information, medical care, and security as needed
▲ Includes a method for documenting the names and numbers of those using shelters

In addition, you must also be sure to follow new laws that relate to sheltering. The Americans with Disabilities Act (ADA) was passed in 1990 to provide those with disabilities the same rights and opportunities as all others. In relation to emergency management, emergency sheltering services now need to accommodate all types of people under this law. The implications of this law are that shelters must "meet the needs of evacuees with disabilities, from providing sleeping arrangements to meeting hygiene and dietary needs, to accommodating for service animals" (Occupational Health and Safety (OHS), 2013). The ADA essentially prevents discrimination against people with disabilities. Lawsuits have been filed against individuals and organizations that have failed to follow this legal regulation.

Finally, you should also be aware that shelters may remain open long after a disaster strikes (and longer than anticipated by their operators). Most disaster victims will desire to leave shelters as soon as possible. However, some people will take advantage of the free housing and food for extended periods of time. These individuals may remain in shelters because they don't have resources to pay rent, or they have nowhere else to go. For instance, one shelter in Miami remained opened for a substantial period after Hurricane Andrew; approximately 400 people were slow to leave even 3 or 4 months after the disaster. For this reason, you must work with others to ensure that temporary shelters do not become permanent shelters. Helping disaster victims find longer-term housing is one way to accomplish this goal. As demand decreases, danger subsides, and recovery proceeds, shelters can be consolidated and shut down one by one. Ultimately, the goal is to get people back in permanent housing as soon as possible.

> ### FOR EXAMPLE
>
> #### Astrodome versus Superdome
>
> Hurricane Katrina provided us with two stark examples of the effectiveness of shelter operations. The Superdome in New Orleans was the first emergency shelter to house evacuees. The roof of the facility was damaged by the hurricane and the Superdome lost electricity due to the storm. The restrooms were also filthy as the water was not running. Furthermore, the Superdome was not staffed with adequate people or resources. Crime also broke out due to inadequate law enforcement. Also, there was not a sufficient volunteer force to address medical needs. What is more, there was not enough food and water for those seeking refuge. The entire shelter was poorly conceived, in part because officials thought they would only need to use it for 1–2 days instead of 4–5 days.
>
> In time, many of the evacuees were sent to the Astrodome in Houston. This shelter was very well organized. People were checked in and documentation of their presence was kept. People received medical care and checkups immediately. The shelter had plenty of cots, blankets, food, and water for everyone. There were also substantial law enforcement personnel on hand. The Red Cross and FEMA also had many people working at the shelter working to reunite families and disperse aid. While problems existed at the Astrodome, they were addressed in an expedited manner.

## SELF-CHECK

- What is sheltering and why is it necessary?
- What are the benefits of sheltering in place, and why should it be considered?
- What are the distinct types of sheltering/housing?
- Will most evacuees use shelters? Why or why not?
- How can the nonprofit sector assist with sheltering?
- What are some issues to consider when running a shelter?

## SUMMARY

Promoting disaster resilience requires the effective implementation of a number of initial response measures. After identifying the hazard, warnings must be issued in a clear and consistent manner. This will require that you work closely with the media. Warnings are typically followed by an evacuation of the population at risk, which helps to protect people from impending hazards. For this reason, you should be aware of the different means to evacuate your population and ensure that this function is performed with typical human behavior in mind. Also, when people leave their homes, they may need a place to stay. You will therefore have to work with others to establish shelters in the short term and recognize that additional efforts may be needed to help victims acquire permanent housing in the future. Performing these functions effectively is the best way to ensure response and recovery operations get off on the right foot.

## KEY TERMS

| | |
|---|---|
| **Disaster plan** | A document that describes how the jurisdiction might respond to a disaster. |
| **Emergency Alert System (EAS)** | A warning system that requires all media providers to comply with any requests from national officials to communicate to the public in the face of an emergency. |
| **Emergency operations center (EOC)** | A central location where leaders can gather information, discuss options, make decisions, disseminate policy, mobilize resources, and communicate with involved parties. |
| **Evacuation** | The movement of people away from potential or actual hazards for the purpose of safety. |
| **Full activation** | The opening of an EOC with all pertinent actors and functions. |
| **Hazard detection** | The process of identifying what hazard is about to occur or has taken place. |
| **Horizontal evacuation** | The movement of people away from a hazard. |
| **Increased readiness conditions** | Rating system that is sometimes based on numerical numbers (e.g., 1–4) and denotes the severity of an event along with appropriate measures to be taken. |
| **Partial activation** | The opening of an EOC with some pertinent actors and functions. |
| **Sheltering** | The location or relocation of evacuees and others to places of refuge, which is a function that is frequently required in many disasters. |
| **Syndromic surveillance** | Tracking the flow of patients in a hospital or clinic to determine trends and consequences of diseases. |
| **Vertical evacuation** | The movement of people from low areas to higher areas (moving from lower floors in a building to those above or the roof if there is a fire or flood). |

**Warnings**                Advanced notifications that allow people to take measures to protect themselves and their property. It indicates that the hazard is imminent, is taking place, or has occurred.

**Watch**                   Notification that conditions are ripe for a hazard to occur.

# ASSESS YOUR UNDERSTANDING

Posttest to evaluate your knowledge of initial response measures.
*Measure your learning by comparing pretest and posttest results.*

## Summary Questions

1. Detecting hazards is one of the first steps for disaster response. True or false?
2. Hazards can be detected by senses but not from increased radio traffic. True or false?
3. ARES and RACES can help you detect a hazard? True or false?
4. A disaster plan is a document that details how a community might respond to a potential disaster. True or false?
5. When activating an EOC, you will need to include all pertinent actors. True or false?
6. According to Quarantelli, warning process typically includes assessment of the hazard and dissemination of the message. True or false?
7. All warnings come from the National Weather Service? True or false?
8. Warnings are likely to be most successful when they are clear, accurate, and consistent. True or false?
9. Horizontal evacuation implies that you move to higher floors. True or false?
10. Fire chiefs, meteorologists, and politicians may have some influence over evacuation decisions. True or False?
11. People can only evacuate by car. True or False?
12. Hazardous material releases may require sheltering in place instead of an evacuation. True or false?
13. Emergency sheltering is likely to include mobile homes and rented apartments. True or false?
14. The incident page network can notify you of:
    (a) Severe weather
    (b) Traffic accidents
    (c) Fires
    (d) All of the above
    (e) Severe weather and fires only
15. Emergency managers:
    (a) Are the only ones that detect hazards
    (b) May be on call on a 24 hour basis, 7 days a week, 365 days a year
    (c) Do not use technology to detect hazards
    (d) Are not able to sense hazards
    (e) Do not communicate with hospitals about disease outbreaks

16. If a hazard is about to occur or has occurred, you will:
    (a) Not need to know the consequences
    (b) Not talk to first responders or fire chiefs
    (c) Need to seek additional information
    (d) Need to avoid communication with nonprofit organizations
    (e) Not focus on the number of people killed but those who are still alive

17. EOC stands for:
    (a) Emergent organization coordination
    (b) Emergent operations center
    (c) Emergency organization chart
    (d) Emergency operations center
    (e) Emergency operations chart

18. Risk identification is:
    (a) Determining if a threat exists
    (b) Determining if protection is needed
    (c) Determining if protection is possible
    (d) Determining what protective action is best and then taking that action
    (e) None of the above

19. Warnings provide information about:
    (a) When a hazard will occur only
    (b) When a hazard will occur, but not how long it will last
    (c) Potential power outages only
    (d) The impact of the disaster and closed streets
    (e) Projected damages to homes and property only

20. A strength of warning sirens is their ability to warn people outside. A weakness is that they:
    (a) Are used by reporters to give advanced notice about a tornado
    (b) Use telephones and computers to issue the warning
    (c) Break down frequently and may not always be reliable
    (d) Take up a lot of manpower to warn people in apartment complexes
    (e) Rely on TV stations that may lose power in a disaster

21. It may take hours and even days to evacuate people away from peril. This is known as:
    (a) The horizontal decision imperative
    (b) Clearance time
    (c) Evacuation shadow
    (d) Risk
    (e) CAMEO/ALOHA index

22. People are less likely to evacuate when:
    (a) They do not take risk seriously.
    (b) They are elderly.

(c) They live in a mobile home.

(d) They live near the threatened area.

(e) All of the above.

23. Staying at a second home or the house of a friend is known as:
    (a) Emergency sheltering
    (b) Disaster sheltering
    (c) Disaster sheltering
    (d) Temporary sheltering
    (e) Temporary housing

24. Shelter use will most likely be highest when:
    (a) There has been a hurricane.
    (b) A hazard affects a rural area.
    (c) The disaster strikes during the day.
    (d) Rich people have been affected.
    (e) The disaster is smaller, rather than larger.

## Review Questions

1. What are four ways you could detect a hazard?
2. What types of technology can help you with hazard detection?
3. What are increased readiness conditions?
4. If there is a large apartment complex on fire, who should you invite to the EOC and why?
5. Why is warning a vital disaster function?
6. What criteria do you consider when issuing a warning?
7. How can you ensure that the warning reaches most people and is acted upon?
8. Why is the media an important partner for warning?
9. What is the difference between a watch and a warning?
10. What steps do you take when you evacuate a population?
11. What can be done to ensure that people with pets evacuate?
12. What are the different types of sheltering/housing?
13. Why is location an important consideration when opening a shelter?
14. Why would medical care, record keeping, and law enforcement be needed when undertaking shelter operations?

## Applying This Chapter

1. The media is reporting that a volcano is becoming active on your Hawaiian island. Who could you contact to get more information about this threat? What questions would you ask this person or agency? What steps might you need to implement and why?

2. The National Weather Service has just notified you that a severe weather system (with the possibility of large hail) is moving through the area. A major sporting event is taking place at an outdoor stadium in the community. Who should you alert?

3. A train derailment requires the activation of your EOC in Santa Fe, New Mexico. The cars are spilling hazardous chemicals onto the ground, and they are running into a nearby river. Other tankers are releasing deadly gasses into the air near an industrial area. Who would you communicate with to get more information about the hazardous materials? Who would you invite into the EOC and why? What other steps might you take to deal with this crisis?

4. You are an emergency manager in Iowa. A serious heat wave is affecting your community, and many of the elderly may be severely impacted. The meteorologists on different stations are giving contradictory advice about the need to stay inside. Should you do anything about this? Why is consistent information necessary?

5. The tsunami warning system has just been activated off of the Washington coast. Expected arrival time is in 30 minutes to 1 hour. If you were the emergency manager in this area, what is the first step you will take to protect people? What could you do as an emergency manager to facilitate their evacuation? What concerns do you have about evacuees as they leave their homes and apartment complexes?

6. You are the emergency manager for Wintersburg, Arizona, and you have been told that in the nuclear plant there has been a small release of hazardous nuclear waste in the air. Do you evacuate or shelter in place? Who could help you make this decision? What factors do you consider when making the decision?

# YOU TRY IT

## Issuing Warnings

You are an emergency manager for Kansas City and you have been told that a tornado was spotted and that it will likely hit your city. What warning systems do you use to issue the warning? What instructions do you give residents?

## Evacuating Miami

You are an emergency manager for Miami and you have been told that a hurricane will likely hit your city. How do you evacuate people? What types of transportation can you use? What is the best way to evacuate the elderly? Children? Families? What types, if any, of transportation would not be used?

## Reasons Not to Evacuate

You are an emergency manager for Miami and you are evacuating the city as a hurricane is approaching. You are going door-to-door to tell people to leave and you hear many different reasons as to why people do not want to evacuate. What are some of the reasons you are most likely to hear? What logic can you use to get the resident to evacuate?

## Shelter

You are an emergency manager for Miami and you are evacuating the city as a hurricane is approaching. You know that not everyone will be able to evacuate, so you set up shelters. What steps do you take to ensure the shelters are adequate?

## Anticipating Disaster

Take 15 minutes to think about the initial measures that must be performed before or immediately after a disaster occurs. Make a list of everything that you think you might need to take care of on the first day of a disaster. In three to four paragraphs, discuss how you would meet these demands and who could help you accomplish that.

# 6

# CARING FOR THE INJURED, DEAD, AND DISTRAUGHT
## Overcoming Physical and Emotional Impacts

## Starting Point

Pretest to assess your knowledge on caring for the injured, dead, and distraught.
*Determine where you need to concentrate your effort.*

## What You'll Learn in This Chapter

▲ The need for and types of search and rescue operations
▲ Behavior of those participating in search and rescue
▲ Emergency medical care and the ethical debate surrounding triage
▲ The challenges regarding mass fatality incidents
▲ The psychological impact of disasters

## After Studying This Chapter, You'll Be Able To

▲ Compare and contrast types of search and rescue operations.
▲ Categorize types of human behaviors in search and rescue operations.
▲ Examine the need for emergency medical care operations.
▲ Determine the steps that can be taken to manage mass fatality incidents effectively.
▲ Understand the common signs of PTSD/CIS.

## Goals and Outcomes

▲ Choose an appropriate search and rescue method.
▲ Predict and respond to human behavior in search and rescue operations.
▲ Estimate potential injuries in disasters the type of medical assistance they will require.
▲ Manage mass fatality incidents.
▲ Evaluate and support victims and personnel who are suffering from PTSD/CIS.

# INTRODUCTION

In a disaster situation, you must understand that emergency workers and volunteers will rush to the scene to rescue anyone who is trapped and assist the injured. In many cases, these emergency medical personnel and rescuers are successful in extracting those who are buried under debris. However, emergency medical responses often require that difficult choices be made in terms of who will be treated first. At other times, the incident creates mass fatalities, and there are several bodies that have to be handled in a sensitive manner. Situations like this can cause posttraumatic stress disorder (PTSD) and critical incident stress (CIS), which are emotional problems that have to be overcome. This chapter will show you a variety of ways to handle these situations and promote resilience.

## 6.1 Search and Rescue Operations

In both routine emergency and non-routine disaster situations, emergency service personnel and volunteers will become involved in search and rescue (SAR) operations. **SAR operations** are response activities undertaken to find disaster victims and remove them from danger or confinement. SAR is necessary so victims may receive urgent treatment such as hydration, basic first aid, or advanced medical care. SAR may include, but is not limited to:

▲ Looking for lost individuals
▲ Determining the whereabouts of disaster victims
▲ Developing and implementing strategies to safely rescue or extract the person in question
▲ Providing immediate and basic care until further medical assistance is provided
▲ Transporting the individual away from the dangerous area to a medical facility for further treatment

### 6.1.1 Types of SAR

If you are working in the emergency management field, you should be aware that there are at least four major types of SAR operations. These include:

1. **Rural SAR.** This occurs when experienced personnel such as forest department workers enter rugged areas to find missing children or lost campers/hikers.
2. **Swift water rescue.** In this case, firefighters or others may inflate rubber rafts and traverse swollen creeks to access people sitting on top of vehicles, perched on roofs, or holding onto trees in order to bring them back to dry land. For example, this technique might be used to rescue people who are trapped in a car by rising floodwaters.
3. **Air-patrolled SAR.** A small plane may be used when another aircraft is presumed to have crashed in an isolated area along its projected flight path. Civil air patrol members or others from the FAA cover large geographic areas looking for wreckage and/or survivors.

Figure 6-1

There are different types of search and rescue operations, including
this water rescue in Kingfisher, OK. Patricia Brach/FEMA.

4. **Urban search and rescue (USAR).** On a regular basis, the Federal
   Emergency Management Agency (FEMA) USAR teams are dispatched to
   major urban areas that are affected by structural collapses. For example,
   multiple individuals and families may need to be extracted from a collapsed
   apartment building after an earthquake (Figure 6-1).

There are additional types of SAR operations as well. Ski patrol or other skilled
individuals look for missing skiers, hikers, and snowmobilers and work to quickly
free those trapped in an avalanche. In different circumstances, highway patrol personnel locate automobiles and passengers trapped as a result of accidents or stuck
as a result of major winter storms. Finally, emergency response personnel put on
wet suits and use ropes to rescue people trapped on thin ice or caught in danger-
ously cold waters. In any of these situations, those involved do all they can to rescue people from dangerous conditions and care for the injured and address their
medical needs.

### 6.1.2 Human Behavior in SAR Operations

As an emergency manager, you must understand how humans behave during SAR
operations. There is a moderate amount of research on this particular subject. One
of the most important studies is by Aguirre et al. (1995). While examining human
behavior after a gas explosion in Guadalajara, Mexico, on April 22, 1992, Aguirre
and his colleagues illustrate many common patterns of activity:

---

**FOR EXAMPLE**

**Saving Themselves**

Many victims actively participate in their own rescue and, by doing so, increase their chances of survival. Aguirre and his colleagues note that victims call attention to their location. In one particular emergency, "a man and his two nephews are having breakfast in their home. The explosion buries them alive. The man reports he is experiencing a great amount of difficulty breathing. He can hear his two nephews near him in the rubble. He talks to them and synchronizes their scream for help at his count of three. Eventually, people hear them and save them" (Aguirre et al., 1995, p. 75).

---

▲ Untrained volunteers are typically the first to engage in SAR operations.

▲ Emergent rescuers will informally or formally assign tasks and create a division of labor during SAR.

▲ Spontaneous rescuers will use anything they can find to help them rescue trapped individuals. This may include bare hands, shovels, or other accessible equipment.

▲ Volunteers will give higher preference to rescuing some victims over others, which will impact survival rates. For example, volunteer rescuers will often first look for their relatives, friends, and neighbors before looking for other possible survivors.

▲ In time, professional SAR teams will arrive on the scene. This may occur within minutes of the incident or several days after occurrence.

▲ Victims will cooperate with each other while entrapped and with rescuers during extraction.

▲ Professional rescuers may or may not integrate their activities with volunteer efforts. Formal organizations are not always able to use volunteers within their own operation.

Thus, both volunteers and professional teams will participate in SAR operations. Their overall objective is to rescue as many victims as possible. Those trapped and injured will likewise work together and do all they can to ensure their survival.

### 6.1.3 Issues to Consider When Carrying Out SAR

SAR operations are both vital and dangerous. In order to ensure success, there are a number of factors that must be considered. If these issues are ignored, not only will the victims be in danger of losing their lives but the rescuers may also be put in harm's way unnecessarily.

### 6.1.3.1 Tools and Equipment

Adequate and appropriate tools and equipment will be needed for SAR. The type of tools needed for the operation depends on the situation. For example, after a vehicle accident, first responders may need the Jaws of Life (equipment used to rip open crushed cars). If people are stranded due to a flood, SAR teams would need boats, ropes, and life preservers. After terrorist attacks involving explosives, cranes will be needed to lift debris so voids can be searched for survivors. Regardless of the type of disaster, there are sometimes cases where supplies are lacking or the equipment is insufficient for the massive SAR effort. For example, after an earthquake in Bam, Iran, killed 50,000 people, the heavy equipment needed to lift debris was not immediately available.

Therefore, tools and equipment are vital in all types SAR operations. It is especially important for responders to wear clothing and use safety equipment appropriate to the task. This equipment includes:

▲ Helmets or hardhats
▲ Goggles
▲ Dust masks (fitted to each responder)
▲ Whistles (to alert others if you get trapped)
▲ Leather work gloves
▲ Steel-toed boots

A failure to have the necessary tools and equipment may ultimately delay rescue and put responders at risk for injury and even death.

### 6.1.3.2  Situational Awareness

Besides having the necessary gear, those involved in SAR must also be aware of the environment they will be working in as well as changing conditions. Different types of buildings will have distinct occupancy levels, which may determine the nature of SAR operations. The occupants will vary in ability and age as well. Rescuing immobile nursing home residents, for example, is logically more difficult than rescuing able-bodied young adults.

There will also be secondary hazards after a disaster that may have a bearing on SAR operations. For example, those who are dispatched to the scene of terrorist attacks may be required to work on top of unstable debris piles that could possibly collapse and cause injury. The FEMA advises rescuers to "be alert for hazards, such as sharp objects, dust, hazardous materials, power lines, leaking natural gas, high water, fire hazards, and unstable structures. If water is present, check the depth before entering" (2003f, p. V-4).

### 6.1.3.3  Rescuer Needs

Rescuer needs and safety must be ensured. The rescue effort will certainly be hampered if the well-being of the rescuers is ignored or overlooked. SAR work is very demanding. Food must be supplied to these first responders and plenty of fresh water should always be available. Crews should also be rotated in and out of service to avoid fatigue. This is often difficult to do, as the rescuers will have a personal and emotional attachment to their work. For example, when the responders were asked to stop searching for their missing coworkers at Ground Zero after 9/11, a minor scuffle broke out between firefighters and police officers. Regardless of how appealing it is to keep working so others can be saved, volunteers and first responders must remember that many rescuers are injured or die when they become tired. In order to maintain an adequate level of safety, breaks and shift rotations should be required. The FEMA also advises rescuers to "always work in pairs, with a third person as a runner" (2003f, p. V-14).

### 6.1.3.4 Time

A major reason why it can be difficult to get rescuers to leave a scene is because the chances for finding someone alive diminish with time. The first hour is the best opportunity for rescuing people alive, but the next 24 hours are also critical. In some disasters, the injured and trapped have an 80% chance of survival if they are rescued within the first day. After this period, the possibility of survival diminishes rapidly. SAR operations may therefore become search and recovery operations if there are credible reasons to believe that people have not survived the incident or disaster.

One of the most miraculous SAR stories is that of Evans Monsignac—a man who survived the Haiti earthquake after being "trapped in the rubble" for 27 days (Goddard, 2013). With no access to food or water, Evans resorted to "sipping sewage" that trickled nearby him. He had no contact with anyone while he was buried under debris, besides hearing "the screams of the dying." Evans was found almost a month later in the rubble as it was being worked through. Doctors are amazed by his survival and worked diligently to restore his health after a long 27 days of malnutrition.

### 6.1.3.5 Medical Care

Once the victims of emergencies or disasters are rescued, they will most likely need immediate medical care. Trapped victims often suffer from life-threatening injuries including the loss of blood and fluids, broken bones, damage to internal organs, and respiratory failure due to the lack of oxygen. Volunteers will often perform basic first aid techniques to save the lives of those they rescue. And these individuals play vital roles in major disasters (when SAR demands are extremely high). However, if rescuers are emergent volunteers, they often have limited—if any—medical training. It is therefore imperative that victims be handed over to trained medical personnel as soon as possible. Volunteer firefighters or professional first responders (emergency medical technicians (EMT) or paramedics) should be sought out as soon as possible to increase the chances of victim survival.

### 6.1.4 Professional USAR Teams

Professional USAR teams are best able to care for the needs of victims who have been crushed under disaster debris. In 1989, after major urban disasters resulted in structural collapses, the FEMA created the National Urban Search and Rescue Response. The **National Urban Search and Rescue Response** is a system made up of 28 FEMA USAR Task Forces that are spread throughout the continental United States. These task forces are comprised of firefighters, engineers, doctors, paramedics, and canine teams from local communities. Each member of the team must be an EMT. Team members must also undergo hundreds of hours of training. Specialties, such as the K-9 unit, are required to have additional hours of preparation.

If a disaster receives a presidential declaration and if the disaster warrants SAR, the FEMA USAR teams may be activated. The team members will be notified and will unite at the specified location (e.g., an airport) with their tools, supplies, and equipment. This includes medical supplies such as:

▲ Medicines
▲ Intravenous fluids
▲ Blankets
▲ Suture sets
▲ Defibrillators
▲ Burn treatment supplies
▲ Bone saws
▲ Scalpels

It also includes SAR supplies and machines like rope, lumber, concrete saws, jackhammers, and drills. Additional gear includes communication and electronic equipment (e.g., radios, cell phones, and laptop computers) or logistic needs (e.g., cots, sleeping bags, food, and water).

After meeting at the staging area, the team members will then load their supplies and equipment onto military transport aircraft (usually C-130 cargo planes) and travel to the disaster site. The deployment and subsequent work will continue until SAR services are no longer needed. At this point, the team will be transported home. Nevertheless, it is important to note that numerous teams will be rotated in and out of major disasters. This helps to prevent crew fatigue and allows others to gain experience.

These professional USAR teams discussed above provide many benefits to emergency management. The responders on such teams are highly trained and fully equipped. They have prior SAR experience in major disasters and receive large amounts of funding from the federal government. Such personnel can be mobilized to distant disaster sites for long periods of time (Figure 6-2).

There are a few significant drawbacks associated with these professional USAR teams however. One of them is their expense. It is very costly to maintain and operate the SAR teams. Each task force has been given 60,000 pounds of equipment (approximately 16,400 pieces) by FEMA. The supplies and equipment for each individual team is worth more than $1.4 million dollars. Also, the teams may be inadequate in terms of numbers for major disasters and for multiple ongoing events. Another problem is that there are not sufficient SAR personnel for major or concurrent disasters throughout the country. In addition, professional SAR teams may arrive too late to save significant numbers of victims. These types of teams are therefore more commonly involved with search and recovery efforts rather than rescue operations. For example, Pakistan suffered an earthquake that registered 7.6 on the Richter scale on October 8, 2005. Within one day, professional SAR teams began to arrive. While the deployment was very quick, the prime time to find survivors had already passed.

Because of the late arrival and insufficient quantity of professional SAR teams, it may become increasingly necessary that volunteers engage in SAR activities. These citizen and emergent groups are advantageous for disaster response. Volunteers

**Figure 6-2**

Professional search and rescue teams play a vital role in disaster response
and recovery operations. Jocelyn Augustino/FEMA.

can perform vital SAR services when professional teams are not present or are insufficient in quantity. These volunteers also have an advantage as they know or are familiar with the area and the victims. Nevertheless, such individuals and groups may create unintentional problems. They lack proper training and equipment for safety. Citizen rescuers may also unintentionally harm victims or aggravate their injuries to the point of death. However, many states have Good Samaritan laws to exempt volunteers from potential lawsuits and liability.

The problems associated with citizen SAR teams can be overcome through community education and training (see Chapter 13). Efforts can also be made to integrate the activities of volunteer and professional SAR teams at the scene of disaster. For example, volunteers can perform simple tasks (e.g., basic first aid) so that trained professionals may focus on more difficult rescue operations (e.g., extraction and/or amputations).

### 6.1.5 Conducting SAR Operations

An elaborate process must be undertaken to ensure a successful SAR operation in urban settings. The FEMA asserts there are several steps in SAR operations (2011). Those participating should:

1. **Gather facts.** One of the first things that must be done is to size up the situation. You will need to consider:
   ▲ The number of potential victims
   ▲ The type and age of construction

▲ The status and potential influence of the weather

▲ The presence of hazards such as sharp objects, downed power lines, and broken gas lines

2. **Assess damage.** Walk around the building, and view the structure from different angles. Consider the following general guidelines:

| If structural damage is: | Then the SAR mission is: |
|---|---|
| Light: Superficial or cosmetic damage, broken windows, fallen plaster, primary damage to contents of structure | To locate, triage, and prioritize removal of victims to designated treatment areas by the medical operation teams |
| Moderate: Questionable structural stability, fractures, titling, foundation movement, or displacement | To locate, stabilize, and immediately evacuate victims to safe areas while minimizing the number of rescuers inside the building |
| Heavy: Obvious structural instability, partial or total wall collapse, ceiling failures | To secure the building perimeter and control access into the structure by untrained but well-intentioned volunteers; seek professional assistance |

3. **Consider probabilities**. Take time to determine if the situation is stable, what could go wrong, and what the situation dictates for SAR operations.

4. **Assess your situation.** Figure out if it is safe to continue the operation. Consider what risks you might face. Identify need for and the availability of personnel, tools, and equipment.

5. **Establish rescue priorities.** Identify the urgency of the situation and verify that it is safe to proceed with the SAR operation. You may need to condemn the building to ensure no one else enters the structure. Afterward, call for additional professional assistance and wait until that help arrives. Easy rescues should be conducted first before proceeding to the rescues that will require additional human or material resources.

6. **Make decisions**. Ascertain where to deploy resources to do the most good while also doing all you can to protect life, property, and the environment.

7. **Develop a rescue plan.** Determine the following:

▲ Who will enter the building?

▲ How will they enter the structure safely?

▲ What can be done to find and free the trapped individuals?

▲ How do you ensure the safety of both the rescuers and trapped victims?

8. **Take action.** Search for people under debris and in voids. This may involve:

▲ Calling out (e.g., asking if people can hear you, if they need help, and where they are)

▲ Covering the entire building

▲ Searching from the bottom up or top down

▲ Following walls on the right until you complete a search of each floor

▲ Looking at debris piles from different angles to fully understand the situations

▲ Listening periodically for breathing, whistling, speaking, whispering, tapping, and any noise that indicates someone is alive

9. **Evaluate your progress.** You need to continually monitor the situation not only to see if your plan is working, but also to prevent any harm to the rescuers.

While performing SAR operations, you may need to use levers, cribbing, and lifting to access the victim. Long pieces of wood (e.g., a 2×4) may be used as **levers** to lift debris off of people. **Cribbing** is the name given to wood stacked under debris to stabilize it after it has been lifted by a lever. The purpose of cribbing is to increase void space so victim retrieval can occur. The use of levers and cribbing should be done slowly and on a rotating basis (e.g., lift the lever one foot, place cribbing under the debris, and repeat). Lifting debris or victims can be dangerous if not done properly. Those involved in SAR should remember to lift in the following way: bend your knees and squat; hold the load close to your body; keep your back straight; and push up with your legs. Monitor the safety of the victim too.

After a victim has been rescued, he or she may need to be moved to safety. The victim should exit the building on their own if he or she is able to do so. If needed, the victim can be assisted by supporting, lifting, or dragging them to safety. Unless there is immediate danger, people with major head, neck, and back injuries should not be removed until professional medical help arrives. Moving them could aggravate such injuries (Figure 6-3).

**Figure 6-3**

Search and rescue personnel are seen here marking a home that has been searched for survivors after Hurricane Katrina. Bob McMillan/FEMA.

During the SAR operation, searched areas may be marked with spray paint so the same area isn't searched twice. Responders often use "/" on the door or façade to denote the building is being searched. They use an "X" to denote the building has been searched. If needed, SAR teams will want to provide additional information near the "X" including searcher initials or team name, time/date, hazards present in the building, and the number of victims found or still inside. An "X" placed inside a box denotes "danger, do not enter." This is a useful symbol to keep people away from unstable structures.

## SELF-CHECK

- Are first responders involved in SAR alone?
- What are the different types of SAR?
- How do people behave in conjunction with SAR operations?
- How can worker safety be ensured?
- What equipment do professional teams have?
- What are the steps to performing SAR effectively?

## 6.2 Emergency Medical Care and Triage

If you are to promote disaster resilience, you should comprehend emergency medical care and triage processes as well. This is because injuries are common to virtually all emergencies and disasters. Some emergency situations may produce a small number of wounds. A collision on the freeway may hurt one or two drivers only. In contrast, an apartment fire may require that a handful of people receive emergency medical care. Other disaster events generate even larger numbers of persons who need medical attention. For instance, between 8,000 and 11,000 individuals sought medical care following the 1994 Northridge earthquake (Shoaf et al., 1998, p. 233). Also, "from 1975 to 1994, natural hazards ... injured some 100,000 in the United States and its territories" (Mileti, 1999, p. 4). More than 250,000 were injured in the Haiti earthquake. Injuries resulting from disasters will vary in terms of seriousness. Some wounds will be minor. For example, victims might receive superficial cuts from broken glass. Other injuries will be very serious or even life threatening. Victims could be crushed under a collapsed building, damaging vital internal organs.

Thus, it is important to realize that different types of disasters may produce unique types of injuries. As an example, flooding will produce hypothermia if victims are in water for an excessive amount of time. Earthquakes and tornadoes cause lacerations (from debris) and fractures (from blunt force trauma). Fires are associated with burns and respiratory problems. A chemical release at a factory may disable one's respiratory or nervous system.

Nevertheless, most disasters will generate a variety of injuries. For example, out of a total of 790 injured victims of the 9/11 terrorist attack, the following problems were treated (Pryor, 2003, p. 9):

| Injury | Number | Percentage |
|---|---|---|
| Inhalation | 387 | 49 |
| Ocular (eye irritation) | 204 | 26 |
| Sprain or strain | 110 | 14 |
| Laceration | 110 | 14 |
| Contusion | 98 | 12 |
| Fracture | 46 | 6 |
| Burn | 39 | 5 |
| Closed head trauma | 14 | 2 |
| Crush | 8 | 1 |

It is obvious, therefore, that disasters create enormous medical challenges. The nature of the injury in a disaster is a result of many factors:

▲ Magnitude of the hazard agent
▲ Location of the victim at the time of the disaster
▲ Availability and performance of protective structures
▲ Age, gender, and prior health status of the disaster victim
▲ Knowledge of what to do when a hazard occurs

However, there is one more thing to remember about emergency medical care: ordinary citizens are not the only ones at risk of injury in a disaster. Thirty-five percent of the people treated after the World Trade Center (WTC) collapse included EMT, police officers, and firefighters (Pryor, 2003, p. 9). Emergency responders work in very dangerous circumstances; they also require medical attention because of on-the-job injuries.

### 6.2.1 Treating the Injured

Emergent groups are typically first to arrive on the scene, and they will often offer emergency medical care to disaster victims (until fire and ambulance services arrive). Emergent groups also provide medical assistance for longer periods of time in major disasters because official medical resources are overstretched. In addition to emergent groups, there are firefighters, EMT, nurses, doctors, and others who will treat the injured. Because disasters generate dangerous conditions and produce secondary hazards (e.g., aftershocks, fires, broken glass, etc.), anyone involved in disaster response should have basic first aid knowledge and skills. Both bystanders and first responders might be put in a situation where they will be required to treat others or even themselves. They must know what to expect in regard to the function of emergency medical care during disaster response.

For instance, it is likely that there may be multiple waves of disaster victims. Many people will be injured immediately when the disaster occurs, and others will be hurt during response and recovery operations. In other words, some people may be hurt from the hazard while others may be injured as they try to help the initial victims. As mentioned earlier, victims will be treated by emergent groups first and then by professional medical personnel. In some cases, the paramedics who arrive can be so numerous that there may be an overabundance of medical personnel. One hospital employee after 9/11 recalled, "one of our problems was crowd control as so many of our medical professional gravitated to the emergency department to observe and offer their services" (in Pryor, 2003, p. 14). This is not the case in every disaster however.

Regardless of the numbers of responders, volunteers and medical personnel will work jointly to meet emergency medical needs. There may be several legal liabilities associated with medical responses to disasters however. Well-intentioned, but untrained, volunteers may inadvertently injure or kill victims that require medical treatment. For example, extracting an individual from debris could lead to a more severe back injury for the victim. It is therefore important that the medical function be transferred to knowledgeable and skilled workers as soon as the situation permits (Figure 6-4).

Because of the chaotic nature of disasters (e.g., many patients requiring the assistance of numerous responders), it is difficult to ensure that all individuals

Figure 6-4

Both citizens and official responders will provide emergency medical care after disasters. Jocelyn Augustino/FEMA.

participating in emergency medical services have sufficient qualifications. Malpractice lawsuits can result if a victim does not receive necessary medical care or if the treatment proves counterproductive. It is therefore necessary to check the credentials of medical personnel on-site or at the hospital. One way to accomplish this is to have EMT, nurses, and doctors check in at a specified location (in the field or at a hospital). Those verifying credentials will then obtain information about training, education, prior experience, current employment, work record, position/title, and area of specialization. The collected data can be stored and sorted to facilitate selection of needed knowledge and skills. For instance, at St. Vincent's hospital after the 9/11 terrorist attack, "personnel were pooled into ready rooms, one for surgeons, physicians, nurses, etc. When a particular talent was needed, supervisors in these ready rooms were contacted" (Pryor, 2003, p. 13).

The nature of disaster will pose other challenges for medical personnel. Victims will typically be brought to hospitals by paramedics who discuss the patient's status with the emergency room while in route to this destination. Nevertheless, many patients will be self-referred (walking wounded) or brought in by others without advanced notification. If medical care and transportation are not promptly furnished, many survivors and victims will not sit idly by. Instead, they will get themselves or others to the hospital quickly. This may mean that they pass up other hospitals and/or go to one that they are most familiar with. As a result, some hospitals may be overwhelmed with patients. For this reason, field hospitals may need to be set up to care for victims near the impacted area or outside hospitals. This measure will ensure that only the most serious patients are admitted to hospitals. Another concern is that hospitals may not have a full understanding of the scope of the disaster. Paramedics and hospitals should contact each other to ensure that the distribution of patients does not overburden any single medical care facility. Emergency managers may even want to inform hospitals about their broad understanding of the unfolding situation.

Another potential problem is that some hospitals may have to be evacuated during the disaster. A major medical center became flooded in Houston after Tropical Storm Allison. This created several logistical challenges when patients had to be transferred to other hospitals (especially those on life-support systems). Hospitals must therefore be ready to evacuate patients, which requires a great deal of foresight as well as trained personnel.

Richard Bievy, Director of the Kansas City Health Department, identified these and other challenges in the medical response to a skywalk (atrium bridge) collapse in a Hyatt Hotel (see Waugh, 1988, pp. 120–121):

▲ "Communication among doctors, paramedics, and ambulance personnel was inadequate because they lacked walkie-talkies, two-way radios, and bullhorns, although some were borrowed from the police and fire units that responded;

▲ Medical supplies, particularly oxygen, splints, and drugs, were in short supply initially, although that problem was solved when supplies arrived from other jurisdictions;

▲ Ambulance drivers left their vehicles, slowing down the pickup line of casualties, because the drivers were curious about the conditions in the hotel;

▲ Life Flight helicopters were withdrawn before all of the critically injured were transported;

▲ Distribution of patients among area hospitals was inefficient and too few casualties were sent to the trauma unit at the Kansas University Medical Center; and;

▲ Ambulance reaction times were too slow because of … the problem of establishing the one-way flow to and from the hotel entrance."

### 6.2.2  Triage

As mentioned, disasters will produce an extremely large number of injuries, and many of them will be life threatening. In many cases, the number of patients will far exceed the number and capacity of medical personnel. For this reason, emergency responders must follow a systematic and efficient approach to emergency medical care. This includes the triage, initial treatment, and transport of the injured to hospitals for additional medical care. It may also include handling of victims who have died as a result of their injuries.

**Triage** is an initial assessment and categorization of victims for treatment based on the severity of their injuries (Figure 6-5). O'Halloran notes (1989, p. 45) that triage means to "choose," and this term "was originally used as an agricultural system for discarding defective produce." Regardless of the precise meaning and source of this term, the goal of triage is to do the most good for the largest number of casualties within the confines of limited medical personnel. Mayer states (1997,

**Figure 6-5**

Field hospitals like this one may need to be set up after disasters. Field hospitals are an important part in triage because they ease the burden on medical facilities when there are many victims. Jocelyn Augustino/FEMA.

p. 2) that the purpose of triage is "to identify severity of illness and injury ... so that patients are seen at the right place at the right time to receive the right level of care." He also lists the five functions of triage (Mayer, 1997, p. 3):

1. Identify severity of illness or injury.
2. Provide appropriate stabilizing clinical and nonclinical supportive care.
3. Communicate clinical and nonclinical information to other emergency providers to transition patient care appropriately.
4. Provide the first best opportunity for customer service to patients, families, and the community.
5. Act as an "ancillary lobby" for the hospital.

Triage is therefore the evaluation, sorting, and treatment of those injured in disasters. As the initial assessment takes place, the medical care provider separates the disaster victims into different groups based on the extent of their injuries. This classification that often requires the attachment of specially marked tags is both categorical and physical. The separation of victims into categories helps paramedics and hospital staff understand which patients are in the most need of medical care and which patients can wait to be treated or for additional help to arrive. There are many other classification schemes and these are summarized below:

| Number | Picture | Color | Word |
| --- | --- | --- | --- |
| 0 | Cross | Black | Dead/dying |
| I | Rabbit | Red | Immediate |
| II | Turtle | Yellow | Delayed |
| III | Ambulance with an "X" over it | Green | Minor |

Once patients are separated, they may be physically moved to different locations. In other words, there will be an area (e.g., room, driveway, portion of the park, segment of the parking lot) for those labeled as dead, immediate, delayed, and others with minor injuries.

The different groups are then treated according to their injuries. For instance, the dead will not receive any attention until the emergency medical needs of others have been addressed. Those with immediate needs will be treated first and sent to hospitals as soon as possible. Others designated as delayed will receive treatment second. Individuals labeled as minor will be treated on-site. Treatment of minor injuries happens after the immediate and delayed patients have received care. Those with minor injuries may be asked to avoid going to hospitals to decrease the burden on these medical facilities.

A commonly made mistake in triage is to send people to the hospital that do not require extra medical care. After the WTC collapse, "of the estimated 1103 survivors that were treated at five hospitals, only 181 (16%) were injured severely enough to be hospitalized" (Pryor, 2003, p. 14). It is therefore important that

---

**FOR EXAMPLE**

**9/11 Injuries**

There are often multiple waves of victims in a major emergency or disaster, and 9/11 is an example of this. The first wave resulted from the impact of the aircraft. These victims were in the building and had burns from jet fuel and injuries from the damaged structure. The collapse of the towers caused a second wave of injuries. People had injuries from falling debris or from breathing in chemicals and hazardous air contaminants. The third wave of injuries was visible during the rescue and recovery effort. These injuries among first responders continued at a low rate for several months after the attack until bodies and debris were removed.

---

medical care providers in the field ensure that triage has been performed accurately. "Over triage can cause hospital emergency departments to be over-run with minimally injured patients, consuming resources and potentially delaying care to more severely injured patients" (Pryor, 2003, p. 14).

### 6.2.2.1 The Ethics of Triage

Although triage is commonly used in emergency and disaster situations, it is controversial. Some scholars and practitioners regard it to be a very important and necessary procedure. It is assumed by some to be the "keystone" to effective medical care in mass casualty situations (Bowers, 1960, p. 59). Triage is also considered by many to be essential for disasters. In fact, ambulance services, hospitals, and FEMA all advocate the use of triage. Others assert that triage is unethical, and they disapprove of it for a variety of reasons.

One of the reasons why triage is controversial is because triage decisions could be made by people with limited medical background. Therefore, some patients may die because of error and mistakes. Triage may also go against EMT and physician oaths of conduct to minimize suffering, care for the injured, and prevent death. Time spent with a few severely injured patients could deprive many patients with less severe but life-threatening injuries and deny them of the medical care they need for survival. Moreover, no responder likes to place a black tag on someone who is dead or expected to die. These points reveal that triage may not be ideal. Regardless, in many cases, it is an unfortunate necessity after disasters occur.

### 6.2.3 Disaster Medical Assistance Teams

In major disasters, local resources for medical care and triage will be completely overwhelmed. Consequently, additional well-trained medical professionals will be required. The National Disaster Medical System (NDMS) has instituted a system to help in these circumstances. This system relies heavily upon disaster medical assistance teams (DMATs). According to the U.S. Department of Health and Human Services, a **DMAT** is "a group of professional and paraprofessional medical personnel designed to provide emergency medical care during a disaster or other event"

Figure 6-6

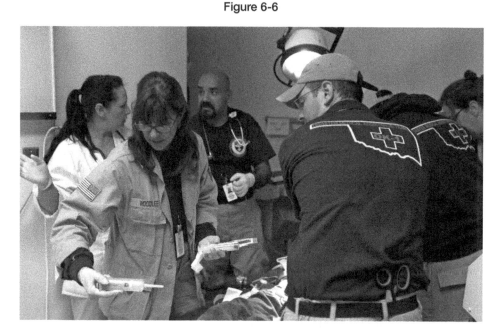

Members of the FEMA disaster medical assistance team, Oklahoma One, assist staff of the Glades General Hospital in Florida after Hurricane Wilma. Jocelyn Augustino/FEMA.

(Figure 6-6). The DMAT concept was generated in 1995 as local and state experts met with the DHHS to discuss the need to improve medical care in disasters. Since this time, 80 DMATs have been created in the NDMS, which includes over 7000 private medical and support personnel.

If local medical resources are stretched beyond limit due to an emergency or disaster, a federal emergency or disaster may be declared (see Chapter 9), and DMAT members are activated as federal (and, in some cases, state) employees. As such, these personnel are paid as temporary employees of the federal (or state) government. They are also protected by the Federal Tort Claims Act in case a malpractice claim arises.

DMATs are sent out to disasters in a process that is somewhat similar to USAR teams. DMATs are dispatched from their home locations to the site of the disaster, and they are capable of functioning for extended periods of time and in difficult conditions. They have their own supplies, which can be replenished by the NDMS. DMATs also provide their own housing and field hospitals (usually tents), thus allowing them to act independently if the housing stock or hospitals have been depleted or damaged in the disaster.

The DMAT members include doctors, nurses, paramedics, pharmacists, and other health-related professionals. In order to participate as a team member, these individuals must maintain the proper medical credentials. They must have immunizations, health clearance forms, and other documents to ensure their safety and that of others. Team members also participate in special drills and exercises to train for medical operations. For example, in July 2000, a disaster medical exercise was conducted in McAllen, Texas. Over 200 U.S. Navy reserves, Texas Army National

Guard members, Texas Department of Health workers, and DMAT representatives participated in the 12-day operation. Free medical and dental services were provided to more than 5600 local residents. The exercise enhanced skills in patient transportation, distribution and medical care, and increased coordination of logistical support.

Because DMATs provide such a valuable service in disasters, team members are required to maintain a 24/7 standby notice. If a disaster occurs and requires deployment, team members will be notified via phone where to report and at what time. DMAT members will leave for the scene no later than 12 hours after being notified. Once at the disaster site, DMATs will perform medical and nonmedical procedures in accordance with established standards and in conjunction with commanding officer requests.

As time goes by, every effort is made to allow members to return home as soon as possible. If needed, other teams or members will be deployed and rotated to backfill or meet the demands until emergency medical care is no longer needed. For instance, after the 9/11 terrorist attacks in New York, at least five DMATs were activated to care for those injured in the incident. They provided medical services at various clinics within five blocks of the WTC site. These DMATs played an important role in caring for some of the 6408 victims injured in the attack and helped to reduce the burden on local healthcare providers.

## SELF-CHECK

- What types of injuries result from disasters?
- How important are volunteers in emergency medical care?
- What is triage?
- Do all scholars and practitioners support triage?
- What medical challenges are faced by hospitals in disasters?
- What is a DMAT and how do they operate?

## 6.3 Mass Fatality Management

Besides creating injuries, mass emergencies and disasters may also generate large numbers of fatalities (Figure 6-7). It is true that fatalities owing to disasters have decreased by 75% over the past 50 years in developed nations (Mileti citing Mitchell, 1999). However, hazards and disasters often result in mass fatalities in many countries around the world and even in the United States. Various hazards (including winter storms, lightning, hail, etc.) produce death, although the number of fatalities is relatively low compared to other types of disasters. A large number of people can also die in structural fires or transportation accidents. The toll of certain major disasters can be staggering—almost beyond comprehension. Some disasters are especially deadly:

Figure 6-7

The earthquake in Haiti killed hundreds of thousands of people, and resulted in a mass fatality management nightmare. Photo courtesy of the author.

▲ Hurricane Katrina produced over 1300 deaths.
▲ The 9/11 terrorist attacks killed about 3000 individuals.
▲ The 1995 Kobe, Japan, earthquake resulted in 5000 fatalities.
▲ The 2011 Japan earthquake/tsunami caused over 15,800 deaths
▲ The Haiti earthquake took about 211,000 lives.
▲ The Indian Ocean Tsunami also left at least 300,000 dead.

In some cases, these disasters show disturbing patterns. Women and children could be disproportionately numbered among the dead in various disasters (e.g., Hurricane Katrina in New Orleans). The vulnerability of women and children is attributed to several factors. Unmarried mothers often do not have the financial resources to evacuate. Also, women and children may not be as physically strong as men to withstand hazard events. In addition, women may be at home caring for children, while the men are at work where they are often better protected from disasters as corporate buildings are often stronger than residences.

As an emergency manager, you should be aware of the fact that disasters may become especially problematic over time. "Some future possible disasters could create victims in the high four or even five figures. Even handling relatively few bodies in most modern societies generates all kinds of problems ... Future disasters with numerous dead bodies will sharply increase those kinds of disasters" (Quarantelli, 1996b, p. 90).

### 6.3.1 Mass Fatality Incidents and Their Challenges

With this in mind, you will need to deal with the consequences of mass fatality incidents. A **mass fatality incident** is any situation where there are more bodies than can be handled using local resources. Mass fatality incidents result in a large number of bodies that stretches the community beyond its capacity and creates several unique challenges (Sadiq and McEntire, 2012). For example, there may not be enough coffins or people to dig graves to keep up with the demand for burial after such an event (Scanlon and McMahon, 2011, pp. 176, 178). Mass fatality incidents often create other management problems for those involved in disaster response operations. Well-intentioned citizens may move bodies to various locations, thereby hindering identification. "After the recent earthquake in Kobe [Japan], private citizens brought bodies to the police stations, temples, schools, gymnasia, health and community centers and private companies, where they were laid out on the floor" (Nishimura as cited by Scanlon, 1998, p. 289). This could create difficulties for investigators. However, major but localized accidents may witness a very different pattern. "After the 12 December 1985, air crash in Gander, for example, the area where the crash occurred was quickly sealed off by Royal Canadian Mounted Police and once the fires were out and dangerous objects removed … all bodies and body parts were marked and tagged before they were moved" (Scanlon, 1998, p. 289).

Bodies can also be obliterated as witnessed by the 9/11 disaster in New York. At ground zero, "fewer than 300 bodies were intact. Only 12 could be identified purely by sight. Searchers recovered 19,893 separate body parts, including a single tooth. One man [corpse] was found in about 200 pieces" (Hamson and Moore, 2003, p. 1B). Because of the condition of bodies, there may be disputes about the number of deaths in a specific incident or disaster. For instance, the actual death count after Hurricane Katrina was much lower than initially anticipated. Even the final death toll at the WTC was not settled for a long period of time:

> On the anniversary, the city counted 2801 victims. A year later, the city now lists, 2792 as lost. That figure still varies from databases assembled by the Associated Press (2775) and USA TODAY (2784). The exact number killed may never be certain, city officials acknowledge. Evidence could surface of a previously unknown victim - a homeless person, perhaps, or an illegal immigrant. Some DNA samples extracted from bones and tissue do not match any genetic profile submitted by victims' relatives. In the medical examiner's freezers may lie the remains of a victim who was never reported as missing (Hamson and Moore, 2003, p. 1B).

Because the identification process may take time, the process cannot occur without the use of modern technology. In New York after 9/11, body identification required samples of DNA. Even then, remains can take years to identify—if they are identified at all. Two years after the WTC attacks, families were still waiting to have their loved ones identified. No trace has been found on 1268 people. Even when there is a body to be identified, the process can be very physically and emotionally disturbing as relatives may have to see the disturbing corpses of their loved ones (e.g., burned or in pieces). Identification, however, is important.

Friends and family will desire to know the fate of their loved ones and have a proper memorial service before burial or cremation.

It is also important to recognize that those in mourning may become frustrated with the procedures of mass fatality management. Some responders may depersonalize the deceased by stacking them up on one another. This aggravates surviving relatives who do not view their loved ones as a "piece of wood." Because of the sheer number of victims, mass fatality disasters may also necessitate the cancellation of normal funeral arrangements. However, "in both the Iranian earthquake and the Italian dam disaster ... public authorities had to abandon plans for mass burials due to the strong public outcry when such a disposition of bodies was proposed" (Blanshan and Quarantelli as cited by Scanlon, 1998, p. 290).

As can be seen, mass fatality events can be very challenging. "Tom Brondolo ... has identified four criteria that can be used to evaluate the complexity of a mass death situation ...:

1. Is there a manifest, a list of the dead?
2. How many dead are there?
3. What condition the bodies in?
4. How fast are bodies being recovered?" (Scanlon and McMahon, 2011, p. 180).

All of these factors should be considered in mass fatality incidents.

### 6.3.2 Responding to Mass Fatality Incidents

Mass fatalities necessitate the involvement of several people including the emergency manager, medical examiners, coroners and forensic investigators, morticians, mental health personnel, funeral home directors, hospitals, and even clergy. Private companies also help to recover the dead after disasters.

There are numerous issues these individuals and organizations must consider when responding to mass fatality incidents:

▲ **Care for investigation/crime scenes.** Accidents, murders, other criminal events, and terrorist attacks leading to death require special treatment of bodies so as to not tamper with evidence or hinder ongoing investigations (Scanlon and McMahon, 2011, p. 173).

▲ **Logistics.** Who will recover bodies? How will they be transported and stored?

▲ **Family assistance.** How will the next of kin be notified? What questions, concerns, and needs might they have, and how can these be addressed?

▲ **Psychological issues.** How will people react to death (both surviving relatives and emergency workers) and what kind of support will they need? What is the best way to communicate with them using tact and sensitivity?

▲ **Cultural and religious issues.** What are the burial customs of different people and groups locally and around the world?

Another recommendation for mass fatality management is to avoid removing bodies immediately (unless that is required in special circumstances). If necessary, a map can be drawn to record the exact location of the deceased. Each body and all personal belongings should be tagged with a unique number. Such record keeping plays an important role in reconstructing the event and identifying the bodies and belongings. Belongings and body parts should be kept near the body or together at all times. In other cases where bodies have been dispersed, efforts should be made to centralize the deceased or maintain meticulous records as to their whereabouts.

After a preliminary investigation has taken place, the deceased should be taken to a central morgue facility. This temporary morgue must be adequate to handle the number of bodies necessary. The facility should be well ventilated and cold and have adequate lighting, sufficient electrical outlets, running water and bathrooms, and furniture for examinations. Clerical, break, and waiting rooms would also be helpful. If no such facilities can be obtained quickly, refrigerated trailers can also be used to store bodies in major mass fatality incidents. However, these trucks should have no visible markings, logos, names, etc. This will help to avoid bad publicity for that particular company.

Mass fatality management includes an effort to determine the cause of death, and victim identification will take place by collecting and analyzing postmortem data. Hooft et al. (1989, p. 6) note that:

1. "The bodies are described as they outwardly appear, recording all significant features, mud, clothing and belongings. The same happens for all loose body parts or belongings.
2. Fingerprints should be taken. Photographs should be taken of the clothed body and all relevant external items.
3. The delicate procedures of examining a human body, even if it is dead, are medical act and should only be performed by a doctor. All relevant marks and signs on the body should be marked. Blood and urine samples or muscle biopsies should be collected for alcohol dosage, blood grouping, and toxicological analysis. As ondontological findings often contribute most to the identification, attention should be given to get complete dental records.
4. If the clothes or any other object are essential for a further investigation or as evidence in court, they should be dried before packing, as wet materials become moldy, change color and disintegrate rapidly, especially in plastic bags.
5. In fire accidents additional airtight blood samples should be taken for the concentration of carboxyhemoglobin and cyanide."

At this point, family members can be brought in to confirm the identification of the deceased. You must ensure that this be done with much care and tact. Will one or multiple families be brought in at a time? Is an escort needed? Will children be allowed to participate? Will the family be required to show personal identification (e.g., a driver's license) before they can be allowed in? These are all important considerations.

FOR EXAMPLE

### 9/11 Victims

The task of identifying remains at the WTC after 9/11 was especially difficult. Tons of debris had to be sorted through for human remains. There was initial sorting at Ground Zero. Afterward, heavy equipment moved debris to Staten Island. This caused some victims to complain that their loved ones were being placed in a trash heap at Staten Island. Debris was then sorted again to search for victims' remains. Many of the deceased were obliterated and badly burned. Some did not have remains to be recovered. Mass fatality management was an emotionally tiring experience for many of the surviving family members.

Final disposition must also be performed under strict guidelines. Before the body is released, a complete postmortem assessment needs to be completed. Unidentifiable bodies should be refrigerated as long as possible or buried separately with the funeral home or coroner keeping a record of their location.

Other steps to successfully respond to a mass fatality incident include:

▲ Ensuring that those responding to a mass fatality incident know where to report, the best route to get to the scene, what type of equipment they will need, where the staging areas are, etc.

▲ Recognizing that the public is watching how bodies are being handled

▲ Flagging or otherwise marking the location of the deceased

▲ Using grids or pictures of the scene for documentation purposes

▲ Ensuring that the trucks that haul remains have metal floors (as wood may retain odors)

▲ Managing personal belongings and identification records in a careful manner

▲ Communicating effectively with the next of kin and helping them cope with the loss of a loved one

▲ Knowing how to deal with the media to prevent the release of sensational photos of the deceased

▲ Opening family assistance centers to address survivor needs and answer questions about lost loved ones and the mass fatality management process

### 6.3.3 Disaster Mortuary Operational Response Teams

In major disasters, local coroners, morticians, and funeral directors will be overwhelmed, unable to deal with the large numbers of dead. In these situations, outside resources should be requested. One of the goals of the U.S. Department of Health and Human Services is to help mortuary services address mass fatality situations (Scanlon and McMahon, 2011, p. 173). Disaster mortuary operational response teams (DMORTs) can be called in to assist. A **DMORT** is a group of private citizens that is activated to process the deceased in mass fatality disasters.

DMORTs are comprised of several licensed and certified experts. These experts include funeral directors, medical examiners, coroners, pathologists, forensic anthropologists, and medical records technicians and transcribers. Others such as fingerprint specialists, forensic odontologists, dental assistants, X-ray technicians, mental health specialists, computer professions, administrative support staff, and security and investigative personnel also play an important part of DMORTs. DMORTs are, in many ways, similar to a USAR teams and DMATs since they are deployed by the federalgovernment. However, a DMORT is in charge of providing victim identification and mortuary services (and not SAR or emergency medical care).

A DMORT can be activated in presidentially declared disasters (see Chapter 9). Once notified and mobilized, DMORT members become federal employees under the Department of Homeland Security. Much like USAR teams or DMATs, DMORTs can be sent to any location and are intended to be relatively self-sufficient. Some even have disaster portable morgue units (DPMU), which are complete and mobile morgues with workstations and prepackaged equipment. However, DMORTs can also respond to circumstances that do not require utilization of the National Response Framework. State emergency management agencies may request a DMORT if the need arises.

As can be imagined, DMORTs provide vital mortuary services after mass fatality incidents, and they operate in a very professional manner. They work with local authorities to process deceased disaster victims with tact and skill. Some of their responsibilities include:

▲ Recovering bodies, body parts, and belongings of the dead
▲ Setting up temporary morgues

**Figure 6-8**

A disaster mortuary operational response team is set up in Gulfport, MS, to respond to Hurricane Katrina. Mark Wolfe/FEMA.

▲ Identifying disaster victims

▲ Answering questions from the family of the deceased and providing comfort as needed

▲ Facilitating death certificate issuance

▲ Preparing and disposing of remains

DMORTs can therefore be a great asset to you and to your community in major mass fatality incidents (Figure 6-8).

## FOR EXAMPLE

### Mass Fatality Management in Haiti

Two days after the earthquake that rocked Port-au-Prince, Haiti, the U.S. Department of Human and Health Services dispatched individuals to assess mass fatality needs in this tiny island country. During the assessment phase, soldiers from the 113th Mortuary Affairs (out of Fort Lee, VA) began to collect the remains of American citizens through search and recovery operations. A DMORT was activated a short time later and established a portable morgue unit at the Port-au-Prince International Airport. The forensic professionals worked on a 24 hour schedule to process over 200 remains. They admitted each corpse, catalogued belongings, and began the arduous task of identification through medical exams and DNA testing. This proved to be difficult since samples of victims' DNA had to be acquired from relatives in the United States. Once a positive match could be made, the bodies and a tracking manifest were flown by the Air Force to Dover, Delaware. Remains were then returned to families for ceremonies and burials. In contrast to these successful mass fatality operations, there were approximately 200,000 Haitians that were never identified after the earthquake. They were picked up by front loaders, carried outside of the city by dump trucks, and buried in mass graves that were dug with backhoes (McEntire et al., 2012).

## SELF-CHECK

- Why do disasters produce a great number of fatalities?
- Are all bodies identified after a disaster? Why or why not?
- What issues need to be considered in a mass fatality incident?
- Do citizens help or hinder mass fatality management?
- What is a DMORT and why are they beneficial after a major disaster?

## 6.4 Stress Management

If you are to respond effectively to a disaster, you must also recognize that people may succumb to problems beyond physical injuries and death. While most people are remarkably resilient, some do face emotional distress. As an example, many people in the United States and around the world were deeply disturbed when watching news reports of Americans being killed on 9/11. This type of psychological harm can have long-term implications and is commonly referred to as PTSD or CIS.

▲ "**Post trauma stress disorder** (PTSD) is the clinical diagnosis given by psychiatrists to the development of specific symptoms following a psychologically traumatic event not generally encountered in human experience" (Corneil, 1989, p. 24). Note: some people advocate the elimination of the word "disorder" from PTSD since stress is a natural reaction to unpleasant events.

▲ **CIS** is defined as unusual work stress resulting from any trauma, crisis, or event that overwhelms available coping mechanisms of emergency service personnel.

There are multiple reasons why some people experience PTSD or CIS. In the aftermath of traumatic events (whether it be a natural disaster, industrial accident, or workplace violence), citizens and first responders will be confronted with many issues. Witnessing death or feeling threats to one's life or the lives of friends, families, and coworkers can lead to PTSD or CIS. Those involved in such events may have no experience in dealing with death and destruction. They could be uncertain of how to act under such circumstances and will often question if their efforts were appropriate or sufficient. First responders may also have to grapple with their actions or inaction during the event. Line-of-duty injuries, mass deaths, and the inability to save others from a horrific situation can all lead to PTSD or CIS. The fact that a community will look to emergency managers to effectively deal with the disaster can also take an emotional toll on you. All of these factors can trigger PTSD or CIS (Figure 6-9).

### 6.4.1 Vulnerability to PTSD/CIS

Stressful situations can happen to anyone at any time. In fact, 60–70% of all people will experience some type of traumatic event at one point or another in their lives (Patterson, 2002, p. 5C). For instance, people in the armed forces will suffer from the emotional toll of combat. Personnel in emergency services will see gruesome injuries and death on a daily or weekly basis. Even regular citizens will be impacted by emergencies and disasters.

While most individuals who experience a disaster or other traumatic event will not suffer any type or long-term psychological distress, some will have to deal with the impact of such stressful events throughout their lifetime. It is estimated that 8–10% of people who experience a stressful situation will suffer from some type of PTSD.

Figure 6-9

The impact of disasters can cause posttraumatic stress in victims and responders alike. Andrea Booher/FEMA.

As discussed earlier, those affected by disaster may experience significant trials such as the death of family members, friends, and coworkers. They may lose personal property (e.g., home or car). Unemployment may result due to business closures. Disaster victims may also have unpleasant dealings with insurance claims adjusters or receive what they regard to be unfair or insufficient federal or humanitarian relief assistance. For many individuals, disasters will result in a feeling that their lifelong dreams have been dashed.

First responders may also become victims of PTSD/CIS. Firefighters, paramedics, and police officers witness many grim realities in their professions. On a frequent basis, they see gruesome injuries and appalling deaths among those in the community and even within their own departments. Rescue workers who see a coworker die often feel "it could have been me." First responders may have an especially difficult time when they weren't able to rescue victims either due to safety concerns or other factors. If traumatic events occur repeatedly, first responders also are confronted with other challenges that lead to PTSD/CIS. Repeated occurrences of traumatic events have a "pileup effect" on rescue workers, and this can prolong or aggravate PTSD (Harris, 1989). For example, a first responder who sees victims of car accidents on a regular basis may develop PTSD after the repeated occurrence of accidents. Rescue workers may also have a difficult time expressing emotions, which aggravates the emotional turmoil.

Both citizens and rescue personnel may be vulnerable in time of disasters. There are some groups that are at particular risk of mental problems following a disaster. Factors leading to such vulnerability include those who:

▲ Had a difficult childhood or past traumatic experiences
▲ Already have acute stress and those who had a preexisting psychiatric disorder
▲ Have lost a loved one or were wounded in the disaster
▲ Were exposed to the trauma intensely and for a long period of time
▲ Are young or advanced in age
▲ Do not have a strong social support system

### 6.4.2  Common Signs of PTSD/CIS

There are many possible signs of PTSD/CIS. These symptoms include weight loss, anger, depression, alcohol/drug use, guilt, chest pains, headaches, and mood swings. Denial, sleeplessness, withdrawal from friends, flashbacks, and memory loss are also signs of PTSD/CIS.

Many of these symptoms are not readily apparent, but may become increasingly visible over time. Some symptoms might last for a few weeks or months, while others will occasionally endure for years. Some symptoms may be age specific. After a disaster, young children could wet their bed or resume thumbsucking and fear of "monsters" and exhibit other behaviors. Older children may rebel and perform poorly in school. Adults may become isolated from others and exhibit anger or resentment. Regardless of the type of symptoms, the traumatic experience could affect people's personal and professional lives for the foreseeable future.

### 6.4.3  Overcoming PTSD/CIS

In light of the psychological problems that result from major emergencies and disasters, it is recommended that posttraumatic stress debriefing/CIS management be implemented by mental health professionals. Critical incident stress debriefing (CISD) has emanated from military experiences such as combat deaths. According to Jeffrey T. Mitchell (1988a, p. 47), the two main goals of debriefing are to:

▲ Reduce the impact of distressing critical incidents
▲ Accelerate recovery from those events before harmful stress reactions have a chance to damage personal and professional lives (Figure 6-10)

As an emergency manager or first responder, you can take steps to minimize the risk of CIS. You and the leaders of response organizations should be aware of possible trauma during response. Surprise can be a dangerous psychological element in the field or EOC, and every effort should be made to cut down on unexpected situations. Frequent breaks for those at the rescue scene or in the EOC will help since people may only be able to work under intense stress for a limited time

**Figure 6-10**

A Red Cross psychologist talks to a victim of the Moore, OK, tornado to let her know that counseling services are available. George Armstrong/FEMA.

before the effects are felt. It is also important to make sure there is plenty of fresh water and food available. Caffeine and sugar should be avoided since they may magnify a stress reaction.

It is also important for emergency and disaster workers to recognize stress reactions. Change in the behavior of one's personnel is a sign that the event has had a significant psychological impact on them. Decisions on whether a distressed person needs to be removed from service at the scene or in the EOC are usually difficult to make. Hasty decisions will usually not be good ones. It is usually best to offer an extended rest break and see if the person improves. If there is not any improvement, keep the person at the scene or EOC but do not assign them to others with other crews or groups. If the distress continues, the worker should be removed from the location.

After the event, defusings can reduce the long-term effects of stress reactions. **Defusings** are short, unstructured meetings that encourage a brief discussion of the events in order to reduce acute stress. Defusings are done anywhere from 3 hours up to 12 hours following the incident. They often take place at the fire or police station and generally last from 30 minutes to an hour. Only those crews most affected are involved; not all emergency responders from the scene need to attend. The same principles holds true for those in the EOC.

Another important activity is to provide ongoing support to those people showing the greatest need and work with their leaders to develop a plan to care for their future emotional needs. Following a crisis, emergency managers or first responders are likely to close ranks, preferring to talk with individuals in the unit or participate in small group conversations related to the event. Peer support personnel, including those involved in the incident, may watch for telltale signs of distress in their fellow workers: irritability, excessive humor, increased derogatory remarks against one another, significant changes in behavior, or social withdrawal.

Well-run defusings and continued support may eliminate further treatment for PTSD or CIS. However, formal debriefing activities may also be necessary (Mitchell, 1988a). A **debriefing** is an extensive and possibly recurring discussion about one's feelings regarding a traumatic stress experience such as a disaster. A full formal debriefing can be conducted approximately three days after the incident. Debriefings may include a joint session with all types of responders as well as multiple one-on-one sessions a few weeks after the trauma. In debriefings, emergency personnel recount the nature of the disaster and the trauma they experienced on the scene. Therapists try to redirect harmful thinking, such as the belief that emergency workers are responsible for the tragedy. Therapists work with survivors to focus on things such as normal reactions to the event, relaxation exercises, and coping strategies. Personnel are given as many practical suggestions for stress management as possible along with an opportunity to ask questions and make comments. The mental health person assigned to their group remains available to privately discuss the situation or their reactions. Talking to the other mental health professionals at the debriefing center is also an option. Chaplains may be present at the debriefing center and are available if an emergency person would prefer to discuss something with them. No one is required to talk unless they choose to.

There are seven phases in critical stress debriefings (Mitchell, 1988b, p. 46):

1. An *introduction* from the members of a CIS team (emergency personnel who are training in psychological counseling), at which point they state that the material to be discussed is strictly confidential.

2. The *fact phase* in which people are asked to describe what happened at the scene.

3. The *thought phase* of the process usually includes the question: "Can you recall your first thoughts once you stopped functioning in an automatic mode at the scene?" The goal of this question is to help people personalize their experiences.

4. The *reaction phase* is when mental health personnel help victims describe the worst part of the event.

5. The *symptom phase* is when the group or individual is asked to describe stress symptoms felt at different times.

6. The *teaching phase* is when people are taught how to cope with and how to reduce their stress. Education should include material on CIS and how it differs from nonemergency stress. This phase also describes CISD team and how to utilize them if the need arises. This segment should include specific information on field strategies for stress control during a crisis.

FOR EXAMPLE

**PTSD Debriefing/CISD**

Rescue personnel often blame themselves for fatalities on the scene. One useful technique to handle this is to put together a timeline of events to show people how quickly people reacted and point out all the things they did right. A fire chief in Hudson, Massachusetts, asked his crew to recount their events and he recorded them. He said, "by using our radio tape recorder I was able to put together a sequential order of events, and the times they had taken place. I found this to be extremely helpful to the overall effectives of the critique because it showed the firefighters how quickly things were done. By the end of the critique the firefighters were openly talking, which made the effects of the incident at least livable" (Garrity, 1989, p. 14).

7. The *reentry phase* is when response personnel may ask whatever questions arise from the session and follow up with each person during the recovery process. Peer supporters may also participate in this phase and assist mental health professionals.

### 6.4.4 The Merit of Defusings and Debriefings

Research often shows the importance of quick psychological treatment. There are a number of studies that reveal that defusings and debriefings have limited CIS in police officers, firefighters, nurses, and others (Mitchell, 2004). In the context of military combat, it has been reported that "approximately 65 percent of those who received immediate psychological treatment for stress were able to return to combat duties, but less than 40 percent of those who were given delayed treatment in distant areas were able to return to combat" (Mitchell, 1988a, p. 48). For this reason, defusings and debriefings should follow the perilous event as soon as possible, but "typically no longer than the first 24 to 72 hours after" (Davis, 1998). The success of these rapid interventions was seen following the 1995 Oklahoma City bombing. Providing CIS treatments to those affected "averted many of the major long-term psychological injuries that could have potentially been experienced from such a traumatizing event" (Davis, 1998).

However, much of this success of these programs may depend on how the treatment is delivered. According to Barnett-Queen and Bergmann (1989, p. 15), effective posttrauma programs seem to require the following four components:

1. **Information**. Personnel who have accurate information about trauma, posttrauma consequences, and productive posttrauma coping skills seem to make more successful recoveries. Those victims of duty-related trauma who do not have recovery information are less likely to recover. In addition, they tend to use inappropriate coping skills to numb or manage their posttrauma consequences (Barnett-Queen and Bergmann, 1989, p. 15).

2. **Support**. Survivors of trauma tend to feel isolated, distrustful, and detached. Where survivors receive consistent support from their peers and families, they feel more positive about themselves, their efforts to recover, and their prognosis (Barnett-Queen and Bergmann, 1989, p. 15).

3. **Ventilation**. Detailed discussion of the incident with others is an important element of posttrauma recovery. Individuals who can talk about their experiences are more likely to feel supported by the listeners and others involved in the incident. They may learn important details of the event from others or may recall more of their own experiences during the incident, which promotes recovery. Finally, survivors who are able to articulate their experiences are more likely to understand what has happened and how it has changed their lives (Barnett-Queen and Bergmann, 1989, p. 15).

4. **Skills**. The coping skills required for day-to-day living may not be those most helpful for a successful recovery. The use of appropriate coping skills enhances the probability of recovery after a traumatic event (Barnett-Queen and Bergmann, 1989, p. 15) (Figure 6-11).

In spite of notable successes (Mitchell, 2009), research also reveals that PTSD/CIS treatments may not always be effective. This is especially the case when personnel are not adequately trained in such interventions and if they do not adhere to published standards (Mitchell, 2009). In addition, posttraumatic stress debriefing/CISD is a relatively new technique to dealing with psychological

**Figure 6-11**

A mental health professional talks to a woman whose home
was damaged from flooding. John Ficara/FEMA.

problems. Emergency medical service organizations began developing psychological support services for staff members in 1972. As a consequence, there are inconsistencies about the benefit of these treatments. Some studies show no relation between CIS management and psychological recovery. For instance, Gibbs et al.'s study of the AVIANCA air crash illustrates that predisaster training on disturbing disaster conditions had no effect on postdisaster symptoms (1996). Other studies have brought to light the possibility of these treatments actually worsening the patient's condition. Some have said, "perhaps the process of debriefing, part of the function of which is to warn participants of emotional reactions that might be expected to develop over weeks and months, actually increases the occurrence of these symptoms" (Wessely and Deahl, 2003). Barnett-Queen and Bergmann have illustrated that there are at least four difficulties associated with individual counseling after traumatic events (1989, p. 15):

1. There can be a stigma in seeking psychological help. Other rescue personnel may believe that coworkers getting counseling are not mentally strong enough for their job.
2. Emergency workers who are referred to counseling may believe that their feelings are not normal and to be expected. They think they are being singled out because they cannot deal with posttraumatic symptoms.
3. Counseling is expensive. One hour of counseling may cost from $40.00 to $120.00. Debriefing sessions that include multiple individuals at once are more economical.
4. Some firefighters hide their true feelings about an incident. If this is the case, some people that need assistance may not receive it.

In short, posttraumatic or CIS treatments have been successful in many cases (Mitchell, 2009), but they are still somewhat controversial. Many scholars agree that CIS management is a complicated matter and that we need more research on the topic. As an emergency manager, you have the responsibility to stay on top of this literature.

## SELF-CHECK

- What is PTSD? What is CIS?
- Why are some people more vulnerable to psychological distress than others?
- What are the symptoms of PTSD or CIS?
- What is the difference between a defusing and a debriefing?
- What are the phases of debriefings?
- Are psychological interventions always advantageous?

# SUMMARY

Disasters are associated with injuries, deaths, and even emotional distress. To deal with these challenges successfully, volunteers and first responders must engage in SAR operations. Medical care must be given to those who have been physically hurt. When deaths result from a disaster, bodies must be collected, identified, and returned to surviving relatives. Those affected psychologically must be evaluated, treated, and supported through understanding and expressions of concern and hope. Meeting people's physical and emotional needs after disaster is required if resilience is to occur.

# KEY TERMS

| | |
|---|---|
| Cribbing | Wood stacked under debris to stabilize it after it has been lifted by a lever. |
| Critical incident stress (CIS) | Unusual work stress resulting from any trauma, crisis, or event that overwhelms available coping mechanisms of emergency service personnel. |
| Debriefing | An extensive discussion about one's feelings regarding a traumatic stress experience such as a disaster. |
| Defusings | Short, unstructured meetings that encourage a brief discussion of the events in order to reduce acute stress. |
| Disaster medical assistance team (DMAT) | A group of private citizens that is activated to process the deceased in mass fatality disasters. |
| Disaster mortuary operational response team (DMORT) | A group of private citizens that are activated under the National Response Plan to deal with mass fatality incidents. |
| Levers | Long pieces of wood (e.g., 2×4) used to lift debris off of people. |
| Mass fatality incident | Any situation where there are more bodies than can be handled using local resources. |
| National Urban Search and Rescue Response | A system made up of 28 FEMA USAR Task Forces that are spread throughout the continental United States. |
| Posttraumic stress disorder (PTSD) | A clinical diagnosis that signifies deep stress that is sometimes debilitating resulting from a traumatic event. |
| Search and rescue operations | Response activities undertaken to find disaster victims and remove them from |

danger or confinement so they may receive urgent treatment such as hydration, basic first aid, or advanced medical care.

**Triage**

An initial assessment and separation of victims for treatment based on the severity of their injuries.

# ASSESS YOUR UNDERSTANDING

Posttest to evaluate your knowledge of caring for the injured, dead, and distraught. *Measure your learning by comparing pretest and posttest results.*

## Summary Questions

1. Search and rescue includes looking for lost individuals but has nothing to do with providing immediate medical assistance. True or false?
2. Emergent groups will use anything they can find to assist them in search and rescue operations. True or false?
3. Those engaged in search and rescue will require sufficient food, water, and rest if they are to be effective and safe. True or false?
4. Before rushing in to conduct search and rescue operations, it is important to assess the situation and determine rescue priorities. True or false?
5. Most hazards will generate the same type of injuries. True or false?
6. People will be injured in a hazard only, and not after one occurs. True or false?
7. The purpose of triage is to limit the impact of mass casualty incidents on the hospitals. True or false?
8. Since first responders are well trained, they will never make mistakes regarding triage. True or false?
9. Emergency managers should not expect that people will move the bodies of those who have died in accidents, emergencies, and disasters. True or false?
10. It is vital that temporary morgue sites be large and refrigerated and have sufficient water and electrical outlets. True or false?
11. The public and media have no interest in mass fatality management. True or false?
12. DMORTs are teams that respond to the medical needs of those who are injured in disasters. True or false?
13. DMORTs may help to issue death certificates. True or false?
14. PTSD and CIS are similar, but they are not exactly the same thing. True or false?
15. Because disasters result in death and destruction of property, some people may become stressed and depressed. True or false?
16. A debriefing occurs in the field right after the accident or disaster. True or false?
17. In the reaction phase, emergency responders engage in search and rescue operations. True or false?
18. Effective posttrauma interventions help disaster victims develop emotional coping skills. True or false?
19. Which type of search and rescue helps to access people and bring them to dry ground?
    (a) Rural search and rescue
    (b) Swift water rescue

(c) Air-patrolled search and rescue

(d) Urban search and rescue

(e) Ski patrol search and rescue

20. Professional search and rescue teams:
    (a) Do not have to undergo training because they work as first responders
    (b) Are transported by bus only to avoid plane accidents
    (c) Are located in three cities in the United States only
    (d) Are well equipped with supplies
    (e) Arrive before emergent groups and first responders

21. Cribbing is:
    (a) Used to lift levers
    (b) A device to stop the bleeding on patients
    (c) A process to help victims recover from CIS
    (d) Used to spray-paint important information on houses that have been searched
    (e) Used to stabilize debris

22. Self-referred means:
    (a) The dispatch of USAR teams
    (b) The dispatch of DMATs
    (c) The arrival of patients at the hospital without a field diagnosis
    (d) The dispatch of DMORTs
    (e) An acknowledgment that one is been affected by PTSD

23. DMAT stands for:
    (a) Disaster medical assistance team
    (b) Disaster medical advice team
    (c) Disaster mortuary assistance team
    (d) Disaster mortuary advice team
    (e) Disaster memorandum assistance terminology

24. Mass fatality management requires:
    (a) That the outward appearance of bodies be recorded
    (b) That fingerprints be taken
    (c) That evidence be kept for investigation and prosecution
    (d) That photographs be avoided to protect privacy
    (e) All of the above except d

25. Which of the following are not members of DMORTs?
    (a) Funeral directors
    (b) Coroners
    (c) X-ray technicians
    (d) First responders trained to perform search and rescue operations
    (e) Administrative support staff

26. Which term is used to describe the impact of disasters on first responders?
    (a) Posttraumatic stress disorder
    (b) Critical incident stress
    (c) Defusings
    (d) Debriefings
    (e) The complex psychoanalysis assumption
27. Which person is most likely to be at risk for mental problems after a disaster?
    (a) An emergency manager
    (b) A fire chief
    (c) Those without strong social support systems
    (d) Those individuals who were slightly injured in the disaster
    (e) Those who did not have a preexisting psychiatric disorder
28. Symptoms of PTSD include:
    (a) Anger
    (b) Guilt
    (c) Sleeplessness
    (d) Flashbacks
    (e) All of the above

## Review Questions

1. Why is search and rescue important?
2. How is urban search and rescue different than other types of SAR?
3. What is situational awareness?
4. Explain the characteristics of professional SAR teams?
5. How are SAR missions conducted?
6. What are the determinants of the number and extent of injuries in a disaster?
7. Do disasters produce waves of victims? What does this mean for hospitals?
8. What are the benefits of triage? What are the drawbacks?
9. How are DMATs deployed?
10. Should we expect more mass fatality incidents in the future?
11. How can those in mass fatality management deal effectively with the surviving family members?
12. Who is involved in DMORTs?
13. Does everyone become affected by PTSD? Why or why not?
14. Why are first responders affected by CIS?
15. Are the signs of PTSD/CIS physical? Emotional? Behavioral? Cognitive?
16. What can be done to limit CIS?
17. What are the four components of successful PTSD interventions?

## Applying This Chapter

1. You are a first responder in a Southern California community that has experienced a major mudslide. Many homes are covered with sediment or are damaged extensively. Volunteers are on the scene to assist but time is running out. What search and rescue concerns do you have and how do you address them?

2. A bus carrying 40 high school students has overturned on a freeway in Oklahoma. Injuries range from minor to major and some students have died. How can triage be applied in this situation?

3. You are the coroner in a small community in North Dakota. An unexpected storm catches many people off guard in the early summer and several campers die from hypothermia as a result. How do you identify the bodies and deal with the next of kin?

4. While responding to a 3-alarm fire at an apartment complex, you become worried about the physical and emotional well-being of your fire department. What can you do to prevent critical incident stress? If some are affected, how do you help them afterward?

5. You are a member of a nonprofit organization in a community that has just experienced a major disaster. Hundreds of people have died and others have lost homes and possessions. Some victims are fighting with insurance companies to settle claims and others believe the federal government is not providing enough disaster assistance. What are your concerns about people in your area? What can you do to help them cope emotionally? Are there things you can do to prevent symptoms of PTSD?

### Volunteer Search and Rescue Teams

You are the emergency manager for your city in the Colorado Rockies and there has been a terrible avalanche in the area. Hundreds of volunteers and upset parents rushed to the local elementary school and begin digging victims out of the snow pile. What concerns do you have about these volunteers? What steps do you take to ensure the volunteers have what they need to be successful and do not injure themselves or others in the process?

### Triage

A chemical or nerve agent has been used in a terrorist attack in Phoenix, Arizona. You are a paramedic and have arrived on the scene to help victims. How do you fulfill the five functions of triage?

### Mass Fatalities

Write a 3-page paper on the following topic: you are the emergency manager for a small town in Ohio when a 747 crashes in a farmer's field, killing everyone on board. What challenges confront emergency responders and others this a mass fatality incident? What concerns do you have about workers, victims, and relatives of the deceased? What can you do to resolve them?

### PTSD/CIS

Many emergency service personnel who worked at the World Trade Center on 9/11 suffered from PTSD/CIS as a result of that disaster. If you were in charge of one of the groups to assist rescue personnel, what steps would you take to prevent PTSD/CIS and to help distraught workers recover? Are there any drawbacks to counseling that you must consider?

# 7

# MANAGING PUBLIC INFORMATION, DONATIONS, AND VOLUNTEERS

## Expected Difficulties and Benefits

## Starting Point

Pretest to assess your knowledge of managing public relations, donations, and volunteers.
*Determine where you need to concentrate your effort.*

## What You'll Learn in This Chapter

▲ The different types of media and typical media behaviors
▲ The goals of public relations after disasters
▲ Problems associated with donations management
▲ The challenges that volunteers create for first responders and emergency managers

## After Studying This Chapter, You'll Be Able To

▲ Handle the media effectively after a disaster.
▲ Examine donations management difficulties.
▲ Prepare for an outpouring of assistance and help from others.
▲ Operate closely with volunteer and volunteer associations.

## Goals and Outcomes

▲ Prepare and provide important disaster information to your community.
▲ Enhance your agency's public image.
▲ Harness outside generosity for the benefit of disaster victims.
▲ Integrate volunteers into disaster response and recovery operations.

*Disaster Response and Recovery: Strategies and Tactics for Resilience*, Second Edition. David A. McEntire.
© 2015 John Wiley & Sons, Inc. Published 2015 by John Wiley & Sons, Inc.

# INTRODUCTION

One measure of resilience is your ability to deal with the expected reactions of people and organizations to disasters. Members of the media rush to the scene to report on what is taking place. Donations pour in from well-meaning individuals and groups that want to help disaster victims. Volunteers arrive to assist the community in its recovery efforts. While the media, donations, and volunteers are essential for response and recovery operations, they will be accompanied with many challenges. You must comprehend the benefits and drawbacks they generate in disasters. Managing all three functions effectively will be one of your top priorities in the aftermath of a disaster.

## 7.1 The Media and Disasters

As an emergency manager, you must understand that the media can be your friend or foe during postdisaster operations (Auf der Heide, 1987d). In the context of emergency management, the **media** includes reporters, camera operators, and news anchors that provide information about disasters to the public. The significance and role of the media cannot be underestimated. The media helps to:

▲ Educate the public about preventive and preparedness measures.
▲ Warn the public about an impending hazard.
▲ Provide information regarding evacuation and sheltering.
▲ Describe what people can do to protect themselves and others.
▲ Relay what the government is doing and how they are responding to the disaster.
▲ List what organizations are providing relief and how assistance can be given or obtained.
▲ Generate support for emergency management personnel and programs.

The media may affect emergency management in other ways as well. At times, the media shares communication equipment with responders when needed (Figure 7-1). They also provide advice to victims on where to go to receive aid. Nevertheless, not everything that the media does is beneficial for emergency management. For instance, the media may issue a request for donations that are not needed. In addition, the media often points out weaknesses of response and recovery operations and is quick to assign blame (regardless of justification). However, the criticisms provided by the media may help you to evaluate and improve response and recovery activities in the future.

### 7.1.1 Types of Media

To be successful in emergency management, you must be aware of the different types of media that exist (Scanlon et al., 1985). Each represents a different level of society and has a unique audience and objective. For example, local media represents the community. Regional medial gives attention to large metropolitan areas or multiple states. National media covers topics pertinent to the entire country. Finally, the international media brings a global perspective to disaster issues.

Figure 7-1

The media will arrive at the scene of disaster and reporters will seek
interviews with emergency management officials, as was the case
in Fayetteville, NC, after Hurricane Earl in 2010. David Fine/FEMA.

Depending on the segment of society they represent, the media has different
goals. For example:

▲ Local media will provide very detailed personal stories, in addition to
specific information for disaster victims.

▲ Regional media are somewhat similar to local media, but they also desire to
report about the response of multiple cities and surrounding states.

▲ National media tend to focus on what the president is doing about the
disaster as well as the activities of federal agencies.

▲ International media gives preference to national responses and global
impacts.

Just as the media has different audiences and goals, it also uses different ways to
convey or deliver information (Scanlon et al., 1985). The type of media often
shapes their style of reporting. As an example, radio stations want to air short
sound bites from victims, scholars, or public officials. Television/cable/satellite stations prefer to include interviews as well as pictures and dramatic video footage of
the scenes of destruction. Photos and videos of the disaster damage will convey a
great deal about the magnitude and extent of the disaster. The Internet and print
media seek in-depth coverage and detailed analysis of the situation.

Each of the media organizations has similar interest in disasters (Scanlon et al.,
1985). The media provides those listening, watching, or reading with human interest

stories. The media will cover loss and death, but it also takes advantage of any opportunity to convey stories about heroism and survival too. Coverage of disasters is common on any given day, but it will dominate the news and preempt normal programming when one is unfolding currently.

Regardless of the type of media, their behavior is generally predictable in normal times as well as in times of disaster. Scanlon and Alldred (1982) have identified the following pattern in disaster reporting:

1. The media will hear of a disaster event.
2. They will immediately report the news of that incident.
3. They will search for additional information via telephone or personal interviews.
4. They will send reporters to the scene. If the event is newsworthy, hundreds of media personnel may descend on the affected area.
5. Once the media is present, it will make demands on local emergency managers. They may pressure you to hold news conferences at specific intervals. The media wants to know the where, what, when, why, and how of the situation. They will also want numbers—the number of dead, the number of casualties, the number of destroyed homes, and the number of dollars that will be spend on response and recovery.
6. The media will likewise put their own spin on the story and will make it fit their perception of what has happened or will occur in the future.

In addition, the media tends to rely on official sources of information. Quarantelli revealed that "one Disaster Research Center study found that local governmental officials were cited in 14 percent of radio, 19 percent of television and 24 percent of newspaper stories; police, fire and relief agencies were also frequently cited.... . Local emergency management officials were [also mentioned in] 8 percent of radio, 2 percent of television and 3 percent of newspaper stories" (1996b, p. 8).

### 7.1.2 Challenges Associated with the Media

It is well known that the media often presents formidable challenges to responders and emergency managers. The problems generated by the media are numerous. Payne (1994) has identified four of the most prevalent problems:

▲ **Inaccurate reporting**. It was widely reported during the early days of Hurricane Katrina that there were rapes and murders at the New Orleans Superdome and Convention Center. There were not always witnesses to these crimes, and many of these reports appear to have been rumors. The media later retracted many of these stories.

▲ **Intrusive manner**. The press wants first-hand accounts of the situation, and they want to beat their colleagues in covering the best story or getting the story on air first. To do this, they will sometimes stoop to unethical activities. For example, in one disaster, reporters went to a hospital and claimed to be relatives of the victims. They then asked the victims to recount their story (Payne, 1994, p. 26).

▲ **Lack of sensitivity**. There is a vivid example of this when a stampede occurred at a soccer game in England. "In 1989 at Hillsborough, Sheffield, there was live filming of people being crushed to death against steel barriers. The horror was brought into the homes of the people who were viewing the football match on television. At the ground, a cameraman who moved around the pitch and terraces filming the scenes was sworn at, spat at, cursed and threatened by the understandably emotional fans. (Later, that cameraman won an award for the best television coverage of the year!)" (Payne, 1994, p. 26).

▲ **Uncooperative attitude**. The media may stop at nothing to get their scoop as witnessed after a boating accident in Europe. "When the *Marchioness* pleasure-boat was being lifted from the Thames, the police positioned a number of police launches to screen the area from the intrusive press. The press moved to another less convenient position and covered the salvage operation in full. They claimed they were able to do so tastefully and without causing widespread offence" (Payne, 1994, p. 26).

In addition to these problems, there are at least eight other problems with the media in times of disaster (see Auf der Heide, 1987d; Scanlon et al., 1985):

1. **Convergence at the scene**. The media will show up in massive numbers at the scene of disaster. As a result, the media can also generate too many volunteers and donations (other problems that will be discussed later on in this chapter).

2. **Additional demands placed on emergency managers and responders** (Figure 7-2). When a disaster strikes and you are in the middle of response and recovery operations, it is difficult to have sufficient time to deal with the media. Not only does the media have an urgent need for information, but they may also need security, supplies, and access to facilities. "Many emergency managers have been frustrated when they have had to divert much needed time and resources to address the demands of the media, while at the same time trying to mount a multi-organizational response under conditions of extreme urgency and uncertainty.....[The media's] demands may completely tie up any surviving transportation and communication facilities, and local officials may find themselves responding more to the needs of the media than to the disaster situation" (Auf der Heide, 1987d).

3. **Interference with response operations**. A good example of this nuisance was visible after the 1983 Coalinga California earthquake. "The California Department of Transportation (Caltrans) was called in to help clear earthquake rubble from the streets. Media personnel reportedly contributed to the crowd problems that made it impossible to safely remove the debris. As a result, Caltrans threatened to remove its equipment altogether unless the traffic could be cleared" (Auf der Heide, 1987d).

4. **Creation of safety problems**. The media often puts their own reporters in danger by asking them to report from cities that are expecting to be hit by hurricanes or affected by earthquake aftershocks. Also, reporters will arrive

Figure 7-2

The media will converge at the scene of disaster and will request information
from public officials as was the case during the Waldo Canyon Fire in
Colorado Springs in June 2012. Michael Rieger/FEMA.

at the scene quickly before security arrangements and other precautionary
procedures can be established. Often, there are so many news helicopters in
the air at the disaster scene that the chance for midair collisions between the
rescue helicopters and those of the media increases. In the case of conflict
disasters, terrorists often want to speak to members of the media. This
communication could hinder law enforcement functions or cause an
escalation of violent behavior.

5. **Lack of technical understanding**. Media personnel, especially television
   personalities, were not hired for their scientific expertise. They are
   intelligent, but they are generalists and not specialists. Many media
   representatives do not understand the technical aspects of stories. They will
   often incorrectly report details or misinterpret statements from experts.

6. **Misrepresentations and perpetuation of myths**. In 1986, the media
   falsely reported that Chernobyl was a simple steam explosion instead of a
   nuclear disaster. This type of mistake led to incorrect speculation about the
   health effects that were to be expected. Other examples took place in
   Hurricane Andrew and Hurricane Katrina. Although looting did occur in
   these events, certainly not everyone was engaged in such behavior. Another

example of this is the coverage of 9/11. During 9/11, the media reported that the State Department had been bombed. This was not true. The story was corrected hours later. There is always a lack of information in disasters and initial details are almost always wrong.

7. **Overstatement of impact**. "Another contention of some disaster researchers is that the media's preoccupation with the dramatic accentuates and exaggerates the destructive magnitude of disasters. This has been labeled the 'Dresden syndrome' (where the media make every tornado-stricken community look like Dresden after it was bombed in World War II). News films and photographs focus on scenes of destruction, but not upon surrounding undamaged areas. The audience is often led to believe that the whole community lies in ruins on the basis of intense coverage of damage which may, in reality, be limited to a few buildings or blocks" (Auf der Heide, 1987d).

8. **Damage to individual or agency reputation**. The media can affect the credibility of leaders and organizations. For example, during Hurricane Katrina, the media was able to report that people had sought shelter in the Convention Center in New Orleans. The media reported on this before FEMA had been notified, making FEMA officials look like they were not as involved as they should have been.

Burkhart summarizes many of the problems the media may create for emergency managers: sensationalizing disasters to build circulation, abusing victims, showing their bias, rushing into print, being less than formal, failing to attribute facts, neglecting to check back with sources, using pseudo experts, omitting important aspects, and failing to admit limitations (Burkhart, 1987). These are a few of the problems the media may create for you after a disaster.

### 7.1.3 Strategies for Working with the Media

Although the media might present formidable problems for those in emergency management, you can take a number of steps to ensure successful public information campaigns. These measures may be taken before, during, and after the disaster (as is the case with many other disaster response and recovery functions). You will want to undertake the following activities so you and others can interact with the media effectively when disaster strikes (Auf der Heide, 1987; Scanlon et al., 1985):

▲ **Appoint a public information officer (PIO)**. PIOs are government employees that have special skills in dealing with the media. A PIO may have a full-time position in this area for the city or for the emergency management office. Alternatively, working with the media could be a part-time role or temporary assignment for some individuals. Regardless, the person may answer phone calls or be on-site during disasters to respond to questions from the press. The PIO should be pleasant, professional, and able to think quickly. This person should be knowledgeable and articulate. In other words, you will want to make sure he or she projects a positive image as a representative of your department. Once appointed, the PIO can help you develop policies on how to handle the media. In time of a disaster, you may need to secure additional personnel to field media requests.

▲ **Get to know the media**. You will want to know what media exist in your jurisdiction and if they are prepared to operate in a disaster. You will also want to know the station manager or owner of the local television stations as well as the publishers of newspapers. "In many communities, media, law enforcement and other emergency service organizations meet regularly to discuss public information issues. These groups often meet bimonthly to discuss how to work together more effectively during complex, major incidents where media is involved (e.g., plane crash). Here it is important to give media personnel some basic understanding of hostage negotiation strategies, the tactical reasons for information dispersement, and other issues that affect media coverage" (Onder, 1999, p. 26). Establishing rapport with the media will go a long way to ease communication difficulties during times of crisis.

▲ **Educate the media about disasters**. Explain to the media, for example, how a dispatch center works. They need to know that dispatchers don't have any additional information than what is heard over the scanner. Also, teach the media about human behavior in disasters—that panic does not occur often. The media should also be told that any adjustments to carefully worded official statements can change the meaning dramatically and cause problems for you as an emergency manager. This should be avoided at all costs.

▲ **Know your audience and media market**. You will want to be sure that you reach everyone through the media. If a large part of your population is Hispanic, for example, be sure to work with the Spanish-speaking stations as well. If your community is rural or suburban, that may also change what is reported and how information is conveyed.

▲ **Establish agreements**. You can enter into agreements with local wire services and Associated Press (AP) and United Press International (UPI) to provide accurate information quickly. In exchange, these services will not bother you as long as they are getting the details they desire.

During response and recovery operations, you also should help the media report the news. But be sure to do so with several points in mind. First, you will need to determine the location of briefings. Will they be at the scene of a disaster or in the emergency operations center (EOC)? Or will a media staging area be established, preferably one that is accessible to all responding agencies (Onder, 1999, p. 26)? Regardless of the specified location, you can establish rules as a condition for media access. This will help to ensure that the media will operate in accordance with your requirements. You will also need to decide how often you will brief them. It is recommended that this take place at least twice a day after a disaster. At times, it will be necessary to brief the media and answer their questions more often, but do not allow them to dictate your schedule. This will take away from other disaster operations you need to be involved in.

Another idea is to ensure the safety of the media and others. Keep close tabs on them in any type of disaster as the location could be extremely dangerous. The last thing that is needed in a disaster is more injuries and deaths. In addition, be sure to monitor media activities during criminal or terrorist incidents. Members of the media shouldn't try to negotiate with terrorists or hostage takers. Any piece of information that could compromise the SWAT team members and police tactics should not be broadcasted.

Another step is to recognize what the media is searching for and avoid providing unnecessary information. Obtain the facts before you communicate with the media and be careful about limiting information. If you do not know the answer to a question, do not hesitate to say, "I don't know, but I will find out." Later on, you can provide the reporter with the correct information. You will likewise want to avoid saying, "no comment." To the media, this implies that you are hiding something. While you may not disclose everything the media wants to know, be sure you don't give them the impression that is exactly what you are doing. Also, know that everything you say will likely be reported or published. Nothing is "off the record." You will want to present any information you give in simple terms. Avoid using jargon and technical terms to ensure accurate and effective communication. Be sure PIOs are visible and that all department leaders are coordinating to ensure a unified voice. Also, ask the media if they understand the message you are trying to convey and clarify if needed.

The final thing you will want to do is to track and periodically evaluate media reporting. Recording your interviews can encourage media to be as careful as possible in how they portray your comments. You may also want to review media reports constantly so you can issue any corrections if needed. Recording media reports also helps you to evaluate how well your department came across in its public relations efforts and if you need to make any changes to your communication plan in the future. Keeping copies of any positive press you receive may be

## FOR EXAMPLE

### Media Briefings in War

War is a conflict disaster that requires unique coordination with the media. In the past, journalists were not allowed to report on wars. What was largely seen as a public relations move by the Pentagon was the process of "embedding" media with infantry units during the Iraqi war. Members of the media were assigned to a unit. They would ride in Humvees and report on the action they witnessed. This gave the media immediate access to the front lines on a very timely basis. The safety of the reporters is a big concern however. Some members of the media lost their lives covering the war. One columnist, Michael Kelly, was killed in Iraq when the Humvee he was riding in was trying to evade enemy fire. Another concern of the armed forces is that they do not want the media to broadcast their position or tactics to the enemy. Geraldo Rivera was a journalist who diagrammed troop movement in the sand while on camera. He was later removed from the infantry unit. The behavior of reporters in war may have similar implications for disaster response and recovery operations. Safety and content of what is being reported are extremely important to you as an emergency manager.

useful during evaluations and assessments of the organization. If other agencies received good press, you could send them copies with notes thanking them for their contribution.

## SELF-CHECK

- Why is the media important to the emergency manager?
- What types of media exist and what type of information or material do they seek?
- What potential problems may result from the media in disasters?
- How can you manage the media in a disaster situation?

## 7.2 Dealing with Donations

When a disaster occurs, relatives, neighbors, and concerned citizens in other cities, states, and nations will send donations to the affected area. You must understand that this outpouring of donations is owing to several factors. People that have survived disaster feel the pains of those who have lost loved ones or material possessions, and they desire to ease the trials others are going through. Those close to the scene have witnessed the trauma inflicted by the event on individuals, families, and the community as a whole, and they desire to do something about it. Victims, PIOs, politicians, and reporters stress the need to get resources to the affected areas. Others far away from the disaster have seen the devastation on national news broadcasts and have heard the media's request for disaster assistance. Sometimes, the request for assistance is not warranted. Kathy Guy, a FEMA donations coordinator, asserts that "the media—particularly television—is pretty bad about sticking a microphone in people's faces right after a disaster so they can film them saying 'We need everything'" (Kim, 1999a). While the generosity is heartwarming, the overabundance of donations creates a second disaster for you as an emergency manager.

A variety of donations will arrive in the disaster-affected community, often in very large quantities. Here are some examples of donations in past disasters (Figure 7-3):

- ▲ Anheuser-Busch frequently supplies pallets of canned drinking water to victims and workers after a disaster (Mravcak, 1994).
- ▲ There was an abundance of ice after a hurricane affected many northeastern states in 2003.
- ▲ The GM Foundation provided numerous vehicles to those in need after an earthquake in California (Mravcak, 1994).
- ▲ After a tornado in Kansas, the Salvation Army received enough clothes to fill a 50 foot warehouse (Kim, 1999a).

Figure 7-3

Donations of all types will be sent to help those in need after a disaster as can be witnessed after Hurricane Sandy in this school in Long Beach Island, NJ. Steve Zumwalt/FEMA.

Another example comes after a tornado struck Fort Worth, Texas, on March 28, 2000. It was reported that pizza, hamburgers, fruit, and other food were delivered by local restaurants and grocery stores to the EOC. Home improvement stores also distributed stacks of plywood to victims and owners who needed to make quick repairs to protect homes and office buildings. Cash was donated to the American Red Cross tornado fund. Calls came in from around the world offering support (McEntire, 2002a, p. 374).

Similar findings were evident after a 2013 tornado in Moore, Oklahoma. Many of the donations were provided by the Red Cross and came from organizations and individuals around the country. Donations included food and "relief items" such as sunscreen and tarps in addition to services provided for health and overnight stays in shelters. After the 9/11 terrorist attacks in New York City, many of the donations were provided by the private sector. For example, a manager of a sporting goods store allowed first responders to use his store as a shelter when the buildings collapsed. The manager then provided swimming goggles and socks to equip responders so they could continue their lifesaving activities. The U.S. Forest Service received containers of coffee from Starbucks for personnel at the staging area near Ground Zero. Likewise, those responding to the terrorist attack dawned overalls and other protective equipment provided by various manufacturers. Respirators and mask cartridges were given to search and rescue teams to alleviate breathing problems created by fire, smoke, and unknown particulate matter.

Gloves, batteries, and other supplies were sent by private companies to help as well (McEntire et al., 2003, p. 452).

Other common donations sent to disaster areas include:

▲ Medicines
▲ Diapers
▲ Baby formula
▲ Coats
▲ Shampoo
▲ Soap
▲ Cots
▲ Sleeping bags
▲ Tents

### 7.2.1 Challenges Resulting from Donations

Donations can prove useful in time of need. However, people's generosity may present several challenges for those involved in disaster response and recovery. Some of the problems may be in regard to the quantity of donations. There are often too many donations. Clothing often falls into this category. An alternative situation is where there may be insufficient donations. For instance, there may be a limited number of generators to meet the high demand for electricity when power is out.

Other problems may result from the quality of the donations (McEntire, 1997). Most donations are not requested or needed. For instance, a pallet of dog food arrived in New York City after 9/11 for the canines involved in body recovery. Unfortunately, the search and rescue dogs have a regimented diet so the food was not used. Some donations are not helpful for other reasons. Medicines arriving at the scene of a disaster may have no labels, are damaged, or are expired. Other goods are not applicable to the disaster context. Coats are sent to warmer regions of the United States. Donations may not be culturally acceptable to some disaster victims. For instance, followers of certain religions may not eat certain types of food (e.g., pork or other meats). Ethnic groups may prefer their own cuisine rather than American food.

Excessive and unwanted donations frequently result in additional work for those involved in emergency management (Neal, 1994). Donations have to be transported from the donors to the disaster area. Donations also have to be stored until they can be given to disaster victims. After a flood in Southwest Texas, a relief organization had to rent a 25,000 square foot warehouse to store donations (Kim, 1999c). Donations also need to be sorted by type, size, purpose, etc. After a 1952 tornado in Arkansas, it took 500 volunteers two weeks to sort through donations to determine what could be used (Neal, 1994, p. 23).

Donations must finally be distributed to those in need. All of this results in incredible logistical challenges for emergency and relief workers. To illustrate these points, three important disaster case studies will be discussed: Hurricane Andrew, the Oklahoma City bombing, and the terrorist attacks of 9/11.

### 7.2.1.1 Hurricane Andrew

On August 24, 1992, a major hurricane struck South Florida. The category 4 hurricane, with sustained winds of at least 141 mph and a storm surge of up to 16 feet, pummeled Miami-Dade County. The hurricane left 170,000 homes in partial or complete ruin, resulting in 250,000 people being homeless. The storm killed over 40 people and injured hundreds more.

As the extent of the devastation was recognized, a massive donations campaign was undertaken. This proved to be problematic at times, however (Neal, 1994). People were encouraged to donate sustenance through food drives that were coordinated by local businesses such as grocery stores and television stations. As a result, too much food was donated and sent to Florida. The thousands of individual cans of food caused distribution, sorting, and cooking problems. Cans of food are difficult to distribute because they are often placed in small boxes without pallets. Then the boxes of food have to be shipped and eventually sorted into logical categories by mass kitchen cooks, which takes a considerable amount of time. Even the process of opening the cans takes valuable amounts of time away from other relief efforts. In disasters where the power is lost, each can has to be opened without the aid of electric can openers.

Whereas these food donations after Hurricane Andrew were useful but labor-intensive, other donations were not needed and may have been counterproductive. Many winter coats, for example, were donated, but they have little use by Miami residents. Other clothing was sent to Florida on trucks, but the drivers sometimes did not know where to deliver them. Under these circumstances, the drivers would dump them on the side of the road. The heat and the rain rotted the clothes, causing a potential health hazard. Volunteers and city workers had to remove the clothing that took time away from other recovery activities. Even when clothing got to its desired destination, some of it was dirty and had to be cleaned. Unfortunately, there was a lack of personnel, electricity, and water to clean them in a time-effective manner.

The management of donations in Hurricane Andrew also damaged public relations efforts. Neal's research reveals that "news reports and videos throughout the US showing rotting clothing, warehouses overflowing with supplies and bulging trucks full of donations being turned back, created two related images. Reports implied that further donations were not needed. This was not the case. Organizations needed money or specific donations (e.g. institutional-sized food) to assist victims. Images of city work crews or the military carting away rotting clothes could imply to viewers that organizations such as the Red Cross or Salvation Army did not appreciate the donations. Simultaneously, organizations continued to request donations (e.g., money)" (Neal, 1994, p. 27).

In time, the amount of donations quickly overwhelmed the ability of disaster organizations to deal with them. The Red Cross became so inundated with donations of goods and food that it began asking for cash-only contributions two weeks after the incident. The Salvation Army had originally requested diapers, food, and cash, but it also altered its request for financial donations. This option has since become popular among nonprofit organizations involved in disaster response and recovery operations. Cash limits sorting and storage issues, increases the speed of disaster assistance, and also supports the local market (because goods are purchased in and near the disaster-affected area). Those involved in emergency management must learn from the problems of and solutions to donations management after Hurricane Andrew.

### 7.2.1.2  Oklahoma City Bombing

On the morning of Wednesday, April 19, 1995, Timothy McVeigh used a 24 foot Ryder rental truck to deliver an ammonium nitrate and diesel fuel bomb to the Alfred P. Murrah Federal Building in Oklahoma City, Oklahoma. A detonation cord was used to set off the explosive mixture about the time he parked and left the vehicle in the drop-off/unloading zone near the structure. The resulting blast destroyed approximately 1/3 of the building. Major portions of the floors in the nine-story building crashed on top of one another as they fell to the ground. A pile of rubble and smoldering debris was left in its wake. Vehicles in the parking lot and in the street were flipped over and caught on fire. Several nearby buildings received heavy damages. Structural impact was extended over a 48 square block area.

The bomb also killed 168 people. Virtually all of the victims were working in or visiting the Murrah Building. However, some of the deaths occurred in surrounding buildings and 1 emergency worker died when debris fell on a nurse as she was responding to the incident. Out of those 168 people, 19 children were killed (the building had an on-site day care facility). This news especially affected people around the world.

As the responders worked to locate survivors, remove victims and process the crime scene, donations began to arrive in the area. Southwestern Bell donated the use of a "cellular-on-wheels" (COW) tower, with free-use phone to anyone responding to the incident. Voluntary organizations brought in food to feed emergency workers. The Oklahoma Department of Civil Emergency Management (ODCEM) noted how this took place:

> The Oklahoma Restaurant Association had just finished their annual conference when the explosion occurred. Subsequently, they quickly established a 24-hour food service operation, at the Myriad Convention Center, to feed all emergency response workers. Eventually, the Myriad was established as a center which met the needs of all personnel responding to the incident. (ODCEM, 1995, p. 8)

The ODCEM also observed that:

> Donated clothing, food, equipment and supplies were available on a 24-hour basis. Other volunteer and donated services included over-the-counter pharmaceutical and personal hygiene items, hair care, optometric, chiropractic, and podiatric care and massage therapy. AT&T provided free telephone calls home for the US&R Task Forces, complimented by a free mail and parcel delivery service provided by the United Parcel Service. (ODCEM, 1995, p. 8)

Several efforts were made to coordinate the reception and distribution of donations. The Red Cross made logistical arrangements for donations management from a nearby U.S. Post Office. The Red Cross also established a warehouse at a Coca-Cola plant for donations staging.

The government was also heavily involved in donations management. On April 22, FEMA sent a Donations Coordination Team to the Disaster Field Office. An In-Kind Donations Coordination Team was established at the Disaster Field Office and included representatives of FEMA, ODCEM, and voluntary organizations. The team's responsibilities were to:

▲ Process information provided by FEMA's toll-free donations hotline.
▲ Establish a single, coordinated, unmet needs list.
▲ Provide direct communication with the multiagency coordination center [MACC].
▲ Address the management of spontaneous volunteers.
▲ Provide a liaison to the local business community.
▲ Share information concerning warehouse space and current inventory (ODCEM, 1995, p. 13).

On April 25, Lt. Governor Mary Fallin participated in the Donations Coordination Team meeting. At this meeting, it is decided that there was no longer a need for mass quantities of goods, and a press release is issued accordingly. On April 26, 1995, a Donations Task Force was identified. Representatives to this task force were state personnel, federal officials, representatives from charities, and members of the local business community. The Donations Task Force was to address items needed by those affected by the blast. They also had to address items needed by individuals and organizations working within the blast area. The task force was not asked to try to meet the long-term needs of victims (ODCEM, 1995, p. 13).

On Saturday, May 6, 1995, the FEMA Donations Team started to return unused goods to original donors. By the middle of May, the donations distribution centers closed down, and an unmet needs committee was formed to deal with long-term disaster assistance issues (see Wedel and Baker, 1998). An **unmet needs committee** is a group of government leaders, concerned citizens, business representatives, and nonprofit organizations who join forces to help collect donations to address long-term needs of disaster victims.

The management of donations after the Oklahoma City bombing was regarded to be a successful operation. The responsiveness, teamwork, and caring incurred on the part of all first responders were a big factor. The American Red Cross and other voluntary organizations' responses were immediate. They continued to meet the needs of all those affected by disaster. Communication support from Cellular One, Southwestern Bell, was superb as they loaned equipment and donated services to the responders. Many officials indicated that city, county, state, and federal response procedures for this incident are a model for future response and recovery operations. Urban Search and Rescue Task Force members commented regularly that they had never been treated so well and that the care and compassion they received had become known as "The Oklahoma Standard" (ODCEM, 1995, p. 18).

In spite of the notable successes, there were a few areas where improvement was needed (ODCEM, 1995). Those dealing with the massive outpouring did not have an adequate plan in place to identify incoming resources. They could not effectively manage the initial staging area for donations during the first two days of the event. Furthermore, it did not appear that there were sufficient personnel to handle the donation challenges this disaster presented. Property accountability at the staging areas and donated goods accountability were virtually nonexistent during the major portion of the incident. In-kind donations management was nonexistent during the initial days of this incident. It was also difficult to send resources to the right place at the right time. Finally, there are complaints even today that not all of the relief has been distributed to the victims in need. Some feel that this is a major problem since so many years have passed since the incident occurred. You should anticipate these types of problems in most disasters.

### 7.2.1.3 9/11 Terrorist Attacks

As mentioned in Chapter 1, several teams of hijackers boarded planes on the morning of September 11, 2001, and began the largest and most coordinated terrorist attack on U.S. soil. An American airlines jet headed from Boston to Los Angeles was overtaken by men with box cutters and intentionally crashed into the north tower of the World Trade Center. A short time later, a United Airlines plane, also departing from Boston to Los Angeles, was hijacked and flown into the south tower at the World Trade Center. A third flight went down in Pennsylvania, with the passengers wrestling control away from the hijackers. A fourth plane hit the Pentagon.

Within minutes, hundreds of people perished. The resulting fires spread throughout the Twin Towers in New York. The massive structures weaken and collapse to the ground and spread fire to other buildings in the area. As the dust settles, the carnage was broadcast on all news networks. World Trade Center employees, firefighters, police officers, and spontaneous volunteers were killed by the hijackings, crashes, fires, and structural failures. Destruction, injury, and death were also seen in Pennsylvania and Virginia (where planes were flown into the ground or the Pentagon).

People we stunned that anyone would desire to perform such a deadly act, and their hearts turned to the heroic efforts of emergency workers and those who have lost loved ones. Over the next few days and months, a large and diverse collection of donations arrived into the area from around the nation and world. The donations included:

▲ A massive blood drive in New York and around the United States for the injured
▲ Food and drinks provided to thousands of emergency personnel
▲ Gear and equipment for search and rescue teams
▲ Computers, phones, fax machines, and other office supplies are given to the new EOC in New York (as the established center was destroyed in the collapse)
▲ Fire apparatus, heavy equipment, and cranes are sent to replace losses or help with debris removal

Recognizing the enormous loss of life and resulting expenses in terms of medical care, funeral costs, and future needs of surviving spouses and children, the American Red Cross welcomed and encouraged financial contributions via cash, check, and credit card donations. The response to the American Red Cross and other charities was overwhelming. According to the Ford Foundation, 58% of all Americans contributed to a fund for the 9/11 victims. By October 31, 2001, donations to the American Red Cross totaled over $543 million. The Red Cross was so overwhelmed that it stopped asking for donations. However, people in the United States and around the world kept giving. By June 2002, an additional $424 million was sent to the Red Cross. Thus, there was a total of $1.3 billion for the victims of the 9/11 disasters. This pool of money became known as the "Liberty Fund."

While this large sum of money rolled in, the Red Cross decided to keep some of the donations as a reserve fund for future disasters. Dr. Bernadine Healy, the chief executive officer of the American Red Cross, announced plans to retain $200 million for potential future terrorist attacks and other disasters. In some ways, the strategy made sense (Harbaugh, 2001). Any potential division of the Liberty Fund would undoubtedly ensure that victims in New York would receive a much larger allotment in comparison to those affected by other disasters. For example, the victims of the U.S. Embassy bombings in Tanzania and Kenya did not receive anything close to the amount of money the 9/11 survivors did; nor did the survivors of the Oklahoma City bombing. Also, resources are always tight for this disaster relief organization. A reserve "rainy day" fund could ensure operations well into the future and help thousands of people in need.

Nonetheless, there was an immediate outcry regarding the decision of the Red Cross. The media quickly publicized the organization's position about the donations. Donors and victims decried the plan as a misuse of funds. They insisted that the decision be reversed. Lawmakers also criticized the misleading of donors and requested that all of the funds be used for the victims of 9/11.

Because of the negative press and pressure to utilize the funds as intended by the donors, the Red Cross immediately changed its position. It promised to spend half of the funds on cash grants for the affected families by December 31, 2001. In particular, the Red Cross would cover up to one year's worth of living expenses for those in need. The remaining funds would be used to hire 200 caseworkers to assist the disaster victims and their surviving families. The Red Cross also agreed to develop a database with other charitable organizations to oversee the distribution of all of the remaining money.

The American Red Cross learned a difficult lesson from the experience. Under significant public scrutiny, Dr. Healy resigned her leadership position. The agency was accused of "using the September 11 tragedies to address long-term fund-raising goals and of siphoning tens of millions of dollars from widows and children" (Henriques and Barstow, 2001). The reputation of the American Red Cross had been tarnished. This resulted in fund-raising problems for several months after the 9/11 disasters. The Red Cross realized that it had to be upfront with its intentions to use donations and make sure that its plans were in conformity with public opinion.

### 7.2.2 Recommendations for Donations Management

As can be seen, donations are not always easy to deal with when a disaster occurs. For this reason, you will need to give extra attention to donations management. **Donations management** is the receipt, sorting, storing, and distribution of goods and monies for the benefit of victims in response and recovery operations. One of the best ways to increase the chance of a successful donations management campaign is to conduct a very thorough needs assessment so that your requests for donations will be accurate. A **needs assessment** is an evaluation of what supplies or services are required in the aftermath of a disaster. Such assessments will help you to request those items that will be most beneficial. The U.S. Army Corps of Engineers has models of what will be needed in the way of water and food after hurricanes of various sizes. The model also discusses how to set up distribution sites, which can help streamline relief operations after disasters (see http://www.englink.usace.army.mil/igp/commodities.htm).

Another major recommendation is to expect and be prepared to deal with massive quantities of both requested and unrequested donations. You will probably get most of what you ask for and even more when you work through the media. The best thing you can do is avoid asking for too many in-kind donations. Cash donations are preferred instead because they allow the most flexibility and can permit you to purchase needed resources locally (and thereby rebuild the affected economy):

▲ **In-kind donations** are physical items such as supplies, equipment, food, etc (Figure 7-4).

▲ **Cash donations** are financial contributions to disaster organizations or the victims themselves.

**Figure 7-4**

In-kind donations may require a great deal of logistical support including large warehouses, sorting, and shipping as was the case after a tornado struck Smithville, MS, in 2011. Howard Greenblatt/FEMA.

It is also vital that you ensure that donors know and agree with your plans for donations. This will help you avoid the public relations problems that confronted the American Red Cross after the 9/11 terrorist attacks.

One of the most important steps is to work closely with the nonprofit sector. They often have unique skills and knowledge to deal with in-kind or monetary donations. Businesses may also provide supplies and equipment in bulk, thereby eliminating the need to seek donations from the general public. Regardless of who you are working with, be sure to hold meetings to coordinate the receipt, storage, distribution, disposal, or return of donations. These can include regular gatherings at warehouses or EOCs or among local, state, and federal donations committees.

It is also advisable that you have forms or computer programs to track donation needs, donor contact information, donation quantities, drop-off/pickup locations, etc. Having adequately trained individuals to receive phone inquiries will also be of great assistance. Make sure they can create shipping agreements, locate storage facilities, operate fort lifts, organize warehouses, etc. It is imperative that donations get to the right place, at the right time, and in the right quantities. Logistical skills are highly coveted by those who are working in donations management (see Chapter 10 for additional information about logistics). If you are involved in donations management, you must pay attention to these types of detail.

## FOR EXAMPLE

### 9/11 Donations from around the World

The 9/11 terrorist attacks touched people in every corner of the word. Even the Masai tribe in Kenya donated 14 cows to the victims in New York. This seems like a strange donation, but cows are among the most cherished possessions for the people of Masai as they are regarded to be sacred animals. The American government initially rejected the donation, not knowing what to do with 14 cows. They later formed a plan and accepted the cows. They were shipped to the Bronx Zoo, where they can be viewed and enjoyed by adults and children alike. This situation was certainly unusual, but emergency managers should always expect the unexpected.

## SELF-CHECK

- Why are so many donations sent to the site of a disaster?
- What donations are likely to be given in a disaster?
- Why do donations create problems for emergency managers?
- What lessons are learned from case studies on donations?
- What is donations management and how can it be performed successfully?

## 7.3 Volunteer Management

As an emergency manager, you must expect that people want to donate their time and services when a disaster occurs. Ordinary citizens become involved in postdisaster operations to assist you, first responders, and victims. As with donations, there are many positive outcomes. There are also challenges associated with the incorporation of volunteers in disaster response and recovery operations. This process of including volunteers in postdisaster operations in such a way as to harness their contributions and avoid their negative impact is known as **volunteer management**.

When a disaster strikes, there will likely be hundreds, if not thousands, of people rushing to the scene to assist in response and recovery activities. Some of these people are referred to as spontaneous or unaffiliated volunteers. **Spontaneous or unaffiliated volunteers** are people that engage in response and recovery efforts with no thought of payment; their efforts are directed toward the benefit of victims, first responders, emergency managers, and the community at large (Lowe and Fothergill, 2003). Such volunteers may have specific skills that can be extremely useful in response and recovery operations. For example, policemen, doctors, translators, and counselors all rushed to the World Trade Center to help after the terrorist attacks. These professionals had specific knowledge and abilities that could be utilized immediately. Others may not possess skills that can be used in disaster operations, but they still have a desire to help nonetheless. Most of these people will come from the impacted or surrounding areas. Other individuals and groups may not be residents of the area. For instance, even celebrities such as Sean Penn, Jamie Foxx, John Travolta, and Harry Connick Jr. arrived at the scene of Hurricane Katrina to bring attention to the plight of victims.

There are also large numbers of volunteers who are affiliated with organizations such as the Red Cross, the Salvation Army, and faith-based organizations. Volunteers who are affiliated with these organizations may have common characteristics, may have been involved in postdisaster operations before, and may become involved in all aspects of postdisaster operations. For instance, many will be women or retired persons. Perhaps these individuals worked with a disaster, charitable, or faith-based organization in the past. Such volunteers help firefighters, public officials, and disaster victims in various response and recovery functions.

Regardless of their background and activities, volunteers have a strong desire to assist in the response and recovery effort. For instance, regarding the 9/11 terrorist attacks, scholars discovered:

…87% of Americans thought it was the "most tragic event in their lifetime" (Kendra and Wachtendorf, 2003, p. 98).

…Volunteers were emotionally impacted by the disaster and personalized the attacks as members of the community affected, which appeared to have contributed to their heightened feelings of victimization. Many of them explained that when they saw the destruction they knew that they had to do something—they needed to help (Lowe and Fothergill, 2003, p. 298).

…the primary motivation for volunteering was a compelling need to help in some way, particularly a need to assist victims, and a desire—even obsession—to "do something" in order to contribute something positive and find something meaningful in the midst of disaster characterized by cruelty and terror (Lowe and Fothergill, 2003, p. 298).

Therefore, volunteering gives ordinary citizens a sense of "interconnection, healing, and empowerment" after a disaster (Lowe and Fothergill, 2003, p. 303).

Significant advantages may result from the integration of volunteers into disaster response and recovery operations. Volunteers can fulfill many functions after a disaster. Here is a partial list that shows the variety of tasks volunteers have participated in in the past disasters:

- ▲ Sandbagging in case of flooding
- ▲ Cleaning up the scene
- ▲ Staffing shelters
- ▲ Keeping records of who is in shelters
- ▲ Handing out water and other supplies to victims
- ▲ Providing healthcare services
- ▲ Counseling victims
- ▲ Preparing food
- ▲ Making beds for emergency workers
- ▲ Setting up websites
- ▲ Working with affected businesses to help them resume activity
- ▲ Work with collection drives
- ▲ Sorting donations

Volunteers are thus crucial to any disaster response and recovery operation. FEMA said this about volunteers: they are involved in all phases of disasters, first to arrive and last to leave (Figure 7-5); are trusted by the public; are community based, flexible, innovative, and resourceful; and complement government services (FEMA, 1999d, pp. 1.5–1.8).

### 7.3.1 Difficulties Associated with Volunteers

As noted previously, volunteers can be very helpful to you as well as victims, first responders, and the community as a whole. However, volunteers are not without potential drawbacks. The challenges they bring to response and recovery operations include:

- ▲ **Lack of skills**. Volunteers may lack the necessary training or skills that are needed for a particular disaster. Some may be willing to help, but they may not be able to operate heavy equipment, drive donations to warehouses, or perform data entry on distinct types of computer programs.
- ▲ **Number**. The sheer number of volunteers can be overwhelming to manage. For example, two and a half weeks after 9/11, the Red Cross had 22,000 people volunteer (Lowe and Fothergill, 2003, p. 294). Each volunteer may be required to complete an application that has to be reviewed and matched up with the needs. Processing the quantity of applications takes a lot of human resources.
- ▲ **Safety**. As with the media, volunteers create additional concerns about safety. Volunteers can put themselves in danger, especially if they rush to

Figure 7-5

Volunteers, including these individuals helping to prevent flooding in
North Sioux City, SD, provide valuable assistance in the time
of disaster. Jeannie Mooney/FEMA.

a site of a disaster immediately. A volunteer could also claim to have skills
that he or she does not have and thereby put the victims at risk. Also, a
terrorist could pose as a volunteer and kill more people when given access
to the scene of an attack or the staging area.

▲ **Frustration**. Volunteers often get frustrated if they cannot help. Part of this
may be due to their lack of skills, their excessive numbers, or restrictions
based on safety concerns. Volunteers become offended if they see a need,
are willing to sacrifice their time, and cannot be successfully incorporated
into the response process. Volunteers may then complain to the media
about their skills not being used, and this will cause poor public relations.
Also, in New York after 9/11, "the spontaneous volunteers ... described
frustrations of long lines, uncoordinated leadership, disorganized lists, and
unclear information about what to do immediately after the attacks" (Lowe
and Fothergill, 2003, p. 300). In some cases, volunteers cut in line or
walked into relief centers without authorization because they didn't want to
wait and they knew their translation skills were needed (Lowe and
Fothergill, 2003, p. 301). Even if volunteers are incorporated into the
response process, they may not be given sufficient direction or supervision.
This can further exacerbate a feeling of frustration on their part or for you
as an emergency manager.

**Figure 7-6**

Giving instructions to volunteers is a great way to ensure safe
and effective relief operations. George Armstrong/FEMA.

### 7.3.2 Strategies for Volunteer Management

The problems associated with volunteers are challenging but not insurmountable. Lisa Orloff (2011), a well-known expert on this subject, has asserted that there are many things you can do to increase the chances for successful volunteer management before and after a disaster. For instance, you should ensure that volunteers are adequately trained for the role they will be fulfilling (Figure 7-6). You must consider the potential liabilities associated with volunteers along with their emotional and physical well-being during response and recovery operations. You must ensure that their shift time is strictly enforced and that they have proper supervision and oversight. In addition to these recommendations for volunteer management, you will specifically need to rely on the expertise of nonprofit organizations, register and care for volunteers, match their skills with disaster needs, and evaluate your progress (Figure 7-7).

### 7.3.2.1 Rely on the Expertise of Nonprofit Organizations and Others

When a disaster occurs, it is important that you work closely with potential partners and volunteer sources. These partners may include your local Red Cross and Salvation Army chapters, churches, the medical staff at hospitals, and other local nonprofit organizations. You should harness their extensive experience in volunteer management, determine what capabilities they have, and identify what skill sets their volunteers offer. You can also create a public campaign with your partners and let citizens know what you may need in terms of volunteers. You will also want to communicate with the media to notify them about the measures that volunteers

Figure 7-7

A leader is seen here sharing important knowledge to those involved
in disaster operations. Mark Wolfe/FEMA.

can take to help you and the disaster victims and to thank them for their service. If used correctly, the media can be another great asset for volunteer management.

### 7.3.2.2 Register and Care for Volunteers

In order to manage volunteers successfully, you will need to implement a logical process to incorporate them into the response and recovery process. You should consider setting up a toll-free, dedicated line for volunteers to call in and inquire about what they can do to help. You will also want to set up a volunteer reception center that is visible, accessible, and close to the disaster site. This on-site registration center should be staffed by experienced employees or volunteers. It may therefore be wise to set up a volunteer coordination team to help the volunteers through the process of registration. During registration, you will want to screen volunteers to learn about their potential contributions and ensure you don't have any criminals take advantage of the situation (e.g., put a sexual offender in charge of a child's day care group). The database of volunteers you create can be used in response and recovery operations as well as in other disasters. If needed, you should provide mental health counseling or healthcare services to volunteers participating in response and recovery operations. You may also need to provide them food, water, and even shelter if that is required.

### 7.3.2.3 Match Their Skills with Disaster Needs

Be sure you develop key documents that include all instructions for volunteers as well as policies and procedures they should follow. The Volunteer Management

Committee recommends that you "develop streamlined registration, screening, and interviewing procedures for unaffiliated volunteers that include: databases that catalogs needed skills, information about individual volunteers (for example: skills, interests, availability, geographic location), contact information for voluntary organizations, tasks, roles and time commitment requirements for individuals and groups of volunteers, approximate number of volunteers needed to perform tasks, compatibility of relevant computer systems, back-up plan for power failures and portability" (2003, p. 7). Such documents can help you match the skills of volunteers to the needs made evident in the disaster. For instance, if a volunteer has work experience in warehouse management, this individual could help with sorting, storing, and shipping donations. Or, if someone is a professional chef, this person could help with cooking.

### 7.3.2.4 Evaluate Your Progress

As with donations management, you will want to review volunteer activities periodically and determine what is being done correctly and what could be improved upon. Be sure to use feedback from organizations and volunteers as they might have special insight into what is taking place. While managing volunteers, you will want to document all important facts about them. For example, you will want to record how many volunteers you had, how many hours they served, and what functions they performed and then assign some kind of dollar figure as to the value of services provided by volunteers. This is especially important as there is a chance your community might be reimbursed for such activities under federal disaster assistance programs. When postdisaster operations conclude, you will also want to write up an after-action report. An **after-action report** is a document that describes what went right and what adjustments you will need to make in the future. It may be useful for volunteer management or any other function after a disaster.

### 7.3.3 Advantages of Volunteer Management

If you are able to manage volunteers effectively, your community will receive many benefits. The Points of Light Foundation has recognized numerous advantages of effective disaster volunteer management. For instance:

> First responders can fulfill their duties without the added responsibility of managing volunteers.
>
> Experienced volunteer coordinators can manage volunteers, to ensure meaningful and quality experiences. As a result, volunteers are more inclined to seek future community service opportunities …
>
> Communities will know how to effectively engage citizens as volunteers in all phases of disasters.
>
> Communities can respond to and heal from disasters more effectively when volunteer efforts are well managed. (Points of Light, 2002, p. 4)

For these and other reasons, "our society can ill afford to ignore the potential capacity of its citizens to help improve conditions in their communities, especially in times of disaster" (Points of Light, 2002, p. 3).

## FOR EXAMPLE

### Red Cross and Hurricane Katrina

The American Red Cross worked closely with thousands of volunteers after Hurricane Katrina. Although the Red Cross was criticized for not meeting the needs of people in a timely manner, the Red Cross had to screen and train thousands of volunteers. It also processed 35,000 requests for aid per day. Here are some additional statistics regarding the services they provided:

▲ Estimated number of Hurricane Katrina victims dispersed across the country: 750,000

▲ Number of surviving families provided Red Cross financial assistance: 929,000

▲ Number of Red Cross shelters open to hurricane victims: 1,150

▲ Number of hurricane victims still provided Red Cross housing at shelters and hotels: 483,000

▲ Amount paid out in Red Cross emergency financial assistance to hurricane survivors: $854 million

▲ Amount Red Cross has spent to date on Hurricane Katrina relief efforts: $1.3 billion

▲ Amount in gifts and pledges received by the Red Cross for hurricane relief: $1.1 billion

▲ Amount the Red Cross expects to need for hurricane relief efforts: $2 billion

▲ Number of Red Cross relief workers mobilized in response to Hurricane Katrina: 177,600

▲ Estimated number of people left homeless in Hancock County, Miss., due to Hurricane Katrina: 30,000 (source: Hancock County Emergency Operations Center)

▲ Population of Hancock County, Miss.: 46,000 (source: U.S. Census Bureau)

Source: The American Red Cross, except as noted; all data as of Oct. 5, 2005.

## SELF-CHECK

- Why are people willing to serve after a disaster?
- What is volunteer management?
- Do volunteers pose any problems in emergency management?
- What recommendations can help with volunteer management?
- What are the benefits of integrating volunteers into response and recovery operations?

# SUMMARY

After a disaster, you will be faced with many challenges. The media will arrive to report on the disaster, and they will want to interview you and others in your community. Citizens and organizations will send tons of donations, which you will have to sort and distribute. Thousands of volunteers will arrive at the disaster to offer their services, and they expect to be put to work. By doing your best to manage public information, donations, and volunteers, you will increase the effectiveness of response and speed of recovery. These steps are keys to resilience.

# KEY TERMS

| | |
|---|---|
| **After-action report** | A document that describes what went right and what adjustments you will need to make in the future. |
| **Cash donations** | Financial contributions to disaster organizations or the victims themselves. |
| **Donations management** | The receipt, sorting, storing, and distribution of goods and monies for the benefit of victims during response and recovery operations. |
| **In-kind donations** | Physical items such as supplies, equipment, food, etc. |
| **Media** | People and news organizations that provide information about disasters to the public. |
| **Needs assessment** | An evaluation of what supplies or services are required in the aftermath of a disaster. |
| **Public information officers** | Members of a department that have special skills in dealing with the media. |
| **Spontaneous or unaffiliated volunteers** | People that engage in response and recovery efforts with no thought of payment; their efforts are directed toward the benefit of victims, first responders, emergency managers, and the community at large. |
| **Unmet needs committee** | A group of government leaders, concerned citizens, business representatives, and nonprofit organizations who join forces to help collect donations to address long-term needs of disaster victims. |
| **Volunteer management** | The process of including volunteers in postdisaster operations in such a way as to harness their contributions and avoid their negative impact. |

# ASSESS YOUR UNDERSTANDING

Posttest to evaluate your knowledge on managing public relations, donations, and volunteers.

*Measure your learning by comparing pretest and posttest results.*

## Summary Questions

1. The media includes reporters, camera operators, and news anchors that provide information to the public. True or false?
2. The local media will focus more than other media on what the president does after a disaster? True or false?
3. The media tends to react to most disasters in the same way. True or false?
4. The media is always sensitive to disaster victims. True or false?
5. It is vital that you know your audience and media market. True or false?
6. People donate supplies because they are eager to help those affected by a disaster. True or false?
7. Baby formula and coats are atypical disaster donations. True or false?
8. The donation of clothing caused major problems after Hurricane Andrew. True or false?
9. Donations management was fairly successful in Oklahoma after the bombing of the Murrah Building. True or false?
10. It is generally advisable that people donate cash instead of in-kind supplies. True or false?
11. Spontaneous volunteers are always related to nonprofit organizations such as the Red Cross. True or false?
12. Volunteers can help with sandbagging but not with food preparation. True or false?
13. Some volunteers may not have skills that can be utilized after a disaster. True or false?
14. In order to manage volunteers successfully, you will need to match their skills with the needs made evident in the disaster. True or false?
15. Television coverage of disasters is most likely to include:
    (a) Interviews only
    (a) Extensive examination of the issues all of the time
    (b) Footage of the disaster scene and what people are doing as a result
    (c) Insights from reporters but not the comments of politicians
    (d) None of the above
16. According to Payne (1994), what are common problems created by the media?
    (a) Intrusive manner
    (a) Lack of sensitivity
    (b) Uncooperative attitude
    (c) Inaccurate reporting
    (d) All of the above

17. As an emergency manager, you should know that the media might:
    (a) Create safety problems for themselves and others
    (a) Fully understand technical information
    (b) Underestimate impact almost all of the time
    (c) Improve your agency's reputation in most cases
    (d) All of the above

18. It is ok to tell the media:
    (a) I don't know.
    (a) I don't know, but I'll find out for you as soon as I can.
    (b) I won't comment on that.
    (c) That is off the record.
    (d) Answers c and d.

19. After disasters, people have donated:
    (a) Vehicles
    (a) Canned drinking water
    (b) Diapers
    (c) All of the above
    (d) Answers b and c only

20. The goal of an unmet needs committee is to:
    (a) Collect donations and address long-term needs of disaster victims.
    (a) Find volunteers to offer crisis counseling only.
    (b) Assist with media relations.
    (c) Assess hazards and their potential impact.
    (d) Warn people of impending hazards.

21. The money raised after the 9/11 terrorist attack was known as:
    (a) The Victims' Account
    (a) The WTC Memorial
    (b) The Freedom Fund
    (c) The Liberty Fund
    (d) The Mutual Fund

22. Supplies, equipment, and food are known best as:
    (a) In-kind donations
    (a) Cash donations
    (b) Donations management
    (c) Disaster relief
    (d) Recovery functions

23. Affiliated volunteers might be associated with:
    (a) The American Red Cross
    (a) The Salvation Army
    (b) Churches
    (c) Nonprofit organizations
    (d) All of the above

24. Difficulties associated with managing volunteers include:
    (a) Too many useful skills
    (a) Their large numbers
    (b) Safety
    (c) Answers b and c
    (d) None of the above
25. When managing volunteers, it is advisable that you:
    (a) Rely on the expertise of nonprofit organizations
    (a) Register and care for victims
    (b) Ignore their skills and put them to work anywhere
    (c) Answers a and b
    (d) Answers b and c

## Review Questions

1. Is the media a friend or foe for the emergency manager?
2. What types of media exist in your community and what do they want?
3. How do the media operate in time of a disaster?
4. What challenges do the media create challenges for the emergency manager?
5. How can you improve public relations in time of disaster?
6. Why do people donate goods and supplies after a disaster?
7. What are common challenges associated with donations?
8. What does 9/11 teach us about donations management?
9. What is a needs assessment?
10. Why are cash donations often preferred over in-kind donations?
11. What is volunteer management?
12. Why did people want to volunteer after the 9/11 terrorist attacks?
13. Do volunteers become frustrated after disasters? Why or why not?
14. What steps can you take to manage volunteers effectively?

## Applying This Chapter

1. On Saturday, September 13, a tropical depression developed in the Atlantic Ocean—nearly 2,000 miles away from the southeastern shores of the United States. Meteorologists at the National Hurricane Center assert that it is far too early to determine the path of this weather system. You know that it will be vital to get information to the public so they can respond effectively. What steps do you take to handle the media? How will you use the media after the hurricane makes landfall?
2. A school has just burnt down in your community. The school district has found a temporary location to hold classes. They need desks and other school supplies. You have been assigned to relay these needs to the media. What concerns do you have? How can you overcome them?

3. You are the emergency manager for a town that just suffered an industrial explosion. The event killed less than 60 people and destroyed many homes and businesses. People are suffering from PTSD and there is a great deal of debris in the roads. What are some of your immediate needs and what skills are you looking for in volunteers?

4. A volcano has erupted in Alaska. It has left a great deal of mud and ash on roads. People in the continental United States are sending you canned food, brooms, gloves, lawn mowers, and heavy equipment. Volunteers have arrived to help. What of these items are useful to you? How can you avoid getting unwanted items? Can the volunteers help you? How would you put them to work?

# YOU TRY IT

## Managing the Media

Divide up into groups of 5 students each. Discuss the following scenario: On Thursday, September 18, the tropic depression is upgraded to a hurricane with sustained winds of more than 82 mph. The location of the storm is 13.0° north and 45.4° east. It continues to travel westward at about 23 mph. Forecasters are still unable to predict the destination of Hurricane Casey. Leaders in Hollywood, Florida, decide to put the emergency operations center on alert. Be sure to identify what questions you should be prepared to answer from the media. Also mention how you might answer them effectively.

## Donating Equipment and Supplies

You work for home depot. A tornado has just ripped through your community, leaving many homes exposed to the elements. What donations could your company provide to help disaster victims? Are there donations that might not be needed? How can you find out what donations are useful and what ones are not?

## Handling Donations

You are the director of the Red Cross. A bomb has just been detonated in St. Louis. It has killed at least 250 people and injured many others at the movie theater. People are starting to donate medical supplies, caskets, and money. What can you do to make sure you help disaster victims? What should you do to avoid offending donors?

## Registering Volunteers

You are the leader of the most important nonprofit organization in your community. A train has derailed outside of your jurisdiction and the passengers who did not sustain major injuries need a place to stay for the night. You will need to open a shelter for approximately 75 people. How can you ensure you have people who can help set up the shelter? Provide food? Provide security? Address the needs of infants and children?

# 8

# MOVING BEYOND IMMEDIATE NEEDS
## Damage Assessment, Disaster Declarations, and Debris Removal

## Starting Point

Pretest to assess your knowledge on additional functions including damage assessment, disaster declarations, and debris removal.
*Determine where you need to concentrate your effort.*

## What You'll Learn in This Chapter

- ▲ The importance of damage assessment
- ▲ Challenges of assessing damages
- ▲ Procedures for conducting damage assessment
- ▲ The benefit of federal disaster declarations
- ▲ The difficulty of dealing with disaster debris
- ▲ Methods and regulations to manage debris effectively
- ▲ Regulations governing debris management

## After Studying This Chapter, You'll Be Able To

- ▲ Compare the different types of damage assessments.
- ▲ Categorize the distinct methods for assessing damages after a disaster.
- ▲ Examine ways to protect those involved in damage assessment.
- ▲ Initiate the process for seeking federal disaster declarations.
- ▲ Explain why debris management is so important after a disaster.
- ▲ Understand the types of debris produced in disasters.
- ▲ Illustrate the steps that can be taken to manage debris effectively.

## Goals and Outcomes

- ▲ Predict typical challenges facing those assessing damages.
- ▲ Formulate damage assessments successfully and safely.

*Disaster Response and Recovery: Strategies and Tactics for Resilience*, Second Edition. David A. McEntire.
© 2015 John Wiley & Sons, Inc. Published 2015 by John Wiley & Sons, Inc.

▲ Assess the importance of federal disaster declarations for disaster recovery.

▲ Request a federal disaster declaration.

▲ Declare how to deal with debris management problems.

▲ Manage debris operations in accordance with federal regulations.

# INTRODUCTION

To promote disaster resilience, you will have to address not only immediate response needs but begin to think about recovery issues. One of the most important things you must do is to assess the damages disasters leave behind. You must overcome the challenges of completing damage assessments and follow procedures meticulously to determine the impact of the event in an accurate manner. Knowing the extent of the impact will then determine if you should declare a disaster at the local and state levels and seek outside assistance from the federal government. Besides understanding how federal declarations take place, you should also comprehend the incredible challenges presented by disaster debris. You must anticipate similar and distinct types of debris in various disasters and consider ways to remove debris quickly and efficiently. Assessing damages, declaring disasters, and removing debris are vital if you are to start on the road to recovery.

## 8.1 Assessing Damages

As an emergency manager, your actions are guided in large measure by the damages and impact of disasters. Therefore, one of the most important functions to be performed during response and recovery operations is damage assessment (Figure 8-1). **Damage assessment** is a process of identifying the extent of destruction, including individual impact as well as overall economic losses in the community. Damage assessment helps to steer response activities and facilitates the acquisition of outside disaster assistance (McEntire, 2002a; McEntire and Cope, 2004). Damage assessment begins immediately after a disaster and even continues into long-term recovery operations. This function:

▲ **Helps identify the immediate needs of disaster victims**. For example, postdisaster evaluations may reveal that victims require emergency medical care or sheltering.

▲ **Influences what material and financial resources will be sent to the disaster area**. Through damage assessments, first responders, emergency managers, and recovery personnel may identify where sandbags are needed and influence where activities should be concentrated.

▲ **Is necessary before federal relief is to be given to disaster-stricken communities**. Without damage assessments, outside assistance will be limited and unwarranted.

▲ **Determines if a structure is habitable**. For example, damage assessments determine if victims can return to their homes. Residences may look safe but could in reality be structurally unsound.

▲ **May assist in the designation of hazardous areas**. Damage assessment may assist in the identification of factors such as poor construction that augment disaster vulnerability.

In short, "after disasters, the damage assessment process is fundamental to relief and reconstruction as it triggers the beginning of formalized disaster relief and recovery aid, beginning with governmental disaster declarations" (Oaks, 1990, p. 6).

Figure 8-1

Federal, state, and local emergency management officials will inspect damages
as was the case after a 7.2 magnitude earthquake in Calexico, CA, that occurred on
June 14, 2010. Adam DuBrowa/FEMA.

> ## FOR EXAMPLE
>
> ### Additional Information on Damage Assessment
>
> If your community was affected by a major earthquake, you would need to assess damages immediately. Should you be unfamiliar with the nature of this function, you should seek recommendations from experts who have knowledge in this area. Useful documents on damage assessment can be ordered from the Applied Technology Council at https://www.atcouncil.org/. Engineers and economists may also provide valuable information about how to conduct damage assessments.

### 8.1.1  Types of Damage Assessment

Not all damage assessments are the same. There are three basic types of damage assessments. These are known as rapid, preliminary, and technical damage assessments.

▲ A **rapid assessment** is the initial survey of the disaster damages.

▲ A **preliminary assessment** is a detailed assessment that is required if federal disaster assistance is sought.

▲ A **technical assessment** is used to determine the cost damages and method for rebuilding structures or the infrastructure.

A rapid or initial assessment is conducted immediately by city personnel and others (e.g., Red Cross) when a disaster occurs. The purpose of a rapid evaluation is to gain quick comprehension of deaths, injuries, victim needs, and general scope of the disaster. It is worth noting that rapid evaluations can be widely inaccurate. For example, the deaths resulting from the 9/11 terrorist attacks were significantly lower than first feared. Nevertheless, rapid damage assessments play a vital role in getting additional resources for the affected community. This may include securing mutual aid agreements from neighboring jurisdictions or requesting additional damage evaluators from nearby areas. When a Missouri levee broke in multiple places along the flooded Black River, a rapid evaluation caused officials to evacuate and shelter thousands of victims.

A preliminary damage assessment (PDA) is performed by governmental officials within days or weeks after the disaster. The goal of this type of evaluation is to determine the extent of the disaster and the need for outside assistance. It is required before a disaster can be declared by the president and federal disaster assistance is made available to your jurisdiction. In obvious cases where federal assets are warranted, the declaration can precede the disaster. However, this type of damage assessment must still be performed as soon as possible to comply with laws and justify expenses.

A technical or engineering assessment is performed days, weeks, or months after the disaster. The goal of this evaluation is to determine the exact value of losses and identify what will be needed for rebuilding. This type of assessment is conducted by engineers, insurance agents, and Federal Emergency Management Agency (FEMA) employees and contractors. It is a necessary step if buildings are to be repaired or completely rebuilt.

In summary, "a rapid or initial damage assessment is undertaken to quickly comprehend the scope of the devastation. This usually involves the collection of

---

**FOR EXAMPLE**

**Assessments after a Disaster**

Each of the different types of damage assessment was employed after the March 28, 2000, tornado in Fort Worth, Texas. Immediately after the tornado struck the downtown area, city personnel in the field immediately reported back to the emergency operations center about the extent of the damages. The American Red Cross, businesses, emergency managers, and the engineering department undertook a more extensive survey of damages and shared findings with FEMA in order to receive a presidential declaration. Engineers and other damage assessment experts worked for insurance companies and FEMA to appraise the value of losses, cut checks, and initiate repair work.

---

data regarding deaths and injuries as well as the number of buildings destroyed or partially damaged. A preliminary damage assessment (PDA) is completed with state and federal emergency management officials for the purpose of obtaining a presidential disaster declaration. This assessment examines the extent of losses and determines the status of property in terms of safety, sanitation and security concerns. A technical damage assessment is performed on structures and infra-structure to view engineering in an in-depth manner. It is conducted to estimate or verify the costs of the disaster and recommend the best approach for repairs, demolition and reconstruction" (McEntire 2002b, p. 9).

### 8.1.2 Methods of Conducting Damage Assessment

After a disaster, you will assess damages in different ways (McEntire, 2002b; McEntire and Cope, 2004). There are three common methods for conducting damage assessments. They are known as windshield, aerial, and walkthrough assessments. Each is common in major disasters.

**Windshield or drive-through assessments** are performed immediately after a disaster and are completed without leaving the vehicle. This assessment allows you to gain a visual of the damages on the ground and from a distance. It is useful in the initial stages of a disaster to determine response priorities and needs. However, sometimes, the debris or water in the roadway may make this type of assessment impossible to conduct.

**Aerial assessments** are conducted in helicopters or planes. The aerial assessment is especially useful when roads are impassible. The footage of aerial assessments is often shown by the media (e.g., the damage caused by hurricanes or earthquakes on the nightly news). As an example, after Hurricane Katrina, President Bush first surveyed the damage from Air Force One as he was flying over the area on a trip from California to Washington, D.C. This method of assessment is popular among politicians and key decision makers as it gives them a broad understanding of the scope of the disaster.

**Walkthrough, or site visits,** are tours of the damaged areas by foot. The walk-through helps determine the amount and type of disaster assistance households, businesses, and the government will need. This method of assessment may require knowledge about demolition and construction (Figure 8-2). "...The technical

## SELF-CHECK

- What is damage assessment?
- What benefits result from assessing damages?
- What are the different types of damage assessment?
- What methods are used to assess damages?

Figure 8-2

Walkthrough assessments, similar to this one after the 1994 Northridge earthquake in Southern California, may be required to understand the exact extent of damages. Andrea Booher/FEMA.

assessment may include a site visit to the affected home, business, road, school or other public building. It is used to verify damage and fill out extensive reports about losses and/or needed repairs (McEntire, 2002b, p. 9)."

## 8.2 Challenges in Damage Assessment

There are several problems or difficulties you will face when involved in damage assessment (McEntire and Cope, 2004). These include accuracy, working with others, and access and safety.

### 8.2.1 Accuracy

There are many reasons why damage assessments are often inaccurate. Some of the damages may not be readily visible or may not be reported immediately. After Hurricane Katrina made landfall, some news headlines reported that New Orleans was spared. This was because the levee failure had not yet been detected. Once the levees gave way, the city was flooded, and the disaster was much worse than initially anticipated. It is also difficult at times to detect the damage to buildings. For example, in the case of a flash flood disaster, buildings may look structurally sound on the outside, but there could be significant damage to the foundation and walls of the building. Another example is from the 2003 San Simeon earthquake in California. "Many people were out of town and were only able to report damages when they returned after the holidays. There were also a significant number of vacation homes in rural areas that could not be assessed until the owners came back to inspect them" (McEntire and Cope, 2004, p. 8).

Damages may also be missed or double counted due to human error. For example, after a tornado roared through downtown Fort Worth, Texas, in March 2000, the numbers from the Red Cross and FEMA did not initially match. Later on, it was determined that one of the organizations miscounted some duplexes, which led to the discrepancy. In addition to damages being missed or counted twice, it is also difficult to know how to identify the monetary value of damages (McEntire and Cope, 2004, p. 10). Should damages be recorded based on purchase price, replacement value, or going market rate? This is an important question you will need to answer.

Another reason for inaccuracy is due to the fact that damage assessments are performed repeatedly after disasters. The Loma Prieta earthquake in San Francisco provides a clear indication of this. "Buildings were reassessed and re-evaluated as changing geologic processes and weather affected the damaged structures, and as city officials tried to balance people's needs for food, fuel, and shelter with safety. Significant factors affecting the damage assessment process included aftershocks, continued ground failure, and secondary hazards, such as the exposure of asbestos in earthquake damage buildings. Significant social, economic and legal concerns also influenced the building evaluation process" (Oaks, 1990, p. 10).

There are also many types of damages, losses, and impacts that may get overlooked in the damage assessment process (French, 1990, p. 18):

▲ Physical and economic damage to the infrastructure, including road, water, sewer, gas, and electric systems

▲ Loss of historical buildings

▲ Diminished ability to carry out emergency response activities

▲ Inconvenience and lost economic revenues due to service interruption

▲ Longer-term economic losses due to limits on recovery

▲ Loss of life

▲ Environmental damages

For this reason, damage assessments should consider not only damages but other anticipated losses and needs as well.

### 8.2.2  Working with Others

Another challenge related to damage assessment pertains to the large number of organizations involved in this postdisaster function. It will be difficult for you to harmonize the activities of everyone that participates in damage assessment. This includes private and public engineers, the Red Cross, local emergency managers, and others from the state and federal government.

Complicating this matter, each organization has divergent purposes for conducting damage assessments. For instance, the Red Cross is involved in assessing residential damages as are insurance claims adjusters. The Chamber of Commerce may be interested in business losses in the community. City and state officials may want to know how government buildings faired in the disaster. FEMA and engineering firms might look at damage to public infrastructure such as roads and bridges.

Furthermore, each organization may use different forms for damage assessments. These distinct documents do not always allow quick and easy integration or summary of the damages. Those evaluating damages may also rely on different coding techniques for the assessment. After the earthquake in Paso Robles, California, some assessors utilized lot numbers, while others noted the complete street address of the damaged structure (McEntire and Cope, 2004, p. 10). This creates additional confusion when trying to compile data or visit the site again. A county emergency management official stated that this discrepancy generated many challenges when he was compiling the PDA numbers after the earthquake (McEntire and Cope, 2004, p. 10).

### 8.2.3  Access and Safety

Because of the widespread destruction associated with disasters, it can be quite difficult to travel to an affected area and complete a damage assessment. Floods, debris, and missing street signs may make travel to the damaged area impossible or difficult. For example, the effects of 1993 Midwest flood was so widespread that those assessing damages could not reach each site. Some areas had so much water that damage assessments had to be postponed for days, weeks, or even longer.

In addition to inaccessibility, damage assessment can be dangerous. Because of the potential for fires or building collapses after disasters, damage assessors can be confronted with various threatening hazards. For example, aftershocks from earthquakes pose serious risks to the damage assessment teams trying to evaluate the integrity of structures. Additional building collapses are common when aftershocks occur after the initial earthquake.

Damage assessments are dangerous activities, but they do ultimately promote a safer environment for the public and those who are involved in demolition or reconstruction. The situation after an earthquake in Paso Robles, California, is illustrative of this point. "When the fire department arrived at the area in Paso Robles with the greatest concentration of damages, the dangerous situation of many buildings was taken into consideration. Roofs and upper floors had collapsed to the ground level. Eves and awnings above the sidewalks had fully or partially separated from numerous edifices. Walls had crumbled, and bricks and concrete were hanging precariously from building facades. Fire fighters therefore used yellow tape to cordon off the areas that were regarded to be the most dangerous. The goal was to keep the public out of harm's way. Over the next few days, the fire and police chiefs met with other city leaders to discuss post-disaster policies. Safety became the number one priority. Anyone entering the area had to have proper safety equipment and had to be accompanied by a fire fighter. Fences were brought in and a perimeter was placed around the damaged buildings in the downtown district. Police officers were stationed in the area to prevent people from entering unsafe areas and buildings (and as a symbolic gesture to discourage possible - but improbable - looting). As the inspections continued, those offices deemed safe were opened to building owners and merchant tenants. Other buildings had to have debris removed, receive shoring, and then be assessed again before access could be granted. Condemned buildings remained closed to the public, although there was at least one report of a building occupant disregarding the fences and entering a damaged structure to gather personal belongings. Nonetheless, damage assessment did play a role in limiting the number of injuries and deaths associated with this disaster" (McEntire and Cope, 2004, pp. 5–6).

---

## FOR EXAMPLE

### Damage Assessment and Businesses

People will often become frustrated with the damage assessment process. Tenants, merchants, business owners, and landlords may be disappointed with damage assessment results. Their buildings may be condemned. Others will want to return to buildings as soon as possible to retrieve their belongings (e.g., purses or computers), but the hazardous situation will not permit it. Business owners facing this situation will be unable to resume their normal operations. They may vent their frustration if a decision is made to condemn buildings or protect their safety. Emergency managers should expect that people will be unhappy with damage assessment even though it may be for their own protection.

## SELF-CHECK

- What difficulties face those who assess damages?
- Why is accuracy of damage assessments challenging?
- What organizations are involved in damage assessment?
- Is damage assessment dangerous?

## 8.3 Damage Assessment Procedures

You must take a number of steps to conduct an effective assessment of damages. Some of these activities will need to be pursued right before the assessment, while others may take place during the evaluation of damages.

### 8.3.1 Preassessment Activities

To effectively assess damages, you will need to meet with others and distribute route assignments. Both of these issues are discussed further below:

▲ **Hold meetings.** After a disaster occurs, all of those involved in damage assessment should meet to discuss various issues. During this meeting, you will need to identify the process for conducting the assessment (Figure 8-3). You will also need to make participants aware of how to fill out the forms correctly and completely. Key distribution (if that is an issue) should be discussed so inspectors can enter buildings. Individuals and teams should know who they should report to and how to communicate concerns or questions. The deadline and location for turning in the assessment should be announced. You will want to make clear the dangers of the job and admonish people to be extremely cautious. You may need to make arrangements for firefighters to participate in damage assessment in case someone becomes injured.

▲ **Plan routes**. During the meeting, it will be necessary that you identify access routes and locations of responsibility. To avoid gaps or duplication in counting, you will want to divide the affected area into geographic districts. The areas should be distributed in a logical manner and clearly assigned to individuals/teams. Maps may be useful when planning route assignments. In some cases, it may be necessary to send someone out to spray paint the street names on the asphalt at intersections. The tornado in Joplin, Missouri, destroyed all signage in and around the impacted area. Without these new markings, the response and recovery operations could be slowed down unnecessarily.

### 8.3.2 Assessment Activities

When you conduct damage assessments, it is imperative that your teams follow all instructions and evaluation methodologies. This will help create as accurate picture of the damages as possible. Be sure participants note damages on forms,

Figure 8-3

After severe storms impacted Findlay, OH, in 2007, federal and state officials met with local damage assessment teams to discuss how they should go about collecting information for their preliminary damage assessments. Mark Wolfe/FEMA.

post results on buildings, cordon off dangerous areas, and educate the public about assessment codes (see McEntire and Cope, 2004). Many assessment codes use a popular color scheme:

▲ **Green**—The building is habitable and residents and businesses are allowed to return.
▲ **Yellow**—The building should only be entered by trained evaluators to continue assessing damages.
▲ **Red**—The building is unsafe and is therefore condemned (Figure 8-4).

You will also need to rely on experts when completing your damage assessment. This may include Red Cross employees and trained volunteers for residential areas or structural engineers for public buildings and businesses. When assessing road damage, you will need the assistance of civil engineers. You will need to work with other specialists to assess water treatment plants, power plants, and phone lines, etc.

Besides working with experts, you may also need to use technology in completing your damage assessments. You will want to use remote sensing for flooded areas, taking aerial pictures from satellites or fixed wing aircraft. Engineers will often place small cameras in water systems (pipes) to see if they are damaged. Computer programs may help you to track damage totals and the locations with the most damage. These tools will help you ensure that data is collected and recorded accurately.

**Figure 8-4**

Some buildings, such as this home that was affected by tornadoes in Tuscaloosa, AL, may have to be condemned because they are uninhabitable. George Armstrong/FEMA.

---

## FOR EXAMPLE

### A Successful Case of Damage Assessment

Damage assessment was effectively performed after an earthquake in 2003. "As volunteer engineers and architects arrived in Paso Robles, they were told to check in at the gazebo at the park in front of City Hall. These experts were then divided into teams (comprised of at least one fire fighter, an architect and an engineer), were assigned geographic areas, were given keys to the buildings that were collected from local businesses, and were briefed about dangerous conditions and the goals and methods of the assessment. Many people commented about how individuals worked together harmoniously to assess the damages. Another major strength made evident during damage assessment was the widespread knowledge of standard operating procedures. Fire fighters spray painted symbols common to the search and rescue community on buildings to denote who evaluated the safety of the structures, when this was done, and what the results were. The Building Department also utilized California's damage codes to track destroyed areas and educate building owners and occupants about their meaning and status. The shift rotation of the Emergency Operations Center appears to have been very smooth, with periodic briefings about the damage assessment function when leadership duties changed. Modern technology such as specialized cameras were utilized to detect damages to the city's water treatment facilities, and Geographic Information Systems helped to track the extent of all types of damages throughout the county" (McEntire and Cope, 2004, pp. 10–11).

When assessments are completed, you will need to collect them in a meticulous manner (noting what has been received and what is still outstanding). As information on damages becomes available, you will also need to ensure the accuracy of damage assessment forms and numbers. In other words, the results should be reviewed on multiple occasions. Once you have complete and accurate data, you can use this information to determine your next actions. For instance, you can inform the city and county leaders about the damages to identify response and recovery priorities. Give information as required to state and federal officials to open up the possibility of outside disaster assistance. As you identify damaged or destroyed buildings, be sure to shore up, repair, demolish, and/or rebuild structures in accordance with prior codes or new emergency permit requirements.

## SELF-CHECK

- What can be done before you complete damage assessment to increase the possibility of success?
- Why is it advisable to plan routes for those assessing damages?
- What are the popular assessment color schemes?
- How can experts assist you in the damage assessment function?
- How can technology facilitate damage assessment?

## 8.4 Disaster Declarations

Once damages, impacts, and needs have been assessed, you will need to share those findings with state and federal officials in the hopes of obtaining a presidential disaster declaration. A **disaster declaration** is a statement that the community or state cannot respond effectively without outside assistance. To receive a presidential or federal disaster declaration, the following events and actions must occur (see Robert T. Stafford Act at http://www.fema.gov/robert-t-stafford-disaster-relief-and-emergency-assistance-act-public-law-93-288-amended):

1. The disaster takes place. City and county initiate response operations. They will assess damages and other negative consequences.
2. If the municipal and county governments determine that the disaster is beyond their capabilities, then a disaster is declared at the local level.
3. When a disaster is declared by city and county officials, the state sends personnel to the scene to evaluate the impact. The state also begins or expands its own response to the disaster.
4. Should state personnel determine that the impact is so severe that additional outside help will be needed, the governor will declare an emergency or disaster. The governor will then request help from the FEMA region responsible for that particular state. At this point,

**Figure 8-5**

If warranted, the president may declare a disaster and become involved in the oversight of response and recovery operations. Aaron Skolnik/FEMA.

FEMA personnel will be deployed for the PDA. If damages warrant a federal declaration, a request will be made through the FEMA regional office, FEMA headquarters, and the Department of Homeland Security.

5. When required, the president will declare a federal disaster, and resources will be dedicated to the jurisdiction(s) in question. If damages do not necessitate a declaration, officials at FEMA and/or the Department of Homeland Security will deny the declaration request (Figure 8-5). The president does not decline the disaster request (in order to avoid blame and the political fallout from that decision).

## 8.4.1 Difficulties Associated with the Process

This process of disaster declarations, and what can go wrong with them, can be examined in the aftermath of Hurricane Andrew in 1992. When Andrew made landfall, local and state governments did the best they could to respond to the event on their own. They addressed immediate medical needs and started to determine what else needed to be done for disaster victims. However, it soon became apparent that the affected communities and the state of Florida would not be able to handle the devastation and debris alone.

The day after Andrew hit, President George H.W. Bush promised storm victims that "help was on the way." But local and state officials claimed that the federal government was not responding quickly enough. "Governor Chiles complained that urgent requests for federal assistance had been delayed or hopelessly lost because of bureaucratic red tape and confusion. Kate Hale, director of Dade County's Emergency Office, stated 'we have appealed through the state to the federal government. We've had a lot of people down here for press conferences. But [in the end] it is Dade County on its own … . Where the hell is the cavalry on this one?'" (Schneider, 1995, p. 95).

FEMA eventually deployed additional personnel and resources to South Florida. However, it could not provide assistance until the damage assessment numbers and formal request for aid came from the state. The federal government asserts that local and state officials asked for everything but failed to follow damage assessment and disaster declaration requirements. Local and state leaders claim they were overwhelmed, and FEMA was too rigid with its standard operating procedures. Regardless of the cause, the mistake or inability of not being specific about needs resulted in a delay of outside disaster assistance. Because similar problems occurred in Hurricane Katrina, emergency management personnel should be very meticulous about the declaration process.

### 8.4.2 Factors Determining Declarations

There are both objective and subjective factors that determine whether a disaster is declared or not. According to the Texas Division of Emergency Management (ftp://ftp.txdps.state.tx.us/dem/recovery/recoverymanual.pdf), these factors include, among other things:

▲ The number of homes destroyed or sustaining major damage
▲ The number of homes sustaining minor damage
▲ The extent to which the damage is concentrated or dispersed
▲ The estimated costs of repairing the damage
▲ The demographics of the affected areas including income levels, unemployment, and concentrations of the elderly
▲ The extent to which the damage is covered by insurance
▲ The extent to which the disaster area is traumatized
▲ The extent of disaster-related unemployment
▲ The level of assistance available from other federal agencies such as loans from the Small Business Administration
▲ The state and local governments' capabilities for dealing with the disaster
▲ The level of assistance available from charities
▲ The availability of rental housing
▲ The extent of health and safety problems
▲ The extent of damage to facilities providing essential services such as hospitals, utility companies, etc.

In addition, FEMA also considers a statewide threshold of $1.39 per capita in estimated eligible disaster costs before it will approve a request for PA help. At the county level, $3.50 per capita is required for disaster declarations.

### 8.4.3 Other Unique Requirements

Emergency managers should be aware of the special requisites pertinent to disaster declarations. For instance, requests for declarations typically include letters and other supporting documents that outline what happened and the resources that are needed. In some cases, phone calls to higher levels of government may initiate the declaration process. For example, a conversation may be enough to request a declaration if there is an obvious need due to the readily apparent magnitude of certain disasters. The U.S. Code of Federal Regulations 44 clarifies when this type of exception may occur: "The requirement for a joint PDA may be waived for those incidents of unusual severity and magnitude that do not require field damage assessment to determine the need for supplemental federal assistance under the Act, or in such other instances determined by the Regional Director upon consultation with the State" (Code of Federal Regulations, 400).

Most federal declarations, if they are given, are issued after a hazard has occurred and damages are verified and deemed significant. However, some declarations can be made before the hazard affects the community or state in question. Advanced declarations can be given if it appears that the hazard is inevitable and if steps can be taken to mitigate damages (e.g., before a hurricane makes landfall). If such declarations occur, FEMA can mobilize staff and resources so they are in place when the disaster occurs. Prepositioning resources can reduce deployment time and increase response effectiveness. Of course, prepositioning personnel and supplies should be pursued only if it is safe to do so.

There are different types of presidential/federal declarations:

▲ An **emergency declaration** is issued by the president for national security situations.

▲ A **disaster declaration** is initiated by the local and state governments but is approved or rejected in accordance to the Stafford Act.

An "emergency declaration" may be issued by the President at any time to mobilize federal resources. This does not require local, state or FEMA involvement. This is directed for events that have national security implications. It is also often used when an incident does not qualify under the definition of a major disaster in the Stafford Act. Emergency declarations may entail "more limited assistance aimed at saving lives and protecting property, public health, and safety" (May 1985a, p. 110).

A "disaster declaration" may be issued by the president under more stringent guidelines. This always requires local and state requests along with FEMA involvement and approval. Such declarations may be given for many different types of natural, technological, and civil disasters. A declaration also "makes available, as necessary, federal grant and loan programs for individuals and public entities" (May, 1985a, p. 110).

Most requests for federal disaster declarations are denied because the damages do not meet minimum threshold requirements. Such requests do not result in federal funding since it is believed that the local and state governments can handle the situation without outside involvement. If a disaster declaration request is denied, the emergency manager should not give up hope. An appeal can be made with additional supporting evidence. Denials can be overturned if federal disaster assistance is warranted. In most cases, however, you will be responsible for dealing with the disaster without federal help.

> **FOR EXAMPLE**
>
> **Politics and Presidential Disaster Declarations**
>
> Politics can play a role in presidential disaster declarations. The president may declare disasters as a way to obtain votes during campaigning and election years. For instance, "during his four years in office, President George H.W. Bush averaged 39 disaster declarations annually. The seven years of the Clinton presidency that Reeves studied averaged 72 disasters per year. When he focused on the presidential election years of 1992 and 1996, Reeves found that President Clinton was about 60 percent more likely than President Bush to declare a disaster in a pivotal, electorally important state" (Tarcey, 2004).

## SELF-CHECK

- What is a disaster declaration?
- How do disaster declarations take place?
- What problems are inherent to disaster declarations?
- What factors determine if a declaration is made or not?
- When are most disaster declarations issued?

## 8.5 Debris Produced by Disasters

As an emergency manager, you must be cognizant of the enormous amount of debris that is generated in disasters (McEntire, 2006) (see Table 8-1). Debris produced by a hazard may be "eight times the usual amount of trash needed to be picked up" (Wright, 2004). Consider the following examples:

▲ 18,000 mobile homes were destroyed in North Carolina by Hurricane Floyd. Floyd also produced over 1,500 tons of animal carcasses.

▲ When a series of tornadoes affected Oklahoma, it was estimated that 500,000 cubic yards of debris was collected.

▲ After the Northridge earthquake, 95,100 tons of debris had to be disposed of.

### 8.5.1 Types of Debris

Debris produced in disasters ranges from broken tree limbs, mud and sediment, and hazardous wastes to broken plywood, twisted metal, shattered glass, and dead animal carcasses (see Table 8-2). However, certain disasters may have specific types of debris (McEntire, 2006). For example, hurricanes may destroy buildings due to storm surge and strong winds. They may also move sand, dirt, and rock on top of roads and parking lots. Moreover, these hazards break tree limbs and damage cars, boats, and household contents.

## Table 8-1: Volume of debris generated by various disasters (Taken from EPA, 1995, p. 2)

| Community | Disaster | Date | Volume of debris |
|---|---|---|---|
| Metro-Dade County, FL | Hurricane Andrew | August 1992 | 43 million cubic yards (CY) of disaster debris in Metro-Dade County alone |
| Louisiana, Mississippi, Alabama, Florida | Hurricane Katrina | August 2005 | More than 100 million CY of disaster debris |
| Jasper County and Newton County, Missouri | Joplin tornado | May 2011 | 3 million CY of debris piles |
| Much of the eastern United States (mid-Atlantic region) | Hurricane Sandy | October 2012 | 5.25 million CY of debris |
| Los Angeles, CA | Northridge earthquake | January 1994 | 7 million CY of disaster debris |
| Kauai, HI | Hurricane Iniki | September 1992 | 5 million CY of disaster debris |
| Mecklenburg County, NC | Hurricane Hugo | September 1989 | 2 million CY of green waste |

Sources:
http://www.fas.org/sgp/crs/misc/RL33477.pdf.
http://www.westonsolutions.com/projects/joplinproject.htm.
http://www.fema.gov/news-release/2013/02/01/
sandy-debris-removal-passes-95-percent-95-days.

## Table 8-2: Type of debris generated by various disasters (Taken from EPA, 1995, p. 3)

| | Damaged buildings | Sediments | Green waste | Personal property | Ash and charred wood |
|---|---|---|---|---|---|
| Hurricanes | x | x | x | x | |
| Earthquakes | x | x | x | x | x |
| Tornadoes | x | | x | x | |
| Floods | x | x | x | x | |
| Fires | x | | | x | x |
| Ice storms | x | | x | x | |

(Adapted from EPA 1995, p. 3).

The violent shaking associated with earthquakes results in structural failures, collapsed brick buildings, broken glass, and sediment from accompanying landslides. Earthquakes likewise damage personal belongings that fall to the ground and break. This hazard produces ash and charred wood from fires that result from gas line breaks.

Other hazards are similarly destructive. The severe winds associated with tornadoes pull trees out of the soil, break limbs off of trees, and create missiles out of lawn mowers, sheds, computers, couches, microwaves, televisions, etc. Flash floods may rip buildings from their foundations as well as carry rock, mud, and tree trunks far downstream. Slow rising waters ruin carpets, furniture, electrical appliances, sheet rock, etc. Fires burn buildings and property, leaving charred debris and ash. Ice storms may break tree limbs and create damage to homes and personal property (Figure 8-6).

The excessive amount and types of debris generated by disasters must be dealt with by the emergency manager. This is known as debris management. **Debris management** is the collection, sorting, storage, transportation, and disposal or recycling of ruble, destroyed materials, and other wastes associated with a disaster. It also incorporates long-term measures to dispose of debris in an environmentally sound manner. Debris management is closely related to damage assessment and disaster declarations. For example, the clearing of debris may help people reach their destinations so they can assess damages. Debris management expenses may be paid in part by the federal government if a disaster declaration is given (Figure 8-7).

Figure 8-6

A resident of Bastrop, TX, looks at what is left of his motorcycle after
a fire devastated the area in September 2011. Patsy Lynch/FEMA.

Figure 8-7

Debris is collected in a front yard for removal after a flood in Ottawa,
OH, on August 27, 2010. Mark Wolfe/FEMA.

---

**FOR EXAMPLE**

**Unique Debris Considerations**

Disasters may be accompanied by unusual types of debris (Ekici et al., 2009). In some cases, human remains and animal carcasses pose major challenges for debris management because they require forensic investigation or special methods for disposition. There are also other types of debris that do not result directly from the physical hazard. Debris is also produced indirectly in and after the disaster. For example, there could be spoiled food (due to power outages) or excessive donations coming from well-meaning citizens and organizations (e.g., expired medicines or clothing that cannot be used). Debris may also include waste created by the response itself. Examples include sandbags that are used to fight flooding and water bottles that are provided to hydrate emergency workers.

---

### 8.5.2 Debris Management Challenges

Because of the large amounts and types of debris generated in disasters, you should be aware of its significance to you as an emergency manager. The presence and removal of debris have bearing on the effectiveness of response and recovery operations (Ekici et al., 2009). For example, police, ambulance, and fire vehicles will get flat tires if glass and splintered wood are not removed from streets and thoroughfares. Conversely, immediate efforts to clear roads of debris will ensure that response organizations may pass without delay.

The presence of debris also leads to concerns about mental well-being, safety, public health, and the environment. Debris creates an eyesore for those in the disaster-affected community. For example, after the 2004 hurricanes passed over Pensacola, Florida, one citizen commented, "it's still kind of depressing to drive around with all of this debris" (Thomas, 2004). After a March 2000 tornado in Fort Worth, Texas, those assigned to clean up broken glass were threatened by lose window panes falling out of office buildings. Residents living near some disposal sites have had trouble breathing because of the ash emitted by debris furnaces (Mariano, 2004). Debris and debris management can adversely affect our natural resources. Burning debris may pollute the air, while burying disaster ruble may adversely affect soil and water conditions. Some people in Palm Beach, Florida, became very upset when public land dedicated as environmentally protected area was used as a dump site (Modzelewski, 2004).

Debris management is also very expensive. "Debris cleanup costs in four states and two territories exceeded $310,000,000 following Hurricane Georges in 1998" (Swan, 2000, p. 222). The removal of debris from Hurricane Andrew cost $585 million. In most disasters, total debris costs may range from 15% to 33% of FEMA's overall disaster expenditures. "Generally, FEMA pays 100 percent of all debris removal costs in the 72 hours following natural disasters. After that, it's agency policy to pay 75 percent of the costs borne by local governments" (Curran, 2004). But the local share is often sizable. And there is no guarantee that every disaster will be declared and permit outside governmental assistance.

Debris management can likewise be very time consuming. After the 2004 hurricanes affected Florida, some city crews worked seven days a week for extended periods of time (Wright, 2004). Other disasters may require ongoing debris management operations for weeks and even months at a time. People often take advantage of disasters to unload unwanted items such as old sinks, couches, mattresses, refrigerators, car doors, and tires. The presence of such debris at the curbside complicates the debris management process for you as an emergency manager.

Oversight of debris management is difficult as there may be no organization that has clear and sole responsibility for this activity. Citizens will place debris near the curb waiting for someone to pick it up and carry it away. The transportation, public works, and park and recreations departments may be involved in cleaning up roads and the ruble from damaged government buildings. Private contractors are utilized to collect debris for some communities. In federally declared disasters, FEMA officials oversee costs and the reimbursement of funds. The EPA ensures that debris management takes environmental protection into account.

Debris and debris management may create other problems for you as well. Debris or debris storage may attract rodents that have to be dealt with. Also, the removal and transportation of debris may create dust and noise and annoy citizens. Roads can also be ruined if they are not able to support the weight of heavily loaded trucks. Some of the impacts of disasters, including the loss of livestock, may also pose special debris management challenges. What should be done when hundreds or thousands of animals are killed in major flooding episodes? These are all important issues that you must address after disasters.

> **FOR EXAMPLE**
>
> **Debris Management, Hazards, and Crime Scenes**
>
> Debris removal was a very difficult task in the aftermath of the 9/11 terrorist attacks on the World Trade Center. The site was not safe because there were fires smoldering among the debris. The air was also unhealthy and filled with dust from the debris. There was a desire to clean up the site as soon as possible as it was psychologically difficult to view the destruction. However, care had to be taken as the site was also a crime scene. Sifting the debris had to be done in such a way as to look for evidence and separate out human remains. The families of victims were very adamant that their loved ones not be placed in trash dumps. It took over eight months for all of the debris to be removed from the World Trade Center site and be sorted for evidence and remains.

## SELF-CHECK

- Can disasters generate a great deal of debris?
- What types of debris are produced in disasters?
- What is debris management?
- What are the challenges associated with debris management?

## 8.6 Dealing with Debris Effectively

A number of steps can be taken to overcome the typical problems associated with debris management (Ekici et al., 2009; McEntire, 2006). Because disaster-generated debris may quickly overwhelm a community, it is imperative that the quantity be reduced as much as possible. Reducing debris can be accomplished after the debris is sorted. Damaged materials may be classified as vegetative, aggregate, and construction/demolition debris:

▲ **Vegetative debris** includes broken tree limbs, tree stumps, brush, leaf, and yard waste.

▲ **Aggregate debris** includes asphalt and concrete from damaged roads and bridges.

▲ **Construction and demolition debris** results from damaged homes, commercial property, and various other types of structures (e.g., barns). This may include wood, metal, wiring, insulation, tar or clay shingles, and other types of materials.

There are at least three ways to reduce the volume of such debris:

1. Vegetative debris can be chipped. This may reduce up to 75% of the total debris volume from certain disasters. The resulting product can be used as mulch for gardens and flower beds.
2. Aggregates can be crushed and later used as road base. Asphalt and concrete can in some cases be reused as well.
3. Construction and demolition debris may be recycled in some cases. Broken 2 x 4s and sheets of plywood can be made into pressboard.

Another way to reduce debris is to burn as much debris as possible in order to reduce the amount sent to community landfills. This will require that special attention is given to the environment however. For instance, the temperature of burning debris may determine the amount of pollution it produces. Recycling and burying debris also has enormous impacts upon the quality of air, water, and soil.

To facilitate oversight of debris management, it is recommended that someone be put in charge of this function and that organizations are made aware of each other's roles in this area. Successful debris management operations are often determined by:

▲ Knowing what equipment is available or needed for debris management
▲ Recognizing the capabilities and limits of departments in the public sector
▲ Being able to communicate to all parties involved after a disaster, including contractors from the private sector
▲ Having the legal department review contracts, "right-of-entry permits, community liability, condemnation of buildings, land acquisition for temporary staging and reduction sites" (Swan, 2000, p. 224)

Individuals and organizations involved in debris removal activities should also understand how debris management activities change over time (Swan, 2000, p. 222). Immediately before and after a disaster, communities should increase readiness by confirming staffing assignments for debris management. This is a great time to remind personnel about proper debris management techniques. During the response phase, attention should be shifted to the removal and storage of debris. Once recovery is underway, debris can be sorted, recycled, burned, or buried (Figure 8-8).

### 8.6.1 Storage Locations and the Environment

To reduce the problems associated with debris management, you should identify the sites for temporary and permanent storage as well as final disposal. "A listing of potential temporary debris management sites should be investigated and evaluated before a major disaster. Public lands should be used first to avoid costly leases. Consider locations with respect to noise, traffic and the environment. Avoid locating near residential areas, schools, churches, hospitals, and other environmentally sensitive areas. Ensure that sites have good ingress/egress to accommodate heavy truck traffic. Sites should be roughly 50 acres in size based on the forecasted quantity of debris" (Swan, 2000, p. 223). In some cases, these staging areas may need to be as

**Figure 8-8**

Heavy equipment may be needed to remove certain types of debris.
Norman Lenburg/FEMA.

---

### FOR EXAMPLE

#### Debris Management in San Bruno, CA

On September 9, 2010, a gas pipeline in a residential neighborhood near the San Francisco Airport ruptured and produced a massive explosion and fire. The incident scene produced significant debris and had far-reaching environmental impacts (McEntire et al., 2013). Debris included charred wood, partially collapsed chimneys, cars gutted by fire, broken glass, sharp nails, and twisted metal. As a result, the city contracted with CalRecycle and Pacific States Environmental Contractors, Inc., to clean up the area. A right-of-entry permit was drafted and signed by property owners to allow debris removal. Small hazardous materials were collected and placed in 10 55 gallon drums. Heavy equipment was then brought in to remove wood, concrete, and metal. Approximately 60% of the debris was recycled, and the remainder was segregated and disposed of in an appropriate manner. Even the ash from the fire was removed from the ground and processed at class II and class III waste management facilities. During debris removal, air and soil samples were frequently monitored, and the streets were cleaned regularly to keep dust levels down. Silt fences, straw wattles, and hydroseed were used to prevent erosion of the charred hillside in Crestmoor Canyon and contaminate the San Francisco Bay water supply. Fortunately, the owner of the pipeline paid for debris removal, which is estimated to have cost $1.8 million.

---

large as 100 acres (Mariano, 2004). Some communities have used fairgrounds and even county airports for this purpose (Moskovitz, 2004).

Protection of the environment can be enhanced during debris management if an environmental specialist or organizations are involved in operations. Experts can provide advice on the methods to dispose of debris in an environmentally sound manner. The public can be made aware of how to assist in debris management by communicating public policies and strategies to media organizations. For instance, NASA and FEMA officials repeatedly advised citizens to stay away from debris laden with hazardous materials after the Space Shuttle Columbia broke up upon reentry. People can likewise be told to cut tree limbs into sections no more than 4 feet long and stack them in a way as to not obstruct roads, utilities, and culverts (Ferrante, 2004).

### 8.6.2 EPA Recommendations for Improving Debris Management

The EPA has similar and additional recommendations to improve debris management (see EPA, 1995, pp. 8–10):

- ▲ **Consider mutual aid arrangements**. Developing compacts with nearby communities may help jurisdictions find needed personnel and expertise and reduce costs associated with purchasing and maintaining equipment.
- ▲ **Implement recycling program**. It is easier to recycle debris if a waste recycling program has been established before a disaster strikes.
- ▲ **Develop a communication strategy**. Government officials must tell citizens about special instructions for reporting and sorting disaster debris, as well as when regular trash collection will resume.
- ▲ **Anticipate increased outreach and enforcement staffing needs**. Additional personnel should be hired after a disaster to answer telephone calls about disaster debris and assist in the removal of disaster-produced ruble.
- ▲ **Obtain equipment and supplies**. Cell phones, chain saws, portable generators, flashlights, batteries, vehicle repair kits (for flat tires), extra work clothing, water, and other materials for debris management personnel should be readily obtained after disaster strikes.
- ▲ **Select collection and storage sites**. Identifying locations for collection, staging, storage, sorting, recycling, landfilling, and burning of debris in advance will eliminate unwanted noise and road damage and increase efficiency of debris management operations.
- ▲ **Determine management options and goals**. Communities should anticipate what types of debris will be produced in a disaster and identify the objectives and methods to appropriately deal with them.
- ▲ **Segregate hazardous waste**. Ensure that everyone involved in debris management understands how to deal with hazardous materials (so it is not mixed with other disaster debris to produce further environmental degradation).
- ▲ **Prepare contracts**. Work with the private sector to seek request for proposals (RFP) to collect, store, sort, process, and dispose of disaster debris.
- ▲ **Plan for FEMA and state reimbursement**. Hire staff to record debris management costs and file reimbursement in accordance with the rules provided by the FEMA.

- How can you sort disaster debris?
- Is it important to reduce the volume of disaster debris?
- What are the characteristics of effective debris management?
- Where should you store disaster debris?
- What recommendations does the EPA have for debris management?

## 8.7 Regulations and Other Considerations

Successful debris management requires that emergency managers are familiar with federal legislation pertaining to this function. There are a host of regulations that pertain to debris management and the reimbursement of debris removal costs. These guidelines suggest that debris expenses may be reimbursed if:

▲ It is a direct result of the disaster.

▲ It is found in the designated disaster area.

▲ It will minimize threats to lives and public health.

▲ It will reduce additional damage to public or private property.

▲ It will help the economic recovery of the area.

Debris must also be removed and disposed of within a definite time period. In certain situations, debris must be identified and a request sent to FEMA within 90 days of the disaster declaration. If FEMA approves payment for removal, debris must be taken care of within 180 days of the federal declaration. Regulations also note that eligible removal expenses are associated with the clearing of debris from roads and also protecting people and the environment from hazardous materials.

Examples of ineligible debris reimbursements include removal of:

▲ Trees and trunks from unaffected forest areas.

▲ Sediment from channels that is not a result of the disaster. For example, this would include natural buildup of sand and rock in a river basin.

▲ Debris from private roads and gated communities.

▲ Extra tree trimmings or trees cut up by contractors.

▲ Yard waste coming from unmaintained lots.

▲ Construction debris created as a result of contractor demolition and repairs.

FOR EXAMPLE

## FEMA and Trash Pickup Rules

As an emergency manager, you should be aware that "some of the rules relating to the federal government's reimbursement for trash pickup can be confusing, even for FEMA Representatives" (Bierschenk, 2004). Differences of opinion regarding debris regulations have led to serious disagreements and even legal actions in some cases (Curran, 2004). Rules may be different for various federal agencies, and some of the laws may be changed in specific disasters. In Alabama, after Hurricane Ivan, "the Federal Emergency Management Agency decided to only pay those communities that entered into contracts with the U.S. Army Corps of engineers" (Curran, 2004). In other cases, the federal government has paid all debris management costs—even the local and state portions. Clarification may be needed to ensure everyone is on the same page.

### 8.7.1 Reducing Expenses

In order to reduce the exorbitant expense of debris management, a number of measures can be taken. For instance, contracts with the private sector can be developed. These contracts may be based on lump-sum, unit price, or time and material agreements:

▲ **Lump-sum contracts** provide payment for completion of a well-defined scope of work (e.g., when debris is concentrated) (Swan, 2000, p. 224).

▲ **Unit price contracts** are based on truckload sizes and are most common in disasters when the exact quantity of debris is unknown (Swan, 2000, p. 224).

▲ **Time and material contracts** are based on labor and equipment costs and are suitable for rights-of-way clearance and should not exceed 70 hours according to FEMA regulations for reimbursement (Swan, 2000, p. 224).

Human and equipment resources can be creatively acquired for debris management, and expenses must always be carefully tracked. One community utilized prison crews to help them meet their debris management demands (Niesse, 2004). Most communities will assign someone the specific duty of recording employee hours, trucks utilized, money spent on fuel, etc. This is crucial since federal reimbursement policies must be followed in a meticulous fashion. Payments will be made in most disasters according to established laws only. Opportunities for reimbursement may be missed if people are not aware of the proper methods to complete and submit paperwork.

### 8.7.2 Preventing Fraud

There are other ways that precious resources can be lost during debris management. This postdisaster function is sometimes associated with scams by public officials and private contractors. "The high dollar value of debris operations can entice Federal officials, local government officials, contractors, and others to step over the line of legal activity in an effort to benefit financially from disaster recovery operations" (FEMA 2003c). Some people intentionally try to include nondisaster-related debris for removal. This may include those clearing land of trees as well as others demolishing or gutting homes to increase debris quantities for reimbursement (Bierschenk, 2004).

Such fraud can be eliminated by working aggressively to stop it. Those participating in debris management should be on the lookout for:

▲ The hauling of ineligible debris (e.g., tree stumps)
▲ Excessive water placed in the bottom of dump trucks to increase weight
▲ Inaccurately specified truckload capacities
▲ Double counting of personnel and equipment
▲ Trucks reentering disposal sites

Taking photographs of debris management activities is another way to discourage would-be criminals. "Monitoring can [also] be accomplished using local government employees or separate contractors. Costs associated with hiring outside contractors to provide monitors are eligible for reimbursement by FEMA … . Contract monitors must be trained before being placed in the field to observe contractor operations. They must have knowledge of techniques that can be used to inflate debris quantities. Moreover, there must be a reporting procedure in place that identifies questionable activities. Documentation should consist of written reports, photographs, and sketches of questionable contractor activities" (Swan, 2000, p. 224). Regulations, expenses, and fraud are important concerns to those involved in debris management.

## FOR EXAMPLE

### Monitoring to Prevent Fraud

The federal government takes its responsibility to monitor fraud seriously. After the 2004 hurricanes in Florida, "the government agencies … [had] monitors riding along with the trucks to try to ensure people don't take unfair advantage of the free service" (Bierschenk, 2004). In other cases, the federal government will send Office of the Inspector General personnel to investigate potential scams, make arrests, and prosecute as necessary. You can help to avoid fraudulent practices by making this a priority during debris removal operations.

## SELF-CHECK

- Is it important for the emergency manager to know debris management regulations?
- What types of debris are eligible or ineligible for reimbursement?
- What types of contracts are used to pay debris removal contractors?
- Is fraud a problem in debris management?

## SUMMARY

The promotion of resilience after disaster requires a number of additional steps after initial emergency management needs are met. Damages must be calculated to determine what additional steps will be required for response and recovery. You will face several challenges regarding accuracy and safety, but these can be overcome if you follow damage assessment protocols. Once you have a good understanding of the impact, you may seek outside assistance by requesting a federal disaster declaration. It will also be necessary that you understand the types of debris that are produced in disasters and take steps to reduce or dispose of them correctly. Each of these functions must be performed in accordance to established regulations if you are to be successful as an emergency manager.

## KEY TERMS

| | |
|---|---|
| **Aerial assessment** | Review of damage conducted in helicopters or planes and is especially useful when roads are blocked or flooding is widespread. |
| **Aggregate debris** | Trash that includes asphalt and concrete from damaged roads and bridges. |
| **Construction and demolition debris** | Trash that includes wood, metal, wiring, insulation, tar or clay shingles, and other types of materials. |
| **Damage assessment** | A process of identifying the extent of destruction, including individual impact as well as overall economic losses in the community. |
| **Debris management** | The collection, sorting, storage, transportation, and disposal or recycling of ruble, destroyed materials, and other wastes associated with a disaster. It also incorporates long-term measures to dispose of debris in an environmentally sound manner. |
| **Disaster declaration** | A statement that the community or state cannot respond effectively without outside assistance. |
| **Lump-sum contracts** | Contracts that provide payment for completion of a well-defined scope of work (when debris is concentrated) (Swan, 2000, p. 224). |
| **Preliminary or detailed assessment** | Review of damage that is performed within days or weeks after the disaster and seeks to determine the need for outside assistance. |
| **Rapid or initial assessment** | Review of damage that is conducted immediately when a disaster occurs and seeks to gain a quick comprehension of deaths, injuries, victim needs, and overall scope of the disaster. |
| **Technical or neering assessment** | Review of damage that is performed days, weeks, or **engi-**months after the disaster to determine the exact value of losses and requirements for rebuilding. |

| | |
|---|---|
| **Time and material contracts** | Agreements that are based on labor and equipment costs and are suitable for rights-of-way clearance and should not exceed 70 hours according to FEMA regulations for reimbursement (Swan, 2000, p. 224). |
| **Unit price contracts** | Agreements that are based on truckload sizes and are most common in disasters when the exact quantity of debris is unknown (Swan, 2000, p. 224). |
| **Vegetative debris** | Trash that includes broken tree limbs, tree stumps, brush, leaf, and yard waste. |
| **Walkthrough or site visit** | A tour of the damaged areas by foot to determine the amount and type of disaster assistance households, businesses, and the government needs. |
| **Windshield or drive-through assessment** | An evaluation performed in a vehicle and is completed without leaving the vehicle. |

# ASSESS YOUR UNDERSTANDING

Posttest to evaluate your knowledge of damage assessment, disaster declarations, and debris removal.

*Measure your learning by comparing pretest and posttest results.*

## Summary Questions

1. Damage assessment looks at destroyed buildings but not economic losses. True or false?

2. A preliminary damage assessment is the first type of damage assessment. True or false?

3. Public officials often view damages from a helicopter or plane. True or false?

4. Buildings may look structurally sound, but they could be unsafe. True or false?

5. The Red Cross often assesses damages associated with homes and apartments. True or false?

6. People may become upset with the damage assessment process or results. True or false?

7. A green paper attached to a house means the house is condemned. True or false?

8. States should declare a disaster only when they cannot deal with the event without outside help. True or false?

9. The number of destroyed homes has a bearing on disaster declarations, but unemployment does not. True or false?

10. A disaster can never be declared before the hazard occurs. True or false?

11. Common debris produced by a disaster may include broken tree limbs, sediment, and broken plywood. True or false?

12. Debris management is not concerned with environmental issues. True or false?

13. Debris management is one of the most expensive postdisaster functions. True or false?

14. Brush, leaves, and yard waste are examples of construction and demolition debris. True or false?

15. A major consideration in debris management is the location of storage and disposal sites. True or false?

16. What is(are) the benefit(s) of damage assessment?
    (a) It helps to identify needs of disaster victims.
    (b) It is required before outside assistance can be given.
    (c) It determines if structures are habitable.
    (d) It identifies areas that might need to be avoided during rebuilding.
    (e) All of the above.

17. A rapid or initial assessment:
    (a) Is performed weeks after the disaster
    (b) Is performed by engineers, insurance agents, and FEMA contractors
    (c) Helps to gain a quick understanding of the scope of the event
    (d) Is the only assessment required for disaster declarations
    (e) Recommends approach for repairs and reconstruction

18. A windshield or drive-through assessment:
    (a) Is performed in a vehicle
    (b) Is common in the initial stages of disaster response
    (c) Requires extensive knowledge about engineering and construction
    (d) Answers a and b
    (e) Answers b and c

19. Reasons why damage assessments are inaccurate include:
    (a) The appearance of buildings can be deceiving.
    (b) Damages may be missed or double counted.
    (c) They are performed repeatedly after a disaster.
    (d) Some types of damages and impacts may be overlooked after a disaster.
    (e) All of the above.

20. Earthquakes pose serious risks to damage assessors because:
    (a) There is a potential for building collapses.
    (b) Fires may result from broken power lines.
    (c) Aftershocks will not occur.
    (d) Answers a and b.
    (e) None of the above.

21. Holding a meeting before conducting damage assessment operations is advisable because:
    (a) Flooding has never destroyed street signs.
    (b) You might need to distribute keys to those involved.
    (c) Route identification is not important.
    (d) Yellow-coded buildings are completely safe.
    (e) Forms do not need to be given to those involved.

22. What steps are required for a federal disaster declaration?
    (a) Local government is affected by a disaster and can't respond alone.
    (b) State government requests outside disaster assistance.
    (c) The FEMA region relays information to headquarters.
    (d) The president agrees that damages warrant federal funding.
    (e) All of the above.

23. Factors determining federal declarations include:
    (a) The number of homes with minor damage only
    (b) Estimated costs of repairing the damages
    (c) The extent to which damage is covered by insurance but not unemployment

(d) The concentration of damages but not cost associated with them

(e) All of the above

24. An emergency declaration:
    (a) Is the same as a disaster declaration
    (b) Requires local and state requests for assistance
    (c) Is used when the definition of a disaster does not fall under Stafford Act guidelines
    (d) Is never used for national security emergencies
    (e) All of the above

25. Disasters may produce what type(s) of debris?
    (a) Ash and charred wood
    (b) Green waste
    (c) Bricks from damaged buildings
    (d) Sediment
    (e) All of the above

26. Debris management:
    (a) Is not very expensive
    (b) Is not very time consuming
    (c) Is performed by a single agency only
    (d) Must be performed in accordance to federal regulations
    (e) Is not related to crime scenes in any way

27. Aggregate debris includes:
    (a) Tree stumps
    (b) Asphalt and concrete
    (c) Asphalt but not concrete
    (d) Metal and wiring
    (e) Metal and wiring, but not wood

28. In terms of debris management, the EPA recommends:
    (a) That mutual aid agreements be developed and used
    (b) The recycling of debris
    (c) That you have chain saws and vehicle repair kits
    (d) All of the above
    (e) Answers a and c only

29. Which debris is ineligible for reimbursement?
    (a) Debris that is a direct result of the disaster
    (b) Disaster that is found within the designated disaster area
    (c) Debris that minimizes threats to lives and property
    (d) Tree trimmings cut up by contractors
    (e) Construction debris only

30. A time and material contract:
    (a) Is based on labor and equipment costs
    (b) Is for well-defined projects
    (c) Can exceed 70 hours

(**d**) Is useful for concentrated debris

(**e**) Is based on truckloads

## Review Questions

1. Why is damage assessment important?
2. What are the different types of damage assessment?
3. What methods are used to conduct damage assessments?
4. What challenges can an emergency manager expect with the damage assessment function?
5. What can be done to perform damage assessment successfully?
6. What is a disaster declaration?
7. What factors determine if a disaster is declared by the president?
8. What are the different types of federal declarations?
9. What type of debris do disasters generate?
10. What is debris management?
11. What are the common problems associated with debris management?
12. What measures can be taken to deal with debris effectively?
13. What regulations need to be followed when performing debris management activities?

## Applying This Chapter

1. You are an emergency manager living near the New Madrid fault. An earthquake has just occurred. How would this hazard affect damage assessment? Suppose your community was affected by flooding. How does this impact damage assessment? Do other hazards create different concerns for damage assessment teams? Why?
2. Different types of disasters produce different types of debris. Can you provide examples that support this statement? Why is it important to know this?
3. You are an emergency manager in the Northwest, and your community has been devastated by a tsunami generated from an earthquake in the Pacific Ocean. Tons of debris have been generated from destroyed homes and businesses. You will have to sort and remove the debris. Why is debris management important, and what considerations should you think about as you implement this postdisaster function?
4. News reports reveal that the declaration process for Hurricane Katrina witnessed similar problems to that of Hurricane Andrew. What were these and how can they be avoided in the future?
5. A flash flood has destroyed many buildings in a rural area and left animal carcasses strewn about the area. The area is well known for its pristine waters and beautiful scenery. What concerns do you have as the emergency manager for this area? How can you ensure debris management is performed successfully?

6. You are the local emergency manager for a community that was devastated by a major tornado. You need to convince officials to declare your jurisdiction a disaster area. What types of facts do you present them with?

7. You are the local emergency manager for a community in Idaho that was adversely affected by landslide. Many homes sustained minor damage, and there is a great deal of vegetative debris as a result also. What scams might be employed by contractors, and how can you prevent them?

### Preassessment Procedures

Write a 2-page paper on the following subject: you are the local emergency manager for a community that has been affected by a volcanic hazard. You now have to assess damages quickly. You have called a meeting with those who will assist. What steps do you take to ensure the safety of those involved in this function? What other things should you make them aware of?

### Assessing Damages

You are the local emergency manager for a community that was severely affected by a major ice storm. You need to assess the impact and damages. How is this different than assessing damage from an earthquake? Who might be involved in this type of assessment?

### Types of Debris

Your community in Arizona has been affected by a major wildfire. Many neighborhoods and small businesses have been ravished in the event. What type of debris will you have to deal with? How does this differ from the debris produced by a hurricane? What concerns do you have about debris management that are common to any type of hazard?

# 9

# PROMOTING RECOVERY AND MITIGATION
## Disaster Assistance and Vulnerability Reduction

## Starting Point

Pretest to assess your knowledge on how to promote recovery and mitigation. *Determine where you need to concentrate your effort.*

## What You'll Learn in This Chapter

▲ The purpose, types, and methods to access individual assistance

▲ The categories of public assistance

▲ The steps to obtain recovery resources for your community

▲ The potential for disagreement during recovery

▲ The special issues that accompany recovery including fraud, preservations of historic buildings, and protection of the environment

▲ How to reduce vulnerability after a disaster

## After Studying This Chapter, You'll be Able To

▲ Examine the goals and categories of public assistance.

▲ Help eligible applicants seek different types of federal disaster relief.

▲ Establish a disaster recovery center.

▲ Determine what possible conflicts could occur among the actors involved in recovery.

▲ Analyze your community's vulnerability to fraud, the loss of historic buildings, and damage to the environment from hazards.

▲ Examine what measures can be taken to decrease future losses.

## Goals and Outcomes

▲ Evaluate the process through which individual assistance may be obtained.

▲ Compare and contrast categories of public assistance.

▲ Synthesize the procedures for obtaining public assistance.

▲ Predict conflict during recovery among internal and external actors.

---

*Disaster Response and Recovery: Strategies and Tactics for Resilience*, Second Edition. David A. McEntire.
© 2015 John Wiley & Sons, Inc. Published 2015 by John Wiley & Sons, Inc.

▲ Argue for greater resources for emergency management using windows of opportunity.

▲ Assess special issues during recovery including ways to minimize fraud, preserve historic buildings, and protect the environment.

▲ Evaluate whether rebuilding or relocating is most appropriate during recovery.

# INTRODUCTION

As an emergency manager, it is your responsibility to help promote resilience during recovery. Victims of a disaster sustain significant losses and may struggle to take care of their immediate and long-term needs. Governments must focus on rebuilding the community as quickly as possible but also think about ways to reduce future disasters. For these reasons, you must help victims understand individual assistance (IA) programs and ways they can apply for relief. You will also need to educate public officials about emergency and permanent public assistance (PA) as well as the process for applying these programs. While pursuing recovery and mitigation after disasters, it will be necessary that you brace yourself for disagreement about policy. You should also endeavor to avoid fraud, protect the environment and historic buildings, and work closely with others. Most importantly, you should do all you can to minimize vulnerability during the window of opportunity disasters provide.

## 9.1 Disaster Impacts and Disaster Assistance

Imagine for a moment that you are the victim of a devastating earthquake. Your home is completely damaged in this disaster. You lose all your possessions and personal belongings. Your company's office building was also destroyed and you become unemployed. Your family might even suffer the loss of loved ones. The normal routines of life—such as bathing, cooking, eating, and doing laundry—would be severely disrupted. Would recovery be difficult? What resources and help would you need? Chances are that you would need a lot of money to help you recover. However, you might also require a host of services such as unemployment assistance and crisis counseling (Phillips, 2009).

A city or state may likewise suffer severe impacts from a disaster. Roads and bridges may be damaged. Schools, courthouses, and government buildings may have collapsed. Municipal or state vehicles could be buried under debris. The destruction of critical infrastructure and key assets may limit the ability of the government to fulfill the functions society has requested they perform. In this sense, local or state governments are also victims of disaster (Figure 9-1). They, too, may require assistance from others if the disaster overwhelms their capacity (Alesch et al., 2009).

As an emergency manager, you must understand the needs of victims and survivors as well as what programs and resources are available to assist them with recovery. Some of this assistance may come from insurance companies, while other help may be provided by the nonprofit sector and faith-based communities. Hopefully,

**Figure 9-1**

Infrastructure, such as these roads and power systems in Tennessee,
may be damaged or destroyed in disasters. David Fine/FEMA.

citizens will have insurance on which they can rely. If people planned ahead and
were able to afford monthly or annual premiums, they can call their insurance
company to file a claim. Insurance adjusters will review the losses and issue a
check to help them begin the process of recovery. In other situations, charitable
organizations like the American Red Cross, Salvation Army, and other nonprofit or
religious agencies will help those with long-standing needs. Such help may include
assistance for housing, money to replace furniture or other belongings, and even
college scholarships for children who have become orphaned in a disaster. In many
cases, victim and survivor needs will be addressed through insurance or the generosity of others. However, as an emergency manager, you may need to work with
these private and nonprofit groups to facilitate recovery in your community
(Phillips, 2009).

    In some situations, governments at the local, county, and state levels may require
outside assistance. Under such circumstances, states or the national government
may also provide relief to those affected by disaster. Some states may have their
own disaster assistance programs to help those in need. When major disasters
occur, federal involvement may begin after damages and needs have been assessed
and if the president has declared a disaster. Such declarations open up the possibility for federal disaster assistance. The resources available from the federal government can be of great benefit to disaster victims.

> ## FOR EXAMPLE
>
> ### Disaster Assistance after the 2007 Southern California Fires
>
> Fires were a major problem in Southern California in the fall of 2007. The fires, which were ignited by human and natural sources, burned more than 500,000 acres and destroyed 1,500 homes. The blazes killed 9 people and injured nearly 100 more. The threat and impact of the fires required the evacuation of nearly 1,000,000 individuals and necessitated the sheltering of 10,000 in Qualcomm Stadium. As a result of the damages, Governor Arnold Schwarzenegger requested a federal disaster declaration on October 21. A few days later, President George W. Bush approved the request and relief was opened up to several counties (Los Angeles, Orange, Riverside, San Bernardino, San Diego, Santa Barbara, and Ventura). As a result, individuals could apply for individual disaster assistance to help them recover from the fires. Cities and counties could also request PA to help with emergency protective measures. This disaster was unique in that it opened up the possibility of federal disaster assistance. The vast majority of emergencies and disasters are not large enough to warrant a national response.

There are two distinct federal disaster assistance programs:

1. **Individual Assistance (IA)** provides relief to citizens, businesses, and others affected by a disaster. Individual assistance is also known as IA.
2. **Public Assistance (PA)** makes available recovery aid for government entities. Public assistance is also known as PA.

Based on the extent of disaster impacts, a community may receive neither, one, or both types of disaster assistance. A FEMA handbook regarding disaster assistance states, "While a wide range of Federal programs are available to aid disaster victims, it should not be assumed that all of them will be activated. The determination as to which programs will be provided is made based on actual needs found during the damage assessment and/or on the basis of subsequent information" (FEMA 1997a, pp. 1–10).

## 9.2 Types of IA

As noted earlier, IA is geared toward individuals, families, and owners of small businesses. IA helps people and private organizations recover from the effects of a disaster. IA may also reimburse nonprofit agencies that provide assistance after disaster. There are different types of IA. Some of these are administered by the federal government, while others are managed by each state. Because each state is unique, you should expect that these programs may be implemented through different departments and agencies. Your state disaster recovery specialist can help you understand how the state is organized to assist individuals who have been impacted by disasters. Regardless of state organization or activities, the federal government often provides the bulk of the funds for such programs.

### 9.2.1 Loans and Grants

IA from the federal government is largely comprised of loans and grants:

▲ **Loan programs** lend money to individuals, families, and businesses that have sustained losses in disasters. Although interest rates are generally lower than the market average, loan rates and repayment schedule are determined by ability of the recipient to repay.

▲ **Grants** are gift funds that do not need to be repaid.

There are six types of loans and grant programs for disaster victims seeking IA:

1. **Disaster loans for homes and individuals**. These are loans available for families and individuals who have sustained losses from disasters. These include home/personal property physical disaster loans. Such loans are for homeowners and renters who lose homes and property. As of January 2014, loans of up to $200,000 can be given for primary residences (secondary residences are not eligible). Loans of up to $40,000 can also be provided to replace personal property lost in the primary residence. In addition, loans can be increased by 20% to implement mitigation measures for future disasters. An example of mitigation measures that can be incorporated while rebuilding is improved engineering so the structure can resist hurricane force winds. The Small Business Administration (SBA) handles these disaster loan programs.

2. **Disaster loans for businesses**. These are loans available for businesses that have sustained losses from disasters. Business physical disaster loans are for small businesses that have been adversely affected by disasters. Loans of up to $1,500,000 are provided to repair or replace structures and machinery. These loans can also be increased by 20% if recovery incorporates mitigation considerations. They are also administered by the SBA.

3. **Economic injury disaster loans**. These are loans for businesses and farming cooperatives that have suffered financial losses or hardship due to the disaster. Loans of up to $1,500,000 may be given to help a business or farm recover. This type of disaster loans is also managed by the SBA.

4. **Farm service agency loans**. This program provides loans for farmers who lose crops or equipment due to a disaster and/or require resources to continue operations. There is also an emergency conservation program to allocate funds to replace fencing, remove debris, and grade and rehabilitate farmland. A haying and grazing program allows the use of conservation reserve land if this is justified. These disaster relief programs are operated under the direction of the U.S. Department of Agriculture.

5. **Individual and households program (IHP)**. This program was formerly known as Individual and Family Grant Program. It provides up to $27,200 for those people who lack homeowners insurance and have uninhabitable

homes. The program has two components. The **disaster housing** portion is for homes that may be uninhabitable due to unsafe, unsanitary, or insecure conditions. This grant is also used by the government to provide mobile homes or help with minor home repairs, hotel/motel stays, and rental/mortgage payments. The disaster housing program is administered by FEMA and is 100% federally funded. This program was formerly known as Temporary Housing Assistance. **Other needs assistance (ONA)** is another program under IHP. It is specifically for those without insurance coverage. ONA makes available grants for home repair, replacement of personal property, and other disaster-related expenses for funeral, medical/dental care, and transportation. This program is administered by the state with a 75%–25% federal–state cost share. The maximum funds for IHP may change annually based on current market adjustments.

6. **Tax assistance**. This program allows for the deduction of uninsured losses if they total over 10% of income. In this case, the Internal Revenue Service provides refunds or tax breaks for victims of disaster.

### 9.2.2 Services

Disaster victims have other needs besides heavy financial burdens. **Services** are government programs that address unique issues or additional needs made evident in the disaster. For example, victims may need crisis counseling to cope with their losses. Another example relates to the rebuilding of homes. As disagreements between property owners and building contractors could arise after disaster situations, homeowners may need consumer services. Examples of services available are described as follows:

1. **Aging services**. This program provides transportation so disaster victims can meet with government officials and obtain answers to questions about all types of disaster assistance. It is administered by the state Department of Aging.

2. **Consumer services**. Under this program, counseling is given to those people dealing with consumer problems such as the lack of products and services after disasters, price gouging, fraud, questionable business ethics, etc. It is administered by the state attorney's office.

3. **Crisis counseling**. This program reimburses mental health centers and Red Cross counselors that provide stress debriefing for emergency responders and disaster victims. This is 100% federally funded. It is administered by the Mental Health Department in each state.

4. **Emergency services**. This program reimburses voluntary organizations for their postdisaster relief expenses. Examples of organizations are the American Red Cross and the Salvation Army. Emergency services provide food, clothing, shelter, medical care, medicines, glasses, home repair, or replacement of other essential items.

5. **Insurance services**. This program helps individuals file and settle claims with insurance agencies. It also helps victims acquire

federal flood insurance coverage or payments. It is administered by the State Department of Insurance and the National Flood Insurance Program.

6. **Legal services**. This program includes free legal counseling for people dealing with disaster-related legal documents, titles, contract problems, insurance, etc. The consulting services are provided by the Young Lawyers Division of the American Bar Association.

### 9.2.3 Benefits

The government also helps people receive or increase benefits that are needed after the disaster. **Benefits** are government welfare programs that can be extended to disaster victims:

1. **Food stamps**. This program assists in the distribution of groceries to those in need after a disaster. In this situation, food stamps are issued by state Human Services Departments.

2. **Unemployment assistance**. This program provides income for up to 26 weeks for people who have lost their job due to the disaster. This program is 100% federally funded. It is administered by state Workforce Commissions or Employment Agencies.

3. **Social security**. This program helps disaster victims complete applications for disability, death, and survivor benefits. It is run by the Social Security Administration.

4. **Veterans assistance**. This program helps retired military personnel obtain answers to questions and process changes regarding Veterans Administration-insured mortgages as well as death, pension, and insurance benefits. The Veterans Administration oversees this program.

---

## FOR EXAMPLE

### Where Is the Help?

Although the federal government offers assistance in many forms, help is not guaranteed. Some disasters do not meet the threshold that is required for federal assistance. Furthermore, IA from the federal government is not immediately given to the victims due to the required application process. The FEMA handbook reads, "Individuals and families will need to plan to use their own resources and financial reserves until Federal funds can be released. An application process must be completed before assistance becomes available. Often, it takes several weeks for the Federal government to review requests for financial assistance and to issue funds to those who meet eligibility requirements. Most Federal assistance is in the form of a loan that must be repaid rather than an outright grant" (FEMA 1997c).

- Do all states operate IA similarly?
- What loans are available to disaster victims?
- What are grants and how are they different from disaster loans?
- What services are available to those who have been affected by disaster?
- What are the benefits available to disaster victims?

## 9.3 Obtaining IA

It is necessary that you understand that the process of obtaining assistance can be frustrating for victims. The application process can take time, it can be confusing, and it may take several phone calls or discussions to resolve questions or get the relief that is needed. If an individual, family, or business has been affected by disaster, they may complete applications for IA by logging on to the FEMA website, calling the National Processing Service Center (NPSC), or visiting a disaster recovery center (DRC).

### 9.3.1 National Processing Service Center (NPSC)

Because of technological advances, people can register for IA online at http://www.fema.gov/assistance/register.shtm. However, because power and Internet lines may not be functioning after disasters, victims can also call a NPSC at a publicized toll-free number: (800) 621-FEMA or TTY (800) 462-7585. The **NPSC** is a location where victims call to apply for government disaster assistance. There are four major and permanent NPSCs around the country. They are located in:

▲ Denton, Texas
▲ Berryville, Virginia
▲ Mt. Weather, Virginia
▲ Hyattsville, Maryland

If a disaster warrants additional processing centers, they may be opened on a temporary basis. Some of these may be located in or near the affected area. NPSCs may offer services in a variety of languages, including Spanish as is the case in Puerto Rico.

At the NPSC, FEMA representatives use a computer program called **National Emergency Management Information System** (NEMIS). This allows FEMA representatives to record personal information about the disaster victim as well as damages, losses, needs, etc. This computer program—along with FEMA employees in the field—determines what types of disaster assistance programs the victim is eligible for. The computer program notes if assistance is available after FEMA employees verify damages to property in the declared disaster area. Within days or weeks, financial assistance in the form of a check is sent to the disaster victim(s).

The use of NPSCs is an increasingly preferred method for taking disaster assistance applications. In this case, disaster victims only have to log onto the Internet or pick up the phone. The application process associated with NPSC increases the speed of assistance delivery, and FEMA's travel expenses are reduced because fewer personnel are needed in the field. Nevertheless, a potential drawback is that victims may prefer to meet with someone in person rather than enter data on a computer or talk to someone on the phone at the NPSC. Phone lines may also be down in the affected community, making it difficult for victims to contact the NPSC.

### 9.3.2  Disaster Recovery Center (DRC)

If disasters render personal phone lines inoperable for a long period of time, the impacted victims may need to seek assistance in other ways. If this is the case, those affected by a disaster may visit a DRC (formerly a disaster application center). A **DRC** is a location where victims go to meet with FEMA representatives and other relief providers to discuss assistance programs and application requirements. A DRC is generally set up in the hardest hit vicinities in a declared disaster area. In large disasters, there may be multiple DRCs (Figure 9-2). DRCs are staffed by state, federal, and nonprofit agencies, which permits easy access to diverse disaster assistance programs and agencies. At the DRC, victims may ask questions and fill out forms (predominantly in electronic copy). Representatives from FEMA, the SBA, the American Red Cross, and other disaster assistance organizations provide detailed answers to technical questions. DRCs often have working phones so victims can call the NPSC from this location. There are even mobile DRCs that can be driven to affected neighborhoods. These have satellite communication capabilities that link victims with NPSC representatives.

**Figure 9-2**

A disaster recovery center is publicized in Pearcy, AR, after tornadoes and flooding resulted in a presidentially declared disaster. Patsy Lynch/FEMA.

The selection of the DRC site is often (but not always) a local and state responsibility. As an emergency manager, you may be tasked with this assignment of identifying a possible location and you should ensure the DRC has the following characteristics:

▲ The building should be sufficiently large. For example, it should be at least 4,500 square ft.
▲ It should have 25–50 tables and 150–250 chairs available.
▲ Air, heating, electricity, water, and restrooms must be available.
▲ The facility should have adequate communication equipment/capability. This includes phones and fax machines.
▲ It must have general office supplies such as paper, pencils, computers, photocopiers, and printers.
▲ The location should allow for adequate parking.

In addition, it is also important that you or other city personnel be present to help answer questions for victims and FEMA officials. You may also need other personnel who can assist victims and survivors in other ways. Some people may have additional needs including transportation requests as well as custodial, medical, security, bilingual, and childcare services. You must likewise ensure that the location of the DRC be publicized. This can be accomplished by handing out flyers in the affected area, by posting information on a local or state emergency management website, or by broadcasting information frequently through the media (Figure 9-3).

**Figure 9-3**

Innovative strategies to publicize the availability of disaster assistance should be pursued. Win Henderson/FEMA.

Regardless if victims apply for disaster assistance over the Internet, on the phone, or in person at the DRC, they must go through a four-step process. Victims must:

1. Rely on personal insurance and go through nonprofit agencies first.
2. Apply for FEMA housing assistance. They must do this even if it is not needed or required.
3. Apply for SBA loans even if they do not anticipate or desire receiving one.
4. Seek unmet needs assistance from additional community-based organizations if federal assistance is insufficient.

Only when all of these conditions are met will the federal and state governments provide disaster assistance. Because there are many factors that may have a bearing on disaster assistance (e.g., losses, insurance claims, income, credit score), not everyone will receive help from the government. And government assistance is not intended to help individuals fully recover. Instead, government relief is only meant to get victims started on the path to recovery. In these situations, victims and survivors may need to work with private companies nonprofit and faith-based organizations to address long-term needs (Figure 9-4). As an emergency manager, you should be aware of what these organizations are doing and share the information with the community as needed.

---

## FOR EXAMPLE

### Insurance Needs

Because federal disaster programs are available, it is tempting for some people to go without insurance. The FEMA handbook states, "Individuals, families and businesses should all carry adequate insurance to meet their needs in the event of a disaster. It is not the purpose of Federal assistance to duplicate protection available through insurance plans. Federal assistance is provided to address only the most basic disaster-related needs not covered by other means. Besides, most disaster events are not Presidentially declared disasters, so Federal disaster assistance is often not available. Disaster assistance may be granted in the form of a loan rather than as an outright cash award. For geographically areas subject to floods … the Federal government ensures that residents of participating communities can receive appropriate insurance coverage through its National Flood Insurance Program (NFIP). In addition, flood insurance coverage is required as a condition to receiving Federal disaster aid for permanent repair or reconstruction within an identified floodplain. You may wish to contact your local emergency preparedness office, the local building or zoning official, or your insurance agent to find out whether your local community is a participant" (FEMA 1997c).

**Figure 9-4**

A private contractor is seen here making repairs to a home in Austell, GA, after floods damaged the residence in September 2009. David Fine/FEMA.

## SELF-CHECK

- What does an NPSC do?
- What does NEMIS stand for?
- Why is a DRC needed after a disaster?
- What issues must be considered when setting up a DRC?
- What issues must be considered when operating a DRC?

## 9.4  Categories of PA

Local and state governments, just like private citizens or businesses, may require disaster assistance from outside sources. For this reason, you should be familiar with federal PA programs. PA is directed toward governments, organizations, and nonprofits with the purpose of helping them react to and recover from a disaster. Eligible public entities include:

1. **Local governments**. This includes city, township, county, and regional governments.
2. **State government agencies**. These agencies consist of the Department of Transportation, Environmental Protection Departments, and so on.
3. **Indian tribes and related organizations**. This includes reservations and other Indian-operated property and facilities.
4. **Private nonprofit organizations**. This covers critical facilities such as hospitals and schools. It may also encompass utility companies, custodial care centers, zoos, museums, community centers, homeless shelters, and so on. These organizations must have tax-exempt status and must provide services to the general public.

PA is divided into emergency assistance and permanent assistance categories:

▲ **Emergency assistance** is financial or other types of assistance to help local and state governments deal with the immediate impacts of disasters.
▲ **Permanent assistance** is financial payments or reimbursements to local and state governments for long-term rebuilding activities.

Each of these will be described in the following.

### 9.4.1  Emergency Assistance

If a disaster is declared at the federal level, emergency assistance is given to communities as soon as possible to help them deal with the immediate impact of disasters. This helps them take care of debris removal and other protective measures.

### 9.4.1.1  Debris Removal

**Debris removal assistance** includes funding to clear disaster-related debris. For example, building rubble or broken tree limbs would need to be cleared from public property. If debris is posing a threat to the public, the federal government may also pay to have it removed from private property if permission is granted by the owner. The removal of certain debris such as tree stumps will not be reimbursed by the federal government because the cost is very high and it is a nonessential activity. To ensure a debris removal activity is eligible for federal assistance, it is vital that you check on all applicable regulations.

### 9.4.1.2  Protective Measures

**Protective measures** are a reimbursement category that has the purpose of reducing losses or eliminating threats to life, public health, and safety. It may include sandbagging to limit property damage in a flood. Another example is shoring up buildings immediately after an earthquake. Creating a backfire to prevent additional loss of property is another form of a protective measure. The goal of protective measures is to limit further injury, death, and destruction after the disaster occurs.

### 9.4.2 Permanent Assistance

Permanent assistance may also be given to local and state governments after a disaster has been declared at the federal level. This includes assistance to repair road systems, water control systems, public buildings/equipment, public utility systems, and other facilities.

#### 9.4.2.1 Road Systems

**Road systems assistance** repays expenses associated with the rebuilding or repairing of bridges, lights, and culverts. Damages must be directly related to disaster (i.e., not preexisting). Repair will conform to current standards and will match current market costs.

#### 9.4.2.2 Water Control

**Water control assistance** deals with repairs to rivers, dikes, levees, and dams. Repairs must fall under U.S. Army Corps of Engineers or Natural Resource Conservation System specifications. Drainage channels will be restored to preflood capacity—assuming there is evidence of prior maintenance. Debris in natural streams will be removed only if there is a threat to public safety. Payment for seeding is used to stabilize slopes only—not for cosmetic purposes.

#### 9.4.2.3 Public Buildings/Equipment

**Public buildings/equipment assistance** is given to repair or replace buildings, supplies, and vehicles. Private or self-insurance must cover all applicable payments before any federal reimbursements are to be made. Payment for rebuilding will conform to preexisting capacity and standards. Buildings and equipment must have been in use before the disaster. Office furniture is replaced with used items only. Trees on public lands are not eligible for reimbursement.

#### 9.4.2.4 Public Utility

**Public utility assistance** includes water, gas, and sewage system repairs. There must be evidence that the disaster caused the damages. Loss of revenue while these systems are down is not eligible for federal reimbursement.

#### 9.4.2.5 Other Assistance

**Other assistance** is for the repair of parks, airports, and recreational facilities. Damages must be in a designated disaster-declared area. Seeding is only covered for stabilization purposes, and trees/plants are not eligible for reimbursement. Expenses for beach repair will be granted if there has been evidence of ongoing maintenance.

## 9.5 Obtaining PA

As a local emergency manager, you will receive many questions about how your government or other eligible organizations may obtain PA. To acquire PA, the affected government entity or organization will need to be aware of the process for obtaining it. Although the steps may vary somewhat in each state, they must conform to federal guidelines.

After an area has been approved for PA (e.g., a presidential declaration has been issued), a briefing will be held. A **briefing** is a meeting that reviews all aspects of federal programs and requirements to give local officials an overview of the entire recovery process. It includes local officials and the State Coordinating Officer. The briefing is often arranged by the state emergency management personnel in charge of recovery. At this point, a kickoff meeting will then be held with the individuals mentioned previously as well as the federal coordinating officer. A **kickoff meeting** covers federal disaster assistance programs and policies in an in-depth manner (Figure 9-5). This meeting will:

▲ Introduce the PA coordinator
▲ Explain the process of applying for and receiving aid
▲ Hand out appropriate forms
▲ Discuss damages and applicant needs
▲ Answer any questions that may arise
▲ Address concerns about mitigation, historical sites, and environmental protection

Once a kickoff meeting has been held, the government affected by the disaster is now able to make a formal request for federal disaster assistance. This must be completed within 30 days after the presidential disaster declaration. Applicants must submit:

1. **Notice of interest and request for PA forms.** These documents show the need for assistance and list damages by category.
2. **A designation of applicant's agent form.** This document notes the point of contact for the government entity seeking federal assistance.
3. **A project worksheet for each category of PA.** This document helps to initiate and record emergency and permanent assistance activities.

Figure 9-5

A FEMA project specialist meets with North Central District Health Department officials in Enfield, CT, to discuss public assistance guidelines. Ed Edahl/FEMA.

Unlike emergency assistance, applications and record keeping for permanent assistance are classified according to one of four types of projects:

▲ **Small projects** are a type of permanent assistance that is typically paid in advance by the federal government. Small projects are those costing less than $66,399. A small project worksheet may combine many projects together (up to the specified amount).

▲ **Large projects** are permanent assistance activities requiring payment over $66,400.

▲ **Improved projects** are assistance programs that make repairs beyond the initial design or expand the building. This may include adding a wing to a building or implementing mitigation measures to prevent a similar occurrence in the future.

▲ **Alternate projects** include permanent projects that require abandonment of an old facility and building in a completely different area. An example of this is demolishing a courthouse in the floodplain and moving it to higher ground.

Once these application materials are received, FEMA/state officials will complete a **Damage Survey Report** (DSR) for each type of assistance being requested to determine the need and validity of the requests. This information is used by federal employees to ensure accuracy. These officials are located in the Joint Field Office (JFO) (formerly known as the Disaster Field Office). A **JFO** is the location where

> ### FOR EXAMPLE
>
> ### Role of Local Government
>
> Despite the many federal programs available after a disaster, the local government plays one of the largest roles in response and recovery operations. The FEMA handbook states, "The local government is primarily responsible for preparing for disasters that might affect a community and helping residents recover from such events. The great majority of disasters are handled successfully at the local level. State and Federal resources are intended to assist the community only when the community's own resources are not sufficient" (FEMA 1997c).

FEMA representatives manage recovery. Local and state representatives may also be housed in the JFO at times. However, the location of the JFO is not announced to the public and should not be confused with the DRC.

The next step is for FEMA to send approved DSRs to the state emergency management department/agency. The state then meets with the applicant(s) (representative or representatives of the affected government or organization) to discuss program requirements further. Once this has occurred, the cleanup and rebuilding may officially begin. When each approved recovery activity is finished, a Project Completion Form will be filled out so local and state governments can seek reimbursement. At times, disagreements about projects and payment amounts will arise and these need to be appealed within 60 days. FEMA officials will determine what adjustments, if any, need to be made. Thus, after a declaration has been issued and orientations about the programs have taken place, the city begins the long process of recovery. The state oversees much of the paperwork and FEMA funds approximately 75% of the costs. The entire process can take months or years, depending on the extent of the disaster losses.

## SELF-CHECK

- What is a briefing and how is it different from a kickoff meeting?
- What forms should be filled out to obtain PA?
- What are the types of projects listed under PA?
- What is a DSR and why is it needed?
- What is a Disaster Field Office and who is located there?

## 9.6 Important Issues for Recovery

As you begin in earnest the process of recovery, there are four additional issues that you must consider. These include the minimization of fraudulent activity, environmental protection, historic preservation, and the mitigation of future disasters.

### 9.6.1 Minimizing Fraud

Because there may be millions of federal dollars pouring in to disaster-affected communities, it is imperative that those working in recovery be vigilant of fraud, waste, and abuse. People have filed IA disaster applications even though they have not been affected by a disaster. For example, a man in Joplin, MO, filed a fraudulent claim after a major tornado. He received $2,750 even though the address he listed for his home was a ministry halfway house. There have even been instances where criminals have sought IA from unaffected jail cells! Public officials have also engaged in fraudulent practices. Some city leaders have filed erroneous paperwork to bring additional monies to their communities or themselves. After Hurricanes Rita and Gustav, a woman, a mayor, and a police chief filed fraudulent time sheets. The woman sought approval and payment for her services even though she was not working at the time. On other occasions, contractors will attempt to get more reimbursement than they are entitled to by misrepresenting their work. Companies removing debris have falsified the amount of fallen trees they removed after a major ice storm in Oklahoma. In such cases, the sentence could include a 5-year prison sentence and come with a fine of $250,000. You should be aware of these potential scams and work closely with the Office of the Inspector General in the Department of Homeland Security to ensure that this behavior is averted or prosecuted. You should also monitor government paperwork and contractor recovery activities carefully. You may need to notify the public through the media about where to report fraudulent activity. FEMA has also set up a toll-free number for you to report fraud. It is 1-866-720-5721.

### 9.6.2 Protecting the Environment

According to the National Environmental Policy Act, the federal government requires an environmental impact statement to be completed before large disaster recovery projects can begin. It is important to note that FEMA will deny funding for projects that have not included an environmental impact statement or obtained the appropriate approvals. An **environmental impact statement** is a complete assessment of

---

### FOR EXAMPLE

**Major Laws and Executive Orders Commonly Involved with FEMA's Environmental Review**

There are a number of laws that deal with environmental protection and disasters. These include: National Environmental Policy Act; Endangered Species Act; National Historic Preservation Act; Coastal Zone Management Act; Rivers and Harbors Act; Coastal Barrier Resources Act; Resource Conservation and Recovery Act; Clean Water Act; Clean Air Act; Marine Mammal Protection Act; Magnuson–Stevens Fishery Conservation and Management Act; CERCLA (Superfund); Farmland Protection Policy Act; Migratory Bird Treaty Act; Bald Eagle Protection Act; Wild and Scenic Rivers Act; Executive Order 11990, Wetlands Protection; Executive Order 11988, Floodplain Management; Executive Order 12898, Environmental Justice; and Executive Order 13112, Invasive Species.

how your recovery actions will affect the air, soil, and water in that area. Environmental impact statements will obviously require the skills and expertise of state officials, environmental professionals, and scholars who understand the physical environment and human interaction with rivers, plant and animal life, and other natural resources. You should work closely with these individuals as well as FEMA officials to ensure that your projects do not harm the environment or create dust, noise, erosion, etc. In some cases, approval of environmental impact statements could take months or even years. Although this may seem like an unnecessary delay, the goal of this requirement is to ensure that recovery does not harm the environment.

### 9.6.3 Preserving Historic Buildings

There are thousands of historic buildings in the United States, and these can be adversely affected by disasters. These structures are especially vulnerable because they are old and not built to current code and regulations (Figure 9-6). Because these buildings carry a legacy of history, there will be many individuals and groups that will oppose their demolition—even if they are severely damaged in disasters. There is consequently a dilemma between historical preservation on the one hand and recovery and future mitigation priorities on the other. For these reasons, you must therefore assess the impact of the disaster on the building and determine what can be done, if anything, to maintain the heritage of the structure. Novel approaches can be undertaken to address multiple concerns simultaneously. After an earthquake in Santa Cruz, California, the façade of a nineteenth-century bank was retained with city redevelopment funds and then

**Figure 9-6**

Historic buildings, such as Fort Johnson that was affected by flooding in New York, may require special consideration during the recovery process. Hans Pennick/FEMA.

attached to a completely new building. In other words, the structure was rebuilt to code, and the original front of the building was reattached. This maintained aesthetic charm but ensured future seismic safety. Should you have questions about historic preservation, it is recommended that you talk to your state agency in charge of disaster recovery or others associated with FEMA's Environmental Planning and Historic Preservation Program. More information can also be obtained from the National Trust for Historic Preservation (see http://www.preservationnation.org/resources/technical-assistance/disaster-recovery/).

### 9.6.4 Mitigating Future Disasters

Recovery is an excellent time to implement more stringent mitigation measures (Public Entity Risk Institute, 2006). In the immediate aftermath of a disaster, interest in mitigation is at an all-time high. You will probably have less resistance against mitigation than before. The city council is likely to be more receptive to change when a disaster occurs. However, this interest does not always stay constant. Over the next few weeks and months, interest wanes since people want to speed up recovery and resume their normal daily activities as soon as possible. In addition, new problems are likely to attract the attention of decision makers. Therefore, it is imperative that you are prepared to implement mitigation measures as soon as a disaster strikes. This may require that a mitigation action plan be written before or after the disaster occurs. A **mitigation action plan** is a document that describes the vulnerabilities of the community and what should be done to correct them in the future. It may also require that proposals for improved warning systems, new building codes, or property buyout programs for low-lying areas be drafted in advance so they can be used when needed. Regarding land-use decisions after disasters, Mileti and Passarini (1996) have noted that there are three options for relocation. These include relocation to a new site, intraurban relocation, and rebuilding in the same area.

### 9.6.4.1 Relocate to a New Site

An example of relocation to a new site occurred in 1964, when the strongest recorded earthquake to ever hit North America struck Valdez, Alaska. The earthquake measured an 8.4–8.6 on the Richter scale, causing the entire town of Valdez to be severely damaged. Shortly thereafter, a tsunami produced by the earthquake caused additional devastation. During damage assessment, it was determined that the ground under Valdez was unstable and at risk of further losses. The federal government would provide financial assistance to the city only if it would relocate to a safer area. The Army Corps of Engineers decided to move the entire town to the delta of Mineral Creek that was much safer. It took about four years for the new city of Valdez to become home to all of the old Valdez residents. Sixty-two buildings were moved from the old town to the new site. Public facilities were replaced by the government and homeowners rebuilt their residences. The advantage of relocating to a new site is a reduction in the vulnerability of the community to disaster. Response and recovery costs associated with future disasters could be minimized. There is also increased employment from relocation after a disaster. However, relocation is very costly and it does disrupt society a great deal.

### 9.6.4.2 Intraurban Relocation

The 6.9 earthquake that shook northwestern Armenia on December 7, 1988, provides an example of intraurban relocation. This earthquake, and an aftershock that followed four minutes later, killed twenty-five thousand people. The city of Leninakan, which had a population of 250,000, was destroyed and other smaller towns were adversely affected as well. Many factors contributed to the disaster including soil conditions and inadequate building design and construction. In addition to the human losses, many medical facilities were destroyed and the medical profession lost capacity as a result. This devastating loss contributed to a difficult rescue and response operation.

After the earthquake, the Armenian government made some modest changes. They altered how the land was used and restricted the rebuilding of certain structures, such as hospitals, in dangerous areas. In addition, a central planning committee decided to modify where replacement housing could be built. An advantage of intraurban relocation is the possibility of increased employment. Intraurban relocation is not as costly as relocating to a new site and does not disrupt society as much either. Intraurban relocation does reduce the vulnerability of the community to disaster, but not to the same extent as relocation to a completely different site.

### 9.6.4.3 Rebuild in the Same Area

A good case of rebuilding in the same area comes from the Whittier Narrows earthquake that struck the San Gabriel Valley in 1987. This disaster resulted in $358 dollars in damages, but the community chose to rebuild in the same area nonetheless. Not only did the citizens and businesses rebuild, but they even expanded and constructed more buildings in dangerous areas.

Mileti and Passarini illustrate that there are many reasons why people wanted to build in the same areas:

▲ **Politics**. Politicians want to rebuild as soon as possible to overcome the negative impact of disasters. Their constituents also want to return to "normal" and have things the way "they used to be."

▲ **Culture**. People have ties to their community and its way of life. Change is socially disruptive and moving is difficult for most people. Relocation may seem impossible and there may not be a clear plan of how that is to be achieved.

▲ **Economics**. Massive federal funding enables communities to rebuild in the same areas. Rebuilding also brings in jobs and income for residents living in the area. The poor are affected most but receive less aid and find it difficult to move. Demolition of damaged structures reduces opportunities for cheap housing elsewhere. Many small businesses cannot handle the shock of relocation either.

▲ **Psychological**. People naturally want to return to their lives as they knew it, and they don't want to feel "beaten" by a disaster. They may be stressed and have a hard time coping with the disaster. Moving would disrupt them even further and cause them to lose their social networks.

Rebuilding in the same area has low immediate costs, but it often increases vulnerability. Unfortunately, rebuilding is most common practice for communities to take after a disaster.

## FOR EXAMPLE

### Change and Disasters

Disasters do not always spur positive change in a community. A case in point was in Centralia, Pennsylvania. In 1961, city officials were getting ready for a parade and they noticed a lot of trash in a certain area. This trash was an eyesore and it was producing odors, insects, and vermin. City leaders decided to burn the trash and did not consult anyone about their action. The trash just so happened to be located on an excavation site of an abandoned coalmine. This area had a rich deposit of anthracite coal underneath. The fire spread to the coal and expanded throughout the mine shafts. Because anthracite burns hot and long, smoke was still rising a year after this incident took place. Carbon monoxide rose into people's basements and foundations (at fatal levels). The heat created massive cracks in the earth above it. Sinkholes appeared and swallowed buildings as the land gave way beneath.

A geological team was brought in to inspect the damage. They determined there was 40 million tons of anthracite coal remaining to be burnt. From 1962 to 1978, the state and federal government spent $3.3 million to control the fire. An additional $10.8 million was spent in 1994 (unsuccessfully). Those responding to the incident tried to pump water into mine shafts, but the fire spread over 450 acres. The water created dangerous steam and also polluted local rivers, streams, and lakes. The sludge that resulted was poisoned with lye and acid. By 1980, the federal government funded a relocation project through the Office of Surface Mining. Route 61 was cut off from the road system and disappeared from the maps. In 1961, there were over 1,200 inhabitants. To date, most residents have moved out of the area. The fire was still burning at the time of this publication. The Office of Surface Mining determined another $663 million would be needed to extinguish it. Most cases do illustrate a better possibility of change after a disaster.

## SELF-CHECK

- Why should you be aware of fraudulent activities?
- How can you protect the environment during recovery?
- Why is historic preservation important to some individuals and groups?
- What are the options for rebuilding after a disaster?
- What is a mitigation action plan?

# CASE STUDY

## Hurricane Katrina, New Orleans, and Community Recovery
### By Kristina Cramb

As one of the largest storms on record, Hurricane Katrina destroyed at least 205,000 homes and 18,750 local businesses in New Orleans (Dawson and McCook, 2006, p. 292). The storm surge, levee breaches, and subsequent flooding also damaged two-thirds of the housing within the city, making it uninhabitable (Vigdor, 2008, p. 146). Prior to this disaster, the population of New Orleans was about 400,000 residents. Immediately after the storm, New Orleans became a virtual ghost town. Even by 2007, only half of the pre-Katrina population returned to New Orleans (Vigdor, 2008, p. 135). As would be expected, New Orleans has had a difficult time recovering from this major disaster (Comfort et al., 2010; Vigdor, 2008). Even today, the city is still finding it difficult to overcome all of the significant impacts of Katrina.

Rebuilding New Orleans following Katrina, has proved to be complex (Comfort et al., 2010), but local, state, and federal levels of government believed it was necessary to reestablish this historic city (Vigdor 2008). One of the first obstacles after Katrina was to repair critical infrastructure. Without repaired roads and utility lines, it would be difficult for the individual citizens and businesses to begin the process of rebuilding. Repairing critical infrastructure was therefore a high priority for those overseeing recovery.

While this was underway, local government officials also decided to focus attention on the least damaged areas of the city first (Comfort et al., 2010). Yet, in many cases, community residents appeared to be fairly resilient and were not content to wait for the government to resolve all of their problems. In fact, many families started to rebuild their homes prior to the creation of formal government building codes, arguing that government failed to promptly create guidelines and procedures in a timely manner. Interestingly, some families even located temporary trailers on their property so that they could live in their neighborhood while rebuilding their homes (Maret, 2006).

At the federal level, FEMA posted recovery and rebuilding guidelines for New Orleans residents about 8 months after Katrina. FEMA wanted to make sure that recovery activities also considered ways to mitigate future flooding disasters. Houses rebuilt in low-lying, flood-prone areas needed to have their foundations raised by a minimum of eleven feet (Maret, 2006). Even the damaged houses that were located on higher ground were also required to have their foundations raised by a minimum of three feet. Fortunately, funds were allocated to help offset the costs of rebuilding the City of New Orleans (Comfort et al., 2010; Maret, 2006; Vigdor, 2008). Homeowners were eligible to receive grant allocations to help elevate their foundations. However, these allotments of funds would not pay the entire cost of the project. The maximum amount of money disbursed to qualified residents was $30,000, but the average cost to raise a foundation ranges from $50,000 to $75,000 (Maret, 2006, p. 17).

A second grant was designed to help offset building costs for homeowners and landlords who want to rebuild housing in New Orleans (Vigdor, 2008).

The Road Home Grant allocations were capped at $150,000 per household, with an average monetary allocation of $66,138 per home (Comfort et al., 2010, p. 672). Another type of grant, Community Development Block Grants, provided approximately $411 million for recovery efforts (Comfort et al., 2010, p. 671). While these sizable grant allocations were set aside for the City of New Orleans and its recovery efforts, several problems became evident. For example, Mayor Ray Nagin was convicted for fraudulent practices regarding the use of federal funds and he was sentenced to prison. In addition, there has been a failure to allocate all of the monies set aside for recovery and rebuilding efforts within the City of New Orleans. Billions of dollars have not been disbursed, leaving the recovery and rebuilding coffers too full.

Another problem associated with the recovery from Katrina involves insurance companies. Because of severe risk, many private insurance providers are raising insurance premiums on housing units within New Orleans or are refusing to insure any new housing within the city itself. In an effort to combat these negative effects, the State of Louisiana has implemented a state program that reduces insurance premiums and grants tax deductions to builders that comply with the state's rebuilding code and mitigation standards (Comfort et al., 2010).

Cost of living is another issue that affects people who desire to return to the City of New Orleans. The price of housing in New Orleans before Katrina was abnormally low due to excess supply of older homes on the market, which allowed for mortgage and rent payments to stay below average costs. However, the destruction of a majority of the homes in the community caused increases in mortgage and rent payments on homes that were not condemned (Vigdor, 2008). Research indicates that these higher property values may make rebuilding damaged and destroyed housing units cost prohibitive for some people.

Many local businesses have also had challenges with recovery (Dietch and Corey, 2011, pp. 320–322). Businesses struggling with recovery are inhibited by certain factors like the decrease in local population, labor shortages, and the loss of the consumer base (Dietch and Corey, 2011). However, this is not universal. Three-fourths of the companies that survived Katrina state that their business is equal to or better than pre-Katrina levels (Dietch and Corey, 320–322). As expected, the strongest post-Katrina businesses revolve around the construction industry (Dietch and Corey, 2011; Vigdor, 2008).

New Orleans has had a long and difficult road toward recovery, and this may be the case for years to come (Comfort et al., 2010). Affordable housing in New Orleans may not be a viable option in the near future since rent and mortgage payments have dramatically increased following the loss of available housing and the rise in costs for rebuilding homes and apartment complexes (Vigdor, 2008). Yet, there are many residents and businesses who are working diligently to rebuild their homes, lives, and places of work. While New Orleans' recovery efforts may be slow, researchers like Vigdor (2008) and Comfort et al. (2010) note that the city is still working hard toward recovery. The city has been marred and battered, yet community residents have fighting spirits and they desire to rebuild New Orleans.

## 9.7 The Potential for Disagreement

Because disaster recovery is characterized by the involvement of many different people and priorities, you should be aware of the potential for disagreement about what needs to be done. Bates and Peacock (1989) have identified several types of disaster recovery. Some of these processes are internal to the community, while others are external.

Internal recovery processes are labeled as indigenous or independent. There are three paths that fall under this category. The **individualistic self-help** mode occurs when the community provides its own labor and supplies for recovery. A community operating under this mode takes sole responsibility for the management of recovery processes. The **collective or cooperative** mode is characterized by victims working together to achieve a common goal. In this situation, agreement is reached about what to do during recovery. The **bureaucratized paternalistic** mode suggests that a person or agency inside the community controls recovery with no input from others. Victims may have little influence over what happens to their damaged homes and community rebuilding.

The exogenous or dependent processes are initiated from outside the disaster-affected community. This category also has three distinct paths. The **independent beneficiary** mode occurs when resources are sent in to the affected community. However, the affected people must still provide their own labor and manage recovery operations. The **collaborative partnership** mode takes place when outsiders and victims work together to facilitate disaster recovery. It is characterized by a great deal of cooperation. The **bureaucratized external paternalism** mode features an outside agency that controls all decisions and recovery activities. Victims seem to have no input on what happens to their community.

Bates and Peacock admit that "the recovery mode usually is mixed with some resources coming from both sources. Nevertheless, the recovery process for a particular social unit in a particular disaster may be dominated by one mode or the other. It is also true that one mode of adaptation may be employed for one type of unit while a different mode is employed by another in the same disaster.

---

### FOR EXAMPLE

#### Research about Disaster Recovery

Disaster researchers have illustrated that most people work together to resolve mutual disaster problems. However, studies also reveal that citizens, businesses, and politicians may disagree about recovery priorities. For instance, a heated debate about what to do with the World Trade Center site occurred once debris was removed from Ground Zero. Some wanted to erect new business towers, while others desired a permanent memorial for victims of the 9/11 terrorist attacks. Scholars have likewise shown that outside assistance is both appreciated and feared. Disaster victims may want federal resources, but they do not like others telling them what to do during recovery. Disagreement about recovery may last a long time after a disaster occurs.

For example, households experiencing a given disaster may receive outside assistance, while in the same disaster organizations (businesses) may be forced to recover on their own. Or, isolated communities may be left to their own devices, while urban centers receive massive outside aid" (1989, p. 359). For these reasons, you should view these modes as ideal types that may occur simultaneously rather than being isolated from one another. Nevertheless, this research is useful because it may help you to recognize possible conflicts during the recovery process. Efforts should be made to integrate efforts rather than work alone or against one another.

## SELF-CHECK

- Is disaster recovery an internal or external process?
- What is the individual self-help mode and how is it different from the independent beneficiary mode?
- Why are the collective and collaborative partnership modes beneficial?
- What are the problems associated with the bureaucratized paternalistic mode?
- Is the bureaucratized external mode different mode advantageous or disadvantageous?

## 9.8 Pressing for Change

Although there are often divergent opinions about what should be done after disasters, local government officials should do their best to implement all types of measures to reduce their community's vulnerability. As the local emergency manager, it is imperative that you take advantage of disasters because they often act as policy "focusing events" (Birkland, 1997). Such focusing events may also be known as a "window of opportunity." A **window of opportunity** is the time immediately after a disaster when leaders and citizens are sensitive to what has happened and are willing to do something to prevent a similar occurrence in the future. For instance, the public outrage after some disasters may cause policy makers to pass and implement new laws (e.g., the Post-Katrina Emergency Management Reform Act and the Sandy Recovery and Improvement Act).

To examine the effects of a disaster on the community, the changes made after the Loma Prieta earthquake in 1998 will be reviewed. On October 17, 1989, a 7.1 earthquake shook San Francisco. It killed 67, injured 2,435, and caused $5.6 billion in damages. Researchers Olson et al. (1998) investigated the policy changes before and after the earthquake. In the mid-1970s, the federal and state government pushed for mitigation activities. However, the City of Oakland rarely considered the need for such legislation. In fact, from 1954 to

1989, earthquake issues appeared only 17 times in the city council meetings. The researchers also determined:

▲ No city meetings discussed unreinforced masonry (URM) buildings.
▲ Building inspectors were given no attention and resources.
▲ Ordinance, SB 547, which was aimed at reducing seismic hazards in existing buildings, was considered another annoying law.
▲ The major issues being discussed and addressed were crime and economic development.

However, after the event (from 1989 to 1995), things changed dramatically. The window of opportunity created by the disaster led to a different environment. Earthquake issues were mentioned 178 times in city agendas. Seven laws were passed that were related to damage from the event. Two laws were passed that focused on URM buildings and the reduction of future risk. These were ordinance 11173 and ordinance 11217.

Ordinance 11173 was an emergency order to deal with damaged buildings. It allowed building officials to assess buildings after the disaster and determine if they posed a risk of collapse or falling objects. This ordinance also recommended that all buildings be upgraded to code. There were some waivers for historic buildings however.

Ordinance 11217 was an act that made the temporary law (ordinance 11173) more permanent. It limited the maximum code for rebuilding. It was also less forceful in wording (e.g., "shall substantially comply") and allowed a way out of compliance if alternative procedures for rebuilding could be found. However, in no case could design specs be 25% below code. Ordinance 11217 brought other changes as well. It made it unlawful to eliminate historic buildings. The code set priority levels based on building location, stories, traffic, use, number of occupants, and complexity of rebuilding. It recommended that walls be attached to the foundation and the roof in order to reduce vulnerability.

### 9.8.1  Lessons from the Loma Prieta Earthquake

As an emergency manager, you can learn a great deal from the Loma Prieta earthquake. Before the Loma Prieta earthquake, building code inspectors and seismic safety advocates were self-suppressed. They recognized their inferior position and did not feel empowered to make changes or suggest them. After the earthquake, this "seismic safety" group gained power and took advantage of situation. One person involved in recovery stated that "the earthquake gave us a window, if we could use it skillfully, to review the entire city approach to building safety in a seismically active area." The building inspectors and seismic safety advocates educated realtors, business owners, and preservationists about earthquakes. They also brought all parties together to hammer out an agreement about what should be done to reduce future vulnerability (Olson et al., 1988).

There are a number of additional lessons from this disaster:

▲ **Education is key**. Make sure everyone understands the logic behind and need for additional mitigation measures (Figure 9-7).

**Figure 9.7**

It is imperative to educate people about mitigation after disasters. David Fine/FEMA.

▲ **Acknowledge different viewpoints**. People have divergent opinions about what should be done. For example, real estate and property owners may argue that there is no danger inherent to current building codes. As an emergency manager, you will desire more stringent building codes and adherence to such regulations. Historic preservationists, on the other hand, will want to protect the buildings from demolition. Find a way to compromise among these groups as it increases the possibility of agreement and compliance.

▲ **Mitigation is as much political as technical**. Information about the science behind mitigation is necessary, but the art of persuasion and political acumen will also be needed to implement change after disasters.

---

## FOR EXAMPLE

### Mitigation Measures for All Disasters

Mitigation measures can protect a community from more than one hazard (Schwab, 1998). In Plainfield, Illinois, a tornado struck late in the season (August 28, 1990). It was an F-5 on the Fujita scale, destroying some homes located in the DePage floodway. Total cost of relocation was $180,500. The city even required building 2 feet above 100 yr plain. In 1996, a major flood hit Plainfield 2 ft. above 100 level. While some sustained damaged, all homes remain standing. Recovery from the tornado linked rebuilding to mitigation for another disaster.

## SELF-CHECK

- Why did public officials not consider mitigation before the Loma Prieta earthquake?
- Did attitudes in city council change after the disaster?
- Do some groups oppose mitigation activities?
- How did the emergency management group promote change?

## SUMMARY

As an emergency manager, you must be aware of the impact of disasters as well as the types of federal disaster assistance programs. You should be aware of IA and how people can apply for it. In addition, you ought to understand the categories of PA and how they can be obtained. Your knowledge about NPSCs, DRCs, NEMIS, JFOs, and required paperwork can help you bring federal assistance to victims and the local government in your community. During recovery, you should also avoid fraud, protect the environment, safeguard old structures, and pursue additional mitigation measures. Knowing how to work closely with others inside and outside of your community and take advantage of windows of opportunity disasters provide is also required for resilience.

## KEY TERMS

| | |
|---|---|
| Alternate projects | Permanent projects that require abandonment of an old facility and building in a completely different area. |
| Benefits | Government welfare programs that can be extended to disaster victims. |
| Briefing | A meeting that reviews all aspects of federal programs and requirements to give local officials an overview of the entire recovery process. |
| Bureaucratized external paternalism mode | A way of operating where an outside agency controls all decisions and recovery activities. |
| Bureaucratized paternalistic mode | A way of operating where a person or agency inside the community controls recovery with no victim input. |
| Collaborative partnership mode | A way of operating that takes place when outsiders and victims work together to facilitate disaster recovery. |
| Collective or cooperative mode | A way of operating that is characterized by victims working together to achieve a common goal. |

| | |
|---|---|
| **Disaster housing** | A government program that helps people find housing for homes that may be uninhabitable due to unsafe, unsanitary, or insecure conditions. |
| **Disaster recovery center (DRC)** | The location where victims go to meet with FEMA representatives and other relief providers to discuss assistance programs and application requirements. |
| **Damage Survey Report (DSR)** | A document that verifies the need and validity of the local and state requests for public assistance. |
| **Emergency assistance** | Financial or other types of assistance to help local and state governments deal with the immediate impacts of disasters. |
| **Environmental impact statement** | A complete assessment of how your recovery actions will affect the air, soil, and water in that area. |
| **Grants** | Gift funds that do not need to be repaid. |
| **Improved projects** | Assistance programs that make repairs beyond the initial design or expand the building. |
| **Independent beneficiary mode** | A way of operating that occurs when resources are sent in to the affected community. |
| **Individual assistance (IA)** | A relief program for citizens, businesses, and others affected by a disaster. |
| **Individualistic self-help mode** | A way of operating that occurs when the community provides its own labor and supplies for recovery. |
| **Joint Field Office (JFO)** | The location where FEMA representatives manage recovery. |
| **Kickoff meeting** | A meeting that covers federal disaster assistance programs and policies in an in-depth manner. |
| **Large projects** | Permanent assistance activities requiring payment over $66,400. |
| **Loan programs** | Funds loaned to individuals, families, and businesses that have sustained losses from disasters. |
| **Mitigation action plan** | A document that describes the vulnerabilities of the community and what should be done to correct them in the future. |
| **National Processing Service Center (NPSC)** | A location that victims call to apply for government disaster assistance. |
| **National Emergency Management Information System (NEMIS)** | A computer program that allows FEMA representatives to record personal information about the disaster victim as well as damages, losses, |

|  | needs, etc. It is an automated system that helps to distribute relief to those in need. |
|---|---|
| **Other assistance** | Category of public assistance funds for the repair of parks, airports, and recreational facilities. |
| **Other needs assistance** | A government program that provides grants for home repair, replacement of personal property, and other disaster-related expenses for funeral, medical/dental care, and transportation. |
| **Permanent assistance** | Financial payments or reimbursements to local and state governments for long-term rebuilding activities. |
| **Protective measures** | A reimbursement category that has the purpose of reducing losses or eliminating threats to life, public health, and safety. |
| **Public assistance (PA)** | A relief program for government entities. |
| **Public buildings/ equipment assistance** | Funds to repair or replace buildings, supplies, and vehicles. |
| **Public utility assistance** | Funds for water, gas, and sewage system repairs. |
| **Road systems assistance** | Funds that repay expenses associated with the rebuilding or repairing of bridges, lights, and culverts. |
| **Services** | Government programs that address unique issues or needs made evident in the disaster. |
| **Small projects** | A type of permanent assistance that is typically paid in advance by the federal government and costs less than $66,499. |
| **Water control assistance** | Funds for repairs to rivers, dikes, levees, and dams. |
| **Window of opportunity** | The time immediately after a disaster when leaders and citizens are sensitive to what has happened and are willing to do something to prevent a similar occurrence in the future. |

# ASSESSING YOUR UNDERSTANDING

Posttest to evaluate your knowledge of promoting recovery and mitigation.
*Measure your learning by comparing pretest and posttest results.*

## Summary Questions

1. Individual assistance is for individuals, but not for families or businesses. True or false?
2. The federal government may provide loans, grants, services, and benefits to disaster victims. True or false?
3. In order to apply for federal disaster assistance, you can only log on to the FEMA's website. True or false?
4. The disaster recovery center is the place where federal officials manage the disaster. True or false?
5. There may be more than one DRC in a major disaster. True or false?
6. Indian tribes are not eligible for public assistance. True or false?
7. Sandbagging is an example of a protective measure. True or false?
8. Permanent assistance deals with road and water systems, but not public utilities. True or false?
9. A briefing is a meeting where federal programs are reviewed by local and state officials. True or false?
10. During recovery, you should be concerned about fraud, environmental protection, historic building preservation, and mitigation. True or false?
11. Some people will not want to relocate after a disaster because of their cultural ties to the community. True or false?
12. The collective or cooperative mode is characterized by external control. True or false?
13. A window of opportunity to promote mitigation often occurs after disasters, but it is not long lasting. True or false?
14. Assistance given to local governments is known as:
    (a) Individual assistance
    (b) Public assistance
    (c) Private assistance
    (d) Self-insured assistance
    (e) None of the above
15. Types of individual assistance includes:
    (a) Disaster loans for businesses
    (b) Other needs assistance
    (c) Tax assistance
    (d) Economic injury loans
    (e) All of the above
16. Services provided after disasters include:
    (a) Crisis counseling
    (b) Food stamps

(c) Social security

(d) Veterans benefits

(e) All of the above

17. DRC stands for:

(a) Disaster response category

(b) Disaster response crisis

(c) Disaster recovery center

(d) Disaster resilience change

(e) Damage reporting category

18. Which is an example of emergency assistance?

(a) Road systems

(b) Water systems

(c) Public utility

(d) Debris removal

(e) Other needs assistance

19. Types of projects for public assistance include:

(a) Small

(b) Large

(c) Improved

(d) Alternate

(e) All of the above

20. Intraurban relocation:

(a) Implies rebuilding in the same location

(b) Implies moving to a different and safer area

(c) Implies moving to a safer area within your community

(d) Does not reduce vulnerability as much as relocation

(e) Answers c and d

21. Which of the following is characterized by a person controlling recovery within the community?

(a) Individualistic self-help

(b) Bureaucratized paternalism

(c) Bureaucratized external paternalism

(d) Independent beneficiary

(e) Collaborative partnership

## Review Questions

1. Why do individuals and businesses require assistance at times after disasters?

2. What is individual assistance?

3. How are loan programs different from grants?

4. What services are available to disaster victims and why are they beneficial?

5. How can food stamps or unemployment services help disaster victims?

6. What is a National Processing Service Center and how does one apply for individual disaster assistance?

7. What is a disaster recovery center used for?

8. What steps should be taken to open an EOC?

9. Who is eligible for public assistance?

10. How is emergency assistance different from permanent assistance?

11. What are the types of permanent assistance?

12. What is a briefing? What is a kickoff meeting? Why are they helpful to the emergency manager?

13. What are the types of projects pertaining to permanent assistance?

14. Who is located at a Disaster Field Office and what do they do?

15. What issues should you consider as you promote recovery?

16. What is a mitigation action plan and why are they useful?

17. What are the different modes for disaster recovery?

18. Why is it important to push for change after disasters?

19. What does Loma Prieta tell us about "windows of opportunities?"

## Applying This Chapter

1. You are the local emergency manager for a town near the Mississippi River. A flood has just devastated the area. Many homes have been affected. There are thousands of people that need to file applications for federal assistance. How does this take place? Can you do anything to help the disaster victims in this process?

2. You are the local emergency manager for a community that has just experience a major hurricane. A great deal of public property has been destroyed as a result. What types of assistance can be obtained for your community? What can you do to help your jurisdiction obtain federal assistance?

3. You are the local emergency manager for a city that was hit by a tornado. Many businesses were destroyed. What advice do you give to businesses in terms of the assistance they are eligible for? What measures can you recommend to reduce their vulnerability to future disasters?

4. Your community has just experienced a major riot. A great deal of public property has been destroyed by fire and acts of vandalism. Leaders and community groups are protesting the decisions of civic leaders concerning immigration issues. What do you need to do to help restore public facilities? Is there a way you could get the different parties to work together to solve mutual problems? If so, how?

5. You are the local emergency manager for New Orleans. The area has just been devastated by Hurricane Katrina. In particular, the low-lying areas of the 9th ward were hit hard as they were completely flooded. What options do you have to reduce the vulnerability of these areas to future disasters?

## Types of Recovery Assistance

Write a 2-page paper on the following topic: You are the local emergency manager for Los Angeles. An earthquake has just devastated the area. What types of IA and PA could be available and how do you get the help you need?

## DRC

You are the local emergency manager for a community in Tennessee. You have experienced a major flood and you need to set up a DRC. What things should you consider when opening up and running a DRC?

## Window of Opportunity

A chemical plant has emitted hazardous materials forcing the evacuation of hundreds of residents. How can you use the disaster to promote mitigation policies? Why will officials be more receptive to policy changes after this major disaster? Will others oppose more stringent policies? Why or why not? What can be done to get people to comply?

# 10

# OVERCOMING TYPICAL CHALLENGES
## Vital Considerations for Response and Recovery

## Starting Point

Pretest to assess your knowledge on overcoming typical challenges.
*Determine where you need to concentrate your effort.*

## What You'll Learn in This Chapter

▲ Importance of communication and coordination
▲ Challenges of making decisions during a disaster
▲ Typical transportation considerations
▲ Potential political concerns
▲ Types of special populations and methods to assist the vulnerable
▲ Legal issues facing emergency managers
▲ The need for record keeping after disasters

## After Studying This Chapter, You'll Be Able To

▲ Examine the importance of working collaboratively with others.
▲ Apply decision-making skills in the context of disasters.
▲ Illustrate the need for public transit in response operations.
▲ Interpret the causes of political conflict after disasters.
▲ Examine the needs of special populations.
▲ Distinguish how to consult with the legal representative of the jurisdiction.
▲ Demonstrate how to record expenses accurately.

## Goals and Outcomes

▲ Appraise how to successfully communicate and coordinate with others.
▲ Design ways to avert decision-making mistakes.
▲ Formulate ways to use transportation resources wisely after a disaster.
▲ Assess how to protect yourself against blame after a disaster.

---

*Disaster Response and Recovery: Strategies and Tactics for Resilience*, Second Edition. David A. McEntire.
© 2015 John Wiley & Sons, Inc. Published 2015 by John Wiley & Sons, Inc.

▲ Predict who requires additional assistance and how to meet their needs.

▲ Propose ways to reduce your legal liability.

▲ Choose strategies to maintain accurate records.

# INTRODUCTION

Ensuring resilience requires that you are aware of the numerous problems that become evident when disaster strikes. Communication is difficult due to technological and human factors, and coordination suffers as a result. Decision making is often challenging because of incomplete and ever-changing information. Transportation systems become disrupted, which complicates response and recovery operations. Organizations don't see eye to eye for political reasons, and blame is placed on those whom are regarded to be responsible for mistakes and failures. Numerous people have unique needs after a disaster, and these must be met in an effective and expeditious manner. Lawsuits may be witnessed as people express anger for the loss of life and property. Record keeping is problematic because of the many activities taking place or because the disaster results in their loss. If you are to overcome these challenges after a disaster, it is imperative that you fully comprehend their causes and what can be done about them.

## 10.1 Communications and Coordination

Two of the most important—and yet most difficult—activities in disasters are communication and coordination. Ironically, there is no widely accepted definition of what communication and coordination mean. Nevertheless, it may be asserted that:

▲ **Communication** is the process of relaying vital information, which has a bearing on the effectiveness of disaster response and recovery operations. This sharing of information can be relayed through verbal and nonverbal forms.

▲ **Coordination** is the harmonization of activities among diverse actors in emergency management with the purpose of overcoming the challenges inherent in disasters. It helps emergency managers work with others to reach and attain goals.

Communication and coordination must occur among all levels of government and with the private and nonprofit sectors in a disaster. They are two fundamental and closely related activities in response and recovery operations.

When an emergency or disaster occurs, communication is needed to understand the impact of the event. Emergency managers must talk among themselves and others so that the needs of the community and disaster victims can be understood and met. For instance, response operations cannot take place unless information has been relayed and received about the location of the incident, the impact of the hazard, and what should be done to care for victims.

There is a close link between communication and coordination. Communication is required if individuals and groups are to be made aware of the need to coordinate. Coordination determines who will respond after the disaster and how this will be accomplished. In other words, if one group is aware of a certain challenge or cannot meet disaster demands alone, this organization will need to relay this information to others. Once this information is shared, personnel and agencies will then need to determine role assignments for response and recovery operations. Agreement is hopefully reached and organizations will work jointly to accomplish such tasks.

Everyone involved in response and recovery should communicate and coordinate with other individuals and groups. It is especially important among certain groups such as dispatch, first responders, fire and police chiefs, EOC personnel, neighboring communities, different levels of government, and pertinent actors in the private and nonprofit sectors.

### 10.1.1  The Importance of Communication and Coordination

Communicating and working with others is crucial in a disaster. Only by sharing information and working with others can you identify the needs of victims and those involved in postdisaster activities. You can inform others about contingencies, goals, and operations by having the lines of communication open. Others can also make you aware of the problems they face, their ongoing actions, and what will be required to bring about a resolution to the issue they are dealing with. It is important that you are able to work collaboratively with others in order to address the demands made evident in a disaster.

A good example of this is the exchange of information and harmonization of activity relating to emergency medical personnel and hospitals. For instance, in order " … to muster their resources, hospitals need to have advanced warning that they will be receiving patients and timely estimates of the types, numbers, and severities of casualties to be expected. This information must come from those at the disaster scene. In addition, hospitals are at the mercy of those at the scene to see that casualties are equitably distributed, so that no one hospital receives an inordinate number" (Auf der Heide 1989, pp. 5–6).

In contrast, the lack of communication and coordination among emergency management organizations may result in "an inability to determine priorities, misunderstandings among organizations, failure to fully utilize equipment and personnel, overly-taxed organizations, delays in service, omission of essential tasks, duplication of effort, safety problems, and counterproductive activity among other things" (Drabek and McEntire 2002, p. 206).

### 10.1.2  Communication and Coordination Barriers

Communication is often difficult during disasters for a number of reasons. Disasters are inherently chaotic, and communications can be hindered because of excessive noise, numerous participating organizations, the overwhelming and dynamic flow information, etc. In addition, equipment and facilities for communications may be disabled or overloaded or fail to operate properly (Auf der Heide, 1989, pp. 49–50). For instance, disasters topple antennas and interrupt electrical power. They may lead to the loss of cell towers. Broadcast stations and radio networks may likewise be adversely affected. After the terrorist attacks on the World Trade Center, police and fire personnel could not communicate due to limited channel capacity as well as radios and repeaters that were unable to penetrate the walls, stairwells, and floors. All of these things could prevent messages from being relayed to the public or other responding organizations.

However, not every communication problem can be blamed on disaster conditions or equipment failures. In fact, "some communications problems are 'people problems,' rather than 'equipment problems'" (Auf der Heide, 1989, p. 5.3). These people problems are broad and numerous. Individuals tend to communicate within the organization first and may fail to share information with others. Someone may have knowledge that another organization requires, but not be aware of the response and recovery needs of other governments or agencies. In addition, there is no agreement about who should be responsible for collecting and distributing information during the response and recovery operations. Do individuals and groups believe it is the sole responsibility of first responders or the EOC? Or should others monitor what is taking place and share it with all pertinent parties? Breakdown in communication networks, simple verbal misunderstandings, and cross-checking to confirm others' messages may also hurt communications (Drabek, 1985, p. 88).

There are a number of reasons why coordination is likewise difficult in times of disasters. A key explanation for this challenge is the nature of disasters. Auf der Heide notes "one of the reasons disaster response is difficult to coordinate is because disasters are different from routine, daily emergencies. The difference is more than just one of magnitude. Disasters generally cannot be adequately managed merely by mobilizing more personnel and material. Disasters may cross jurisdictional boundaries, create the need to undertake unfamiliar tasks, change the structure of responding organizations, [and] trigger the mobilization of participants that do not ordinarily respond to local emergency incidents … . As a consequence of these changes, the normal procedures for coordinating community emergency response may not be adapted well to the situation" (1989).

There are many other factors that make coordination problematic. Because of political values and organizational culture, people do not always see eye to eye. A fire chief is likely to have very different priorities than a representative of a faith-based organization. Interorganizational rivalry also hinders the harmonization of activity. Some individuals may try to be the sole "hero," while other groups may operate independently in order to highlight their respective successes. This type of competition is extremely damaging to collaborative efforts. McEntire (2002a) has identified additional factors that inhibited or discouraged coordination after a tornado hit the city of Fort Worth, Texas:

▲ Insufficient, incomplete, inaccurate, or an overabundance of information
▲ Lack of communication among first responders and those in the EOC
▲ Language barriers among responders and victims
▲ Controlling or domineering attitudes on the part of individuals responding to the disaster

### 10.1.3 Enhancing Communication

There are a number of ways you can overcome people's problems associated with disaster communications (Figure 10-1). Bill Swan, Section Emergency Coordinator (SEC) for the North Texas Section of the American Radio Relay League, provides several recommendations. He asserts that communication is most effective when

**Figure 10-1**

Getting all relevant parties in a room to discuss policy options is one way to improve coordination in disasters. Dan Watson/FEMA.

information sharing is calm, courteous, correct, and concise. Here are some of his tips for communication:

▲ Do not get too caught up in the excitement of the disaster.
▲ Be respectful to the others you talk with.
▲ Ensure that the information you share is as accurate as is possible.
▲ Keep your discussions short and simple if possible.

### 10.1.4 Improving Coordination

Communication and coordination can likewise be enhanced by establishing trust within the organization and between organizations. To foster confidence with others, Auf der Heide (1989) encourages the maintenance of formal and informal contacts between personnel within the organization and with members of different responding organizations. He also recommends the implementation of agreements regarding the division of emergency responsibilities, response and recovery procedures, performance criteria, and resource sharing.

Coordination may be improved through other methods too. In one study of response, it was observed that coordination was facilitated when there is a "team" orientation, experience in prior disasters, and effective EOC management (McEntire, 2002a). McEntire also suggests that coordination is more likely to occur when there is contact,

Figure 10-2

Getting all relevant parties in a room to discuss policy options is one way
to improve decision making in disasters. George Armstrong/FEMA.

communication, and cooperation among responding organizations. Networking
frequently with other organizations, relaying information constantly, and being willing
to collaborate with others are all positively correlated to coordination (Figure 10-2).

In addition, Tom Drabek, a well-known disaster sociologist, recommends that
emergency manager employ five key methods to coordinate disasters (2003).
These include:

1. **Core strategies.** You may enhance coordination by clarifying agency roles
   before a disaster. Know what resources can be accessed for the response.
   Determine who should be given authority in a certain circumstance.
2. **Consequence strategies.** Those involved in the response can promote
   coordination by keeping track of needs and how they are being met.
3. **Customer strategies.** Coordination can be increased when an effort is
   made to serve partner agencies, stakeholders, and the victims of a disaster.
4. **Control strategies.** Responders and emergency managers can improve
   coordination by reminding those they are working with of approved
   agreements, experiences from past disasters, the need to share authority, the
   value of departing from established procedures, and the advantages of
   working with emergent organizations.
5. **Cultural strategies.** Helping other agencies understand the cultural
   differences of different responding agencies, viewing multiagency responses
   critically, and celebrating successes may also help organizations to
   coordinate.

---

**FOR EXAMPLE**

**"Give Me Everything You Got"**

According to many published reports, Louisiana Governor Blanco asked President Bush to give Louisiana "everything you've got" the night Hurricane Katrina made landfall. The governor, however, did not specifically request the 82$^{nd}$ Airborne, which is what she should have done to receive the immediate assistance she was looking for. According to one of her unnamed staff members, Governor Blanco "wouldn't know the 82$^{nd}$ Airborne from the Harlem Boy's Choir." The lack of awareness impacted communication and resulted in an impasse between the state and federal government (Thomas, 2005).

---

The degree of success or failure of coordination can also be determined by two other factors (Drabek, 2003). The first is the frequency of communications. The more often an organization communicates accurately with others the better. The second factor is the breadth of coordination. This includes the number of organizations an individual, department, or agency collaborates with. Thus, coordination is most likely to occur when organizations go out of their way to work with others.

## SELF-CHECK

- What is communication?
- What is coordination?
- How is communication related to coordination?
- What are the benefits of communication and coordination?
- Why are communication and coordination difficult in disasters?
- What is interoperability and how can it be promoted?
- What steps can be taken to improve coordination?

## 10.2 Decision Making

Decision making can be extremely challenging — even in routine or normal situations. People and organizations typically try to make rational choices as they go about their daily activities. They attempt to apply logic to decision making when confronted with problems. This **rational decision making** implies a search for alternative solutions and selection of the one that is deemed most appropriate for the situation at hand. In other words, rational decision making is a careful and deliberate review of options in order to maximize benefit and minimize negative consequences.

The rational decision-making model is rarely applicable to disasters. Decision making in disasters exhibits, at best, "bounded rationality." **Bounded rationality** implies that the attempt to be rational is never fully achieved because of the constraints disasters present to the decision maker.

Yehezkel Dror has identified a number of reasons why rational decision making under disaster conditions is difficult (1988):

▲ *Facing adversity.* Disasters are characterized by injury, death, and destruction. These events will demand the immediate attention you as an emergency manager. In the aftermath of a disaster, functions to be performed include fire suppression, search and rescue, emergency medical care, damage assessment, public information, etc. Not only are there many things to do, but the consequences of failure to fulfill duties are very serious. For instance, a failure to sound the siren during severe weather may result in the death of numerous citizens. The sheer number and importance of things to address during and after a disaster will be overwhelming to you.

▲ *Image production.* During a disaster, information acquired by you may come from the media, first responders, or other sources. The perception relayed or received may be inaccurate. News organizations may show pictures from one area and not show the impact of another neighborhood. The advice of responding organizations in the field may lead to an over- or undercommitment of resources. Interpretations of radio traffic may also be inaccurate when you are working in emergency management positions. The false images produced in disasters complicate decision making.

▲ *Compressed time.* Because people's lives and well-being are at stake in a disaster, there is incredible pressure for decision makers to act quickly and even prematurely. The failure to evacuate an area due to an approaching hurricane may result in the loss of many lives. Acting early can create complications however. This is because the track of hurricanes often changes direction. Acting early can also create other problems in response and recovery. For example, requesting donations without considering the best way to obtain them could create additional problems for you as an emergency manager.

▲ *Tragic choice.* Disasters are often accompanied by situations where there are drawbacks to nearly every decision that needs to be made. Helping one person by following medical triage procedures may result in the death of another. Answering questions for television news programs may mean that people in cars will not immediately have vital information about disasters. Connecting electricity to one neighborhood may result in the delay of assistance to another. It is impossible for you to resolve all disaster problems at any given time.

▲ *Fuzzy gambling.* Decision making during response operations is challenging as uncertainty is an expected correlate of disasters. The full extent of a disaster may not be known for hours, days, or even weeks. There may be too much information, a lack of information, or both. Disaster events unfold in unpredictable ways, hindering decisions and the development of future policies. For instance, moving residents out of a nursing home after a chemical release could be deadly if winds shift unexpectedly.

▲ *Strain and stress.* The demands placed on you and others involved in response and recovery are physically and emotionally taxing that they impair decision making. Disaster response and recovery operations require long hours and tiresome work for days, weeks, and even months. The trauma you witness and the pressure you face may result in impaired judgment. The strain and stress of disasters may overwhelm you, first responders, city leaders, and others involved in response and recovery operations (Figure 10-3).

▲ *Group processes.* The interaction of individuals and organizations in the decision-making process often leads to suboptimal results. Failure to come to an agreement on decisions delays required response and recovery operations. Therefore, there may be incredible pressure to find consensus when more discussion is in order. However, coming to an agreement in order to appease elected leaders or going along with the crowd may have negative consequences. For instance, disregarding the need for traffic control may hurt the ability of firefighters to rescue those affected by an earthquake. Thus, a decision by one organization may undermine the goals of another if all actors and consequences are not considered.

**Figure 10-3**

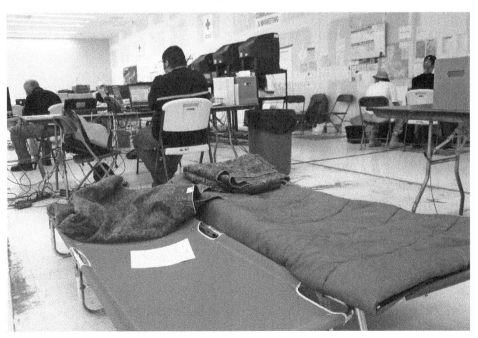

Working in a disaster can be physically and emotionally draining and may require you to sleep less or in undesirable circumstances. Robert Kaufmann/FEMA.

### 10.2.1 Overcoming Decision Errors

Because there is such a great probability of making poor choices during disaster response and recovery operations, you must do all you can to overcome decision errors. Dror (1988) has identified two methods.

The first method is similar to attempts to pursue rational decision making. It is known as "designing preferable models." **Designing preferable models** entails studying the situation or problem in detail, determining the gap that exists between the goal and the current situation, and implementing a decision to adapt the process to the desired outcome. Obviously, this approach is not easy. There will be many factors you must consider during a disaster. An example of this is spending sufficient time and resources to determine the best routes for evacuation before a hurricane approaches. This is difficult under the best of circumstances; it is even more challenging under conditions of disasters. Put differently, there would be no time to conduct a major study about evacuation if it is not completed before the hurricane reaches the coast.

The second method is "debugging." **Debugging** is a method that includes a keen observation of the decision process in order to correct potential weaknesses and mistakes as the situation unfolds. For instance, if one person in the EOC observes that the request from the fire chief is not being given sufficient attention, he or she may wish to state that there is a need to reconsider the appeal. Another example is a mayor that makes decisions based on political factors rather than practical objectives. In this case, you might ask him or her to review response and recovery priorities again.

There are additional steps that can be taken to improve decision making in time of disaster:

- ▲ Increase situational awareness. **Situational awareness** suggests a need to be vigilant of circumstances in the environment in order to understand the context of what is taking place. Look for clues and signals in the disaster as well as options and alternatives.

- ▲ Listen to the information provided by others and pay extra attention to the tone of voice when they communicate. Rely upon your gut instincts, modern technology, and other support systems to help you make choices.

- ▲ Determine if your perception is accurate and if you comprehend the events of the disaster correctly as it unfolds.

- ▲ Examine the disaster from different viewpoints. Ask yourself or others periodically if you have made any mistakes or if you have addressed all current and future contingencies.

- ▲ Take care of physical needs. Getting sufficient rest and adequate nutrients can help improve the level of alertness and mental sharpness. Be aware that some food and drink can be detrimental to your performance. For example, sugars, carbonated drinks, and caffeine inhibit performance.

- ▲ Accept the need to adapt and be creative. There is a tendency in disasters to follow plans, established guidelines, and widely accepted norms— sometimes to the detriment of the success of response and recovery operations.

**FOR EXAMPLE**

### Instructions from the World Trade Center Tower

Poor decisions can have fatal consequences. After the North Tower of the World Trade Center was hit by a hijacked airplane, someone using the public announcement system in the South Tower advised everyone to stay in the building and not evacuate. Although it is unknown who gave this order, the person or persons may have been under the impression that the first plane was an accident and therefore saw no reason for people to leave the building. In hindsight, the order to evacuate should have been given immediately to protect additional lives. Perhaps more information should have been sought before making decisions about remaining at work.

In short, you will need to think critically during response and recovery operations. People often fail to "think outside the box." Ask yourself or others if the policy, decision, or course of action has or will have any negative consequences. Seek fresh thinking from outside the organization. Determine if there are other options that have not yet been considered. Find an alternate way of viewing or addressing the problem, and assess its feasibility and desirability. Laws and rules are there to protect the decision maker, limit liability, and ensure safety, effectiveness, and efficiency. However, there are times when flexibility is what is needed to get the job done. Disasters will always throw curves at you and other decision makers.

## SELF-CHECK

- Why is decision making difficult in disasters?
- How is bounded rationality different than rationality?
- What can be done to improve decision making in disasters?
- What is a "preferable model?"
- What is debugging?
- What is situational awareness and how does it relate to decision making?

## 10.3 Transportation Issues and Logistics

Other common challenges you will face in disasters relate to transportation and logistics. Transportation systems can be severely disrupted in disasters. One example comes from the 1995 Kobe earthquake in Japan. Roads were blocked by debris, which inhibited the movement of firefighters and their equipment. In another case, the collapse of the World Trade Center on 9/11 affected subway operations and tunnel traffic in New York. Because of road and subway closures, people had difficulty traveling around the city. There are additional problems related to transportation.

---

**FOR EXAMPLE**

**Transportation Systems Can Be the Site of Disasters**

As we saw in 9/11, the Madrid train attacks, and the London subway bombings, transportation systems are rapidly becoming the target of choice for terrorists. Transportation systems are vulnerable due to the large number of people that use them and their ease of access. This situation suggests an increased need for training for transportation workers so they can identify suspicious activity and determine what actions should be taken in an emergency.

---

For instance, one of the failures in the response to Hurricane Katrina in New Orleans was the lack of public transportation for those who were not able to evacuate on their own. In contrast, during Hurricane Rita, there were too many commuters leaving the Houston area. Roads were jammed. Fuel stations ran out of gas because of the unusually high demand. In other cases, it is difficult to keep people out of unsafe areas or quickly ship needed supplies to affected areas because of logistics challenges. Transportation and logistics problems are likely to abound in disasters.

### 10.3.1 Dealing with Transportation Problems

If transportation systems and resources are severely disrupted, alternate means for travel can be found. For instance, if roads are blocked, planes, helicopters, and boats might come in handy to move people and supplies around. You may also use other available transportation systems and resources effectively when disasters occur. In many situations, transit companies and "school buses are called on for … service especially in smaller communities where they may be the only form of mass transportation" (Scanlon, 2003, p. 431).

You should also be aware of others that can help with transportation functions. In Fort Worth, Texas, police officers used barricades to control access to the downtown area affected by the March 2000 tornado. The goal was to keep people out of dangerous locations and thereby speed up the process of recovery. After 9/11, the police department, public works, and transit authorities also worked jointly to keep people out of the Ground Zero area while concomitantly ensuring the continued movement of traffic around the area.

Of course, everything in your power should be done to inform residents where transportation will be available in case of a disaster. And, if needed, you should ensure that sufficient fuel is available when people evacuate from hurricanes or other disasters. For this reason, some states will dispatch courtesy patrols to fill up tanks and get cars and trucks moving again. Also, the high demand for fuel and the loss of power at gas stations requires constant communication with the private sector. Service stations should anticipate these problems and plan in advance to prevent or respond to them.

In some cases, the response from transportation companies will be ad hoc in nature. However, the companies that react to disasters are generally very effective. There are several reasons as to why transportation companies are so responsive in disaster situations. "The first is that transportation companies are always dealing with minor problems that disrupt their schedules, such as those cause by traffic accidents, spills and, most important, weather. Second, most such companies have experience with special events... . Disasters create the same kind of demands [repeatedly so] ... the required response is a familiar one even though the timing is unexpected. Third, most transportation companies operate during two peak periods: if the demand for assistance comes at any other time, they have staff and equipment available. Fourth, it would appear that transportation systems treat requests for emergency assistance as a priority, and are willing to adjust their regular service if this is required. Perhaps more important, when transportation systems are called on to provide help in an emergency, they are doing, for the most part, what they normally do, taking persons from one place to another" (Scanlon, 2003, p. 436).

Transportation therefore has a close relation to disasters as well as response and recovery operations. This is because transportation systems commonly deal with unexpected changes, special events, and severe weather. In addition, transportation systems are required for effective evacuations.

### 10.3.2 Logistics in Disasters

The transportation systems discussed above carry vital personnel and supplies from far around the world or country to the scene of a disaster. For example, food and equipment were delivered from many different countries after the earthquakes in Pakistan in 2005. In light of disasters, many transportation companies will offer their road, rail, or air services to emergency managers voluntarily. They will also contract with you or nonprofit organizations to deliver water, food, ice, or other supplies to affected areas. This brings up the topic of logistics.

**Logistics** is "the process of planning, implementing and controlling the efficient, cost-effective flow and storage of goods and materials as well as related information, from the point of origin to the point of consumption for the purpose of meeting the end beneficiary's requirements" (Tatham and Hughes, 2011, p. 67). In other words, logistics implies moving resources from where they are available to where they are needed. Collecting supplies, loading shipping containers, unloading semitrucks, storing supplies, breaking down large bundles into smaller units, and distributing relief to those in need are all part of logistics.

The process of logistics is not quick or painless. Disasters often pose intense logistical challenges. As already mentioned, transportation systems will be disrupted (due to road closures, damaged bridges, and traffic congestion). In addition, there will also be other problems—unavailability of storage facilities, insufficient trucks or cargo vans, and an inability to track resources.

There are measures and equipment that can be utilized to minimize these problems however. Personnel trained and certified on logistical issues can be employed to assist with such operations. Storage facilities, forklift operators, drivers, and semitrucks can be identified during an incident, but it is always better to plan for such needs in advance. There is also a software that can help logistics operations (e.g., HELIOS) and radio-frequency identification (RFID) that can pinpoint the location of specific boxes and pallets. Finally, it is vital that you monitor every segment of the supply chain to identify bottlenecks and find ways to overcome them. Effective logistics are essential for resilient response and recovery operations (Figure 10-4).

**Figure 10-4**

Storing and moving supplies effectively and efficiently
are the goals of logistics. Bob McMillan/FEMA.

## SELF-CHECK

- How can transportation be affected by disasters?
- What problems are evident in evacuation? Traffic control? Service delivery?
- Is transportation important to the emergency manager?
- What can be done to overcome transportation problems?
- How vital is the mass transit system or the private sector in disasters?
- What is disaster logistics and how can it be improved?

## 10.4 Special Populations

Another challenge in disasters concerns individuals and groups who are vulnerable (Phillips et al., 2010). Different people have varying capacities to cope with disasters. For example, some are more likely than others to be affected by disasters. This is because of the location of their home, the construction of their residence, the nature of their employment, their socioeconomic status, cultural attitudes and practices, and so on. These people may not be able to react quickly or effectively to (or after) a disaster because of physical, mental, emotional, economic, and other reasons.

Those persons that are susceptible to disasters and are least able to deal with their impact are known as "**special populations**" (Pickett and Block 1991, p. 287). A special population is a group of individuals that are prone to become victims of disasters. They also lack the capability to respond alone and/or have requirements for additional assistance to fully recover (Figure 10-5). Special populations may also be referred to as special needs groups, those with functional needs, or vulnerable populations.

A special population is comprised of people that sometimes have limited self-sufficiency after a disaster strikes. They require extra or unique aid, additional resources, and follow-up care and attention from others. Although all people may be vulnerable to some degree to a disaster, specific individuals and groups are especially susceptible to disasters. They are also the least resilient in the aftermath of the event. For this reason, it is vitally important that you and other responders know who may be regarded as a special population. You must then take steps to ensure that their needs are met after a disaster.

Research literature has devoted a great deal of attention to gender, ethnic groups, and the poor. Less is known about others that may be considered special populations. We will examine each group in turn.

**Figure 10-5**

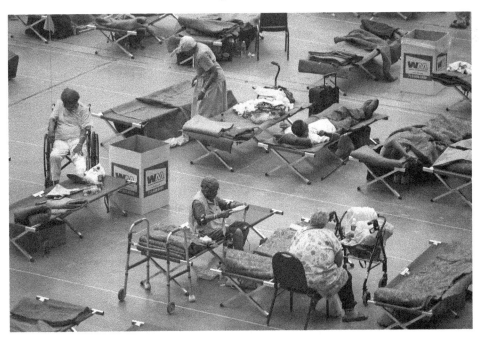

For a variety of reasons, some individuals and groups are more
vulnerable to disaster than others. Andrea Booher/FEMA.

### 10.4.1 Gender

Research reveals that gender may have a close relation—in some instances—to special needs groups. Researchers have illustrated, for instance, that women are classified at times as special populations for a variety of reasons including:

▲ **Socioeconomic status**. Women, single women, and single mothers often have a lower socioeconomic status than men. This often places women at risk. "Women in public housing are especially at risk. While projects vary in the degree to which they are safely located, retrofitted, or maintained, on balance the rising maintenance costs in aging structures have resulted in deterioration of the nation's public housing stock" (DeParle, 1996, p. 43).

▲ **Their role as mothers**. Women will often protect their children in time of disaster. Women put their children's needs first, which jeopardizes their own safety. Childcare can also require staying indoors, which is dangerous in some disasters such as earthquakes (Fothergill, 1996).

▲ **The likelihood of suffering from posttraumatic stress disorder (PTSD)**. Caregivers often have higher incidents of stress and fatigue than other people after disasters (Fothergill, 1996).

▲ **Domestic violence after disasters**. Research shows that domestic violence increases in times of disasters due to the stress of the devastating and disruptive experience. Women are most likely to be the target of such attacks.

▲ **Poorly designed government relief programs**. "Government-provided temporary housing communities were not designed around the needs of women and children. During their long stays in temporary trailers, women's day-to-day efforts to cook, clean, and care for their families, often in combination with paid jobs and unpaid community work, were complicated by the physical limitations of temporary accommodations, e.g., lack of privacy, few play spaces for children or activities for teens, insufficient laundry facilities, and social isolation" (Enarson, 1999, p. 48).

Although most of the research has focused on women's issues in disasters, this should not imply that women are helpless or that men have no vulnerabilities. As an example, women are often heavily involved in recovery efforts, and they make significant contributions toward disaster resilience. Also, many—but not all—of the first responders are men, and they fulfill very dangerous roles in disasters. Furthermore, men are less likely to have social support networks that are helpful during recovery. Therefore, both women and men may be vulnerable to disasters but in different ways.

### 10.4.2 Race and Ethnic Groups

The proportion of minorities in the United States is on the rise (e.g., Hispanics, African-Americans, Native Americans, and Asians). Demographers estimate that by 2050, perhaps over one-half of the population will be comprised of ethnic and racial minorities. In general or at least in specific situations, these ethnic groups may have additional disaster needs and are therefore referred to as special populations. Ethnic groups are considered vulnerable owing to several factors:

▲ **Housing in risk-prone groups**. In the United States, many minorities live in old apartment buildings and unreinforced masonry structures, which are the most susceptible to damage in a disaster (Fothergill et al., 1999, p. 161).

▲ **Risk perception**. Ethnic groups are not always as sensitive to risks as others in the population are. This may be due to cultural factors or socioeconomic constraints that limit their ability to protect themselves.

▲ **Response actions**. Minority groups, including Mexican-Americans and African-Americans, are less likely to evacuate than Caucasians (Fothergill et al., 1999, p. 160). In some cases, this may be due to distrust in government authorities based on prior experience.

▲ **Discriminatory practices**. It is believed that some African-Americans and Hispanics may receive less aid than whites after a disaster. Undocumented workers will be reluctant to apply for aid for fear of deportation. Ethnic groups are also less likely to receive government loans. This is because of qualification requirements. "Members of racial and ethnic minorities are less likely to qualify and receive various types of aid, including Small Business Administration (SBA) loans, and to have trouble with the housing process" (Fothergill et al., 1999, p. 167).

▲ **Language barriers**. Research also shows problems with language and translations. For example, warnings are often not repeated correctly in other languages. In one disaster, the radio operator used the phrase "aviso de tornado." "The operator's use of 'aviso' probably was not correct, for the word means to give news, advice or information. The technical meaning of the word 'warning,' representing a materialized, impending disaster, has no direct translation into Spanish and its meaning is not conveyed by 'aviso'" (Aguirre, 1988, p. 72). In addition, relief information for some disaster victims (e.g., those affected by Hurricane Andrew) is provided in English only. Disaster-related agencies may have little or insufficient bilingual staff to address language needs. This may slow down recovery for those affected by disasters.

▲ **Cultural sensitivities**. "In Miami, immigrants from countries with a history of political repression, such as El Salvador and Guatemala, were averse to getting help (Enarson and Morrow, 1997). In California, some residents of Central America origin found the National Guard tents and fences to be reminders of death camps in their native countries and refused to use them (Phillips, 1993)" (Fothergill et al., 1999, p. 166).

▲ **Higher rates of PTSD.** Minority groups also have higher rates of PTSD, and they may have a harder time rebounding emotionally from disasters. "Green et al. (1990) performed a ... study on ... the dam collapse and found that more blacks had delayed post-traumatic stress disorder (PTSD) than whites" (Fothergill et al., 1999, pp. 162–163). This may be a result of ethnic groups being located in more hazard-prone areas. It may also result from insufficient financial reserves, a lack of insurance, and an inability to qualify for government loans.

▲ **Other factors**. Undocumented aliens are likely to live in substandard housing. They may not seek or receive federal disaster assistance due to their illegal entry in to the United States. Beggs, Haines, and Hurlbert illustrate that some of the temporary migrants and permanent immigrants do not have sufficient social networks so they are unable to tap into formal disaster assistance programs (1996).

In summary, minorities may be vulnerable to hazards for a variety of reasons. Also, "many minorities had greater difficulties recovering due to lower incomes, fewer savings, greater unemployment, less insurance and less access to communication channels and information" (Fothergill et al., 1999, p. 164).

### 10.4.3 The Poor

The poor are especially vulnerable to disasters because they have few resources. Because they lack sufficient income, the poor are more likely to live in hazard-prone areas and dilapidated buildings/homes that do not meet current building code requirements. The poor will not have vehicles or discretionary spending to facilitate evacuation and sheltering. They will also lack insurance or savings to help them recover after a disaster. For instance, the lack of resources makes it difficult for the poor to find suitable housing solutions after a disaster (because rent may rise when available housing becomes scarce). Those with limited wealth will typically lack education also, so they will most likely have trouble working through the government relief system. Without help to fill out forms and meet crucial deadlines, the poor will receive less government aid. The homeless are especially vulnerable as they have the least resources of any group. Many aid programs could be based on the erroneous assumption that disaster victims have a physical address.

## FOR EXAMPLE

### Poverty and Disasters

In times of relative wealth for the United States, poverty is not in many people's consciousness. When Hurricane Katrina hit New Orleans, it was clear that the majority of the victims were poor. The hurricane raised the economic status of disaster victims as a national issue. Since Hurricane Katrina, there have been many discussions about how to combat poverty and help the poor. Some argue that a culture of entitlement to welfare programs needs to be changed. Others assert that society exploits poor and powerless individuals, so economic structure must be altered. Regardless of the cause and proposed solutions, it is clear that poverty exacerbated Hurricane Katrina. It remains to be seen if any new federal or state programs will be proposed or implemented to address this issue, but there is a growing realization that emergency managers cannot ignore poverty in the future.

### 10.4.4 Tourists

Tourists are vulnerable to disasters. The main reason is because many tourist destinations are located in hazard-prone areas. For example, coastlines with beautiful beaches are likely to be impacted by hurricanes and tsunamis. Mountain resorts may witness landslides or forest fires. Tourists are also unfamiliar with the surroundings they find themselves in and therefore do not know how to take actions to protect themselves. At times, they may not speak the local language either. Unfortunately, insufficient attention has been given to disaster preparedness and response in tourist destinations around the world.

### 10.4.5 The Elderly

The elderly are often regarded to be a special or vulnerable population. Because of vision limitations, the elderly may not be able to drive and will need assistance with evacuation. The elderly are more likely than others to be injured in a disaster because of their frail bodies. The proportion of the injured among the 65–74 age group is higher in disasters than for any other segment of the population. Not only will their injuries be greater, but extremes in temperature and weather conditions will affect the elderly more than others as their immune systems are weakened. In addition, disasters can restrict access to medications or medical treatments that the elderly desperately need (Eldar, 1992). The aged may also lack financial resource needs for recovery due to limited retirement incomes.

### 10.4.6 Children

Another group that is vulnerable to disasters is children. Babies, infants, and children have high casualty rates in many disasters. Because they are young, they may not be able to make and implement proper decisions to protect themselves when disasters occur. For this reason, children are also more likely to be injured than most adults. Moreover, children may also suffer intensely from the emotional strain of disasters. Children could require extra attention to ensure that they do not suffer from PTSD.

### 10.4.7 The Disabled

The percentage of people with a disability has increased over time. They now comprise one-quarter of the country's entire population (Rahimi, 1993, p. 59). The disabled (physically and/or mentally) are vulnerable to disasters. They may need additional help to understand warnings and evacuate safely. There are many buildings and spaces that are difficult for the disabled to navigate even during normal times. This is complicated in disasters when buildings collapse. Wheelchair-bound people have an especially difficult time evacuating when the elevators do not work in times of emergency. In these cases, wheelchair-bound people have to rely in their coworkers or rescue workers to carry them down the stairs to safety. The blind, hearing impaired, and others have similar needs.

### 10.4.8 Other Special Needs Groups

There are many other special groups who are vulnerable to disasters. Some of these people include:

▲ **Prisoners**. Prisoners may require extra attention for warning and evacuation. This is due to their numbers as well as their confined and inaccessible locations. It is also due to the requirement for supervision by law enforcement personnel.

▲ **Patients in hospitals and nursing homes**. Hospital and nursing patients necessitate special attention. This is due to their lack of mobility, reliance on medications, need of medical care, requirement of power supply for life support, etc.

▲ **Homebound**. Those who are homebound may not be able to protect themselves or evacuate to safer areas. They may have to remain at home for physical, mental, emotional, or other reasons.

▲ **Migrant workers**. Migrant workers may live in temporary housing in hazardous areas and be least able to cope with disaster due to poverty and language barriers.

▲ **People with pets**. Individuals and families may not want to evacuate without their pets. Accommodations must also be made when sheltering these people.

▲ **Farmers/ranchers**. People living in secluded areas may be overlooked by emergency management personnel. Farm animals may also have unique needs in a disaster (e.g., food or rescue from floodwaters).

As can be seen, there are many categories of vulnerable populations. However, you should recognize that certain populations may have compounded needs

## FOR EXAMPLE

### Hurricane Katrina and Special Populations

If there ever was a disaster that illustrated the challenges of dealing with special populations, it was Hurricane Katrina. A large number of deaths were reported among women and children. They were in many cases unable to escape from the rising floodwaters. Most of those seeking shelters were poor African-Americans. They did not have their own vehicles to leave New Orleans. The elderly and patients in hospitals and nursing homes would not or could not evacuate when warned. This created enormous problems for healthcare providers and resulted in many deaths. Prisoners were sent by bus to various cities including Dallas, Texas. However, insufficient communications and coordination allowed some of them to escape during the evacuation. Some people in New Orleans would not leave their homes or enter designated shelters. They did not want to leave their pets and required search and rescue assistance as a result. Each of these problems illustrates the importance of addressing special population needs during disasters.

because they fall into a number of the above categories. For instance, a woman of color might be poor, elderly, and disabled. Emergency managers should be particularly cognizant of those who are chronically vulnerable and work to assist them.

### 10.4.9 Meeting the Needs of Special Populations

As can be imagined, you should take a number of steps to ensure that the needs of special populations are met in disasters. Recommended actions are as follows:

1. Identify the special populations that exist in the community and understand the needs they have in relation to responding organizations.
2. Recognize the need to promote further social and economic equality in society.
3. Approach the disaster with special populations in mind. Considering the needs of women, ethnic groups, and the poor in mind is essential. The same could be said for all other special population groups.
4. Seek resources as needed to effectively respond to the needs of special populations. For example, you will probably need to work with bilingual employees or volunteers.
5. Ensure responders and the community are aware of special populations. For example, you will want to ensure disaster personnel are providing appropriate assistance to the elderly (Eldar, 1992). You could also contact hotel personnel to make them aware of the procedures they should take after a disaster to help tourists (Burby and Wagner, 1996).
6. Address the needs of special populations when disaster strikes. A good way to ensure that this occurs is by communicating with special needs groups and nonprofit disaster relief organizations.

### FOR EXAMPLE

#### Neglect of the Disabled

There is not only a moral responsibility to take care of those in need. In many cases, neglect of the vulnerable could also lead to legal liability. After Tropical Storm Irene and Hurricane Sandy, many of the disabled brought a lawsuit against the government in New York. Several buildings lacked water, heat, and power, and this had an adverse effect on those with disabilities. The city failed to develop evacuation plans for the disabled in high-rise buildings and did not open enough shelters. According to a federal judge who reviewed the case, the neglect violated the rights of about 900,000 people. Emergency managers must therefore remember the Americans with Disabilities Act and respond accordingly in a disaster.

**SELF-CHECK**

- What is a special population?
- Why are ethnic minorities and the poor particularly vulnerable to disasters?
- Why are tourists considered special populations?
- Why are the elderly most likely to die or be injured in disasters?
- What are the unique needs of the disabled in disasters?
- How do pets impact their owners and emergency managers during response and recovery operations?
- What can be done to assist special populations after disasters?

## 10.5 Politics

Politics is another common problem in disaster response and recovery operations. For instance, after Hurricane Katrina, we all saw that the needs of many disaster victims were not met. The disturbing footage of people stuck in shelters or on the interstate without any food or water angered many Americans. Hurricane Katrina quickly became a hot button political issue. Some argued that the needs of certain individuals and groups were not met because of racism. Others argued that the government was just inept or that people need to do a better job of caring for their own needs. Regardless of the cause of these difficulties, these cases show that disasters are undoubtedly a political phenomenon. Politics are exhibited in disaster response operations in at least three distinct ways. Political turmoil or favoritism may be seen in interorganizational conflict, blame, and disaster declarations and assistance delivery.

When disaster strikes and the response operations begin, you should not be surprised if there is some or a significant degree of interorganizational conflict. There may be disagreement about several issues pertaining to the response. For instance, who will be given authority over the incident? Which organizations will be assigned central roles or menial and less visible tasks? Which organizations will be given additional resources and responsibilities? Who will get credit for their role and success in the event?

Some organizations will limit their interaction or stop working with others simply because interorganizational rivalries exist. For example, police and fire departments often exhibit this type of competition. An example is a discussion that takes place between the police chief and fire chief in an attempt to determine whether or not to close a freeway as a result of a major traffic accident. The firefighters may want to protect their workers, but the police officers desire to keep traffic flowing. There are many cases where different departments or levels of government may not agree on response and recovery priorities.

You should also expect that an individual or a group will be blamed after a disaster (see Neal, 1984). For instance, there was a significant amount of discussion about who was at fault for the 2001 terrorist attacks (see the 9/11 Commission Report 2004). Some claimed that President Clinton did not do enough to respond to terrorist bombings of the embassies in Africa and attack on the USS Cole. Others suggested that President Bush was too concerned about China and failed to notice the growing threat of terrorism from nonstate actors. Fingers were also pointed to a number of other organizations for a variety of reasons:

▲ Why did the CIA and FBI fail to integrate clues about an imminent attack from various intelligence reports?
▲ How did the terrorists manage to get into the country past customs and border patrol agents?
▲ Did the aviation schools fail to adequately report suspicious terrorist behavior?
▲ How did airport screeners miss the weapons smuggled on board by terrorists?
▲ Who issued contradictory evacuation orders in the South Tower?
▲ Why was communication between the police and fire departments inadequate?
▲ Why did the World Trade Center structures collapse and could this have been prevented by architects, engineers, and building inspectors?

Such blame may seem distant or not applicable to state and local emergency management agencies or personnel. However, you may also receive excessive and undo blame for the impact of disasters or subsequent response and recovery operations. In fact, there is a very large chance that you will be seen as the "scapegoat" after disasters. Politicians will often do this because they are interested in protecting their own image in the media and popularity among voting citizens. Many emergency managers have lost their jobs after disasters for both justified and unjustified reasons.

Politics are also prevalent when disasters are declared and when relief assistance is distributed. Local and state officials may exaggerate damages in order to obtain additional federal assistance. As an illustration, presidents have provided disaster relief without going through the regular declaration process (Sylves, 1996). There may likewise be disagreement about who should be given aid or assistance first. Politicians may assist major corporations and wealthy neighborhoods initially in order to gain votes in upcoming elections. They may do this instead of helping smaller businesses and poorer communities because of their lack of political power. Even if there is no intentional malfeasance, some individuals and groups will complain that preference is being given no matter what is taking place. This may be due to the fact that they do not understand that there are limited resources and excessive needs that must be met. As can be seen, politics will certainly be a concern for you as an emergency manager.

### 10.5.1 Overcoming Political Problems

You should not feel powerless in light of the political forces at work in disasters. Steps can be taken to overcome interorganizational conflict, limit blame, and use politics to one's advantage. For instance, in order to reduce interorganizational conflict, you can do several things both before and after a disaster strikes. Get to know departmental leaders in the city and those of all other organizations. Try to develop a rapport with them and encourage them to do the same among others. Work together and clarify responsibilities before disaster strikes. It is much easier to find consensus during normal, routine times rather than resolve disagreements after a disaster occurs. It is also important to reason with organizations. Show the merit of collaboration. Illustrate how other's involvement and assistance will help disaster victims and speed up response and recovery operations. If all else fails, go to the political leader for assistance. Ask the mayor, county commissioner/judge, or governor to settle differences or enforce decisions.

You can also reduce the amount of blame you could receive and protect your career by:

▲ **Keeping minutes**. Tracking the policy and budget proposals you submit to the mayor and city council and noting the degree of support given or withheld by such decision makers can help you in the long run. For instance, note in a journal that funding for a new warning system was denied by city officials. File the proposal for later retrieval if needed. This could be helpful if warning is seen as problematic in future disasters.

▲ **Monitoring progress**. Review the progress of response and recovery operations, make adjustments as required, record successes, and work swiftly to address lessons learned. Communicate accomplishments of response operations to key political leaders and diligently resolve problems made evident in the management of the disaster.

▲ **Going to the media if needed**. As a last resort, you can try to keep your job by expressing your viewpoint with the press. Note: this could create even more animosity for you or it may help you retain employment. Therefore, this recommended should be a last resort and should be approached with extreme caution.

---

## FOR EXAMPLE

### Hurricane Katrina and the Blame Game

The anger and disappointment that many Americans felt about the response to Hurricane Katrina encouraged politicians to place blame. Local and state politicians argued that the federal government did not respond quickly enough. National politicians asserted that state and local governments were not prepared to deal with such an obvious risk. In reality, all three levels of government made mistakes that were compounded by a failure to integrate decisions and policies among them. The head of FEMA, Michael Brown, lost his job because of the poor response. This occurred even though some believe that the Department of Homeland Security (DHS) had set FEMA up for failure (because of changes that were made when DHS was created). In short, too many changes had been made to a system that appeared to work effectively before 9/11. The mistakes visible during Hurricane Katrina were taken into account when the Post-Hurricane Katrina Reform Act was implemented a shortly thereafter.

Lastly, emergency managers can also use politics to their advantage after a disaster. Disasters generate an incredible amount of interest on the part of the media, citizens, and politicians. As mentioned in Chapter 9, disasters are unique "focusing events" that can influence the policy agenda (Birkland, 1996). You should harness the interest in disasters to improve the ongoing response, seek recovery aid, and promote additional mitigation and preparedness activities.

## SELF-CHECK

- Do emergency managers need to be concerned about the politics of disasters?
- What political problems face the emergency manager?
- How can the emergency manager overcome interorganizational conflict and the politics of declarations?
- What can be done to reduce blame after disasters?
- Are disaster declarations and postdisaster activities political?
- What is a focusing event?

## 10.6 Legal Concerns

Legal issues are a typical problem in certain disasters. Nevertheless, some emergency managers may not sufficiently understand disaster law since "FEMA educational materials are noticeably lacking when it comes to coverage of legal issues" (Nicholson, 2003a, p. 17). However, it is a fact that response and recovery activities are shaped in large part by disaster law. You must be aware of the fact that lawsuits may arise due to disaster impacts or the way they are handled. For instance, after the West, Texas, fertilizer plant explosion in 2013, some citizens of this small community questioned why schools, nursing homes, and residences were allowed to be built so close to such a hazardous industry. In another case, some critics of the response to the Mt. St. Helens eruption asserted that politicians and scientists drew up illogical evacuation zones near the volcano. While some people stayed in or ignored danger zones, it is believed that the limited size of the zones on one side of the volcano was at least partially responsible for the deaths of 64 people. Should the government be held liable because of the impact of such decisions? Regardless of the justification, civic leaders may be taken to court for the impact of disasters and outcome of response and recovery activities. It is therefore important that emergency managers understand the disaster law and how to protect against possible lawsuits.

### 10.6.1 Disasters and Law

Postdisaster operations have a close connection to the law. **Laws** are rules that are established by the government to maintain order and perform important functions in society. Laws pertaining to disasters must be understood and followed by emergency managers. Many federal laws have been passed after disasters to permit the disbursement of funds to those affected. Laws have also been established to manage response and recovery efforts.

The Congressional Act of 1803 was the first disaster law in the United States. It was established to provide relief to a New Hampshire town that was damaged by a fire. From 1803 to 1950, there were scores of disasters that received similar ad hoc decrees. In 1950, the Federal Disaster Act established permanent legislation to ensure more structured relief programs. In 1969, Hurricane Camille led to the creation of the Federal Disaster Assistance Administration in the Department of Housing and Urban Development (HUD). The Disaster Relief Act of 1970 was introduced to minimize the fragmentation of federal recovery programs. In 1974, the Disaster Relief Act of 1974 streamlined the presidential disaster declaration process. Legislation was passed again in 1979, this time to create FEMA by integrating several organizations from HUD and the Defense Department's Defense Civil Preparedness Agency. In 1988, the Robert T. Stafford Disaster Relief and Emergency Assistance Act expanded the definition of what events could be considered as a disaster and specified who could receive assistance, for what purposes, and how it should be administered. There are other laws that have been past in recent years. In 2002, the federal government passed the Homeland Security Act, which combined 22 federal agencies into the DHS. Recent disasters have also led to the creation of the National Response and Recovery Frameworks and other measures that have had a dramatic impact upon the direction of emergency management in this country.

Laws are applicable to disasters in other ways as well. For instance, there are numerous statutes that have to be followed in response to hazardous material incidents. These include:

▲ The Comprehensive Environmental Response, Compensation and Liability Act (CERCLA)
▲ Title 29, Section 1910.1200 of the Code of Federal Regulations
▲ Federal Food, Drug, and Cosmetic Act
▲ Toxic Substances and Control Act (TOSCA)
▲ The Superfund Amendments and Reauthorization Act (SARA).
▲ The Emergency Planning and Community Right to Know Act (EPCRA)
▲ The Federal Insecticide, Fungicide, and Rodenticide Act (FIFRA)

States and local government have similarly passed a number of laws for disaster response and recovery operations. For example, states have enacted legislation to create emergency management agencies and endorse federal disaster laws and regulations. The laws are not uniform across all states, however, because of the unique disaster contexts in different parts of the country. Local jurisdictions have also established ordinances concerning disasters. Some of the city ordinances mandate the creation and operation of emergency management offices and programs. Others discuss local disaster declarations and the management of recovery activities.

There are additional organizations that have created semibinding legal resolutions, which may have an impact on current and future emergency management activities. For example, the National Fire Protection Association (NFPA) created NFPA 1600: Recommended Practices for Disaster Management. "**NFPA 1600** establishes a shared set of norms for disaster management, emergency management, and business-continuity programs... . One vital aspect of NFPA 1600 is its requirement that all emergency management and business-continuity programs comply with its relevant laws, policies, and industry standards" (Nicholson, 2005b, p. 44). NFPA 1600 has been recommended or endorsed by professional entities. These include the 9/11 Commission, the National Emergency Management Association, and others.

There has also been growing recognition and support of other semi-legal documents or programs. These include the Capability Assessment for Readiness (CAP) and the Emergency Management Accreditation Program (EMAP). You should ensure that you are familiar with these and any other pertinent legislation that may impact your job as an emergency manager. It is possible that lawsuits could arise if these programs are not meticulously followed.

As an emergency manager, you should also be aware of the possibility of lawsuits and other types of legal claims. It is true that "units of government enjoy immunity, or protection from legal liability, for many of their activities" (Nicholson, 2005a, p. 12). However, liability is not unlimited. Before 1960, few states allowed civil suits against public organizations. However, this has changed over time and governments are not fully immune from legal liability (Pine, 1991).

### 10.6.2 Constitutional Rights

Legal claims against emergency managers may involve constitutional rights or federal statutory violations (Pine, 1991). In terms of constitutional rights, Congress passed civil rights legislation in 1871. Such laws hold accountable public officials who deny rights established by the U.S. Constitution. "In disasters, local officials sometimes limit freedom of association, the use of public communication channels, or entry into evacuated areas, all of which pose the potential for violation of First Amendment rights" (Pine, 1991, p. 300).

Other possible legal liabilities include discrimination. The Civil Rights Act of 1964 and Equal Employment Act of 1972 prohibit any form of discrimination. Emergency managers cannot discriminate based on race, color, sex, religion, and national origin. An example of this is treating employees or disaster victims in a preferential or discriminatory manner. This may result in costly lawsuits.

### 10.6.3 Negligence

**Negligence** occurs when the policies, actions, or inactions of politicians, emergency managers, or responders cause injuries or damage to people and their property. Negligence is the failure of emergency managers and responders to do what a reasonable and prudent person would have done under similar circumstances (Pine, 1991). "For example, a state statute may require state and local agencies to prepare and keep current an emergency preparedness plan for natural, technological, or civil disasters. If a local government failed to prepare a plan and a disaster occurred, a citizen could file a suit claiming that the governmental unit had failed to carry out a statutory duty and was therefore liable for losses. In the field of emergency management, for example, a tort could involve a failure to warn citizens of a known hazardous materials release or a failure to provide adequate time for an evacuation order in a natural disaster" (Pine, 1991).

Medical lawsuits could also occur after a disaster if victims have been treated inadequately or misdiagnosed. Lawsuits are also common if there are problems with consent, record disclosures, reporting requirements, or other issues (Hafter and Fedor, 2004; Mancini and Gale, 1981). Legal action may likewise be taken against nearby jurisdictions if there have been problems with mutual aid agreements. For example, a first responder from another jurisdiction was killed when he was dispatched to a fire in Fort Worth, Texas. A dispute arose between the cities regarding who would pay death benefits to the surviving family members.

There are other reasons why lawsuits and prosecution might occur after disasters. These include (Nicholson, 2003b):

▲ Vehicle accidents involving government or emergency vehicles
▲ Slow 911 dispatch
▲ Delayed emergency response operations
▲ Failure to follow response protocols

The failure of emergency management personnel to follow laws and regulations regarding the use of disaster funds can also lead to legal troubles. Lawsuits may occur if there is an unwillingness to comply with statutes pertaining to hazardous material record keeping and disclosure. Even emergent groups could be held liable for their noble actions after disasters in some cases (e.g., unintentionally harming someone during search and rescue operations). However, most states have passed "**Good Samaritan laws**," which protect citizens who do what they can to provide medical and other services to those affected by accidents and disasters. The diverse nature of legal problems is so serious that one expert on disaster law states, "I firmly believe that liability issues are the great unplanned-for hazard faced by emergency managers" (Nicholson, 2003a, p. 17).

### 10.6.4 Minimizing Liability

Since you will be involved in response and recovery operations, it is vital that you are aware of what can be done to minimize legal liability. Some measures have to be taken at the state level. "State disaster or emergency statutes often contain … specific immunity provisions to protect government officials engaged in critical decision-making procedures in emergencies. Some states have gone further, putting into place broad immunities shielding a variety of players (i.e., the state, political subdivisions, or local government entities) who act during an emergency response rather than just the individuals involved in decision making" (Nicholson, 2005a, p. 12).

There are also things you can do to protect yourself at the local level:

▲ Develop and follow standard operating procedures that address various legal subjects. These topics may include employment practices and negligence.
▲ Be a proactive risk manager. Work with legal counsel in the community to discuss hypothetical scenarios. Discuss how they should be addressed.

> ### FOR EXAMPLE
>
> **The Station Nightclub Fire**
>
> The Rhode Island Night Club fire that killed at least 100 people on February 3, 2003, was the result of at least two illegal activities. First, a rock band used pyrotechnics inside the nightclub. Second, flammable material was installed on the ceiling. Both of these mistakes were not prevented by the band manager, those overseeing the club, and building inspectors. Numerous lawsuits were filed as a result of the tragedy. This is one example of why it is important to always consider legal issues in your community.

▲ Consult with a city attorney or legal staff to discuss response and recovery actions. Identify how your ongoing operations could conflict with citizens' rights or result in negligence.

▲ Pursue a policy of "litigation mitigation." **Litigation mitigation** is an active effort with city attorneys to prevent legal liabilities and accept the need to spend time, effort, and money now to avoid future lawsuits (Nicholson, 2003b).

## SELF-CHECK

- What is a law?
- How is law related to disasters and emergency management?
- Can first responders or emergency managers be held liable in disasters?
- What rights should emergency managers protect?
- What is negligence and how can it be avoided?
- What is "litigation mitigation?"

## 10.7 Record Keeping

Record keeping is vitally important in response and recovery operations. Accurate records help you make better decisions, and they are important for other reasons as well. As a disaster unfolds, you and other organizations may need to know who is missing. You must also find out how many people may be trapped or injured. Record keeping is required to track damages as well as human and material resources. You will need to keep records of response and recovery activities for federal reimbursement. Insufficient records can also hurt the reconstruction of the sequence of events that lead to the disaster and curtail organizational learning about the response. A failure to compile records hinders preventive activities and the improvement of future postdisaster operations. Ironically, and despite the importance of such histories and documents, record keeping is sometimes neglected by disaster scholars and emergency management practitioners (Figure 10-6).

**Figure 10-6**

Whether it is about personnel, supplies, individual and public assistance, or any other issue, record keeping is extremely important in disasters. Jocelyn Augustino/FEMA.

### 10.7.1 Record Keeping Problems

There are several problems associated with record keeping and disasters. Scanlon (1996) has provided the most extensive study on the matter. He suggests:

▲ **Records do not exist before the disaster**. There may be limited or no records regarding individuals who are affected in disasters. For instance, there may be no names for people who are impacted by disasters at sporting events, outdoor concerts, and papal masses. This is also true in cases where disaster affect public transportation systems such as subways and ferries. Record keeping is lacking regarding disaster victims in libraries and museums.

▲ **Emergence makes record keeping difficult**. The initial search and rescue operations are often carried out by friends, neighbors, and coworkers. These individuals are not professional emergency personnel. They do not keep records, and they rarely tell anyone what they have witnessed before taking victims to the hospital(s).

▲ **Records are not reliable**. Subways, airlines, ferries, apartments, and public buildings often have inaccurate records of their occupants at any given time. A business or government agency that is affected by a disaster may have records of their employees, but not which employees were on vacation or out ill. They probably also won't have records of those visiting their facilities. Also, hospitals that receive large numbers of victims at one time will be too overwhelmed to keep accurate and up-to-date records.

▲ **Access to records is restricted.** The buildings where the records are located may be damaged in the disaster. People may not be able to physically get to the records because the building has been condemned. Additionally, records may have restricted access due to their contents. The problems associated with secrecy may be more prevalent in the future due to homeland security concerns.

▲ **Records are lost or destroyed**. Records may be destroyed due to the damage sustained in the disaster. For example, the terrorist attacks on 9/11 completely destroyed the city EOC, and some businesses lost records if they had no electronic backups. Another example is from the Fort Worth tornado. This hazard destroyed many computers in downtown office buildings. The strong winds broke windows and sucked away corporate documents and even classified FBI files (McEntire, 2002a).

▲ **Records may be toxic**. Many disasters involve hazardous materials, and "it follows that documents recovered after such events will be contaminated" (Scanlon, 1996, p. 275).

▲ **Record keeping fails after a disaster**. In the midst of the numerous response and recovery activities that take place after a disaster, there is often not enough time to accurately record the details of what has occurred (Hatfield 1990, 28 as cited by Scanlon, 1996).

### 10.7.2 Keeping Accurate Records

Although record keeping is challenging after a disaster, the problems are not insurmountable. There are a number of actions that can be taken to improve record keeping after disasters. For instance, the emergency manager must recognize the importance of records. He or she should take the time to jot down or compile names, contact information, contract documents, and expenses accurately during response and recovery operations. The following questions may also help the emergency manager keep more complete and accurate records:

▲ If an incident happens, what types of records would be of value?
▲ How could such records be compiled?
▲ How can such valuable records be stored safely?
▲ Who should have access to these records?
▲ What are the costs of record keeping and is it worth it (Scanlon, 1996)?

The emergency manager may obtain vital data and create pertinent disaster records from a variety of sources. There are a number of records and ways to save information (Killian, 1956). These useful documents and means of recording data include tape-recorded material (e.g., dispatch conversations and interviews), personal documents (e.g., diaries), agency and official letters (e.g., police reports, situation reports), and notes from EOC meetings and operations (e.g., after-action reports). Pictures may also be important to refer to at a later date.

> **FOR EXAMPLE**
>
> **Using Records to Solve Terrorist Attacks**
>
> After 9/11, the United States became aware of the fact that Al-Qaeda and Osama Bin Laden were behind the terrorist attacks. They knew this in part thanks to the information provided by a flight attendant on the first hijacked airplane. After the terrorists took over the airplane, she called the flight control tower. She told the authorities what seat the terrorist was sitting in. Using the airliner's records, the authorities could see that the seat belonged to Mohammed Atta, one of the masterminds of 9/11. Other terrorists were tracked by apartment contracts, driver's licenses, flight school documents, etc.

Putting someone in charge of records can also be helpful. If you are unable to carefully keep records in the immediate aftermath of a disaster, it is imperative that you review the response and recovery operations with others as soon as it is feasible to reconstruct incomplete notes or elaborate on details. As mentioned earlier, the failure to compile records about disasters could have far-reaching negative implications.

## SELF-CHECK

- Is record keeping important to the emergency manager?
- Why is it difficult to keep complete and accurate records after disasters?
- What steps can be taken to improve record keeping?
- What sources information can emergency managers pursue to facilitate record keeping.

## SUMMARY

There are numerous challenges that you will face after disasters. Communication is difficult because of technological failures or human error. This leads to coordination problems among organizations. The lack and dynamic nature of information in disasters make decision making problematic. Road bridges will be destroyed and traffic will be disrupted severely. Politics will enter response and recovery operations as interorganizational conflict occurs, blame is placed, and people express frustration with postdisaster activities. Numerous people will require special attention because they are the most vulnerable in disaster situations. There is also a chance that you or your city might be held liable after a disaster. Records will need to be kept, but this is difficult in light of the many other activities that must be performed after a disaster occurs. Overcoming these challenges through carefully crafted operations is necessary if you are to promote resilience after a disaster.

# KEY TERMS

| | |
|---|---|
| **Bounded rationality** | The attempt to be rational is never fully achieved because of the constraints disasters present to the decision maker. |
| **Communication** | The process of relaying information that has bearing on the effectiveness of disaster response and recovery operations. |
| **Coordination** | The harmonization of activities among diverse actors in emergency management with the purpose of overcoming the challenges inherent in disasters. |
| **Debugging** | A method that includes a keen observation of the decision process to correct potential weaknesses and mistakes. |
| **Design preferable models** | Studying the situation or problem in detail, determining the gap that exists between the goal and reality, and intervening to adapt the process to the desired outcome. |
| **Good Samaritan laws** | Statutes that protect citizens who do all they can to provide medical and other services to those affected by accidents and disasters. |
| **NFPA 1600** | A shared set of norms for disaster management, emergency management, and business continuity programs. |
| **Interoperability** | The ability to communicate and operate across and with various disaster organizations. |
| **Laws** | Rules that are established by the government to maintain order and perform important functions in society. |
| **Litigation mitigation** | An active effort with city attorneys to prevent legal liabilities and accept the need to spend time, effort, and money now to avoid future lawsuits (Nicholson, 2003b). |
| **Logistics** | "The process of planning, implementing and controlling the efficient, cost-effective flow and storage of goods and materials as well as related information, from the point of origin to the point of consumption for the purpose of meeting the end beneficiary's requirements" (Tatham and Hughes, 2011, p. 67). |
| **Negligence** | Policies, actions, or inactions of politicians, emergency managers, and responders that cause injuries or damage to people and their property. |

**Rational decision making**   Searching for alternative solutions and selecting the one that is deemed most appropriate.

**Situational awareness**   A need to be vigilant of circumstances in order to understand the context of what is taking place.

**Special populations**   People that are susceptible to disasters and those who may be least able to deal with them.

# ASSESS YOUR UNDERSTANDING

Posttest to evaluate your knowledge of overcoming challenges after a disaster. *Measure your learning by comparing pretest and posttest results.*

## Summary Questions

1. One reason why communication is problematic in disasters is because disasters destroy communication equipment. True or false?

2. Reminding others about the need to focus on disaster victims is one way to improve coordination. True or false?

3. Coordination implies an ability to work together to resolve mutual disaster concerns. True or false?

4. Disasters pose coordination challenges because they are dramatically different than routine emergencies. True or false?

5. Interoperability means that organizations are not capable of communicating effectively one with another. True or false?

6. Emergency managers will not face decision-making challenges after disasters. True or false?

7. Tragic choice suggests there will be drawbacks to nearly every decision made in a disaster. True or false?

8. Disasters permit bounded rationality at best. True or false?

9. Designing preferable models is similar to rational decision making. True or false?

10. Eating right and getting sufficient rest can improve decision making. True or false?

11. School busses may be used to evacuate large populations. True or false?

12. Police and public works departments may play a role in traffic control. True or false?

13. Logistics is about getting people and resources to the right place at the right time. True or false?

14. Hurricane Katrina illustrated the potential for blame after a disaster. True or false?

15. Emergency managers should recognize that they may be a convenient scapegoat for politicians if postdisaster operations are ineffective. True or false?

16. Clarifying responsibilities when disasters strike will not reduce interorganizational rivalry. True or false?

17. While all people may be vulnerable to disaster, some people are more vulnerable than others. True or false?

18. Women may constitute special populations in disasters because they often have to care for children. True or false?

19. Language issues are not a concern for the emergency manager. True or false?

20. Prisoners may be considered special populations because they have to be monitored closely after a disaster. True or false?

**21.** Keeping records can help the emergency manager retain his or her job. True or false?

**22.** Mt. St. Helens is a good example of possible lawsuits resulting from the government's handling of disasters. True or false?

**23.** Laws are rules that guide government behavior and the performance of tasks for the public good. True or false?

**24.** Disasters have no bearing on the creation of emergency management law. True or false?

**25.** Record keeping is vital for federal reimbursements of disaster expenses. True or false?

**26.** Even though you will be busy after a disaster, it is imperative that you give sufficient attention to record keeping. True or false?

**27.** Situation reports can help you with record keeping, but tape recording communication with others will not. True or false?

**28.** Keeping a diary of your activities could help you remember what steps were taken to respond to a disaster. True or false?

**29.** Hazardous materials may limit the availability of certain records after a disaster. True or false?

**30.** Communication problems result from:
   **(a)** Damaged communication equipment
   **(b)** People problems
   **(c)** An understanding of who needs your information
   **(d)** Answers a and b
   **(e)** A failure to recognize the negative impact of situational awareness

**31.** Communication is most likely to be successful when it is:
   **(a)** Calm
   **(b)** Courteous
   **(c)** Correct
   **(d)** Concise
   **(e)** All of the above

**32.** Coordination will:
   **(a)** Limit duplication of service
   **(b)** Limit gaps in service
   **(c)** Increase the effectiveness of response
   **(d)** Increase the effectiveness of recovery
   **(e)** All of the above

**33.** Tracking needs and how they are met is an example of what type of coordination strategy?
   **(a)** Consequences
   **(b)** Control
   **(c)** Cultural
   **(d)** Customer
   **(e)** Core

34. Facing adversity implies:
    (a) Emergency managers have compressed time to make decisions.
    (b) Disasters kill people and injure others.
    (c) First responders are tired.
    (d) No decision will be optimal.
    (e) None of the above.

35. Situational awareness:
    (a) Is closely related to tragic choice
    (b) Cannot be construed as a decision-making challenge
    (c) Implies one is aware of what is taking place during response and recovery operations
    (d) Is a result of fuzzy gambling
    (e) Is a trait to be avoided by the emergency manager

36. Which disaster illustrated problems with insufficient fuel?
    (a) The Northridge earthquake
    (b) The Asian Tsunami
    (c) Hurricane Andrew
    (d) Hurricane Rita
    (e) The Fort Worth tornado

37. Public transit authorities may be helpful after a disaster because:
    (a) They deal with traffic problems on a regular basis.
    (b) They provided transportation to thousands of people for special events.
    (c) They operate at peak traffic periods.
    (d) They are eager to help emergency managers.
    (e) All of the above.

38. Interorganizational rivalry can be increased when:
    (a) Organizations dispute authority over a given domain area.
    (b) Questions about tasks arise.
    (c) It is unclear who will get resources or credit.
    (d) All of the above.
    (e) Answers a and b only.

39. A focusing event:
    (a) Helps bring political attention to disaster issues
    (b) Is a major problem for decision making
    (c) Was evident in a small earthquake in Idaho
    (d) Was evident in a tornado in Cincinnati
    (e) Cannot be related to the strain and stress of disasters

40. Tourists may be considered special populations because:
    (a) They are always poor.
    (b) They can always speak the language.
    (c) They are minority populations only.
    (d) They often lack sufficient information about local hazards.
    (e) None of the above.

41. In order to deal effectively with special populations:
    (a) It is advisable that you avoid nursing homes and prisons.
    (b) It is advisable that you work closely with nonprofit organizations.
    (c) It is necessary that you communicate with the fire department only.
    (d) It is recommended that you coordinate with prisons but not schools.
    (e) Answers b and c.
42. The standards and norms for emergency management and business continuity are contained in:
    (a) IEMSA 2210
    (b) IAEM 3622
    (c) NFPA 1600
    (d) NFPA 763
    (e) UNLS 7350
43. Immunity implies:
    (a) A government employee can be held liable for an action or inaction
    (b) A government employee cannot be held liable for an action or inaction.
    (c) The situational awareness has led to core coordination strategy.
    (d) Litigation mitigation has not succeeded.
    (e) The government has made a mistake in response and recovery operations.
44. Negligence occurs when:
    (a) Something is done that a reasonable person would not do.
    (b) Something is not done that a reasonable person would do.
    (c) An action or inaction hurts others or destroys their property.
    (d) All of the above.
    (e) None of the above.
45. Emergent groups cannot be held liable in some states because of:
    (a) Interoperable immunity
    (b) Negligent immunity
    (c) Litigation mitigation
    (d) Good Samaritan laws
    (e) Rational decision making
46. Reasons why record keeping is problematic after disasters include:
    (a) Records are not reliable.
    (b) Records have been lost or destroyed.
    (c) Records may be hazardous.
    (d) Access to records has not been granted.
    (e) All of the above.

## Review Questions

1. What is communication and why is it important for emergency managers?
2. How would you define coordination?
3. Are communication and coordination related to each other? Why or why not?

4. What are typical communication and coordination problems?

5. How can the barriers to communication and coordination be overcome by the emergency manager?

6. How can interoperability be promoted after disasters?

7. Disasters pose serious challenges for decision makers. Why is this the case?

8. Is it possible to make fully rational decisions in disasters? Why or why not?

9. What problems hinder decision making in disaster situations?

10. There are two major recommendations for disaster decision making. What are they?

11. Can disasters impact transportation systems? If so, how?

12. What transportation related issues are evident in disasters?

13. Why is logistics critical for emergency management?

14. Are disasters political? Why or why not?

15. How can emergency managers avoid blame placement?

16. What is a special population?

17. Why are some people more prone to disasters than others?

18. Do all disaster victims have the same capabilities?

19. What can you do to help special populations after disasters?

20. Do laws have a bearing on emergency management?

21. What legal issues should be taken into account by the emergency manager?

22. Who can help the emergency manager make decisions to avoid legal liability?

23. What is litigation mitigation?

24. Is record keeping important after disasters?

25. What factors make record keeping problematic for the emergency manager?

26. What are some novel ways to save information after disasters?

## Applying This Chapter

1. A major hailstorm has just affected your community in Mississippi. It is unclear what neighborhoods have been affected and what needs your citizens have. How does this situation affect your decision making? What can be done to overcome such problems?

2. A terrorist attack caused a major evacuation of your city initially and resources are needed to help affected businesses in the jurisdiction. How can you utilize transportation systems and related personnel to respond effectively?

3. Two of the departments in your community are not working together after a flood because of priority conflicts among the leaders of these organizations. In particular, the search and rescue team in the fire department is not happy with the traffic control provided by the police department. What can you do to ensure that this conflict does not hinder postdisaster operations?

4. You are the local emergency manager in a community that has a state run school for the mentally retarded. This state is also prone to tornadoes. What concerns do you have about the individuals in this facility? What activities do you undertake during an event to care for those who are most vulnerable?

5. While working in the EOC, you notice that the different organizations are not resolving disaster problems in a coordinated fashion. What can you do to improve communication across organizations and facilitate an effective response?

6. During recovery, a question has arisen regarding the relocation of homes from the flood plain. The action would reduce community vulnerability but is not popular among many residents. Who can you talk to in your jurisdiction ensure your decisions are within the parameters of the law?

7. Your city's response to a winter storm is unfolding. A great deal of money is being spent on sand and chemicals to keep the roads from freezing. In addition, it is expected that drivers will be required to work on a rotating basis over the next several days. What records can you keep to track expenses?

## YOU TRY IT

### Working with Others

You are the chapter manager for the American Red Cross in your community. A train has derailed and spilled chemicals near an apartment complex. What organizations and levels of government do you want to work with and why in this situation? What are the benefits of coordination? How can you improve coordination among all of the groups?

### Decision Making

You are a local emergency manager for a city that has just experienced a major power outage. Information about the cause is nonexistent. What possible explanations could there be for the outage? Who could help you determine what happened? What decisions do you need to make to resolve the issue?

### Transportation Groups

You are a transportation official for a city that has been targeted by terrorists in the past. You need to anticipate response and recovery operations should terrorists attack your city. How does transportation fit into emergency management?

### Disasters and Politics

You are the local emergency manager in the Midwest and the response to a flooding episode was less than perfect. The media is pointing out the failures and city leaders are calling for your resignation. While you know you committed errors, you also know that many other organizations made mistakes as well. What do you do to protect your job and avoid alienating others who participated?

### Using Politics to Your Advantage

You are the risk manager for an industrial facility that has recently experienced a chemical explosion. In the past, the CEO has been less than supportive of your efforts to keep the business safe. How can the increased interest in this disaster be used to your advantage?

### Special Populations

You are an emergency manager in a city that has just experienced a major fire at a nursing home. The building has been severely damaged and cannot be inhabited. What concerns do you have about the residents? How can you evacuate patients and the elderly safely? Where could they go? What considerations should be included in your decisions?

### Limiting Liability

After monitoring a storm moving in your direction and communicating with the National Weather Service, you decide to sound the outdoor warning system. You later learn that some of the sirens did not function properly and citizens in that area are expressing their frustrations to the media. What can you do as an emergency manager to protect the legal interests of the city?

### Keeping Records

You are the local emergency manager for a city that has just experienced a major plane crash. Most passengers have been killed and their belongings have been strewn about the crash site. Survivors have been taken to several nearby hospitals. Families are calling you to get information about their loved ones who are believed to have been on the flight. The media wants to know how the event unfolded. The state is asking if they can help in any way. What types of records do you need to keep and why?

### Research Paper

Collect literature on at least two disaster cases. Write a 6-page paper on the challenges encountered by the emergency manager in these events. Explain what could be done differently to overcome them in the future.

# 11

# HARNESSING TECHNOLOGY AND ORGANIZATION
## Tools for Effective Operations

## Starting Point

Pretest to assess your knowledge on how to harness technology and organization. *Determine where you need to concentrate your effort.*

## What You'll Learn in This Chapter

- ▲ Importance of technology for emergency managers
- ▲ The benefit of decision support systems
- ▲ Principles of incident command and the nature of emergency operations centers (EOCs)
- ▲ Value of mutual aid, the Standard Emergency Management System (SEMS), and the Emergency Management Assistance Compact
- ▲ Principles of the National Incident Management System (NIMS), the National Response Framework, and the National Recovery Framework

## After Studying This Chapter, You'll Be Able To

- ▲ Apply technology in response and recovery operations.
- ▲ Examine the usefulness of geographic information systems.
- ▲ Use incident command in time of a disaster.
- ▲ Demonstrate how to run an EOC.
- ▲ Employ mutual aid, SEMS, and NIMS.
- ▲ Appraise the National Response Framework and the National Recovery Framework.

## Goals and Outcomes

- ▲ Evaluate how technology is used after disasters.
- ▲ Compare different types of technological tools.
- ▲ Manage the scene of a disaster in an effective manner.
- ▲ Work closely with others in the EOC.
- ▲ Organize response operations with nearby jurisdictions.
- ▲ Request disaster assistance from other state governments.
- ▲ Oversee municipal recovery with federal disaster assistance.

---

*Disaster Response and Recovery: Strategies and Tactics for Resilience*, Second Edition. David A. McEntire.
© 2015 John Wiley & Sons, Inc. Published 2015 by John Wiley & Sons, Inc.

# INTRODUCTION

Resilience is increased when you harness technology and organization after a disaster. It is imperative that you, as an emergency manager, understand the importance of technological tools in response and recovery operations. Communication equipment, decision support systems (DSSs), and geographic information system (GIS) will help you work with others, make good choices, track the impact of disasters, and identify where resources are located and needed. Although you will not be deployed to the field in most disasters, it is useful that you understand the principles and limitations of the incident command system (ICS). Being able to run an emergency operations center (EOC) is also a vital skill that you must acquire. Besides these steps, you must at times seek mutual aid assistance from nearby jurisdictions. It is likewise advisable that you recognize the operational characteristics of the Emergency Management Assistance Compact (EMAC), the National Incident Management System (NIMS), the National Response Framework (NRF), and the National Disaster Recovery Framework (NDRF). Such measures will help you manage the disaster effectively and work closely with local, state, federal, and tribal governments.

## 11.1  The Importance of Technology

The role that technology plays in response and recovery cannot be overestimated. Innovations in technology are occurring rapidly, and the new technological tools should improve the effectiveness of postdisaster operations. For instance, a revolution has occurred in communications, with the advent of two-way radios, cell phones, and the Internet. Because of advances in technology, new tools are increasingly available to emergency managers. And, in some cases, the cost of such equipment has come down, making it more accessible for those who need and use it. Not all communities or government agencies have the same technology resources though. In fact, some jurisdictions and organizations may possess very few technological tools. However, federal grants are helping many cities, states, and tribal governments acquire technological improvements. Although each jurisdiction and agency does not use every tool, there are many examples of technology that can be utilized in emergency management:

▲ Doppler radar improves the forecasting of severe weather such as tornadoes, and CASA radar systems are better able to predict the approximate time the severe weather will arrive and in what specific locations.
▲ Reverse 911 systems warn thousands of people about impending hazards within a short amount of time. These recorded emergency notifications can be delivered via telephone with the use of computer programs that target neighborhoods and potentially affected areas.
▲ Computers are used to manage dispatch centers and assist responders in reaching the destinations of emergencies and disasters quickly. A computer-aided dispatch system can be used to guide first response vehicles to the scene of an emergency in the most expedited manner possible.

▲ Traffic signal preemption devices use high-frequency strobe lights to change lights and allow responders to arrive at the scene of an incident without unnecessary delay.

▲ Detection equipment can determine the presence of weapons of mass destruction to keep responders safe and alert citizens to danger. Special sensors have been installed in major metropolitan areas throughout the country to make this possible.

▲ Cardiac defibrillators help to save lives when people are in medical distress. Most public buildings are now equipped with these lifesaving devices.

▲ Listening devices and extraction equipment help search and rescue teams locate and remove those crushed under disaster debris. These and other tools have helped to save the lives of those who normally would have perished in prior disasters.

▲ Cell phones now permit the delivery of emergency warnings from government officials. They also increase the ability of people to communicate in more and more remote locations.

▲ Ham radios use short waves to permit the sharing of information when many other communication systems fail to operate (cell towers may go down and other frequencies might be overloaded).

▲ The Global Positioning System (GPS) is a navigation system that relies on satellites. GPS can help to plot damages and locate the position of victims, first responders, and other critical assets.

▲ Video cameras help law enforcement agencies investigate acts of terrorism. As an example, authorities were able to quickly identify the 2013 Boston bombing suspects from nearby surveillance and security cameras.

▲ Remote sensing uses aerial photographs to obtain data about the earth from above. It can provide information about the track of storms and extent of disaster damages.

▲ Text messaging and e-mail are additional ways to communicate when information needs to be shared in real time or through larger and more detailed documents.

▲ Tablets are small portable phones that have computer. They contain phone numbers and addresses, calendars, and to-do lists. These can help you to contact resources and schedule functions that need to be performed.

It is important to keep in mind that some of this technology is not always useful, applicable, or even beneficial. Technology can be rendered useless if the power goes out. Technology can also become unavailable in some cases if phone lines or towers are damaged. Sometimes, technology can provide so much information that it is easy to get overwhelmed. However, it is also true that "innovative technological advances are transforming the practice of emergency management" (Sutphen and Waugh, 1998, p. 9). If you are to be successful, you must acquire knowledge and expertise in the technological realm.

> ### FOR EXAMPLE
>
> **Technology and 9/11**
>
> Many technology tools were used at Ground Zero after 9/11. One of them was LIDAR. LIDAR is an acronym for Light Detection and Ranging. **LIDAR** is an airborne laser system that was used to detect heat and dangerous debris accumulations after the World Trade Center Towers collapsed on 9/11. The technology helped authorities understand the extent of the disaster, including rubble accumulations, dangerous voids, and debris that were hanging precariously. It helped responders react safely in spite of extremely dangerous circumstances.

## SELF-CHECK

- Why is technology important for emergency managers?
- How has technology or its accessibility changed over time?
- How can technology help with warning?
- How does technology help dispatch and responders?
- How can technology help with other postdisaster functions?

## 11.2 Communication Equipment and Interoperability

As noted in Chapter 10, being able to talk to co-workers and those in other agencies is necessary in disasters. Seeking and sharing information are the major functions common in emergency management. In general, there are three types of equipment used for communications:

- ▲ **Transmitters** are communication instruments that convey information through radios, sirens, television stations, and cable override systems.
- ▲ **Receivers** are equipment devices that obtain signals from transmitters. They include stereos, pagers, police scanners, and televisions.
- ▲ **Transceivers** are able to both transmit and receive information. Examples of transceivers include telephones, satellites, smartphones, two-way radios, citizen band radios, 800 MHz radios, and ham radios.

There are several specific pieces of equipment that will assist you with communications. Some of this technology may even span different types of communication devices (Figure 11-1).

**Figure 11-1**

Modern communication equipment, including this mobile incident command post, may facilitate communication. Marilee Caliendo/FEMA.

### 11.2.1 Trunked Radio Systems

The history of communication equipment reveals steady progress in technological advances for those involved in response and recovery operations. Traditionally, emergency communications took place through transceivers. They used low-band VHF or UHF. This usually required a radio tower, repeaters, and an uninterrupted power supply. In time, communications were improved by using common radio channels or relaying information through a designated dispatcher. By 1977, the Association of Public-Safety Communications Officers created minimum standards for what is known as an 800/900 MHz trunked radio system. A **trunked radio system** is a computer-controlled network. It searches for a clear channel for users to use to talk to each other (Dees, 2000, p. 8). The major advantage of trunked radio systems is their ability to serve a number of users. Put differently, these systems allow a variety of "talk groups." A **talk group** is a unit with its own designated channel to facilitate communications regarding particular topics or subjects. Today, some radio systems have digital coding to identify the source of communication and rely on encryption in the case of high-security operations (e.g., response to terrorist attacks). Although advances like these are beneficial, many of the systems across jurisdictions do not work well with each other. Each community has equipment based on their own needs, preferences, and budgets.

### 11.2.2 The Internet

The Internet has become a useful tool for response and recovery operations. The Internet makes a vast amount of information available to a large group of people at one time. As an emergency manager, you can use the Internet to research the unique features of specific types of hazards. The Internet may help you to compare notes with others on the best equipment for your city's needs. For example, you can use the Internet to get opinions on which rain gauges are the most reliable. Also, you can identify the features and cost of various types of communication equipment.

From the Internet, you can also access vital information from research centers and government disaster-related agencies (Fischer, 1998a). The Internet allows you to read case studies to determine how other professionals in the field handled the same threats you face. It can also help you to determine where to acquire much needed resources when disaster occurs.

The Internet may also allow you to communicate with colleagues during response operations. The "Internet communication has radically changed the relay of information so that in most cases the 'generals' hear the news about road closures and flood gauge readings at precisely the moment the data are first available and at the same time as the 'underlings'" (Gruntfest and Weber, 1998, p. 58). E-mail is one way you can share and receive this type of information. The Internet may similarly help you videoconference with other remote agencies as you determine recovery priorities.

Finally, the Internet is likewise a great tool for citizens to use to obtain information. For example, citizens can print off instructions on what to do in case of a hurricane or tornado. Before or after a disaster, you could set up a page on your city's website to give people all kinds of information including evacuation routes, emergency numbers, shelter options, and other recommendations.

### 11.2.3 Voice over Internet Protocol and Other Equipment

Another system, **Voice over Internet Protocol** (VoIP), routes communications over the Internet. It uses a packet-switched set of lines instead of circuit-switched voice transmission lines. The possibility of communication through VoIP has increased over the years. VoIP is used in cell, radio, and computer networks. Wireless systems also help to overcome communication problems, and they became a reality with cell and satellite systems. Of course, some equipment may be damaged or overloaded after a disaster. In addition, it should be restated that many communication problems cannot be blamed on equipment only.

### 11.2.4 The ACU-1000

At times, there is an inability to communicate across departments and jurisdictions. Because of different needs, preferences, and budget allocations, agencies and communities purchase distinct types of communication equipment. Sadly, one piece of equipment may not be compatible with others in disasters (e.g., a radio from one community may operate distinctly than another radio in a different community). In light of this inability to communicate across departments and jurisdictions, numerous vendors invented radio bridges and other interfaces.

A very valuable piece of equipment is the ACU-1000. The **ACU-1000** is type of interface equipment that links mobile radios, cell phones, satellite technology, and regular phones in a single real-time communication system. It is now common in many EOCs and mobile command posts (a vehicle with EOC capabilities). During emergencies and disasters, ACU-1000 allows different radio systems to be cross-connected and routed over wide area networks. Local, state, and federal agencies can then coordinate response with multiple organizations. You should become familiar with this equipment as it will facilitate interoperability across departments and jurisdictions.

### 11.2.5 Interoperability

The ACU-1000 is a device used to increase interoperability. **Interoperability** is the ability to communicate and operate across and with various disaster organizations. Interoperability became an important priority after 9/11. The Department of Homeland Security (DHS) created an Office for Interoperability and Compatibility to overcome the problems witnessed after 9/11. This office was established in response to the 9/11 Commission Report that detailed a number of communication problems that were evident among responders. This office is working on the development of equipment to improve communication capabilities. The DHS is partnering with first responders and industry to improve cross communications across frequencies or across manufacturers.

It should be remembered that interoperability requires not just the necessary communication equipment. A willingness to work harmoniously with partner agencies is essential too. As an example, the 9/11 Commission Report illustrated that the police and fire departments in New York City had at least some equipment prior to the terrorist attack that would have allowed interoperability. However, the organizations disagreed about who would be responsible for maintaining it. Even after this tragic incident, Dwyer and Flynn (2005, p. 60) discovered that attempts for interoperability among the police and fire departments after 9/11 were not fully or quickly resolved. Such attitudes must be avoided at all costs to improve communications in disasters.

## SELF-CHECK

- What are the three types of communication equipment?
- How can **trunked radio systems** aid communications?
- How can the Internet improve disaster response and recovery?
- What is the **ACU-1000**?
- What is interoperability and why is it important?

## 11.3 Decision Support Systems (DSSs)

There are a number of computer programs to assist those involved in disaster response operations. These are commonly known as **DSSs**—software applications that help the emergency manager determine priorities and respond to a disaster.

"Decision support systems (DSSs) are computer information systems that have evolved from existing but disparate information pathways used by decision makers. The computer allows for instantaneous links among the database … simulation models, and management tools. Other components may be part of a DSS, such as optimization of routines for resource allocation or artificial intelligence and expert systems. … The DSS ties together spatially and temporally based information with simulation models that depict a spatial/temporal reaction to a response and allows problem-specific information to be reported. … [They may include] historical data (losses, physical events, trends), current data (weather, demographics, and political information), simulation tools (environmental, economic, and socio-political models), and report tools (statistical analyses, maps)" (Mileti, 1999, p. 248).

There are several types of DSS including:

▲ **SoftRisk** (http://www.softrisk.com/). SoftRisk is a software program for critical incidents and emergency management. It has a large database for resource lists and relevant contacts. The software supports call taking and the assignment of tasks and responsibilities. It helps with e-mail and fax communications. SoftRisk integrates with ArcView for spatially referenced mapping.

▲ **CoBRA** Chemical Biological Response Aide (http://www.cobrafirstresponder. com/). This software is designed for incidents involving chemical, biological, radiological, nuclear, and explosive materials. It has an extensive database and checklists to help manage response operations. CoBRA tracks user activities to facilitate an after-action incident log. It also relies on various reference books such as the DOT Emergency Response Guide and DOJ Crime Scene Investigation for improved evacuations/sheltering and prosecution.

▲ **WEBEOC** (http://www.esi911.com/esi/index.php/products-mainmenu-68?id=377). **WEBEOC** is a DSS that can be used in your EOC. With a computer and modem, you are able to access information about the weather, satellite images, and maps. WEBEOC also allows you to track resources deployed by local, state, and federal governments. WEBEOC is touted as the first DSS for emergency managers.

▲ **E-Team** (http://www.eteam.com/). E-Team facilitates the management of crises and disasters. The software enables the user to gather information. It helps the user to assess damages and notify agencies of the status of the incident. E-Team is designed to request and deploy resources. It is anticipated that E-Team will soon be able to assist with the management of volunteers and donations.

▲ **EPlan** (http://www.eplanonline.com). EPlan is a secure web system. It provides vital information to firefighters such as access to hazardous material (HazMat) inventories. It provides access to material safety data sheet (MSDS) site maps—maps that note the location of HazMat. EPlan also has links to the DOT Emergency Response Guide and can help you with many other disaster functions.

▲ **Disaster Management Interoperability Services** (http://www.cmi-services.org/). This program includes Internet service for improved communication among first responders. It helps facilitate awareness and coordination among local, state, and national emergency response organizations. One of the strengths is its ability to ensure security due to passwords and encryption.

▲ **CAMEO** (http://www2.epa.gov/cameo). This program was created by the EPA's Chemical Emergency Preparedness and Prevention Office with the assistance of the National Oceanic and Atmospheric Administration's Office of Response and Restoration. The entire program includes a database of over 6000 hazardous chemicals and supports regulatory compliance on reporting chemical inventories. CAMEO also provides important response information regarding health hazards, firefighting strategies, plume modeling for evacuation, personal protective equipment, and cleanup. CAMEO is a combination of three programs. It includes a chemical database, Areal Locations of Hazardous Atmospheres (ALOHA), and Mapping Applications for Response, Planning, and Local Operational Tasks (MARPLOT).

---

## FOR EXAMPLE

### Other DSS

There are many other DSSs that support a variety of disasters and functions. Some include SLOSH, HURREVAC, and the Health Alert Network. SLOSH stands for Sea, Lake, and Overland Surges from Hurricanes. It is a computer model that helps you predict storm surge heights from tropical cyclones. HURREVAC is another program that examines storm surge, but it also predicts the time it will take to evacuate an area that is expected to be affected by a hurricane. The Health Alert Network is used by hospitals and public health agencies. It is a program that tracks disease outbreaks and bed availability in medical facilities. As an emergency manager, it is your responsibility to determine what programs are available and how this software can assist you in disasters.

---

## SELF-CHECK

- What is a decision support system?
- What are the features of SoftRisk?
- How is CoBRA different than WEBEOC, EPlan, or CAMEO?
- What does E-Team do for the manager?
- Can you think of other software that might be useful for disaster response or recovery operations?

# 11.4 GIS

A geographic information system is an "organized collection of computer hardware, software, geographic data, and personnel designed to efficiently capture, store, update, manipulate, analyze, and display all forms of geographically referenced information" (ESRI as cited by Dash, 1997). GIS can help emergency managers determine what is at or near a certain location. GIS can also be used to show how the use of an area has changed over time as well as patterns in spatial analysis (Dash, 1997). Organizing geographic information in a computer database has many applications. The information available can be very helpful to the emergency manager. For example, many emergency management personnel use GIS on a regular basis. GIS specialists can help others understand a neighborhood through electronic maps. The information displayed may include the languages spoken by the population in that particular area. This type of knowledge will allow authorities to tailor a warning message based on the predominant and other languages of that specific location.

GIS-based spatial analysis is important for mitigation and preparedness as well as postdisaster operations. It has been argued that "spatial data analysis is the most exciting technological development in emergency management in the past decade" (Waugh, 1995). There are numerous powerful software programs developed by the federal government. **HAZUS**, for example, is an assessment software tool that is used to predict potential losses from floods, hurricane winds, and earthquakes. In HAZUS, scientific and engineering information is combined with GIS. This information works together to produce estimates of hazard-related damage. Such assessments may include physical damage, economic loss, and social impacts including the estimated shelter and medical needs of the citizens. These calculations can be made before or after a disaster occurs.

GIS programs have also been used widely in postdisaster operations, including hurricanes and oil spills. For example, after a hurricane, GIS can show the emergency manager destroyed areas and needs for rebuilding. GIS can also illustrate what utility lines are down and where service needs to be restored. GIS helps you determine what the priorities should be during response and recovery activities. For instance, "after the first shock of a catastrophic event … the focus … will be on one thing: understanding all that has happened. Of all the tasks of disaster management, it is this one at which GIS excels. Its visualization and data consolidation capabilities allow GIS to convey large amounts of information to a large number of people in a short period of time – exactly what is needed in the immediate aftermath of a disaster" (Greene, 2002, p. 42).

One of the first applications of GIS was after Hurricane Andrew in 1992. "The initial use of GIS was in mapping damage and analyzing community demographics…. Later, as the potential of GIS was better understood, its use grew in areas like Public Assistance….Projects included tracking (1) debris and debris removal, (2) ….damaged homes, and (3) the location of trailers used for temporary housing" (Dash, 1997).

Other uses of GIS after a disaster include:

▲ Assessing the extent of floods, fires, and earthquakes
▲ Showing the path of tornadoes
▲ Plotting the location of fire stations

▲ Locating fire hydrants and other critical infrastructure (e.g., water mains)
▲ Noting the geographical need for emergency personnel
▲ Finding where the American Red Cross has shelters open
▲ Understanding what field hospitals are in use
▲ Conveying where to go to be fed at mass disaster kitchens
▲ Conveying information about incident command posts (ICPs) and EOC locations
▲ Relaying how to access disaster sites or secure zones
▲ Viewing what buildings have been condemned
▲ Transmitting the location of donation sites
▲ Denoting where to go for disaster assistance

To utilize GIS effectively, accurate information must be put into the computer program before a disaster occurs (Dash, 1997, p. 140). Relevant disaster information must be inputted correctly and completely, which is a time-consuming process. Data can be entered into a computer after a disaster occurs, but this will require that the emergency manager or other city personnel be familiar with the program and its capabilities. Fortunately, many cities have designated GIS departments today so data entry can occur before a disaster and not just in the aftermath.

## FOR EXAMPLE

### GIS and 9/11

Prior to the terrorist attacks on the World Trade Center, New York was already developing a detailed spatial system to track parcel information and street centerlines. When the towers collapsed, GIS was modified to track the physical changes of Manhattan (e.g., affected buildings, search and rescue grids, utility outages, and new transportation routes). The hundreds of maps that were produced identified not only the impact but also resource allocation during response and recovery operations (Thomas et al., 2002, p. 4). So many maps were produced that it was difficult to ensure that everyone had the latest information. Nevertheless, GIS is a great tool for you as an emergency manager.

## SELF-CHECK

- What is a GIS?
- How does spatial analysis help with response and recovery?
- What is HAZUS?
- How has GIS been used in past disasters?
- Can GIS help with damage assessment or building condemnation?
- How can GIS help track shelters, field hospitals, or donation sites?

## 11.5  Managing Disasters at the Local Level

In addition to the technological tools that help improve response and recovery operations, organizational structures will also assist you to be more successful. The incident command system and the emergency operations center are two means by which you can more effectively work with other agencies at the local level. Incident command is used for most emergencies or disasters. EOCs, on the other hand, are used mainly for large disasters or catastrophes. Mutual aid, another collaborative arrangement, may also help jurisdictions collaborate successfully after a disaster.

### 11.5.1  ICS

Incident command, or the ICS, has become the most important field-level operations strategy for first responders. **ICS** is "a set of personnel, policies, procedures, facilities and equipment, integrated into a common organizational structure designed to improve emergency response operations of all types and complexities" (Irwin, 1989, p. 134). The purpose of incident command is to "allow its user(s) to adopt an integrated organizational structure equal to the complexity and demands of single or multiple incidents without being hindered by jurisdictional boundaries" (Gordon, 2002, p. 12). Incident command is therefore an organizational strategy for management. If implemented properly, it may facilitate a more successful field response to emergencies and disasters.

Incident command was created after firefighters had significant challenges while responding to wildfires in California in 1970. After a dry and hot summer, at least 13 large fires were ignited in Southern California. Sixteen lives were lost as a result and more than 600,000 acres was burned. Nearly 800 structures were destroyed over a 13-day period. The fires affected property and land in local, county, state, and federal jurisdictions.

The efforts to deal with the fires were heroic. However, a number of interrelated shortcomings were made evident during the response. These problems were investigated by Congress and the U.S. Forest Service. Local, state, and federal authorities also formed the Firefighting Resources of California Organized for Potential Emergencies (FIRESCOPE) to review the incident. The final reports highlighted various problems that were evident during the response to the 1970 fires (FEMA, 1998a, pp. 1–2; Irwin, 1989, pp. 135–136). The documents noted that more than 100 local, state, and federal agencies participated in the fire suppression. The difficulty of integrating all of these agencies into a coherent response system was recognized as these organizations did not always work together to accomplish goals. In most cases, the agencies performed their functions in isolation from others. There were four reasons for this:

▲ **Poor communications**. Supervisors could not always contact subordinates. They had difficulty reaching other agencies. This was a result of limited channel capacity on radios and different frequency usage. Unfamiliar terminology also complicated the reception and interpretation of conveyed messages.

▲ **Insufficient intelligence and prediction**. None of the responding organizations were asked to gather information about the size and movement of the fires. Information that did exist was incomplete and late.

Expertise was not always available to help make decisions about the number of threatened structures, available evacuation routes, and possible shelter arrangements.

▲ **Lack of joint planning**. The responding agencies did not meet to discuss the fires and outline a coordinated strategy to deal with them. This jeopardized safety and resulted in duplication of effort and gaps in service.

▲ **Inadequate resource management**. All of the above problems resulted in overstaffing of firefighters in some areas. At the same time, there was a scarcity of personnel for other fires. Resources such as fire apparatus, bulldozers, and airplanes were lost, underutilized, or overcommitted.

The investigations revealed that response operations must be based on standard criteria. Those involved in the disaster realized that a system was needed to aid the operations of single agencies and allow them to work closely with other partner organizations. It was argued the new system "… must be readily adaptable to new technologies that may become available to support emergency response and management. It must be able to expand from the organizational requirements of simple, daily incidents up to the needs of a major emergency. It must have basic common elements in organization, terminology, and procedures" (Irwin, 1989). All of this led to the development of ICS.

### 11.5.2 Principles of Incident Command

ICS is based on a common organizational structure (Figure 11-2). It includes the incident commander(s) and the information, safety, and liaison officers. There are also four supporting sections under incident command. These four sections are planning, operations, logistics, and finance/administration (FEMA, 1998). **Incident command**, or the incident commander, is the on-scene leadership for the disaster. Initially, this may be the first person to respond to the incident. Incident command may also be given to the person(s) with the most expertise in certain disasters or those who have extensive knowledge of certain response functions. Later on, command will often be taken over by the highest-ranking official. Command can also be shared among the leadership of several responding agencies. Whether command is given one person or shared among many others, it has the goal of facilitating coordination.

Three officers work closely with the incident commander(s). The **information officer** works with the media to answer their questions about the event. He or she releases information to the public. The **safety officer** monitors the hazardous conditions of the disaster to ensure protection of responding personnel. The **liaison officer** is the point of contact with other organizations responding to the incident. Each of these officers reports to the incident commander(s) to provide an update of the situation as it unfolds.

If needed, the incident commander(s) establishes and works with four organizational sections:

1. The **planning section** collects and evaluates information about the disaster. This section also defines operational priorities. Planning disseminates information about the incident and the use of resources during response

**Figure 11-2**

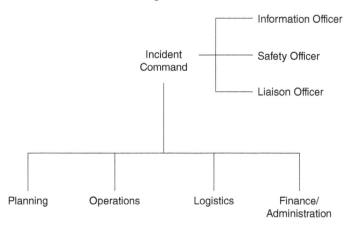

The Incident Command System includes the incident commander(s), liaison officer, safety officer, public information officer, and planning, operations, logistics and finance/administration sections.

operations (e.g., the location of the fire and how many crews have been dispatched to fight it).

2. The **operations section** is responsible for implementing the strategy to respond to the incident as determined by the incident commander and the planning section. For instance, fire suppression or search and rescue may be located under operations.

3. The **logistics section** acquires and provides materials, services, and facilities to support the needs of responders as directed by the incident commander and the operations section. Seeking additional firefighters and fire engines is an example of a logistics activity.

4. The **finance/administration section** tracks costs, completes and files paperwork, and records expenses of operations and logistics. This is especially important for payment purposes and especially if there is hope of being reimbursed by the federal government in a presidential declaration (Figure 11-3).

The ICS is not just an organizational structure. It is based on a number of vitally important principles:

▲ *Common terminology.* Because there are so many response organizations involved in the response, common vocabulary should be used instead of "ten" codes (i.e., 10-4).

▲ *Modular organization.* Depending on the nature and scope of the disaster, ICS consists of the incident commander and one responding unit. In other cases, ICS may be comprised of the incident commander(s), liaison officers, support sections, and additional layers as needed. For example, you may need divisions, branches, and strike teams. The system is designed to be flexible.

Figure 11-3

The incident commander has responsibility to oversee an emergency,
but he or she must be sure to collaborate with all relevant organizations
to make sure the response is successful. Robert Rose/FEMA.

▲ *Integrated communications.* To accommodate each of the participating agencies, a common communication plan is used. Assigned frequencies are clearly identified.

▲ *Unity of command.* As a way to limit organizational confusion, each person reports to one commanding officer only.

▲ *A unified command structure.* When there is more than one responding organization, the command structure expands to include all major agencies. This facilitates joint decision making.

▲ *Consolidated incident action plans (IAPs).* The incident commander(s) and planning section identify operational goals. They produce written IAPs to guide operations. This typically happens over recurring 12-hour periods.

▲ *A manageable span of control.* Each supervisor should manage between three and seven people. Five is the best number of people to manage.

▲ *Designated incident facilities.* All of those responding to disaster should be made aware of the location of the ICP. They should know the location of the following: staging areas, camps, helibases, helispots, casualty collection points, etc.

---

**FOR EXAMPLE**

### ICS in Action

On September 15, 1999, a disgruntled man walked into a youth rally at a Baptist Church in Fort Worth, Texas. He opened fire killing several of those attending the event and then turned the gun on himself. A policeman lived across the street and was notified of the incident. The fire department showed up and sounded a second alarm, indicating the need for additional resources. As the response unfolded, the area was divided up by battalions (e.g., sectoring off the room, building, and treatment and transportation areas). A command post was also set up, and it included police officers, firefighters, and other department heads including the ambulance company.

These departments worked closely to respond to the situation. Police were initially the first responders and their goal was to protect civilians from the gunman. The fire department then took care of emergency needs, and the ambulance transported the wounded to nearby hospitals. Later on, the police conducted the preliminary investigation and requested the assistance of the fire department (since they had a well-trained bomb squad). The police then finished the investigation. This event illustrated how incident command principles can be applied effectively.

---

▲ *Comprehensive resource management.* Human, material, and equipment resources are always checked in. They are given assigned, available, or out-of-service status. This designation maximizes the effective use of resources.

### 11.5.3 Strengths and Weaknesses of Incident Command

It is vital that you are aware of the advantages and disadvantages of incident command. Strengths of incident command include (Figure 11-4):

- ▲ Closer contact among key decision makers
- ▲ An ability to adapt to the size of events
- ▲ Increased safety for responders
- ▲ Improved information flow to the public and from other organizations
- ▲ A logical system of organization that addresses many important disaster functions
- ▲ Joint planning and operations for emergencies and disasters
- ▲ Enhanced communication due to common terminology
- ▲ More realistic expectations for management processes (e.g., span of control)
- ▲ Increased ability of supervisors to work with subordinates (e.g., unity of command)
- ▲ More efficient acquisition of resources and improved management of personnel and equipment

Figure 11-4

Federal officials meet with the incident commander to coordinate the response
after the 2001 terrorist attack on the Pentagon. Jocelyn Augustino/FEMA.

Donald Moynihan asserts that ICS has a unique blend of different management
approaches. On the one hand, ICS combines hierarchical and network management together to foster coordination among network actors responding to crisis
situations (Moynihan, 2008). On the other hand, ICS maintains a unified command
structure, with a central authority, that allows for autonomy between individual
responding agencies (Moynihan, 2008, 2009).

ICS is not without its critics however. Wenger et al. (1990) question if ICS is
applicable to all types of disaster situations. Dynes (1994) shows that incident
command models are often based on false assumptions about human behavior in
disasters. Neal and Phillips (1995) illustrate that the command and control
approach may be too rigid for disaster situations. Other weaknesses of incident
command are also notable (Buck et al., 2006; Decker, 2011; Jensen, 2011):

▲ The focus on "command" may imply excessive authority in
  multiorganizational disaster responses (Drabek, 2003). Department heads
  may sometimes fight over who is in charge rather than recognizing that they
  need to coordinate joint efforts. For this reason, it might be better to use the
  term "incident management" instead of "incident command."

▲ Emergency mission-oriented organizations (e.g., police and fire) are more
  comfortable with using ICS than emergency-relevant organizations (e.g.,
  public works and social services) (Lutz and Lindell, 2008). In other words,
  organizations that use ICS on a daily basis will be more familiar with ICS in
  emergency or disaster situations.

▲ ICS loses strategic importance in larger emergencies and disasters
(Moynihan, 2006; Neal and Webb, 2006). The larger and more
heterogeneous the composition of the hierarchical network, the more
difficult it will be to properly coordinate and collaborate all of the network
actors. In widespread events, the EOC becomes more critical for effective
management of response and recovery operations.

### 11.5.4 EOC

As noted in Chapter 5, "the Emergency Operations Center is the central direction,
control, and coordination point for emergency operations. It is the place to decide
what specific information should go to persons carrying out an 'emergency service'
operation" (FEMA, 1981). The EOC is the facility where key decision makers gather
information and assess policy options regarding the event. It supports field operations for emergency service and other disaster personnel and agencies by acquiring
needed resources. EOCs are crucial for effective response and recovery operations.

Historically, there has been very little known about EOCs in the research literature (Perry, 1995, p. 37). We do know, however, that in any major disaster, the
emergency manager and other key leaders are likely to open and manage the
response and recovery operations from the EOC. What is more, in major disasters,
multiple EOCs may be open at any given time. There is the possibility that EOCs
will be opened by the affected community and nearby jurisdictions. There may be
EOCs for utility companies, nonprofit organizations, and state and federal levels of
government. Each of these EOCs may interact with other EOCs to determine how
to manage response and recovery operations. Personnel in the field also communicate with those in the EOC on a frequent basis. Therefore, it is vitally important
that everyone understand what the EOC is and what it does for you in a disaster.

### 11.5.5  Characteristics of an EOC

According to Ronald Perry (1991), the EOC is a place, a structure, and a function.
First, the EOC is a location where the disaster is managed. It is typically a permanent facility, often at a department headquarters, city hall, or another publicly
owned building. There can be temporary units also. An example is an EOC that is
quickly set up after a disaster in a room that has multiple purposes (e.g., a conference or training room in the county office building). Some EOCs can be taken to
the scene of a disaster. They are nothing more than a mobile coordination center
made out of a bus, recreational vehicle, or semitrailer. For these reasons, EOC
setup or organizational arrangements will vary dramatically. There is no correct
floor plan for every community. "A wide array of types and designs of emergency
command and control centers exists within the United States. These range from
simple, inexpensive single or adjoining rooms with several telephones and radios
to multimillion-dollar, stand-alone facilities with the latest warning and communications technology" (Moore, 1998, p. 2).

Regardless of significant differences, many EOCs have a large open room. This
room is where most of the representatives gather to manage response and recovery
activities. EOCs also have desks, chairs, computers, TVs, phones, and other communication equipment (Figure 11-5). EOCs do not usually consist of a single room

**Figure 11-5**

This Regional Response Coordination Center in Atlanta, Georgia, is an EOC utilized by FEMA Region IV to mobilize resources and communicate effectively with local and state partners. Tim Burkitt/FEMA.

only however. EOCs often have a series or cluster of closely positioned and interconnected rooms. These rooms have various designated functions. For example, the EOC may have a separate room for key decision makers. This conference room can be used by political leaders to analyze the information from the field, declare a state emergency or disaster, and develop policy options for response and recovery operations (Moore, 1998, p. 5). The EOC may also have restroom facilities, a break area, and a room to assess hazards and issue warnings.

The EOC also has a structure. This means EOC includes an organization of many different agencies that are involved in postdisaster operations. Some EOCs may have a single large table where each agency leader meets to discuss the disaster and how to respond to it. Other EOCs may have a series of individual desks for each participating agency. "In this organizational design ... resources are merely titled under very general disciplines, such as fire, law enforcement or police, utilities, and so on" (Moore, 1998, p. 7). Many EOCs are now organized in accordance with the sections of incident command (e.g., planning, operations, logistics, and finance/administration). Other EOCs are arranged according to emergency support functions or ESFs. An **ESF** is an activity that must be performed in the aftermath of a disaster. This brings up the last characteristic of EOCs.

EOCs perform several important functions in disasters. According to Quarantelli (1979), these functions include:

▲ **Information gathering**. After a disaster occurs, one of the primary functions of the EOC is to gather information. This information includes what happened, why it happened, how many people are injured/dead, what areas are affected, what resources are needed, and how to respond most effectively.

▲ **Policy making**. Public officials will meet with the emergency manager and key department leaders to identify what needs to be accomplished in the aftermath of a disaster. They will discuss what options there are for accomplishing those goals. Leaders will also discuss which alternative is most likely to remedy the situation.

▲ **Operations management**. EOCs help to meet agent- and response-generated demands. For instance, a heat wave may require that fans be given to the elderly. An earthquake will require ongoing assessments of damages. A disease outbreak will require doctors and medical treatments. All of these activities will require a great deal of logistical support.

▲ **Coordination**. Another task the EOC performs is coordination of response-generated demands. If fans are needed, the EOC may help to acquire them. If an assessment of damages is required, the EOC may organize teams for that purpose. If doctors and medicines are needed, the EOC may communicate with hospitals and special teams from local, state, and federal public health departments.

▲ **Hosting visitors**. Politicians and public servants from various levels of governments may visit the EOC to determine what is going on. They may also provide recommendations or offer assistance that can benefit response and recovery operations.

▲ **Public information**. To keep citizens apprised of the status of the disaster and what they can do to protect themselves, the EOC will communicate with the media to relay vital information.

▲ **Record keeping**. Disaster response and recovery operations are costly. Because they include hundreds of personnel from numerous agencies, the EOC will track expenses as well as the deployment human and material resources.

Besides these functions, EOCs may also help to oversee recovery activities and the paperwork that is required for federally funded disaster aid programs.

### 11.5.6 Challenges Facing EOCs

The management of EOCs presents many problems (Scanlon, 1994). One challenge is that the EOC may be rendered inoperable in a disaster. On 9/11, Building #7 was damaged and caught on fire when the Twin Towers collapsed. For this reason, EOCs located in the area of impact will have to be reestablished elsewhere when disaster strikes. Also, access to the EOC may be inadequately controlled. Too many individuals in the EOC can hamper, rather than help, response and recovery operations. In addition, there is high turnover in the EOC on a daily basis and it isn't always clear who is managing the EOC itself.

There are other difficulties associated with the EOC environment (Perry, 1991, p. 210). As mentioned in Chapter 10, disasters produce a great deal of stress in EOCs. This is a result of the many tasks that have to be accomplished in disasters and significant constraints on time. There is an emotional toll after disasters because people's lives are at stake. There may also be too little or inaccurate knowledge about what is occurring as the disaster unfolds. This complicates decision making in the EOC. There will also be shifting priorities. As new information arrives in the EOC or as incorrect or incomplete messages are clarified, the goals of response may quickly change.

During response and recovery operations, there will likewise be overlapping lines of authority and responsibility. The presence of numerous agencies could at times create organizational confusion, conflict, and competition over who has jurisdiction over geographic areas, response functions, etc. Communication problems are frequent in the EOC. Misunderstandings and technological failures are possibilities. However, "the concern with problems and difficulties should not obscure the fact that the concept of an EOC for disasters is an extremely valid one. In most emergencies DRC [Disaster Research Center] has studied, EOCs have functioned relatively well" (Quarantelli as cited by Scanlon, 1994, p. 70).

### 11.5.7  Using EOCs

There are many things that can be done to overcome typical EOC problems. There are several steps that will also ensure successful response operations:

1. Have a backup location in mind for the EOC in case it is needed.
2. Control access to the EOC with guards or identification cards. Allow essential personnel in to the EOC only.
3. Require people working in the EOC to take frequent breaks in order to reduce stress.
4. Ensure everyone is familiar with more than one single function. This allows people to take breaks or go home to rest for a shift and still cover all of the important functions.
5. Be sure to communicate effectively with all of the parties involved in response and recovery operations.
6. Put someone with clear authority in charge of the EOC. "The most common management situation was to have the EOC run by the political head of the affected community, either the mayor or someone equivalent" (Scanlon, 1994, p. 60). This eliminates questions of power and delegation of responsibility.

### 11.5.8  Comparison of ICS and EOCs

As an emergency manager, you must recognize that ICS and EOCs do not operate in isolation from one another. Both may function in the same incident, emergency, or disaster. The incident commander will likely radio the EOC for additional assets. These resources may include personnel, mutual aid, barricades, sandbags, and so on. The EOC then attempts to acquire the requested items and updates incident command on their arrival. In addition, there are similarities between ICS and the EOC. Both ICS and EOC have the common goal of coordinating the response. They work together to minimize disruption, save lives, and protect property and the environment. They may also have common organizational structures. In other words, both may include people from the fire department, police department, etc.

Nonetheless, there are substantial differences between ICS and EOC. First, it should be underscored that incident command is utilized in most emergencies or disasters. These events range from car accidents to major earthquakes. In contrast, EOCs are not generally used in small incidents. They are typically staffed and utilized for larger events only. Second, incident command is a field-level coordination point. It is concerned with operations at the scene of an emergency or disaster. EOCs, in contrast, are located at the headquarters level. They coordinate much larger and more complex response and recovery operations. Third, incident command generally includes emergency service personnel such as first responders. Police and fire service leadership can be represented in most EOCs (Scanlon, 1994, p. 58). However, EOCs may also include city leadership (emergency managers, politicians, and other decision makers) and others from the private and nonprofit sectors (e.g., utility and Red Cross representatives). Fourth, incident command generally involves a limited number of organizations. On the other hand, EOCs may include a much broader number of departments and agencies. These organizations include representatives from parks and recreation, the engineering department, utility companies, nonprofit organizations, and so on.

Finally, incident command is concerned with tactical decisions and operations. For example, ICS deals with fire suppression at a specific location. EOCs focus on strategic issues instead. Rather than giving attention to the needs of a specific geographic area, EOCs are more likely to oversee the deployment of resources based on all types of response and recovery needs. Thus, "an EOC is an effective way to achieve coordination among agencies responding to a major emergency or disaster. The absence of an EOC seems to encourage the opposite" (Scanlon, 1994, p. 70).

### 11.5.9  Memorandums of Understanding and Mutual Aid Agreements

Memorandums of understanding (MOUs) and mutual aid agreements are other ways to organize operations and gain assistance and cooperation from different agencies. Both of these documents are developed by different departments and communities to promote interagency and interjurisdictional assistance in a disaster. MOUs are less formal that mutual aid agreements. MOUs tend to be agreements that may be activated if it is possible to do so. In contrast, mutual aid agreements have to be approved by the city/county attorney and the mayor/judge/commissioner. The mutual aid agreement could be legally binding. They may open up liabilities in terms of who will be responsible for injuries, fatalities, and expenses.

Despite the potential drawbacks, MOUs and mutual aid agreements are beneficial to you for many reasons. MOUs and mutual aid agreements open up the possibility of acquiring much needed resources after disasters. Communities may not be allowed to request certain types of federal disaster assistance unless they have entered into and activated mutual aid arrangements. Equipment supplied by the federal government is also based on the assumption that it will be shared with nearby communities. Mutual aid agreements improve the coordination of disaster responses because they resolve concerns about joint operations. For all of these reasons, emergency managers should consider participating in MOUs and mutual aid agreements.

> **FOR EXAMPLE**
>
> ### EOCs and Disasters
>
> Multiple EOCs may be opened after a disaster. Hurricane Sandy provided a vivid example of this. Affected communities opened EOCs to manage response and recovery operations. Nearby but unaffected communities opened EOCs in order to provide mutual aid. Cities and states that received evacuees also opened EOCs in order to manage shelter operations. FEMA opened EOCs in Region II and at national headquarters. Such EOCs interact one with another and may look at times like a complex network system.

## SELF-CHECK

- What is ICS and what are the different components?
- What are the principles of incident command?
- What are the strengths and weaknesses of ICS?
- What is an EOC?
- EOCs have been described as a place, structure, and function. What does this mean?
- What is the relationship between ICS and EOCs?
- What is an MOU? Mutual aid agreement?

## 11.6 Managing Disasters at the State Level

When disasters exceed the capability of local jurisdictions, state resources may be utilized. California is one state that bases its response on the Standard Emergency Management System (SEMS). **SEMS** is the systematic adoption of incident command by all political jurisdictions in a given state. States may also support one another by participating in the EMAC. The EMAC is a mutual aid agreement for states.

### 11.6.1 SEMS

The federal government now mandates that the ICS principles be established and used everywhere. However, the federal government was not the first to promote standardization. The SEMS was developed by California before ICS was a national requirement. SEMS was established after the Oakland Hills firestorm in 1991. On October 19th, a series of fires broke out in a residential area in Northern California because of dry weather conditions and inadequate mitigation activities. Within the first hour of the fire, 790 structures were destroyed. The firestorm eventually destroyed 2449 homes as well as 437 apartment and condominiums. Numerous individuals were killed or injured by the event as well.

During the ensuing blaze, firefighters had communication and coordination problems. They had difficulty talking within their own organization and especially with those mutual aid partners from other fire departments. The units that arrived from outside the area also had hoses that did not connect to Oakland's hydrant system. In response to these and other problems, Senator Dominique Petris introduced Senate Bill 1841. This proposal called for the integration of response operations among all jurisdictions in California. The bill was approved on January 1, 1993. It mandated that the California Governor's Office of Emergency Services implement a strategy to improve communication and coordination among all responding agencies. SEMS was the resulting strategy. It is based on ICS but has other unique features as well.

Specifically, SEMS mandates ICS as the standard for emergency and disaster operations in California. All cities must use this system while assessing damages, requesting mutual aid, and managing resources. SEMS also integrates all organizational levels involved in disaster response. These five organizational levels are:

▲ **Field response**: First responders from local agencies.
▲ **Local government**: Subdivisions in each county.
▲ **Operational area**: County governments.
▲ **Regional levels**: Regional governments offer assistance.
▲ **State levels**: State governments offer assistance.

SEMS also requires a great deal of education and awareness. First responders have therefore improved responses to disasters as a result of SEMS. It has helped to improve interoperability of organizations in California disasters such as the Northridge earthquake. Nonetheless, it is possible that some local jurisdictions may feel that state-mandated approaches are to too rigid and don't take into account unique circumstances and limitations.

### 11.6.2 EMAC

EMAC owes its existence to one of the most devastating disasters in the early 1990s. Hurricane Andrew made landfall over Florida on August 24, 1992, and then traveled to south central Louisiana. It was one of the most destructive hurricanes ever to hit the United States. This disaster was responsible for at least 23 deaths and $45 billion dollars in damages. Hurricane Andrew was similar to Hurricane Katrina in that there were many complaints that federal help did not arrive soon enough. The delay in federal resources causes states to believe that they would also need to rely on each other for personnel, supplies, and equipment.

After several states joined together to respond to Hurricane Andrew, Congress proposed and ratified EMAC in 1996. Fifty states, the District of Columbia, Puerto Rico, Guam, and the Virgin Islands now participate. States are asked to donate $1000 as a membership fee to maintain and build system operability. The goal is to provide quick assistance to states in need.

EMAC has proved useful and has facilitated the sharing of ferryboats, police, and other resources in disasters. In 2004, EMAC had one of the largest deployments of state-to-state mutual aid in history (Figure 11-6). Over a span of 85 days and as a result of Hurricanes Charley, Frances, Ivan, and Jeanne, EMAC deployed more than 800 state and local personnel from 38 states. The cost in personnel, equipment, and National Guard expenditures was $15 million. See http://www.emacweb.org/.

**Figure 11-6**

EMAC members from Minnesota and Washington State meet in New York to provide assistance after Hurricane Irene in 2011. Elissa Jun/FEMA.

## FOR EXAMPLE

### EMAC and Hurricane Katrina

EMAC was an important part of the response to Hurricane Katrina. EMAC deployed more than a thousand doctors, nurses, emergency medical technicians (EMTs), and dentists. It also resulted in the sharing of ambulances and medevac helicopters. In addition, EMAC assisted in the deployment and management of other resources in the response effort. These resources include National Guard troops, law enforcement personnel, search and rescue teams, HazMat teams, communication dispatchers, and satellite phones (http://www.emacweb.org, "Emergency Management Assistance Compact Deploying Help Across Disciplines," September 12, 2005).

## 11.7 Managing Disasters on a Federal Level

Unfortunately, there are many disasters that overwhelm local and even state resources. In these cases, the federal government must step in and provide assistance. Adding another layer of bureaucracy and even more agencies further complicates response and recovery operations. However, there are strategies employed at the federal level to facilitate coordination. We will discuss each one of these.

### 11.7.1 NIMS

The NIMS "is a comprehensive, national approach to incident management that is applicable to all jurisdictional levels and across functional disciplines" (FEMA, 2004c). It is somewhat similar to SEMS in that it adopts ICS as a standard. However, NIMS was promoted at the federal level, whereas SEMS was developed at to the state of California only. In addition, both SEMS and NIMS go beyond ICS and include other recommendations for disaster management.

NIMS owes its existence to at least three sources. First, NIMS is an offspring of the National Interagency Incident Management System (NIIMS). This system was developed in 1980 by the Forest Service in the U.S. Department of Agriculture to fight fires and deal with other types of disasters. The command and management component of NIMS emanates from the on-scene model developed by FIRESCOPE. Second, NIMS is based off of the principle of interoperability as espoused by SEMS. One common goal among NIMS and SEMS is improved communications and coordination. Finally, NIMS was an outgrowth of unique, well-publicized, complicated, and deadly disaster incidents like 9/11. This disaster underscored the need for an improved approach to disasters. The heroic efforts of first responders saved the lives of a number of tenants and visitors in these buildings. Nevertheless, a variety of problems confronted emergency personnel and many perished as a result. Under pressure from victims' families, a bipartisan committee was formed to review the response operations. The committee reviewed mistakes made in intelligence gathering, counterterrorism operations, and emergency response to the terrorist attacks. After months and even years of investigation, the committee released its findings in the 9/11 Commission Report. The 9/11 Commission Report identified many interrelated weaknesses:

▲ **Communication technology**. The radio equipment, for example, could not penetrate the steel and concrete floors that separated firefighters. Also, most Port Authority police used local channels that did not work.

▲ **Communication procedures**. "There were no standard operating procedures covering how different [Port Authority] commands should communicate via radio during such an incident" (National Commission on Terrorist Attacks, 2004, p. 282).

▲ **Information management**. Responders had inaccurate information or no information at all. For example, "The deputy fire safety director in the lobby, while immediately aware that a major incident had occurred, did not know for approximately ten minutes that a commercial jet had directly hit the building" (National Commission on Terrorist Attacks, 2004, p. 286).

▲ **Interorganizational coordination**. There was a lack of communication and coordination between the Port Authority police, the firefighters, and the police. There was no unified command structure in place to deal with this event.

▲ **Public information**. People did not receive information because the public address systems were not heard. In other cases, people were given conflicting information. For instance, some people were advised to wait for further instructions, while others were advised to evacuate the Twin Towers.

▲ **Incident management**. There was a breakdown in issuing and following orders. Many off-duty firefighters rushed to the scene and did not have radios. Others were ordered to evacuate because the other tower had crumbled to the ground. In spite of this request, many refused to out of a desire to help the citizens get to safety. There were also areas of the buildings that were searched twice. This occurred because of the lack of communication and coordination.

As a result of these weaknesses, the Commission wrote that "The lesson of 9/11 for civilians and first responders can be stated simply: in the new age of terror, they … are the primary targets. The losses America suffered that day demonstrated both the gravity of the terrorist threat and the commensurate need to prepare ourselves to meet it" (National Commission on Terrorist Attacks, 2004, p. 323). 9/11 encouraged many firefighters and military personnel to push for national standards for disaster management (FEMA IS-700, 2004).

### 11.7.2 Goals of NIMS

Aware of the problems identified by the 9/11 Commission, President George W. Bush issued two Homeland Security Presidential Directives (HSPD). HSPD-5 called for standardization among responders. HSPD-8 reiterated the importance of disaster preparedness.

HSPD-5 was issued on February 28, 2003, and stressed the need to "enhance the ability of the United States to manage domestic incidents by establishing a single, comprehensive national incident management system." This Presidential Directive:

1. Encourages the integration of local, state, and federal disaster responses
2. Seeks to coordinate government activities with the private and nonprofit sectors

3. Promotes information sharing with the public, the private sector, local and state authorities, and federal departments and agencies
4. Provides for improved interoperability and compatibility among local, state, and federal governments
5. Recommends the development of a National Response Plan

HSPD-8 was issued on December 17, 2003, and it has undergone revision when President Obama entered the White House. According to its stated goals, HSPD-8 was to establish "policies to strengthen the preparedness of the United States to prevent and respond to threatened or actual domestic attacks, major disasters and other emergencies." This Directive:

▲ Requires the development of a national domestic all-hazard preparedness goal.
▲ Ensures continuous efforts to prepare first responders for major events. This is mainly for terrorist attack prevention and response.
▲ Describes the allocation of funds to states to strengthen capabilities. The distribution is based on population, infrastructures, and other risk factors.
▲ Points out that the federal government will support state and local entities in planning, interoperability, and equipment acquisition.
▲ Establishes national standards for preparedness.
▲ Develops a system to collect, analyze, and disseminate lessons learned, research, and best practices to improve response operations.
▲ Maintains adequate teams, stockpiles, and caches in accordance with national preparedness goals.
▲ Encourages active citizen participation in preparedness measures.
▲ Demands periodic assessment of progress made and areas needing improvement.

NIMS was created with the goals of these Presidential Directives in mind.

### 11.7.3  Principles of NIMS

NIMS has the purported goal of helping the nation prevent, prepare for, respond to, and recover from all types of disasters including domestic terrorist incidents. It intends to facilitate government and private entities at all levels working together to deal with disasters. NIMS is supposed to allow a flexible response regardless of cause, size, location, or complexity of a disaster. At the same time, NIMS provides a set of standardized organizational structures. It also specifies requirements for processes, procedures, and systems designed to improve interoperability (FEMA IS-700, 2004).

NIMS includes six key components:

1. **Command and management**. NIMS is based on three organizational/operational systems. The first is the **ICS**. This defines the management structure and operations at the scene of a disaster. This may include unified command, which is comprised of more than one responding agency or

multiple jurisdictions. It may also incorporate **area command**. Area command oversees the management of multiple incidents. Each organizational structure requires ICS. The second system is the **multiagency coordination systems**. These define the structure and management principles for those working with or supporting incident command. Such systems facilitate logistics. They also allocate and track resources. They share information. They coordinate interagency and intergovernmental issues regarding policies, priorities, and strategies. These may be EOCs and Multiagency Coordination Entities that take a strategic perspective. They also provide support to incident and area commanders. The third system concerns **public information**. This includes ways for communicating timely and accurate information to citizens. Such systems include public information officers (PIOs). They advise incident command about public information matters. It also includes Joint Information Centers. This is a system where PIOs from multiple agencies meet to provide critical information, crisis communications, and public affairs assistance.

2. **Preparedness.** Under NIMS, "preparedness is implemented through a continual cycle of planning, training, equipping, exercising, evaluating, taking action to correct and mitigate" (FEMA IS-700, 2004). Preparedness involves all levels of government. Preparedness also involves the public and nonprofit sectors. Such readiness efforts are based on standards and certification for planning, training, equipment, mutual aid, emergency assistance compacts, etc. Preparedness efforts require the involvement of "a wide variety of committees, planning groups" to create plans, integrate activities, promote interoperability, establish priorities, and improve coordination.

3. **Resource management**. Resource management involves four primary tasks:
   ▲ Describing, inventorying, requesting, and tracking resources
   ▲ Activating those systems prior to, during, and after an incident
   ▲ Dispatching resources prior to, during, and after an incident
   ▲ Deactivating or recalling resources during or after an incident
   Resource management also operates under five key principles. It recommends advanced planning among agencies before disaster strikes, resource identification and ordering using standard processes and methods, and resource categorization based on size, capacity, capability, skill, or other characteristics. Effective resource management also requires use of agreements for resources before an incident occurs as well as effective management (implying the reliance on validated practices such as credentialing and other forms of standardization).

4. **Communications and information management.** NIMS recognizes that responses require effective communications. Responses also require successful information management strategies. This is facilitated by "a common operating picture that is accessible across jurisdictions and agencies" (FEMA IS-700, 2004). It is also fostered through common communication terminologies, processes, and standards.

## FOR EXAMPLE

### Policy Changes after 9/11

The impact of 9/11 shifted the direction of federal emergency management policy in dramatic ways. First, terrorism has become the hazard of priority among policy makers. Additional funding has been given to the DHS. This has been done sometimes by cutting FEMA's budget. Furthermore, the focus has shifted away from more collaborative approaches to incident command structures like NIMS and the NRF. These changes have hurt—at least initially—the nation's ability to deal with natural disasters. Some experts believe that the response to Hurricane Katrina was so poor because of the policies enacted by the DHS after 9/11. The argument is that FEMA has been marginalized even though it is (or should be) the agency in charge of disaster response operations.

5. **Supporting technologies.** NIMS recognizes the importance of technology but recommends:

   ▲ Interoperability and compatibility. Systems must work together.

   ▲ Technological support. Communication equipment and expertise are vital in response.

   ▲ Technology standards. Common rules will enhance interoperability.

   ▲ Broad-based requirements. All types of technology, procedures, protocols, and standards must be recognized and incorporated.

   ▲ Strategic planning and research and development (R&D). This signifies that an agenda for technological R&D has been identified and prioritized.

6. **Ongoing management and maintenance.** To provide direction as well as routine review and refinement of NIMS, the DHS established a NIMS Integration Center. Its purpose is to serve as a resource to better coordinate responses to all types of disaster incidents.

### 11.7.4 Strengths and Weaknesses of NIMS

NIMS has several strengths that you should consider. One of the main benefits is that it incorporates the lessons we have learned from prior disasters such as the 9/11 terrorist attacks (e.g., the need for interoperability). NIMS also recognizes the need to include the public, private, and nonprofit sectors in response operations. It has other possible advantages because it suggests the need to focus on all hazards, desires to address each phase of emergency management, promotes proactive measures for preparedness, and wants to improve interagency communications. NIMS likewise gives extra attention to resource management, recognizes the need for flexibility and standardization, is based on the ICS, and updates emergency management in the United States.

However, research reveals that NIMS has numerous weaknesses that you must acknowledge as well (Buck et al., 2006; Jensen, 2008, 2009, 2011). NIMS illustrates an overlearning from 9/11 events. For instance, it has an evident bias toward terrorism as opposed to natural or technological disasters. NIMS discusses government operations more than the role of the private and nonprofit sectors. It is not utilized uniformly by each organization or in all types of disasters. In addition, many jurisdictions do not have the intent or capability to implement NIMS. NIMS also:

▲ Does not give sufficient attention to prevention activities
▲ May downplay mitigation and recovery activities
▲ Focuses too heavily on technology for improved coordination
▲ Possibly marginalizes functions other than resource management
▲ May stress standardization at expense of adaptability and flexibility
▲ Does not adequately capture a strategic perspective as it is based on the ICS
▲ Reinvents the wheel, rather than addressing more fundamental problems in emergency management

### 11.7.5 NRF

As mentioned in Chapter 2, the NRF is a guide to help the nation respond to all types of disasters and emergencies. The document, which was put into effect in 2008, is somewhat similar to prior federal-level plans (e.g., Federal Response Plan, National Response Plan) in that it addresses what the federal government will do to deal with a disaster (Figure 11-7). However, the NRF attempts to be much more inclusive than prior plans. The NRF recognizes that the federal government cannot react to a disaster alone. It requires the help and assistance of tribal government, state government, local government, private sector, nonprofit organizations, and others. The NRF is based on five key principles:

1. **Engaged partnership**: Communication helps to engage in partnerships in order to create common goals and sharing capabilities through all levels of government and NGOs so that the disaster will not become overwhelming. All levels of government and NGOs will be able to work together and will be prepared for impending incidents.
2. **Tiered response**: Disaster incidents will be managed at the lowest level of government that can handle the situation. Resources will be provided to the jurisdiction as needed. Local governments and the private sector are unified in disaster response. The federal government limits the amount of disasters they get involved in.
3. **Scalable, flexible, and adaptable operational capabilities**: Response must be able to adapt to changes of size and complexity.
4. **Unity of effort and unified command**: All entities involved must have a clear understanding of the roles and responsibilities of the participating organizations.
5. **Readiness to act**: All entities involved must understand that disasters have the ability to change; all entities involved must be prepared for any and all disaster scenarios.

**Figure 11-7**

The National Response Framework was introduced at a press conference in January 2008. The National Disaster Recovery Framework was created one year later. Bill Koplitz/FEMA.

### 11.7.6  ESFs in the NRF

The NRF also outlines 15 ESFs that must be performed after a disaster. Each ESF is a grouping of government and private sector capabilities into an organizational structure to provide support, resources, and services during response and recovery operations. Each ESF is composed of primary and support agencies. A **primary agency** has ultimate responsibility for a particular ESF. A **support agency** has the role of assisting the primary agency in the fulfillment of ESFs. These designations are made on the basis of authorities, resources, and capabilities of each federal department or agency. The 15 ESFs are listed below:

▲ **ESF 1: Transportation**
Includes federal and civil transportation support, safety, restoration of the infrastructure, restricting movements, and an impact assessment (Department of Transportation)

▲ **ESF 2: Communications**
Comprises coordination with the telecommunications industry, repair of the infrastructure, and protection and restoration of cyber and information technology resources (National Communications System)

▲ **ESF 3: Public Works and Engineering**
Consists of engineering services, construction management, and repair and protection of the infrastructure (Department of Defense—U.S. Army Corps of Engineers)

▲ **ESF 4: Firefighting**
Incorporates firefighting activities and support to urban and rural firefighting operations (Department of Agriculture—U.S. Fire Service)

▲ **ESF 5: Information and Planning**
Involves coordination of incident management efforts, incident action planning, resource management, and mission assignments

▲ **ESF 6: Mass Care, Emergency Assistance and Temporary Housing, and Human Services**
Includes mass care, housing, and human services (Department of Health and Human Services)

▲ **ESF 7: Logistics**
Covers resource support such as facility space, office equipment, and contracting services (General Services Administration and DHS)

▲ **ESF 8: Public Health and Medical Services**
Comprises public, medical, and mental health and mortuary services (Department of Health and Human Services)

▲ **ESF 9: Search and Rescue**
Covers lifesaving assistance (DHS—FEMA)

▲ **ESF 10: Oil and Hazardous Materials**
Includes HazMat response, environmental safety, and short- and long-term recovery (Environmental Protection Agency)

▲ **ESF 11: Agriculture and Natural Resources**
Captures nutrition assistance, animal disease, plant disease, food safety, and natural and cultural resource protection and restoration (Department of Agriculture)

▲ **ESF 12: Energy**
Includes energy infrastructure assessment, repair, and restoration, energy industry utility coordination, and energy forecast (Department of Energy)

▲ **ESF 13: Public Safety and Security**
Consists of facility and resource security, security planning, public security support, and support to access, traffic, and crowd control (Department of Justice)

▲ **ESF 14: Long-Term Community Recovery and Mitigation**
Covers social and economic community impact assessment; long-term recovery assistance to states, local government, and the private sector; and mitigation analysis (DHS—FEMA)

▲ **ESF 15: External Affairs**
Includes media and community relations, congressional and international affairs, and emergency public information (DHS)

The ESFs listed in the NRF are logical divisions of labor. However, the fulfillment of ESFs does not necessarily guarantee that the federal government responds in a successful manner. For this reason, an Area Field Office (AFO) is established in the disaster-affected area. The **AFO** is like an EOC, but it coordinates the efforts of federal, state, local, tribal, nongovernmental, and private sector organizations. The AFO is a central location where response and recovery are managed at a federal level. When needed, an AFO can be open before or after a disaster. It can also be activated during an event of national

---

## FOR EXAMPLE

### Federal Deployment for Special Events

A JFO was used in the presidential inauguration for the first time in 2005. The JFO housed dozens of officials from 50 federal, state, and local agencies in a high-tech command center. The JFO was located in Northern Virginia and had 120 work stations and several giant video screens. Law enforcement and security personnel watched the cameras that monitored downtown Washington streets. They kept track of aerial surveillance flights. They checked sensors scanning for evidence of biological or chemical weapons. The JFO also commanded the Coast Guard cutters and helicopters. The JFO oversaw canine bomb-sniffing units, customs aircraft, bicycle patrols, and crowd control issues.

All the federal agencies that handled security, law enforcement, and crisis response were housed in the JFO. The federal agencies participating in the JFO were under the command of a single federal officer. The officer was Tim Koerner, the top deputy of the Secret Service. Koerner reported directly to Homeland Security Secretary Tom Ridge. The JFO and the reporting structure had the goal of improving communication and coordination among the federal agencies. Jim Rice, the FBI supervisory agent said, "When an incident first happens, in the first 30 minutes probably about 75 percent of the information you get is wrong. Being able to look the guy in the eye that you're talking to, that eliminates a lot of problems" (Associated Press, "Security Goes High Tech for Inauguration," January 18, 2005).

significance (e.g., Olympics) for prevention and preparedness activities. The AFO is mainly for federal authorities. However, the AFO may include representatives from local and state agencies and other organizations when they visit to coordinate policy.

The AFO uses the organizational structure of NIMS for both preincident and postincident management activities. However, the AFO does not manage on-scene operations. Instead, the AFO provides support to on-scene efforts and also addresses a broader range of response and recovery concerns. The broader support operations will most likely extend beyond the incident site and encompass multiple JFOs. Additionally, threat situations or incidents that affect multiple states or communities may require separate AFO. In these circumstances, one of the AFOs may be identified to provide strategic leadership and coordination for the overall incident management effort. The AFO that is identified as lead is usually the one that is in the most heavily impacted area.

### 11.7.7 The National Disaster Recovery Framework

The **National Disaster Recovery Framework** (NDRF), as discussed in Chapter 2, is another plan to guide operations after large-scale disasters, but it is concerned with recovery and not response. Like the NRF, the NDRF provides guidance to local, state, and tribal governments who have experienced a disaster and are attempting to reestablish the normalcy that existed prior to the event (Figure 11-8). The NDRF was created in 2009 and takes over responsibility from the NRF at ESF 14 (Long-Term Recovery).

There are nine core principles of the NDRF. These include:

1. **Individual and family empowerment**: Community members must have equal opportunity to participate in local recovery efforts. The community cannot discriminate against any person wanting to help with recovery efforts.

2. **Leadership and local primacy**: In order for leadership to be successful, leaders in all levels of participating government and NGOs should use coordinated leadership. Local, state, and tribal government have primary responsibility for recovery; the federal government is only a partner in recovery efforts and will take on a larger role in recovery if the disaster occurs within federal jurisdiction.

3. **Predisaster recovery planning**: Stakeholders should be involved in and work together toward both pre- and postdisaster planning and coordination.

4. **Partnership and inclusiveness**: Partnership and collaboration promote successful recovery efforts. The recovery process should include people who are diverse culturally, ethnically, etc.

5. **Public information**: Inclusive communication should incorporate a diverse community where information is accessible to everyone. It is important to ensure that everyone within the community has equal access to recovery information and resources.

Figure 11-8

A deputy associate administrator addresses 300 attendees in Salt Lake City, UT, and discusses the National Disaster Recovery Framework. Cynthia Hunter/FEMA.

6. **Unity of effort**: All stakeholders involved in recovery efforts must stay united and work toward common recovery objectives. All recovery objectives are based upon group consensus and should be transparent.

7. **Timeliness and flexibility:** Successful recovery should practice recovery efforts that are efficient in nature. Recovery efforts should also be flexible in nature in order to deal with unforeseen obstacles.

8. **Resilience and sustainability**: Stakeholders should minimize the community's risk to hazards while still effectively recovering from the disaster.

9. **Psychological and emotional recovery**: Recovery efforts need to address the psychological and emotional needs of the community while recovering from disaster.

## 11.7.8 Recovery Support Functions in the NDRF

The NDRF also outlines fifteen Recovery Support Functions (RSFs) that must be performed after a disaster. Each RSF is a grouping of government and private sector capabilities into an organizational structure to provide support, resources, and services during response and recovery operations. Like the NRF, the RSFs are composed of primary and support agencies. The six RSFs are listed below with the primary agency responsible for this function:

▲ **RSF 1: Community Planning and Capacity Building**
Support and build recovery capacities and community planning resources of local, state, and tribal governments needed to effectively plan for, manage, and implement disaster recovery activities in large, unique or catastrophic incidents (DHS—FEMA; Department of Health and Human Services).

▲ **RSF 2: Economic**
The mission of the Economic RSF is to integrate the expertise of the federal government to help local, state, and tribal governments and the private sector sustain and/or rebuild businesses and employment and develop economic opportunities that result in sustainable and economically resilient communities after large-scale and catastrophic incidents (Department of Commerce).

▲ **RSF 3: Health and Social Services**
The Health and Social Services RSF mission is for the federal government to assist locally led recovery efforts in the restoration of the public health, healthcare, and social service networks to promote the resilience, health, and well-being of affected individuals and communities (Department of Health and Human Services).

▲ **RSF 4: Housing**
Address pre- and postdisaster housing issues and coordinate and facilitate the delivery of federal resources and activities to assist local, state, and tribal governments in the rehabilitation and reconstruction of destroyed and damaged housing, whenever feasible, and development of other new accessible, permanent housing options (Department of Housing and Urban Development).

▲ **RSF 5: Infrastructure Systems**
Facilitate the integration of the capabilities of the federal government to support local, state, and tribal governments and other infrastructure owners and operators in their efforts to achieve recovery goals relating to the public engineering of the nation's infrastructure systems (Department of Defense—U.S. Army Corps of Engineers).

▲ **RSF 6: Natural and Cultural Resources**
Integrate federal assets and capabilities to help state and tribal governments and communities address long-term environmental and cultural resource recovery needs after large-scale and catastrophic incidents (Department of the Interior).

Emergency managers should be aware of these RSFs and determine how they relate to state and local efforts to promote recovery.

## SELF-CHECK

- What is NIMS and how is it related to ICS?
- Why did NIMS come about?
- What is crisis management? What is consequence management?
- What are the six components of NIMS?
- Is NIMS beneficial or detrimental for emergency management?
- What are some ESFs under the National Response Plan?
- What is an AFO and how is it different than a JFO?

## SUMMARY

Technology and organization are tools that you can use to improve response and recovery operations. Knowing what technology is available is a crucial responsibility you will have in emergency management. Understanding communication equipment and DSSs will help you manage postdisaster operations. Incident command can facilitate communication and coordination at the scene of an emergency or disaster. EOCs should also be utilized to harmonize response and recovery activities among a myriad of organizations. If a disaster overwhelms your jurisdiction, you may seek help from mutual aid partners or the state EMAC. You should also be aware of NIMS, the NRF, and the NDRF if federal initiatives are to be integrated seamlessly into local and state efforts. Harnessing these tools will help you promote resilience after a disaster.

## KEY TERMS

| | |
|---|---|
| ACU-1000 | A type of interface equipment that links mobile radios, cell phones, satellite technology, and regular phones in a single real-time communication system. |
| Area Field Office (AFO) | An office like an EOC or JFO, but it is responsible for coordinating the entire effort of federal, state, local, tribal, nongovernmental, and private sector organizations. |
| Decision support systems | Software applications that help the emergency manager determine priorities and respond to a disaster. |
| Emergency Management Assistance Compact (EMAC) | A mutual aid agreement for states. |

**Emergency support function (ESF)**  An activity that must be performed in the aftermath of a disaster.

**Finance/administration section**  An organizational division under ICS that tracks costs, completes and files paperwork, and records expenses of operations and logistics.

**Geographic information systems (GIS)**  An "organized collection of computer hardware, software, geographic data, and personnel designed to efficiently capture, store, update, manipulate, analyze, and display all forms of geographically referenced information" (ESRI as cited by Dash, 1997).

**HAZUS**  An assessment software tool that is used to predict potential losses from floods, hurricane winds, and earthquakes.

**Incident command**  The on-scene leadership for the disaster.

**Incident command system (ICS)**  It is "a set of personnel, policies, procedures, facilities and equipment, integrated into a common organizational structure designed to improve emergency response operations of all types and complexities" (Irwin, 1989, p. 134).

**Information officer**  A professional who works with the media to answer their questions about the event and release information to the public.

**Liaison officer**  The point of contact with other organizations responding to the incident.

**Light Detection And Ranging (LIDAR)**  An airborne laser system that is used to detect heat and dangerous debris accumulations.

**Logistics section**  An organizational division under ICS that acquires and provides materials, services, and facilities to support the needs of responders as directed by the incident commander and the operations section.

**National Incident Management System (NIMS)**  It is "a comprehensive, national approach to incident management that is applicable to all jurisdictional levels and across functional disciplines" (FEMA, 2004c).

**Operations section**  An organizational division under ICS that is responsible for implementing the strategy to respond to the incident as determined by the incident commander and the planning section.

| | |
|---|---|
| **Planning section** | An organizational division under ICS that collects and evaluates information about the disaster to determine operational priorities. |
| **Primary agency** | A department that has ultimate responsibility for a particular ESF. |
| **Receivers** | Equipment devices that obtain signals from transmitters. They include stereos, pagers, police scanners, and televisions. |
| **Safety officer** | A professional who monitors the hazardous conditions of the disaster to ensure protection of responding personnel. |
| **Standard Emergency Management System (SEMS)** | The adoption of incident command by all political jurisdictions in a given state. |
| **Support agency** | A department with the role of assisting the primary agency in the fulfillment of ESFs. |
| **Talk group** | A unit with its own designated channel. |
| **Transmitters** | Communication instruments that convey information through radios, sirens, television stations, and cable override systems. |
| **Transceivers** | Instruments that are able to both transmit and receive information. Examples of transceivers include telephones, satellites, PDAs, two-way radios, citizen band radios, 800 MHz radios, and ham radios. |
| **Trunked radio system** | A computer-controlled network that searches for a clear channel for users to use to talk to each other. |

# ASSESSING YOUR UNDERSTANDING

Posttest to evaluate your knowledge of harnessing technology and organization. *Measure your learning by comparing your pretest and posttest results.*

## Summary Questions

1. A Doppler radar helps the emergency responders find victims trapped after a disaster. True or false?
2. A talk group is a unit with its own designated communication channel. True or false? VoIP stands for Vector Organization Incident Plan. True or false?
3. E-Team helps the emergency manager request and deploy resources. True or false?
4. ICS was developed after Hurricane Andrew. True or false?
5. The logistics section acquires and provides materials for the operations section. True or false?
6. In order to improve coordination, it may be advisable to change the name of incident command to incident management. True or false?
7. EOCs are places where leaders get together to discuss response priorities. True or false?
8. Controlling access to EOCs is not needed since you actually want all departments to be represented. True or false?
9. Mutual aid agreements are beneficial in that they resolve concerns about joint operations. True or false?
10. Operational area is not included as one of the five organizational levels of SEMS. True or false?
11. NIMS is similar to SEMS in that it mandates the use of ICS in disasters. True or false?
12. The first AFO was set up to deal with the shuttle disaster. True or false?
13. What device can help responders arrive at the scene of a disaster quickly?
    (a) Video cameras
    (b) Detection equipment
    (c) Traffic signal preemption devices
    (d) Remote sensing
    (e) All of the above
14. Trunked radio systems:
    (a) Get their names from vehicle trunks, where they are stored
    (b) Do not permit communications among different organizations
    (c) Cannot overcome the VoIP
    (d) Search for clear channels for the user
    (e) Answers a and c

15. Internet communications:
    (a) May help generals get information as quickly as underlings
    (b) Are not related to VoIP
    (c) Cannot overcome the ACU-1000
    (d) May help responders use the DOT 250
    (e) None of the above

16. Decision support systems:
    (a) Do not allow for instantaneous links among the database
    (b) Include SoftRisk but not E-Team
    (c) Include GIS but not CoBRA
    (d) Include EPlan only
    (e) None of the above

17. GIS may assist with:
    (a) The tailoring of warnings for a specific population
    (b) The identification of tornado paths
    (c) The identification of fire hydrants
    (d) All of the above
    (e) Two of the above

18. ICS and mutual aid are geared specifically for:
    (a) Local governments
    (b) State governments
    (c) The federal government
    (d) The private sector
    (e) The nonprofit sector

19. Problems leading to the creation of ICS included:
    (a) Poor communications
    (b) Insufficient intelligence and prediction
    (c) Lack of joint planning
    (d) Inadequate resource management
    (e) All of the above

20. Which officer is in charge of relaying information from other organizations
    to the incident commander?
    (a) Incident command
    (b) Safety officer
    (c) Liaison officer
    (d) Information officer
    (e) Planning officer

21. Which section would be involved in carrying out debris removal?
    (a) Planning
    (b) Operations

    (c) Logistics

    (d) Finance/administration

    (e) Incident command

22. What are the strengths of ICS?

    (a) Closer contact among decision makers

    (b) Improved information flow to the public

    (c) Enhanced communication due to common terminology

    (d) More realistic expectations for managers over employees

    (e) All of the above

23. Research reveals:

    (a) EOCs are less useful than incident command posts.

    (b) EOCs are extremely valuable for coordination.

    (c) EOCs cannot overcome the VoIP.

    (d) EOCs should subsume ICU-1000 statutes.

    (e) EOCs do not host visitors.

24. ICS focuses on tactical issues, whereas EOCs focus on:

    (a) Planning only

    (b) Field operations

    (c) Strategic issues

    (d) Small disaster issues

    (e) Simple disaster issues

25. NIMS includes:

    (a) Command and management

    (b) Preparedness

    (c) Resource management

    (d) Supporting technologies

    (e) All of the above

26. NIMS:

    (a) Suggests the need to focus on all types of hazards

    (b) May downplay recovery issues

    (c) Focuses too heavily on technology for effective response management

    (d) Answers a, b, and c

    (e) Answers b and c only

27. AFOs:

    (a) Are not associated with the federal government

    (b) Are associated with the federal government

    (c) Are associated with the federal government only

    (d) Are not associated with the NRF

    (e) Cannot be opened for anything but a natural disaster

## Review Questions

1. Do all communities have the same technological tools? Why or why not?
2. How can technology help with emergency medical care or search and rescue?
3. How is a transmitter different than a receiver?
4. Can any equipment be used to improve interoperability?
5. What are the benefits of the Internet for emergency managers?
6. What is a decision support system?
7. How can CAMEO assist with a hazardous material response?
8. GIS has been described as "the most exciting technological development in emergency management." Why is this the case?
9. What problems were evident in the response to the 1970 fires in California?
10. What are the four sections listed under ICS?
11. How can "common terminology" help response operations?
12. Is ICS beneficial? Is it without drawbacks?
13. What are the three characteristics of EOCs?
14. What are the seven functions of EOCs Quarantelli mentions?
15. Why are mutual aid agreements helpful for response and recovery operations?
16. What is SEMS and how is it related to ICS?
17. Why did states develop EMAC?
18. Why did 9/11 lead to the creation of NIMS?
19. What is the relationship between crisis and consequence management?
20. What are the six components of NIMS?
21. What are the goals of the National Response Plan?
22. What is the difference between a primary and support agency?
23. How is an AFO different than an EOC or JFO?

## Applying This Chapter

1. You are a business continuity specialist for a Fortune 500 company. The company stores data for the mortgage industry. Your role is to get the business up running after a disaster and ensure that employees can continue to serve their clientele. What types of technology would you need to fulfill your responsibilities if a power outage disables your operations?
2. You are the emergency manager for a city that has hazardous waste transported on its interstate highways every day. One of the semitrucks carrying the waste turned over and is threatening a nearby residential area. Traffic needs to be controlled and evacuees need to be sheltered. The media has arrived and the Department of Transportation is seeking answers. What principles of incident command do you use and why are they important?

3. A major drought has affected your community and jurisdictions in the nearby state. Farmers are losing cattle at an astonishing rate because of the heat and lack of rain. Hay and veterinary care for animals are needed immediately or further deaths with result. How can mutual aid or EMAC be applied in this situation?

4. You work for FEMA and have just been deployed in San Jose, California. A major earthquake occurred and affected the community in almost every way imaginable. How can the ESFs from the NRF help you to respond and recover? Would a JFO be necessary? Why or why not?

5. You are the director for Homeland Security. Terrorists have threatened an attack against the Super Bowl, and it appears that the evidence is credible. Should you set up an Area Field Office? If so, why? Who should be involved?

6. You are the emergency manager in a city that is having a parade. You are concerned about protestors or terrorist attacks because controversial groups are participating. What kind of technology do you want at your disposal to respond to the situation and why? What equipment would be useful if the situation turns violent?

7. You are the emergency manager in Washington State. In the early hours of the morning, an earthquake occurs in the central business district. There is significant damage to roads and businesses. Fires have spread throughout various neighborhoods. How do you activate the emergency operations center and who do you want to involve?

# YOU TRY IT

## Using Technology after a Terrorist Attack

You are the emergency manager for New York City. During the afternoon rush hour, terrorists unleashed multiple bombs on four different subway systems. You are worried about the presence of dangerous chemicals and would like to apprehend the suspects. What kind of technology would you use to respond to the situation and why?

## Applying Incident Command

You are the emergency manager in Kansas. You have been alerted by the National Weather Service that a tornado unexpectedly touched down in your moderately sized community. Under incident command, what four sections do you activate at the scene of a disaster to facilitate emergency and disaster management?

## Class Presentation

Select a disaster that has occurred in the past. Prepare a 10–15 minutes presentation on how technology or organization was used during response and recovery. Be sure to highlight successes and failures. PowerPoints or handouts are preferred.

# 12

# FORESEEING THE FUTURE
## Prior Lessons, Unrecognized Threats and Rising Vulnerability

## Starting Point

Pretest to assess your knowledge of how to deal with future disasters.
*Determine where you need to concentrate your effort.*

## What You'll Learn in This Chapter

▲ The different hazards and threats that face the United States
▲ The interaction of primary, associated, and secondary hazards
▲ The nature of industrial hazards
▲ How to prepare for and respond to acts of violence
▲ What to expect after a terrorist attack
▲ New threats and insufficiently recognized hazards
▲ Reasons for rising vulnerability

## After Studying This Chapter, You'll Be Able To

▲ Examine the complexities inherent in disasters.
▲ Appraise the danger of HazMat incidents.
▲ Question the similarities of mass shootings and other types of disasters.
▲ Employ methods to protect evidence and first responders after a terrorist attack.
▲ Demonstrate an ability to take steps to prepare for biological threats.
▲ Compare and contrast the different technological hazards.
▲ Analyze additional causes of vulnerability.

## Goals and Outcomes

▲ Manage natural disasters effectively.
▲ Respond successfully after technological disasters.
▲ Assess how to collaborate with law enforcement after mass shootings.
▲ Select ways to coordinate with public health officials after terrorist attacks.
▲ Estimate the different biological threats that currently face the United States.
▲ Plan steps to take to deal with new threats.
▲ Evaluate alternative ways to reduce vulnerability.

---

*Disaster Response and Recovery: Strategies and Tactics for Resilience*, Second Edition. David A. McEntire.
© 2015 John Wiley & Sons, Inc. Published 2015 by John Wiley & Sons, Inc.

# INTRODUCTION

As an emergency manager, you must not only foster resilience before, during, and after the current disasters you are confronted with. It is vital that you think critically about how to improve response and recovery in the future as well. You must realize that disasters are on the rise in terms of frequency and impact. This disturbing fact suggests that we will have to deal more effectively with the complex nature of natural disasters. It is imperative that you also recognize the unique challenges of technological disasters. Furthermore, you will need to understand how to deal with violent activity and take precautionary steps to protect your personnel and community during and after terrorist attacks. There are also new or unrecognized hazards that threaten us. These include environmental degradation, meteor strikes, disease outbreaks, and computer-related disasters. Vulnerability is also increasing around the world, and it is your job to help everyone in the community to take steps to reverse such trends. You must have an understanding of the factors that will have a bearing on future disasters if you are to respond to and recover from them successfully.

## 12.1 Disasters on the Rise

There is a growing perception among many scholars and practitioners that disasters are becoming more frequent and intense as compared to the past (Block, 2014; Quarantelli, 1992). For instance, the 1980s witnessed major events such as the Mt. St. Helen's eruption, the Bhopal chemical release, the Chernobyl nuclear accident, and the Loma Prieta earthquake. In the 1990s, Hurricane Andrew, the Midwest flooding, the Northridge earthquake, the bombing of the World Trade Center, the Oklahoma City bombing, and the Tokyo sarin gas release were also noteworthy events. The new millennium appears to be continuing this trajectory of major disasters. Catastrophes have certainly taken their toll in recent years.

The terrorist attacks of September 11, 2001, for example, were costly in terms of physical damage, lives lost, and economic impact. These well-orchestrated events also had global implications due to the deposing of the Afghanistan government and subsequent military conflict in Iraq. During the late summer and early fall of 2004, Florida was hit by several hurricanes and a tropical storm. This severely tested the emergency management capacity in that state and the government at the federal level. A few months later, an extremely strong earthquake occurred off of the coast of Indonesia. The quake produced a tsunami in the Indian Ocean, which took over 300,000 lives and cost billions in damage. This event illustrated the power of nature and lack or failure of warning systems. In 2005, Hurricane Katrina struck New Orleans and other communities off the Gulf Coast area. The wind, storm surge, and flooding resulting from breached retaining walls killed over 1300 people and produced billions of dollars in damages. The response by local, state, and federal authorities was harshly criticized by citizens and politicians. The government appeared to be unable to react effectively to this major calamity.

There are two other cases that illustrate the catastrophic nature of disasters. A major earthquake occurred in January 2010, and it had a devastating impact on

Haiti, the poorest country in the Western Hemisphere. Overall, about 211,000 individuals were killed as a result of the 7.0 quake and its aftershocks. The main challenge with the response and recovery was the lack of equipment to rescue victims from the rubble and treat their medical needs.

Hurricane "Superstorm" Sandy occurred in October of 2012 and affected the northeastern United States. New York and New Jersey were hit particularly hard, but 24 states were impacted in the region. Fatalities numbered nearly 300 from direct and indirect causes. Damages amounted to $65 billion, and this prompted a major concert by famous musicians to generate relief funds. Because of the extent of the disaster, recovery efforts have not progressed as fast as many would prefer (Figure 12-1).

Such events lead many people to wonder if disasters are on the rise. Some scholars point out that our record keeping has improved over time and this accounts for the new perspectives on the matter. It has also been suggested by others that the media is better able to report disasters than in the past (the CNN effect). Other researchers point out that hazards are both more numerous and severe than they were in prior decades. Several scholars are now recognizing that human attitudes and activities are augmenting disasters (Mileti, 1999).

Although there are many possible explanations for more and worse disasters, evidence does suggest that we may be experiencing more flooding hazards as compared to the past. Flooding is occurring at rates and intensities in areas that previously were not affected by such hazards. This may be due, in part, to the extensive use of concrete and asphalt in locations that were formerly undeveloped. The use of these materials in urban areas covers soil (the earth's natural sponge) and causes

**Figure 12-1**

Events like Hurricane Sandy indicate the power of nature and the extent of human vulnerability. Patsy Lynch/FEMA.

runoff water to flow rapidly in low-lying areas. Besides more flooding hazards, it is possible that hurricanes witness increased activity at times. Some researchers believe this is a naturally occurring cycle, while others credit the spike to global climate change. Regardless of the cause or legitimacy of arguments, weather patterns have always fluctuated, and this trend will continue to impact the probability of both flooding and drought episodes domestically and abroad.

Apart from these hazards, the increased use of hazardous materials (HazMat) will likely create more technological hazards in the future. There is simply more industrial activity, so such disasters may also increase over time. With the emergence of militant terrorist groups like Al-Qaeda, terrorist incidents will continue to occur around the world. These often involve suicide bombings in places like Israel, but it is likely that a variety of attacks may occur in the United States (and not just by foreign terrorists). There is also a higher probability of environmental degradation, climate change, pole reversals, meteor strikes, disease outbreaks, and computer-related disasters in the future. As an emergency manager or responder, it will be imperative that you understand how to deal with these types of events. You must be aware of the new hazards and rising vulnerability that will have bearing on future disasters. Without this knowledge, you will not be able to reverse such trends and promote resilience.

## FOR EXAMPLE

### Terrorists and Weapons of Mass Destruction

Terrorist leaders have clearly indicated their desire to obtain weapons of mass destruction (WMD) and use them against the United States. There is at least some evidence that Iran is also pursuing a program to develop nuclear weapons. This, combined with the hostility of some radical groups and our porous borders, creates an extremely vulnerable situation. It is an unfortunate probability that the United States will be attacked with WMD in the future. This could include conventional, biological, chemical, radiological, or nuclear weapons. Even an electromagnetic pulse is possible, and it would render modern electronic equipment useless. Emergency managers and others in homeland security must anticipate, prevent, and prepare for such contingencies.

## SELF-CHECK

- Are disasters on the rise?
- What are the causes of more and worse disasters?
- What is the CNN effect?
- Are there more natural hazards than in the past?
- Why is it important to think critically about the future?

## 12.2 Understanding Natural Disasters

Natural disasters are becoming increasingly complicated, and the primary hazard that triggers them may generate other types of hazards. A **primary hazard** is a natural hazard agent that interacts with vulnerabilities and therefore produces a disaster. An **associated hazard** is a natural hazard agent that typically occurs at the same time as the primary hazard (e.g., hurricanes produce flooding). A **secondary hazard** is a hazard (natural, technological, or otherwise) that occurs as a result of the initial hazard. Some associated and secondary hazards are immediate; others are delayed. Sometimes, it is difficult to distinguish between associated and secondary hazards. Examples of these hazards are listed in Table 12-1.

Natural (and other types of) hazards may also lead to complex, cascading, synergistic, or na-tech (natural and technological hazards) disasters.

▲ A **complex or compound disaster** is an event that involves multiple variables. An earthquake that is accompanied with a landslide, structural collapse, and fires is an example of this.

▲ A **cascading disaster** is an event that triggers additional hazards or impacts. A good illustration of this is 9/11. A hijacked plane hit the trade center towers. These buildings, in turn, caught on fire and collapsed. As a result of the collapse, the infrastructure and subway systems were damaged.

### Table 12-1: Primary, Associated and Secondary Hazards

| Primary hazard | Associated hazard(s) | Secondary hazard(s) |
|---|---|---|
| Volcanic eruption | Earthquakes | Wildfires, fires, flooding, and mudslides |
| Earthquake | Landslides | Structural collapse, fires, chemical releases or explosions, landslides, tsunamis |
| Hurricane | Tornadoes and flooding | Structural collapses |
| Lightning strikes | Thunderstorms | Urban and rural fires |
| Flooding | Hurricanes, tornadoes, and other forms of severe weather | Structural collapse, mold, and diseases such as cholera and diphtheria |
| Winter storms (snow and ice) | Traffic accidents | Fires (as people try to keep warm) and avalanches |
| Tornadoes | Hurricanes, hail, flooding, and other forms of severe weather | Structural collapse |
| Wildfire | Thunderstorms, lightning strikes | Landslides due to loss of vegetation |

▲ A **synergistic disaster** is an event where one resulting impact seems to magnify others. For instance, the loss of power or water in a disaster may limit the ability to communicate or fight fires.

▲ A **na-tech disaster** occurs when a natural hazard interacts with technology to produce or magnify adverse effects (Cruz et al., 2001). A tornado that overturns a train full of HazMat is an example of this type of event.

Hurricane Katrina is a good example of these types of disasters. The hurricane was the initial hazard. It was associated with flooding due to the breaching of the levees. As the water settled in New Orleans, gas lines and fuel storage tanks were broken. Fires erupted as a result. Hazardous chemicals and sewage also ended up in the floodwaters, causing an environmental nightmare. The impact of the hurricane was therefore more severe than would normally be the case in most disasters. Another example of the complexity of disasters is the Tōhoku earthquake that occurred in March 2011 in Japan. The earthquake subsequently triggered a powerful tsunami. The tsunami then caused nuclear accidents in the Fukushima Daiichi Nuclear Power Plant complex. The combined disasters produced over 15,000 deaths. The lack of expertise to deal effectively with radiation leaks made response and recovery efforts more difficult. The nature of today's hazards and disasters necessitates that you and others approach response and recovery operations in a much more cautious and holistic manner.

### 12.2.1 Responding to a Natural Disaster

Every type of disaster creates both common and unusual challenges for you as an emergency manager or responder. To examine these challenges, one incident will be reviewed to see what lessons can be acquired from it. The case to be discussed is the East Bay Hills fire that occurred in California in 1991.

As mentioned in Chapter 11, the East Bay Hills fire was a devastating event that occurred from October 19 to 22, 1991. The event started out as a brush fire that was reported on a hillside at 12:12 p.m. on October 19. The cause of the fire is unknown, but there is some speculation that it was a result of arson. In time, five alarms were sounded as firefighters tried to get control of the situation. This included 12 engine companies, 2 ladder companies, and other emergency resources and personnel. A number of helicopters were brought in as well. Because the wind was very light that day, the firefighters were eventually able to get control of the fire and extinguish it.

Unfortunately, a number of flare-ups occurred throughout the night due to embers that remained hot. Most of these small fires were quickly quenched. But at 10:40 a.m. on October 20, another major flare-up occurred and cinders were carried elsewhere by strong winds. Within a few minutes, a new fire started, crowning trees on another hillside. Superheated gasses from the fire would dry out vegetation; the shrubbery and trees would then explode on fire. The blaze was so hot that even the power poles far from the actual fire would ignite. When all was said and done, the fire:

▲ Covered 1500 acres

▲ Destroyed more than 3000 houses and 2000 vehicles

▲ Killed 25 people and injured 150 others

▲ Left 10,000 people homeless

▲ Necessitated the evacuation of 20,000–30,000 people

▲ Resulted in $1.5 billion in damages and losses

▲ Was declared a presidential disaster

This disaster shows the complex interaction of systems Mileti discusses in *Disasters by Design* (1999). Natural disasters are obviously closely associated with the natural environment. The **natural environment** is the physical milieu in which many disasters occur. For instance, the East Bay Hills area is very hazard prone. There have been many fires in this area over the past 70 years. Since 1930, there have been 14 large-scale fires. In 1923, a fire destroyed 640 structures. In 1970, a fire destroyed 37 homes. In the 1980s, another fire destroyed 5 buildings.

Not only is the area hazard prone, but the nature of hazards has changed over time. In the 1800s, most of the wood in the East Bay Hills was consumed by citizens from the area. As a result, people imported *Eucalyptus* from Australia. Monterey pine was also brought in from other parts of California. These trees grow rapidly and are extremely vulnerable to fires and produce flying brands and embers. Furthermore, because the west side of the hills gets more rain than the east side, the vegetation became thick and lush in this area. Complicating the matter further is the fact that the East Bay Hills experienced five years of drought prior to 1991. In addition, a severe winter also killed many *Eucalyptus* trees and underbrush. Consequently, there was lots of flammable vegetation after a long, hot summer. At this time, the Diablo Winds (Santa Ana) were growing in strength (which are very common in September and October due to a high-pressure system in the Great Basin and a low-pressure system off the coast in the Pacific Ocean). Making matters worse, there was low humidity at the time of the fire. The terrain was also steep, making fires burn much faster than in flat areas.

The built environment exacerbated vulnerability to the natural hazard conditions. The **built environment** includes the structures, technology, and infrastructure created by humans. After the 1906 San Francisco earthquake, the East Bay Hills area began to be developed. Cities expanded dramatically again during the 1960s and 1970s. A 456-unit apartment complex was built in the area at this time. 340 densely built condominiums were placed here as well. Homes were expensive and had multiple floor levels. Homes also had garages, decks, and short bridges, mostly made of wood. Roofs included shake (wood) shingles. New roads were constructed to further develop the area. However, some neighborhoods only had one entrance/exit, and roads were narrow and included many switchbacks. Water systems installed in the area relied on electricity to pump supplies from storage tanks. Electric lines erected in the area often arc in high winds; this actually occurred in the East Bay Hills fire.

The social environment was also to blame for the impact of the disaster. The **social environment** includes the social, political, economic, cultural, and demographic activity or characteristics of the community. In the past, the grazing of animals on the hillside required the introduction of new grasses, oats, and barley. These plants were allowed to grow even when grazing ceased. People in

San Francisco, Oakland, and San Jose moved to the area because they prefer the beautiful views due to the 1300 feet elevation of the East Bay Hills.

As the area transitioned from a rural to suburban area, fire suppression activities were utilized as a way to protect property (thus permitting further growth of plants and trees in the area). New regulations on shingles were proposed after a fire in 1923, but these were not implemented as they were not politically popular. Similar regulations were recommended in a study in 1959, and these same regulations were suggested again in 1970. In both cases, the regulations were bypassed. After a fire in 1980, an ordinance for fire control was passed in Berkeley, but it was soon rescinded due to popular outcry. In 1982, a Blue Ribbon Committee studied the need for fire breaks, but these recommendations fell victim to the poor economic performance at the time. In the 1980s, the fire department lost 40% of its staff due to fiscal constraints and 10 companies were discontinued. Local and state governments did not spend money on fuel thinning and fire breaks because of limited budgets.

Adding to the aforementioned problems, some property deeds in the East Bay Hills residential neighborhoods restricted removal of trees, thereby adding fuel for future fires. In addition, people built decks connected to their homes, but didn't clear brush underneath. One expert observed that there was no warning of the residents about the rising dangers of the threat: "If the Oakland Hills had been part of a national park or forest, instead of a commercial neighborhood, the area would have been evacuated during the Red Flag weather conditions." Unfortunately, no one addressed the growing urban–wildland interface issues and the disaster that resulted. In short, the natural, built, and social environments combined to produce a vulnerable situation.

The Oakland Hills fire also provides important lessons that you should consider when dealing with a natural disaster:

▲ **Be sure to finish the job.** The initial fire on October 19th was extinguished, but hot embers reignited the next day. Fire officials and firefighters should do all they can to douse hot spots and monitor potential flare-ups.

▲ **Give extra attention to communications in disasters.** Because of the large numbers and diverse nature of responders who helped to fight this fire, communications were overwhelmed immediately in the field. In light of the large volume of calls and inadequate communications with those at the scene, the 911 center could not process calls or tell people where to go for the purpose of evacuation. It took a great deal of time to locate and utilize public information officers as the fire occurred on a Sunday.

▲ **Expect a chaotic and dangerous incident area, and do all you can to protect the safety of your personnel**. When police warned people to evacuate, the narrow roads became clogged as up to 5000 people tried to leave the area. Firefighters had to protect themselves from the rapidly moving flames. Some were even forced to take refuge in swimming pools when the fire jumped roads and freeways. One firefighter commented, "It's hard to get organized [to respond] and run for your life at the same time!"

▲ **Be sure not to repeat mistakes regarding mutual aid**. All local resources were quickly committed to the fire. Unfortunately, a request for mutual aid was either delayed or the arrival of outside personnel took longer than anticipated. Besides this error, planes were restricted by strong winds, turbulent updrafts, and heavy smoke. By the time mutual aid personnel arrived at their assigned location, their areas to protect were already burned. In another situation, one captain reported to a command post as instructed but was then told that he was actually supposed to be elsewhere (thus delaying his contributions further). Scores of strike teams were used (some from 99 to 350 miles away). However, some mutual aid teams did not have the right hose connectors. Oakland and San Francisco opted to maintain 3″ lines when the rest of the state went to 2½″ lines. Adapters were available in a warehouse, but these could not be acquired quickly because the fire occurred over the weekend.

▲ **Advise the public on appropriate response activities**. Some people turned on sprinklers to protect their homes from the fire. The water remained on even if homes were burned to the ground. This caused a shortage of water and water pressure for firefighters.

▲ **Harness technology to help you respond**. As the incident unfolded, a helicopter with an infrared monitor and a GPS system pointed firefighters to hot spots that needed to be extinguished. Because power lines were down, firefighters obtained generators to pump water out of wells to fight the raging fires.

▲ **Be sure to address victim needs.** Instead of establishing a disaster recovery center, a community restoration and development center was established in a vacant grocery store. This venue provided access to federal and state disaster assistance, city permitting, psychological and financial counseling, and other victim support services.

▲ **Be sure to consider all options in recovery.** Rather than rebuilding as quickly as possible, a great deal of planning should go into recovery policy and implementation. For instance, decision makers faced with this situation should grapple with important questions. Should the homes in this incident be rebuilt or relocated? If they are to be rebuilt, should the new neighborhood be planned first? Are new restrictions needed to achieve greater safety? What retrofit requirements should be applied to repairs? What restrictions should be put on nearby vacant land? Would it be safer to move these homes to a new area?

▲ **Take advantage of opportunities after the disaster**. A new task force on emergency preparedness and community restoration was created after the East Bay Hills fires, and it pushed through a $50 million bond election for safety improvements. This resulted in the acquisition of new water supplies, the seismic reinforcement of fire stations, the establishment of an EOC, and the purchase of a GIS system to mark natural fire breaks. The task force pushed through new (class A) roofing requirements and additional restrictions on siding, eaves, decks, and balconies. The task force could not address street issues (relating to the size of roads and cul-de-sacs). The large cost per property ($6000–10,000 for each lot) made this prohibitive. However, they were able to implement more stringent parking restrictions. Such steps may reduce risk in the future.

The East Bay Hills fire is significant because the event teaches us to complete the job, ensure first responder safety, plan for mutual aid, acquire adequate equipment for responders, utilize technology in our response operations, and think critically about recovery options and opportunities. These lessons must be incorporated into emergency management if we are to avoid a repetition of the problems in the response to the East Bay Hills Fire.

## FOR EXAMPLE

### Complex Disasters

The Northridge earthquake is an example of a complex disaster. The earthquake occurred in an extremely hazardous area in Southern California. The infrastructures, including roads and industrial facilities, were seriously impacted in the event. Many of those affected in the disaster were poor minorities who lived in vulnerable residential structures. Lives were lost, properties were damaged, and the response was complicated due to fires resulting from broken gas lines. Language barriers among emergency management personnel and victims slowed down response and recovery operations. The natural, built, and social environments interacted in unique ways to produce a complex disaster (Figure 12-2).

## CASE STUDY

### Joplin Tornado
### By Kristina Cramb

Joplin, Missouri, a city of approximately 50,000 people, was ravaged when an EF-5 tornado occurred on May 22, 2011. The tornado destroyed nearly one-third of the city (Johnsson, 2011). This disaster produced wind gusts of 200 plus miles per hour, traveled a destruction path of approximately 22 miles, and had a maximum width of one mile (NOAA, 2011, p. 1; Paul and Stimers, 2011, pp. 1512–1513). The tornado destroyed 8000 buildings (Johnsson, 2011; Zagier et al., 2012). It killed at least 158 people (Doswell et al., 2012, p. 88; Paul and Stimers, 2012, pp. 1511–1512; SPC, 2012). At least 17,000 individuals were directly affected by the twister (Zagier et al., 2012).

As the tornado approached, multiple warnings and alarms were sounded for the residents of Joplin. The first tornado warning was issued at 5:09 p.m. CDT, and the first siren was sounded at 5:11 p.m. The tornado touched ground at 5:34 p.m. just outside of Joplin's city limits (NOAA, 2011, p. 2), and this was followed up with a subsequent sounding of the siren system at 5:38 p.m. At 5:41 p.m., the city of Joplin, Missouri, was hit by the tornado. Fortunately, approximately 90% of Joplin's residents received the tornado warning in spite of the fact that sirens are not always heard inside of a house (Paul and Stimers, 2011, pp. 1517–1518).

The tornado dissipated at 6:12 p.m. CDT (Paul and Stimers, 2011, p. 1512), but it left over 1000 people injured. Medical responders volunteered their services in treating those in need. Though local hospitals lost power and technology due to the disaster, staff were still able to verify the credentials of the medical personnel who volunteered to provide medical care to the victims (O'Brion, 2011).

The Joplin tornado had left behind damages estimated to be between $2.8 billion and $3 billion (Smith and Sutter, 2013, p. 1; Zagier et al., 2012). Cleaning up from the tornado was a massive undertaking in that 1.5 million cubic yards of debris was removed from Joplin (Smith and Sutter, 2013, p. 8). Following the debris removal, new buildings were constructed with the help of $1.8 billion in insurance claims (Zagier et al., 2012). Most new homes have incorporated some type of tornado protection such as safe rooms (Shagets, 2013).

An impressive number of individuals, community groups, and nonprofit agencies volunteered their services following the tornado. By the end of 2011, there were more than 92,000 people registered to help with disaster relief and recovery at Joplin, including nearly 750 community groups. In order to promote recovery, the Red Cross collected and donated money to help the survivors, and the local area YMCA provided free day care services for those in need (Smith and Sutter, 2013, pp. 8–9). The interest in promoting recovery after this tornado has made Joplin resilient.

**Figure 12-2**

Seismic activity, like the Northridge earthquake, may damage hundreds of thousands of buildings and result in billions of dollars in damages. However, it is also important to remember the social impacts resulting from disasters. FEMA News Photo.

## 12.3 Understanding Technological Disasters

While working in emergency management, you will most likely be required to respond to various types of technological hazards. Some of these hazards appear to have characteristics similar to natural hazards. For example, fires can be produced by lightning or through electrical short circuits. There can be structural failures resulting from dams that have been affected by earthquakes or buildings that collapse because they have been poorly designed and constructed. Other technological hazards and disasters may result from transportation accidents such as plane crashes or train derailments. However, one of the most common technological agents emanates from industrial hazards and HazMat.

As an emergency manager, you should be aware of the nature of industrial hazards so you can respond effectively to their consequences (Mitchell, 1996). Such disasters may include fires, explosions, chemical leaks, hazardous material spills, and other forms of environmental degradation. Industrial disasters may occur when companies convert raw materials into usable products for society. These events may happen during the extraction, processing, manufacturing, transportation, storage, use, and disposal of HazMat. Industrial disasters also take place at the intersection of people, place, property, and product. That is to say, humans are typically involved at a location where buildings and equipment are affected by HazMat. Such incidents have been classified by Mitchell (see Table 12-2).

If you work in emergency management, you should also recognize that no two disasters are exactly alike. However, evidence from a number of industrial disasters (e.g., Bhopal, Chernobyl, Challenger, West Texas explosion, etc.) reveals several similarities:

▲ **Risk is often underestimated**. CEOs, engineers, and plant operators often ignore the probability of accidents and disasters.

## Table 12-2: Industrial Disasters as Classified by Mitchell (1996, p. 11)

| Experience | Unsuspected hazards (unknown) | Improperly managed hazards (mistakes) | Instrumental hazards (war and terrorism) |
|---|---|---|---|
| One of a kind | Ozone depletion: chlorofluorocarbons | Kyshtym: nuclear wastes | Hiroshima, Nagasaki: atomic bombs |
| First of a kind | DDT: pesticide | Metal fatigue: Comet aircraft | World War I: poison gas |
| Worst of a kind | Minamata: methyl mercury biomagnification | Chernobyl: nuclear power station | Kuwait: oil well fires |

▲ **Planning and design are frequently faulty.** Engineers may not consider all possible negative outcomes of technological equipment.

▲ **Operation is improper.** Maintenance may be neglected and regulations or policies are not followed.

▲ **Denial of wrongdoing or the hiding of evidence is commonplace.** Corporate public relations specialists sometimes place the blame on others, and company leaders do not fully disclose everything they know about the incident.

▲ **Knowledge is lacking about hazards and materials involved.** Employees and first responders do not fully comprehend what they are dealing with.

▲ **People are killed and health is jeopardized.** The disaster might kill people and threaten the physical well-being of others.

▲ **The environment may be adversely impacted.** The natural habitat can be degraded and rendered unusable due to an industrial hazard.

▲ **Lawsuits and fines typically result.** Victims seek compensation from the company and the government imposes penalties to prevent recurrences.

### 12.3.1 Responding to HazMat Incidents

Because it is unlikely that all technological hazards will be completely avoided, first responders and emergency managers should respond to HazMat incidents in a very cautious and deliberate manner. HazMat releases are probably the most common type of technological or industrial disasters, and they are extremely dangerous and even life threatening (Figure 12-3). There are several steps that can be taken to respond effectively:

1. **Ensure everyone has the proper background and personal protective equipment.** If firefighters, police, medical technicians, public works employees, and others do not have the proper credentials and gear, they should not be allowed to respond to the HazMat incident.

**Figure 12-3**

Because of the danger they pose, hazardous material incidents require special training, equipment, and procedures. Win Henderson/FEMA.

2. **Obtain as much information when in route and while on scene.** When the call comes in, responders can obtain information from 911 call centers and material safety data sheets (MSDS). Knowledge about the contents of containers can be gathered from employees and witnesses to the event.

3. **Approach cautiously and maintain a safe distance from the scene.** Do not rush in! Doing so could kill or injure you. Stay upwind (opposite of wind direction) and uphill from most HazMat.

4. **Determine what you are dealing with.** Use binoculars and look for placards to know what HazMat has been released. The DOT Emergency Response Guidebook (ERG) lists HazMat in terms of class. The ERG also has useful indexes of dangerous goods in numerical and alphabetical order. It also helps responders understand potential hazards, public safety measures, emergency response actions, and how the material reacts with water.

5. **Seek expert advice if needed.** There are thousands of types of HazMat, and many of them are complex and volatile. If you do not know what to do with the situation, find someone who does.

6. **Evacuate or shelter in place, and seal off the area.** Determine if it is best to evacuate people from the area or have them shelter in place. Work with the police and media to implement the decision. Use barricades and public safety officials to keep people from entering the danger zone.

7. **Be aware of the dynamic nature of the disaster scene**. One HazMat may interact with another in complicated ways. Temperature, humidity, wind, and other variables can cause HazMat to react differently at any given time.

8. **Contract with remediation companies.** If needed, consult your resource lists and network to seek the assistance of corporations that specialize in HazMat response and recovery. Examples include CURA Emergency Services for road spills and Hulcher Services for trail derailments (see http://www.spillsolutions.com/Spills/Index.htm and http://www.hulcher.com/).

9. **Follow all regulations for reporting and cleanup**. State and federal transportation and environmental agencies have several rules that must be followed in order to avoid fines or prosecution. This includes a quick time frame to notify authorities of the spill as well as cleaning up the contaminated soil and disposing of HazMat in an acceptable manner.

Only by following these guidelines can you reduce the risk facing personnel, rescue those affected, limit property damage, protect the environment, and avoid costly legal fees.

---

### FOR EXAMPLE

#### HazMat Incident on the Railways

On April 14, 1983, one of the rail cars on a train traveling through Arizona began to emit smoke. The engineer brought the train to a stop on the west side of the city of Casa Grande. Recognizing the potential for a major HazMat incident, emergency response personnel tried to determine what was on board. Information from the rail operator was slow in coming, so there was a great deal of confusion regarding the need to evacuate people from the nearby area. Police and fire also had difficulty communicating effectively during the response and notifying each other of potential dangers and proposed solutions. The delay in requesting assistance from the state HazMat coordinator further complicated the response to the incident. This case illustrates the potential for uncertainty and the need to rely on expertise for effective decision making (see Pijawka et al., 1988).

---

## SELF-CHECK

- What are some examples of technological disasters?
- What are the common features of technological disasters?
- What should be done to respond effectively to a HazMat incident?
- What recovery considerations are witnessed after HazMat releases?

## 12.4 Understanding Acts of Violence

As an emergency manager you may have the unfortunate task of dealing with acts of violence. War among countries is the most devastating type of violence, and it results in the death of hundreds, thousands, and even millions of people. War also devastates the infrastructure of the warring parties and disrupts their economies significantly. In some countries, there may be significant bouts of civil conflict where internal factions vie for power. The cases of Syria and Egypt come to mind. Civil wars are often characterized as complex emergencies. A **complex emergency** is a humanitarian crisis that involves an extreme amount of violence among different ethnic groups coupled with political instability, poor economic conditions, weak law enforcement capabilities, and disaster conditions of some sort (e.g., drought and famine). The genocide in Rwanda and ethnic fighting in the former Yugoslavia are visible examples of this type of activity that approximates total anarchy. These incidents are especially problematic in that the warring factions disapprove of humanitarian aid sent to their enemy. Many external disaster relief providers have been killed as a result. Conveys of humanitarian aid have also been hijacked by warlords in countries with failed governments. Such situations present serious challenges for relief workers from the United Nations (UN), the U.S. Office of Foreign Disaster Assistance, or the International Red Cross.

The United States may not have to deal with complex emergencies directly, but it is currently involved in a military campaign against insurgents in Afghanistan and elsewhere around the world. It is also feasible that the United States could be involved in a major war if Iran obtains and threatens the use of nuclear weapons. Internal conflict could also result if the ideological friction between political parties widens in the future or if class or ethnic strife worsens. Although war and internal conflict are possible, the United States is most likely to be affected with mass shootings or terrorist attacks.

### 12.4.1 Responding to Acts of Violence

There have been episodes of mass shootings at the workplace, in restaurants, or in schools. In the Maryland and Washington, D.C., areas, two snipers killed several people over a multiple-week period. Disgruntled employees or deranged individuals may also enter a facility or hide in secluded areas. They will then begin to fire their weapons intentionally or randomly as was the case in the Navy Yard shooting in 2013. Incidents of mass violence (such as the shootings at Fort Hood or Sandy Hook Elementary School) produce several injuries and deaths. Emergency medical personnel and law enforcement officials will play significant roles in the response to each of these acts of violence. To learn how to better respond to these incidents, a case study of the events surrounding the Columbine school shootings will be discussed.

In 1999, Columbine High School students Eric Harris and Dylan Klebold carried out a shooting rampage. These students felt they were mistreated by their peers in high school. To seek revenge, the students planned an attack involving bombs and guns. The students planted bombs in the school cafeteria and other locations in advance. Harris and Klebold then entered the school and killed 12 of their peers and

1 teacher. The shootings also wounded 24 others before the gunmen committed suicide. It is to date the deadliest act of violence at a school in American history.

The response to the shootings was heavily criticized even though the police and firefighters arrived only 12 minutes after the first 911 call. The most significant problem responders had was that they did not know who the perpetrators were. Any of the exiting students first responders came in contact with could have been carrying weapons discretely. Eric Harris and Dylan Klebold could have also put down their guns and blended into the crowd. Those responding to the situation also lacked information about the layout of the school. Needing this, they had to first interview some students and ask for help to draw a rough schematic of the school floor plan.

The unfolding and dangerous situation at Columbine did not allow responders to get sufficient or accurate intelligence they needed. This delayed the police and medical response for what seemed to be an eternity. Thirty minutes after the shootings began, 10 officers from three agencies assembled into teams and finally entered the building with sufficient force to do so safely. During the next 90 minutes, additional help arrived. Three SWAT teams made up of 50 officers from four jurisdictions walked through the hallways (Macko, 1999). They found hundreds of students and their teachers hiding in classrooms and hallways to protect themselves. As they were discovered, the students and teachers were evacuated from the premises. Many of the students needed both protection from the assailants and medical care from paramedics.

There were many other difficulties associated with these active shooter events, including:

- ▲ *A failure to recognize warning signs.* Both Eric Harris and Dylan Klebold were in trouble with law enforcement before the Columbine massacre occurred. They both also searched on websites and posted messages about murder, hate, and revenge. Eric Harris is also said to have had bombs under his bed. If the parents would have known this, the tragedy could have been prevented. School officials also should be made aware that they needed to look for antisocial behavior in Harris and Klebold.
- ▲ *Inaccurate information.* The SWAT teams received incomplete or incorrect information during initial moments of the event. They heard that there are eight gunmen, that there were snipers on the roof, that the killers were mingling with the students, and that they were located in the classrooms (Macko, 1999).
- ▲ *Lack of intelligence.* Because the SWAT teams were not thoroughly familiar with the school, they did not know how to operate the building's emergency systems. Alarms, strobe lights, and sprinklers added to the chaos. A SWAT team member incorrectly entered the code to turn off the alarm. In frustration, he hit the panel with the butt of his rifle that made the system inoperable.
- ▲ *Lack of communication.* Distinct agencies operated on radios set at different frequencies and vital information from outside the building did not reach

the SWAT teams on the inside (Macko, 1999). No one seemed able to grasp the full nature of this incident initially.

▲ *Dangerous bombs.* The planted pipe bombs, $CO_2$ bombs, and propane bombs were all unstable and required careful removal since many were antipersonnel devices. SWAT members could not enter some areas until the explosives were removed and defused by bomb technicians. If the bombs had gone off, the casualties could have been much higher—perhaps in the hundreds.

▲ *Difficult choices.* During the incident, one teacher, Dave Sanders, was shot in a classroom and was bleeding to death. A student put a sign in the window that read, "1 bleeding to death." Police spotted this sign before noon, and yet no one reached Sanders until after 3:00 p.m. Many argue that the SWAT team should have rushed in and saved Sanders. However, the SWAT team was being cautious since they could have been ambushed in the dangerous situation (Macko, 1999).

▲ *Problematic media coverage.* As the response unfolded, the media filmed the entire event with helicopters overhead. Their footage could have given vital information about police activities that could have jeopardized their security.

▲ *Distribution of victims.* Hospitals had some difficulty coordinating 2 helicopters and 48 ambulances for the injured. Medical rescue efforts in mass emergencies are often problematic because of the large numbers of victims.

▲ *Lengthy investigation.* Because of the presence of bombs and the need for a thorough investigation into the incident, over 1000 backpacks had to be examined. Approximately 2000 lockers were searched as well. The search for bombs and evidence was a long and tedious process.

There are several lessons we can glean from the response to the Columbine massacre. The most important point is that you should work closely with law enforcement officials, the media, and the medical community when dealing with these types of situations. Personnel trained in **tactical emergency medical service (EMS)** (emergency medical technicians that also skilled in the use weapons) may be particularly useful in cases where there are both threats and medical needs. Careful efforts must also be taken to track down, negotiate with, or neutralize the perpetrator by force if necessary. At the same time, emergency responders must protect potential victims, treat the injured, and distribute patients to medical facilities before initiating the investigation (Figure 12-4). Media relations will take on a new importance, because of the highly charged situation. It is likely that you will need to help your community recover psychologically after these disturbing incidents. FEMA has produced documents to help you respond to active shooter situations. See http://www.dhs.gov/xlibrary/assets/active_shooter_booklet.pdf.

> ### FOR EXAMPLE
>
> #### Protest of the World Trade Organization
>
> There are many types of violent activity that an emergency manager must be aware of. Even civil protests must be considered by today's emergency managers. On November 29, 1999, people unhappy with the economic policies of the World Trade Organization (WTO) gathered in Seattle to protest an economic summit that was being held there. Most protesters held signs and expressed their views peacefully. There were some that began to act violently by pestering police and burning vehicles. Those involved in this behavior exploited police procedures as well as the lack of equipment and trained personnel in law enforcement agencies. The city did not have the ability to deal with all of the situations relating to this event effectively. The experience taught city officials about the importance of being ready to deal with protests that could turn violent.

## SELF-CHECK

- What is a complex emergency?
- Do emergency managers need to be concerned about international political conflicts?
- What is the most likely act of violence to be committed in the United States?
- Why did first responders have difficulty after the Columbine School shooting?
- What lessons are gleaned from the mass emergency situation at Columbine?

## 12.5 Understanding Terrorism

As we have sadly learned from first-hand experience in this country, terrorist acts pose serious challenges to those involved in response and recovery activities. Terrorists—whether individuals, groups, or states—instill fear in others as a way to reach their aims and intentions. According to the FBI, **terrorism** is defined as "the unlawful use of force against persons or property to intimidate or coerce a government, the civilian population, or any segment thereof, in the furtherance of political or social objectives." The Department of Defense defines terrorism as "the calculated use of violence, or the threat of violence, to inculcate fear, (and is) intended to coerce or to intimidate governments or societies in the pursuit of goals that are generally political, religious or ideological."

McEntire et al. (2001) note that terrorists use the drug trade, burglary, or other illegal activities to finance their operations. In other cases, terrorist activity will be

**Figure 12-4**

The FBI has knowledgeable and trained agents who can deal with active shooters and defuse improvised explosives. Courtesy of FBI.

sponsored by wealthy individuals, corporations, or governments. Terrorists actively recruit people who adhere to their ideology, and they use the Internet to spread their message to others. Sometimes, terrorist groups like Al-Qaeda set up camps and conferences where recruits are taught to raise funds, stake out targets, forge passports, use weapons, and carry out attacks. Common terrorist tactics include threats, assassinations, and suicide bombings. Terrorists also use weapons such as knives, guns, and computer viruses to carry out these attacks. They may likewise seek WMD (including biological, nuclear, incendiary, chemical, and explosive devices).

Terrorists select a variety of targets for maximum exposure and impact. Their preferences include:

▲ Public venues such as malls, restaurants, stores, and sporting stadia
▲ Information and communication technology
▲ Water and electricity utilities
▲ Buss and subway systems
▲ Petroleum/chemical facilities
▲ Business districts
▲ Emergency and government services

### 12.5.1 Responding to Terrorist Disasters

As an emergency manager, you should be aware of the similarities and differences of terrorist attacks as compared to natural disasters. Webb (2002) has provided an excellent description of the common patterns of human behavior in both terrorist attacks and other types of disasters. Similarities among both types of events include:

1. **Very little looting, if any**. Most people have no intention of taking other people's property after a terrorist attack.
2. **Emergence of therapeutic communities**. Individuals and groups almost always help victims who are in need.
3. **Convergence of people and resources at the scene**. People come to the site of a disaster and send supplies to assist with the response and recovery operations.
4. **Adaptability of organizations**. Emergency response agencies are able to deal with difficult challenges.
5. **Reliability of emergency workers**. Police and firefighters typically overwork themselves after terrorist attacks (e.g., in New York after the 9/11).
6. **People do not panic**. The evacuation of the World Trade Center was, for the most part, orderly.
7. **Certain groups are more vulnerable than others**. For example, in the 9/11 attacks, first responders were most at risk.
8. **Placement of blame and litigation**. There is always a belief that we can do more than what we are doing to prevent and respond (e.g., the 9/11 Commission Report identified a number of steps that can be taken to reduce vulnerability to terrorism).
9. **Reemergence of societal conflict**. President Bush has been criticized for the war on terrorism even though the response to 9/11 was seen as a success.

In spite of notable similarities, you must be cognizant of possible differences that may have significant implications for postdisaster operations. In comparison to certain types of natural disasters, there may be no warning before a terrorist attack. Terrorists—especially lone wolf terrorists—operate on the principle of surprise. Terrorist attacks, particularly those that involve WMD, could conceivably generate a larger number of casualties than some natural disasters in the United States. For instance, an attack involving biological weapons could kill millions of people. Another area of concern is human behavior. Although there is little or no evidence to expect that humans will react differently after a terrorist attack, it is unclear if typical responses will remain the same in possible catastrophic terrorist attacks. For instance, the use of biological weapons may necessitate isolation practices, which could be controversial. Victims may also have a more difficult time coping emotionally if terrorists attack critical infrastructure as the event was an intentional act rather than a natural hazard. In addition, citizens may not always be able to protect themselves in a terrorist attack since this might require national security, law enforcement measures, or advanced medical knowledge. Moreover, evacuation may or may not be advantageous depending on the nature of the situation (e.g., an attack involving hazardous chemicals). The circumstances of the agent and weather will determine whether people should leave or shelter in place.

In addition to these complications, there are other challenges associated with terrorist disasters. Emergency services may need to communicate through secure radio channels so their operations will not be overheard by terrorists. It may be wise to stop citizen involvement in search and rescue activities as soon as possible because terrorists may blend into the civilian population (one or more of the volunteers might be a terrorist in disguise). Even donations might not be safe as the generosity of others may include secondary devices that cause more destruction. Debris removal could be complicated as well. Debris is evidence and may be contaminated in the case of nuclear, biological, or chemical weapons. Victims may also require decontamination before they can be given medical care. Environmental restoration may be impossible in the short term for certain types of attacks. For example, a dirty bomb (a conventional explosive packed with radioactive material) may spread hazardous substances in a vital commercial district. The affected area may not be habitable for months, years, or even decades. Those responding to terrorist incidents must therefore be aware of the extreme dangers and unique impact associated with these types of disasters.

There are other more specific things to consider when dealing with these situations. For instance, it is important for you to recognize that any disaster other than a natural disaster could be a terrorist attack. A structural fire may be due to arson. An explosion may result from a bomb. A disease outbreak may occur in conjunction with bioterrorism. A plane crash may accompany due to hijacking or bombing. In addition, the scene of a terrorist attack may be very dangerous. A terrorist incident may include one or more of six types of harm you can encounter (based on the TRACEM acronym) (FEMA, 1999f):

▲ **Thermal**—excessive heat from a fire
▲ **Radiological**—emission of alpha/gamma particles and gamma rays
▲ **Asphyxiative**—blood poisons or agents that displace oxygen
▲ **Chemical**—toxic materials and corrosive materials
▲ **Etiological**—biological living agents
▲ **Mechanical**—an explosive device

For this reason, it is imperative that responders look for identifiers of WMD before rushing into the scene of a terrorist attack. FEMA (1999f) has listed a number of clues that should be considered. For instance, in a biological attack, there might be unusual numbers of sick or dying people. A nuclear attack might be accompanied by the presence of placards and labels on canisters or the presence of radioactive material that could trigger Geiger counters. An incendiary device might produce multiple fires, odors of accelerants, and heavy burning. An incident involving dangerous chemicals might generate an unusual dispersion of mists and gasses, odors and tastes, and the onset of similar symptoms in a large group of people. Attacks involving explosives may result in damage to buildings, scattered debris, and victims with shrapnel or shock-like symptoms.

The scene of a terrorist attack may also include secondary devices. There may be bombs designed to take out emergency responders. Terrorists may target police, fire, and EMS personnel in order to add to the loss of life. Terrorists may want to limit the effectiveness of first responders when they arrive at the scene. They may also attempt to create a mood of confusion and fear. There are a number of examples of terrorists using secondary devices. As responders showed up to a 1997 abortion clinic bombing in Atlanta, a bomb was detonated in a dumpster. In Ireland, terrorists called in a bomb threat for a public building, but the device was actually detonated at the evacuation site. Finally, the scene of any terrorist attack is therefore a crime scene. Physical evidence will be present and it is crucial for prosecution.

### 12.5.2 Protecting First Responders

You should be extremely cautious during responses to terrorist attacks. Responders should be aware at all times of the circumstances in which they find themselves. A particular concern is to ensure the scene is as secure as possible. Police may be needed to block off roads and limit access to the area. All personnel entering the site should be screened and have a justified reason for being there. This may necessitate the showing of identification, contacting the affiliated organization to verify employment, and verifying licenses and working permits. Incident commanders and emergency managers may need to refuse donations if they appear suspicious or come from unknown sources. Fences may be needed to keep citizens out of the area. Patrol of the area on the ground, in the air, or by the sea may be needed to detect and deter potentially harmful terrorist activities.

According to FEMA (1999f), emergency responders should take other measures to protect themselves at the scene of a terrorist attack. This can be accomplished by limiting time at the incident scene to minimize exposure to hazards, keeping a safe distance between you and agent to also prevent or minimize exposure (e.g., stay uphill and upwind), and utilizing shielding (e.g., personal protective equipment and self-contained breathing apparatus). Waiting for HazMat teams to arrive (if you do not have the proper training or equipment), creating a site safety plan, and ensuring there is a safety liaison officer to monitor activities at the incident scene will also help to protect first responders.

All personnel, equipment, and victims must be decontaminated if there is an indication that WMD are used in the attack. The decontamination process should include hot, warm, and cold zones.

- ▲ The **hot zone** is the affected (or contaminated) area.
- ▲ The **warm zone** is the washing (or decontamination) area.
- ▲ The **cold zone** is not affected and can only be accessed by clean (or decontaminated) individuals.

Zones should be set up in such a way so that wind blows toward the hot zone. The warm zone should include tents or plastic sheeting to protect the privacy of victims as they are being decontaminated.

When undertaking decontamination procedures, you will also need to ensure that first responders take the following steps (see Figure 12-5):

1. Put on necessary personal protective equipment.
2. Have responders enter the cold zone first before entering the warm and hot zones.

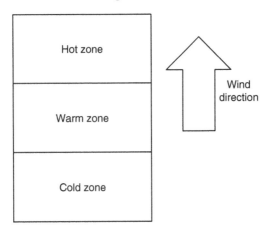

Decontamination zones.

3. Remove victims from the hot zone and transfer them to the warm zone.

4. Decontaminate individuals and equipment using water, bleach or mild soap, brushes, and plastic pools (to retain the contaminated solution in the warm zone).

5. Extract victims to cold zone and give proper medical care (including transportation to hospital).

6. Ensure all responders are decontaminated before entering cold zone again.

7. Dispose of contaminated solution and other contaminated items properly.

Once this process is completed, be sure to decontaminate all first responders and clean or properly discard all clothing, supplies, equipment, gurneys, blankets, etc.! If applicable, ensure that hospitals also follow the same decontamination process before admitting patients. Failing to do so may render the hospital emergency room useless after a terrorist attack.

### 12.5.3 Protecting Evidence

As terrorist acts are criminal acts, all evidence around the scene is important. Emergency responders should do all they can to protect evidence and collect information vital for prosecution (FEMA, 1999f). When and if possible, responders and officials should try to avoid disrupting the scene (e.g., leave things as they are), be aware of persons entering or leaving the area, and record the license plate numbers of vehicles that were present. It would also be useful if responders jot down descriptions of people and make of cars, encourage witnesses to remain at scene until investigators come (if safe to do so), and take photos of the impact when possible. Other steps include drawing a map of the scene and writing an after-action report. Video footage may also help you discover who was involved in the attack, as was the case in the Boston bombing in April 2013. Security cameras, personal cameras, cell phone cameras, and news coverage all helped to reveal, neutralize, or capture the perpetrators. Ensuring the evidence is protected (e.g., through a chain of custody) and testifying in court are other activities that can improve the chances for apprehension and prosecution.

### 12.5.4 Relying on Other Organizations

Because terrorist events require technical knowledge and special skills, it is imperative that you know who can assist at the local, state, and federal levels. At the local level, you may request the assistance of the fire department, EMS, the police department, hospitals, public health officials, and the coroner's office (see Perry, 2003b) (Figure 12-6). The organization and roles of these groups are mentioned in Table 12-3.

States may also have a highly trained team to assist in the detection of WMD and subsequent response operations. For instance, there are 57 special military units around the nation that have the purpose of identifying what weapons have been used and how to deal with them effectively. The 6th Civil Support Team in Texas is a specially trained National Guard unit that can be activated as needed. This and similar teams have WMD detection capabilities that can help you identify what hazard agent you are dealing with (e.g., poison gas vs. radioactive material). The federal government also has additional teams to assist in terrorism response. The Centers for Disease Control (CDC) and Department of Homeland Security can help with WMD detection. The FBI will mobilize its response units to neutralize threats, protect evidence, and begin investigation for prosecution purposes. Under the Metropolitan Medical Response System, the federal government may also send pharmaceutical supplies to the scene of a terrorist event. The National Disaster Medical System (NDMS) response teams may also deploy for WMD events or provide medical standby support for National Special Security Events (NSSEs). A Special Event Assessment Rating (SEAR) is used to determine the priority status of events like the Super Bowl, NCAA Final Four, Republican or Democratic conventions, etc. The EPA and CDC may also have expertise to help you deal with chemical or biological attacks.

**Figure 12-6**

Law enforcement officials and the military will play a larger role in terrorist incidents than in natural disasters. Robert Rose/FEMA.

**Table 12-3: Roles and Responsibilities of Emergency Response Organizations**

| Organization | Roles and responsibilities |
| --- | --- |
| Fire | Isolate impact area and set up perimeter<br>Position equipment and responders upwind, uphill, and upstream from the incident site<br>Assess downwind hazards and implement evacuation or shelter in place decisions<br>Identify agenda and adjust scene layout if required<br>Respond to victim needs with appropriate PPE<br>Decontaminate all victims, responders, and equipment as needed |
| EMS | Implement mass casualty triage procedures<br>Provide medical treatment as dictated by the incident<br>Transport victims to definitive care facilities<br>Determine mental health impact and treat accordingly |
| Police | Share preliminary intelligence data with incident command and the EOC<br>Notify and interact with the FBI<br>Deploy law enforcement personnel, including bomb squads and tactical operations teams<br>Assure incident security for first responders<br>Collect and control evidence<br>Apprehend and assume custody of suspects at the scene |
| Hospitals | Implement lockdown of facility to ensure security<br>Decontaminate and triage all arriving patients<br>Track patients, including their symptoms, and communicate with public health officials<br>Decide where to treat patients (internally or externally)<br>Treat as dictated by nature of injuries |
| Public Health | Conduct surveillance for evidence of epidemics<br>Identify and control agent<br>Determine and implement protective measures for the population, including immunizations or prophylactic medicines<br>Work with police to implement quarantines if needed |
| Coroners | Receive human remains<br>Safeguard personal property<br>Identify the deceased and notify next of kin<br>Prepare and complete file for each decedent<br>Photograph, fingerprint, and collect DNA specimens as appropriate<br>Provide death certificates<br>Coordinate and release remains for final disposition |

The federal activities in relation to terrorism have been categorized previously as crisis management or consequence management:

▲ **Crisis management** is a law enforcement activity that includes intelligence gathering to prevent terrorist attacks or evidence collection for the purposes of interdiction and prosecution. The FBI was designated as the lead agency for crisis management.

▲ **Consequence management** concerns typical emergency management response and recovery operations that also take place after terrorist attacks. FEMA is in charge of consequence management.

In light of the operational problems made evident across crisis and consequence management after the 9/11 terrorist attack, the Department of Homeland Security is now downplaying the use of these terms or at least trying to minimize the distinction of these functions. Both crisis and consequence management are now viewed as integrated activities that cannot be separated operationally.

## FOR EXAMPLE

### Oklahoma City Bombing

After the Oklahoma City bombing in 1995, there was a swift response on the part of many different organizations. At the scene of the destroyed Murrah Federal Building, local police, fire, and medical units arrived quickly. They took care of immediate life safety issues. Various agencies from the state and federal government also arrived to assist. For instance, the state law enforcement agency monitored highways to capture potential suspects. FEMA showed up with resources and personnel to help with search and rescue as well as long-term recovery operations. The Red Cross also assisted with donations management. When the vast majority of bodies had been recovered, the FBI took over the scene for investigation. Many different individuals and organizations will respond to terrorist attacks.

## SELF-CHECK

- How do terrorists operate?
- What are the likely targets for terrorists?
- Are terrorist attacks similar or different than other types of disasters?
- What are the important considerations when responding to a terrorist attack?
- How can you protect first responders after a terrorist attack? Evidence?
- Who can help you deal with terrorist attacks?

## 12.6 Insufficiently Recognized Hazards

In the immediate years after the attacks in September 2001, the United States was focused primarily on future acts of terrorism. However, Hurricane Katrina, the meteor strike in Russia, and the West Texas fertilizer explosion all illustrate why it is unwise to focus on one hazard alone. As an emergency manager, you must recognize that there are other hazards that could be neglected by decision makers. These include environmental degradation, pole reversals, meteor impacts, biological threats, and computer/information technology hazards.

### 12.6.1 Environmental Degradation, Global Warning, and Climate Change

As humans attempt to provide for their needs, the earth's resources are constantly being polluted or depleted. This can have extremely negative consequences. For instance, the dumping of toxic chemicals into rivers and the ocean may limit the supply of fresh water or food such as fish. In the next few decades, oil and petroleum products may become scarce, which may make it difficult to deliver needed products and heat homes during the winter. Such **environmental degradation** is serious and should not be ignored or downplayed. The emergency manager must be conscious of the impact of human activity on the environment.

In addition to focusing on the protection of natural resources, many are calling for further attention to be given to global warming. **Global warming** is the rise of temperatures in the earth's atmosphere. According to the National Science Academy, the temperature of the earth has risen one degree Fahrenheit within the last century. The sun provides heat for our planet, but the earth also produces heat. This heat is trapped within the atmosphere by the heat-retaining greenhouse gasses. Global warming is attributed to the buildup of three of such gasses: methane, carbon dioxide, and nitrous oxide. This naturally occurring process, called the greenhouse effect (see Figure 12-7), allows the earth to maintain temperatures hospitable for humans, animals, and plant life. However, scientists are concerned because the amount of greenhouse gas in the environment is increasing. The assertion is that the combustion of fossil fuel is augmenting greenhouse gasses.

Global warming has drawn concern from the scientific community for many reasons. As the earth warms, climate changes could be noticeable. **Climate change** is an alteration of the earth's temperature and weather patterns (Figure 12-8). For instance, according to the EPA, extreme rainfall across the United States has increased in recent years, while snowfall and ice accumulation in the Arctic has decreased. However, scientists still do not know exactly how global warming will affect the climate. The U.S. National Assessment of Climate Change Impacts (NACCI) has issued several reports that conclude that humans will be able to adapt to their changing climate, but not without significant regional effects. Their best estimations are that warmer weather will cause an increase in evaporation. Some regions will become more arid, while others will see a drastic increase in rainfall. Agriculture, forestry, and land and water management may all be affected. There is also an indication that coastal areas could be flooded if the earth warms and ice caps continue to melt.

Figure 12-7

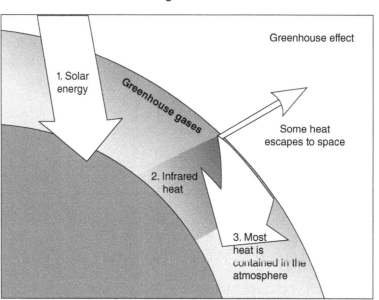

The greenhouse effect. Accessed at http://yosemite.epa.gov/oar/ globalwarming.nsf/content/climate.html on January 23, 2006.

Figure 12-8

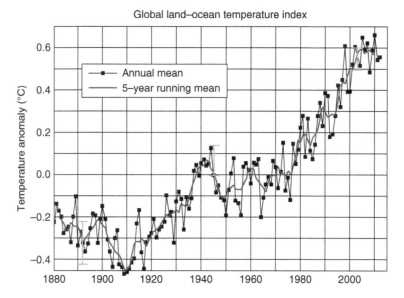

Global temperature changes from 1880 to present. Accessed at http://www.roperld. com/science/GlobalWarmingGraphs.htm#ModTemp on January 29, 2014.

Findings about global warming and climate change are not without criticism. Some scholars argue that the earth's temperatures have always varied over time. Others assert that while temperatures on the earth's surface have been rising in recent decades, the temperature in the upper level of the atmosphere has shown very little change. Moreover, scientists are still determining exactly how much human behavior such as driving influences global warming. Others assert that the warming trend has ended and even noted that some of the research on global warming is blatantly false (e.g., some data has been manipulated in an erroneous manner for political purposes) (Ferrara, 2013).

In spite of these divergent findings and disagreement, there are several implications for disaster scholars and you as a practitioner. Climate change may lead to a situation where more rainfall increases the prominence of waterborne vectors, leading to disease outbreaks in areas where the disease was formerly unheard of. Flood mitigation would also have to be addressed for the communities facing extreme rainfall or coastal areas affected by rising sea levels. Drought and famine would also become more prevalent issues as well.

Ambiguity and controversy surrounding global warming will make it difficult to establish mitigation and emergency management protocols. For this reason, it will be imperative that research on the matter continues in order to solidify trends and reduce uncertainties about future predictions. You should take steps to ensure that you are monitoring research data produced by reputable agencies. Moreover, it would be beneficial for you to establish relationships with environmental organizations in order to increase understanding and awareness. Prevention and precautionary actions, within reason, should be implemented as recommended.

### 12.6.2 Pole Reversals

Another unsuspected hazard is a pole reversal. A **pole reversal** is a change in the earth's magnetic fields. Our planet is surrounded by a magnetic field, which is generated by a magnet that runs through the center of the earth, called a dipole. The dipole has a north and south end, but it does not correspond with the geographic north and south. The poles of the dipole are offset from true north and south bearings approximately 11 degrees (NGDC, 2006). This magnetic field is measured according to vertical intensity, horizontal intensity, and magnetic declination. The force is not uniform across the globe, but varies according to location.

Scientists are closely monitoring the intensity of earth's geomagnetism. By analyzing minerals in the earth's magma and crust, geophysicists have determined the orientation and strengths of the dipole (Glatzmaier and Olson, 2005). The information gathered indicates that the magnetic orientation of the dipole has repeatedly reversed itself over time. What comes into question is the frequency and time frame that these reversals take place. Some scientists believe that a pole reversal has occurred approximately every 200,000 years over the last 100 million years. It is also believed that the most recent reversal would have taken place 750,000–780,000 years ago (NGDC, 2006). Other scientists refute this theory by stating that pole reversals happen much quicker. They assert reversals take place nearly 1000 times faster than previously observed (Coe et al., 1995).

Scientists do not have any conclusive evidence as to the cause or speed of pole reversals. They now know that lava flows have a connection with the magnetic fields. Researchers have used cooled lava to study the changes in direction and frequency of a reversal (NRC, 2005). The theories about reversals are generally divided into two groups. The first is based on the hypothesis that intense volcanic eruptions can alter the regeneration of the earth's magnetic field (Jacobs, 1984). The second theory states that reversals occur as a result of "irregular oscillations" of the earth's magnetic field (Jacobs, 1984). Research is currently underway to test both theories.

In any case, evidence seems to suggest that the strength of the magnetic field is decreasing. The deterioration of earth's magnetic field does not indicate that a reversal is imminent however (Hoffman, 1995). Scientists have stated that even with the unknown variables and conflicting timetables surrounding polarity reversal, a reversal would take at least 1000 years (NGDC, 2006). Should this occur, it is speculated that the magnetic field would weaken and produce several or different poles.

Animals that rely on magnetism for navigational purposes would be impacted by a pole reversal (NGDC, 2006). Pole reversals may not produce catastrophic impact for humankind. However, technology that depends on geomagnetism would be affected. Luckily, technology can be adapted if the changes of the field are monitored and acted upon. Dealing with possible pole reversals is somewhat similar to the response to global warming. Research on the phenomena must continue. Measures must also be taken to anticipate possible problems and react effectively.

### 12.6.3 Asteroid Strikes

Viewing meteor impact as a hazard is relatively recent. Prior to the 1960s, researchers did not believe that there was any threat of extraterrestrial collisions. However, this view began to change as means were developed to expose scientists to the history and effects of cratering across the earth as well as on other planets. As science progressed, researchers began to identify the presence and movement of objects that could pose a threat to our well-being (French, 1998).

Every day, foreign objects enter earth's atmosphere. The majority of them burn up quickly and do not pose a threat to humans (NASA, 2006a, b). However, researchers seem to feel that a major terrestrial impact is not a matter of "if" but "when." There are several types of terrestrial impact structures (see Figure 12-7). Scientists call those structures nearest to the earth near-earth objects (NEOs). An **NEO** is made up of mostly ice and dirt particles. Gravitational pull is attributed as the cause of NEOs entering earth's atmosphere (NASA, 2006a, b). The measure of their proximity to earth is based on astronomical units (AU). One AU is equivalent to approximately 92,955,807.5 miles. An asteroid that comes within 0.05 AU or less of the earth is deemed a **potentially hazardous asteroid** (PHA). As of February 3, 2006, 3933 NEOs have been discovered. 748 of these are classified as PHAs (NASA, 2006a, b).

There are many issues surrounding meteorite impact that make it difficult to mitigate and prepare for. One expert in this area addresses three (French, 1998) (Figure 12-9). First, large meteorite impacts are rare. As such, it is challenging for researchers to study their effects. More vital to emergency managers, it is hard for people to comprehend the danger of an impact. With no perceived threat, those involved in emergency management must go to greater lengths to legitimize the significance of an impact. Secondly, the predicted energy a major impact would produce is greater than that produced by earthquakes or volcanoes. French (1998) points out that "the impact of an object only a few kilometers across (still smaller than many known asteroids and comets) can release more energy in seconds than the whole Earth releases (through volcanism, earthquakes, tectonic processes, and

**Figure 12-9**

| Asteroid | A relatively small, inactive, rocky body orbiting the Sun. |
|---|---|
| Comet | A relatively small, at times active, object whose ices can vaporize in sunlight forming an atmosphere (coma) of dust and gas and, sometimes, a tail of dust and/or gas. |
| Meteoroid | A small particle from a comet or asteroid orbiting the Sun. |
| Meteor | The light phenomena which results when a meteoroid enters the Earth's atmosphere and vaporizes; a shooting star. |
| Meteorite | A meteoroid that survives its passage through the Earth's atmosphere and lands upon the Earth's surface. |

Types of terrestrial impact structures. Accessed at http://neo.jpl.nasa.gov/faq/#diff.

**Figure 12-10**

The Barringer Meteor Crater illustrated how damaging even a small meteor can be if it strikes earth. Photo courtesy by author.

heat flow) in hundreds or thousands of years." The final issue differentiates meteoroid impact from other energy-expending disasters and their instantaneous effects. Upon impact, major energy is expended and a massive crater is formed (Figure 12-9). The striking of the earth would produce a massive crater such as the Barringer Meteor Crater in Arizona (Figure 12-10). It would also send shock waves out, causing "immediate and catastrophic changes" (French, 1998). A few of the predicted repercussions could include massive earthquakes, volcanic eruptions, and even tsunamis (if it were to hit the ocean). The Chelyabinsk meteor, for example, entered the earth's atmosphere undetected over Russia in February 2013. The accompanying shock wave caused enough damage to over 7000 building structures in six cities to indirectly injure about 1500 people.

Scientists have created the **Torino Scale** in an attempt to predict the impact of a meteoroid strike. The Torino Scale describes the possibility of collision along with the resulting impact. Contingency planning by emergency managers becomes vital if the impact of a PHA becomes imminent. Astronomers and emergency managers need to increase their relations in order to devise warning and preparedness measures for the possibility of such a catastrophic occurrence.

### 12.6.4 Biological Threats

Because of globalization, disease can spread rapidly throughout the entire world. The ease of travel and international economic relations could easily trigger a pandemic in other nations. In other words, disease spreads at the speed and extent of travel and commercial activities. Below are a few of the biological threats that must be considered by emergency management and public health personnel.

**Severe Acute Respiratory Syndrome (SARS). Severe acute respiratory syndrome (SARS)** is a viral respiratory disease caused by a coronavirus (SARS-CoV). The incubation period for SARS is 2–14 days. During this time, it is not believed that the person is infectious. After symptoms develop, the person is considered highly infectious until at least 10 days after their fever breaks. The symptoms of SARS are similar to the flu. Patients who contract the disease have a high fever and suffer from chills, headaches, and body aches. They usually develop a dry cough and eventually pneumonia (CDC, 2006b).

Medical personnel have been looking into the variations through which this disease is transmitted (CDC, 2006b). However, it is believed that SARS is spread through person-to-person contact. Individuals can contract the disease from others who are infected. This may be through physical contact with bodily fluid through holding hands or kissing. Physical contact does not mean sharing the same space environment however. Germs may be spread via droplets from a person's cough or sneeze.

The CDC registered the first outbreak in Southern China in November 2002. SARS quickly spread and was considered a global threat in March 2003. During the 2002–2003 epidemic, 8098 people contracted SARS, and all of them were reported in people living or traveling to Asia. Probable cases were reported in 31 countries including Vietnam, China, Taiwan, Singapore, Canada, the United States, and Germany (Lipsitch et al., 2003). Of those infected, 774 individuals died.

By July 2003, the outbreak began to temper and the World Health Organization declared the end of the epidemic (WHO, 2006). Nonetheless, the CDC reports that they are monitoring several potential SARS cases throughout the world. The National Intelligence Agency concurs with a report that states that while SARS has not killed as many people as more common diseases, it is still a threat because it tends to outbreak in areas "with broad commercial links," which would accelerate the spread of the disease and exacerbate its effects worldwide (NIA, 2006).

Measures taken to deal with SARS vary dramatically based on the current threat. Doctors recommend that basic hygiene measures are always followed, such as washing hands and avoiding the touching of the mouth, eyes, and nose. However, once SARS has been identified, other steps must be taken. The National Institute for Occupational Safety and Health recommends that a respirator be worn by personnel in contact with a patient (NIOSH, 2006). The respirator should be rated N-95. Immediate intervention should also be made to isolate any confirmed cases. This is known as a **quarantine**. Quarantines should be set up for those that are suspected to have come in contact with the disease. Lipsitch et al. makes the point that quarantine and isolation will be beneficial only as long as the number of cases present can be contained (2003). Quarantine numbers may initially be high. However, these numbers will begin to drop as individuals are either sent for treatment in isolation or confirmed healthy. Isolation will allow for treatment without spreading the disease further.

**West Nile Virus.** The **West Nile virus** (WNV) is a flavivirus that is dependent upon mosquitoes as vectors. It is a seasonal disease that is more common when mosquitoes begin to breed and thrive during spring, summer, and early fall. WNV affects people in different ways. There are three severe diseases caused by the virus: West Nile encephalitis, West Nile meningitis, and West Nile meningoencephalitis. These are classified as neuroinvasive because they attack the nervous system. West Nile fever is another less invasive reaction to the virus (CDC, 2006i).

As its name implies, West Nile originated in the Middle East, but it has also affected West Asia and parts of Africa. It is unknown how the virus was introduced to the United States. The CDC believes the disease was introduced in early 1999. In 2002, the World Health Organization tracked an outbreak of WNV across thirty-nine states. Moreover, evidence of the virus has been found in 43 states (WHO, 2002).

The most common transmission of WNV is the bite of an infected mosquito. Mosquitoes become infected when they feed on infected birds. They may then transmit the disease to other animals or humans. CDC has also tracked the transmission of the disease through blood transfusions, organ transplants, and breastfeeding. However, they note that these methods are infrequent and comprise a small proportion of WNV cases (CDC, 2006b).

WNV primarily affects birds, but it is also a threat to humans, horses, and some other types of mammals (NBII, 2006). In areas where the WNV is more common, birds and other affected mammals have developed the necessary antibodies to fight off the disease. In North America, where the disease is relatively new, WNV has proved particularly virulent. Of the 3737 people reportedly infected, 214 people have died. The disease seems to affect persons over the age of 50 more severely, but all people are at risk.

Proper outbreak prevention and control measures require a vector monitoring system. Mosquitoes and birds must be effactually monitored for WNV. If these systems are in place, then the amount of time before human infections occur can be increased (CDC, 2003). Response to WNV must include the prevention of mosquito bites. When spending time near mosquito-infested areas, it is important to apply repellent to exposed skin. People can also reduce the chances of being infected by removing standing water or other elements that may attract mosquitoes. Installing or repairing door and window screens will also prevent bites (CDC, 2006c).

There is no specific treatment for WNV. At the present time, there is no human inoculation available, though several laboratories are conducting pertinent research and hope to introduce a vaccine shortly (CDC, 2006e). Medical care involves "intensive support therapy"; this can include hospitalization and prevention of secondary infections such as pneumonia (CDC, 2006d).

**Avian Influenza** (Bird Flu). **Avian flu** is an infection that stems from viruses commonly found in birds. The disease is frequently found in the intestines of wild birds, although it typically has no effect on undomesticated fowl. However, the viruses can be contracted by domesticated birds through excretions and secretions. Birds may come in contact with the disease by exposure to excrement in things such as dirty cages. As more virulent strains infect domestic flocks, the birds become sick and begin to die. This has serious impact on bird farms as well as bird feed producers and distributors. Outbreaks of avian flu have been reported in birds in 14 European and Asian countries. For these reasons, the USDA has an embargo in place preventing the import of birds from countries reporting the disease (CDC, 2005).

Avian flu is differentiated from seasonal flu in that its viruses come from birds. There are other significant differences that must be taken into account as well. Seasonal flu comes from influenza viruses, but there are only three subtypes of seasonal flu found in humans (CDC, 2006d). In contrast, avian flu has 25 known subtypes, and these can combine to form different influenza strains (CDC, 2006d).

Because of the many subtypes of the avian flu, it is not known exactly how the disease is contracted by humans. At this point, doctors believe that the confirmed cases all resulted from contact with infected birds or contaminated areas (CDC, 2006d). Prevention measures should therefore include staying away from areas of known outbreak, limiting the handling of birds, or avoiding surfaces where birds have been present. Regardless of this admonition, avian flu has been found in humans in seven European and Asian countries. In 2006, there were 165 confirmed cases of humans with avian flu, of which 88 have reportedly died (WHO, 2006). The disease also has serious economic consequences. As an example, economists estimate that the avian flu would cause a decrease of 29% in exports, 8% in tourism, and 2% in private consumption in Thailand alone (PECC, 2005). In November of 2005, the World Bank issued a statement saying that avian flu "poses one of the biggest uncertainties in the generally positive outlook for East Asian economies" (World Bank, 2005). The U.S. State Department has also issued travel advisories for any American planning to spend time in one of the reported countries. They warn that in the case of a pandemic, Consular Affairs will be severely restricted in any aid they can provide (State Department, 2005).

World Health officials are monitoring current outbreaks in Europe and Asia. The current fear among them is that a strain of the avian flu may mutate and make itself easily transmittable between humans. This could prove disastrous as humans have no natural immunity toward this type of virus (CDC, 2006g). In addition, there is no vaccine to protect humans from the avian flu. The CDC reports that scientists have been researching the development of a vaccine since 2005 (CDC, 2005).

Patients that present themselves for treatment and display symptoms of avian flu should be questioned as to their recent travel history. If avian flu is suspected, the patient should be treated in isolation following the prescribed treatment for a SARS patient. However, because the disease is so new, the CDC is reviewing their treatment recommendations.

**Hoof and Mouth Disease. Hoof and mouth disease** (HMD, also known as foot and mouth disease) is a highly infectious disease that occurs among livestock—not people. Animals such as goats, cows, sheep, and other cloven-hoofed mammals are particularly susceptible to the disease. However, camels, llamas, and alpacas have an established natural defense against HMD (Merck Veterinarian Manual, 2003). HMD symptoms consist of fever and blisters that develop on the hooves, in the mouth, and in some cases on the snout of the infected animal. The disease is caused by *Apthovirus*. Its affects result in high mortality among young livestock (FAO, 2002). The disease is very rarely transmitted to humans, and human symptoms are generally mild.

HMD can be spread through a variety of ways. The most common means of transmission is interaction of infected animals with healthy animals. An infected animal can spread the virus by breathing as well as through any excretions or secretions (Merck Veterinarian Manual, 2003). Nursing animals are at risk of passing the disease on to their young through their milk. The virus can survive apart from a carrier for any number of days depending on the host material. The disease has an incubation period of 2–14 days (Merck Veterinarian Manual, 2003).

The UN has declared HMD endemic throughout Africa, Asia, the Middle East, and parts of South America. Europe, North America, the Caribbean, and Pacific nations remain free from the disease, with noted exceptions that have been quickly contained (FAO, 2002). The major concern with HMD around the world is its economic impact. The ease of transmission and loss of animals can severely constrict trade.

The countries in which HMD is endemic attempt to protect their animals through vaccinations. The vaccinations are not a foolproof method, however, as they do not protect against every strain of HMD (Merck Veterinarian Manual, 2003). When the disease has been identified, the reaction is usually to eradicate it by killing the entire stock. Slaughtered animals should be burned or buried immediately (Merck Veterinarian Manual, 2003). However, James and Rushton examine alternate approaches different communities have taken in attempts to identify the most cost-effective method of prevention and/or eradication (2002).

Emergency managers and public health officials have not paid much attention to this type of disease in the past. Part of this is due to the fact that it is an agricultural disease rather than a public health crisis. However, it is now becoming more important to control HMD and protect agricultural economics interests of potentially affected communities. A system should consequently be in place that will:

1. Detect and manage an outbreak
2. Prevent introduction of a foreign disease
3. Respond to and eradicate an outbreak

As with other types of diseases, success of this system depends on proper coordination among local, state, national, and international governments (Torres et al., 2002). It is also important to note that the diseases described earlier are less

> ## FOR EXAMPLE
>
> ### HMD
>
> During the 2001 outbreak of HMD in the United Kingdom, more than 6.5 million animals had to be slaughtered. The country took special precautions in disposing the carcasses. Nevertheless, it became impossible for farmers to bury all of their animals, and communities were concerned about emissions released from pyre burnings (Scudamore et al., 2002). Many farmers were adversely affected from the temporary loss of their livelihoods.

probable than the common flu or other infections that inflict animals. They also may be less deadly than nearly eradicated diseases like the plague. However, you should be aware that these diseases may appear naturally or in conjunction with a terrorist attack. They will require close collaboration among you and the medical, public health, and veterinary personnel.

One of the important steps to take after an outbreak affects humans is to request resources from the **Strategic National Stockpile**. This is a collection of antibiotics, vaccines, antiviral drugs, and other pharmaceuticals stored by the federal government. When requested, this can be sent from one of several undisclosed locations around the United States to an affected area within 12 hours. The community will then be required to break down the supplies and transfer them to sites for treatment (points of distribution). This will require a great deal of coordination among emergency managers, public health organizations, and volunteers.

### 12.6.5 Computer/Information Technology Hazards

Another underestimated hazard concerns computers and information technology. In his very important study on the matter, E.L. Quarantelli (1997a) uncovers several social problems resulting from the information/communication revolution. The problems he discusses may have a significant impact on disaster response and recovery operations. The challenges are as follows:

▲ New computers and communication technology will undoubtedly result in information overload. The ease of communications often exceeds human capacity to absorb information.

▲ Technological advances will likely result in information that is lost or outdated. For instance, you may seek information to assist with your response operations, but these websites may be outdated or defunct.

▲ Improved technology will likely lead to the diffusion of inappropriate information. Rumors about or after disasters could spread quickly because of modern computers and today's communication equipment.

▲ Advanced computer equipment may lead to the diminution of nonverbal communication. This could hinder your ability to understand the information being relayed after a disaster.

▲ Technology may make intra- and intergroup communication more difficult in the future. The sharing of information and coordination of actors is difficult at best in most disaster situations. Computers and communication technology could conceivably magnify this problem in the future.

▲ Today's technology is not supported by an adequate infrastructure and culture. For instance, some organizations or communities do not develop backup systems for computerized data bases. This information will most likely be lost after a disaster.

▲ Computers will produce new types of disasters that we will have to deal with in the future. For example, a small fire at a Bell Telephone switching center in Chicago caused severe disruption in the transportation, retail, and financial sectors (Quarantelli, 1997a, p. 103).

In addition to the problems described by Quarantelli, you should be aware of other threats relating to computers. A **computer virus** is a program that contains malicious codes. It reproduces itself and overloads the infected computer, causing it to run slowly or ineffectively. **Worms** are similar to viruses, but they are generated over many computer systems due to Internet, networks, and e-mail connections. **Hackers**, individuals that log into others' computers illegally, may also enter programs to run or disrupt them from afar. Cyberterrorism is another threat that must be considered. **Cyberterrorism** is the use of computers and the Internet to plan or carry out attacks.

Such problems could create additional problems or disasters for you and your communities. These threats can hinder response and recovery operations (as technology and computers are becoming increasingly vital in emergency management today). Furthermore, hackers and cyberterrorists may enter computers to disrupt postdisaster operations. These individuals have already managed to enter government computers on occasion to dispatch fire personnel to false calls or meddle with Department of Defense records. There is also the possibility that they could control gas lines, water mains, and other critical infrastructure remotely. The unintended negative consequences of computers and information technology must therefore be considered by you as an emergency manager. In fact, this hazard has probably not received the attention it deserves for the future.

### 12.6.6 Responding to Computer/Information Technology Disasters

Because of the newness of computer and information technology problems, there are no definitive solutions for emergency managers. However, the following steps can be taken to minimize the negative impact of the information/communication revolution on your organization or community. Some of these measures may include:

1. Filtering incoming information to prevent an overload of information about disasters

2. Ensuring information provided or received is as accurate and up-to-date as possible

3. Halting the distribution of incorrect information and using the media, Internet, and social media to correct false reports

4. Attempting to be as clear as possible in nonverbal communication (e.g., especially when you are communicating via e-mail or text messaging)

5. Acknowledging the drawbacks of technology and creating redundant systems to prevent overreliance on computers and modern communication equipment

6. Being aware of new types of technological disasters and understanding how these might adversely impact subsequent response operations

7. Using antivirus software and firewalls to reduce the possibility that hackers and cyberterrorists will enter your systems and create denial of service impacts

8. Finding experts who can help you address the problems created by hackers and cyberterrorists

By addressing the negative aspects of the computer/information revolution, you will be able to foster resilience as an emergency manager. This will require closer contact with information technology specialists in the future. It will also be imperative that you consider the need for continuity of operations (COOP) in your community. **COOP** is a goal to maintain the functioning of government in time of disasters and is somewhat similar to business continuity. It deals with computer systems as well as personnel staffing, alternate EOC locations, and lines of succession. If the emergency management office and other government departments cannot operate after a disaster, response and recovery activities will surely be limited, delayed, or ineffective.

## SELF-CHECK

- What is environmental degradation and how is it related to global warming and climate change?
- What is a pole reversal and what are the possible effects of one occurring?
- Are meteor impacts probable? Are they possible?
- What are the different types of biological threats facing us today?
- Has technology produced new disasters?
- What can be done to deal effectively with the new hazards that threaten us?

## 12.7 Increased Vulnerability

As an emergency manager, you should recognize that hazards are not the only concern regarding future disasters. As society changes over time, our vulnerability to disasters may increase as well. Augmented vulnerability comes from poverty, population changes, increased diversity, industrialization, improper land use and construction, and weak emergency management institutions. There are also many other factors that increase our vulnerability to hazards. Interestingly, it is this vulnerability that we are most able to limit and control to reduce future disasters.

### 12.7.1 Persistent Poverty

Although poverty has been reduced around the world, it is still is a major problem in many countries. In 2010, for example, 1.22 billion people in the developing world lived on less than $1.25 a day (World Bank, 2013). Today, the annual salary in East Asian countries is only $1,000. Others in some developing nations are found in more dire situations. Individuals finding themselves in these circumstances are living in conditions of **absolute poverty**. This means that they do not have sufficient resources to take care of basic needs such as food and shelter.

In contrast to these situations, the salaries in industrial countries are much higher. They average $20,000 or even more. Those living in the United States are very well off, and their income has increased dramatically over time. However, there are still large segments of the population that are poor. The overall poverty rate in our country is 16%. Minorities comprise a larger share of those found in poverty. For example, 24.7% of African-Americans and 21.9% of Hispanics live at or below the poverty line.

The causes for poverty are highly political, ranging from capitalist exploitation to a poor work ethic. People also view a lack of education, overspending, and addiction to vices as culprits. Regardless of the source, poverty has a bearing on disaster vulnerability. The lack of resources limits one's ability to buy safe housing and ensure personal and family preparedness. Poverty constrains choices regarding insurance and hinders effective family response activities. It is one of the many factors that make some people more vulnerable than others.

### 12.7.2 Growing Population and Urbanization

Changes in population are having a huge impact on vulnerability. As of 2013, the world population is estimated to be at about 7.11 billion people. This growth has not stopped. Population experts expect enormous growth through the year 2050. It is anticipated that total world population will soar over 9.3 billion at the midpoint of this century. But what does population size have to do with disasters? Vulnerability is increased when more people are exposed to hazards. Also, with the increased demand for water and food, droughts and famine will likely increase. When resources are scarce due to large populations, there is the possibility of conflicts over resources as well.

While the population is growing, it is also changing as well. The elderly segment of the population is much larger than in the past. In most cases, the elderly are not as able to protect themselves when earthquakes, floods, and tornadoes occur. Although the elderly segment is larger than in the past, the largest proportion of the population is in the age range of 15–24. Youth may be better able to protect themselves from different hazards than the aged populations. However, younger individuals, especially infants and children, will not have sufficient knowledge to deal with hazards. Many are particularly vulnerable if their parents are not present when a disaster occurs.

Population growth also pressures people to migrate to new areas. Many families are leaving the rural communities where their family had lived for generations and are moving to the cities to seek jobs. Numerous cities are located in seismically active areas, along the coast, or in the path of potential lava flows. But such urbanization has a bearing on disaster vulnerability. These areas are obviously vulnerable to major earthquakes, hurricanes, or volcanic activity. When buildings are placed closely together, fires will also spread more quickly. Buildings that house a large number of residents or workers will also kill more people when they are damaged or collapse. Population growth and urbanization should be recognized as major concerns to you as an emergency manager.

### 12.7.3 Increased Diversity

Many United States cities are now quite diverse with large representations of immigrants from all over the world. Even smaller cities are collectively home to hundreds or thousands of immigrants. This diversity is what makes the United States the "melting pot" of the world. Such diversity may have an impact upon disaster vulnerability however. Many ethnic groups see hazards differently. Some may adopt a fatalistic attitude or fail to take any precautions for disasters (Quarantelli, 1992, p. 21).

Diversity can also affect disasters in a variety of other ways (Quarantelli, 1992, p. 21). The most obvious difficulty is that the different languages spoken by ethnic groups complicate warning processes. Many of the immigrants do not speak or read English fluently. Because not everyone will understand the recommended protective actions, notifications must be given in several languages. Language barriers also complicate the delivery of disaster relief and recovery assistance. The deaf and blind are also vulnerable to disasters because of their inability to hear or see.

Furthermore, some ethnic groups may have extended friends and family in the area that they can turn to for support. However, other immigrant groups may be small and distrustful toward outsiders (Quarantelli, 1992, p. 21). All things being equal, the more heterogeneous a society is, the more difficult it will be to manage disasters (Quarantelli, 1992, p. 21).

### 12.7.4 Further Industrialization

The increased use of technology may also add to our vulnerability. In one study on the matter, Quarantelli wrote that "there are new and escalating kinds of technological accident and mishap which were almost non-existent prior to the Second World War and which will increasingly result in disasters [sic]" (1992, p. 12). Since this time, the world has become even more industrialized. There are now greater risks to nearby populations. Possible vulnerabilities are in the chemical and nuclear areas.

The widespread use of chemicals also has an impact on vulnerability. As mentioned in Chapter 1, the 1984 Bhopal disaster was an example of a very serious industrial disaster. A pesticide production plant located in India accidentally released 40 tons of methyl isocyanate (MIC). The gas rolled along the ground through the streets and killed thousands instantly. People did not know what they were dealing with and could not take necessary precaution measures. Even doctors did not know how to treat those who were affected in the incident. Although final numbers are in dispute, it is estimated that over 15,000 people were killed in the short term and another 15,000 died due to related illnesses over time. It is argued that an additional 200,000–600,000 people were injured due to the chemical release. Even though the accident occurred over 20 years ago, reports in 2004 suggest that contamination is still present. Chemicals provide many advantages for life, but they may present complications for first responders, medical care providers, emergency managers, and environmental specialists.

Nuclear material is also a concern today. Before the nuclear bomb was developed in the 1940s, we did not have to worry about such problems. Today, the manufacturing, transportation, and use of nuclear material all pose threats to people in the United States and around the world. The Three Mile Island accident illustrated the extreme difficulties associated with people's concern about nuclear material. Citizens did not trust the information provided by government officials and the evacuation was problematic. Another example involving nuclear material is the Chernobyl accident near Kiev. As mentioned in Chapter 1, this disaster occurred in 1986 and is the worst accident in the history of nuclear power. Because the plant was not properly constructed, maintained, and operated, a plume of radioactive fallout drifted from parts of the Soviet Union all the way around the world in the Northern Hemisphere. Fifty-six people (including some children) died in the short term. Forty-seven of these deaths were emergency responders who did not have sufficient knowledge about radioactive material. There has been debate as to the long-term effects of Chernobyl, although some scientists worry the fallout will cause cancers and lead to the early deaths of many others. What is also worrisome is that there are many more nuclear power plants in operation today. More plants might be anticipated in the future as fuel costs continue to rise. While most have or will have adequate safeguards, the dangerous nature of nuclear material complicates response and recovery operations for emergency managers and first responders.

### 12.7.5 Internationalization

The world truly is a global village. The shrinking of distance and disappearance of national borders are beneficial in that it allows for additional trade and commerce. However, globalization is not without its drawbacks. A disaster in one part of the world may adversely affect those in other countries. For instance, when an earthquake affected Japan in 1995, computer markets in other countries were severely disrupted. The same could be said of the 9/11 disaster in New York City. It had serious implications for international finance corporations. Globalization could also increase the spread of other disasters such as infectious disease outbreaks. Travel to and from exotic places may augment the possibility of epidemics.

Internationalization also has a bearing on vulnerability to conflict-type disasters. Improved communication and media capabilities are able to relay different cultural viewpoints around the world. Unfortunately, this could create animosity among some extreme Islamic fundamentalists and others in western nations. Such clashing attitudes and values were responsible for the terrorist attacks in the United States on September 11, 2001. This, in turn, led to the war in Afghanistan and the war in Iraq. More of this type of conflict is possible in the future.

### 12.7.6 Improper Land Use and Construction

Vulnerability has also increased due to location and building decisions. In some situations, the most hazardous land is also the most desirable real estate. For instance, people are moving to coastal areas for the warm weather and beautiful scenery. This has a significant impact upon future disasters however. Coastal property is more vulnerable to flooding and hurricanes than other land. Not only are there homes in these areas, but there are also large hotels, casinos, restaurants, bars, and other gathering places such as clubs. People also like to live close to mountains, which can cause complications when there are landslides or wildfires. In 2006, a town in the Philippines was buried due to a landslide and 1500 people were killed. Insufficient attention is given to slope stability. Major forest fires have broken out in Arizona, New Mexico, and California in recent years. Hundreds of homes have been destroyed as a result. Location choices therefore have a significant impact upon vulnerability. Unfortunately, we seem to overlook this important lesson.

Construction also plays a role in disaster vulnerability. The devastation of Hurricane Andrew was not universally felt. Neighborhoods built by certain contractors or developers faired better or worse than others. In many cases, the design of the buildings was flawed (e.g., because of ornamental roofs and too many gables). In other cases, shortcuts in building processes or materials were taken. For instance, roofs were not properly fastened to walls and the foundation. Material such as chipboard often loses its strength when exposed to excessive wind and rain. This, in addition to poor inspection practices, left many homes and businesses vulnerable to the hurricane. Ironically, our nation has yet to universally adopt more stringent building code standards.

### 12.7.7 Weak Emergency Management Institutions

Increased vulnerability also results from the intentional or unintentional neglect of emergency management institutions. There are a number of reasons why this occurs (McEntire, 2007). Politicians do not always take disasters seriously. They are often more concerned about short-term priorities and choose not to see beyond the next election. Citizens do not think much about disasters until they occur, so priority is often given to other issues such as transportation systems, law enforcement, or education. Emergency management also has to compete with scores of other governmental programs, and it often fails to gain the attention and resources needed to prevent or deal effectively with disasters. Other departments will sometimes ignore your requests to prepare for disasters since they have their own issues to worry about.

There are also far too few emergency managers in the United States (McEntire, 2012). Many cities do not have a full-time designated emergency manager. The vast majority fail to hire one emergency manager for every 25,000 people residing in their jurisdiction (as has been recommended by FEMA). Emergency managers also lack adequate EOCs, equipment, and operating budgets. These problems are especially detrimental in that the workload of emergency managers has increased dramatically over the past few years due to more frequent and severe disasters, new homeland security concerns and programs, the preference of cities to obtain additional resources through grants, and increased desires to prevent disasters and mitigate their effects. The capacity of emergency management institutions has not kept pace with the expectations they are to meet.

In addition, our vulnerability is increased when politicians appoint unqualified persons to positions of great responsibility. Historically, the post of FEMA Director or Administrator has been given to a colleague of the president or to someone who had supported the campaign or party of the administration. This can cause major problems for policy direction and morale in this emerging profession. This mistake is not limited to the federal level however. The New Orleans Levee Board was comprised of people who were political appointees as well. After Hurricane Katrina, it was revealed that the board spent money on fountains and other projects for casinos, but not for the levees as intended. As we saw with Hurricane Katrina, even the most powerful country in the world can be unprepared for a disaster when emergency management institutions are dismissed as unimportant or otherwise neglected.

### 12.7.8  Other Factors

Not all of the activities and changes taking place in society increase disaster vulnerability. In fact, there are several positive transformations that are reducing vulnerability. For instance, there are more democracies today than there were just 30 years ago. This is good for emergency management as this type of government is less able to cover up the causes of disasters. Politicians cannot keep information from people as was the case in the Soviet Union in the immediate aftermath of the nuclear accident of Chernobyl. Events like 9/11 and Hurricane Katrina have also brought further support and funding to emergency management. Improved engineering practices and advances in technology facilitate mitigation and the development of better warning systems. Regional approaches to emergency management are also improving the possible uses of mutual aid.

While there are many positive changes taking place, there are numerous other factors that are augmenting disaster vulnerability. Many of these have yet to be recognized but may have significant impact upon disasters and emergency management. For instance:

- ▲ The National Flood Insurance Program (NFIP) may be augmenting vulnerability to this hazard instead of decreasing it (because NFIP allows development in flood-prone areas if certain criteria are met).
- ▲ The age and condition of dams and levees are expected to lead to more breaches in the future.
- ▲ The focus on terrorism at the expense of other hazards has caused our vulnerability to rise in regard to natural disasters.
- ▲ Increasingly complicated and intertwined infrastructure systems raise the probability of more complex disasters in the future.
- ▲ An overreliance on technological solutions to the disaster problem masks other more fundamental causes of vulnerability in society.
- ▲ The reorganization of FEMA after 9/11 has created considerable confusion, at least initially, regarding the workings of the National Response Plan.
- ▲ The consolidation of dispatch centers across many cities may prohibit their capacity to answer calls in major emergency or disaster situations.

▲ The rising dropout rate of students in high school hinders community education (a disturbing fact since knowledge is positively related to disaster preparedness).

▲ The increasing reliance on cell phones and VOIP may complicate the location of victims after emergencies and disasters (as this equipment does not always tell exactly where the call is coming from).

▲ The federal government is starting to delegate disaster responsibility to local and state governments, but officials at these levels have not recognized the impact this will have on emergency management.

▲ Urban development (which results in the destruction of agricultural land) and further reliance on foreign nations to produce food for the United States could increase the chance of famine in major drought episodes in the future.

▲ The additional layers of bureaucracy under the Department of Homeland Security have increased the organizational distance between the FEMA administrator and the president of the United States.

▲ The overreliance of Americans on fast food and neglect of cooking skills may complicate people's ability to care for nutritional needs when disasters occur.

▲ Additional use of antibiotic medicines and soaps may cause diseases to mutate and become increasingly resistant to medical treatment.

▲ The cutting down of trees will lead to more flooding and mudslides as there are insufficient root systems to absorb water and maintain soil stability.

▲ People's expectations that the government should care for them in time of disaster decrease their ability to take care of their own needs and those of others.

▲ The building of new jumbo jets (holding over 500 passengers) will place extra burdens on responders, emergency medical care providers, and coroners if they are involved in crashes.

▲ Weak border control (due to corporate desires to keep wages low and the promotion of a better way of life for illegal aliens) increases the vulnerability of our nation to terrorist attacks.

▲ Further obesity in the United States may complicate rescue operations from confined spaces, lead to poor health, and increase susceptibility to various diseases.

▲ The presence of more children and adults in care centers today may limit the ability of such providers to ensure the well-being of their residents after disasters.

▲ The reduction of back stock in supermarkets may limit the presence of needed supplies before and after a disaster takes place.

▲ The de-emphasis of close-knit family and neighborhood relationships may hold back community recovery after disaster.

▲ Federal disaster assistance for victims and communities may subsidize risk and discourage increased attention toward mitigation.

These causes of vulnerability, along with many others not mentioned here, must be addressed if disasters are to be reduced in the future. As an emergency manager, you must develop an ability to see and correct the linkages that have bearing on the probability and impact of disasters. This skill is imperative if disaster resilience is to be promoted in the future.

---

### FOR EXAMPLE

#### Is There a Doctor in the House?

The 2003 heat wave in France illustrated the deadly consequences of not assisting vulnerable populations. During France's vacation holiday, temperatures soared to record highs. The elderly could not support the excessive heat, and over 14,000 elderly people died as a result. The deaths sparked a major public debate. Surviving friends and relatives criticized the government for not ensuring that sufficient care was given to those who passed away. The government suggested that family members did not take care of their own elderly parents. The government also blamed the doctors and family practitioners who were on vacation in August during the heat wave. In return, the doctors argued that the government did not issue an emergency recall of all physicians. One thing was not debated however. The elderly were severely affected by the extreme temperatures and human behavior and activities.

---

## SELF-CHECK

- What are some social factors that are leading to increased vulnerability?
- Does population growth impact urbanization? What does this mean for the emergency manager?
- Do different languages add complications to disaster response and recovery operations? If so, how?
- How does internationalization, land-use, and construction practices impact vulnerability?
- What concerns should you have regarding the status of emergency management in the United States today?
- What are the other unrecognized causes of vulnerability? Can you think of any other factors that augment the probability of disaster?

---

## SUMMARY

As an emergency manager, you must recognize that disasters are becoming more frequent and intense. You must be able to deal with all types of events and foresee new hazards that will certainly threaten us. Natural disasters, technological disasters, and violence and terrorism have unique and complicated features. It is imperative that you learn from prior response and recovery operations and anticipate new hazards and how disasters will change in the future. In addition, it is vital that you understand the predominant and multiple causes of vulnerability so you can work with others to address them. Only by learning from the past and anticipating the future will you be able to promote resilience in your community.

## KEY TERMS

| | |
|---|---|
| **Absolute poverty** | A condition where people do not have sufficient resources to take care of basic needs such as food and shelter |
| **Associated hazard** | A natural hazard agent that typically occurs at the same time as the primary hazard (e.g., hurricanes produce flooding). |
| **Avian flu** | An infection that stems from viruses commonly found in birds. Also known as the "Asian flu" or the "bird flu." |
| **Built environment** | The structures, technology, and infrastructure created by humans. |
| **Cascading disaster** | An event that triggers additional hazards or impacts. |
| **Climate change** | An alteration of the earth's temperature and weather patterns. |
| **Cold zone** | An area not affected and can only be accessed by clean (or decontaminated) individuals. |
| **Continuity of operations** | A goal to maintain the functioning of government in time of disasters. |
| **Complex or compound disaster** | A disaster event that involves multiple variables. |
| **Complex emergency** | A humanitarian crisis that involves an extreme amount of violence among different ethnic groups coupled with political instability, poor economic conditions, weak law enforcement capabilities, and disaster conditions of some sort (e.g., drought and famine). |
| **Computer virus** | A program that contains malicious codes. |
| **Consequence management** | Typical emergency management response and recovery operations that also take place after terrorist attacks. |
| **Crisis management** | A law enforcement activity that includes intelligence gathering to prevent terrorist attacks or evidence collection for the purposes of interdiction and prosecution. |

| | |
|---|---|
| **Cyberterrorism** | The use of computers and the Internet to plan or carry out attacks. |
| **Environmental degradation** | The depletion or pollution of the earth's natural resources. |
| **Global warming** | The rise of temperature of the earth's atmosphere. |
| **Hackers** | Individuals that log into others' computers illegally and run or disrupt them from afar. |
| **Hoof and mouth disease** | A highly infectious disease among livestock caused by *Apthovirus*. Also known as foot and mouth disease. |
| **Hot zone** | The affected (or contaminated) area. |
| **Na-tech disaster** | A disaster that occurs when a natural hazard interacts with technology to produce or magnify adverse effects. |
| **Natural environment** | The physical milieu (earth's systems) in which disasters occur. |
| **Near-earth object (NEO)** | A terrestrial impact structures made up of mostly ice and dirt particles. |
| **Pole reversal** | A change in the earth's magnetic fields. |
| **Potentially hazardous asteroid (PHA)** | An asteroid that comes within 0.05 AU or less of the earth. |
| **Primary hazard** | A natural hazard agent that interacts with vulnerabilities and therefore produces a disaster. |
| **Quarantine** | The isolation of people who have contracted a communicable disease. |
| **Secondary hazard** | A hazard (natural, technological, or otherwise) that occurs as a result of the primary hazard. |
| **Severe acute respiratory syndrome (SARS)** | A viral respiratory disease caused by a coronavirus (SARS-CoV). |
| **Social environment** | The social, political, economic, and cultural activity or characteristics of the community. |
| **Strategic National Stockpile** | This is a collection of antibiotics, vaccines, antiviral drugs, and other pharmaceuticals stored by the federal government. |
| **Synergistic disaster** | An event where one resulting impact seems to magnify others. |
| **Tactical EMS personnel** | Emergency medical technicians that are also trained to use weapons |
| **Terrorism** | Violent acts committed by individuals or groups seeking to disrupt society, instill fear, and promote objectives that are ideological in nature. |

**Torino Scale**  A measurement tool scientists created in an attempt to predict the impact of a meteoroid strike.

**Warm zone**  The washing (or decontamination) area.

**West Nile virus**  A flavivirus that is dependent upon mosquitoes as vectors.

**Worms**  Similar to viruses, but they reproduce over many computer systems due to Internet, networks, and e-mail connections.

# ASSESS YOUR UNDERSTANDING

Posttest to evaluate your knowledge of how to deal with future disasters.
*Measure your learning by comparing pretest and posttest results.*

## Summary Questions

1. Because emergency management has improved over the years, there are fewer disasters today than in the past. True or false?

2. A secondary hazard occurs as a result of the primary hazard. True or false?

3. A na-tech disaster is disaster that results from a computer malfunction only. True or false?

4. The introduction of trees, the building of narrow roads, and personnel shortages in the fire department were some of the factors that led to the East Bay Hills fire. True or false?

5. Mutual aid teams had no problem responding to the East Bay Hills fire. True or false?

6. After the East Bay Hills fire, a number of improvements in emergency management were made. True or false?

7. Natural and technological hazards may share many similarities. True or false?

8. People will often deny wrongdoing or hide information after an industrial disaster. True or false?

9. If you don't know how to deal effectively with a hazardous material incident, it is ok to respond anyway because people's lives are at stake. True or false?

10. Chemicals always react the same way—regardless of the weather. True or false?

11. Acts of violence will require close coordination between emergency medical personnel and law enforcement officials. True or false?

12. Planted bombs may complicate emergency response operations or criminal investigations. True or false?

13. Terrorists may launch attacks with the use of knives, guns, computer viruses, or weapons of mass destruction. True or false?

14. Although the initial period after a disaster is characterized by a "therapeutic community," it is not long lasting as societal conflict often reemerges during recovery activities. True or False?

15. Unusual numbers of sick or dying people may be an indicator of the use of a biological weapon. True or false?

16. Terrorists will only target civilians and not first responders. True or false?

17. A hot zone is the place where decontamination takes place. True or false?

18. Hospitals may need to lock down their facilities after terrorist attacks in order to avoid contamination. True or false?

19. If you need assistance in dealing with terrorist attacks, the state and federal governments may have specialized teams that can help you. True or false?

20. Scientists agree on the cause and speed of pole reversals. True or false?

21. Avian flu is exactly like seasonal flu. True or false?

22. Hoof and mouth disease affected humans and not animals. True or false?

23. SARS is spread by droplets from a person's cough or sneeze. True or false?

24. Modern computer equipment may prohibit the sharing of nonverbal communication. True or false?

25. The population is only growing; it is not changing. True or false?

26. There is no single cause of vulnerability. True or false?

27. Disasters are increasing because:
    (a) We have undoubtedly entered a period of more active hurricanes.
    (b) Global climate change may alter episodes of rain and drought.
    (c) Urbanization may lead to more flooding.
    (d) Answers a and b.
    (e) Answers a, b, and c.

28. An example of a cascading disaster is:
    (a) Hurricane Iniki
    (b) The 9/11 terrorist attacks
    (c) Hurricane Andrew
    (d) The Oklahoma City bombing
    (e) The Bhopal chemical release

29. The social environment before the East Bay Hills fire:
    (a) Promoted and encouraged the development of emergency management
    (b) Discouraged development in hazard-prone areas
    (c) Incorporated all of the findings of the Blue Ribbon Committee
    (d) Opposed new regulations that could have limited the impact of the event
    (e) None of the above

30. During the response to the East Bay Hills fire:
    (a) The first responders made sure they put out all embers.
    (b) Did not have problems with mutual aid.
    (c) Firefighters had to protect themselves by diving into a pool.
    (d) Did not rely on technology.
    (e) Failed to address all options for recovery.

31. Types of technological hazards include:
    (a) Electrical short circuits
    (b) Dam failure
    (c) Train derailments
    (d) Hazardous material releases
    (e) All of the above

32. Which of the following is not often a problem in technological disasters?
    (a) Emergency responders have full and complete information about what they are dealing with.
    (b) Lawsuits and fines typically result.
    (c) Risk is often underestimated.

(d) Operation is improper.

(e) All of the above.

33. When responding to a HazMat incident, it is imperative that:

(a) Everyone is wearing personal protective equipment.

(b) You approach the scene cautiously.

(c) You seek expert advice if needed.

(d) You be aware of the dynamic nature of the scene.

(e) All of the above.

34. An environmental remediation company:

(a) Is only useful in after a terrorist attack

(b) Can help you clean up after a hazardous material incident

(c) Will never follow regulations after a hazardous material incident

(d) Is beneficial for law enforcement agencies

(e) None of the above

35. The response to Columbine:

(a) Was regarded as a complete success

(b) Showed no problems regarding the identification of the perpetrator

(c) Illustrated the dangers of live camera footage of police operations

(d) Illustrated that the police had ample intelligence about what was taking place

(e) Did not include the planting of any dangerous bombs

36. Terrorists:

(a) Seek targets with maximum exposure

(b) Avoid the intimidation of others

(c) Do not pursue ideological goals

(d) Do not pursue social or religious goals

(e) Cannot utilize WMD

37. The T in TRACEM stands for:

(a) Terrorism

(b) Technology

(c) Trunked radio systems

(d) Thermal

(e) Temperatures

38. What is an indicator of an explosive device?

(a) Blown-out windows

(b) Dead animals and fish

(c) Mass casualties with no obvious trauma

(d) Mass casualties that are associated with unscheduled sprays

(e) None of the above

39. To enter a contamination zone, you should:

(a) Approach from the hot zone

(b) Approach from the cold zone

    (c) Approach from the warm zone

    (d) Bypass medical screening

    (e) Bypass law enforcement personnel

40. In order to protect evidence:

    (a) You must secure the scene of the crime.

    (b) You must avoid interaction with terrorists.

    (c) You must deny entry to authorized personnel.

    (d) Answers b and c.

    (e) None of the above.

41. Responsibilities of the coroner in after a terrorist attack include:

    (a) Receiving human remains

    (b) Identifying the deceased

    (c) Notifying next of kin

    (d) Providing death certificates

    (e) All of the above

42. Global warming is attributed to:

    (a) Natural processes

    (b) Automobiles

    (c) The buildup of three greenhouse gasses

    (d) Answers a, b, and c

    (e) Answers b and c only

43. Which type of biological disease is spread by birds?

    (a) Hoof and mouth disease

    (b) Avian flu

    (c) SARS

    (d) AIDS

    (e) West Nile virus

44. PHA stands for:

    (a) Prime hazard assessment

    (b) Potentially hazardous avalanche

    (c) Potentially hazardous asteroid

    (d) Perspective hazard adjustment

    (e) Probably hazard association

45. In order to prevent computer/information technology disasters, you should:

    (a) Filter incoming information to prevent information overload

    (b) Avoid up-to-date information

    (c) Avoid e-mails all of the time

    (d) Harness antitechnology firms

    (e) Rely on backup systems only

46. Why are emergency management institutions weak?

   (a) People downplay the possibility of disasters.

   (b) Politicians frequently ignore long-term issues.

   (c) There are not enough emergency managers.

   (d) Demands placed upon emergency managers are excessive compared to their resources.

   (e) All of the above.

## Review Questions

1. What disaster events occurred in the 1980s and 1990s that have impacted emergency management in the United States? Have events in the last 15 years given additional attention to emergency management? If so, why?

2. What are the associated and secondary hazards associated with primary hazards?

3. How did the natural, built, and social environments produce the East Bay Hills fire?

4. What are the types of industrial hazards that may occur and what are their consequences?

5. What steps must be taken to respond effectively to hazardous material incidents?

6. What lessons does Columbine have for first responders and emergency managers?

7. Are responses to terrorist attacks similar or different than response to natural disasters?

8. What are the different types of harm that could be encountered at the scene of a terrorist attack?

9. How can time, distance, and shielding keep you safe after a terrorist attack?

10. What steps need to be taken to decontaminate victims effectively?

11. What other organizations can help you deal with terrorist disasters?

12. Is global warming controversial? How do you feel about the possibility of rising temperatures? How could this influence future disasters?

13. Why is it difficult to encourage people to prepare for possible meteor impacts?

14. What are the symptoms of avian flu? SARS? West Nile virus?

15. Are advances in computers and information beneficial and detrimental?

16. What are the causes of vulnerability and how can they be corrected?

## Applying This Chapter

1. You are the emergency manager for a small town in Tennessee. You have just been advised by the National Weather Service that a severe thunderstorm is likely to occur in about 12 hours. What are some associated and secondary hazards that you should be concerned about? What should you

be ready to do if the inclement weather produces flooding, hail, or tornadoes?

2. You have been hired as the risk manager at a chemical plant outside of Houston, Texas. You have been asked to review your company's operations with an eye on potential safety problems. What types of industrial accidents could occur and why? If an explosion took place and it emitted dangerous chemicals into the atmosphere, what should you do to respond effectively?

3. You are the emergency manager for Seattle where there has been a terrorist attack with nerve gas. What measures should be taken to protect first responders? What can be done to help law enforcement officials obtain evidence and prosecute the guilty party?

4. As the president of the International Emergency Management Association, you have been asked to testify before congress regarding some of the new threats our nation should be aware of. What would you convey in your briefing? Can you think of any other hazards or threats that have not been identified in this chapter?

5. A wildfire has just erupted in Arizona and it is moving toward a small mountain city. You are the emergency manager. Keeping the lessons of the East Bay Hills incident in mind, what steps can you take to respond effectively?

6. You are the emergency manager for Miami, Florida, and you have been assigned to review your ability to implement disaster response and recovery operations. What areas in and around Miami are vulnerable to natural disasters and why? What population segments are more vulnerable than others and why? What other factors could augment vulnerability in this area?

7. You work for the city of Cleveland, Ohio. You have a son who is in high school and he shows you a website where students express their views on a variety of subjects. Some of the students espouse affinity toward violence and how much they hate minority groups. From an emergency management perspective, why should this concern you? What should you do to alleviate your fears?

### Responding to HazMat

You are the emergency manager in Chicago where there has been a spill of hazardous material on a major interstate highway. The spilled product has shut down traffic and is draining into a nearby river. What measures should be taken to safely respond to this incident? What else should be done to protect the environment?

### Responding to Biological Hazards

You are the emergency manager for Washington, D.C., an international city that welcomes thousands of visitors from other countries every day. What information can you give to people in a public education campaign that will prevent them from being infected with diseases such as SARS and West Nile virus?

### Technological Hazards

Quarantelli asserts that computer and information technology is producing new types of disasters. What steps can you take to minimize the negative impact of the technological revolution? How could this technology help or hinder response and recovery operations?

# 13

# ENHANCING DISASTER RESILIENCE
## Preparedness, Spontaneous Planning, Improvisation, Leadership, and Professionalism

## Starting Point

Pretest to assess your knowledge of how to enhance disaster resilience. Determine where you need to concentrate your effort.

## What You'll Learn in This Chapter

▲ The need for preparedness and methods for acquiring resources
▲ EOC activation and management
▲ The importance of hazard and vulnerability assessments
▲ The components of emergency operations plans (EOPs)
▲ The benefit of training and types of exercises
▲ Ways to promote community education
▲ The value of spontaneous planning and improvisation
▲ Principles of leadership

## After Studying This Chapter, You'll Be Able To

▲ Apply the concept of preparedness and be aware of different resources.
▲ Understand how to establish an EOC.
▲ Examine who can help you assess hazards and vulnerability.
▲ Analyze the benefit and limitations of planning, training, and exercises.
▲ Recognize the value of disaster education.
▲ Explain why departing from plans and SOPs could be advantageous.
▲ Illustrate the importance of professionalism.

## Goals and Outcomes

▲ Propose ways to increase preparedness in your community.
▲ Write grants and manage budgets.

*Disaster Response and Recovery: Strategies and Tactics for Resilience*, Second Edition. David A. McEntire.
© 2015 John Wiley & Sons, Inc. Published 2015 by John Wiley & Sons, Inc.

▲ Design and operate an EOC.

▲ Formulate a hazard and vulnerability assessment.

▲ Create an EOP.

▲ Propose training and exercise programs for your community.

▲ Prepare the public for disasters.

▲ Plan ways to improvise when the situation requires it.

▲ Evaluate the benefit of leadership and professionalism.

# INTRODUCTION

As has been illustrated throughout this book, effective response and recovery operations often result from the decisions and activities taken after disasters occur. While this fact is technically true and will be reiterated again toward the end of this final chapter, it is imperative that you do not wait until after a disaster to promote resilience. There are many proactive steps emergency managers can take to facilitate a strong emergency management program. Creating an ordinance and establishing a preparedness council are some of the first obligations you will have as an emergency manager. Obtaining resources from internal and external sources will help to fund your emergency management program. Establishing an emergency operations center (EOC) will help you to coordinate postdisaster functions during response and recovery operations. Beyond these steps, you should assess the hazards and vulnerability in your community and write an emergency operations plan (EOP) to anticipate and guide your activities after a disaster. Training can help build capabilities in first responders and among the heads of the various departments in your jurisdiction. Exercises should be held to verify understanding of the plan and to ensure equipment is operating properly. Public education will also be needed if you are to enlist the support of citizens in your community. When a disaster occurs, you can also increase resilience by carefully planning how you will react and adapting to the unusual circumstances that inevitably arise during response and recovery operations. Finally, professionalism and leadership skills will help you to promote emergency management and make disasters a bigger priority in your jurisdiction.

## 13.1 Preparing Your Community

As an emergency manager, you must work tirelessly to prepare your community. Preparedness is defined by the Department of Homeland Security/Federal Emergency Management Agency (DHS/FEMA) as "a continuous cycle of planning, organizing, training, equipping, exercising, evaluating, and taking corrective action in an effort to ensure effective coordination during incident response" (DHS, 2013). Preparedness has also been described as one of the twin foundations of emergency management (Kreps, 1991a, p. 31). Interestingly, there is little agreement on what preparedness actually means. Some scholars see preparedness as "planning, resource identification, warning systems, training, simulations, and other pre-disaster actions taken for the sole intent of improving the safety and effectiveness of a community's response during a disaster" (Gillespie and Streeter, 1987, p. 155). Others assert that preparedness has the goal of foreseeing potential disaster problems and projecting possible solutions (Kreps, 1991a, p. 34). An alternate perspective is that **preparedness** builds capabilities to improve the effectiveness of response and recovery operations (McEntire and Myers, 2004).

In spite of this disagreement about meaning, you should recognize the value of preparedness. Preparedness activities include anticipation and the development of a variety of resources for response and recovery. It identifies important functions to be performed after a disaster. It also facilitates the assignment of roles and responsibilities among organizations (Auf der Heide, 1989, pp. 39–41). Communication and coordination are improved when preparedness is pursued in a serious manner (Auf der Heide, 1989, p. 39). Because preparedness generates additional options for first responders and emergency management personnel, it also allows for increased flexibility during response and recovery operations (Kreps, 1991a, p. 34). Creating an ordinance and establishing a preparedness council are some of the first steps you will take to prepare for disasters.

### 13.1.1  Creating an Ordinance

One of the first things you will need to do to facilitate preparedness is to develop an emergency management ordinance or law. This gives the emergency management program legitimacy and authority in your community. Such ordinances illustrate the jurisdiction's commitment to preparedness, and these laws typically include a number of sections:

- ▲ **Justification**. This illustrates why emergency management is needed.
- ▲ **Relation to state and federal law**. This reiterates that the local ordinance will comply with state and federal statutes pertaining to emergency management.
- ▲ **Powers and duties**. This indicates who is in charge of emergency management in terms of approving plans or declaring local disasters.
- ▲ **Organization**. This denotes how the functions will be assigned among leaders and various departments.
- ▲ **Joint operations and mutual aid**. This permits agreements with other jurisdictions in case outside assistance is required after a disaster.
- ▲ **Expenditures and contracts**. This describes who can make purchases and for what purposes.
- ▲ **Violations and penalties**. This outlines the enforcement of emergency management laws and regulations.

The ordinance therefore sets the foundation for everything else you will do as a local emergency manager.

### 13.1.2  Establishing a Preparedness Council

While the legal foundation has been or is being set, you should establish a preparedness council. Depending on the jurisdiction, preparedness councils may be called by different names (Figure 13-1). For example, in Denton, Texas, this organization is

## FOR EXAMPLE

### The Ordinance in Highland Village

The preamble to Ordinance Number 97-761 describes the purpose of the law in the city of Highland Village, Texas: "An ordinance of the city council for the city of Highland Village, Texas, establishing a municipal emergency management program; organizing the emergency management program; providing for the offices of an emergency management director, an emergency management coordinator and an emergency management committee; requiring an oath of office; providing for duties and responsibilities: authorizing a survey of hazards, development of a plan, and ordering an emergency curfew. Providing for joint operations and mutual aid; providing for emergency override; providing for exemptions from liability; providing for restricted expenditures and contracts; providing for conflict with other provisions and with the state and federal law; providing for obstruction of authority; providing for impersonation of personnel. Prohibiting unauthorized warning and all-clear signals; providing a severability clause. Repealing in its entirety ordinance No. 87-503 of the city relating to emergency management; providing for a review; making violations punishable by fine not to exceed $2,000.00; and providing an effective date."

**Figure 13-1**

It is advisable to create a preparedness council and meet with them periodically to guide planning efforts. Robert Kaufmann/FEMA.

known as the Denton Emergency Preparedness Advisory Council (DEPAC). The Council of Governments in Washington, D.C., labels their committee as the National Capital Region Emergency Preparedness Council (NCREPC). While each community may have one central committee and a unique name, it should be recognized multiple committees may be utilized. These various organizations may be based on the hazards threatening the jurisdiction, functions to be performed, needs to be addressed, and agencies to be involved. Members of the council may include:

▲ The mayor, city manager, and emergency manager
▲ Department leaders from the local government
▲ Representatives from public health agencies, utility providers, insurance companies, universities, the FBI, and nursing home units
▲ Others from the American Red Cross, Salvation Army, churches, and nonprofit groups, and so on

The most well-known preparedness councils are **Local Emergency Planning Committees** (LEPCs) (Lindell, 1994). LEPCs were created in the late 1980s in response to the Emergency Planning and Community Right-to-Know Act (SARA Title III). This law had the goal of helping communities prepare for hazardous material (HazMat) releases and other disasters. Constituting agencies vary by jurisdiction but typically include the emergency manager(s) and representatives from the fire department, hospitals, environmental protection agencies, and petrochemical facilities. These advisory councils have been studied extensively by Michael Lindell. He affirms that they have a positive impact on disaster preparedness since they reject the isolated planning undertaken by former civil defense directors (1994, p. 103). Other factors that facilitate LEPC preparedness and response to industrial disasters include the ability to:

▲ Acquire funding
▲ Maintain the organization
▲ Incorporate highly committed members
▲ Assess risks accurately
▲ Identify evacuation routes
▲ Develop knowledgeable HazMat teams

## SELF-CHECK

- What is preparedness?
- Why is preparedness necessary?
- What is an ordinance?
- How can a preparedness council help you prepare your community for disaster?

## 13.2 Acquiring Financial Resources

Without resources, you will not be able to maintain an effective emergency management program or increase the chances for successful postdisaster operations. It is vital that you identify resources that can be obtained in a disaster and seek funding from internal and external sources. You will want to ask yourself three questions:

1. What resources does the community have that will aid response and recovery operations?
2. What external resources can the community obtain, and how can you access them?
3. What other needs might arise, and how will you find required resources (McEntire and Myers, 2004)?

### 13.2.1 Resource Lists

A good way to begin to answer the above questions is to develop a resource list. A **resource list** is a database that includes human and material resources that can be deployed in a disaster. Such a list should include equipment, supplies, and services that are available on a 24 hour basis. Resource lists, which may be recorded electronically on a spreadsheet, may also have names, phone numbers, fax numbers, physical addresses, e-mail addresses, and a description of the service to be provided. This may include city officials, department leaders, private companies, and nonprofit organizations. Such lists may also have information about those who can assist with vehicle towing, sandbagging, power generation, sheltering, mass care operations, etc. Other common elements of resource lists include:

▲ An inventory of government vehicles and heavy equipment
▲ Preapproved contracts with vendors and expense estimates for certain services such as debris removal

The resource list should be updated at least on an annual basis. Having a list with incorrect names, old phone numbers, and expired contractual agreements will hurt your ability to respond to disasters and recover from them effectively. Conversely, an extensive and well-maintained list will help you acquire resources on a moment's notice.

### 13.2.2 Annual Budgets

Another way to ensure the availability of resources is to seek a large budget for your organization. A **budget** is an allocation of monetary support for a given department by city or county leadership. Budgets are typically requested and approved on an annual basis. They may pay for office space, equipment, personnel, and operating costs such as phone lines and electricity. Such funding may also help to acquire computer decision support systems or upgrade warning systems. Financial support can also improve dispatch and EOCs.

Besides concentrating on specific budgets for emergency management offices, it is important that you recognize that funding allocated to police, fire, and public health departments may positively influence overall community preparedness as well.

Because resources are always scarce, denials for increased funding may be common. However, you should not give up on your efforts to obtain internal funding. Persistence will pay off over time. In addition, it is recommended that you remember that the best time to ask for additional funding is immediately after a disaster. When a disaster occurs, begin conversations with authorities about how to prevent or prepare for disasters in the future. Be sure to take advantage of the increased interest in emergency management that disasters provide.

### 13.2.3 Grants

Funding can also be sought from outside agencies (McEntire, 2009). Many grants are provided by the federal government. You can find grant opportunities through:

▲ Emergency management associations
▲ Emergency management newsletters or bulletins
▲ Federal agencies
▲ The state administrative agency in charge of emergency management grants
▲ Websites such as www.grants.gov
▲ The Catalog of Federal Domestic Assistance at www.crda.gov/default.htm
▲ A city or county grant manager or coordinator

Some federal grants, such as the Emergency Management Performance Grant (also referred to as EMPG or Emergency Management Preparedness Grants), are vital for emergency management. This grant is allocated to the states on the basis of population and with consideration given to hazard and vulnerability assessments. The state may keep some or all of the money, but most pass much of the financial assistance to local governments. Local governments are given the funds based on needs and efforts to promote disaster preparedness.

EMPG often funds the emergency manager's salary or portions thereof. In addition to providing salaries for those in emergency management, the money also pays for travel, equipment, insurance, and supplies. The money can be shared with other departments who assist in emergency management activities. Although the EMPG funding is useful, it does not pay for everything. For example, the EMPG will not pay for rent on EOCs. It will not cover expenses associated with advertising, convict labor, benefits for volunteers, or motor vehicles.

There are many other grants besides EMPG, and these help acquire equipment or fund special programs. Examples include:

▲ National Urban Search and Rescue Response System
▲ First Responder Counter-Terrorism Training Assistance
▲ Fire Suppression Assistance
▲ Predisaster Mitigation Grants

▲ Chemical Stockpile Emergency Preparedness Program

▲ State and Local All-Hazard Emergency Operations Planning

▲ Interoperable Communication Equipment and Port Security Grants

▲ State Homeland Security Grant Program (SHSGP)

▲ Community Emergency Response Teams (CERT) Grants

▲ Information Technology Evaluation Program (ITEP)

Most of these grants are available from the FEMA in the DHS. However, certain grants have match requirements. For instance, many federal grants require that the local jurisdiction fund 25% of the total cost of the project in order to be eligible.

### 13.2.4 Applying for and Managing Grants

When applying for grants, you will first need to request an application package or download one from the Internet. Once you access the document, you should follow all directions as outlined. If needed, you may want to involve others in the writing of the grant. Your jurisdiction may have a full-time grant writer that can help you develop the proposal. Whether writing the grant alone or with others, it is imperative to remember that concise, clear writing is critical. Your proposal should include the goals of the proposal, the team to be involved in the project, the work plan, deliverables, a budget, and information on matching funds, performance measures, and the frequency of activity reporting.

Getting the grant isn't the end objective of course. It is only the beginning. If you are awarded the grant, you will need to accept the funds in a letter. You will also need to set up a grant budget and set up an account for electronic bank deposits. Be aware that funding may be given up front, in intervals, or after the activity has been performed and documented. Regardless of how funding takes place, you will need to have a strong management team to accomplish the goals of the grant. You should consider hiring additional employees to complete the work of the grant contract if that is necessary. You will also need to complete the activities that you outlined in the proposal and issue regular reports. Failing to do so, or using the funds for fraudulent purposes, could lead to a revocation of the grant or even prison terms and fines.

---

### FOR EXAMPLE

#### Local Grants

States often give grants to local governments. For example, Florida distributes grants to local governments to mitigate repetitively flooded structures. Flooding is Florida's most prevalent natural hazard. Many structures in Florida were built before flood-resistant design, and construction techniques were implemented. In 2006, Florida had over $4 million dollars to distribute to local governments for mitigation. Grants can be used for prevention and not preparedness activities alone.

## 13.3 Establishing an EOC

As mentioned in prior chapters, one of the most important resources for your community is an EOC (Figure 13-2). Therefore, another important step is to design and build an EOC. There are several things you should keep in mind while establishing an EOC:

▲ Locate the EOC in a safe area (FEMA, 1995, pp. 1–6), and have an alternate location in case the primary EOC is affected in the disaster (FEMA, 1995, pp. 1–6).

▲ Determine the best space configuration for the community EOC. For example, you will need to determine how many rooms you will need. You will also need to determine what personnel or organizations will participate.

▲ Identify and acquire the equipment and supplies that will be needed (FEMA, 1995, pp. 2–4). This may include computers, phones, fax machines, desks, tables, chairs, paper, pencils, and so on.

▲ Address life support requirements. These include sleeping accommodations, food service, water sources, sanitary facilities, medical supplies, heating, and air conditioning (FEMA, 1995, pp. 3–12).

▲ Ensure backup power and communications (FEMA, 1995, pp. 1–6). Examples include generators and ham radios.

▲ Maintain and update EOC personnel contact list (FEMA, 1995, pp. 2–6). This includes representatives of the public, private, and nonprofit sector.

▲ Clarify under what criteria the EOC will be opened. For example, will the EOC be opened for a tornado watch or warning?

Once the EOC is ready to be activated in an actual disaster, be sure that all of the personnel are familiar with the appropriate plans and protocols. An EOC will be of no use to the emergency management personnel if they do not know how to use it. Therefore, a quick review of procedures may be required to ensure training.

Figure 13-2

It is advisable to establish an EOC before a disaster strikes, because it will be difficult to set one up during an emergency. Jacinta Quesada/FEMA.

## FOR EXAMPLE

### Collin County's Fusion Center

One county in North Central Texas has created a fusion center that integrates many different departments and other organizations that have interest in emergency management and homeland security. If required, this EOC may include the actual presence of people from various government departments as well as others from the private and nonprofit sectors. Participating stakeholders include police, fire, EMS, public health, and other agencies. The fusion center also allows the sharing of information with the military, intelligence agencies, and the department of transportation. It is novel in terms of organization and technological capabilities.

## SELF-CHECK

- Why is an EOC an important resource for your community?
- Should cities and counties have a backup EOC? Why?
- What equipment and supplies are needed in EOCs?
- Is backup power and communications necessary for EOCs?
- What else should you do to establish an EOC?

## 13.4 Hazard and Vulnerability Assessment

In order to prepare adequately, you will need to know what types of disasters are most likely to occur in your jurisdiction. While working with the preparedness council and other experts, you will need to assess the threats facing the community and your ability to address them. This is often known today as a Threat and Hazard Identification and Risk Assessment (THIRA). Such **hazard and vulnerability assessments** are an evaluation of the risks facing your community along with your capability for dealing with them. These assessments should explore:

▲ All natural, technological, and civil hazards and rank them according to their predictability, speed of onset, magnitude, duration, seasonality, and so on

▲ The location of buildings, property, and critical infrastructure near hazardous areas

▲ The status of building codes and a measure of their enforcement

▲ Demographic patterns including race/ethnicity, age, and income levels

▲ Potential impact of a disaster and expected ability to deal with needs, problems, and functions to be performed

There are many resources available to help you complete your THIRA or hazard and vulnerability assessment. These resources include historical data on prior disasters, FEMA and state websites, and other emergency managers that work in the field. You may also want to meet with geographers, floodplain managers, and meteorologists to understand risks. Scholars and state/federal emergency management personnel can likewise help you determine what could happen in your community. These assessments play an important role in steering the direction of hazard mitigation action plans (HAZMAPs). They also determine the content of the EOP, first responder training, disaster exercises, and public education.

---

### FOR EXAMPLE

#### The Importance of Assessments

Many federal homeland security grants are awarded if the threat of terrorism has been illustrated through various kinds of assessments. If a community is unable to demonstrate that it is a possible target and that it has vulnerabilities that need to be addressed, it will not receive funding. Conversely, if a community can effectively convey ample hazards and vulnerabilities, it will be in a better position to obtain money for prevention, protection, and preparedness activities. In recent years, the allocation of federal funding has been altered because some states have not been able to demonstrate risk.

## SELF-CHECK

- What is a hazard and vulnerability assessment?
- What do these assessments examine or look at?
- Are hazard and vulnerability assessments important?
- Who can help you complete a hazard and vulnerability assessment?

## 13.5 Writing an EOP

After the hazards and vulnerabilities have been identified, you should work with others to create the EOP. As mentioned in Chapter 5, the **EOP** is a document that describes what the community will do in the aftermath of a disaster. The EOP should address all functions pertinent to response and recovery operations (McEntire and Myers, 2004). EOPs must also give extra attention to EOC management, interdepartmental coordination, mutual aid, and interaction with private companies, nonprofit organizations, and different levels of government. Typical sections include:

- ▲ **Authority**. This section describes the legal basis of emergency management and the plan. It may cite laws, decrees, or other documents.
- ▲ **Purpose**. This section discusses the objectives of the plan. This part of the plan will often mention the four phases of emergency management. It may also state that the plan is an overview of who does what, where, when, how, and why.
- ▲ **Situation and assumptions**. The situation part of the plan discusses what hazards the unit is faced with and the potential disruption, injuries, deaths, and damages that can result. It may also discuss how one hazard can interact with another. The assumptions section of the plan mentions things such as an ongoing presence of hazards, the unpredictability of disasters, how officials will recognize and respond to the event, difficulties that might arise, and that plan implementation may limit the loss of life, property, and the environment.
- ▲ **Concept of operations**. This section discusses who will do what and how. It discusses the fact that departments will respond based on their daily activities and areas of expertise that are also similar to emergency functions. This section does not have many details.
- ▲ **Organization and assignment of responsibilities**. This part of the plan describes the roles of each responding department. It is more specific than the concept of operations section.
- ▲ **Direction and control**. This portion describes the management of the entire operation. The roles of the top official and those in the EOC are mentioned.

▲ **Plan development and maintenance**. This section describes plan revisions and who will be in charge of them. It may also state who gets copies of the plan. This section notes that each department should give input to the plan, even if you are ultimately responsible for the entire document.

Other sections may form part of the plan as well. These possible sections include increased readiness conditions and administration and support.

The development of the EOP should be based on collective decision making. That is to say, you should work with your preparedness council and other department leaders to write the EOP. Meetings might be held to determine the best way to respond to and recover from disasters. Notes from these discussions can then be incorporated into the EOP. Drafts of the plan should be circulated to make sure that the document addresses response and recovery operations in a logical fashion. If needed, templates can be acquired from state and federal emergency management websites. In addition, it would be wise to follow FEMA's Comprehensive Preparedness Guide (CPG 101). However, it is imperative that you tailor your plan to the community that you serve. Each city and county has different organizational arrangements, distinct hazards, and unique vulnerabilities. Above all, remember than planning is only one part of the preparedness process. In fact, having a plan is of little benefit if you have no capabilities to implement it.

## FOR EXAMPLE

### Avoiding Fantasy Documents

Planning, if it is to be effective, must be based on accurate assumptions (Dynes, 1994). It is imperative that emergency managers think about what they will do under worst-case scenarios rather than engage in wishful thinking about likely disasters. The document should be seen as a part of preparedness—but not the only indicator of increased readiness. Writing an EOP without building capabilities amounts to the creation of a fantasy document (Clarke, 1999). Emergency managers must not get caught up in the "paper plan syndrome" (Auf der Heide, 1989).

## SELF-CHECK

- What is an **EOP**?
- What are the typical sections of EOPs?
- Should you write the EOP alone?
- Is planning the only step you have to take to prepare for a disaster?

## 13.6 First Responder and Organizational Training

Training is another way to prepare communities for disaster response and recovery operations. **Training** involves a review of emergency procedures as well as their application in a nonthreatening situation. Training is important as it compensates "for the limited opportunities available for acquiring actual disaster response experience" (Jackson and Paton, 2002, p. 115). Training must ensure:

▲ Firefighters can don and doff appropriate bunker or HazMat gear.

▲ Department leaders understand the incident command structure.

▲ EOC personnel are familiar with their roles and responsibilities in disasters.

▲ City officials know how to assess damages, declare a disaster, and seek federal disaster assistance.

Training can be conducted at the local level, across multiple jurisdictions, by the state, or through FEMA and other agencies. For instance, FEMA operates a training facility in Emmitsburg, Maryland. A series of dorms and classroom buildings are located on what used to be a former Catholic girls' school. First responders and emergency managers travel to this location and attend classes for several days and weeks at a time. Participants may learn more about incident command, EOC management, or how to deal with acts of terrorism.

Public health agencies and the FBI also provide several training courses. Training should be seen as a process to maintain first responder certifications. It is another way to promote disaster resilience.

---

### FOR EXAMPLE

#### The Center for Domestic Preparedness

The Center for Domestic Preparedness (CDP) is a federally funded entity that provides advanced training to first responders, emergency managers, public health officials, public works directors, and other personnel. It is located in Anniston, Alabama, and focuses heavily on weapon of mass destruction. Training covers many different topics including HazMat, incident command, crime scene management, and pandemic planning. To register for classes at the CDP, you will need to obtain a FEMA Student Identification Number, fill out a training course application, and submit the paperwork through your state coordinator.

---

## SELF-CHECK

- What is training?
- How can training impact your level of preparedness?
- What type of training opportunities exist for first responders, emergency managers, and department leaders?
- Where can you learn more about training opportunities?

## 13.7  Disaster Exercises

Conducting disaster exercises is another way to increase the effectiveness of postdisaster operations (Figure 13-3). An **exercise** is a simulation of a crisis, emergency, or disaster that has the goal of improving response and recovery operations in an actual event. There are a number of reasons why exercises are beneficial. Exercises:

▲ Help all responders become familiar with the EOP.

▲ Test the plan to ensure that no functions or assignments have been overlooked.

▲ Provide an opportunity to verify the availability and utility of equipment and resources.

▲ Provide a non- or less-threatening atmosphere to hone skills and practice disaster response operations.

### 13.7.1  Types of Exercises

According to FEMA, there are five types of exercises:

1. An **orientation** is an informal introductory meeting. It familiarizes people about the plan and motivates active participation in response operations. It covers policies and procedures in addition to roles and responsibilities. Orientations are typically geared to new agency representatives, and they last about 1 hour in an office setting. Orientations do not involve any equipment, and they do not create stress for the participants.

**Figure 13-3**

Healthcare workers participate in a disaster exercise in Anniston, AL.
Shannon Arledge/FEMA.

2. A **drill** is a small and limited exercise to improve a single function in response and recovery operations. It typically includes first responders in the field to test their use of equipment. A drill may last one or two hours, and it may produce limited stress.

3. A **tabletop** is an informal discussion of a mock emergency or disaster situation. This improves problem solving and facilitates coordination. Tabletop exercises usually involve department leaders in an office or EOC setting. Tabletops are usually a few hours in duration and may or may not involve equipment. These types of exercises lead to low stress among the participants.

4. A **functional exercise** is a moderately sized drill to test a limited number of response and recovery capabilities. Functional exercises may involve one or a few agencies, and they occur at the EOC, in the field, or at both locations. These types of exercises will often test the use of equipment. They may take up to a half day and evoke a medium degree of stress among those involved.

5. A **full-scale exercise** is a very large simulation that tests nearly all response and recovery capabilities. It requires the inclusion of most organizations and incorporates dispatch, field, and EOC components. Full-scale events utilize equipment to an impressive degree, last nearly an entire day, and create a significant degree of stress since they appear to be real-life incidents.

### 13.7.2 Managing Exercises

The aforementioned types of exercises do not just happen by themselves. A great deal of work goes into exercises. As an example, you will need to review the hazards and vulnerabilities that confront you, the EOP, and the current capabilities to determine what should be exercised. You will also need to schedule the date for the exercise in advance as well as the location, equipment, and personnel. It is also imperative that you decide upon the purpose, objectives, narrative, events, expected actions, messages, evaluation criteria, and enhancements for the exercise. For instance:

▲ The purpose of the exercise identifies the functions to be tested, the agencies to be involved, the type of exercise, the simulated hazard, and the location of the event.

▲ The objective of the exercise is a statement of what will be tested according to a simple, clear, achievable, and measurable standard.

▲ The narrative is an introduction of the event. It often covers where, when, and why the hazardous event takes place.

▲ The events portion of the exercise lists the problems or challenges all participants will face as they respond to the hypothetical emergency or disaster. Events may be labeled as major or minor. A major event, for example, might be an explosion resulting from an earthquake. A minor event could include a resulting fire that creates the need for emergency medical care.

▲ Expected actions list how participants might react to the problems or challenges that they encounter in the exercise.

▲ Messages describe the problems or challenges to be encountered as a result of the major and minor events. They evoke expected actions. Messages include the source of the message, the content and means of transmission, and the position of the designated recipient.

▲ Evaluation criteria may include a list of things to assess along with forms to verify compliance with emergency management policies and procedures.

▲ Enhancements are the props needed to bring realism to the exercise. For example, if you want to simulate the experience of being in a collapsed building, you will need props such as scattered debris or smoke.

Failing to include these components will limit the effectiveness of exercises.

### 13.7.3 Exercise Participants and Other Considerations

Participants in the exercise may include the design team, players, victims/simulators, controller, and evaluators. The **design team** helps to develop the purpose, objectives, narrative, events, expected actions, messages, evaluation criteria, and enhancements for the exercise. **Players** are the responders or department leaders that are evaluated in the exercise. **Victims** are simulators who provide opportunities to test the players' knowledge and skills. The **controller** runs the exercise by initiating the events and distributing messages to be acted upon. **Evaluators** determine if the players responded to the exercise effectively and in accordance to established policies and procedures.

Exercises are not finished when they are completed. They require a significant amount of follow up. Paperwork should be filled out and sent to state and federal emergency management agencies to illustrate compliance with exercise requirements. This is important since funding may be tied to the number and type of exercises undertaken in a given year. The recommendations of after-action reports also need to be acted upon in order to improve response and recovery operations for actual disaster events.

---

### FOR EXAMPLE

#### Tabletop Drills

The Office of Emergency Management (OEM) in New York City carries out a variety of drills and exercises. OEM conducts tabletops to determine the effectiveness of its plans and degree of preparedness. One such exercise, which dealt with a hypothetical biological attack on New York City, involved several agencies. Participating in this drill were the commissioners of the NYPD, FDNY, and the Department of Health and Mental Hygiene. Also participating were several city and state agencies. Even the mayor took part in this particular drill. Exercises such as this help all pertinent actors in the community prepare for disasters.

Strong exercise programs have the following characteristics:

▲ They are progressive, meaning that a current exercise builds upon the strengths and corrects the weaknesses of prior exercises.

▲ They are programs, implying that they are carefully planned and conducted to meet goals and objectives.

▲ They involve the community, suggesting that all other organizations should participate. First responders and the emergency manager will logically be involved. Every effort should be given to get local officials, businesses, and nonprofit agencies involved as well.

## SELF-CHECK

- What is an exercise?
- Why are exercises beneficial?
- What are the different types of exercises?
- What are the various components of exercises?
- Who are the participants in exercises?
- What makes an exercise program strong?

## 13.8 Public Education

Citizens may not always understand what types of hazards threaten their community. They may not know what to do in time of a disaster. For this reason, public education programs are vital if response and recovery is to be effective. **Public disaster education** can be considered a concerted effort to inform people about hazards and what to do if a disaster should occur. The education of citizens can be directed toward individuals, schoolchildren, community groups, families, and businesses. It may describe the nature of hazards, what can be done to prepare for them, and how to react should a disaster occur. For example, public education can outline the need to store food and purchase a first aid kit. It can also tell people to rotate flashlight batteries and pay attention to weather reports. Education programs can also instruct people on how to evacuate or where it is safe to seek shelter. Disaster education materials can be obtained from FEMA or the American Red Cross. Other brochures and pamphlets can be developed by the jurisdiction and distributed at fairs, parades, sporting events, or public speaking engagements or in utility bills.

For those jurisdictions that want to include the public in further proactive efforts, CERT can be established (Figure 13-4). As mentioned in Chapter 2, **CERTs** are groups of citizens that have received detailed information and specialized training to improve self-sufficiency in disasters. First responders will be overwhelmed in major disasters. State and federal assets may not arrive for 72 hours.

Figure 13-4

The director of FEMA Region IX reminds Sacramento residents to be prepared for possible disasters, including earthquakes. Barbara Pritchard/FEMA.

---

**FOR EXAMPLE**

### Educating our Youth

If emergency managers are to improve disaster response and recovery operations in the future, it will be imperative that they educate children. Children often encourage parents to take greater precautionary measures. They are also the best hope for implementing change. For this reason, the emergency manager should visit schools to educate youth about disasters. Schools, Girl Scouts, Boy Scouts, and churches would be logical locations and groups to target for public disaster education programs.

---

Therefore, it has been decided that the public should be able to care for themselves until outside help arrives. CERTs have been created in cities around the United States. CERT members are taught about potential hazards, disaster preparedness, urban search and rescue, fire suppression, basic first aid, psychological effects of disasters, and appropriate responses to terrorist attacks. These teams require continuous education and training.

## SELF-CHECK

- What is public education?
- Why is educating the public beneficial for emergency management?
- Who can help you educate the public about disasters?
- What are CERTs and why are they valuable after a disaster?

## 13.9 Spontaneous Planning, Improvisation, Creativity, and Flexibility

In addition to preparing before a disaster, you may also need to take steps during response and recovery operations to ensure success. As stated earlier, planning is one important way to help foster resilience before a disaster occurs. However, it is necessary that you recognize that you may need to develop a new or more detailed plan on how you will react when a disaster unfolds. This is because disasters present unforeseen challenges and because existing EOPs lack sufficient detail for unique circumstances. This exigency brings up the recently introduced concept of spontaneous planning.

**Spontaneous planning** is planning that occurs immediately before, during, or after a disaster to inform and shape response and recovery operations (McEntire et al., 2013). It is a process of evaluating the disaster context, determining solutions, and implementing those decisions. Spontaneous planning may be based at times on existing EOPs, but it will often depart from agreed-upon procedures and result in novel postdisaster actions. In other words, spontaneous planning is planning during the crisis period of disaster that is undertaken to implement preexisting emergency operations plans or to determine what to do when such plans are not adequate for the situation at hand. Several actions may be included in spontaneous planning:

▲ Pursuing situational awareness
▲ Assessing environmental cues
▲ Reflecting on prior plans and experience
▲ Entertaining hunches about the future
▲ Identifying emergent goals
▲ Developing mental models of what needs to be done
▲ Learning on the job
▲ Seeking the assistance of potential collaborators
▲ Communicating or meeting with others during or about response operations
▲ Presenting, critiquing, and negotiating options for problem resolution
▲ Determining how to accomplish new priorities
▲ Coordinating the activities of pertinent agencies

---

**FOR EXAMPLE**

### Spontaneous Planning and Neighborhood Reentry

After a gas pipeline in a residential neighborhood exploded and caught numerous homes on fire, city officials in San Bruno, California, recognized that the area was in a dangerous condition. However, they wanted to allow homeowners back on their property as soon as possible to file insurance claims and begin the process of recovery. Over a period of two days, those in the local EOCs planned how reentry would occur. The plan included the staging of homeowners at an off-site location. Property owners would then be verified (by showing identification) and given a permission tag to allow a few of them in the area at one time. The plan included mandatory training for property owners (regarding what was to occur for reentry) and required them to wear protective clothing. The plan specified that each property owner would be accompanied by building inspectors for a two hour period. The reentry process after the San Bruno gas explosion was a great example of spontaneous planning in action.

---

The notion of spontaneous planning was first introduced after the September 9, 2010, gas pipeline explosion in San Bruno, California (McEntire et al., 2013). While exploring the factors that facilitated disaster resilience in this event, researchers discovered that emergency managers frequently plan operations while response and recovery unfold. Several of those interviewed noted that they planned various functions (including firefighting, mass care, public relations, damage assessment, neighborhood reentry, and debris removal) on the fly. Where this type of spontaneous planning occurred, operations were deemed to be more successful. For instance, one respondent commented:

> I mean, literally, we had though through every possible contingency and had addressed it. The operation was so smooth that people didn't even believe it themselves – that they had been able to pull it off.   (McEntire et al., 2013, p. 20)

In contrast, where spontaneous planning was not fully evident, the operations were less effective. This was especially the case in regard to donations management.

Although much more logically needs to be learned about the process and value of spontaneous planning, it is clear that this type of behavior has close relation to improvisation. **Improvisation** can be defined as adapting to an unfolding situation. It is one of the key foundations of emergency management (Kreps, 1991a). Improvisation requires both creativity and flexibility:

"Considered as a noun, an improvisation is a transformation of some original model. Considered as a verb, improvisation is composing in real time that begins with embellishments of a simple model, but increasingly feeds on these embellishments themselves to move farther from the original melody and closer to a new composition. Whether treated as a noun or a verb, improvisation is guided activity whose guidance comes from elapsed patterns discovered retrospectively." (Kendra and Wachtendorf, 2003b, p. 126)

When the preparedness is inadequate, improvising becomes critical (Kreps, 1991a, p. 31). Planning and exercises may take place in an artificial environment.

Since this is the case, real-world problems create a need for creativity. Kreps, (1991a, p. 32) provides an excellent, but perhaps fictitious, example of improvisation, creativity, and flexibility:

> *A city is hit by a tornado. It causes major damage to homes. There are not many staff members available to perform damage assessment. The building commissioner seeks the assistance of a regional building association. To limit legal liability, the volunteers from the building association are hired immediately with a salary of one dollar each. After being trained on damage assessment, the teams are divided up. They are assigned different sections of the city. The teams categorize buildings as: lightly, moderately, and severely damaged. When the assessments are completed, repairs begin on the buildings with light and moderate damage. Those with heavy damage are condemned and destroyed. This quick thinking and novel approach enables the city to meet the needs of insurance claim adjustors and private contractors, and helps victims be eligible for disaster assistance.*

As witnessed in this case, thinking outside the box can be extremely beneficial. During a disaster, you will have to respond to circumstances that you have never considered or trained for. You will have to be creative and flexible. Creativity is one part of improvisation (Kendra and Wachtendorf, 2003, p. 126). **Creativity** can be described as the development of "new alternatives with elements that achieve fundamental objectives in ways previously unseen. Thus, a creative alternative has both elements of novelty and effectiveness" (Kendra and Wachtendorf, 2003, p. 123).

**Flexibility** is similar to creativity and could be described as a willingness to depart from widely accepted standards and practices of doing things (improvising solutions) in order to react effectively to unforeseen problems. "Under some circumstances … , emergency organizations need to preserve an ability to respond flexibly, and, where necessary, an ability to improvise appropriate counter-measures for the special needs of an unanticipated situation which threatens to become a crisis" (Turner, 1994, p. 87).

---

### CASE STUDY

#### Response to 9/11 Terrorist Attacks

Kendra and Wachtendorf illustrate the importance of improvisation in their study of response to the terrorist attacks on the World Trade Center (WTC). The reestablishment of the EOC on this fateful date and many other postdisaster activities required creativity and flexibility (Kendra and Wachtendorf, 2003a).

For instance, building #7 of the WTC collapsed as a result of a fire ignited by WTC Tower 1. Unfortunately, this building housed the EOC for the city. All officials and key personnel were able to evacuate safely. But they lost scores of computer-equipped stations, video monitoring devices, and GIS capabilities. Emergency managers now had no conference room or press briefing room due to the loss of the EOC. Since there was no designated backup facility, New York officials therefore had to respond to one of the largest disasters in U.S. history without a functioning EOC.

Fortunately, a training room served as the temporary EOC until a decision was made to move to pier 92. Having scheduled this pier on the Hudson

**Figure 13-5**

After losing its EOC due to the collapse of WTC #7 and a subsequent fire, New York created this improvised EOC (with a layout similar to the prior EOC) on pier on the Hudson River. Andrea Booher/ FEMA News Photo.

River for a bioterrorism drill after September 11, the OEM decided to make it the designated EOC for the 9/11 terrorist attacks. Desks, chairs, computers, and other office supplies were delivered within 36 hours. The American Red Cross provided hot meals to those working in the EOC. Sleeping arrangements were made with nearby hotels. Security was tightened to protect the facility against possible attacks.

Although EOC personnel were initially scattered and disorganized, over 700 people were working each day in the EOC. The makeshift EOC mirrored the old one and was fully functional. Thus, "… although the EOC was destroyed, the emergency management organization was not. Rather, the organization in New York City exhibited robust, adaptive behavior, demonstrating considerable improvisation, evidence of goal-directed solution-seeking and incorporating resources from diverse sources" (Kendra and Wachtendorf, 2003a, p. 45) (Figure 13-5).

Mapping and GIS functions were also adapted after 9/11 (Kendra and Wachtendorf, 2003b, p. 130). The collapse of numerous buildings at the WTC altered the cityscape. It resulted in several road closures and detours. The destruction created a need for a tracking system to monitor all of the people involved in response. The OEM developed a map creation and distribution system based on GIS. It was developed with local students and professors, technology specialists from New York, and software representatives from the ArcInfo vendor. With this new system, emergency managers and responders were able to request and pick up maps. These maps included the locations of command posts, warehouses, food serving stations, sanitation facilities, etc. "The activities related to mapping and spatial analysis [therefore] illustrate ... entrepreneurial creativity ..." (Kendra and Wachtendorf, 2003b, p. 131).

Improvisation was also evident in the massive waterborne evacuation (Kendra and Wachtendorf, 2003b, p. 133). When the attacks on the WTC occurred, the government feared that additional terrorist events could take place on bridges or in tunnels. The collapse of the buildings also rendered some of the subways inoperable. Citizens and government officials recognized the need to leave the affected area and return home, but there were limited transportation systems available for this purpose. Tour boats, military vessels, passenger ferries, and private craft worked in an ad hoc basis with the Coast Guard to evacuate people from Lower Manhattan. Coast Guard inspectors permitted vessels to exceed normal passenger capacities. They relied on their experience and judgment to determine the extent to which regulations could be safely loosened. Emergent self-organization, and flexibility from the Coast Guard, resulted in an impressive evacuation of 500,000 people from Manhattan. Such an evacuation may never have occurred to this extent by water before, although some might say that the Dunkirk experience in World War II came close to or exceeded it.

Creativity and flexibility were also prevalent features of the credentialing system (Kendra and Wachtendorf, 2003b). "Not only was the September 11th incident a high-impact disaster that produced numerous casualties, it was also a complex emergency with added ambiguous dimensions such as the ongoing terrorist threat, the criminal investigation, an ongoing process of remains recovery and identification that persisted more than six months after the attack, and a very dangerous collapse site situated within close range of an extremely densely populated urban area" (Kendra and Wachtendorf, 2003b, p. 134).

## FOR EXAMPLE

### Departing from Standard Operating Procedures

Adapting to disasters is beneficial in many situations. It gives you flexibility to adjust to any contingency you might face. However, some standard operating procedures (SOPs) are created for a very specific reason—the protection of emergency workers. If emergency responders rush into the scene of an incident without considering their own vulnerability, they may become victims of the disaster. This is sure to complicate response operations. Checking in with incident command, working with others, and taking breaks frequently can enhance safety in addition to following SOPs.

These facts, along with the loss of standard OEM visitor badges, suggested that a check-in procedure would be needed to allow access and maintain safety and security at the same time. At first, anyone needing to enter Ground Zero would be given a blue and yellow badge. Later on, white badges were issued. These were photo IDs. The badges had codes for different levels and locations of access. Other temporary badges were distributed to contractors and volunteers who needed to enter the site for a limited time only. Only a limited number of these temporary badges were issued, usually 20 at a time. Contractors found ways to skirt the system. For instance, one worker would take the badges from 19 individuals who already entered the site. He then gave them to new workers so they could also gain access. The credentialing system was an example of creativity to determine who would have access to Ground Zero. They ascertained who required access. They instituted a system for issuing and tracking badges. And they improved the system over time (Kendra and Wachtendorf, 2003b, p. 135). These cases of improvisation, creativity, and flexibility illustrate how response operations can be successful in spite of significant challenges.

## SELF-CHECK

- What is improvisation?
- Why are creativity and flexibility important after disasters?
- What lessons are learned from the response to the 9/11 terrorist attacks?
- Why is improvisation regarded to be one of the twin foundations of emergency management?

## 13.10 Leadership and Professionalism

Besides preparing communities for disasters, planning spontaneous operations, and being willing to improvise when needed, it will be vital that you take a leadership role during response and recovery operations (Urby and McEntire, 2013). Leadership and its attributes have been the focus of many scholarly studies. **Leadership** is often described as an ability to motivate others to reach a goal or complete a task. Claire Rubin outlines the importance of leadership in emergency management in her book, *Community Recovery from a Major Natural Disaster*. Her research reveals that there are several qualities associated with respected leaders in emergency management.

Rubin states that leaders are able to decide what to do when a disaster occurs. In time of disaster, you must determine who you want to participate in the recovery planning and implementation (Rubin, 1991, p. 45). The quicker you are able to put resources to work and let people know what their tasks are, the more effective recovery operations will be. It is much easier to do this quickly if you have overseen the development of an EOP. It is also easier if you have experience in a prior disaster.

Rubin also points out that effective leaders understand governmental relationships. She states, "since the quality of intergovernmental relations is of paramount importance to efficient recovery, it is necessary to attend to the many intergovernmental activities entailed in recovery promptly and efficiently after a major disaster" (Rubin, 1991, p. 46). Recovery is most successful when local officials use their status as leaders to work closely with their governor, congressional representatives, and other federal officials. Strong leaders know how to obtain resources from the state and federal governments (Rubin, 1991, p. 50).

Another important attribute of leadership is having a vision of what the community should look like after a disaster. When officials have ideas on how the community can rebound, it is then much easier to reach those goals (Rubin, 1991, p. 49). Rubin asserts, "if you view a heavily damaged area as a site for 'instant urban renewal,' a broader perspective and a wider array of reconstruction options will be maintained during the recovery and planning process" (1991, p. 47). Her research reminds us that leadership is vital if you are to be an effective emergency manager (Figure 13-6).

**Figure 13-6**

Leadership and professionalism are vital attributes for today's
emergency managers. Catherine Belfi/FEMA. Photo by Kenneth Wilsey.

> **FOR EXAMPLE**
>
> ### Rudy Giuliani and Leadership
>
> After the terror attacks on September 11, 2001, New York Mayor Rudy Giuliani was widely praised for his leadership acumen and skills. Giuliani was widely recognized for his close oversight of response and recovery efforts. He coordinated the response of many different city departments. He communicated to the state and federal authorities the support that New York would need. He used the support not only for the WTC but also for citywide antiterrorist measures and rebuilding. At the end of 2001, *TIME* magazine named him as Person of the Year.

### 13.10.1 Becoming a Professional Emergency Manager

In addition to being a leader, you should develop your own professional characteristics if you are to promote disaster resilience. Until recently, emergency managers were not regarded to be professionals. Those individuals who had posts in civil defense and emergency management did not have formal training or education in their field. Many obtained their positions because of their political connections, experience in the military, and knowledge of response operations. Things began to change in the 1990s. People with specific emergency management credentials were appointed to important leadership positions. For example, James Lee Witt, an emergency manager from Arkansas, was the first professional emergency manager to lead the FEMA. Witt served under President Clinton and was one of many individuals who helped to advance the profession of emergency management.

A **profession** is an occupation that is based on scientific knowledge and is respected by the community. Such professions involve specialized training and coveted qualifications. Emergency management is certainly moving in this direction. For instance, there are now undergraduate and graduate degrees offered in emergency management. There are also continuing education requirements and expectations for those employed in this career. Professional associations (like the International Association of Emergency Managers) now exist too. As natural hazards and terrorism continue to confront the United States, emergency managers are increasingly recognized for the vast knowledge and skills they possess.

Developing professionalism should be a top priority for future emergency managers. An important study about this topic was published in 1987. The well-known disaster sociologist Thomas Drabek interviewed government officials and other personnel from 62 cities. The responses from those interviewed revealed that successful emergency managers are regarded as professionals. They have unique individual qualities. They perform vital services. Professional emergency managers are individuals who have specialized knowledge about disasters and what to do to deal with them in an effective manner. Those regarded to be professionals can motivate others to action. They integrate diverse organizations into the emergency management system. They can also resolve interorganizational conflict through mediation.

They understand disaster legislation as well as response and recovery processes and are highly committed to their work (Drabek, 1987).

The unique qualities of successful emergency managers are consistent in many cases. Some of the most frequently mentioned characteristics include skills in communications, managing human resources, and maintaining a calm personality while under duress. Other qualities varied. They included technical training, educational background and experience, or an ability to work with volunteers (Drabek, 1987).

According to Drabek, there are three types of activities performed by successful emergency managers. First is the ability to shift from a narrow focus on civil defense issues to a more comprehensive form of emergency management. In other words, successful emergency managers acknowledge the diversity of hazards that threaten their communities. Second, professional emergency managers are able to elevate the visibility and respect others had for the emergency management program. This means that they have gained the same recognition as other government departments and agencies in the community. Finally, successful managers are able to accomplish important goals. For example, they are able to establish a new EOC, purchase a warning system, undertake a training program, or educate the community about disasters (Drabek, 1987).

There are three additional principles associated with professionalism that you should understand and incorporate. The first is knowing the science of the field. To be a good emergency manager, you will need to understand the hazards and vulnerabilities threatening your jurisdiction as well as the functions that need to be performed when a disaster strikes. This understanding comes with education and experience. The second principle is networking with others. You will need to work with others in different agencies and at different levels of government. Collaboration is built on good communication and the fostering of a relationship of trust. Finally, you will also need to be a successful advocate for your emergency management program. You will need to think strategically and push for change. You can do this by helping to put emergency management on the political agenda. You will need to use your knowledge and networking ability to influence policy and increase funding and support for emergency management. Being a professional emergency manager is the fundamental way to promote disaster resilience.

## SELF-CHECK

- What is a profession?
- Is emergency management a profession?
- What are the qualities of professional emergency managers?
- What is leadership?
- What are the characteristics of strong leaders in the field of emergency management?

## SUMMARY

Disasters pose serious problems for communities. Emergency managers and many others are needed to effectively respond and recover when disasters occur. For this reason, it is imperative that those working in the field understand human behavior in disasters, alternative management approaches, and the many response and recovery functions that must be performed in emergency management. In addition, it is vital that emergency managers understand the challenges disasters present as well as tools and strategies that can improve postdisaster management. However, it should be recognized that effective response and recovery operations are most likely to be facilitated when four conditions are met: the community has built capacity through preparedness, those responding to disasters are willing to improvise if needed, those working in emergency management possess strong leadership skills, and the emergency manager seeks to become a highly educated and trained professional. If these steps are taken, they will most likely facilitate effective response and recovery operations when disasters occur. Resilience is a very important goal to be sought by today's emergency manager. As a professional emergency manager, it is your responsibility to promote it!

## KEY TERMS

| | |
|---|---|
| **Budget** | An allocation of monetary support for a given department by city or county leadership. |
| **Community Emergency Response Teams (CERTs)** | Groups of citizens that have received detailed information and specialized training to improve self-sufficiency in disasters. |
| **Controller** | Person who runs the exercise by initiating the events and distributing messages to be acted upon. |
| **Creativity** | Finding ways to resolve problems through unanticipated means. |
| **Drill** | A small and limited exercise to improve a single function in response operations. |
| **Emergency operations plan (EOP)** | A document that describes what the community will do in the aftermath of a disaster. |
| **Exercise** | A simulation of a crisis, emergency, or disaster that has the goal of improving response and recovery operations in an actual event. |
| **Evaluators** | People who determine if the players responded to the exercise effectively and in accordance to established policies and procedures. |
| **Flexibility** | A willingness to depart from widely accepted standards and practices of doing things (thinking creatively and improvising solutions) in order to react effectively to unforeseen problems. |

| | |
|---|---|
| **Full-scale exercise** | A very large simulation that tests nearly all response and recovery capabilities. |
| **Functional exercise** | A moderately sized drill to test a limited number of response and recovery capabilities. |
| **Hazard and vulnerability assessment** | An evaluation of the risks facing your community along with your capability for dealing with them. |
| **Improvisation** | Adapting to an unfolding situation. |
| **Leadership** | An ability to motivate others to reach a goal or complete a task. |
| **Orientation** | An informal introductory meeting. |
| **Players** | The responders or department leaders that are evaluated in the exercise. |
| **Preparedness** | The building capabilities to improve the effectiveness of response and recovery operations. |
| **Profession** | An occupation that is based on scientific knowledge and is respected by the community. |
| **Public disaster education** | A concerted effort to inform people about hazards and what to do if a disaster should occur. |
| **Resource list** | A database that includes human and material resources that can be deployed in a disaster. |
| **Spontaneous planning** | Planning that occurs immediately before, during, or after a disaster to inform and shape response and recovery operations. |
| **Tabletop** | An informal discussion of a mock emergency or disaster situation. |
| **Training** | A review of emergency procedures as well as their application in a nonthreatening situation. |
| **Victims** | Simulators who provide opportunities to test the players' knowledge and skills. |

# ASSESS YOUR UNDERSTANDING

Posttest to evaluate your knowledge about how to promote disaster resilience. *Measure your learning by comparing pretest and posttest results.*

## Summary Questions

1. Preparedness has been described as one of the twin foundations of emergency management. True or false?
2. Creating an ordinance is one of the first steps you will take to prepare your community for disasters. True or false?
3. An LEPC is an example of a preparedness council. True or false?
4. Resources needed for emergency management include financial budget allocations only. True or false?
5. A resource list should be updated at least once each year. True or false?
6. Emergency managers can find out more about grants by talking to colleagues or searching government websites. True or false?
7. There are no grants that help to improve mitigation measures. True or false?
8. Once you've been awarded a grant, you will not need to submit any additional paperwork. True or false?
9. Life support requirements for EOCs include food service and sanitary facilities. True or false?
10. Geographers can help you with a hazard and vulnerability assessment, but not scholars or meteorologists. True or false?
11. Direction and control addresses the role of the top officials in the given jurisdiction. True or false?
12. Training courses are available through the state only. True or false?
13. A full-scale exercise does not produce any stress for the participants. True or false?
14. The narrative is an introduction to a disaster exercise. True or false?
15. The controller is the person that manages the disaster exercise. True or false?
16. Citizens always know what to do when a disaster occurs. True or false?
17. Spontaneous planning implies efforts to implement the plan with additional details or plan for improvisations. True or false?
18. Improvisation, creativity, and flexibility are closely related. True or false?
19. There was improvisation in the reestablishment of the EOC after 9/11, but not in mapping and GIS functions. True or false?
20. Leaders can use their status to obtain additional assistance for disaster recovery. True or false?
21. Professional emergency managers have special knowledge and skills and know what to do when a disaster occurs. True or false?

22. Preparedness may be defined as:
    (a) Planning and resource identification
    (b) Training
    (c) Foreseeing potential problems and finding solutions
    (d) Building capabilities to respond and recover
    (e) All of the above

23. Which of the following is not included in a city ordinance?
    (a) Justification
    (b) Concept of operations
    (c) Powers and duties
    (d) Expenditures and contracts
    (e) Violations and penalties

24. Who is included on a preparedness council?
    (a) The mayor and city manager
    (b) Department leaders from local government
    (c) Private and nonprofit organizations
    (d) All of the above
    (e) All of the above except private organizations

25. In order to develop a resource list, you should:
    (a) Include names and contact information
    (b) Inventory equipment and vehicles
    (c) Answers a and b
    (d) Not worry about updating the list periodically
    (e) Avoid preapproved contracts with vendors and other service providers

26. A budget is:
    (a) An operation performed during disaster response
    (b) An allocation of monetary support given by the city leadership
    (c) A function in disaster recovery
    (d) A grant administrated by the federal government
    (e) An exercise program that is run by the controller

27. EMPG money:
    (a) Covers travel and equipment only
    (b) May pay a portion of your salary
    (c) Will fund the purchase of vehicles
    (d) Will pay for convict labor
    (e) None of the above

28. Grant proposals often include:
    (a) The goals of the grant
    (b) The team involved in the project
    (c) The work plan
    (d) Information on matching funds
    (e) All of the above

29. An EOC should:
    (a) Be located in a safe area
    (b) Have a backup location
    (c) Have a clearly identified opening procedure
    (d) Answers a, b, and c
    (e) Answers a and b only

30. Resources to help you complete a hazard and vulnerability assessment include:
    (a) Floodplain managers only
    (b) Scholars but not emergency management colleagues
    (c) Historical data on prior disasters
    (d) All of the above
    (e) None of the above

31. Which component of a plan describes the hazards faced by the community?
    (a) Authority
    (b) Purpose
    (c) Situation and assumptions
    (d) Concept of operations
    (e) Direction and control

32. Training courses are offered:
    (a) At the local level only
    (b) Across multiple jurisdictions
    (c) By the federal government alone
    (d) By the FBI but not FEMA
    (e) None of the above

33. Which type of exercise is an informal introductory meeting?
    (a) An orientation
    (b) A drill
    (c) A tabletop
    (d) A functional exercise
    (e) A full-scale exercise

34. An expected action of an exercise:
    (a) Identifies what functions are to be tested
    (b) Includes a clear statement of what is to be tested
    (c) Introduces the disaster event
    (d) Lists how participants might respond to the problems they encounter
    (e) All of the above

35. Who is in charge of determining if the exercise participants are responding effectively?
    (a) The controller
    (b) The evaluators
    (c) The players

(d) The simulators

(e) The victims

36. Who should be educated about disasters?
    (a) Individual citizens
    (b) Schoolchildren
    (c) Families
    (d) Businesses
    (e) All of the above

37. What is one of the foundations of emergency management?
    (a) Improvisation
    (b) Exercises
    (c) Grant management
    (d) Public education
    (e) Leadership

38. Leadership may be defined as:
    (a) An ability to improvise
    (b) An ability to motivate others to a common goal
    (c) An ability to increase your proportion of the city budget
    (d) A willingness to be flexible in disasters
    (a) None of the above

39. Professional emergency managers:
    (a) Focus on more than just one type of hazard
    (b) Gain respect from their coworkers
    (c) Can accomplish the programmatic goals
    (d) All of the above
    (e) Answers a and b only

## Review Questions

1. What is disaster preparedness?
2. Why is preparedness important?
3. What is an ordinance?
4. How can you establish a preparedness council?
5. What resources are needed to increase your community's level of readiness?
6. How can budgets support your emergency management program?
7. What types of grants exist and how can you apply for and manage them effectively?
8. How would you establish an EOC if you did not have one?
9. What type of information is included in a hazard and vulnerability assessment?
10. What are the various sections of an EOP?

11. How does one go about writing an EOP?

12. Why does training improve your emergency management capabilities?

13. What are the five types of exercises?

14. How can exercises be managed effectively?

15. What are the major participants in disaster exercises?

16. What can you do to educate the public about disasters?

17. What is improvisation and how does it relate to plans and spontaneous planning?

18. What lessons do we learn from the response to the 9/11 disaster?

19. What skills should you develop to be an effective leader after disasters?

20. What are the common characteristics of professional emergency managers?

## Applying This Chapter

1. You are the emergency manager on an Indian reservation in Oklahoma. Your tribe operates several casinos that are located somewhat close to an interstate where hazardous waste is transported. What steps do you take to prepare for a hazardous material incident?

2. You are an emergency manager in Kansas. Spring is right around the corner, and the possibility of severe weather will be increasing. What can you do to promote preparedness in your community?

3. The city manager in your community has asked you to obtain additional funding for emergency management in light of recent revenue shortfalls. Where can you learn about grants? What steps do you have to take to apply for them?

4. As a new emergency manager in Los Angeles, you have been asked to revise the city's hazard and vulnerability analysis. Where do you start? Who can help you with this task?

5. You are an emergency manager in Atlanta. A major power outage has occurred, and your EOC backup generation system is not working properly. How can you find out what is going on with the electrical grid? What options do you have to communicate with others? Why would it be necessary to improvise in this situation?

6. One of your major responsibilities as an emergency manager is to update the emergency operations plan annually. Who can you include in the process of accomplishing this assignment?

7. You work for the American Red Cross headquarters near Washington, D.C. You have been assigned to develop a training program for all of the employees and volunteers associated with this organization. What types of programs and materials could help you fulfill this goal?

8. You have just been hired as an emergency manager in Lincoln, Nebraska. Why is it important that you approach your career in a professional manner? What can you do to be regarded as a professional emergency manager?

9. As an emergency manager in Pueblo, Colorado, you are supposed to put in at least 10 hours of public education every month. Who or what organizations might benefit from your knowledge? What would you teach them?

10. Terrorists have just shot scores of people in a busy shopping mall. There are several deaths, a number of injuries, and a great deal of concern on the part of the public. Would leadership be important in this situation? How can you lead the community through the response and recovery operations in an effective manner?

### Hazard and Vulnerability Assessment

You were recently appointed as the emergency manager for a small city in South Carolina. Your mayor has asked you to conduct a hazard and vulnerability assessment. What do you need to consider when performing such an assessment?

### Aoquiring Rooouroco

You are the public health official in charge of preparing Pittsburg for a bioterrorism attack. You need funding for all phases of emergency management. What sources do you look to for funding? What else can you do to acquire equipment, supplies, and personnel?

### Leadership

You are the emergency manager in Laguna Niguel, California. A major earthquake has just occurred, waking you up in the middle of the night. Because the earthquake has caused some minor damage in your home, you get in your car to drive to the EOC. On the way, you make a few phone calls to get a status on the situation. What other steps do you need to take to ensure all necessary functions are being completed in this disaster?

# BIBLIOGRAPHY

Accardi RT. (1997) Search operations at building explosion and collapse. Firehouse, 22 (October):88–92.

Aguirre BE. (1988) The lack of warnings before the Saragosa Tornado. Int J Mass Emerg Disasters, 6 (1):65–74.

Aguirre BE. (2002) Can sustainable development sustain us? Int J Mass Emerg Disasters, 20 (2):111–125.

Aguirre B, Wenger D, Glass T, Murillo M, Vigo G. (1995) The social organization of search and rescue: evidence from the Guadalajara gasoline explosion. Int J Mass Emerg Disasters, 13 (1):67–92.

Alexander D. (2002) From civil defense to civil protection—and back again. Disaster Prev Manage, 11 (3):209–213.

Alesch DJ, Arendt LA, Holly JN. (2009) *Managing for Long-Term Community Recovery in the Aftermath of Disaster*. Fairfax: Public Entity Risk Institute.

Allan LW. (2003, December 31) City Hall sustains $10 million in damages. *Atascadero News*, p A1.

Allison E. (1984) Media relations at major response situations. J Emerg Med Serv, 9 (December):39–42.

Amdahl G. (2001a) *Disaster Response: GIS for Public Safety*. Redlands: ESRI Press.

Amdahl RL. (2001b) Identifying hurricane induced hazardous materials release scenarios in a petroleum refinery. Nat Hazards Rev, 2 (4):203–210.

American Academy of Experts in Traumatic Stress. (2002) Trauma Response (Special Edition for Survivors of Traumatic Events and Those Who Care for Them), 13(1).

Anderson MB, Woodrow PJ. (1998) *Rising from the Ashes: Development Strategies in Times of Disaster*. Boulder: Lynne Reiner.

Aptekar L. (1994) *Environmental Disasters in Global Perspective*. New York: G. K. Hall.

Armstrong E, Rosen H. (1986) *Effective Emergency Response: The Salt Lake Valley Floods of 1983, 1984 and 1985*. Chicago: Public Works Historical Society.

Auf der Heide E. (1987a) The apathy factor. In: *Disaster Response: Principles for Preparedness and Coordination*. St. Louis: CV Mosby. Retrieved June 25, 2008. Available at http://orgmail2.coe-dmha.org/dr/flash.htm. Accessed June 28, 2014.

Auf der Heide E. (1987b) The paper plan syndrome. In: *Disaster Response: Principles of Preparation and Coordination*. St. Louis: CV Mosby. Retrieved June 25, 2008. Available at http://coe.dmha.org/dr/flash.htm. Accessed June 28, 2014.

Auf der Heide E. (1987c) Triage. In: *Disaster Response: Principles and Practices for Coordination*. St. Louis: CV Mosby. Retrieved June 25, 2008. Available at http://www.coe-dmha.org/dr/flash.htm. Accessed June 28, 2014.

Auf der Heide E. (1987d) The media: friend and foe. In: *Disaster Response: Principles of Preparation and Coordination*. St. Louis: CV Mosby. Retrieved June 25, 2008. Available at http://coe.dmha.org/dr/flash/htm. Accessed June 28, 2014.

Auf der Heide E. (1989) Disaster Response: Principles of Preparation and Coordination. St. Louis: CV Mosby. Available at http://coe.dmha.org/dr/flash.htm. Accessed June 28, 2014.

Austin LS. (1992) *Responding to Disaster: A Guide for Mental Health Professionals*. Washington, DC: American Psychiatric Press.

Baker EJ. (1990) Evacuation decision making and public response in Hurricane Hugo in South Carolina. Boulder: Natural Hazards Research and Applications Information Center, University of Colorado. Quick Response Research Report #39.

Bardo J. (1978) Organizational response to disaster: a typology of adaptation and change. Mass Emerg, 4:145–149.

Barnett-Queen T, Bergmann LH. (1989) Counselling and critical incident stress. *The Voice* (August/September), p 15–18.

Barsky L, Trainor J, Torres M. (2006, February) Disaster Realities in the Aftermath of Hurricane Katrina: Revisiting the Looting Myth. Quick Response Research Report #184. Disaster Research Center, University of Delaware. Miscellaneous Report #53. Available at http://udspace.udel.edu/bitstream/handle/19716/2367/Mis?sequence=1. Accessed on June 27, 2014.

Bates FL, Peacock WG. (1989) Long term recovery. Int J Mass Emerg Disasters, 7 (3):349–365.

Bates FL, Peacock WG. (1992) Measuring disaster impact on household living conditions: the domestic assets approach. Int J Mass Emerg Disasters, 10 (1):133–160.

Bathos S, Russell L, Williams G. (1999) Crisis management to controlled recovery: the emergency planning response to the bombing of Manchester City Centre. Disasters, 23 (3):217–231.

Beggs JJ, Haines VA, Hurlbert JS. (1996) The effects of personal network and local community context on the receipt of formal aid during disaster recovery. Int J Mass Emerg Disasters, 14 (1): 57–78.

Berke PR. (1995) Natural hazard reduction and sustainable development: a global reassessment. Working Paper No. S95-02. Chapel Hill: University of North Carolina, Center for Urban and Regional Studies.

Bevelacqua A, Stilp R. (2002) *Terrorism Handbook for Operational Responders*. Albany: Delmar Publishers.

Bierschenk E. (2004, October 14) Rules for collecting storm waste confusing even to FEMA reps. Vero Beach Press J.

Bigley GA, Roberts KH. (2001) The incident command system: high-reliability organizing for complex and volatile task environments. Acad Manage J, 44 (6):1281–1299.

Birkland TA. (1996) Natural disasters as focusing events: policy communities and political response. Int J Mass Emerg Disasters, 14 (2):221–243.

Birkland TA. (1997) *After Disaster: Agenda Setting, Public Policy, and Focusing Events*. Washington, DC: Georgetown University Press.

Blanchard Wayne B, Canton LG, Cwiak CL, Goss KC, McEntire DA, Newsom L, Selves MD, Sorchik EA, Stenson K, Turner III JE, Waugh Jr WL, West D. (2007) *Principles of Emergency Management Supplement*. Emmitsburg: Federal Emergency Management Agency. Available at http://training.fema.gov/EMIWeb/edu/emprinciples. asp. Accessed June 18, 2014.

Block B. Natural disasters becoming more frequent. Worldwatch Institute. Last modified February 1, 2014. Available at http://www.worldwatch.org/node/5825. Accessed February 1, 2014.

Bogard WC. (1989) Bringing social theory to hazards research: conditions and consequences of the mitigation of environmental hazards. Sociol Perspect, 31:147–168.

Bohle HG, Downing TE, Watts MJ. (1994) Climate change and social vulnerability: the sociology and geography of food insecurity. Global Environ Change, 4:37–48.

Bolin R, editor. (1990) The Loma Prieta Earthquake: studies of short-term impacts. Program on Environment and Behavior #50. Boulder: Institute of Behavioral Science, University of Colorado.

Bolin R, Stanford L. (1991) Shelter, housing and recovery: a comparison of U.S. disasters. Disasters, 15 (1):24–34.

Bolin R, Stanford L. (1998) The Northridge earthquake: community-based approaches to unmet recovery needs. Disasters, 22 (1): 21–28.

Borden FW. (1989, July) Urban search and rescue: the need for command and control [Applied Research Project Submitted to the National Fire Academy]. Emmitsburg: National Fire Academy.

Bowers WF. (1960) *Surgical Philosophy in Mass Casualty Management*. Springfield: CC Thomas.

Boyer D. (2003) Disaster donations: manage or 'be managed.' Kentucky Division of Emergency Management. Available at http://www.kyem. dma.state.ky.us/donation.htm. Accessed June 18, 2014.

Brand C. (2004, October 14) Debris removal discussed at meeting. *Enterprise Ledger*.

Bridges A. (2003) Earthquake claims a building that wasn't upgraded to meet safety standards. Available at http://www.azcentral.com/news/articles/1223Calif-Qua. Accessed December 22, 2003.

Brillman JC, Doezemma D, Tandberg D, Sklar DP, Davis KD, Simms S, Skipper BJ. (1996) Triage: limitations in predicting need for emergent care and hospital admission. Ann Emerg Med, 27 (4):493–500.

Britton NR. (1989a) Anticipating the unexpected: is the bureaucracy able to come to the party? Working Paper #1. Sydney: Disaster Management Studies Centre, Cumberland College of Health Sciences, University of Sydney.

Britton NR. (1989b) *Reflections on Australian Disaster Management: A Critique of the Administration of Social Crisis*. Sydney: Disaster Management Studies Centre, Cumberland College of Health Science, University of Sydney.

Britton NR. (1991) Constraint or effectiveness in disaster management: the bureaucratic imperative versus organizational mission. Canberra Bull Public Admin, 64:54–64.

Britton NR. (1999) Whither the emergency manager? Int J Mass Emerg Disasters, 17 (2):223–235.

Britton NR, Clark GJ. (2000) From response to resilience: emergency management reform in New Zealand. Nat Hazards Rev, 1 (3):145–150.

Britton NR, Moran CC, Correy B. (1994) Stress coping and emergency disaster volunteers: a discussion of some relevant factors. In: Dynes RR, Tierney KJ, editors. *Disasters, Collective Behavior, and Social Organization*. Newark: University of Delaware Press. p 128–144.

Brooks ER. (1964, May 25) Post attack damage assessment for civil defense. Operations Research Division Research Memorandum. Durham: Research Triangle Institute.

Buck G. (1998) *Preparing for Terrorism: An Emergency Services Guide*. Albany: Delmar Publishers.

Buck DA, Trainor JE, Aguirre BE. (2006) A critical evaluation of the incident command system and NIMS. J Homeland Security Emerg Manage, 3 (3).

Buckle P, Mars G, Smale S. (2000) New approaches to assessing vulnerability and resilience. Aust J Emerg Manage, 15 (2):8–14.

Bullock JA, Haddow GD, Coppola D, Ergin E, Westerman L, Yeletaysi S. (2005) *Introduction to Homeland Security*. New York: Elsevier.

Burby RJ, Wagner F. (1996) Protecting tourists from death and injury in coastal storms. Disasters, 20 (1):49–60.

Burkhart FN. (1987) Experts and the press under stress: disaster journalism gets mixed reviews. Int J Mass Emerg Disasters, 5 (3): 357–367.

Bush GW. (2003a) Homeland security presidential directive/HSPD-5. Available at http://www.whitehouse.gov/news/releases/2003/02/20030228-9.html. Accessed August 15, 2008.

Bush GW. (2003b) Homeland security presidential directive/HSPD-8. Available at http://www.whitehouse.gov/news/releases/2003/12/20031217-6.html. Accessed August 15, 2008.

Campbell Public Affairs Institute. (2002) *Governance and Public Security*. New York: Syracuse University.

Cannon T. (1993) A hazard need not a disaster make: vulnerability and the causes of natural disasters. In: Merriman PA, Browitt CWA, editors. *Natural Disasters: Protecting Vulnerability Communities*. London: Thomas Telford.

CDC. (1998, April–July) Deaths among children during an outbreak of hand, foot, and mouth disease—Taiwan, Republic of China. Available at http://www.cdc.gov/mmwr/preview/mmwrhtml/00054640.htm. Accessed February 6, 2006.

CDC. (2003) Epidemic/epizootic West Nile virus in the United States: guidelines for surveillance, prevention, and control. Available at http://www.cdc.gov/ncidod/dvbid/westnile/resources/wnv-guidelines-apr-2001.pdf. Accessed May 13, 2003.

CDC. (2005) Quarantine questions and answers on the executive order adding potentially pandemic influenza viruses to the list of quarantinable diseases. Available at http://www.cdc.gov/ncidod/dq/qa_influenza_amendment_to_eo_13295.htm#authority. Accessed February 7, 2006.

CDC. (2006a) Avian influenza (bird flu). Available at http://www.cdc.gov/flu/avian/index.htm. Accessed February 7, 2006.

CDC. (2006b) Frequently asked questions about SARS. Available at http://www.cdc.gov/ncidod/sars/faq.htm. Accessed January 29, 2006.

CDC. (2006c) Embargo of birds from specified countries. Available at http://www.cdc.gov/flu/avian/outbreaks/embargo.htm. Accessed June 21, 2011.

CDC. (2006d) Avian influenza infection in humans. Available at http://www.cdc.gov/flu/avian/gen-info/avian-flu-humans.htm. Accessed May 23, 2008.

CDC. (2006e) Avian influenza vaccines. Available at http://www.cdc.gov/flu/avian/gen-info/vaccines.htm. Accessed February 7, 2006.

CDC. (2006f) Interim recommendations for infection control in health-care facilities caring for patients with known or suspected avian influenza. Available at http://www.cdc.gov/flu/avian/professional/infect-control.htm. Accessed February 7, 2006.

CDC. (2006g) Avian influenza: current situation. Available at http://www.cdc.gov/flu/avian/outbreaks/current.htm. Accessed February 7, 2006.

CDC. (2006h) Hand, foot, and mouth disease. Available at http://www.cdc.gov/ncidod/dvrd/revb/enterovirus/hfhf.htm. Accessed January 1, 2006.

CDC. (2006i) Key facts. Available at http://www.cdc.gov/flu/avian/geninfo/facts.htm. Accessed February 6, 2006.

CDC. (2006j) Overview of West Nile virus. Available at http://www.cdc.gov/ncidod/dvbid/westnile/qa/overview.htm. Accessed January 31, 2006.

CDC. (2006k) Prevention. Available at http://www.cdc.gov/ncidod/dvbid/westnile/qa/prevention.htm. Accessed January 31, 2006.

CDC. (2006l) Testing and treating West Nile virus in humans. Available at http://www.cdc.gov/ncidod/dvbid/westnile/qa/testing_treating.htm. Accessed January 31, 2006.

CDC. (2006m) Transmission. Available at http://www.cdc.gov/ncidod/dvbid/westnile/qa/transmission.htm. Accessed September 10, 2010.

CDC. (2006n) West Nile virus vaccine. Available at http://www.cdc.gov/ncidod/dvbid/westnile/qa/wnv_vaccine.htm. Accessed January 31, 2006.

Champion HR, Sacco WJ, Gainer PS, Patow SM. (1988) The effect of medical direction on trauma triage. J Trauma, 28 (2):235–239.

Chan KP, Goh KT, Chong CY, Teo ES, Lau G, Ling AE. (2003) Epidemic hand, foot and mouth disease caused by human Enterovirus 71, Singapore. Available at http://www.cdc.gov/ncidod/EID/vol9no1/02-0112.htm. Accessed February 6, 2006.

Changnon SA. (1996) *The Great Flood of 1993: Causes, Impacts and Responses*. Boulder: Westview Press.

Changnon SA. (2003) Shifting economic impacts from weather extremes in the United States: a result of societal changes, not global warming. Nat Hazards, 29 (2):273–290.

Charles MT, Kim JCK. (1988) *Crisis Management: A Casebook*. Springfield: Charles C. Thomas Publisher.

Christian Science Monitor. (2012) Available at http://www.csmonitor.com/USA/Latest-News-Wires/2012/0521/One-year-later-Joplin-ison-the-mend. Accessed June 25, 2013.

City of Paso Robles. (2004) Demographics, damage assessment, earthquake repair funding, earthquake information. Available at http://www.prcity.com/government/departments/commd. Accessed June 18, 2014.

Clark County Fire Department. (no date) The MGM Grand Hotel fire investigation report. Available at http://www.co.clark.nv.us/firedept/ccfd_mgm.htm. Accessed February 3, 2004.

Clarke L. (1999) *Mission Improbable: Using Fantasy Documents to Tame Disaster*. Chicago: University of Chicago Press.

Clifford RA. (1983) *The Rio Grande Flood: A Comparative Study of Border Communities*. National Research Disaster Study #7. Washington, DC: National Academy of Sciences.

Cochrane H. (1990) The damage assessment process: an overview. In: Bolin R, editor. *The Loma Prieta Earthquake: Studies of Short-Term Impacts*. Program on Environment and Behavior Monograph #50. Boulder: Institute of Behavioral Science, University of Colorado.

Cochrane H. (1991, July 10–12) The principles of damage assessment applied to the Loma Prieta earthquake and Hurricane Hugo. Paper Presented at the International Conference on the Impact of Disasters, University of California, Los Angeles.

Code of Federal Regulations. (2007) Available at http://www.gpo.gov/fdsys/pkg/CFR-2007-title44-vol1/xml/CFR-2007-title44-vol1-sec206-33.xml. Accessed on June 27, 2014.

Coe RS, Prevot M, Camps P. (1995) New evidence for extraordinarily rapid change of the geomagnetic field during a reversal. Nature, 374:687–692.

Coile RC. (1994) Emergency managers mutual aid in California. ASPEP J, 57–62.

Coile RC. (1997) The role of amateur radio in providing emergency electronic communication for disaster management. Disaster Prev Manage, 6 (3):176–185.

Cole E, Buckle P. (2004) Developing community resilience as a foundation for effective disaster recovery. Aust J Emerg Manage, 19 (4):6–15.

Comfort LK. (1993) Integrating information technology into international crisis management and policy. J Contingencies Crisis Manage, 1 (2):15–26.

Comfort L. (1996) *Self Organization in Disaster Response: The Great Hanshin, Japan Earthquake of January 17, 1995.* Quick Response Report No. 78. Boulder: Natural Hazards Research and Applications Information Center, University of Colorado.

Comfort L, Wisner B, Cutter S, Pulwarty R, Hewitt K, Oliver-Smith A, Wiener J, Fordham M, Peacock W, Krimgold F. (1999) Reframing disaster policy: the global evolution of vulnerable communities. Environ Hazards, 1:39–44.

Comfort LK, Birkland TA, Cigler BA, Nance E. (2010) Retrospectives and perspectives on Hurricane Katrina: five years and counting. Public Admin Rev, 70 (5):669–678.

Connor SJ, Thomson MC, Flasse SP, Perryman AH. (1998) Environmental information systems in malaria risk mapping and epidemic forecasting. Disasters, 22 (1):39–56.

Cook S, Sinclair D. (1997) Emergency department triage: a program assessment using the tools and continuous quality improvement. J Emerg Med, 15 (6):889–894.

Corneil W. (1989) Firefighters suffer critical incident stress: stress in the aftermath of disasters. Emerg Preparedness Digest, 16 (1):24–27.

Cosgrave J. (1997) Estimating the capacity of warehouses. Disasters, 21 (2):155–165.

County of San Luis Obispo. (2004) Summary of financial damage estimates for the San Simeon earthquake, January 8. San Luis Obispo County Office of Emergency Services.

Cowan F. (1996) Make them go away! The media/dispatch conflict. *9-1-1 Magazine* (July/August), p 26–31.

Craine R, Bagdasarian T. (2003) Early identification and management of critical incident stress. Crit Care Nurse, 23 (1):59–65.

Cruz AM, Steinberg LJ, Luna R. (2001) Identifying hurricane induced hazardous materials release scenarios in a petroleum refinery. Nat Hazards Rev, 2 (4):203–210.

Cuny FC. (1983) *Disasters and Development*. New York: Oxford University Press.

Cuny FC, Hill RB. (1999) *Famine, Conflict and Response: A Basic Guide*. New West Hartford: Kumarian Press.

Curran E. (2004, September 19) FEMA to pay for mobile cleanup, not Baldwin. *Mobile Register*.

Cutter SL. (1993) *Living with Risk*. London: Edward Arnold.

Daines GE. (1991) Planning, training and exercising. In: Hoetmer GJ, Drabek TE, editors. *Emergency Management: Principles and Practice for Local Government*. Washington, DC: ICMA.

Dash N. (1997) The use of geographic information systems in disaster research. Int J Mass Emerg Disasters, 15 (1):135–146.

Davis JA. (1998) Providing critical incident stress debriefing (CISD) to individuals and communities in situational crisis. The American Academy of Experts in Traumatic Stress. Available at http://www.aaets.org/article54.htm. Accessed January 4, 2014.

Dawson A, McCook KDLP. (2006) Rebuilding community in Louisiana after the hurricanes of 2005. Ref User Serv Q, 45 (4):292–296.

Dececco J. (1986) Is triage ethical? Emergency, 18 (April):60–63.

Decker RJ. (2011) Acceptance and utilization of the ICS in first response and allied disciplines: an Ohio study. J Bus Contingencies Emerg Plan, 5 (3):224–230.

Dees T. (2000) *Information and Communications Technology for Public Safety*. IQ Service Report, Vol. 32, no. 1. Washington, DC: ICMA.

Denis H. (1997) Technology, structure, and culture in disaster management: coping with uncertainty. Int J Mass Emerg Disasters, 15 (2):293–308.

DeParle J. (1996) Slamming the door. *New York Times*, 20, p. 52.

DHHS. (2000) *Field Manual for Mental Health and Human Service Workers in Major Disasters*. Rockville: U.S. Department of Health and Human Services, Substance Abuse and Mental Health Services Administration, Center for Mental Health Services.

DHHS. (2001) Emergency response: disaster medical assistance teams (DMATs) and disaster mortuary operational response teams (DMORTs). Available at http://www.hhs.gov/new/press/2001pres/20010911c.html. Accessed June 18, 2014.

DHHS. (2003) What is a disaster mortuary operational response team?. Available at http://www.ndms.dhhs.gov/NDMS/About_Teams/about_teams.html#dmort. Accessed June 18, 2014.

DHS. (2013) Preparedness. Available at http://www.fema.gov/preparedness. Accessed June 28, 2014.

Dietch EA, Corey CM. (2011) Predicting long-term business recovery four years after Hurricane Katrina. Manage Res Rev, 34 (3):311–324.

Division of Emergency Management. (2000a) *Local Emergency Management Planning Guide*. Austin: Texas Department of Public Safety.

Division of Emergency Management. (2000b) *Preparedness Standards for Texas Emergency Management*. Austin: Texas Department of Public Safety.

DOD. (2000) *Improving Local and State Agency Response to Terrorist Incidents Involving Biological Weapons, Interim Planning Guide*. Washington, DC: Department of Defense. Available at http://www2. sbccom.army.mil/hld/downloads/bwirp/bwirp_interim_planning_guide.pdf. Accessed September 29, 2002.

Doepel DG. (1991) Crisis management: the psychological dimension. Ind Crisis Q, 5:177–188.

Donaldson MW. (1998) The first ten days: emergency response and protection strategies for the preservation of historic structures. In: Spennemann DHR, Look DW, editors. *Disasters Management Programs for Historic Sites*. San Francisco/Albury: Association for Preservation Technology and the Johnstone Centre, Charles Stuart University.

Doswell CA III, Carbine GW, Brooks HE. (2012) The tornadoes of spring 2011 in the USA: an historical perspective. Weather, 67 (4):88–94.

Dow K, Downing TE. (1995) Vulnerability research: where things stand. Hum Dimens Q, 1:3–5.

Drabek TE. (1985) Managing the emergency response. Public Admin Rev, 45 (January):85–92.

Drabek TE. (1986) *Human System Responses to Disaster: An Inventory of Sociological Findings*. New York: Springer Verlag.

Drabek TE. (1987) Emergent structures. In: Dynes R, Marchi B, Pelanda C, editors. *Sociology of Disasters: Contribution of Sociology to Disaster Research*. Franco Angeli: Milan.

Drabek TE. (1991) The evolution of emergency management. In: Hoetmer GJ, Drabek TE, editors. *Emergency Management: Principles and Practice for Local Government*. Washington, DC: ICMA.

Drabek TE. (2003) *Strategies for Coordinating Disaster Response*. Program on Environment and Behavior Monograph #61. Boulder: Institute of Behavioral Science, University of Colorado at Boulder.

Drabek TE. (2004) Media in disaster. In: *Social Dimensions of Disaster*. 2nd ed. Emmitsburg: FEMA.

Drabek TE, McEntire DA. (2002) Emergent phenomena and multiorganizational coordination in disasters: lessons from the research literature. Int J Mass Emerg Disasters, 20 (2):197–224.

Drabek TE, McEntire DA. (2003) Emergent phenomena and the sociology of disaster: lessons, trends and opportunities from the research literature. Disaster Prev Manage, 12 (2):97–112.

Dror Y. (1988) Decision making under disaster conditions. In: Comfort L, editor. *Managing Disasters: Administrative and Policy Strategies*. Durham: Duke University Press. p 255–273.

Dwyer J, Flynn K. (2005) *102 MINUTES. The Unforgettable Story of the Fight to Survive Inside the Twin Towers*. New York: Times Books.

Dynes R. (1970) *Organized Behavior in Disaster*. Lexington: Lexington Books.

Dynes R. (1988) Cross-cultural international research: sociology and disaster. Int J Mass Emerg Disasters, 6 (2):101–129.

Dynes R. (1994) Community emergency planning: false assumptions and inappropriate analogies. Int J Mass Emerg Disasters, 12 (2): 141–158.

Dynes R. (2003) Finding order in disorder: continuities in the 9-11 response. Int J Mass Emerg Disasters, 21 (3):9–23.

Dynes RR, Quarantelli EL, Kreps GA. (1972) *A Perspective on Disaster Planning*. Newark: University of Delaware. Disaster Research Center Report Series #11.

Ebert CHV. (1993) *Disasters: Violence of Nature, Threats by Man*. Dubuque: Kendall Hunt.

Edwards-Winslow F. (2002) Changing the emergency management paradigm: a case study of San Jose, California. Emmitsburg: U.S. Emergency Management Institute. Available at https://www.hsdl.org/homesec/docs/dhs/nps23-091207-12.pdf&code=0cbc7a245f0e458d31fd8c5387bc3821. Accessed October 1, 2007.

Eisenberg D. (2003) Do laypeople and emergency management officials subscribe to disaster mythology? A comparative analysis [Masters thesis]. Illinois: Illinois State University.

Ekici S, McEntire DA, Afedzie R. (2009) Transforming debris management: new essentials to consider. Disaster Prevent Manage, 18 (5): 511–522.

Eldar R. (1992) The needs of elderly persons in natural disasters: observations and recommendations. Disasters, 16 (4):355–357.

EmergencyNet News Service. (1999, August 20) Services Report, Volume 3, p 232.

Enarson E. (1999) Women and housing issues in two U.S. disasters. Int J Mass Emerg Disasters, 17 (1):39–63.

Enarson E, Morrow BH. (1997) A gendered perspective: the voices of women. In: Peacock WG, Morrow BH, Gladwin H, editors. *Hurricane Andrew: Ethnicity, Gender and the Sociology of Disasters*. New York: Routledge. p 116–137.

EPA. (1995) Planning for disaster debris. EPA530-K-95-010. Washington, DC: Office of Solid Waste.

EPA. (2006a) Global warming. Available at http://yosemite.epa.gov/oar/globalwarming.nsf/content/index.html. Accessed January 18, 2006.

EPA. (2006b) Changing climate. Available at http://yosemite.epa.gov/oar/globalwarming.nsf/content/climate.html. Accessed January 18, 2006.

Everly GS. (1999) Toward a model of psychological triage: who will most need assistance? Int J Emerg Mental Health, 3:151–154.

Everly GS. (2000) The role of pastoral crisis intervention in disasters, terrorism, violence and other community crises. Int J Emerg Mental Health, 2 (3):139–142.

Falkenrath RA, Newman RD, Thayer BA. (1998) *America's Achilles' Heel: Nuclear, Biological and Chemical Terrorism and Covert Attack*. Cambridge: MIT Press.

Falkiner L. (2005) Availability of Canadian social science disaster management education. Int J Mass Emerg Disasters, 23 (1):85–110.

FAO. (2002) Preparation of foot-and-hand disease contingency plans. Available at ftp://ftp.fao.org/docrep/fao/005/y4382E/y4382E00.pdf. Accessed February 1, 2006.

Farazmond A. (2001) *Handbook of Crisis and Emergency Management*. New York: Marcel Dekker, Inc.

Fauchereau N, Trzaska S, Rouault M, Richard Y. (2003) Rainfall variability and changes in Southern Africa during the 20th century in the global warming context. Nat Hazards, 29 (2):139–154.

Faulkner S, McLean A, Othan-Chande M, Hassan Quoreshi A, Alvaro Ruiz J, Taylor J, Wenger A. (1989) *The Things We Give: A Critical Look at Donations in Kind*. Geneva: Henry Dunant Institute.

Faupel CE, Kelley SP, Petee T. (1992) The impact of disaster education on household preparedness for Hurricane Hugo. Int J Mass Emerg Disasters, 10 (1):5–24.

FEMA. (1981) *Disaster Operations: A Handbook for Local Government*. Washington, DC: FEMA.

FEMA. (1983) Emergency Manager: An Orientation to the Position. IS-1. Emmitsburg: Federal Emergency Management Agency. Available at http://training.fema.gov/EMIWeb/is/crslist.asp. Accessed June 18, 2014.

FEMA. (1994) Inspection of FEMA's debris removal mission. Available at http://www.fema.gov/ig/i-01-94.shtm. Accessed June 18, 2014.

FEMA. (1995) An Orientation to Community Disaster Exercises. IS-SM 120. Emmitsburg: Federal Emergency Management Agency. Available at http://training.fema.gov/EMIWeb/is/crslist.asp. Accessed June 18, 2014.

FEMA. (1996) Guide for All-Hazard Emergency Operations Planning. SLG-101. Emmitsburg: Federal Emergency Management Agency. Available at http://training.fema.gov/EMIWeb/is/crslist.asp. Accessed June 18, 2014.

FEMA. (1997a) *Debris Management Course*. Emmitsburg: Emergency Management Institute, National Emergency Training Center.

FEMA. (1997b) *Multi-Hazard Identification and Risk Assessment: A Cornerstone of the National Mitigation Strategy*. Washington, DC: FEMA.

FEMA. (1997c) A Citizen's Guide to Disaster Assistance. IS-7. Washington, DC: FEMA.

FEMA. (1998a) Incident Command System. Independent Study—195. Emmitsburg: Emergency Management Institute.

FEMA. (1998b) Emergency preparedness U.S.A. IS-2. Emmitsburg: Federal Emergency Management Agency. Available at http://training.fema.gov/EMIWeb/is/crslist.asp. Accessed June 18, 2014.

FEMA. (1998c) Introduction to Mitigation. IS-393. Emmitsburg: Federal Emergency Management Agency. Available at http://training.fema.gov/EMIWeb/is/crslist.asp. Accessed June 18, 2014.

FEMA. (1998d) Public Assistance Policy Digest. FEMA 321. Washington, DC: FEMA.

FEMA. (1999a) Public Assistance Guide. FEMA 322. Washington, DC: FEMA.

FEMA. (1999b) The Professional in Emergency Management. IS-513. Emmitsburg: Federal Emergency Management Agency. Available at http://training.fema.gov/EMIWeb/is/crslist.asp. Accessed June 18, 2014.

FEMA. (1999c) The Role of Voluntary Agencies in Emergency Management. IS-288. Emmitsburg: Federal Emergency Management Agency.

FEMA. (1999d) *When Disaster Strikes … Donated Goods and Volunteers May Be Needed … How You Can Help.* Washington, DC: Federal Emergency Management Agency.

FEMA. (1999e) *Public Assistance Debris Management Guide.* Washington, DC: Federal Emergency Management Agency.

FEMA. (1999f) Emergency Response to Terrorism, Self Study (ERT:SS-Q534). Washington, DC: FEMA. Available at www.usfa.fema.gov/applications/nfacsd/display.jsp?cc=Q534. Accessed July 2, 2014.

FEMA. (2000a) Equipment cache list. Available at http://www.fema.gov/pdf/usr/tfcache2000.pdf. Accessed June 18, 2014.

FEMA. (2000b) Urban search & rescue response system operations manual. Available at http://www.fema.gov/usr/usrdocs.shtm. Accessed September 3, 2003.

FEMA. (2001a) Local governments should be aware of fraudulent debris contractors. Available at http://www.fema.gov/diz00/d1354n24.shtm. Accessed June 18, 2014.

FEMA. (2001b) Urban search & rescue field operations guide. Available at http://www.fema.gov/usr/usrdocs.shtm. Accessed June 18, 2014.

FEMA. (2002a) Mass fatalities incident response, course G386, March 4–5, 2013. Doral: Miami-Dade Department of Health.

FEMA. (2002b) Introduction to Debris Operations in FEMA's Public Assistance Program. IS-632. Available at http://training.fema.gov/emiweb/IS/is632.asp. Accessed June 18, 2014.

FEMA. (2003a) Full array of disaster assistance programs available to help you. Available at http://www.fema.gov/rt/1044-1d.shtm. Accessed June 18, 2014.

FEMA. (2003b, November) Proceedings, Volunteers in Homeland Security Conference, Austin.

FEMA. (2003c) Debris removal management issues, OPM circular A-102. Available at http://www.fema.gov/doc.ig/debrisremoval.doc. Accessed June 18, 2014.

FEMA. (2003d) Disposing of debris and removing hazardous waste. Available at http://www.fema.gov/regions/iii/env/debris.shtm. Accessed June 18, 2014.

FEMA. (2003e) Public assistance. Available at http://www.fema.gov/rrr/pa/. Accessed July 26, 2013.

FEMA. (2003f) Light search and rescue. In: *Community Emergency Response Teams Training Manual*. Emmitsburg: Emergency Management Institute, Federal Emergency Management Agency. Available at http://training.fema.gov/EMIWeb/cert/mtrls.asp. Accessed June 18, 2014.

FEMA. (2003g) Emergency Planning. IS-235. Emmitsburg: Federal Emergency Management Agency. Available at http://training.fema.gov/EMIWeb/is/crslist.asp. Accessed June 18, 2014.

FEMA. (2003h) Principles of Emergency Management. IS-230. Emmitsburg: Federal Emergency Management Agency. Available at http://training.fema.gov/EMIWeb/is/crslist.asp. Accessed June 18, 2014.

FEMA. (2004a) Department of homeland security establishes national incident management system integration center. Available at http://www.fema.gov/news/newsrelease.fema?id=12385. Accessed June 18, 2014.

FEMA. (2004b) Fact sheet: national incident management system (NIMS). Available at http://www.dhs.gov/dhspublic/display?theme=14&content=3697. Accessed December 7, 2004.

FEMA. (2004c) National incident management system (NIMS): an introduction. IS-700. Available at http://training.fema.gov/EMIWeb/IS/is700.asp. Accessed November 22, 2005.

FEMA. (2004d) The national incident management system (NIMS) integration center. Available at http://www.fema.gov/news/newsrelease.fema?id=12385. Accessed June 18, 2014.

FEMA. (2004e) Are you ready? An in Depth Guide to Citizen Preparedness. IS-22. Emmitsburg: Federal Emergency Management Agency. Available at http://training.fema.gov/EMIWeb/is/crslist.asp. Accessed June 18, 2014.

FEMA. (2011) *CERT Training Manual*. Washington, DC: Federal Emergency Management Agency. Available at http://www.fema.gov/media-library-data/20130726-1839-25045-8729/pm_combined.pdf. Accessed June 18, 2014.

FEMA. (2012a, October 25) Glossary of terms. Federal Emergency Management Agency. Retrieved August 7, 2013. Available at http://www.fema.gov/vii-glossary-terms. Accessed June 18, 2014.

FEMA. (2012b, June 16) Whole community. Federal Emergency Management Agency. Retrieved August 7, 2013. Available at http://www.fema.gov/whole-community. Accessed June 18, 2014.

FEMA. (2013a) New FEMA guidance for sheltering disabled in emergencies. Occupational Health & Safety. Available at http://ohsonline.com/articles/2010/11/04/new-fema-guidance-forsheltering-disabled-in-emergencies.aspx. Accessed June 18, 2014.

FEMA. (2013b) Community Hurricane Preparedness. IS-324. Emmitsburg: Federal Emergency Management Agency. Available at http://training.fema.gov/EMIWeb/IS/courseOverview.aspx?code=IS-324.a. Accessed June 18, 2014.

FEMA. EMI workshop E270.1, Workshop in emergency management: asking for help. Available at http://www.nh.gov/safety/divisions/hsem/Training/trainingemdesc.html. Accessed on June 28, 2014.

FEMA. Introduction to Community Emergency Response Teams. IS-317. Emmitsburg: Federal Emergency Management Agency. Available at http://training.fema.gov/EMIWeb/is/crslist.asp. Accessed June 18, 2014.

FEMA. State Disaster Management. IS-280. Emmitsburg: Federal Emergency Management Agency. Available at http://training.fema.gov/EMIWeb/is/crslist.asp. Accessed June 18, 2014.

FEMA/National Donations Management Steering Committee. (1985) *Donations Management Guidance Manual.* Washington, DC: Federal Emergency Management Agency.

Ferrante J. (2004, October 13) Clear out storm debris by Friday. *Tampa Tribune.*

Ferrara P. (2013) Your move, global warming alarmists. Science has exposed your unwarranted hysteria. *Forbes.* Available at http://www.forbes.com/sites/peterferrara/2013/09/22/your-move-global-warming-alarmists-science-has-exposed-your-unwarranted-hysteria/. Accessed June 28, 2014.

Firth C. (2003) Mapping gets mobile: new solutions in public safety mapping systems—and new challenges. 9-1-1 Magazine, 16 (1): 46–48.

Fischer HW III. (1998a) *Response to Disaster: Fact Versus Fiction and its Perpetuation: The Sociology of Disaster.* Lanham: University Press of America.

Fischer HW III. (1998b) The role of the new information technologies in Emergency mitigation, planning, response and recovery. Disaster Prev Manage, 7 (1):28–37.

Fischer HW III. (1999a) Hurricane Georges: The Experience of the Media and Emergency Management on the Mississippi Gulf Coast. Quick Response Report #117. Boulder: Natural Hazards Research and Applications Information Center, University of Colorado.

Fischer HW III. (1999b) Dimensions of biological terrorism: to what must we mitigate and respond? Disaster Prev Manage, 8 (1):27–32.

Fischer HW III. (2000) Mitigation and response planning in a bio-terrorist attack. Disaster Prev Manage, 9 (5):360–367.

Fischer HW, Stine GF, Stoker BL, Trowbridge ML, Drain EM. (1995) Evacuation behaviour: why do some evacuate, while others do not? A case study of the Ephrata, Pennsylvania (USA) evacuation. Disaster Prev Manage, 4 (4):30–36.

Flannery R. (2003) Psychological trauma and post-traumatic stress disorder: a review. Int J Emerg Mental Health, 77–82. Available at http://www.icisf.org/articles/Acrobat%20documents/TerrorismIncident/PsyTrauPTSD.pdf. Accessed June 18, 2014.

Flannery R, Everly GS. (2003) Crisis intervention: a review. Int J Emerg Mental Health, 119–125. Available at http://www.icisf.org/articles/acrobat%20documents/TerrorismIncident/CrsintRev.pdf. Accessed June 18, 2014.

Flin R. (2002) *Incident Command: Tales from the Hot Seat.* Burlington: Ashgate Publishing Company.

Florida Commission on Community Service. ( no date) *Unaffiliated Volunteers in Response and Recovery.* Tallahassee: Florida Commission on Community Service.

Flynn K, Dwyer J. (2002, August 3) Fire department lapses on 9/11 are cited. *New York Times.* Available at http://www.story.news.yahoo.com/n...s_nyt/fire_dept__lapses_on_9_11_are_cited.     Accessed June 18, 2014.

Fothergill A. (1996) Gender, risk and disaster. Int J Mass Emerg Disasters, 14 (1):33–56.

Fothergill A, Maestas EGM, Darlington JD. (1999) Race, ethnicity and disasters in the United States: a review of the literature. Disasters, 33 (2):156–173.

Fowler AM, Hennessy KJ. (2003) Potential impacts of global warming on the frequency and magnitude of heavy precipitation. Nat Hazards, 11 (3):283–303.

Fox M, Bowlus D. (1996, March) Critical incident stress effects on wildland firefighters. Wildfire, p 41–46.

French, SP. (1990) The damage assessment process: an overview. In: Bolin R, editor. *The Loma Prieta Earthquake: Studies of Short-Term Impacts.* Program on Environment and Behavior Monograph #50. Boulder: Institute of Behavioral Science, University of Colorado.

French BM. (1998) *Traces of Catastrophe: A Handbook of Shock-Metamorphic Effects in Terrestrial Meteorite Impact Structures.* LPI Contribution No. 954. Houston: Lunar and Planetary Institute. pp. 120.

Fritz CE, Marx E. (1954) The NORC studies of human behavior in disaster. J Soc Issues, 10:26–41.

Fritz CE, Mathewson J. (1957) *Convergence Behavior in Disasters.* National Research Council Disaster Study #9. Washington, DC: National Academy of Sciences.

Fritz CE, Eli JH, Marks S. (1954) The NORC studies of human behavior in disaster. J Soc Issues, 10:26–41.

Gant DB. (1996) The Potential Impact of Information Technology on the Structure of Interorganizational Relationships During Crisis Response: The Pennsylvania Floods of 1996. Quick Response Report # 85. Boulder: Natural Hazards Research and Information Applications Center, University of Colorado.

Garrity TE. (1989, August/September) The need for psychological assistance in the fire service. *The Voice.* p 14.

Geis D. (2000) By design: the disaster resistant and quality of life community. Nat Hazards Rev, 1 (3):151–160.

General Accounting Office, Project SAFECOM. (2004) *Key Cross-Agency Emergency Communications Efforts Requires Stronger Collaboration.* Washington, DC: United States General Accounting Office.

Gibbs M, Lachenmeyer JR, Broska A, Deucher R. (1996) Effects of the AVIANCA aircrash on disaster workers. Int J Mass Emerg Disasters, 14 (1):23–32.

Gillespie DF, Streeter CF. (1987) Conceptualizing and measuring disaster preparedness. Int J Mass Emerg Disasters, 5 (2):155–176.

Glatzmaier G, Olson P. (2005) Probing the geodynamo. Sci Am, 292 (4):51–58.

Goddard J. (2013, August 15) Buried for 27 days: Haiti earthquake survivor's amazing story. *The Telegraph.* Telegraph Media Group Limited. Available at http://www.telegraph.co.uk/news/worldnews/centralamericaandthecaribbean/haiti/7530686/Buried-for-27-days-Haiti-earthquake-survivors-amazing-story.html. Accessed September 15, 2013.

Godschalk DR. (1991) Disaster mitigation and hazard management. In: Hoetmer GJ, Drabek TE, editors. *Emergency Management: Principles and Practice for Local Government.* Washington, DC: ICMA.

Golden J, Adams CR. (2000) The tornado problem: forecast, warning and response. Nat Hazards Rev, 1 (2):107–118.

Gordon JA. (2002) *Comprehensive Emergency Management for Local Governments: Demystifying Emergency Planning.* Brookfield: Rothstein Associated Inc.

Gordon M. (2004) Climate change and extreme weather: a basis for action. Nat Hazards, 31 (1):177–190.

Governor's Committee on Disaster Planning and Response. (1993) *The Lewis Report* (Hurricane Andrew). Tallahassee: Florida Division of Emergency Management.

Graham H, Graham J. (1989) CARDA dogs are search-and-rescue superstars. Am Fire J, 41 (February):28–31.

Green S. (1977) *International Disaster Relief: Towards a Responsive System.* New York: McGraw-Hill.

Green W. (2001) *Command and Control of Disaster Operations.* Richmond: Universal Publishers.

Greene RW. (2002) *Confronting Catastrophe: A GIS Handbook.* Redlands: ESRI Press.

Gruntfest E, Weber M. (1998) Internet and emergency management: prospects for the future. Int J Mass Emerg Disasters, 16 (1):55–72.

Gryzkewicz R. (1996) Preparation and teamwork key to mass fatality situations. *The Director* November, p 57–59.

Haddow GD, Bullock JA. (2003a) *Introduction to Emergency Management.* Burlington: Butterworth-Heinemann.

Haddow GD, Bullock JA. (2003b) The disciplines of emergency management: recovery. In: Haddow GD, Bullock JA, editors. *Introduction to Emergency Management*. Burlington: Butterworth-Heinemann. p 95–114.

Hafter JL, Fedor VL. (2004) *EMS and the Law*. Boston: Jones and Bartlett Publishers.

Hall MJ, Norwood AN, Ursano RJ, Fullerton CS, Levinson CJ. (2002) Psychological and behavioral impacts of bioterrorism. PTSD Res Q, 13 (4):1–8.

Hamada M. (1991, November 13–15) Damage assessment of lifeline systems in Japan. In: Proceedings of the 3rd United States/Japan workshop on Urban Earthquake Hazard Reduction; Honolulu, Hawaii; USA/Japan: Earthquake Engineering Research Institute/ Institute of Social Safety Science; 1991.

Hammond DJ. (1989) Urban search and rescue: an engineer's view. *Response*, (Winter), p 18–20.

Hampson R, Moore MT. (2003, September 4) Two years after Sept. 11, NYC couple to bury son. *USA Today*. p 1A–2A.

Hancock L, Michaels D. (2003) Search for wreckage, remains just starting. *Dallas Morning News*, p 1A, 9A.

Handmer J. (2006) American exceptionalism or universal lesson? The implications of Hurricane Katrina for Australia. Aust J Emerg Manage, 21 (1):29–42.

Harbaugh B. (2001, November 11) So the red cross tugged hearts to raise money after the Sept. 11 attacks; the cause is worthy and donors, however well-intentioned, don't know what's best. *Oregonian*. Available at http://www.oregonlive.com/commentary/oregonian/ index.ssf?/x.../10053969102097322.xm. Accessed September 13, 2001.

Harrald JR, Stephens HR. (2001) From Texas City to Exxon Valdez: what have we learned about managing marine disasters. In: Farazmand A, editor. *Handbook of Crisis and Emergency Management*. Public Administration and Public Policy 93. New York: Marcel Dekker Inc. p 231–244.

Harris V. (1989, August/September) Beyond critical incident stress. *The Voice*. p 16–18.

Harris M, Baloglu M, Stacks JR. (2002) Mental health of trauma-exposed firefighters and critical incident stress debriefing. J Loss Trauma, 7:223–238.

Hart P'T. (1997) Preparing policy makers for crisis management: the role of simulations. J Contingencies Crisis Manage, 5 (4):207–214.

Hartman C. (2005, 15 October) Evicted by the storm. *New York Times*, editorial desk. p. 20.

Hawley CD. (2003) *Hazardous Materials Incidents*. Cliften Park: Thomson Delmar Learning.

Henriques DB, Barstow D. (2001, November 15) Red cross pledges all of terror fund to Sept. 11 victims. *New York Times*. Available at http://nytimes.com/2001/11/15/nyregion/15CROS.html? todaysheadlines. Accessed September 13, 2001.

Hewitt K. (1983) *Interpretations of Calamity: From the Viewpoint of Human Ecology*. Boston: Allen & Unwin.

Hoetmer GJ. (1991) Introduction. In: Hoetmer GJ, Drabek TE, editors. *Emergency Management: Principles and Practice for Local Government*. Washington, DC: ICMA.

Hoffman K. (1995) How are geomagnetic reversals related to field intensity? EOS, 76:289.

Hogan LJ. (2001) *Terrorism: Defensive Strategies for Individuals, Companies and Governments*. Frederick: Amlex, Inc.

Holt F. (1990) State-of-the-art emergency communications: Rhode Island's statewide enhanced 911 system. *Fire Engineering*, November, p 33–39.

Hooft PJ, Noji EK, Van De Voorde HP. (1989) Fatality management in mass casualty incidents. Forensic Sci Int, 40:3–14.

Hopkins J, Jones C. (2003, September 23) Disturbing legacy of rescues: suicide. *USA Today*. p 13A.

Hunt J. (1989, June) Citizen sheltering for a safe haven from the Haz Mat Storm. Am Fire J, 28–40.

Ingleton J, editor. (1999) *Natural Disaster Management*. Leicester: Tudor Rose.

Intergovernmental Panel on Climate Change. (2006) Available at http://www.ipcc.ch/. Accessed January 23, 2006.

International Critical Incident Stress Foundation, Inc. (2004) CISM Information Pamphlet. Ellicott City.

Irving P, Long A. (2001) Critical incident stress debriefing following traumatic life experiences. J Psychiatr Mental Health Nurs, 8 (4): 307–314.

Irwin RL. (1989) The incident command system (ICS). In: Auf der Heide E, editor. *Disaster Response: Principles of Preparedness and Coordination*. St. Louis: CV Mosby Company. p 133–161.

Iwai S, Kameda H. (1998, September 6–11) Post-earthquake reconnaissance and disaster information management methodologies. In: Proceedings of the 11th European conference on Earthquake Engineering, Paris.

Jackson D, Paton D. (2002) Developing disaster management capability: an assessment center approach. Disaster Prev Manag, 11 (2): 115–122.

Jacobs JA. (1984) *Reversals of the Earth's Magnetic Field*. Bristol: Adam Hilger, Ltd.

James A. (1992) The psychological impact of disaster and the nature of critical incident stress for emergency personnel. Disaster Prev Manage, 1 (1):63–69.

James AD, Rushton J. (2002) The economics of foot and mouth disease. Rev Sci Tech Off Int Epiz, 21 (3):637–644.

Jenkins SR. (1998) Emergency medical workers' mass shooting incident stress and psychological recovery. Int J Mass Emerg Disasters, 16 (2):181–197.

Jensen J. (2008) NIMS in Action: A Case Study of the System's use and Utility. Quick Response Report #203. Boulder, CO: Natural Hazards Center, University of Colorado at Boulder. Last modified August 2008. http://www.colorado.edu/hazards/research/qr/qr203.pdf. Accessed on January 31, 2014.

Jensen J. (2009) NIMS in Rural America. Int J Mass Emerg Disasters, 27 (3):218–249.

Jensen J. (2011) The current NIMS implementation behavior of United States Counties. J Homeland Security Emerg Manage, 8 (1):Article 20.

Jensen J. (2013, August 15) Report of the 2013 disciplinary purview focus group: scholarship and research to ground the emerging discipline of emergency management. Available at http://www.ndsu.edu/fileadmin/emgt/Jensen_-013_REPORT_DISCPLINE_ISSUES_WHITE_PAPER_FOCUS_GROUP__2_.pdf. Accessed June 27, 2014.

Jigyasu R. (2005) Cultural heritage concerns in WCDR. Int J Mass Emerg Disasters, 23 (1):141–160.

Jocius P. (1994) Critical incident stress: what to look for and what to do. ASPEP, 163–169.

Johnson WH, Matthews WR. (1997) Disaster plan simulates plane crash into high-rise building. Disaster Prev Manage, 6 (5):311–317.

Johnsson P. (2011) Joplin Tornado: with one-third of Homes Gone, where will residents live? *Christian Science Monitor*. Available at http://www.csmonitor.com/USA/2011/0531/Joplin-tornado-With-one-third-of-homes-gone-where-will-residents-live. Accessed June 25, 2013.

Jones T. (1994) Cellular phones: playing an increasing role in public safety. APCO Bull, 60 (February):10–14.

Jones RN. (2001) An environmental risk assessment/management framework for climate change impact assessments. Nat Hazards, 23 (2–3):197–230.

Kaiser R, Spiegel P, Henderson A, Gerber M. (2003) The application of geographic information systems and global positioning system in humanitarian emergencies: lessons learned, program implications, and future research. Disasters, 27 (2):127–140.

Kartez JD. (1982) Emergency Planning Implications of Local Governments' Responses to Mount St. Helens. Working Paper #46. Boulder: Environmental Research Center, Washington State University.

Kartez JD, Lindell MK. (1987) Planning for uncertainty: the case of local disaster planning. Am Plann Assoc J, 53:487–498.

Kates RW. (1977) *Managing Technological Hazard: Research Needs and Opportunities*. Program on Technology Environment and Man

Monograph #25. Boulder: Institute of Behavioral Science University of Colorado.

Kates RW. (1985) The interaction of climate and society. In: Kates RW, Ausubel JH, Berberian M, editors. *Climate Impact Assessment.* New York: Wiley.

Kemp RL. (2003) *Homeland Security: Best Practices for Local Government.* Washington, DC: ICMA.

Kendra JM, Wachtendorf T. (2003a) Elements of resilience after the World Trade Center disaster: reconstituting New York City's emergency operations center. Disasters, 27 (1):37–53.

Kendra JM, Wachtendorf T. (2003b) Creativity in emergency response to the World Trade Center disaster. In: Monday JL, editor. *Beyond September 11th: An Account of Post-disaster Research.* Program on Environment and Behavior Special Publication #39. Boulder: Institute of Behavioral Science: Natural Hazards Research and Applications Information Center: University of Colorado. p 121–146.

Kendra JM, Wachtendorf T. (2003c) Reconsidering convergence and converger legitimacy in response to the World Trade Center disaster. In: Clarke L, editor. *Terrorism and Disaster: New Threats, New Ideas.* Research in Social Problems and Public Policy 11. New York: Elsevier. p 97–122.

Kent RC. (1987) *Anatomy of Disaster Relief.* New York: Pinter Publishers.

Ketcham J. (1998, November 17) The trouble with trousers. Available at http://www.disasternews.com/disasters/clothing.shtml. Accessed September 13, 2001.

Khaleej Times Staff Journalist (2005) Gretna residents support decision to ban entry of blacks in wake of Katrina. Dubai: Khaleej Times.

Killian LM. (1956) *An Introduction to Methodological Problems of Field Studies in Disasters.* Washington, DC: National Academy of Sciences, National Research Council.

Killian L. (1994) Are social movements irrational or are they collective behavior? In: Dynes R, Tierney K, editors. *Disasters, Collective Behavior and Social Organization.* Newark: University of Delaware Press.

Kim S. (1999a) Making disaster donations count. Retrieved May 20. Available at http://www.disasternews.com/howtohelp/greenbeans.shtml. Accessed June 15, 2014.

Kim S. (1999b) Needed donations can change lives. Retrieved April 14. Available at http://www.disasternews.com/howtohelp/gettingitright.shtml. Accessed June 15, 2014.

Kim S. (1999c) Unwanted donations are second disaster. Retrieved April 5. Available at http://www.disasternews.com/howtohelp/inappropriate.shtml. Accessed June 15, 2014.

Kim PS, Lee JE. (2001) Emergency management in Korea. In: Farazmand A, editor. *Handbook of Crisis and Emergency Management.* Public Administration and Public Policy 93. New York: Marcel Dekker Inc.

Kipp J, Loflin M. (1996) *Emergency Incident Risk Management.* New York: ITP.

Kirschenbaum A. (2002) Disaster preparedness: a conceptual and empirical reevaluation. Int J Mass Emerg Disasters, 20 (1): 5–28.

Kreps GA. (1991a) Organizing for emergency management. In: Hoetmer GJ, Drabek TE, editors. *Emergency Management: Principles and Practice for Local Government.* Washington, DC: ICMA.

Kreps GA. (1991b) Organizing for emergency management. In: Drabek T, Hoetmer G, editors. *Emergency Management: Principles and Practice for Local Government.* Washington, DC: International City Management Association. p 30–54.

Kriner S. (2000) Red Cross caseworker helps Oklahoma City move on. Retrieved April 24. Available at http://www.disasterrelief.org/ Disasters/000420Oklahoma2/. Accessed June 15, 2014.

Kripalani RH, Kulkarni A, Sabade SS, Khandekar ML. (2003) Indian monsoon variability in a global warming scenario. Nat Hazards, 29 (2):189–206.

Krüger GC, Leckebusch ML, Iwona Piskwar M, Kurexzka AW. (1996) Critical incident stress in law enforcement. FBI Law Enforcement Bull, 65 (2/3):10–16.

Kundzewicz ZW, Ulbrich U, Brücher T, Graczyk D, Krüger A, Leckebusch GC, Menzel L, Pinskwar I, Radziejewski M, Szwed M. (2005) Summer floods in Central Europe—climate change track? Nat Hazards, 36:165–189. DOI: 10.1007/s11069-004-4547-6.

LaPlante JM. (1988a) Recovery following disaster: policy issues and dimensions. In: Comfort LK, editor. *Managing Disaster: Strategies and Policy Perspectives.* Durham: Duke University Press. p 217–235.

LaPlante JM, Kroll-Smith JS. (1988b) Centralia: the Nightmare which would not end. In: Charles MT, Kim JCK, editors. *Crisis Management: A Casebook.* Springfield: Charles C. Thomas Publisher. p 85–100.

Larsson G, Enander A. (1997) Preparing for disaster: public attitudes and actions. Disaster Prev Manage, 6 (1):11–21.

La Trobe S. (2005) Tearfund. Int J Mass Emerg Disasters, 23 (1):141–160.

Leibovici D, Gofrit ON, Heruti RJ, Shapira SC, Shemer J, Stein M. (1997) Interhospital patient transfer: a quality improvement indicator for prehospital triage in mass casualties. Am J Emerg Med, 15 (4):341–344.

Lesser I. (1999) *Countering the New Terrorism.* Santa Monica: RAND.

Lin C, Siebeneck LK, Lindell MK, Prater CS, Wu H, Huang S. (2011) Evacuees' information sources and reentry decision making in the aftermath of Hurricane Ike. Nat Hazards. 70 (1):865–882.

Lindell MK. (1994) Are local emergency planning committees effective in developing community disaster preparedness? Int J Mass Emerg Disasters, 12 (2):159–182.

Lindell M, Perry RW. (1992) *Behavioral Foundations of Community Emergency Planning.* Washington, DC: Hemisphere Publishing Company.

Lipsitch M, Cohen T, Cooper B, Robins J, Ma S, James L, Gopalakrishna G, Chew SK, Tan CC, Samore M, Fisman D, Murray M. (2003) Transmission dynamics and control of severe acute respiratory syndrome. Science, 300:1966–1970.

Lloyd C, Creson DL, D'Antonio MS. (1993) A petrochemical plant disaster: lessons for the future. J Soc Behav Pers, 8 (5):281–298.

Lowe S, Fothergill A. (2003) A need to help: emergent volunteer behavior after September 11th. In: Monday J, editor. *Beyond September 11th: An Account of Post-disaster Research.* Special Publication #39. Boulder: Natural Hazards Research and Applications Information Center, University of Colorado.

Lutz LD, Lindell MK. (2008) Incident command system as a response model within Emergency Operation Centers during Hurricane Rita. J Contingencies Crisis Manage, 16 (3):122–134.

Lynem J. (2004, January 9) Artifacts are broken, but not beyond repair. *The Tribune.* p A1.

Macko S. (1999, August 20) Lessons learned from the Columbine massacre. ERRI Emergency Services Report-EmergencyNet News Service-Friday, Vol. 3, p 232.

Maniscalco PM, Christen HT. (2001) *Understanding Terrorism and Managing the Consequences.* Upper Saddle River: Prentice Hall.

Mancini MR, Gale AT. (1981) *Emergency Care and the Law.* Rockville: Aspen Systems Corp.

Mariano W. (2004, October 9) Hurricane debris burdens neighbors. *Orlando Sentinel.*

Maret I. (2006) Washed away by Hurricane Katrina? J Archit Edu, 60 (1):15–17.

Massell BF, Winter SG Jr. (1961) *Post Attack Damage Assessment: A Conceptual Analysis.* Memorandum RM-2844-PR. Santa Monica: Rand Corporation.

May PJ. (1985a) Mount St. Helens: a case study. In: *Recovering from Catastrophes: Federal Disaster Relief Policy and Politics.* Contributions in Political Science, 128. Westport: Greenwood Press. p 71–86.

May PJ. (1985b) Political influence, electoral benefits and disaster relief. In: *Recovery from Catastrophe: Federal Disaster Relief Policy and Politics.* Contributions in Political Science, 128. Westport: Greenwood Press. p 104–128.

May PJ. (1988) Disaster recovery and reconstruction. In: Comfort L, editor. *Managing Disasters: Strategies and Policy Perspectives.* Durham: Duke University Press. p 236–251.

Mayer TA. (1997) Triage: history and horizons. Top Emerg Med, 19 (2):1–11.

McCuen GE. (1999) *Biological Terrorism and Weapons of Mass Destruction.* Hudson: GEM Publications.

McEntire DA. (1997) Reflecting on the weaknesses of the international community during the IDNDR: some implications for research and its application. Disaster Prev Manage, 6 (4):221–233.

McEntire DA. (2000a) Sustainability or invulnerable development? Justifications for a modified disaster reduction concept and policy guide [Ph.D. Dissertation]. Denver: University of Denver.

McEntire DA. (2000b) Coordinating multi-organizational responses to disaster: lessons from the March 28, 2000, Fort Worth Tornado. Disaster Prev Manage, 11 (5):369–379.

McEntire DA. (2000c) Understanding and improving damage assessment. IAEM Bull, 19 (May):9–12.

McEntire DA. (2003a) The community dispatch center: an assessment of neglected component of emergency management. J Emerg Manage, 1 (1):41–61.

McEntire DA. (2003b) Causation of catastrophe: lessons from Hurricane Georges. J Emerg Manage, 1 (2):22–29.

McEntire DA. (2004a) The status of emergency management theory. Paper presented at the FEMA Higher Education Conference; Emmitsburg.

McEntire DA. (2004b) Tenets of vulnerability: an assessment of a fundamental disaster concept. J Emerg Manage, 2 (2):23–29.

McEntire DA. (2006) Managing Debris successfully after disasters: considerations and recommendations for emergency managers. J Emerg Manage, 4 (4):23–28.

McEntire DA. (2007) The historical challenges facing emergency management and homeland security. J Emerg Manage, 5 (4):17–23.

McEntire DA. (2009) *Emergency Management Grant Administration for Local Government*. IQ Service Report. Vol. 41, no. 2. Washington, DC: ICMA.

McEntire DA. (2012) The current crisis and impending disaster. J Emerg Manage, 10 (5):317–318.

McEntire DA, Cope J. (2004) Damage Assessment after the Paso Robles (San Simeon, California) Earthquake: Lessons for Emergency Management. Quick Response Report 166. Boulder: Natural Hazards Center, University of Colorado at Boulder. Available at http://www.colorado.edu/hazards/qr/qr166/qr166.html. Accessed December 9, 2011.

McEntire DA, Myers A. (2004) Preparing communities for disasters: issues and processes for government readiness. Disaster Prev Manage, 13 (2):140–152.

McEntire DA, Robinson R, Weber R. (2001) Managing the Threat of Terrorism. IQ Service Report. Vol. 33, no. 12. Washington, DC: International City/County Management Association.

McEntire DA, Fuller C, Johnson CW, Weber R. (2002) A comparison of disaster paradigms: the search for a holistic policy guide. Public Adm Rev, 62 (3):267–281.

McEntire DA, Robinson RJ, Weber RT. (2003) Business responses to the World Trade Center disaster: a study of corporate roles, functions, and interaction with the public sector. In: *Beyond September 11th: An Account of Post-Disaster Research*. Special Publication #39. Boulder: Institute of Behavioral Science, Natural Hazards Research and Applications Information Center, University of Colorado. p 431–459.

McEntire DA, Sadiq A, Gupta K. (2012) Unidentified bodies and mass fatality management in Haiti: a case study of the January 2010 earthquake with a cross-cultural comparison. Int J Mass Emerg Disasters, 30 (3):301–327.

McEntire DA, Kendra JM, Kelly J, Long L. (2013) Spontaneous planning in the San Bruno gas pipeline explosion: a case study of anticipation and improvisation during response operations. J Homeland Security Emerg Manage, 10 (1):1–25.

McGlown KJ. (2004) *Terrorism and Disaster Management: Preparing Healthcare Leaders for the New Reality*. ACHE Management Series. Chicago: Health Administration Press.

McKay GA. (1991) The changing atmosphere: a review. Nat Hazards, 4 (4):353–372.

McLuckie BF. (1970) *A Study of Functional Response to Stress in Three Societies*. Columbus: Ohio State University.

McNally V, Solomon R. (1999) The FBI's critical incident management program. FBI Law Enforcement Bull, 68 (2):20–25.

McWhirter EH, Linzer M. (1994) The provision of critical incident stress debriefing services. J Mental Health Counsel, 6 (4):403.

Merck Veterinarian Manual. (2003) Foot-and-mouth disease: introduction. Available at http://www.merckvetmanual.com/mvm/index. jsp?cfile=htm/bc/51000.htm&word=foot%2cand%2cmouth. Accessed February 1, 2006.

Merriman PA, Browitt CWA. (1993) *Natural Disasters: Protecting Vulnerable Communities*. London: Thomas Telford.

Mileti DS. (1989) Catastrophe Planning and the grass roots: a lesson to the U.S.A. from the U.S.S.R. Int J Mass Emerg Disasters, 7 (1):57–67.

Mileti D, Passarini E. (1996) A social explanation of urban relocation after disasters. Int J Mass Emerg Disasters, 14 (1):97–110.

Mileti DS. (1999) *Disasters by Design: A Reassessment of Natural Hazards in the United States*. Washington, DC: Joseph Henry Press.

Mileti DS, Sorensen JH, O'Brien PW. (1992) Toward an explanation of mass care shelter use in evacuations. Int J Mass Emerg Disasters, 10 (1):25–42.

Ministry of the Interior. (2011) *Red Sludge: Hungary 2010*. Budapest: Ministry of the Interior.

Minear L. (2002) *The Humanitarian Enterprise: Dilemmas and Discoveries*. Bloomfield: Kumarian Press.

Minear L, Weiss TG. (1995) *Mercy Under Fire: War and the Global Humanitarian Community*. Boulder: Westview Press.

Mitchell JT. (1987) Effective stress control at major incidents. MD Fire Rescue Bull, 16 (June):36.

Mitchell JT. (1988a) Stress: the history, status and future of critical incident stress debriefings. JEMS, 13 (11):47–52.

Mitchell JT. (1988b) Stress: development and functions of a critical incident stress debriefing team. JEMS, 13 (12):43–46.

Mitchell JT. (2004) Critical incident stress management (CISM): a defense of the field. Last modified January 9, 2004. Available at http://www.cism.cap.gov/files/articles/CISM_Defense_of_Field. pdf. Accessed February 1, 2014.

Mitchell JT. (2009, September) Developments in the critical incident management stress field. Paper presented at the Irish National Critical Incident Stress Management conference, National University of Ireland, Maynooth.

Mitchell JK. (1996) *The Long Road to Recovery: Community Responses to Industrial Disaster*. New York: United Nations University Press.

Mitchell JK. (1999) *Crucibles of Hazard: Mega-cities and Disasters in Transition*. New York: United Nations University Press.

Modzelewski E. (2004, October 9) Despite objections, storm debris going to Allapattah. *Palm Beach Post*.

Moore W. (1998) *Developing an Emergency Operations Center*. IQ Service Report. Vol. 30, no. 7. Washington, DC: ICMA.

Moskovitz D. (2004, October 10) St. Lucie County's pockets hit hard by debris cleanup. *Port St. Lucie News*.

Mravcak A. (1994, March 10) From the general to the specifics: National Donations Management Policy. Presentation at the Donated Goods and Services Workshop, National Hurricane Conference.

Moynihan D. (2006, November 2–4) What makes hierarchical networks succeed? Evidence from Hurricane Katrina. Madison.

Moynihan DP. (2008) Learning under uncertainty: networks in crisis management. Pub Admin Rev, 68 (2):350–365.

Moynihan D. (2009) The network governance of crisis response: case studies of incident command systems. J Pub Admin Res Theory, 19 (4):895–915.

Murray LS. (1995, March/April) Mass Fatality Management. *Street Skills*. p 30–31.

NASA. (2006a) Frequently asked questions. Available at http://neo.jpl. nasa.gov/faq/. Accessed February 14, 2006.

NASA. (2006b) Target Earth. Available at http://neo.jpl.nasa.gov/neo/ target.html. Accessed February 14, 2006.

National Academy of Sciences. Understanding and responding to climate change. Available at http://dels.nas.edu/basc/climate-change_ final.pdf. Accessed January 18, 2003.

National Advisory Council to the Congressional Fire Services Caucus Urban Search and Rescue Task Force. (1991) Urban search and rescue in the United States. White Paper for The Honorable Elton Gallegly, California Chairman, Urban Search and Rescue Task Force, Congressional Fire Service Caucus and The Honorable Curl Weldon, Pennsylvania Chairman, Congressional Fires Services Caucus.

National Biological Informational Infrastructure. (2006) West Nile virus: overview. Available at http://westnilevirus.nbii.gov/diseasehome.jsp?disease=West%20Nile%20Virus&pagemode=submit. Accessed January 31, 2006.

National Commission on Terrorist Attacks Upon the United States. (2004) *The 9/11 Commission Report*. New York: W.W. Norton.

National Institute for Occupational Safety and Health. (2006) Understanding respiratory protection against SARS. Available at http://www.cdc.gov/niosh/npptl/topics/respirators/factsheets/respsars.html. Accessed January 29, 2006.

National Intelligence Agency. (2006) Available at http://www.cia.gov/nic/special_sarsthreat.html. Accessed January 29, 2006.

National Oceanic and Atmospheric Administration. (2011) *NWS Central Region Service Assessment Joplin, Missouri, Tornado-May 22, 2011*. Kanas City: U.S. Department of Commerce.

National Symposium on Medical and Public Health Response to Bioterrorism. (1999) Emerging infectious diseases. Emmitsburg: National Center for Infectious Diseases, 5 (4). Available at http://www.cdc.gov/ncidod/eid/vol5no4/pdf/v5n4.pdf. Accessed June 18, 2014.

National Voluntary Organizations Active in Disaster. (2002) *NVOAD Newsletter* (Summer), Burtonsville.

Natural Hazards Research and Applications Information Center, University of Colorado. (2002) Public/Private Collaboration in Disaster: Implications from the World Trade Center Terrorist Attacks. Quick Response Report No. 155. Boulder: Natural Hazards Research and Information Application Center, University of Colorado.

Neal DM. (1984) Blame assignment in a diffuse disaster situation: a case example of the role of an emergent citizen group. Int J Mass Emerg Disasters, 2 (2):251–266.

Neal D. (1990) Volunteer organizations following the Loma Prieta earthquake: a look at tasks, organizational networks, and effectiveness. In: Bolin RC, editor. The Loma Prieta Earthquake: Studies of Short Term Impacts. Program on Environment and Behavior, Monograph #50. Boulder: Institute of Behavioral Science, University of Colorado at Boulder. p 91–97.

Neal DM. (1994) The consequences of excessive unrequested donations: the case of Hurricane Andrew. Disaster Manage, 6 (1):23–28.

Neal DM, Phillips BD. (1995) Effective emergency management: reconsidering the bureaucratic approach. Disasters, 19 (4):327–337.

Neal DM. (1997) Reconsidering the phases of disaster. Int J Mass Emerg Disasters, 15 (2):239–264.

Neal DM, Webb GR. (2006) Structural Barriers to Using the National Incident Management System. Learning from Catastrophe. Natural Hazard Center Special Publication No. 40. Boulder: Natural Hazards Center, University of Colorado at Boulder.

Neely KW, Spitzer WJ. (1997) A model for a statewide critical incident stress (CIS) debriefing program for emergency services personnel. Prehosp Disaster Med, 12 (2):114–118.

New York City Fire Department. (2002) McKinsey report: increasing FDNY's preparedness. Available at http://www.ci.nyc.ny.us/html/fdny/html/mck_report/toc.html. Accessed June 18, 2014.

NGDC. (2006) Geomagnetic field frequently asked questions. Available at http://www.ngdc.noaa.gov/seg/geomag/faqgeom.shtml. Accessed February 20, 2006.

Nicholson WC. (2003a) Litigation mitigation: proactive risk management in the wake of the West Warwick club fire. J Emerg Manage, 1 (2):14–18.

Nicholson WC. (2003b) *Emergency Response and Emergency Management Law: Cases and Materials.* Springfield: Charles C. Thomas Publishers, Ltd.

Nicholson WC. (2005a) Immunity law: protection for emergency responders. J Emerg Manage, 3 (1):12–13.

Nicholson WC. (2005b) NFPA 1600: The new standard for emergency management. J Emerg Manage, 3 (2):44–46.

Niesse M. (2004, October 9) County debris removal just 15% complete, official says. *Palatka Daily News.*

Nigg JM. (1994) Emergency response following the 1994 Northridge earthquake: intergovernmental coordination. In: Proceedings of the NEHRP Conference and Workshop on Research on the Northridge, California Earthquake of January 17, 1994.

Noji EK. (1997) *The Public Health Consequences of Disasters.* New York: Oxford University Press.

Noll GG, Yvorra J. (1995) *Hazardous Materials: Managing the Incident.* Stillwater: International Fire Service Training Association.

North Carolina Division of Emergency Management. (2002) North Carolina disaster debris planning manual: local government guide for Debris Management Planning, Raleigh.

North Dakota, Division of Emergency Management. (1998) *After Action Report of Donations Management.* Bismarck: North Dakota Division of Emergency Management.

North SC. (2002) Coping function and adjustment of rescue workers after Oklahoma City Bombing. J Trauma Stress, 15 (3):171–175.

NRC. (2005) Geomagnetism. Available at http://gsc.nrcan.gc.ca/geomag/nmp/reversals_e.php. Accessed June 18, 2014.

Oaks SD. (1990) The damage assessment process: an overview. In: Bolin R, editor. *The Loma Prieta Earthquake: Studies of Short-Term Impacts.* Program on Environment and Behavior, Monograph #50. Boulder: Institute of Behavioral Science, University of Colorado. p 6–16.

O'Brion C. (2011) Slow healing in Joplin, Missouri. Physician Exec, 37 (5):4–9.

O'Brien GO, Read P. (2005) Future UK emergency management: new wine, old skin? Disaster Prev Manage, 14 (3):353–361.

O'Brien PO, Mileti DS. (1992) Citizen participation in emergency response following the Loma Prieta earthquake. Int J Mass Emerg Disasters, 10 (1):71–89.

Occupational Health and Safety (OHS); New FEMA guidance for sheltering disabled in emergencies. (2010) Last modified November 4, 2010. Available at http://ohsonline.com/articles/2010/11/04/new-fema-guidance-for-sheltering-disabled-in-emergencies.aspx. Accessed on January 31, 2014.

Office of the Federal Register, National Archives and Records Administration. (2001) Code of Federal Regulations 44, Emergency Management and Assistance. (as of October 1, 2001). Washington, DC: U.S. Government Printing Office.

Office of Homeland Security. (2002) National Strategy for Homeland Security. Washington, DC: Office of Homeland Security.

O'Halloran P. (1989) Triage: issues and ethics. Emergency, February. p 45–47.

O'Keefe P, Westgate K, Wisner B. (1976) Taking the naturalness out of natural disasters. Nature, 260:566–567.

Oklahoma Department of Civil Emergency Management (ODCEM). (1995) Donations management case study of the Alfred P. Murrah Federal Building Bombing: 19 April 1995 in Oklahoma City, Oklahoma. Summary and lessons learned. Available at http://www.ok.gov/OEM/documents/Bombing%20After%20Action%20Report.pdf. Accessed June 27, 2014.

Oliver-Smith A. (1986) Natural Disasters and Cultural Responses. Williamsburg: William and Mary College.

Oliver-Smith A. (1994) Peru's five hundred year earthquake: vulnerability in historical context. In: Varley A, editor. Disasters, Development and Environment. London: Belhaven Press.

Olson RS, Drury AC. (1997) Un-therapeutic communities: a cross-national analysis of post-disaster political unrest. Int J Mass Emerg Disasters, 15 (2):221–238.

Olson RS, Olson RA, Gawronski VT. (1998) Night and day: mitigation policy making in Oakland, California before and after the Loma Prieta Disaster. Int J Mass Emerg Disasters, 14 (1):97–110.

Onder JJ. (1999, January) Media and law enforcement relations during hostage-taking terrorist incidents: a cooperative decision. Responder. p 26–32.

Oregon 1 Disaster Medical Assistance Team. (2001) Oregon disaster medical team standard operating procedure. Available at http://www.odmt.org/procedures.html. Accessed June 18, 2014.

Orloff L. (2011) Managing Spontaneous Community Volunteers in Disasters: A Field Manual. Boca Raton: CRC Press.

Oyola-Yemaiel A, Wilson J. Three essential strategies for emergency management professionalization in the U.S. Int J Mass Emerg Disasters 2005;23 (1):77–84.

Pan American Health Organization. (1994) *A World Safe From Natural Disasters: The Journey of Latin America and the Caribbean.* Washington, DC: PAHO.

Paton D, Smith L, Violanti J. (2000) Disaster response: risk, vulnerability and resilience. Disaster Prev Manage, 9 (3):173–179.

Patterson K. In disaster's wake use of 'Debriefing' to help people cope may not work, experts say. *Dallas Morning News,* September 30, 2002, p 1C, 5C.

Paul BK, Stimers M. (2012) Exploring probable reasons for record fatalities: the case of 2011 Joplin, Missouri, Tornado. Nat Hazards, 64 (2):1511–26.

Payne CF. (1994) Handling the press. Disaster Prev Manage, 3 (1):2–32.

Payne CF. (1999) Contingency plan exercises. Disaster Prev Manage, 8 (2):111–117.

Peacock WG. (1997) Cross-national and comparative disaster research. Int J Mass Emerg Disasters, 15 (1):117–133.

Peacock W, Morrow BH, Gladwin H, editors. (1997) *Hurricane Andrew and the Reshaping of Miami: Ethnicity, Generate and the Socio-Political Ecology of Disasters.* Gainesville: University Press of Florida.

PECC. (2005) Thailand, Pacific food system outlook 2004–05. Available at http://www.pecc.org/food/papers/2004-05/thailand-0405-profiles.pdf. Accessed February 7, 2006.

Peek LA, Sutton JN. (2003) An exploratory comparison of disasters, riots and terrorist acts. Disasters, 27 (3):319–335.

Pelling M. (2005) King's college London. Int J Mass Emerg Disasters, 23 (1):141–160.

Pepe PE, Kvetan V. (1991) Field management and critical care in mass disasters. Crit Care Clin, 7 (2):401–420.

Perlstein M, Lee T. (2005) Many New Orleans cops emerged as heroes. Some fled, while a few joined looters. Battle-scarred but intact, the NOPD now has a rare chance to reshape its future. The good & the bad. Available at http://www.nola.com/crime/stories/good_bad.html. Accessed August 6, 2014.

Perrow C. (1999) *Normal Accidents: Living With High-Risk Technologies.* New Jersey: Princeton University Press.

Perry RW. (1991) Managing disaster response operations. In: Drabek TE, Hoetmer GJ, editors. *Emergency Management: Principles and Practice for Local Government.* Washington, DC: ICMA. p 201–223.

Perry RW. (1995) The structure and function of emergency operations centers. Disaster Prevent Manage, 4 (5):37–41.

Perry RW. (2003a) Incident management systems in disaster management. Disaster Prev Manage, 12 (5):405–453.

Perry RW. (2003b) Municipal terrorism management in the United States. Disaster Prev Manage, 12 (3):190–202.

Phifer FJ. (1990) Psychological distress and somatic symptoms after natural disaster: differential vulnerability among older adults. Psychol Aging, 5 (3):412–420.

Pijawka DA, Radwan E, Soesilo JA. (1988) Emergency response to a hazardous materials rail incident in Casa Grande Arizona. In: Charles MT, Kim JCK, editors. *Crisis Management: A Casebook*. Springfield: C.C. Thomas. p 43–61.

Phillips BD. (1986) The media in disaster threat situations: some possible relationships between mass media reporting and voluntarism. Int J Mass Emerg Disasters, 4 (3):7–26.

Phillips BD. (1993) Cultural diversity in disasters: sheltering, housing and long term recovery. Int J Mass Emerg Disasters, 11 (1): 99–110.

Phillips BD. (2003, October 22) Disasters by discipline: necessary dialogue for emergency management education. Paper Presented at the Workshop, Creating Educational Opportunities for the Hazards Manager of the 21st Century, Denver.

Phillips BD. (2009) *Disaster Recovery*. Boca Raton: CRC Press.

Phillips BD, Deborah SKT, Fothergill A, Blinn-Pike L. (2010) *Social Vulnerability to Disasters*. Boca Raton: CRC Press.

Phillips BD, Neal DM, Webb GR. (2012) *Introduction to Emergency Management*. Boca Raton: CRC Press.

Pickett JH, Block BA. (1991) Day-today management. In: Hoetmer GJ, Drabek TE, editors. *Emergency Management: Principles and Practice for Local Government*. Washington, DC: ICMA.

Pijawka KD, Radwan AE. (1985) The transportation of hazardous materials: risk assessment and hazard management. Dangerous properties of Industrial Materials Report, (September/October). p 2–11.

Pijawka DA, Radwan E, Soesilo JA. (1988) Emergency response to a hazardous materials rail incident in Casa Grande Arizona. In: Charles MT, Kim JCK, editors. *Crisis Management: A Casebook*. Springfield: Charles C. Thomas Publisher. p 43–61.

Pine J. (1991) Liability issues. In: Drabek TE, Hoetmer GJ, editors. *Emergency Management: Principles and Practice for Local Government*. Washington, DC: ICMA. p 289–310.

Pinkowski J. (2001) Potential for disaster: case study of the Powell Duffryn chemical fire and hazardous material spill. In: Farazmand A, editor. *Handbook of Crisis and Emergency Management*. Public Administration and Public Policy 93. New York: Marcel Dekker Inc. p 433–450.

Platt RH. (1999) *Disasters and Democracy: The Politics of Extreme Natural Events*. Washington, DC: Island Press.

Pohl D, Bouchachia A, Hellwagner H. (2013, August 10) Automatic sub-event detection in emergency management using social media. In: SWDM '12 Workshop; 2012 Apr 16–20; Klagenfurt: Klagenfurt University. Available at http://www2012.wwwconference.org/proceedings/companion/p683.pdf. Accessed June 18, 2014.

Points of Light Foundation & Volunteer Center National Network. (2002) *Preventing a Disaster within the Disaster: The Effective Use and Management of Unaffiliated Volunteers*. Washington, DC: Points of Light Foundation & Volunteer Center National Network.

Porfiriev B. (1996) Social aftermath and organizational response to a major disaster: the case of the 1995 Sakhalin earthquake in Russia. J Contingencies Crisis Manage, 4:218–227.

Porfiriev B. (1999a) Development policy: a driving force of environmental hazard in Russia. Environ Hazards, 1:45–50.

Porfiriev B. (1999b) Emergency and disaster legislation in Russia: the key development trends and features. Aust J Emerg Manage, 14 (1): 59–64.

Portsea LJO. (1992) Disaster relief or relief disasters? A challenge to the international community. Disasters, 16 (1):1–8.

Poverty Overview. (2013) World Bank. Available at http://www.worldbank.org/en/topic/poverty/overview. Accessed on June 28, 2014.

Principles Focus Group. (2007) Emergency Management. FEMA.gov. Federal Emergency Management Agency. Web. 8 Aug. 2013. Available at http://training.fema.gov/EMIWeb/edu/docs/emprinciples/0907_176%20EM%20Principles12x18v2f%20Johnson%20(w-o%20draft).pdf. Accessed June 18, 2014.

Poulin TE. (2005) National threat—local response: building local disaster capacity with mutual aid agreements. PA TIMES, 28(3), p 3.

Powell M. N.Y. (2002, August 20) rescuers disorganized in 9/11 attack. *Washington Post*. p A01.

Pryor JP. (2003) The 2001 World Trade Center disaster. Int J Disaster Med, 1:6–18.

Public Entity Risk Institute. (2006) *Holistic Disaster Recovery: Ideas for Building Local Sustainability after a Natural Disaster*. Fairfax: Public Entity Risk Institute.

Quarantelli EL. (1966) Organization under stress. In: Brictson R. editor. *Symposium in Emergency Operations*. Santa Monica: System Development Corp. p 3–19.

Quarantelli EL. (1970) The community general hospital: its immediate problems in disasters. Am Behav Sci, 13:381–391.

Quarantelli EL. (1972, February) Conventional beliefs and counterintuitive realities. Social Res Fall 2008;75 (3):873–904.

Quaranteli EL, Dynes RR. When disaster strikes it isn't much like what you've read about. *Psychology Today*. p 67–70.

Quarantelli EL. (1979) *Studies in Disaster Response and Planning*. Newark: Disaster Research Center, University of Delaware.

Quarantelli EL. (1982) *Sheltering and Housing after Major Community Disasters: Case Studies and General Observations*. Washington, DC: Federal Emergency Management Agency.

Quarantelli EL. (1983) *Delivery of Emergency Medical Services in Disasters*. New York: Irvington.

Quarantelli EL. (1984) *Organizational Behavior in Disasters and Implications for Disaster Planning.* Monograph Series. Vol. 1, no. 2. Emmitsburg: National Emergency Training Center.

Quarantelli EL. (1986) Disaster studies: an historical analysis of the influences of basic sociology and applied use on the research done in the last 35 years. Available at http://www.researchgate.net/publication/26990342_Disaster_Studies_An_Historical_Analysis_of_the_Influences_of_Basic_Sociology_and_Applied_Use_on_the_Resarch_Done_in_the_Last_35_Years. Accessed June 27, 2014.

Quarantelli EL. (1987) Disaster studies: an analysis of the social historical factors affecting the development of research in the area. Int J Mass Emerg Disasters, 5 (3):285–310.

Quarantelli EL. (1989) Human behavior in the Mexico City Earthquake: some implications from basic themes in survey findings. Preliminary Paper #37. Newark: Disaster Research Center, University of Delaware.

Quarantelli EL. (1990) The warning process and evacuation behavior: the research evidence. Preliminary Paper #148. Delaware: Disaster Research Center, University of Delaware.

Quarantelli EL. (1992) The environmental disasters of the future will be more and worse but the prospect is not hopeless. Disaster Prev Manage, 2 (1):11–25.

Quarantelli EL. (1995) Patterns of sheltering and housing in US disasters. Disaster Prev Manage, 4 (3):43–53.

Quarantelli EL. (1996a) Emergent behaviors and groups in the crisis time of disasters. In: Kwan KM, editor. *Individuality and Social Control: Essays in Honor of Tamotsu Shibutani.* Greenwich: JAI Press. p 47–68.

Quarantelli EL. (1996b) Local mass media operations in disasters in the USA. Disaster Prev Manage, 5 (5):5–10.

Quarantelli EL. (1997a) Problematical aspects of the information/communication revolution for disaster planning and research: ten non-technical issues and questions. Disaster Prev Manage, 6 (2): 94–106.

Quarantelli EL. (1997b) Ten criteria for evaluating the management of community disasters. Disasters, 21 (2):39–56.

Quarantelli EL. (2006) Catastrophes are different than disasters: some implications or planning and management drawn from Hurricane Katrina. In: *Understanding Katrina Perspectives from the Social Sciences.* New York: Social Science Research Council.

Quinn A. (2003, December 31) Los Robles mobilehome estates hit hard by quake. *Paso Robles Press.* p A1.

Rahimi M. (1993) An examination of behavior and hazards faced by physically disabled people during the Loma Prieta earthquake. Nat Hazards, 7:59–82.

Reginald L, Langford R. (1990) *Fundamentals of Hazardous Materials Incidents.* Baca Raton: CRC Press.

Rice GE, Graham B. (2001) KC Teams to assist in disaster response efforts. The Star. Available at http://www.kestar.com/item/pages/home.pat,local/3accf.... Accessed June 18, 2014.

Richter LK, Waugh WL. (1991) Terrorism and tourism as logical companions. In: Medlik S, editor. *Managing Terrorism*. Oxford: Butterworth-Heinenmann Ltd. p 318–327.

Rigg NJ. (1997, May/June) Come rain or come slide: Yosemite search and rescue. *911Magazine*. p 30–33.

Roberts B. (1997) *Terrorism with Chemical and Biological Weapons: Calibrating Risks and Responses*. Washington, DC: Chemical and Biological Arms Control Institute. Available at http://www.cbaci.org/. Accessed June 18, 2014.

Rodríguez H. (2005) Reflections on the United Nations World Conference on disaster reduction: how can we develop disaster resilient communities? Int J Mass Emerg Disasters, 23 (1):141–160.

Ross GA. (1978) Organizational innovation in disaster settings. In: Quarantelli EL, editor. *Disasters: Theory and Research*. London: Sage. p 215–232.

Routley JG. (no date) *The East Bay Hills Fire, Oakland-Berkeley, California (October 19–22, 1991)*. Emmitsburg: Federal Emergency Management Agency, United States Fire Administration.

Rubin CB. (1991) Recovery from disaster. In: Drabek TE, Hoestmer GJ, editors. *Emergency Management: Principles and Practices for Local Government*. Washington, DC: ICMA. p 224–262.

Ruchelman L. (1988) The MGM Grand Hotel Fire. In: Charles MT, Kim JCK, editors. *Crisis Management: A Casebook*. Springfield: Charles C. Thomas Publisher. p 101–113.

Russell GW, Mentzel RK. (1990) Sympathy and altruism in response to disasters. J Soc Psychol, 130:309–316.

Sadiq A, McEntire DA. (2012) Mass fatality management challenges: a case study of the Haiti Earthquake. J Emerg Manage, 10 (6):459–471.

Salter J. (1997/98) Risk management in the emergency management context. Aust J Emerg Manage, 12 (4):22–28.

Saulny S. (2002, August 6) Credit Union Says A.T.M. Users Stole Millions After 9/11. *New York Times*. Available at http://www.nytimes.com/2002/08/06/nyregion/credit-union-says-atm-users-stole-millions-after-9-11.html. Accessed August 6, 2014.

Scanlon J. (1988) Disaster's little known pioneer: Canada's Samuel Henry Prince. Int J Mass Emerg Disasters, 6 (3):213–232.

Scanlon J. (1991) Reaching out: getting the community involved in preparedness. In: Hoetmer GJ, Drabek TE, editors. *Emergency Management: Principles and Practice for Local Government*. Washington, DC: ICMA.

Scanlon J. (1994) The role of EOCs in emergency management: a comparison of American and Canadian experience. Int J Mass Emerg Disasters, 12 (1):51–75.

Scanlon J. (1996) Not on the record: disaster, records and disaster research. Int J Mass Emerg Disasters, 14 (3):265–280.

Scanlon J. (1998) Dealing with mass death after a community catastrophe: handling bodies after the 1917 Halifax explosion. Disaster Prev Manage, 7 (4):288–304.

Scanlon J. (1999) Emergent groups in established frameworks: Ottawa Carleton's response to the 1998 ice disaster. J Contingencies Crisis Manage, 7 (1):30–37.

Scanlon J. (2003) Transportation in emergencies: an often neglected story. Disaster Prev Manage, 12 (5):428–437.

Scanlon J. (2005) Research about the mass media and disaster: never (Well Hardly Ever) the Twain Shall Meet. FEMA. Available at http://training.fema.gov/emiweb/downloads/ScanlonJournalism.pdf. Accessed June 18, 2014.

Scanlon TJ, Alldred S. (1982) Media coverage of disasters: the same old story. Emerg Planning Digest, 9:13–19.

Scanlon J, McCullum C. (1999) Media coverage of mass death: not always unwelcome. Aust J Emerg Manage, 14 (3):55–59.

Scanlon J, McMahon T. (2011) Dealing with mass death in disasters and pandemics: some key differences but many similarities. Disaster Prev Manage, 20 (2):172–185.

Scanlon J, Alldred S, Farrell A, Prawzick A. (1985) Coping with the media in disasters: some predictable problems. Public Adm Rev, 45 (January):123–33.

Scawthorn C, Wenger D. (1990) *Emergency Response, Planning and Search and Rescue.* HRRC Publication 11P. College Station: Hazard Reduction and Recovery Center, College of Architecture, Texas A & M University.

Schaper FC. (1991, September) PIOs enhance media relations. *Fire Chief.* p 68–69.

Schneider SK. (1992) Governmental response to disasters: the conflict between bureaucratic procedures and emergent norms. Public Adm Rev, 52 (2):135–145.

Schneider SK. (1995) *Flirting with Disaster: Public Management in Crisis Situations.* Armonk: M.E. Sharpe.

Schwab J. (1998) Tornado case study: Plainfield, Illinois. In: Schwab J, Topping KC, Eadie CC, Deyle RE, Smith RA, editors. *Planning for Post-Disaster Recovery and Reconstruction.* Chicago: American Planning Association. p 229–234.

Schwarzenegger.com. (2004) Governor Schwarzenegger Tours Paso Robles, declares state of emergency in San Luis County. Available at http://www.schwarzenegger.com/en/news/uptotheminut... Accessed June 18, 2014.

Scudamore JM, Trevelyan GM, Tas MV, Varley EM, Hickman GAW. (2002) Carcass disposal: lessons from Great Britain following the foot and mouth disease outbreaks of 2001. Rev Sci Tech Off Int Epiz, 21 (3):775–787.

Selves MD. (2002) Local emergency management: a tale of two models. Emergency Management Institute, Federal Emergency Management Agency. Available at http://www.training.fema.gov/emiweb/edu/localEM1.html. Accessed June 18, 2014.

Shagets FW. (2013) Thoughts on the May 2011 Joplin, Missouri Tornado. South Med J, 106 (1):113–14.

Sheehan DC. (1999) Stress management in the Federal Bureau of Investigation: principles for program development. Int J Emerg Mental Health, 1 (1):39–42.

Shoaf KI, Ngyyen LO, Sareen HR, Bourque LB. (1998) Injuries as a result of California earthquakes in the past decade. Disasters, 22 (3):218–235.

Showalter PS, Myers MF. (1994) Natural disasters in the United States as release agents of oil chemicals or radiological materials between 1980–1989: analysis and recommendations. Risk Anal, 14 (2): 169–182.

Siebeneck LK, Lindell MK, Prater CS, Wu HC, Huang SK. (2013) Evacuees' reentry concerns and experiences in the aftermath of Hurricane Ike. Nat Hazards. 65 (3):2267–2286.

Sikich GW. (1995) Incident command systems: a perspective on strategic and tactical applications. ASPEP J, 107–116.

Simpson DM. (2001) Community emergency response training (CERTS): a recent history and review. Nat Hazards Rev, 2 (2): 54–63.

Simpson G. (2005, November 22) In year of disasters, experts bring order to Chaos of relief. *Wall Street Journal*. Available at http://online.wsj.com/news/articles/SB113262454249603760. Accessed August 6, 2014.

Sinha DK, editor. (1992) *Natural Disaster Reduction for the Nineties: Perspectives, Aspects and Strategies*. Calcutta: International Journal Services.

Smith K. (1995) *Environmental Hazards: Assessing Risks and Reducing Disaster*. New York: Routledge.

Smith DJ, Sutter D. (2013) Response and recovery after the Joplin Tornado: lessons applied and lessons learned. Available at http://ssrn.com/abstract=2261353. Accessed May 6, 2013.

Snow M. (2003, December 31) Fire department's quick actions prevented fires. *Paso Robles Press*. p A1.

Snow M, Quinn A. (2003, December 31) Downtown Merchants face an uncertain future. *Paso Robles Press*. p A1.

Sorensen JH. (1981) Emergency Response to Mount St. Helens' Eruption: March 20 to April 10, 1980. Working Paper #43. Boulder: Energy Division, Oak Ridge National Laboratory.

Sorensen JH. (2000) Hazard warning systems: review of 20 years of progress. Nat Hazards Rev, 1 (2):119–125.

Sorensen JH, Mileti DS. (1988) Warning and evacuation: answering some basic questions. Ind Crisis Q, 2:195–209.

Stallings RA, Quarantelli EL. (1985) Emergent citizen groups and emergency management. Public Adm Rev, 45 (Special Issue):93–100.

State Department. (2005) Avian Flu fact sheet. Available at http://travel.state.gov/travel/tips/health/health_1181.html. Accessed February 7, 2006.

State/Federal Hazard Mitigation Survey Team. (1990) Description of the disaster. In: *State and Federal Hazard Mitigation Survey Team Report for the October 17, 1989, Loma Prieta Earthquake, California.* San Francisco: FEMA. p 5–27.

Stehr S. (2002) Victim Identification and Management Following the Collapse of the World Trade Center Towers. Quick Response Report #148. Boulder: Natural Hazards Research and Applications Information Center. Available at http://www.Colorado.EDU/hazards/qr/qr148/qr148.html. Accessed June 18, 2014.

Steinberg LJ, Cruz AM. (2004) When natural and technological disasters collide: lessons from the Turkey earthquake of August 17, 1999. Nat Hazards Rev, 5 (2):121–130.

Steinberg LJV, Basolo R, Burby LJN, Cruz AM. (2004) Joint seismic and technological disasters: possible impacts and community preparedness in an urban setting. Nat Hazards Rev, 5 (4):159–169.

Stephens HW. (1997) *The Texas City Disaster, 1947.* Austin: University of Texas Press.

Stephenson R, Anderson PS. (1997) Disasters and the information technology revolution. Disasters, 21 (4):305–334.

Stilp R, Bevalacqua A. (1996) *Emergency Medical Response to Hazardous Materials Incidents.* Cliften Park: Thomson Delmar Learning.

Storm Prediction Center (SPC). (2011) Annual U.S. Killer Tornado Statistics. Available at http://www.spc.noaa.gov/climo/torn/fatalmap.php?yr=2011. Accessed June 26, 2013.

Suarez-Villa L, Walrod W. (1999) Losses from the Northridge earthquake: disruption to high-technology industries in the Los Angeles Basin. Disasters, 23 (1):19–44.

Sutphen S, Waugh WL Jr. (1998) Organizational reform and technological innovation in emergency management. Int J Mass Emerg Disasters, 16 (1):7–12.

Swan RC. (2000) Debris management planning for the 21st century. Nat Hazards Rev, 1 (4):222–225.

Sylves R. (1996) The Politics and Administration of Presidential Disaster Declarations: The California Floods of Winter 1995. Quick Response Report 86. Boulder: Natural Hazards Center, University of Colorado at Boulder. Available at http://www.colorado.edu/hazards/qr/qr86.html. Accessed June 18, 2014.

Sylves RT, Waugh WL Jr. (1990) *Cities and Disaster: North American Studies in Emergency Management.* Springfield: Charles C. Thomas Publisher.

Sylves RT, Waugh WL Jr. (1996) *Disaster Management in the U.S. and Canada: The Politics, Policymaking, Administration and Analysis of Emergency Management.* Springfield: Charles C. Thomas Publisher.

Tatham P, Hughes K. (2011) Humanitarian logistics metrics: where we are and how we might improve. In: Christopher M, Tatham P, editors. *Humanitarian Logistics: Meeting the Challenge of Preparing for and Responding to Disasters*. Kogan Page: London. p 65–84.

Terry FR. (2001) The 1989 rail disaster at Clapham in South London. In: Farazmand A, editor. *Handbook of Crisis and Emergency Management*. Public Administration and Public Policy 93. New York: Marcel Dekker Inc.

Texas Department of Health, Division of Emergency Preparedness. (2013, May 21) Stress reactions to traumatic events, Austin. Available at http://www.dshs.state.tx.us/mhsa-disaster/cism/stress-reactions/. Accessed on June 28, 2014.

Texas Division of Emergency Management. (2001) Disaster recovery manual. Available at ftp://ftp.txdps.state.tx.us/dem/recovery/recoverymanual.pdf. Accessed June 18, 2014.

The National Academies. (2006) A closer look at global warming. Available at http://www4.nationalacademies.org/onpi/webextra.nsf/44bf87db309563a0852566f2006d63bb/f6335bf011038bb185256a84005838c7?OpenDocument. Accessed January 18, 2006.

The World Bank. (2005) Economic impact of Avian Flu. Available at http://web.worldbank.org/WBSITE/EXTERNAL/NEWS/0,,contentMDK:20709923~pagePK:64257043~piPK:437376~theSitePK:4607,00.html. Accessed February 7, 2006.

The World Health Organization. (2006) Cumulative number of confirmed human cases of Avian influenza A/(H5N1) reported to WHO. Available at http://www.who.int/csr/disease/avian_influenza/country/cases_table_2006_02_06/en/index.html. Accessed February 7, 2006.

Tholkes BF. (1996) Ethical concerns in the field of wilderness search and rescue. J Natl Assoc Search Rescue, 15 (Winter):3–5.

Thoma K. (2004, October 13) Community works on debris cleanup. *Pensacola News Journal*.

Thomas E. (2005, September 19) How Bush blew it. *Newsweek*. Available at http://www.newsweek.com/how-bush-blew-it-118257. Accessed August 6, 2014.

Thomas D, Mileti DS. (2003) Designing Educational Opportunities for the Hazards Manager of the 21st Century. Working Paper No. 109. Boulder: Natural Hazards Research and Applications Information Center, University of Colorado.

Thomas DSK, Cutter SK, Hodgson M, Gutekunst M, Jones S. (2002) Use of Spatial Data and Geographic Technologies in Response to the September 11 Terrorist Attack. Quick Response Report #153. Boulder: Natural Hazards Research and Information Applications Center, University of Colorado.

Tierney KJ. (1985) Emergency medical preparedness and response in disasters: the need for interorganizational coordination. Public Admin Rev, 45 (Special Issue):77–84.

Tierney K. (2003) Disaster beliefs and institutional interests: recycling disaster myths in the aftermath of 9–11. In: Clarke L, editor.

*Terrorism and Disaster: New Threats, New Ideas.* Research in Social Problems and Public Policy, Volume 11. Amsterdam: Emerald Group Publishing Limited. p 33–51.

Tierney KJ, Lindell MK, Perry RL. (2001) *Facing the Unexpected: Disaster Preparedness and Response in the United States.* Washington, DC: Joseph Henry Press.

Timmerman P. (1981) *Vulnerability, Resilience and the Collapse of Society.* Toronto: Institute of Environmental Studies.

Torres A, David MJ, Bowman QP. (2002) Risk management of international trade: emergency preparedness. Rev Sci Tech Off Int Epiz, 21 (3):493–498.

Tracey B. (2004, January 7) The politics of disaster. *Harvard Magazine* (March-April). Tribune Staff Reporter. Local officials continue to push for FEMA funds. *The Tribune,* p A1, A6.

Trainor J, Barsky L. (2011) Reporting for duty? A synthesis of research on role conflict, strain, and abandonment among emergency responders during disasters and catastrophes. Available at http://udspace.udel.edu/handle/19716/9885. Accessed June 28, 2014.

Turner BA. (1994) Flexibility and improvisation in emergency response. Disaster Manag, 6 (2):84–89.

Turner S. (2004, October 14) Dumping at Allapattah Ranch in Stuart might soon be prohibited. *Stuart News.*

Tyler M. (1994) Demolitions in Fillmore after the Northridge earthquake. In: *Proceedings of the NEHRP Conference and Workshop on Research on the Northridge, California Earthquake of January 17.* Richmond: California Universities for Research in Earthquake Engineering.

UNISDR. (2013) Global assessment report on disaster risk reduction. Available at http://www.preventionweb.net/english/hyogo/gar/2013/en/home/index.html. Accessed on June 18, 2014.

United States Fire Administration. (1994) *Search and Rescue Operations Following the North Ridge Earthquake.* Technical Rescue Incident Report. Emmitsburg: Federal Emergency Management Agency.

United States Geological Survey. (2004) Preliminary earthquake report, magnitude 6.5 – Central California, 2003 December 22 19:15:56. Available at http://earthquake.usgs.gov/recenteqsUS/Quakes/nc4014. Accessed June 18, 2014.

Urby H, McEntire DA. (2013) Applying public administration in emergency management: the importance of integrating management into disaster education. J Homeland Security Emerg Manage, 10 (3):1–22.

US Department of Labor. (2005) Bureau of labor statistics, occupational employment statistics. Available at http://bls.gov/oco/oco20051.htm. Accessed August 10, 2005.

US Global Change Research Program. Available at http://www.globalchange.gov/. Accessed on January 23, 2006.

Vigdor J. (2008) The economic aftermath of Hurricane Katrina. J Econ Perspect, 22 (4):135–154.

Vigo G, Wenger D. (1994) Emergent behavior in the immediate response to the 1985 Mexico City earthquake and the 1994 Northridge earthquake in Los Angeles. In: Proceedings of the NEHRP Conference and Workshop on Research and the Northridge, California earthquake of January 17, 1994, Social Science and Emergency Management, 20–22 August, Los Angeles. Vol. 4. p 237–244.

Vigo G, Prater C, Pramanik P, Beeson JE, Hall M. (1993) *Search and Rescue & Emergency Medical Services: A Multidisciplinary Annotated Bibliography*. Second ed. College Station: Hazard Reduction and Recovery Center, College of Architecture, Texas A&M University.

Villagran De Leon JC. (2005) WCDR in Kobe and the way forward, the unspoken challenges!. Int J Mass Emerg Disasters, 23 (1): 141–160.

Volunteer Management Committee. (2003) *Managing Unaffiliated Volunteers: Concepts of Operations*. Alexandria: National Voluntary Organizations Active in Disasters (NVOAD).

Volunteer Management Committee. (no date) *Managing Spontaneous Volunteers in Times of Disaster: The Synergy of Structure and Good Intentions*. Washington, DC: Points of Light Foundation & Volunteer Center National Network.

Wagman D. (2005, January/February) Well-intentioned, sometimes misguided: spontaneous, or unaffiliated, volunteers have big hearts, but without proper planning and guidance, they can impeded, not help, disaster response and recovery efforts. *Homeland Protection Professional*. p 34–38.

Wallace WA, De Balogh F. (1985) Decision support systems for disaster management. Public Adm Rev, 45 (Special Volume):134–146.

Walton L. (2004, October 13) Cities looking forward to extra cleanup cash. *Daytona Beach News-Journal*.

Warn G, Berman J, Whittaker A, Bruneau M. (2003) Investigation of a damaged high-rise buildings near ground zero. In: Monday J, editor. *Beyond September 11th: An Account of Post-Disaster Research*. Special Publication #39. Boulder: Natural Hazards Research and Applications Information Center, University of Colorado.

Watts MJ, Bohle HG. (1993) The space of vulnerability: the causal structure of hunger and famine. Prog Hum Geogr, 17:43–67.

Waugh WL Jr. (1988) The Hyatt Skywalk disaster. In: Charles MT, Kim JCK, editors. *Crisis Management: A Casebook*. Springfield: Charles C. Thomas Publisher.

Waugh WL Jr. (1993) Coordination or control: organizational design and the emergency management function. Disaster Prev Manage, 2 (4):17–31.

Waugh WL Jr. (1995) Geographic information systems: the case of disaster management. Soc Sci Comput Rev, 13 (4):422–431.

Waugh WL Jr. (2000) *Living with Hazards, Dealing with Disasters: An Introduction to Emergency Management*. Armonk: M.E. Sharpe.

Waugh WL Jr. (2001) Managing terrorism as an environmental hazard. In: Farazmand A, editor. *Handbook and Crisis and Emergency Management.* Public Administration and Public Policy 93. New York: Marcel Dekker, Inc.

Waugh WL Jr. (2004) The all-hazards approach must be continued. J Emerg Manage, 2 (1):11–12.

Webb GR. (2002) Sociology, disasters, and terrorism: understanding the threats of the new millennium. Sociol Focus, 35 (1):87–95.

Webb GR, Chevreau FR. (2006) Planning to improvise: the importance of creativity and flexibility in crisis response. Int J Emerg Manag, 3:66–72.

Webb GR, Beverly M, McMichael M, Noon J, Patterson T. (1999) Role Improvising Under Conditions of Uncertainty: A Classification of Types. Preliminary Paper #289. Newark: Disaster Research Center, University of Delaware.

Wedel KR, Baker DR. (1998) After the Oklahoma City bombing: a case study of the resource coordination committee. Int J Mass Emerg Disasters, 16 (3):333–362.

Weichselgartner J. (2001) Disaster mitigation: the concept of vulnerability revisited. Disaster Prev Manage, 10 (2):85–94.

Wenger D. (1989) The Study of Volunteer and Emergent Organizational Response in Search and Rescue: Approaches and Issues for Future Research. HRRC Publication 5P. College Station: Hazard Reduction and Recovery Center, College of Architecture, Texas A&M University.

Wenger D, James T. (1990) Convergence of Volunteers in a Consensus Crisis: The Case of the 1985 Mexico City Earthquake. HRRC Publication 13P. College Station: Hazard Reduction and Recovery Center, Texas A&M University.

Wenger DE, Dykes JD, Sebok TD, Neff JL. (1975) It's a matter of myths: an empirical examination of individual insight into disaster response. Mass Emerg, 1:33–46.

Wenger D, Quarantelli EL, Dynes RR. (1990) Taking a critical look at the incident command system. Hazard Monthly, 10 (3):8–12.

Wessely S, Deahl M. (2003) Psychological debriefing is a waste of time. Br J Psychiatry, 183:12–14. The Royal College of Psychiatrists, 2003. Web. 23 Aug. 2013. Available at http://bjp.rcpsych.org/content/183/1/12.full. Accessed June 18, 2014.

Wikipedia Kiss Nightclub Fire. (2013, August 17) Wikipedia. Wikimedia Foundation. Available at http://en.wikipedia.org/wiki/Kiss_nightclub_fire. Accessed June 18, 2014.

Wilson J, Oyola-Yemaiel A. (1998, February 23) Emergent Coordinative Groups and Women's Response Roles in the Central Florida Tornado Disaster. Quick Response Report No. 110. Boulder: Natural Hazards Research and Applications Information Center, University of Colorado at Boulder; 1998.

Winslow FE. (2001) Lessons learned from Three Mile Island and Chernobyl reactor accidents. In: Farazmand A, editor. *Handbook of*

*Crisis and Emergency Management*. Public Administration and Public Policy 93. New York: Marcel Dekker Inc.

Wise CR. (2002) Organizing for homeland security. Public Adm Rev, 62 (2): 131–144.

Wisner B, Blaikie P, Cannon T, Davis I. (2004) *At Risk: Natural Hazards, People's Vulnerability and Disasters*. New York: Routledge.

Wisner B. (2005) Circus of hope. Int J Mass Emerg Disasters, 23 (1):141–160.

Witt H. (2005, April 18) Tragedy haunts the heroes. *Chicago Tribune*. Available at http://www.chicagotribune.com/classified/jobs/chi-0504180178 apr18,0,2770766.story. Accessed August 6, 2014.

Woodman RW, Sawyer JE, Griffin RW. (1993) Toward a theory of organizational creativity. Acad Manage Rev, 18 (2):293–321.

World Bank, Turkey Country Office. (1999, September 14) *Turkey Marmara Earthquake Assessment*. Turkey: World Bank.

World Health Organization. (2002) West Nile virus in the United States-Update 10. Available at http://www.who.int/csr/don/2002_11_27/en/index.html. Accessed January 31, 2006.

World Health Organization. (2006) Update 95-SARS chronology of a killer. Available at http://www.who.int/csr/don/2003_07_04/en/index.html. Accessed January 29, 2006.

Wright T. (2004, October 9) Massive amount of yard debris Overwhelms City. *Tallahassee Democrat*.

Zagier AS, Clark C, Lieb DA. (2012) One year later, Joplin is on the mend. Available at http://www.cnn.com/2012/05/21/us/joplin-tornado-one-year-later/. Accessed on June 28, 2014.

Ziaukas T. (2001) Environmental public relations and crisis management: two paradigmatic cases—Bhopal and Exxon. In: Farazmand A, editor. *Handbook of Crisis and Emergency Management*. Public Administration and Public Policy 93. New York: Marcel Dekker Inc.

## Web Cites

http://training.fema.gov/emiweb/edu/aem_courses.asp

http://westnilevirus.nbii.gov/diseasehome.jsp?disease=West%20Nile%20Virus&pagemode=submit. Accessed January 31, 2006.

http://www.cdc.gov/flu/avian/gen-info/facts.htm. Accessed February 6, 2006.

http://www.cdc.gov/ncidod/dq/qa_influenza_amendment_to_eo_13295.htm#authority. Accessed February 7, 2006.

http://www.cdc.gov/ncidod/dvbid/westnile/qa/overview.htm. Accessed March 24, 2003.

http://www.cdc.gov/ncidod/dvrd/revb/enterovirus/hfhf.htm. Accessed January 1, 2006.

CDC. (1998) Deaths Among Children During an Outbreak of Hand, Foot, and Mouth Disease—Taiwan, Republic of China, April–July 1998. http://www.cdc.gov/mmwr/preview/mmwrhtml/00054640.htm. Accessed February 6, 2006.

http://www.who.int/csr/don/2003_07_04/en/index.html. Accessed June 18, 2014.

# INDEX